# Exit Stalin

MARK B. SMITH

# Exit Stalin
*The Soviet Union as a Civilization, 1953–1991*

ALLEN LANE
*an imprint of*
PENGUIN BOOKS

ALLEN LANE

UK | USA | Canada | Ireland | Australia
India | New Zealand | South Africa

Allen Lane is part of the Penguin Random House group of companies whose addresses can be found at global.penguinrandomhouse.com

Penguin Random House UK
One Embassy Gardens, 8 Viaduct Gardens, London SW11 7BW

penguin.co.uk

First published 2026
002

Copyright © Mark B. Smith, 2026

The moral right of the author has been asserted

Penguin Random House values and supports copyright. Copyright fuels creativity, encourages diverse voices, promotes freedom of expression and supports a vibrant culture. Thank you for purchasing an authorized edition of this book and for respecting intellectual property laws by not reproducing, scanning or distributing any part of it by any means without permission. You are supporting authors and enabling Penguin Random House to continue to publish books for everyone. No part of this book may be used or reproduced in any manner for the purpose of training artificial intelligence technologies or systems. In accordance with Article 4(3) of the DSM Directive 2019/790, Penguin Random House expressly reserves this work from the text and data mining exception.

Set in 10.5/14pt Sabon LT Std
Typeset by Six Red Marbles UK, Thetford, Norfolk
Printed and bound in Great Britain by Clays Ltd, Elcograf S.p.A.

The authorized representative in the EEA is Penguin Random House Ireland, Morrison Chambers, 32 Nassau Street, Dublin D02 YH68

A CIP catalogue record for this book is available from the British Library

ISBN: 978–0–241–40085–2

Penguin Random House is committed to a sustainable future for our business, our readers and our planet. This book is made from Forest Stewardship Council® certified paper.

*Dedicated to the memory of Larisa Shikova*

# Contents

| | |
|---|---|
| List of Illustrations | ix |
| Map | xi |
| Prologue: 2 June 1962 | 1 |
| 1 Nikita Khrushchev's Revolution of Multiple Futures (1917–53) | 17 |

### PART ONE
## *The Dictatorship that Loves You (1953–64)*

| | |
|---|---|
| 2 The Man of the People with Blood on His Hands | 51 |
| 3 Gagarin's Conquest | 73 |
| 4 The Glittering Metropolis | 93 |
| 5 The Boundary Between Two Environments | 113 |
| 6 Slush | 133 |

### PART TWO
## *Eternal Red Star (1965–74)*

| | |
|---|---|
| 7 New Year with Brezhnev | 155 |
| 8 People in Uniform | 177 |
| 9 To the Square | 197 |
| 10 Socialist Bodies | 217 |
| 11 A String Bag | 237 |
| 12 On Stage, Off Stage | 257 |

## CONTENTS

### PART THREE
## *Faded Paradise (1975–84)*

| | | |
|---|---|---|
| 13 | Oil Fields and Silver Birches | 279 |
| 14 | Hammer and Sickle as Far as the Eye Can See | 299 |
| 15 | *Homo Sovieticus* | 319 |
| 16 | The Danger Society | 339 |
| 17 | Misfits | 361 |
| 18 | The Life Cycle of Eternal Socialism | 383 |

### PART FOUR
## *The Country That Committed Suicide by Accident (1985–91)*

| | | |
|---|---|---|
| 19 | The Last Revolutionary | 405 |
| 20 | Phone Call to Gorky | 427 |
| 21 | The End of Soviet Civilization | 449 |
| | Afterword | 473 |
| | *Notes* | 483 |
| | *Acknowledgements* | 531 |
| | *Index* | 533 |

# List of Illustrations

Photographic credits are shown in italics.

p. xvi. Lenin Monument, Komsomolskaya Square, Ufa, 1969. *ITAR-TASS/Boris Klipinitser/Imago.*

p. 16. Nikita Khrushchev in Kyiv, 1945. *Keystone/Gamma-Rapho/Getty Images.*

p. 50. A prisoner of the Vorkuta Gulag (Vorkutlag), Komi Republic, 1945. *Laski Diffusion/Getty Images.*

p. 72. Yuri Gagarin, Helsinki, 1962. *ullstein bild/Rudolf Dietrich/TopFoto.*

p. 92. Construction of new apartment buildings, Krasnoyarsk, Siberia. *Oleg Ivanov/RIA Novosti/TopFoto.*

p. 112. World Festival of Youth, Moscow, 1957. *ullstein bild/Klaus Rose/Getty Images.*

p. 132. Leonid Brezhnev and Ekaterina Furtseva, 1956. *Lisa Larsen/The LIFE Picture Collection/Shutterstock.*

p. 154. New Year Ball at the Kremlin, Moscow, 1964. *Imago/SNA.*

p. 176. Marshal Kliment Voroshilov and Marshal Semyon Budenny, Moscow, 1968. *TopFoto.*

p. 196. Elena Bonner and Andrei Sakharov in their apartment, Moscow, 1974. *Christian Hirou/Gamma-Rapho/Getty Images.*

p. 216. Observing a patient, Lermontov Sanatorium, Odesa, 1973. *Sovfoto/Universal Images Group/Getty Images.*

p. 236. Inspecting a VAZ-2101, Tolyatti, 1968. *TASS/Valentin Sobolev/A. Bryanov/TopFoto.*

LIST OF ILLUSTRATIONS

p. 256. Vladimir Vysotsky as Hamlet, with Valery Lvanor as Laertes, at the Taganka Theatre, Moscow, 1970s. *TopFoto.*

p. 278. Harvesting in the Svaneti region, Georgia, undated photo. *Mark Redkin/FotoSoyuz/Getty Images.*

p. 298. Cotton farmer near Samarkand, Uzbekistan, 1970s. *Keystone/Gamma-Rapho/Getty Images.*

p. 318. Party meeting in a car factory, Moscow, 1980. *TASS/Anatoly Morkovkin/TopFoto.*

p. 338. Aeroflot ticket counter, Tashkent, undated photo. *Richard Harrington/Three Lions/Hulton Archive/Getty Images.*

p. 360. Hippy commune, Gauja, Latvia, 1984. Photographer unknown. Genadii Borisovich Zaitsev Collection, Wende Museum, Culver City (Acc. No. 2013.1029.1624). *Photograph by courtesy of the Wende Museum.*

p. 382. Natalia Gundareva (and Oleg Basilashvili) in *Autumn Marathon*, 1983. *Sputnik/RIA Novosti/TopFoto.*

p. 404. Raisa Gorbacheva and Mikhail Gorbachev, Moscow, 1989. *AP Photo/Boris Yurchenko/Alamy.*

p. 426. Andrei Sakharov during the 1st Congress of People's Deputies, Moscow, May 1989. *Sergei Guneyev/Getty Images.*

p. 448. The Baltic Way, 23 August 1989. *Ullsteinbild/TopFoto.*

p. 472. In the USSR, c. 1991. *Collection of the author.*

# Exit Stalin

The Soviet Union as a civilization? Ufa, 1969

# Prologue: 2 June 1962

'Are you out of your mind?' the young man said. 'They don't shoot people these days!' They were out walking when his friend thought she heard gunfire. A few moments later, they took the wrong turning and were caught up in a massacre.[1] In this life-and-death disagreement between friends, *she* was proved right. The bullets were incontrovertible evidence. But was he wrong?

Two days earlier, on 31 May 1962, the Soviet government had announced that the price of meat was to rise by 30 per cent and butter by 25 per cent. Although wartime rationing had long since ended, the Soviet economy was still run by central planning. The planners set production targets, wage levels and prices, and distributed resources around the country. They worked for the State Planning Authority, Gosplan, in a massive Stalin-era edifice two minutes from the Kremlin.

Six hundred miles to the south, in Novocherkassk, news of the price rises was met with disquiet. This medium-sized town, the historic capital of the Don Cossacks, had a proud Soviet heritage, with its locomotive works which employed 13,000 people. Across the USSR, citizens registered their disapproval about the price rises in mostly quiet ways. But it was at this factory that the real trouble in June 1962 began and ended.

It was no wonder. Five months earlier, on New Year's Day, the Novocherkassk management cut wages by one-third in real terms, increasing the work required to earn each ruble. Now workers could buy less with their already depleted income. When they showed up at the locomotive works on 1 June, they gathered on the square outside the factory. The atmosphere became tense. The plant director,

B. N. Kurochkin, came down to talk it over. A bruising conversation followed, but there was no accounting for the stupidity of his conclusion. 'If you can't afford meat and sausage,' he told them, 'eat pies instead.'

And so Kurochkin opened the floodgates to an unlikely whole-town strike that ended in a massacre. Even the drop in wages and rise in prices, which together threatened disaster for household budgets, might not have made people down tools. This was no easy task anyway, given that Soviet trade unions were banned from striking. But the contempt of oily bosses turned popular anger into mass protest.

The strike which began at Novocherkassk was spontaneous. Protestors did not seek the end of Soviet power, but drew on the same instincts of social justice and personal entitlement as their ancestors of 1917. Their dissent was expressed as a howl of rage, indifferent to the consequences. Breaking into the works boiler room, two strikers set off the factory siren, and people from across town began to gather, wondering what disaster was befalling them.

Over the next two days, citizens went to the public spaces of Novocherkassk to debate the failures of socialist justice and lambast those in power. In general, they invoked the values of the Russian Revolution of 1917, on which the government's legitimacy was formally based, but their demand was precise: end the price rises. The local authorities were poleaxed. Such events were off the scale of their experience. Within hours, the head of the regional Party, in the nearby town of Rostov, requested that the local army command, the North Caucasus Military District, bring troops to Novocherkassk. Plain-clothes KGB were already infiltrating the mêlée. They photographed faces in the crowd using cameras the size of cigarette lighters. Tanks blocked the entrance to the factory. More workers joined the strike. But not all did. Among those who stayed at work or away from trouble were Party members, Young Communists, honoured workers, volunteer-busybodies who patrolled local neighbourhoods, not to mention the people with something to lose, the indifferent, nervous and conformist, as well as the contrarians who performed their scepticism only behind closed doors. Throughout the afternoon and evening, anger transmitted itself across the town. A mass public meeting continued into the small hours of 2 June. People gathered again at first light, by which time 3,000 regular soldiers and 300 troops from the Ministry of Internal Affairs were waiting in the town.

Khrushchev had known what was happening since lunchtime on 1 June. His instinct was to fly down himself to restore common sense. Convinced he was on the side of ordinary people, he could not imagine they would not see the reason of his case. In the end he despatched a delegation headed by two members of the Presidium, as the Politburo was called between 1952 and 1966: Frol Kozlov and Anastas Mikoyan. Patience and face-saving concessions should have brought events to a close. Nothing could stop the KGB arresting the noisiest troublemakers in due course. Bad as that was, it could have been an end of it.

On the morning of 2 June, between 5,000 and 12,000 men and women moved peacefully through the town, towards the main square that housed government and Party buildings. Many protestors carried banners that looked radical in the context of a demonstration, but were actually Soviet in their entirety. Attacking the protestors, even with water cannon, seemed unthinkable. Firing on unarmed strikers, many of them women, was precisely what the Tsarist government had done several times in its last years. The memory of Bloody Sunday, when Cossack troops charged through a peaceful march and provoked the 1905 revolution, was unmistakable. Following discussions with local bosses, the Moscow delegation seemed unsure. Although Mikoyan was a conciliator by temperament, Kozlov was a hardliner, and he had the armed force at his disposal to prove it.

The demonstrators crossed the river, elbowing soldiers aside on the bridge or wading through the water. They reached the town square. A handful forced their way into Party HQ. One of them found slices of the finest sausage on a table. He went to the balcony and displayed them as a trophy. This is what they're keeping for themselves while they're stealing our scraps! But the demonstrators were not seizing government buildings; they were merely trespassing and making speeches, coming and going. Twenty-five years later, one politicized worker, Pyotr Siuda, whose father had joined the Party in 1903, said that the two days were 'a joyous time, a time of spiritual emancipation'.² Meanwhile, a different group of protestors entered the police station, looking for arrested comrades. This crossed a line. Troops opened fire. Five strikers were killed, while two sixteen-year-olds, caught up in events, were also shot, dying shortly after.

At midday, in the town square, workers faced troops. It was a stand-off, but there were jokes between the two sides. Members of the crowd asked for a speech from Mikoyan. The general in charge of the detachment came to the balcony of the Party building and called for people to go home.

Then he gave them an ultimatum. Leave the square or the troops will shoot. The soldiers were in the firing position. They shot a warning in the air. Few thought that their fellow countrymen would look them in the eye and pull the trigger. Then the real shooting started. Crushed against each other, screaming and panicking, people tried to flee.

Back at the office, a 33-year-old engineer was at work. N. P. Bredikhin had a place on the board of honour. He was the father of two young children. Suddenly he heard what he thought was the noise of carts rattling over cobbles. He looked up. Someone had come in, saying they'd started to shoot. He dismissed this as a rumour. But then a senior engineer burst in and said he'd seen them firing into the crowd. A female technician started crying, frightened for her mother. Bredikhin, who had never put a foot wrong, walked across the room, took the portrait of Khrushchev from the wall and threw it out of the window.³

Afterwards, the KGB carried the sixteen corpses into trucks. They ignored the wailing and screaming, and the last expressions of defiant fury. The hospital was overflowing. Including the seven killed in the police station shooting, twenty-four people were dead. The twenty-fourth was on a work secondment from Lviv, caught on the street after the emergency curfew, and shot when he ran off. Most of the dead were male workers from the locomotive plant, such as V. K. Karpenko, aged eighteen, but forty-year-old A. D. Gribova was a hairdresser, and A. N. D'iakonov, forty-seven, was a manager from another factory. In one of the most horrible aspects of the cover-up that followed, the KGB quietly buried some of these victims miles from town, misleading and tormenting the bereaved. Trials would follow later – of strikers, not secret policemen. A few of the 'ringleaders' were executed or imprisoned.

Nothing was quite clear. The general on the balcony had not given the order to shoot. And the deaths of sixteen people in the square seemed too few for several minutes of semi-automatic shooting from a line of soldiers. Evidence exists that KGB officers or members of military intelligence orchestrated the shooting from other parts of the square, and that the regular soldiers and senior officers from the North Caucasus Military District were out of the loop and not responsible. Despite the 'Caucasus' designation, most of those troops were ethnic Russians, like the inhabitants of the town. Some of them – including non-Russians – were in tears shortly afterwards, their officers not challenging locals who called them 'fascists', perhaps the worst insult in the postwar Soviet Union. On 2 June 1962, the local military leadership was capable of questioning a political order to fire on civilians.[4] But even if Frol Kozlov had bypassed the regular military command and made them look like stooges, the army's troops did not rise to the moment and stop the KGB. At Novocherkassk, it was an exaggeration to distinguish between good men in army uniforms and KGB villains in plain clothes. Perhaps 'who pulled the trigger?' was only an academic problem.

Yet 'who is to blame?' is an eternal Russian question. The Soviet Union had changed dramatically since Stalin died in 1953. No longer were people shot in the hundreds of thousands on trumped-up charges, as they had been in the 1930s. Instead, they enjoyed better living conditions and even a form of rights. But there were still powerful men and women in the USSR who thought their fellow-citizens were 'shit' and could be denied a stable life, or framed-up and incarcerated, or even killed.

The search of Soviet people for a kind of normality in the decades after Stalin's death is the story I tell in this book. But the ultimate truth of Soviet civilization was the atrocities of Stalinism, of unaccountable power arbitrarily destroying innocent individuals in the pursuit of communist utopia. If I could only tell one story about Soviet history, I would choose Masha's.

*

The story was written by the great novelist Vasily Grossman. It is part of an unfinished novel that he wrote sporadically during the Khrushchev era until his own death in 1964. Only published during *perestroika*, *Everything Flows* describes a series of encounters that follows a man's release from the Gulag.

Masha is one of the people he remembers. She is a gentle young woman. In the late 1930s, she lives a quiet, happy, honest life with her husband and three-year-old daughter in Moscow's Arbat district. Suddenly, one day, her husband is arrested in their home. Then the secret policemen – the men of the NKVD – come back for her. Their daughter Yulya is abandoned, probably taken to a children's home. Masha is imprisoned in the Lubyanka, the NKVD HQ not far from her home. Her interrogation makes no sense. She is sentenced for counter-revolutionary political crimes, as a spy who failed to denounce her equally innocent husband. Then she is transported 6,000 miles across Siberia to Magadan. She endures typhus, hunger, exhaustion, filth, endless work and constant fear of the brutish criminals who surround her. In the camp, she is taken under the protection of a guard, who rapes her at will. She endures, thinking of nothing apart from how Yulya might be eating, keeping clean, getting enough sleep. This life goes on for years. One day, coming back to the camp after their exhausting shift, she and her fellow convicts suddenly hear dance music, unexpectedly broadcast from a speaker outside the timber store. The women convicts are overcome by the unaccustomed music. They cannot stop weeping. While the guards yell obscenities, Masha has an epiphany. The music moves her to accept that her husband has been shot and she will never find her daughter.

> A year later Masha left the camp. Before returning to freedom, she lay for a while on some pine planks in a freezing hut. No one tried to hurry her out to work, and no one abused her. The medical orderlies placed Masha Lyubimova in a rectangular box made from boards that the timber inspectors had rejected for any other use. This was the last time anyone looked at her face. On it was a sweet, childish expression of delight and confusion, the same look as when she had stood by the timber store and listened to the merry music, first with joy and then with the realization that all hope had vanished.[5]

## PROLOGUE: 2 JUNE 1962

Anyone who wants to explore the later decades of Soviet civilization must first encounter Masha. You cannot go straight to 1953 without making the journey from 1917. However much the Soviet Union changed after 1953, Masha's fate is the inescapable truth of the country's history. And any historian – including the author of this book – who argues that a kind of normal life emerged during and after Khrushchev's Thaw must first look Masha in the eyes.

'They don't shoot people these days,' the young man said as the shooting got underway. He meant that Stalin's Terror was over. And he was right: the mass incarceration and murder of innocent citizens ended in the USSR with the death of Stalin. Yet he also meant that what was about to happen on that devastating Saturday was unthinkable. He was wrong about that.

The young man's two judgements lie at the heart of this book. By 1962, the Soviet Union had transformed over the course of the previous nine years, developing a regularized, partly rights-based relationship between citizens and the authorities, which allowed the living standards of ordinary people – their housing, pensions and working conditions – to have a new priority. And yet the Soviet Union remained a dictatorship, even a police state. By the 1970s, it could not sustain rises in the standard of living, especially in the provinces, where shortages, corruption, exhaustion and isolation sometimes predominated. This only became a crisis, though, when Mikhail Gorbachev began to reform the system radically and all at once in the late 1980s. His dramatic changes to the Soviet Union's political system, economy and diplomatic agenda lost him the support of the Party elites, who went on to form a different kind of country starting in December 1991.

Over the last three or four decades of Soviet life, following Stalin's death in 1953, a distinctive civilization emerged. ('Civilization' is here a neutral term, used in the sense that we apply it, say, to the Aztecs; the value-laden word 'civilized' and the rhetorical counterposing of 'civilization' and 'barbarism' are avoided in this book.)[6] This was a civilization in the sense of a complex, urbanized society. It was modern:[7] a consequence of the industrialization that took place on a mass scale from the late 1920s onwards. According to the American historian Stephen Kotkin, interwar Soviet modernity 'constituted a quintessentially Enlightenment utopia' whose aim, like in all modern utopias, was 'to impose a rational ordering on society' but with the addition of 'overcoming the wrenching class divisions' of a previous, capitalist era of industrialization. Kotkin wrote of 'Stalinism as a civilization' in his microhistory of the city of Magnitogorsk in the 1930s.[8] He showed how the ideology and discourses of Bolshevism, and the practices of central planning, played out in the everyday lives of Soviet citizens and in their relationship to 'power'. My book draws on this way of understanding Soviet civilization in its analysis of the *post*-Stalin period. By then, the USSR possessed a highly developed culture in the broadest sense, across the arts, sciences and everyday relationships. The Soviet Union had its own distinctive apartment buildings, consumer goods, films, rituals, hobbies, cars, curtains and underground culture. It was its own universe of political practices, 'spiritual' values and material goods. By exploring the cultures, discourses and practices of everyday life – captured by the Russian word *byt* – and their connection to politics, ideology and the arts, this book describes Soviet life on a civilizational scale.[9] It borrows from the way that Svetlana Alexievich, the Belarusian Nobel Prize-winning author, used the term in her polyphonic oral history of the end of the Soviet Union.

> Soviet civilization ... I'm rushing to make impressions of its traces, its familiar faces. I don't ask people about socialism. I want to know about love, jealousy, childhood, old age. Music, dances, hairdos. The myriad sundry details of a vanished way of life. It's the only way to chase the catastrophe into the contours of the ordinary and try to tell a story ... There are an endless number of human truths.[10]

This was a *post-Stalinist* civilization. Stalinism was the version of Marxism-Leninism that dominated Soviet life between 1928 and 1953. It always sacrificed individuals for the sake of the revolutionary goals of building socialism (before 1941), defending it against mortal threat (during the war) or reconstructing it (after 1945); it subordinated the present to the future; and it consistently used extreme violence against the population as an intrinsic element in the revolutionary project. After 1953, and especially after Khrushchev's epoch-defining Secret Speech of 1956, when he condemned Stalin and some of his policies, Soviet life became post-Stalinist and sometimes driven by de-Stalinization. The revolutionary project changed tack. Fulfilling the goals of the revolution now meant benefiting the people, not sacrificing them, though this remained a dictatorship with a secret police and a privileged elite. Building communism in the future was still the goal, but no longer was future paradise more important than the interests of people in the present – and so, by definition, state violence was dramatically dialled down. Urban life became more diverse, culture more varied and consumer goods more important. The distinctive forms that Soviet civilization took became increasingly polyvocal and physically recognizable *after* 1953, not before. One of the most striking elements in this polyvocality was the dissidents, such as Andrei Sakharov, whose mentalities emerged from within the USSR and were one more element in Soviet civilization, not something extraneous to it.[11]

Soviet civilization, as I present it in this book, was not coterminus with the Soviet state. It depended on the state but, in the last two years of the USSR, the state developed in a different direction and abandoned its animating civilization. Between 1917 and 1990, the Soviet state was attempting to put the Bolshevik Revolution into practice, and the civilization that resulted was infused with this goal. This meant that Soviet civilization had a careful ideological vision – an adapting and evolving set of interpretations of Marxism-Leninism – and a rhetorical commitment to the cause of ongoing revolution. In the late 1980s, Gorbachev's reforms increasingly hollowed Soviet civilization out; its sense of revolutionary time collapsed, and its popular legitimacy dissolved. When Gorbachev effectively abandoned Marxism-Leninism and the revolution in 1990, Soviet *civilization* came to an end. But the Soviet *state* lasted until the end of 1991. It was likely that the end of Soviet civilization in any generally understood sense made the Soviet state more vulnerable, less instinctively accepted by the population; but it was the inadvertent consequences of particular economic and political reforms initiated by Gorbachev that brought the Soviet Union to an end. In this sense the Soviet Union committed suicide by accident, a process made much quicker by the unanticipated rise of republican nationalisms inside the USSR and the improbable international context of the end of the Cold War.

The Soviet Union violently imposed its civilization on other places during the Stalin period and retained a forcible hold on these territories even after 1953 and through to 1991. During the Second World War, it annexed Estonia, Latvia, Lithuania and Moldavia (Moldova) as union republics, and incorporated parts of Poland, including Lviv, into its existing Ukrainian republic. With the onset of the Cold War, East Germany, Czechoslovakia, Hungary, Poland, Romania and Bulgaria fell within the Soviet sphere of influence, behind the Iron Curtain, and became 'people's democracies': Party dictatorships whose cultures, discourses, economic practices and structures of coercion were analogues of the Soviet model. They were not part of the Soviet Union but, as Warsaw Pact allies, they had no option but to remain fraternal republics until Gorbachev let them go in 1989. If there was any room for doubt, the crushing of the Hungarian Revolution in 1956 and the Prague Spring in 1968 showed conclusively that their Soviet-type socialism rested on coercion. Soviet civilization was also found in many parts of what was then called the 'Third World', where revolutionary socialist dictatorships sprang up from Cuba to Mozambique to North Vietnam. Immediately recognizable imprints of Soviet civilization were found in their health systems, urban form, art and institutions.[12] This book does not extend to this wider hinterland, apart from when its existence shaped experiences inside the USSR.

In 1953, Soviet borders stretched north towards the Arctic, east through Siberia, south to the Caucasus and Central Asia and westwards to Moldova and the Baltics. The new socialist federation of the Soviet Union, which was formally constituted in 1922, was unmistakably an empire, but it was also a driver of development and ethnic emancipation. But even 'liberations' had their 'orientalizing' and coercive aspects. Studying this paradox requires Soviet history to be decolonized, as scholars from different backgrounds observe the view from diverse perspectives and listen to forgotten voices on their own terms. This book seeks out this decolonized sensibility while describing the civilization that unified Soviet experiences, which means that the Russian republic and the USSR's capital receive the most attention.

Soviet civilization changed over time and was transformed after Stalin died. It was then that Soviet civilization assumed its clearest and most sustainable form. Under the collective leadership and then government of Khrushchev (1953–64), the Soviet project became post-Stalinist and even anti-Stalinist, though in renewing its commitment to Lenin and the revolution of 1917, it was by definition never 'liberal'. For the German historian Jörg Baberowski, the de-Stalinization of the Khrushchev era was so fundamental that it was 'a civilizational accomplishment'.[13] This book follows that reasoning. But this is to argue an historical, not a moral or political, point. It does not mean that the Soviet Union was a place to be envied at any point in its existence or that it was more 'civilized' than other places. Until shortly before its collapse, the government denied its citizens reliable public information, suppressed consumption, ran elements of a police state, did not submit to the rule of law, governed certain nations against their will, kept borders closed and stopped nearly all of its citizens from visiting the outside world. This book presents readers with a new picture of Soviet life and leaves them to make a judgement on it.

I make six interrelated claims about Soviet civilization before it became an empty vessel in the last two years of the Gorbachev period. They relate to periodization, revolution, decolonization, personhood, normality, and culture. Each of these categories rests on a paradox of some kind – the endless revolution, the decolonized empire – and throughout this book it will become clear that unresolved paradoxes sustained Soviet civilization rather than undermined it.

First, Soviet civilization was never static because it changed so much over time. Turning points, above all in 1953, marked out the process of evolution and transformation. Development was unpredictable and contingent, subject to sudden and deep changes. The events of 1917 contained many different possible futures, and some of them took place; the revolution lasted for more than seventy years, and on the way it created not one but several different Soviet dictatorships. At stake in this book are the remarkably different Soviet periods of the Thaw (c.1953 to c.1968), a richly suggestive term that was used at the time; 'late socialism', a historiographical shorthand for the 1960s, 1970s and 1980s (the 'long 1970s'), though here more specific labels familiar to contemporaries, such as 'developed socialism', are used instead; and *perestroika*, the term associated with the changes that followed Gorbachev's rise to power in 1985.

Second, the Soviet Union was a revolutionary civilization from beginning to end. Even though at certain points it appeared unchanging, the USSR came into being as the result of a revolutionary seizure of power; its people experienced several decades of extremely fast, unpredictable and violent change across the range of social, cultural, economic, political, family, community and personal experience; and Marxism-Leninism was the basis of policy, politics and political culture for seven decades until the year before the collapse. Soviet history can reasonably be interpreted as a sequence of attempts to complete the revolution, to carry it through to a conclusion.

Third, no group, not even the Politburo, had a monopoly on the meaning of the revolution or the definition of Sovietness. It was clear to citizens throughout the republics that the Soviet Union was an empire, but it was simultaneously unthinkable, as the anthropologist Serguei Oushakine maintains, for them to articulate that they lived in colonies.[14] (There were exceptions, especially in the Baltic.) This meant that each republic developed its own multiple ways of being Soviet. A diversity of Soviet mentalities, across provinces, in subaltern groups and in the republics, decolonized the master narratives of Sovietness in real time. Most people automatically sensed the complexity of possessing multiple and overlapping identities, though the centre sometimes acted coercively to simplify the sense of Sovietness.

The implication of this – and this is my fourth claim about Soviet civilization – was that individual persons were central to the Soviet project. Before 1953, the Soviet person consisted of human matter that could be reshaped, put to work and destroyed. For all the mass violence that this principle engendered, the exercise of remoulding took place on an individual level. The Bolsheviks built their civilization by maintaining the twin pressures of their revolution – liberation and elimination – upon each citizen. They created and destroyed on a massive scale but also one person at a time. After 1953, de-Stalinization normalized the relationship between citizens and the state by removing the threat of arbitrary arrest and death, while social policy allocated a form of rights to citizens.

This combination of factors seemed to give Soviet civilization – this is the fifth point – some measure of legitimacy after 1953. It is impossible to make this claim in quantitative terms in the absence of competitive elections. But in the decades after 1953, this legitimacy was based on a growing sense of normality in Soviet life. 'Normality' was not an international index or a value judgement, but a generally accepted range of practices, relationships, experiences and mentalities. Like in other modern societies, it was an environment in which people constantly made judgements about how to be themselves, and how to overcome the frustrations they encountered.

And sixth, this legitimacy was debated inside permitted Soviet culture, which was capacious and which developed in the tension between creator and censor, and which in turn modified reality in an engaging performance. Culture was understood in broad terms. Films, novels, songs and other items of cultural production fitted alongside 'cultured' (*kul'turnyi*) behaviour. Creating and refining civilization and civilized conduct took place across this cultural territory. Many of the people responsible for cultivating Soviet civilization in this sense were members of the intelligentsia, which itself was a large category, denoting educated people who professed a commitment to personal sincerity and, at some level, to cultural and intellectual pursuits.[15]

Together, these six categories, which are revisited throughout the book and analysed at the end, create a substantially new framework for describing and interpreting Soviet civilization. The novelty is an interpretive one, as the book rests on a synthesis of the ideas and evidence that many other historians have contributed to the growing scholarly field of post-1953 Soviet history; but it is also a substantially empirical novelty too, drawing on many years of primary research in archives and libraries in Moscow. It is precisely the extent of my research that makes me want to emphasize the nuance of the picture I present. In other words, this book presents a version of Soviet civilization that cannot be decoded as a 'system', but whose multiple, changing realities were contingent, overlapping and experienced differently. It is a history perhaps best captured in fragments arranged chronologically.¹⁶ The structure of the book therefore mirrors the structures of Soviet civilization that I want to present. It tells stories that most often relate to society and culture, and sometimes to politics and economics, but only to international events when they directly affected everyday lives. The general secretaries themselves are of course important figures, affecting Soviet civilization, shaped by Soviet civilization, and also making the decisions which provide the basic chronology on which the book rests. But the book is not a comprehensive thematic account or a high political chronicle of the later Soviet Union. Instead it is a montage of perspectives, linked together as a narrative that explores the experience of Soviet civilization.[17]

At the heart of this book is the unlikely figure of Nikita Khrushchev. Made by the revolution of 1917, he went on to reinvent it. Many possible futures were encoded into 1917. They ranged from socialist equality to massive terror. No one observed, participated in and created more of those revolutionary futures than Khrushchev, Stalin's heir and nemesis.

Khrushchev in Kyiv, 1945

# I
# Nikita Khrushchev's Revolution of Multiple Futures (1917–53)

The Soviet Union was built from the outside in. All its leaders were outsiders. Lenin was the son of a school inspector from Kazan. Stalin was a Georgian seminarian-turned-bank-thief. Khrushchev hailed from a village near Kursk. Brezhnev was born into the skilled working class of eastern Ukraine. Andropov came from very modest origins in the south of Russia. Chernenko was raised in a Siberian village. And then there was Gorbachev, a peasant boy from Stavropol Region, and nobody let him forget it.

Nikita Sergeyevich Khrushchev was the biggest outsider of all. In April 1894, he was born amid poverty in the large village of Kalinovka. This corner of Kursk province was 300 miles south of Moscow. It was deep within the Russian rural heartlands but also on the road towards the western borders of the empire. Khrushchev was an ethnic Russian. Nearby, just to the west, were many peasants who were identifying themselves more clearly as Ukrainian, as well as many town-dwelling Jews.

Khrushchev spent almost thirty years of his life in what today is Ukraine, during an extended period of which he was the boss of the Soviet Ukrainian republic. Even though he could not have conceived of it as a separate country – in the 1950s only a very small number of committed nationalists could – he possessed a deep sense of it as its own place, existing in a way that was its own. In April 1954, when he was back in Moscow and aiming for the very apex of Soviet power, Khrushchev met a group of Ukrainian writers who were visiting the capital. 'The Russian and Ukrainian peoples are the most numerous in the Soviet Union,' he told them, 'the closest in all relations. We must strengthen this friendship.'[1]

The men from the periphery who built and ran Soviet civilization came not just from the edges and provinces of 'Russia' but also from the Caucasus and Baltic regions, from Poland, and, not least, from the Ukrainian lands themselves. When Khrushchev was first appointed to the Politburo in 1939, not one of his colleagues was from Moscow or any other major city, and they had all got to their seats in the Kremlin by the unlikeliest of routes. Even from inside the Kremlin, he and his colleagues did not build Soviet civilization from the inside out, but from the outside in.

Origins, circumstances and temperament made Nikita Khrushchev an outsider. Until he was fourteen, he lived a peasant life in Kalinovka. This intimate knowledge of poverty defined Khrushchev's politics and temperament. All his life he made the case for how capitalism, empire and monarchy caused the mass of people to be held back in unhappy surroundings while a small minority trampled on them. His early life was his primary case study in Marxism-Leninism.

Khrushchev's mother carried the burden of non-stop work, inside and outside the family household, not least as a cleaner in the home of a local landowner. Her consolations were conscience, faith, commitment and responsibility. She passed them on to her son, though in forms she could never have imagined. Nikita's father, Sergei, worked seasonally in the emerging industrial centre of Yuzovka. This nearby city, in what became Ukraine, was later called Donetsk. It was named after the Welsh industrialist John Hughes, whose New Russia Company won the contract from the imperial government to develop the region in 1869. An industrial revolution was going on. In two spurts, one at the end of the nineteenth century, one after the 1905 revolution, Moscow and St Petersburg doubled in size, and other major centres, from Kyiv to Nizhny Novgorod, also grew out of all recognition. In the meantime, Nikita helped out in the fields and looked after animals. He spent no more than two years at school. His work as a shepherd disrupted even this abbreviated education.

Khrushchev was born a villager but he was a natural city-dweller. When he followed his father to Yuzovka in 1908, he too became an employee of the Uspensky mine on the edge of town. With two sets of wages, father's and son's, it was plausible to bring the female members of the family to join them. They came a few weeks later to communal barracks rooms – shared not just with their own menfolk, but with another family.

It was three years after the revolution of 1905. The government had only overcome the rebels by combining unprecedented concessions with deadly violence. On the one hand, it promised a version of constitutional government, with a parliament, or Duma, elected on a fairly wide (but only male) franchise; and, on the other, at the end of the year, it crushed the Moscow Uprising, killing more than 1,000 people in street battles. During 1905, 'soviets', or spontaneous, grass-roots councils of revolutionary democracy, emerged across the empire. The factions of the far-left Russian Social Democratic and Labour Party (RSDLP) were astonished beneficiaries. Established underground in 1898, the party split in 1903 between the Bolsheviks and Mensheviks. Both were extremists, though the Bolsheviks were more prone to violence and conspiracy. Mensheviks and Bolsheviks were elected to the Duma in 1906.

Khrushchev established himself as an apprentice fitter and became a skilled metalworker. Life in Yuzovka was tough, even brutal, but the provision of services for workers was improving.[2] For the radicals of late imperial Russia, it was disgracefully inadequate. On the outbreak of the First World War, the Bolsheviks and Mensheviks together had around 400 members in Yuzovka. Khrushchev, aged twenty, was not one of them, but he was awakening politically.

His ability to charm a room, seek out girlfriends, make more friends and entertain his expanding social network was not especially fuelled by alcohol or cigarettes – his mother's faith warned him about those vices – but by a need for company, a pleasure in personal connections, and by the extrovert's anxiety: that solitude made you vulnerable. He also craved the sense of responsibility that eluded him at work. In 1914, he married Yefrosinia, who had completed a grammar school (*gymnazium*) and came from a more confident and stable household. Khrushchev had outgrown his origins. He no longer lived in a patched-up self-built hutment in the sticks, or in shared barracks accommodation in the city, but in a respectable apartment into which he and his wife moved on their marriage in 1914. It consisted of a bedroom and a kitchen-dining room, with a wooden floor and its own vestibule.³ They had two children. Yulia was born in 1915, and Leonid in 1917.

In better times, Khrushchev's ambition for his own betterment might have extended less quickly to his desire to elevate his class as a whole. But as 1917 approached, the interests of his peers seemed opposed to those of the bosses in a zero-sum game. And revolution became an ethical commitment because of the experiences of his childhood and youth.

One unclear cause was Orthodox instruction in the village. During his two years of elementary education, he attended two schools, one of which was an Orthodox institution, and he went to church at least occasionally. More significant perhaps was the example of his mother, a committed believer. Although Bolshevism and Christianity were in some senses poles apart, they possessed common cultural elements. The Bible shaped the Bolshevik worldview, partly because of the habit it conferred of analysing, debating and accepting the value of texts, and partly because of its characters, stories and narrative shape. Like Christianity, Bolshevism was a story that went from darkness to light. Faith was tested by tribulation. Both had an eschatology: the promise of heaven or of communist utopia. Both could be fervent and millenarian. And both, too, offered a theodicy, a compelling explanation for suffering.⁴ In terms of real-world politics, believers existed in a sect that became a great international Church. Perhaps the instinctive Christian framework with which Khrushchev grew up, and which he soon dropped, made Marxism easy for him to absorb. The example of his mother worked upon him in another way, too. This was her sticking power, her refusal to give up.

During the First World War, the coal, steel and industrial products of the Donbass were essential to the imperial war effort. Much of the workforce, including Khrushchev, was not called up. More women and youths worked in the factories. The place became combustible. Khrushchev made speeches in support of his fellow-workers, especially the local miners who regularly went on strike. He even helped organize stoppages. It was a red-letter day in the Khrushchev household when they heard that the Tsar had abdicated in February 1917.⁵

*

Following Lenin's return from exile in April, the Bolsheviks' message was clarified as 'bread, peace and land', a set of promises that united workers, soldiers and peasants. Khrushchev was sympathetic to the principle though not yet a Party member. Support for the Bolsheviks swelled as 1917 went on. Yet another far-left party, the Socialist Revolutionaries (SRs), with their support in the countryside, were the most popular of all, but the Bolsheviks had the clearest message and the most inspired leadership. Where the Mensheviks were conscientious Marxists, applying theory to events, the Bolsheviks took their chances.

In the Donbass, support for the Bolsheviks (as opposed to the Mensheviks) grew more slowly than in the capital. Khrushchev was voted in by workers at the Rutchenko mine. In March 1917, he was their representative at a regional Donbass conference in Bakhmut, as one of 138 delegates who represented a total of 187,000 electors.[6] By the autumn, the Bolsheviks were winning big majorities in several Donbass centres. More open to compromise than the exclusivist Bolsheviks in Petrograd, Bolsheviks in Yuzovka entered coalition government through the executive committee of the city's Duma. But in other parts of the region, such as that covered by the Gorlovka-Shcherbinovka soviet, Bolsheviks were aggressively intolerant and obsessively pure-minded.[7] Khrushchev witnessed more political compromises than he would have seen in some other places.

On 25 October 1917, according to the old-style Julian calendar that was then still in use, the Bolsheviks grabbed power while their rivals dithered, and used violence to keep it. From the start, their rule looked in two directions: creation and destruction, liberation and imprisonment, legitimacy and coercion. In week one, they gave all the land to the peasants while forming a new secret police force, the Cheka.

It took some time for the effects to be felt in Yuzovka. At the point of the Bolshevik takeover, Party membership in the town had grown to 2,000. Over the next weeks, the Bolsheviks took over one soviet in the region after another until their core measures, including workers' supervision (*kontrol'*) of industry, were in place. In early 1918, back in Petrograd, the Bolsheviks dissolved the democratically elected Constituent Assembly even as it was being convened. Opposition was intolerable. Impurity was an infection. Coming second in the poll behind the Socialist Revolutionaries, the Bolsheviks closed the would-be parliament by force.

The German Army came to Yuzovka in April 1918 as part of the occupation of the western Russian empire that followed the Treaty of Brest-Litovsk. The treaty only temporarily denuded Bolshevik Russia of large swathes of its western lands but permanently shaped the Soviet world. It forever defined the communist anxiety about the western border. Brest-Litovsk offered a model of national independence and sovereignty that was a compelling alternative to the Russian Revolution. Suggesting self-determination in theory – and lethal nationalism in practice – it was a complement to the Treaty of Versailles.[8]

Opposition to the Bolsheviks coalesced. Some people fled for good, not least members of the nobility. Civil war began. Remnants of the Imperial Army were reshaped in the north and the south, as well as in Siberia. For Khrushchev, fear and opportunity combined. With many other refugees, he left the region in 1918, escaping from Cossack forces as well as imminent German occupation. Now a Bolshevik, he was drafted into the Reds' Ninth Army. He saw some military action, and served in a construction battalion. Everything about his experience was political: not just ideological polarization and politicized bloodletting, but also the worlds and people he encountered, from barracks to mansions, and peasants to the high intelligentsia. He was secretary of the Party cell in his military unit. He saw Nikolai Bukharin, author of the *ABC of Communism*, and from 1924 a member of the Politburo, give a speech in 1919.[9] It was an ideological inspiration and a career example. He witnessed horrors. Trotsky had given orders for the torture of captured White officers. 'Enemy of the People' was born as a defining label for Soviet experience.[10] Khrushchev was brutalized, and he pushed back against his own brutalization.

Meanwhile, the Red Army faced a 'Green Army' as well as a White one, thanks to a peasant rising in Tambov. Over the decades, the Bolsheviks never really understood the peasantry and did much to destroy it. In 1920, the Reds enjoyed favourable geography. They worked out how to transport materials and resources. Their propaganda was positive and accessible. Lenin was a tireless centralizer with a grip on every aspect of governance. Trotsky designed and ran the Red Army.

## NIKITA KHRUSHCHEV'S REVOLUTION OF MULTIPLE FUTURES

By 1920, the Whites could not avoid defeat. Red victory illuminated a mosaic of nations and ethnicities which complicated the idea of a united revolution – or a united opposition. 800,000 people died directly because of the Civil War, while indirect victims, including from famine, brought the total to as many as ten million.

The socialist dictatorship was now secure, but this was an uneasy basis on which to build a new civilization. Victory came at a terrible cost. The ends justified the means. It became a familiar message. Breaking eggs to make an omelette, chips flying when you cut wood – it was the ultimate revolutionary ethic, in time almost the definition of Stalinism.

Yefrosinia was dead. Fleeing Yuzovka in 1918, Khrushchev had brought his wife and children to his home village of Kalinovka. It was much safer there and wasn't very far from his own unit. But while Khrushchev survived military service, his wife succumbed to typhus. It left him shocked and 'greatly saddened', a single father of two small children.

In March 1921, Khrushchev was about to turn twenty-seven. The Civil War was over. No one knew what would happen next. Since October 1917, the revolution had been neither a coherent nor a predictable thing. It was a force of nature, of history, not a force of logic. From the start, the revolution contained multiple possible futures, only some of which came to pass, and then only in a sequence determined by contingency. When leading Bolsheviks from across the country gathered at the time of their victory, at the Tenth Party Congress of March 1921, they had two items on the agenda. One: to set the people free. Two: to incarcerate them.

The New Economic Policy (NEP), introduced at the Congress, facilitated the liberations of the 1920s. War Communism, the previous Bolshevik economic policy, had been a catastrophe; lacking management, investment and expertise, all branches of economic life had failed. The NEP, by contrast, promised a mixed approach to economic development, with private trade coexisting with a vast state. But the Congress also coincided with the tragedy of Kronstadt.

If Petrograd was the heart of the Bolshevik revolution, Kronstadt was its conscience. Kronstadt had been a naval base since just after

Peter the Great founded St Petersburg. From early 1917, its sailors were among the most radical socialists in Russia. In September 1917, they founded a Military Revolutionary Committee. The base became a vital redoubt during the Civil War. But on 27 February 1921, sailors at Kronstadt rose up against the Bolsheviks. They joined the protests that were taking place in major cities. Demonstrators in all these places were calling for an end to Bolshevik 'dictatorship'. They insisted that the Bolsheviks were selling out the cause of socialism. But a riot in a distant outpost was one thing; the sailors of Kronstadt were another. On 7 March, Trotsky coordinated Red Army attacks on the Kronstadt base.

The following day, Lenin opened the Bolsheviks' Tenth Party Congress in Moscow. Meeting in power and in peace, it was the Party gathering that defined Soviet 'democracy'. While the Kronstadt rising was being crushed by force, the Workers' Opposition was outmanoeuvred in debate. The Congress voted in favour of a ban on factions. Lenin carried the idea of democratic centralism to its logical conclusion. There could be disagreement and debate, but decisions were always final. Formal groups that adopted specific ideological stances were outlawed.

Khrushchev was demobilized from the Red Army into the world of the NEP. For some, it was a roaring twenties of cabarets, nightclubs and avant-garde poets. Quick divorces and abortion were legalized. In the Donbass, to which he returned, Khrushchev encountered the travelling traders – the 'bagmen' – who oiled the wheels of the economy. Retaining his connections to village life, he could see close-up the attempts of policymakers to solve the 'scissors crisis', by bringing into alignment supply and demand across the rural and urban sectors. Unemployment was permitted. Broadly speaking, the economy had recovered to pre-1914 levels by 1926, but the outlook was unstable and prone to crisis.

Some people, often students or young workers, lived in experimental communes, sharing a 'common pot' and idealizing the possibilities of revolutionary communism.[11] The 'former people' who had benefited most from imperial rule lived at the rough end of property expropriation, affirmative action, psychological crisis and sometimes arrest.[12]

Since 1917, the authorities had resettled people in apartments vacated by the previously privileged, or in which the original occupant had retreated to a single room. This was the start of the communal apartment, or *kommunalka*. Each family had its own room but shared everything else: the bathroom, kitchen, hallway and front door, with its worn panels and multiple bells. The several stoves in the kitchen; the food stored in one's own room; the artfully stacked furniture, piled books and hung curtains that created niches for family members and deadened noise; even the toilet seats hanging on the lavatory wall, one per family: it all spoke of carving out private territory wherever possible. Evidence suggests, too, that *kommunalkas* resulted from lack of government investment in housing rather than a deliberate attempt to remake the Soviet person. Whenever resources allowed, from the 1920s to the 1980s, housing blocks were built with separate family apartments.

In 1922, the Soviet Union itself came into existence as the USSR, or Union of Soviet Socialist Republics. It was the successor state of the Russian empire, but it was also something brand new: a communist federation of several republics, in the first instance Russian, Transcaucasian, Ukrainian and Belorusian (Central Asia emerged from the shadow of Russia to become its own Soviet republic of Turkestan within a couple of years, while Armenians, Georgians and their neighbours remained unified administratively for now within 'Transcaucasia'). In line with Lenin's wishes, the format of the union was less Russia-focused and 'chauvinistic', and offered more decentralized national rights, than Stalin – the Commissar of Nationalities – had sought.

As the USSR was coming into being, Khrushchev was restarting his career. He enrolled in a workers' college, or *rabfak*, and continued to study in his spare time for the next three years. He also began work for the Soviet administration in Yuzovka. Across the urban centres of the Soviet Union, young men and women with proletarian backgrounds were given disproportionately favourable access to higher education. Completing the autobiographical sections of application forms, candidates saw that the route to success in the workers' state was to define oneself and one's heritage as working class. They moulded their identities accordingly.[13]

Meanwhile, the government promised to electrify the whole country. It also vowed to eliminate illiteracy. Grass-roots cultural programmes, such as that sponsored by the 'Proletkult', and funded by the Commissariat of Enlightenment, encouraged workers and peasants to write, paint and act. The same 'affirmative action' imperative guided nationalities policy, with the aim of making non-Russian national identities across the USSR stronger and the life chances of national minorities better, on the principle that peoples had to become national before they could achieve communism. Education, publishing and government all discriminated in favour of non-Russian languages. The personnel of local administrations became increasingly dominated by members of national groups, though these formed their own local hierarchies. Identity coalesced in places such as Ukraine, while new forms of national identity were created in such territories as Kazakhstan.[14] The programme was called *korenizatsiia*, or indigenization.

Lenin was confined to a house just outside Moscow following a stroke in 1922. He died two years later. Even during this period of serious illness, his influence was profound, and his legacy, for nearly seventy years, even more so. All Soviet politicians said they were Leninists.

Politics attracts observers, enthusiasts, activists, cynics, careerists, visionaries and people who change the world. Khrushchev was all of these in turn.

He was a true politico. He thirsted after politics. The thrill of politics went to his head, kept him up late and got him up early. In April 1925, he was part of the Yuzovka delegation to the Fourteenth Party Conference in Moscow. This was a major event, which gave him a ringside seat on Kremlin politics. Stalin was already the one that everybody wanted to see. 'I would get up early and go by foot to the Kremlin,' Khrushchev said in his memoirs, 'to get there earlier than the other delegates and get a decent place.'[15]

The drama of choice still ran through Soviet politics. Before 1927, Stalin still had to win arguments and make a substantive case in Party meetings. The preliminary debate permitted by 'democratic centralism' still existed. It was the same from the top to the bottom of Soviet politics. Khrushchev was in the Yuzovka delegation because he had been elected, shunting aside the favourite, Konstantin Moiseyenko. In the 1920s, there was a democratic aura around Stalin himself. Khrushchev later told the story of how Stalin came over to join the Yuzovka delegation for a team photo during the conference. Stalin insisted that the photographer was in charge of proceedings; he himself was following orders while the frame was being composed. According to Khrushchev, at that moment, though they later changed their minds, 'it seemed to us that Stalin really was a democratic person.'[16]

In April 1922, Stalin had become Party general secretary, with an office in Old Square. Late at night, after a day of meetings, decisions and paperwork, Stalin and his deputy Molotov would walk back to the Kremlin, where they both had apartments. During the long working day, Stalin's personal charisma softened up the comrades he met in meetings. Stalin sat on the Politburo, the Orgburo and the Secretariat, the three senior branches of Party and government administration. One meeting extended into another. He mastered politics as the management of cadres, remembering people's names and the details of their lives, knowing when to slap someone's back or look someone else in the eye.

Khrushchev returned to Moscow in December 1925 for the Fourteenth Party Congress, a bigger and more formal event than the recent ad hoc conference, with more than 1,300 delegates charged with greater decision-making powers. Stalin used the occasion to out-manoeuvre Grigory Zinoviev, Lev Kamenev and their supporters, especially those from Leningrad. Trotsky was exiled in 1928. They were all later killed.

Stalin's mastery of Soviet politics was multi-dimensional and derived from several causes – ideological, political, personal – and was always conditioned by chance. He was a true believer in communism. A ruthless set of ethics laced through his ideological, policy and career commitments. Launching the USSR towards communism required terror. The ends justified the means. Lacking the cosmopolitan and multilingual intellectualism of Lenin and Trotsky, he was nevertheless sharply intelligent, with a sense for both practical problems and intellectual abstracts. When it came to analysing revolutionary texts and finding the right justifications from Marx, he was a match for most.[17] And when it came to navigating and using bureaucracy, he was *nonpareil*. It gave him the personal capacity to undertake work of great evil. And in the 1920s he was also good company. He was a convivial leader of the team, putting his arms around his comrades, even if the squeeze was sometimes too pressing for comfort.

Lazar Kaganovich, a Jew from the Donbass and a member of the Politburo from 1930, had attended the same public meetings as Khrushchev in Yuzovka at the time of the February Revolution. Six months his senior but a lifelong revolutionary, Kaganovich observed Khrushchev's progress as a Party official in Yuzovka in the mid-1920s. In 1928, when Khrushchev rose out of the Yuzovka Party apparatus and was transferred to a more responsible post in the bigger centre of Kharkiv, it was Kaganovich who pulled the strings, and who brought him to Kyiv shortly thereafter when the Kharkiv job proved uncongenial. Patronage was central to Soviet politics from the start.

Stalin reached the leading position in Soviet politics by taking up a platform on the extreme left, one that Kaganovich respected and wanted to join. At the end of the 1920s, Stalin launched his 'great break' in Soviet life, a vast, accelerated construction of industrial modernity, apparently devised according to Marxist-Leninist principles, with paradise as the ultimate destination, and any number of victims permitted as collateral damage or even welcomed as proof of social transfiguration. It was a far-left swing away from the New Economic Policy, though Trotsky denied it had much to do with socialism. Trotsky was right that it had nothing in common with a humane socialism, but it had everything to do with the cold, modernizing imperatives which were inherent also in Trotsky's own vision of revolution. As the 1930s went on, Trotsky claimed to be witnessing from exile 'the Soviet Thermidor', whose effect was to give 'complete independence and freedom from control to a bureaucracy possessing little culture'.[18] Kaganovich and his comrades, the men in Stalin's Politburo, were Trotsky's alibi. They put his terrible Civil War crimes, which he neither admitted nor apologized for, in perspective.

Their aim was to build a true workers' state inside ten years – a place of enormous factories, new cities and unparalleled industrial production. Either that, Stalin warned, or the capitalists would invade and crush the revolution for good. The number of industrial workers approximately tripled between 1928 and 1941. A new way of life emerged in this heavily industrialized landscape. Labour was celebrated as the cardinal virtue, but only on the Party's terms. Experiments in equal wages did not last long. Instead, to incentivize production and weaken independent working-class solidarity, shock workers (*udarniki*) were venerated on honour boards and given bonuses for overfulfilling their targets. In 1935, Aleksei Stakhanov mined more coal in a single shift than anyone could plausibly imagine, no less than 102 tons, and the feat was indeed rehearsed and confected for the benefit of the media. Top-performing workers were thereafter known as Stakhanovites.[19] Their many privileges – big apartments, motorbikes – went far beyond the dreams of usual factory workers. Ordinary men and women lived in overcrowded, communal and sometimes scarcely habitable conditions.[20] They might time-share a bunk, sleep under their workbench, or extract some privacy with their family behind a hooked-up sheet in the corner of a dormitory.

Central planning lent the process a 'total' feel. The successive five-year plans began in 1928. Economists, statisticians, clerks and managers devised the plans at their desks in central Moscow. Gosplan (the State Planning Agency) gathered data from across the USSR, formulated targets and distributed resources. It looked scientific, but the mega-targets of the first five-year plan were impossible to meet, even when they were revised downwards. Their purpose was to inspire gigantic efforts and excessive visions, and serve as a hostage to fortune for the industrial managers who failed to meet them. Huge projects, such as the Turksib railway, a 1,000-kilometre line through Siberia to Central Asia, had a civilizational and frontier quality, at once revolutionary and primeval. Across the USSR, migration was chaotic. Planlessness vied with planning. The urbanization of open land took place alongside the 'ruralization of the cities'.[21] Tension between central control and its absence defined Soviet civilization.

Yet Trotsky warned that Bolshevism had given way to a 'great retreat': that Stalin betrayed the revolution again in the middle 1930s, not least for women.[22] The reality was that the revolution in women's lives never stopped, and would continue for decades to come. It just never had nearly as much to offer women as the idealists of 1917 claimed. The revolutionary equality and international feminism of the years after 1917 transformed the proletariat. By 1935, women made up 42 per cent of the industrial workforce. Yet pro-natalist policies, dating from 1936, outlawed abortion and channelled benefits to 'hero mothers' who gave birth to multiple children. Such women had little chance of working outside the home, at least for extended periods. Others did, but faced the double burden of restricted promotion chances plus shopping and housework in an economy of shortages and poverty.

In December 1929, agricultural collectivization was rolled out across the country. The aim was to increase the state's access to grain, extract capital from the countryside and push investment to industry and cities. State procurement of grain tripled between 1929 and 1935.

It was a war against the peasantry.[23] Bolsheviks rushed to the countryside to enforce their urban revolution on a recalcitrant rurality. Their task was to 'persuade' peasants to join the new collective farms. Peasants were no longer to be autonomous persons, anchored in the self-governing communes that had lasted for centuries. The communes had sought to guarantee subsistence and protect their members through a network of mutual responsibility while offering the consolations of tradition and place, though they were also patriarchies that were often brutal. Instead, peasants became *kolkhozniki*: workers in large, hierarchically managed farms that impoverished and alienated them. They were answerable to a collective farm chairman who managed them with an iron fist.

Many peasants resisted, aggressively or passively, hiding their grain and refusing to cooperate. They risked losing a season's food. Those peasants who were least enthusiastic about collectivization, or protested about it too much, or were slightly more prosperous or energetic than their peers, were labelled 'kulaks', after the Russian word for (grasping) fist. 'Dekulakization' was the forcible removal of these people and their families from the communities in which they lived. 'Either we destroy the kulaks as a class,' Kaganovich said, 'or the kulaks will ... liquidate the dictatorship of the proletariat.'[24] This zero-sum tension between creation and destruction was the signature of Soviet civilization in the Stalin era: economic transformation and political violence were the inseparable imperatives of the ongoing revolution.

'Kulaks' were moved to 'special settlements', which could be thousands of miles away from their lost homes. They might be abandoned in the middle of nowhere and required to set up a makeshift township.[25] Or they might be sent direct to the camps of the Gulag. Others were executed. Millions died prematurely. The prison camp network grew out of the Civil War, but it dramatically expanded under Stalin's rule. In 1926, 7,547 people were sentenced to time in a camp or a prison for political crimes; in 1930, 114,443 were; and in 1937, 429,311.[26]

Dekulakization and the expansion of the Gulag in the early 1930s were mutually indispensable. Turning people into 'kulaks' and incarcerating them was the primary method of stocking the country's labour camps. In turn, these camps made a crucial economic contribution to industrialization. They opened up, for instance, new seams of coal, new stocks of metals or new reserves of minerals in remote and inhospitable parts of the country to which it was difficult and expensive to attract free labour.

At its most extreme, the violence led to famine in parts of the Ukrainian republic, southern RSFSR, north Caucasus and present-day Kazakhstan. In Ukraine alone, 3.9 million peasants died in the terror-famine, or *Holodomor*; a disproportionate number of them were Ukrainian rather than Russian, and Ukrainian cultural elites were separately targeted. These events were deliberately engineered. Kaganovich played a major role as a leading Politburo member; Stalin trusted him more than any other colleague. In his frequent letters to Stalin about Politburo business when the boss was away on summer holidays in Crimea, Kaganovich showed a full knowledge of policy but zero concern for the people who suffered its consequences. He was worried about something else. 'After reading my letter I see that I failed to fulfil your directive to master punctuation marks, I started to, but it didn't take, despite the workload it can be done,' he wrote in August 1931. 'I will try to have full stops and commas in future letters.'[27]

In 1930, Khrushchev petitioned Stanislav Kosior, his boss in the Ukrainian Party, to allow him to complete some extra education. 'I am already thirty-five,' he remembered saying to him. 'I want to study.'[28]

He wanted to train as a metallurgist. Kosior, himself of worker heritage, said yes. Kaganovich facilitated the transfer. Khrushchev was one of the highest-flying promotees – *vydvyzhentsy* – in the whole country, the men and women who rose out of their proletarian and peasant backgrounds, turning the world upside down, to become the professionals and politicians who ran the USSR in the biggest and quickest exercise in social mobility the world had hitherto seen.[29] He was an obvious promotee: his natural intelligence allowed him to grasp the range of policy; his workaholism and outsize amiability equipped him for the world of patron–client machine politics; his ambition allowed him to see opportunities before they arose; and his true belief in the cause was obvious to his bosses.

In the autumn of 1930, Khrushchev started at the Industrial Academy on Novo-Basmennaya Street in Moscow. He had recently remarried, to Nina Kukharchuk, although the marriage was not formally registered. In 1929, a daughter, Rada, was born in Kyiv. She was more than a dozen years adrift from her step-siblings. Khrushchev lived in Moscow by himself, while his new young family remained in Kyiv. He took lodgings in a comfortable hostel not too far from where he was studying and received a good stipend. Khrushchev's fellow students were people like himself, on a fast-forward march through the Party or trade union apparatuses, aspiring, for example, to be 'red directors' in industrial plants. Some of the students were Old Bolsheviks, taking a break from more senior positions. Khrushchev studied a range of subjects, from mathematics to Marxism-Leninism, but what he really received was a political education.

He put himself at the forefront of the Academy's Party cell, standing for election. In the middle of the first five-year plan, any dissent was seen as 'right-wing'. Those who questioned the pace of industrial development or advised caution about agricultural collectivization were pushed down in debate, and many of them perished in 1937. Elections for Party office at the Academy were scarcely routine student politics. Unlike most Soviet electoral contests, they were bitterly contested. Their winners – notably Khrushchev – were given a seat at higher Party conferences and might even have the chance to make the acquaintanceship of Stalin. The losers, eventually, suffered the ultimate punishment. In 1931, Khrushchev was promoted to second Party secretary of two of Moscow's most famous districts: Baumansky and Krasnopresnensky. The former was named after Karl Bauman, the revolutionary hero of Latvian heritage who had recently been elected to the Politburo – and who would in a few years be consumed by the Great Terror. Krasnopresnensky was the site of the desperate Moscow Uprising of December 1905.

In 1934, he was transferred to the city's central Party apparatus. After serving there as second secretary for two years, he rose to the top, appointed first secretary in 1936. The year before, he had already assumed the position of head of the Party in Moscow's greater region. He succeeded Kaganovich. The combination of Moscow city and region was one of the top appointments across all of Soviet politics. In 1935, the new grand plan for the city of Moscow was introduced. The most 'charismatic' aspect of the plan was the Moscow Metro. It was a transformational blueprint that shaped Soviet urban space for a generation – and Khrushchev was in charge of it. Three of his passions – for politics, Marxism and construction – intertwined, allowing him to make a mark on the ultimate socialist metropolis.

At the newly convened Union of Writers, in 1934, the country's culture boss, Andrei Zhdanov, announced the Soviet Union's new cultural order: socialist realism. Zhdanov tasked writers, directors and other cultural producers with creating accessible works, in direct contrast to the confusing 'formalism' of modernism and the avant-garde. The aim was to represent 'reality in its revolutionary development'. An apparently realistic image on screen or canvas – a peasant table groaning under a village banquet – did not show something that really existed, but something that was being constructed, or should exist in the future, thanks to the revolution. It was an immersive aesthetic, incorporating the viewer or reader through familiarity, accessibility, layout or staging; in painting, the colour red and Soviet iconography were ubiquitous. Readers encountered characters who were tested by betrayal or doubt, moving from darkness to light, acknowledging their failures and learning from their mistakes. Novels such as *Time, Forward!* by Valentin Kataev or *How the Steel was Tempered* by Nikolai Ostrovsky contained unvarnished prose, exciting plots and recognizable characters. Celebrating workers like themselves, the films and books of the 1930s were popular among the newly literate working class.

Socialism realism was both a distraction and a source of hope. Workers' conditions were unimaginably harsh. Stories, paintings and films had little in common with real life. But that was the point. In the Stalin era, Soviet civilization told its stories about the future, not about the truth.

Meanwhile, far from the rough, poor life of so many of their countrymen, the Khrushchev family moved into apartment number 206 in the new House of Government in Moscow.[30] Built on marshy ground across the river from the Kremlin during the first five-year plan, this landmark complex contained 505 large flats and the full range of amenities, from a theatre to a post office and a hairdresser's. Khrushchev's apartment was a five-room dwelling. His neighbours were generals and commissars, top managers and officials – men like himself – as well as leading cultural figures and record-busting Stakhanovite workers. They were elite figures, a boss class.

One by one they disappeared during the Great Terror.

Until the 1950s, conspiracy laced through the Bolshevik worldview. Imagined webs of domestic and international conspiracy; tendencies to extreme suspiciousness; worries about the weakness of a state that was actually firmly in control: these were the frameworks in which Stalin ordered the Great Terror. Atrocities 'cleansed' or 'purged' the top levels of Party and government. The senior ranks of the army were also cleared out. Industrial managers who were not keeping up with the plan were destroyed. 'Sabotage' was everywhere. Denunciations followed. Ordinary people were caught up in the cycles of suspicion, condemnation and fear. The Great Terror was an overlapping sequence of atrocities that were not necessarily connected with each other. Decrees also targeted national groups, such as Poles. In some cases, ordinary policemen had instructions to sweep people off the streets. The security services were given arrest quotas.

Between late 1936 and 1938, about 692,000 innocent people were arrested and shot dead. Many of them were convicted under article 58 of the criminal code, a catch-all clause for counter-revolutionary, political crimes. Stalin personally started and stopped the Terror. But systemic, ideological and personal guilt were also dispersed more

## NIKITA KHRUSHCHEV'S REVOLUTION OF MULTIPLE FUTURES

widely. Top of the list were the men and women of the NKVD. Much of the Great Terror was headed by Nikolai Yezhov. These events were known as '1937' or 'the repressions' or the Yezhovshchina (using a suffix that can mean 'reign of terror').

Khrushchev had his own share of responsibility. As chair of Party and government in Moscow city and region, he headed an office where lists of potential arrests were drawn up. At Yezhov's express request, Khrushchev's office contributed lists with thousands of names. 'By eliminating one, two or ten, we are doing the work of millions,' Khrushchev said at a Moscow Party plenum in August 1937. 'Therefore we must not hesitate. We must step over the corpses of the enemy for the good of the people.' Killing one enemy, he argued, saved thousands of lives.[31] Khrushchev was a true believer in the revolution. It is likely that he really did think that the revolution was under siege from enemies, even if he was alarmed and sometimes overwrought about the terrible fate of obviously decent comrades. Khrushchev retained some commitment to Party democracy in the 1930s, and saw the damage that the Terror was inflicting on the Party; yet it was precisely the vision of revolutionary democracy – the triumph of the people who shouted loudest, the whipping up of a crowd to transcend the individual moral sense of each person within it, the hostility towards the minority – that made possible the mass nature of the Terror, with the participation of many people. The revolution had many futures within it, but there was a straight line between the democracy of terror in 1917 and 1937.

Nikita Khrushchev said that his overall knowledge of the Terror was limited at the time, even though he joined the Politburo shortly after, in 1939.[32] But he was a significant participant in the episodes of the Terror that he encountered. He admitted it, even faced up to it. In 1937, the revolution was the source of Soviet civilization's unlimited sins; nineteen years later, the revolution was the route towards partial redemption. Khrushchev was a true revolutionary: he wanted to be redeemed, but he was a guilty man.

Khrushchev had been transferred to Ukraine in 1938 as first secretary of the republic. On the Saturday evening of 21 June 1941, Khrushchev was in his house in Kyiv. At some point between ten and eleven o'clock, the phone rang. It was the staff of the city's military district. A document had come from Moscow. The first secretary was urgently needed in the offices of the Ukrainian republic's Central Committee. Khrushchev travelled the short distance and began the first of many top-pressure wartime nights, when personal survival and the revolution itself were at stake. In the early morning of Sunday, 22 June, the Germans invaded the Soviet Union with unimaginable force. As Khrushchev paced around, he knew that the front line was perilously close, that he himself was in the enemy's sights, and that Soviet civilization might be a few weeks at best from total annihilation.

The Wehrmacht pummelled its way across the north and south of Khrushchev's Ukraine, encircling four Soviet armies in the area around Kyiv. Unable to retreat because of Stalin's orders, the soldiers were destroyed. Some civilians (not least the families of officers who were stationed in advanced areas) raced to safety. The roads were full. That motif of Soviet civilization – mobility – was ever present. Khrushchev and the generals – future household names like Zhukov and Konev – were ordered to return to Kyiv. Khrushchev's wife, young children and other relatives were evacuated to Moscow, and then to Kuibyshev, together with many other officials and their families. Khrushchev did not see them for the next two-and-a-half years. His older son, Leonid, was a pilot who was injured during that summer's fighting. He was killed in operations in 1943. There was no respite: his widow Lyuba was arrested (by her own side) and sent to a camp.

Kyiv fell on 19 September. Khrushchev ignored Stalin's orders and allowed his command to be evacuated from the city. The transgression caused trouble for him, but he was not arrested. For Moscow, Ukraine was a devastating loss. But if Barbarossa was to be a success, every day counted in the summer and autumn of 1941, and the fighting at Kyiv held up the Wehrmacht. For ten weeks, between 5 August and 16 October, Odesa was fought over at abominable costs to local people and Soviet soldiers, but it diverted much of the Germans' Army Group South away from other targets. Still, within weeks, by the middle of October, Army Group Centre was at the gates of Moscow. It seemed that the capital was there for the taking. Stalin himself was still in the Kremlin. Could the Russian Revolution withstand the loss of Moscow? Kyiv had already gone and Leningrad was in mortal peril.

The city held on. But in the spring of 1942, the Wehrmacht renewed its drive through the Soviet Union, defeating the Red Army at Kharkiv in May and dismembering the last Soviet redoubt in Crimea – Sevastopol – in July. The Germans unleashed a new hell on the road south. Khrushchev saw it all as a military commissar – the top political official serving in an army group at the front – and never recovered. Voroshilovgrad (Luhansk) was captured on 19 July, Rostov the following week. Krasnodar fell in August. The north Caucasus was in reach. But by then the Germans were already attacking Stalingrad. Between September and November, the battle raged inside the city itself. From 19 November, Soviet forces launched an offensive whose aim was to encircle and strangle the enemy. On 2 February 1943, the exhausted remnants of the German Sixth Army and its Romanian allies surrendered inside the Stalingrad cauldron. Khrushchev was there. As commissar, he was the political counterpart to the commander of the south-western front, General Yeryomenko.[33]

After this, it was possible to imagine the route to Berlin. The long journey there saved Soviet civilization and required the crossing of many moral boundaries.

The first of these, the Nazi–Soviet Pact, had pre-dated the war itself. Many Soviet people, committed to socialism, were aghast that their government had come to terms with fascists. The openly published sections of the pact could be explained as a way of preserving peace, protecting Soviet borders and therefore defending the revolution. Britain, France and the USSR had failed to form an anti-Nazi alliance in summer 1939; by counterintuitively making terms with its greatest enemy, the Soviet Union seemed temporarily to head off the threat from the West. The pact's *secret* clauses, which permitted annexations of neighbouring territory, posed a much bigger moral problem, though. Ever since the early 1920s, the Soviet government had foregone its commitment to world revolution in favour of building 'socialism in one country'. This strategy remained integral to Soviet civilization thereafter, though in 1939 (and again in 1945), the USSR took advantage of events to occupy a western buffer zone and impose its lethal variant of socialism on the local population. On 17 September, sixteen days after the Nazi invasion and in line with the pact, the Soviets invaded Poland from the east, occupying and incorporating the eastern part of the country, as well as the Baltic states and Bessarabia. They attacked Finland a few months later. Occupation and Sovietization were extremely brutal. The massacre at Katyn, where almost 22,000 Poles were murdered in the spring of 1940, became globally famous, but it was not exceptional. Large numbers of potential 'enemies' were deported from these territories to Siberia, where they were imprisoned in camps or restricted in special settlements and in many cases died.

Among them at least 157,000 Polish Jews – but possibly as many as 375,000, as the data are difficult to reassemble – were deported into the Soviet interior between 1939 and 1941. This meant that they found themselves deep inside the USSR rather than in Nazi-occupied Poland after Operation Barbarossa. It was emblematic of Soviet civilization's particular antisemitism. A terrible haven resulted. They avoided the Holocaust, but they endured appalling working and living conditions. Some of them were allowed to join Allied armies fighting in Italy in 1943, and eventually to make lives in Israel. Some continued to live in the USSR as Soviet citizens, while others returned to Poland after the end of the war.[34]

Another uncomfortable moral truth of the war was the violence that the Soviet government used against its population. In 1941–2, 95,000 people were convicted under the counter-revolutionary statute of the criminal code. In the last quarter of 1941, 41.5 per cent of these convictions resulted in execution: the peak number during the war.[35] A decree of 26 December 1941 made civilian labour subject to some of the same regulations as military service. Unauthorized absence from work was equated with desertion. Yet Procuracy offices only passed on half of cases to the courts, which pursued cases with variable severity, dropping many or only giving suspended sentences. In other words, wartime labour regulation was extremely coercive, but corrections were built into it, including purposeful inefficiencies and deliberate turning of blind eyes by administrators. They blunted its worst effects and allowed the economy to function.[36]

Evacuating civilians and industrial plant away from the danger zones was predicated upon a similar paradox, of simultaneously tightening and loosening control, of deploying coercion and permitting autonomy. As many as 16.5 million evacuees set off between the invasion and the autumn of 1942, travelling from eight of the republics to sites much deeper in the interior. The classic destination was Tashkent.[37] Nearly all had very tough experiences, but some remembered it as the freest period of their lives. Amid the migrations of tens of millions were also deportations. As many as 1.2 million members of suspect national groups, often located in the western borderlands, fell under suspicion and were forcibly removed wholesale in a sequence of operations between 1941 and 1944. These included 89,000 Finns, moved from the far north-west, near Leningrad, to Kazakhstan; 183,155 Crimean Tatars, moved from the peninsula to the region near Arkhangelsk; and 496,460 Chechens and Ingush, transported from their north Caucasus homelands to Central Asia.[38]

Occupation posed its own moral problems. People living under German rule had to work out how to survive. Old tropes like 'collaboration or resistance' do little to explain the complex, high-risk judgements that people made on a daily basis.[39] In treason trials after the war, the authorities responded with a blend of retributive justice and pragmatic accommodation, as communities continued to live under the clouds of their wartime experiences.[40]

Soviet civilization seemed especially fragile in villages from which the Red Army had retreated but through which the Wehrmacht had not yet advanced. They were in a period of *bezvlastiye*, 'the time without authority', or 'non-control'. Research on Ryazan district, which had no government in November and December 1941, shows that peasants and the inhabitants of small towns quickly made pragmatic judgements, taking what they could from state enterprises and cutting themselves off from state institutions. In the absence of the NKVD and other forms of coercion, the inner sense of Sovietness, to the extent that it had existed, began quickly to dissolve. The Red Army was back within a few weeks, and a process of re-Sovietization had to take place. In 1941, in a provincial, rural part of the country, only 200 kilometres from Moscow and almost completely Russian in ethnic terms, Soviet civilization turned out to have conspicuously shallow roots.[41]

Among soldiers, desertion was a comparable moral decision which exposed how much Soviet civilization had really penetrated a serviceman's mentality. A decree of August 1941 equated surrender or capture with treachery, and another, of July 1942, criminalized retreat. And if the Germans did take them, Soviet soldiers faced the worst of conditions in Nazi prisoner of war camps. Even so, significant numbers of them accepted all these risks and surrendered to the Germans. Very often they were trapped in the colossal battles, fluid fronts and rapid manoeuvres of 1941 and had no choice. In total, of the 34.5 million who at one time or another enlisted during the war, 5.8 million were captured. Of these, between 117,000 and 251,000 gave themselves up deliberately, crossing the lines as deserters. Some of them went on to fight against their country in volunteer units made up of Soviet citizens. The most famous of these was commanded by General Vlasov. A further 1.5 million drifted away when they had the chance, hiding, becoming refugees, changing identities or making money inside the USSR in the second economy. All of these numbers were high by international comparison. Some deserters were unmistakable adversaries of the Stalinist turn in Soviet life. Unsurprisingly, large numbers came from national minorities in the western borderlands, but many were ethnically Russian; there were intellectual foes of Stalinism, but also very many proletarians and peasants.[42]

On 20 April 1945, Hitler's last birthday, Vasily Grossman was heading west. The war correspondent was still embedded with the Red Army. He had seen every shade of horror. Soon he would witness the deaths in battle, just hours before the end of the war, of men who had fought their way from Stalingrad to Berlin. Within four years, he turned his experience into high art. In 1948, Grossman completed his epic novel *For a Just Cause* (*Za pravoe delo*, though he preferred the title *Stalingrad*). It is a sweeping narrative of the Soviet Union at war that focuses on the looming battle of Stalingrad. Its equally long sequel, *Life and Fate*, is more famous. The two books had much in common, but contained aesthetic differences: the first, which was published in part at the end of the Stalin period, had a loose claim to socialist realism, while the second, which was only published during *perestroika*, did not.

In his dispatches from the front line during the war, Grossman did not hesitate to say what he believed: the Germans were monsters who deserved to be destroyed. His mother had lived in Ukraine, had existed under German occupation and then been murdered in the Holocaust.

But Grossman saw a moral equivalence, even a family resemblance, between the violent acts of the Nazis and the Bolsheviks. The Nazis mostly killed outside German borders, while the Bolsheviks targeted their own citizens. Between 12 and 14 million civilians were killed under Nazi occupation during the war (including Jews), while 500,000 to 600,000 Germans were killed by their own policemen during the period of the Third Reich. In the Soviet Union, across the twenty-five years of the Stalin era, between 1 and 1.2 million people were executed, of whom 692,000 met their fate during the Great Terror of 1936–8. Deportation accounted for 1.5 million deaths. Around 1.6 million people died in the Gulag (out of 17 million who were at one time or another incarcerated, 3 million were 'political' rather than criminal convicts).[43] In the famines of 1932–3, which were a direct consequence of collectivization, as many as 3.9 million people died in Ukraine, 2 million in Kazakhstan, and more than a million inside the Russian republic. Soviet rule was negligent as well as outright destructive of human life. For example, the avoidable famine of 1946–7 that struck Russian, Ukrainian and Moldavian (Moldovan) territory directly caused at least a million deaths from hunger and perhaps as many more from indirect impacts, such as disease.

There is a *prima facie* case that Nazi Germany and the Stalin-era Soviet Union were united by a common totalitarianism of comparable brutality. In *Life and Fate*, Grossman describes the interrogation of Mikhail Mostovskoi, an Old Bolshevik, inside a German concentration camp in the middle of the war. His interrogator is Liss, an SS officer, who acts as a provocateur, but whose words force Mostovskoi, the passionate Marxist, to reflect on the apparent mutual dependence between the two dictatorships.

> Two poles of one magnet! Of course! If that wasn't the case, then this terrible war wouldn't be happening. We're your deadly enemies. Yes, yes... But our victory will be your victory. Do you understand? And if you should conquer, then we shall perish only to live in your victory. It's paradoxical: through losing the war we shall win the war – and continue our development in a different form.[44]

Yet while the aerial view of recent history that Grossman was composing in his novels was bold and clear, his description of life on the ground was messy and layered. Grossman admired the Soviet men and women who had fought and suffered in the war. He could see these people's individuality, and also the different characters of the small collectives to which they belonged. The way that people related to their country and their nation – to the USSR, Russia, Ukraine – and also to the revolution was strikingly varied. This was not a totalitarian quality. It was quite different from the way that he described the lives and mental worlds of Nazis.

For Grossman, the moral complexity of the Russian Revolution and its legacy was as true as the moral equivalence between Stalinism and Nazism. Grossman recognized that the war had been worth fighting and the terrible sacrifice of defeating the Nazis had been worthwhile. Jews suffered during the Great Terror not directly because of their Jewishness, but because so many of them had risen to positions where they became targets. During the Second World War, as many as two million Soviet Jews were killed because they were Jews – but they died at the hands of the Nazis, and others survived because they were transported to the Soviet Union. The moral differences between Stalinism and Nazism were difficult to draw – after all, every life and death has the same value – but the analytical distinctions were more obvious. Stalinism was the maximally coercive variant of the Russian Revolution. This meant two things. First, Stalinism destroyed individual people with equal ferocity to Nazism. Second, Stalinism was committed to the revolutionary project. It sought to build socialism. National Socialism had aims that were only destructive; territorial expansionism was a requirement, not a bonus. The whole direction of policy and ideology was towards the killing of the Jews, the purification of the German nation and the simultaneous expansion of German territory.

Soviet civilization was unmistakably modern, but Nazism had an awkward relationship to modernity. Nazi ideologists insisted that their era marked a clean, forward break with the immediate Weimar past. German engineers and scientists continued to develop the modern technologies for which they were famous and on which Nazi rule depended. But the Nazis were not interested in progress. They looked to the deepest reaches of the past for inspiration, for the confirmation of their ethnic purity.[45] The dynamic of the Russian Revolution was in the opposite direction. Past, present and future were connected by a new and total focus on progress. Unlike Hitler's Germany, Stalin's

Soviet Union was a landscape of unimaginable newness. New cities rose up on the empty steppe; new factories were legion; a new way of writing literature was devised. The 'new Soviet man and woman' walked the streets of the new world. It was a 'new civilization'. This manic construction of the new and strong implied destruction of the old and weak. Agricultural collectivization was a civil war against old peasant ways, while breakneck industrial development sacrificed citizens in unsafe working conditions and unsanitary, overcrowded dwellings.

Modernity in the Stalinist sense was not something to be envied. But it was the paradigmatic difference with Nazism. After the death of Stalin, when the destructive aspects of Soviet forward-movement were reduced, it would become possible to see Soviet civilization as an extreme variant of Enlightenment progress. The Cold War linked the Soviet Union on a continuum not with Nazi Germany, but with the United States. America and the USSR were dramatically different in almost all ways. But they were united by a sense, in theory at least, that they were carrying half the world with them on a progressive trajectory towards the future.

At the end of 1943, Khrushchev was back in Kyiv, installed in a large house on Herzen Street, formerly the residence of a merchant in pharmaceuticals. His old house, which was also grand, had not survived the war.[46] He had decisions to make about how to reconstruct Ukrainian territory. Soon after he was back in post, he spoke at a conference on welfare for the elderly in December 1944. 'And what about the state?' he asked his audience. 'First of all, it must make things better for the people.' Prefiguring the tenor of his own social reforms of the following decade, he went on: 'The state must supply reasonable living conditions, some kind of minimum of housing space,' though he accepted that it was impossible to make progress immediately.[47] Shortly after the end of the war, he made another major speech on the social consequences of the fighting. 'Comrades,' he started, 'the issues of giving assistance to invalids of the Fatherland War, to families of servicemen, is a first-rank question, which has been put by our Party, by comrade Stalin, and by all Party and Soviet organizations.'[48] Khrushchev saw the war as an opportunity to return to the spirit of

Leninism and 1917: to improve living standards for their own sake, to lighten people's load and to open their horizons. As Khrushchev then saw it, this did not mean abandoning Stalinism, but reforming it. All the Stalinist tools of mobilization were still required. Khrushchev repeatedly talked about mobilizing postwar society to overcome the challenge of reconstruction. Just as in the 1930s and during the war, he called for 'the mobilization of all resources for the fulfilment and overfulfilment of the plan'.[49]

The Great Fatherland War changed the Soviet Union. Following victory, a new version of Stalinism emerged: 'late Stalinism'. It was another of the revolutionary futures of 1917. It was recognizably Stalinist – the ends continued to justify the means, and individuals had little value in their own right – but the government was adopting new policies to face new challenges. No longer did socialism have to be built from scratch, or defended from invasion. It had to be reconstructed.

Following a law of 23 June 1945, the Red Army began to release its wartime recruits to civilian life. A second wave followed in September and a third in March 1946. The process was generally dependent on the year of a soldier's birth; older veterans were demobilized first. In Leningrad alone, 143,003 service personnel had come home by 31 December 1945, and a total of 268,378 by July 1947. And yet Stalinist society was always mobilized, before, during and after the war. After 1945, the high tempo of life continued, thanks to the dynamic of reconstruction, the relaunch of heavy industry and the demands of the Cold War. During the late Stalinist era, demobilization and mobilization were two sides of the same coin.[50]

In the first few years after 1945, the Soviet Union faced a physical and moral crisis of mass destruction. Soviet civilization did not have clear answers to it. In Smolensk, an exemplar of fought-over territory, the housing stock in 1945 had 19 per cent of its 1940 level.[51] The Soviet authorities often claimed, not unreasonably, that the Nazis had razed 70,000 towns and villages to the ground. Exhausted urbanites hauled water from the standpipes of their apartment courtyards, waited in turn at the bath house, endured the lack of soap and struggled to protect vulnerable family members amidst food and drug shortages.[52] Life in some villages was even more apocalyptic.

Millions of people – returning veterans, homeward-bound evacuees, vagabonds and orphans – were on the move. Everything was fluid, transient and full of risk. Teenagers who were too young to have fought in the war grew up in the absence of fathers and developed sharp-edged cultures of their own.[53] The so-called *stilyagi* were tough young men with fashionable haircuts and clothes who privileged style above other virtues.

The late Stalinist agenda was to reconstruct industry and advance national security. But the population was so depleted and malnourished, scarred by bereavement and unbalanced by illness and disability that policymakers had to pay attention to living standards in order to achieve their bigger goals. This made late Stalinism different from the 1930s. More than three times as many dwellings were built per thousand population in the postwar decade than in the 1930s. In Minsk, which had been utterly destroyed during the war, the number of square metres of housing had already recovered by 1950 to its prewar extent.[54] Resources were also diverted to pensions and disability payments for injured veterans and bereaved families. Spending on healthcare increased.

As ever, Khrushchev personified the ambiguities of Soviet life. At the same time as he began to rebuild his republic, he also used great violence to solve the new problem of the Ukrainian western border, the unwilling lands around Lviv that had been incorporated from Poland during the war. The 'cleansing' of partisans and nationalists was merciless. Many were killed or arrested. He stayed in post in Kyiv until December 1949, after which he returned to Moscow to run Party and government in the city and the surrounding region (the job he had held between 1936 and 1938). These were terrifying times. In 1949, the so-called Leningrad Affair, an inflated conspiracy, blew up and led to the execution of 200 top officials the following year. There was no re-run of the Great Terror, but the mood was very tense. In the years that followed, Khrushchev spent exhausting nights socializing with fellow Politburo members at Stalin's so-called 'nearby' dacha, just to the west of Moscow. Here the taunts and humiliations and extreme suspiciousness of the boss were getting worse: it was quite different from the charismatic Stalin of the 1920s. Sometimes the gramophone came on, and Stalin made Khrushchev dance with

Molotov or Malenkov. One had to make the best of it or be ready for the worst. No one was really safe. For these men, the Gulag was a constant presence.

Its camps had made an important contribution to wartime victory. Through to the end of 1944, prisoners manufactured, for example, twenty-five million shells. It came at a deadly cost: 932,000 people died inside the camps between 1 January 1941 and 1 January 1946. Wartime Gulag enterprises, such as the Chkalov Aviation Factory, remained embedded in the western Siberian economy. The total population of the Gulag reached its highest level in 1950: just over 2.5 million. It stayed at approximately that number through to early 1953.[55] Although the number of new arrests and deaths inside the camps seemed to fall, the number of re-arrests and deaths immediately following release did not.[56] Yet the Gulag changed. The high-tempo mobilization of the wartime period could not be sustained. Production and productivity fell. Conflict within the camps rose, not least because of their more ethnically diverse composition, which was a result of deportations, republic-focused arrests, and the growing emphasis on nationality in public life.[57]

In January 1953, the radiologist Lydia Timashuk became a national figure. Her claims about the apparent misdiagnosis of Andrei Zhdanov, the Politburo member who had died of a heart attack while at a sanatorium four years earlier, suddenly resurfaced. They were splashed across *Pravda*. The news agency Tass announced on 13 January that 'the agencies of state security have uncovered a terrorist group of doctors who made it their aim to cut short the lives of active public figures of the Soviet Union by means of sabotaged medical treatment'.[58] The doctors were all Jewish. Timashuk was given the Order of Lenin for her efforts. In January and February 1953, the temperature of anti-semitism in Soviet society was unmistakably increasing. It had been rising steadily since 1946, when the director of the Jewish Theatre, Solomon Mikhoels, had been murdered in Minsk. The foundation of the State of Israel in 1948 had initially been welcomed by the USSR, but Israel's growing association with the United States caused unease in the Kremlin. When Golda Meir arrived in Moscow as Israeli ambassador later that year, her rapturous welcome in the city's synagogues escalated the personal suspicions of Stalin. Meanwhile, the wartime Jewish Anti-Fascist Committee had been broken up and some of its members put on trial. They were executed in 1952. Antisemitism in the workplace and on the street seemed newly acceptable. Fears were widespread among Jews that they stood on the threshold of a terrible future.

The Doctors' Plot exemplifies the moral awfulness that infested Soviet civilization in early 1953. In 1917, the Russian Revolution had also been a Jewish revolution. Many Jews had been active revolutionaries. As keen Bolsheviks or Mensheviks, they had a reasoned faith in Marxism and were active builders of the new world. As loyal Bolsheviks, they were promoted through the system. Late Stalinist antisemitism betrayed them. No betrayal was more acute than Molotov's for his beloved wife Polina Zhemchuzhina, a Jew who was arrested in 1948 and did not return from the camps until 1953. Molotov remained in the Politburo, as if revolutionary was a higher calling than husband. Antisemitism exemplified the late Stalinist shift in emphasis from class to nationhood as a marker of identity. A class revolution was still underway in the Soviet Union, but it had been deflected by the demands of nationality, ethnicity and religion. In certain situations, it seemed that 'nationality' trumped class as the presumed source of loyalty and privilege. Again, this seemed like a betrayal of the revolution.

Yet the moral crisis was more fundamental. Late Stalinist society was dramatically varied. It contained sub-cultures and generated dissent, some of it quietly expressed among comrades in the 'Blue Danube' bars that proliferated in these years. For a time, though, a uniting assumption was that wartime losses must not be in vain.[59] Party leaders should re-energize the revolution. The Stalinist theodicy – its doctrinal explanation for suffering – was that mass death and stunted life today were justified by the utopia that would come tomorrow: that the fruits of the revolution would grow out of the graveyard of the present generation. But that was no longer enough. It was an insult to the twenty-seven million who had perished and to the survivors who were clinging to life. Even Andrei Zhdanov recognized this. 'Things are difficult, and more difficulties lie ahead,' he said in a private conversation in mid-September 1947. 'Our people showed self-sacrifice and heroism that defies description. Now they want to live well … People want to reap the fruit of their victory, live well – have good apartments like they saw in the West [while fighting the Germans], eat well, dress well.' He went on: 'And we are duty-bound to give them all that.'[60] It was true that this was an era of new social policies, but their purpose was instrumental, to bolster the Stalinist economy and security state. Stalinism had changed, but not that much, and Zhdanov remained one of the ultimate Stalinists.

Late Stalinist society could not stitch together the threads of moral sadness and revulsion and make out of them a common desire to start the revolution again. 'We now have two classes,' commented a skilled weaver in the wake of price rises in September 1946, 'the rich and the poor.'[61] The weaver, of course, had no public audience. Zhdanov's words in September 1947 were uttered in a private conversation, not a public speech, and in any case they were hypocritical. In January 1947, Zhdanov wrote to Stalin from Sochi, where he was undergoing treatment for the serious heart condition that would kill him in 1948. 'The conditions of rest are excellent,' he pointed out; he requested a further ten days' leave in the resort.[62] Even during the Blockade of Leningrad, when he was the city's Party boss, Zhdanov had ensconced himself in the Bolshevik HQ at Smolny. While famine ravaged the city, he enjoyed pies, beef, peaches and pancakes.[63] During the years of late Stalinism, it even seemed like a hereditary ruling elite might be developing. The year after the death of Andrei Zhdanov, his son, Yuri, married Stalin's daughter, Svetlana.

Even on its own terms, let alone the norms of reasonable humanity, Soviet civilization had become corrupt and immoral. It was yet another of the many futures, across the full socialist spectrum from liberation to elimination, that were encoded into 1917. Leading voices whispered that its foundations were creaking. And then everything changed in a moment. Stalin died on 5 March 1953. One Soviet Union was replaced by another. The civilization of post-Stalinism began to emerge, building on the complex foundations of a terrible past. Khrushchev, short and fat, addicted to politics, ambitious for advancement, afraid of being liquidated, disturbed by Stalinism, committed to Leninism, was only a few steps away from the greatest office.

PART ONE

# The Dictatorship That Loves You (1953–64)

The late Stalin-era Gulag

# 2
# The Man of the People with Blood on His Hands

In the 1950s, Aleksandr U. lived in Tbilisi and worked for the Georgian Construction Trust. He and his colleagues were tasked with modernizing infrastructure in the republic of the leader's birth. When he heard the news of Stalin's death, Aleksandr U. wrote on 9 March to Kliment Voroshilov, a veteran of Stalin's inner circle. The two men were acquainted. 'This letter comes from sunny Georgia,' he wrote, 'though there is little sun here.' Amid the ritualistic phrasing – 'the most loved one of our motherland', 'the eternal Stalin' – Aleksandr U. hinted at a varied response towards the death of their leader. 'I cannot,' he went on, 'especially in these grief-filled days, come to terms with the thought that there are still people who recoil from his teachings.'[1]

It is one of the enduring clichés of Soviet history that the people of the USSR heard the news of Stalin's death and began simultaneously and ostentatiously to grieve. Mikhail Gorbachev was a law student at Moscow State University when he heard. He wrote later that 'the overwhelming majority' of his comrades were upset and fearful. Gorbachev himself set off with some friends to pay their respects. The dictator was lying in state in the Hall of Columns. Millions trod the same route. Nearby, in Trubnaya Square, dozens were killed in a crush. Gorbachev's party queued through the night and eventually got their chance to walk past the coffin.[2]

Mass grief was orchestrated across the Soviet Union in set-piece locations, big and small: crowds around the Hall of Columns and then the Mausoleum, where the embalmed Stalin was positioned next to Lenin; a head-teacher informing a group of schoolchildren at assembly; a forlorn group of workers at the entrance to their factory. Newspapers, public addresses and letters to the authorities drew on a repertoire of phrases that expressed deep sadness and gratitude. Even sceptical citizens found themselves falling for it, speaking highly of Stalin, and then bitterly regretting it. 'Very soon I would be blushing every time I recalled these sentiments of mine,' wrote none other than the distinguished physicist and soon-to-be dissident Andrei Sakharov.[3] There were all shades between true believers and total haters, but the ubiquity of Stalin in twenty-five years of Soviet iconography had an immersive effect.

Even so, many people, at least after the event, said they felt cold at the news and incredulous at the displays of grief. Some swallowed the temptation to laugh when everyone else in a hall or office was bowing their head or weeping. Pushing back against apparent unanimity seems a plausible human response. Extravagant public feeling also sublimated other emotions, especially grief for one's own losses in the Stalin era, in a sudden moment of collective release. Anxiety about what could happen next was also common; there was widespread worry at this time about war with the United States and Britain. People cry at moments of helpless despair and utter frustration. Stalin at least was the devil they knew. And there were many instances of contempt and loathing for the dead dictator, as Aleksandr U. was hinting in Tbilisi. Such feelings might be expressed in private as a shared understanding between trusted friends or a spontaneous outburst (sometimes ill judged). S. V. Vasil'ev, a railway worker in the Murmansk region, turned up at the apartment of his foreman on 6 March just as they were tuning in to the news. 'The *vozhd'* is dead,' he exclaimed, 'so now everybody will be free, the collective farms will be disbanded and the land will be given out to the people.' A. N. Tarasova, who worked in the telephone exchange at Leningrad's port, turned to a colleague during the days of mourning on 6 and 7 March and said: 'What are you crying for? Has your son died?'[4] In the Gulag, there were tears of sadness and joy alike. Celebration gave way to unrest. One prisoner spoke for many about 'the unforgettable spring of 1953!'[5]

Unlimited grief for a person who had no idea of one's existence tilted quickly towards hysteria. 'I very, very much, from all my soul, want to know something about the family of comrade Stalin,' wrote a schoolteacher to the authorities, in a sentiment of celebrity-obsession rather than communist revolutionism.[6] Others made use of the moment, deploying its discourse to seek redress for loss. On 11 March, a woman wrote in to describe her thirteen-year-old son, sentenced to three years for petty theft, and suggested that now was the time for a general amnesty for those aged twelve to sixteen, in honour of Stalin's love for children, and in line with the Party's care for the next generation.[7]

The story of Stalin's death has been told many times. He collapsed on 1 March, following a late night of work and socializing with members of the Presidium at his 'nearby dacha', just outside Moscow. When he didn't emerge from his room the next day, his guards tarried. They did not enter until they had the highest authorization to do so. During the days that followed his stroke, news gradually filtered out, and members of the Presidium jostled for position. Beria, Malenkov and Molotov were the most likely successors.

Following Stalin's death on 5 March, Lavrenty Beria seized the political initiative. A fellow Georgian, he had been Stalin's security chief for nearly fifteen years. Not only did he know where all the bodies were buried – so much so that all his political rivals were uneasy around him – but he had a strategic vision for the future of the USSR and a willingness to achieve it by pursuing radical reforms partly akin to 'de-Stalinization'. Mass amnesties led to a halving of the population of the Gulag within weeks, though it was criminals who were released; 'politicals', for the most part, continued to languish behind the wire. Beria was curious about the reunification of a completely demilitarized and neutral Germany. The fiction of the Doctors' Plot dissolved overnight; the 'plotters' were freed. Soviet culture began to diversify.

Beria was the worst of men. For years, he had run an industrialized machine for the incarceration and humiliation of innocent persons. In his spare time, he abused young women. One of his many hunting grounds was the company of the Bolshoi Theatre. Among his victims was the singer Nina Nelina, who soon became the wife of the novelist Yuri Trifonov. The daughter of Trifonov and Nelina described the devastating repercussions that this caused for their family over many years.[8] And Nina was just a quick encounter on an endless list, soon forgotten by the rapist-in-chief.

He was also an enforcer-manager with a unique understanding of the interlocking practices and institutions that made up Soviet rule, a boss who was capable of designing and pursuing complex policies. In early 1953, the aim of these policies was to stabilize the dictatorship and to project his own position within it. He failed. Molotov was no rival: his star quickly fell. But Malenkov, head of the government, and Khrushchev, head of the Party, became politically stronger in the summer of 1953. Their agendas for reform were not dissimilar, and they shared a sense of the danger that Beria posed. They plotted to disarm him. It was not easy. Beria oversaw the country's security officers. His ears were everywhere. On June 26, on an afternoon of the highest drama, agents loyal to the plotters entered the Kremlin room in which the Presidium was meeting, while friendly troops moved towards Red Square. Beria was the most powerful and dangerous man in the communist world. The hard men of the Presidium, who had lived through the Terror, signing the death warrants and waiting for the meat grinder to take its turn on them, were shaking. Not quite seeing the depth of his predicament, Beria allowed himself to be ushered away. He was executed by firing squad in December. It was the last political killing of its type in Soviet history, an epilogue to Stalinism.

Beria had wanted to eliminate Stalinism from the surface of Soviet life. His aim in cutting the Gulag back was to keep the Soviet Union going, even relaunch it, and precisely not to acknowledge the irreducible value of individual people. Keeping the most innocent incarcerated – leaving the Article 58ers inside – left the Stalinist core of the system intact. Beria's power ensured a Stalinist sensibility at the top of politics. By definition, though, shrinking the Gulag began the process of de-Stalinization. It would have been impossible while Stalin was alive. Mass incarceration was the keystone of Stalinism. The Gulag and collectivization were inextricably linked; the contribution of the Gulag to the wartime economy was immense; and the Gulag was at its maximum size between 1950 and 1953 – 2.5 million at its peak – with no obvious signs of becoming smaller.

Beginning in March 1953, de-Stalinization was a literal process, too, as Stalin's image and words were removed from Soviet society.

This was a contested, spasmodic and emotional task. For twenty-five years, the cult of Stalin accumulated political and cultural traces across Soviet public life. It left deposits in the mentalities of Soviet people. Never had the iconography and language of Stalin been more ubiquitous than in early 1953 (though his image in *Pravda* was much more selectively printed after the war than before).[9] Stalin was in films, novels and plays; he was constantly in the newspapers; his portraits, statues and busts were everywhere; and his name was forever sloganized in publications and speeches, on posters and on the side of buildings. Although Stalin had considerable personal power and became if possible ever more suspicious of those around him, the cult was a component of the propaganda system rather than a manifestation of personal self-regard. The aim was not to turn Stalin into an omnipresent, irreplaceable deity, but to give accessible human form to things that were otherwise abstract, or existed only in memory: the revolution, the state, Marxism-Leninism, 'Sovietness'. The products of the cult were secular, masculine and based on a democratic myth of popular sovereignty. They were generated in modern ways by the new mass media.[10] In the cult, 'Stalin', the 'man of steel', was a political creation, a personification of all the virtues rather than a recognizable human being. 'You're not Stalin and I'm not Stalin,' the dictator is famously reported to have said during an argument with his son. 'Stalin is Soviet power. "Stalin" is what is in the newspapers and the portraits, not you, no, not even me!'[11] In March 1953, then, the cult of personality collapsed overnight. Stalin's successors understood this.[12] Despite the opposition of Molotov and Kaganovich, there was no coherent alternative to some kind of de-Stalinization, which was driven from above and below.

Ordinary citizens did not need an official decree to wonder whether the ubiquitous flummery of the personality cult was still appropriate and whether the slogans still made sense. People were shocked and frightened, wondering what to do next. For years, Soviet citizens had been invited to condemn many of their comrades as 'enemies', but now the categories were changing their value and people were understandably confused. More than a million had been released from the camps, but a significant number of returnees were genuine criminals, convicted for acts of theft or violence. It was not easy to incorporate them back into their communities or to understand why they were no longer enemies. One tram conductor in Moscow wrote to the authorities about the 'bandits' and 'gangsters' who were creating disorder on her line and inverting the guiding moral principles of Soviet life, lacking the 'honour' of the people who had so recently defeated the Germans.

Public discourse emphasized terms like 'legality' and 'humaneness', but society lacked the political or cultural guidance to reach a consensus about what these might mean.[13] The authority of the teacher, which was so important in Soviet culture, remained, but aspects of the curriculum were renegotiated, and students seemed more autonomous. Compulsory classes in Marxism-Leninism needed to be tweaked. Subjects across the arts and sciences paid more attention to 'truth'. At the Gnesin Institute in Moscow, one of the country's most prestigious establishments for the study of music, the academic council nervously debated how to incorporate 'creative individualism' into their teaching and how to deal with growing indiscipline among the student body.[14]

Excising Stalin and Stalinism was an epochal change. It derived from the conjunction of political chance and the personal need of many citizens to restore the values of the revolution, and humane values in general, to Soviet life. Making the USSR a morally habitable environment was an urgent task precisely because people had nowhere else to go and only a single life to live. The core values at stake were truth and justice (defined in one word, *pravda*) and sincerity (*iskrennost'*). They were given unique shape by the Thaw but of course had a much longer lineage. As cultural concepts they emerged from the Russian and other national traditions, and they were expressed in the language of the revolution.

In December 1953, the critic Vladimir Pomerantsev published an influential article, 'On Sincerity in Literature', in the leading reformist journal, *Novyi mir*. He excoriated some of the writing of the Stalin period for 'fabricating' and 'varnishing' reality. Such works did not display the 'Party's truth', which by definition was the same as truth in general. Books were only works of truth if their authors wrote with the grain of conscience. If many previous authors had failed this test, it was not because socialist realism itself was to blame, it was because too many authors had worked as mere 'constructors', not true writers. A few months later, the journal *Znamya* published *The Thaw* by Ilya Ehrenburg, a famous writer with an international reputation and a fine apartment on Moscow's Gorky Street; he had been a journalist and author since the revolution. It was the novel that gave its name to the era. Describing professional and personal conflicts that were resolved in favour of love, individuality and conscience, it used the symbolism of the complex winter–spring transition, long familiar to Russian readers, to critique the cynicism of officials and to demand a better status for the person within the collective. It was a humdrum book whose keen sense of the public mood made it wildly popular.

The annual thaw in many Soviet republics was a major event. Over several weeks, temperatures fluctuate above and below zero. Huge reserves of snow melt. Water flows and then freezes again. Streets become filthy. Rural roads turn impassable. From beneath the ice, lost items and old waste appear. This is a time of awkwardness and uncertainty. It lacks the pristine qualities of winter or the joy of spring. Yet the general direction, from winter to spring, is unmistakably optimistic. 'The Thaw' of the 1950s and 1960s had all the qualities of the metaphor. And the metaphor itself took on a life of its own, shaping the period into an historical process, emphasizing its fluctuating relationships to the past and the future, and self-consciously moulding a new generation, the 'people of the sixties'.[15] It was no accident that literature itself conceptualized the era. Just like a century earlier, during the reforms of Alexander II in the 1860s, literature was called upon to promote conscience and hold power to account, even though the scope for achieving this was much smaller in the post-Stalin dictatorship than in the Tsarist autocracy.

Ehrenburg's themes flowed through the writings of the Leningrad author Daniil Granin. From his base in the northern capital, whose cultural milieu had been targeted by Stalin and Zhdanov a few years before, Granin became an explainer of the Thaw. In the mid-1950s, he was launching himself on one of the most successful literary careers of the post-Stalin period and was still writing sixty years later. He exemplified tendencies of the Thaw: he was ambitious but anti-totalitarian, embraced by the authorities yet loved by many reform-minded readers. Granin was born with the surname Gherman on New Year's Day,

1919, in the countryside of Kursk province. His father worked for the forestry authorities. The family moved around with his itinerant work, arriving eventually in Leningrad when the boy was seven. He attended school in the city's Smolny district; his father was later arrested and sent to Siberia. Granin said it was a gentle household, where his mother loved to sing, or it was before the Soviet state ripped into it by incarcerating his innocent father. He went on to study electrical engineering, focusing on one of the priorities of the early Soviet state, power stations; he continued as a graduate student.

Granin was twenty-two when the Germans invaded. He volunteered to fight immediately and served in the 1st Leningrad Rifle Division. Although he spent time as a political officer (a *politruk*), he fought like everyone else. Later in the war he commanded a tank company. In some ways, the war decided everything for him, just as it did for everyone else who lived through it. Starting again and becoming someone else was central to Soviet civilization. It was part of the aesthetic of socialist realism and private reality alike. 'Was it me that was fighting?' Granin asked himself. 'Perhaps it was someone else, and perhaps I was killed, and someone else remained?'[16]

The possibility of reinvention was indispensable to the ethos of the Thaw. After the war, he was back in devastated Leningrad and working for the city's energy authority. He began to write and adopted his pseudonym. Already married, he and his wife had a daughter in 1945. His first novel, *The Seekers*, was published in 1954, catapulting him to prominence. It was a Thaw classic: an engineer who has designed a new locating device is stymied by bureaucrats, careerists and Party busybodies; unlike them, he is committed to pure research and social progress. The narrative is shaped by his desire for sincerity and openness in all aspects of his life, not just at work, but also in his relationship with the lost fiancée who now comes back into his life after she has married someone else. Like so many aspects of the Thaw, the book (and the film that shortly followed) was simultaneously non-political and entirely political. It was becoming possible to debate politics by apparently not raising political controversy at all.

Across the Soviet Union, dozens of readers' groups held meetings to discuss the themes and characters of *The Seekers*. They met in the

## THE MAN OF THE PEOPLE WITH BLOOD ON HIS HANDS

Agricultural Academy in Kyiv; in an MVD office in North Ossetia; in a trade school for train drivers in Smolensk; in the public library in Irkutsk.[17] Reports described lively disputes about the implications of the book. Granin received hundreds of letters. Like many others, Galina F., a young teacher of Russian language and literature in the town of Kazandzhik in the Turkmen republic, praised the book's 'candour' (*otkrovennost'*) and 'truthfulness' (*pravdivost'*). 'The author possesses good powers of observation,' Galina wrote, 'and can talk about everything simply and warmly.' These were the values of the Thaw. And yet *The Seekers* was in some ways a conventional work, too, with themes and motifs that were recognizable to readers of Stalin-era fiction. This was still socialist realism, as Galina recognized. Granin's book was, she thought, 'about struggling with difficulties and overcoming them', and 'it teaches us not to choose the easy path'. She wanted him to write a new book about students, 'the wonderful family of builders of communism'. Galina simultaneously embraced the personal sensibility of the Thaw and the collective endeavour of the communist project itself. Still only a young teacher, she was in the Komsomol. Students, for her, were the ones who 'will create this radiant future with their own hands!' In the meantime, 'they are arguing, dreaming about the future, making friendships, loving others.'[18] Galina was a long way from the salons of literary Leningrad, but she hit the nail on the head. The individual was inviolable, but only when the collective was mobilized. Her point sounded like a paradox, but it was the logic of the Thaw.

Stalin was dead, Beria was in jail, and Molotov was a busted flush. The Soviet Union was ruled by a collective leadership, the senior members of the Presidium. Every modern political system produces a top person: a chancellor, a president, a *Caudillo*. The collective leadership, though, lasted for years. Some of them had been working together for decades: Molotov, Mikoyan, Kaganovich and Voroshilov had been comrades since the 1920s; Khrushchev had joined the higher ranks in the late 1930s; and Malenkov and Bulganin entered the most trusted realm of top politics in the 1940s. Despite the persistence of Stalin-era figures, only two of them were conspicuously Stalinist, looking backwards: Molotov and Kaganovich. Voroshilov was a weaker figure, easily demoted upstairs to be the toothless head of state, or chair of the Presidium of the Supreme Soviet. Mikoyan was the great survivor, whose flexible approach to power kept him in high office for forty years, into the Brezhnev era. Bulganin was slightly more junior and more willing to bend with the wind. Together, they pursued an agenda that reduced the Gulag, brought the security services under control, made the country more open and introduced social reforms. Their agenda also cemented control of the Eastern bloc, sometimes with awful violence, and allowed a 'tamed' police state to endure in the USSR. Their aim was to make the Soviet Union function indefinitely as a viable polity at home and abroad, and to help it flourish in a recognizably revolutionary way.

The two most energetic members of the collective leadership were Malenkov and Khrushchev. Together they read out Stalin's report at the Nineteenth Party Congress in December 1952. As chair of the Council of Ministers, Georgi Malenkov had a powerful base from which to develop policy and coordinate strategy. Born in 1901 in Orenburg, he had joined the Bolsheviks and fought in the Civil War, before receiving a scientific education at Moscow's Bauman Institute in the 1920s and then joining the Party administration. He was a natural functionary, a virtuoso politician of meeting rooms and memos, not crowds and speeches. Foreign governments saw him as Stalin's successor. Khrushchev was the first secretary of the Party, backed by Moscow-based ideologists and union-wide communist officials. This released him from the demands of devising policy in a major ministry or coordinating policy across government, while still giving him a commanding view of Kremlin politics, a sense of strategy and regular contact with major figures from every region.

Khrushchev and Malenkov had similar agendas. Malenkov supported overtures to NATO and releases from the camps. Grateful peasants gave him the credit for the collective farm reform of August 1953. They now had enhanced rights to grow and sell their own crops, and more rights of personal mobility. It was remembered as a kind of liberation. At the same time, economic investment shifted from heavy to light industry, giving greater priority to consumer goods. Khrushchev retained special interests in urban policy and technology. In December 1954, he called for an end to 'excess' in architecture in favour of cheaper buildings for the use of ordinary people. It signalled a major change in official attitudes to popular living standards and revealed Khrushchev's growing power. In February 1955, Malenkov lost his position as chair of the Council of Ministers. He was demoted to minister of power stations. His replacement was Nikolai Bulganin, who was intelligent and experienced but more pliable. For Khrushchev, the best way to cement his political advantages was by calling a Party Congress. At a major national occasion he could lend de-Stalinization clarity and momentum by associating it irrevocably with himself. He called the Twentieth Congress of the Communist Party of the Soviet Union for February 1956.

The first three years of the Thaw had tested Soviet society. Tensions were high. Moods were brittle. People were uncertain, but Khrushchev was a true believer. Although he knew all about the exceptions and the irreconcilables, not least in the western borderlands, he was convinced that unity defined Soviet life. Facing the crisis of post-Stalinism, this sense of unity gave him the confidence to roll the dice. He was about to gamble the whole future of the revolution on finding out how united Soviet civilization really was.

Old Bolsheviks, survivors of the camps, widows, orphans: many of them wanted to know more clearly what had happened to themselves, their comrades and their family members, especially between 1936 and 1938. Facing up to past tragedies – if only to some of them – seemed to Khrushchev a necessary way of seeking solace for individuals and relaunching the revolution for society as a whole. Khrushchev was a participant in the Great Terror, but not a first-rank decision-maker. He knew the essence of what took place. He himself was responsible for many appalling cases. But he could not describe a complete picture or know the data. Without numbers, it was difficult to calibrate de-Stalinization. Conscience, politics and curiosity gave him a burning interest in knowing exactly what had happened: who, how many, where, when.

In December 1955, the Presidium formed a commission to investigate the repressions. It was led by Pyotr Pospelov, the historian, journalist and publicist who had co-written *The Short Course*, Stalin's book about the origins of Bolshevism, and gone on to edit *Pravda*.

Under Pospelov's direction, researchers went through the archives and within a few weeks compiled a comprehensive report about the Great Terror. He summarized its findings in an emotional Presidium meeting on the eve of the Twentieth Congress. It was another pin-drop moment of the highest drama in the Kremlin. In secrecy, in a closed room, Pospelov himself read out the shocking data to the country's top eleven politicians. He cited 1,920,635 arrests between 1935 and 1940 for counter-revolutionary crimes, and 688,503 executions, most of which were shootings in 1937 and 1938. Stalin knew everything and played the major role in the violence, but other leading figures, including two who were sitting round the table – Molotov and Kaganovich – were also substantially guilty. Pospelov was as tough-minded as any Stalin-era functionary, but he made no bones about the fact that these were atrocities and that they cast a moral blight on the present day.[19]

This was the burden of knowledge which Khrushchev took into the Congress. A minority of the Presidium – the old Stalinists of Molotov, Kaganovich and Voroshilov – argued that the information was tendentious, that it masked the achievements of the Stalin years, and that violence against the guilty and innocent alike was an inevitable, even desirable, component of the revolution. They thought that too much public introspection placed the Soviet Union itself in jeopardy. Yet most Presidium members accepted that a public conversation of some kind was necessary, and that there was a moral need to tell a version of the truth.

From across the USSR, 1,349 delegates with full voting rights came to Moscow, representing the Party's almost seven million members; they were joined by eighty-one delegates with only limited votes, as well as visitors from abroad. As the Congress was coming to an end, on 25 February 1956, delegates were called back to the Kremlin for a final, closed session. Visitors from outside the Eastern bloc were excluded, radio microphones were switched off, and newspaper reporting was not permitted. A few Bolshevik survivors of the Terror and the camps were admitted instead. The speech that Khrushchev gave that day was therefore 'secret'. It was secret because its content seemed so explosive that it could only be released cautiously to Soviet society.

*

## THE MAN OF THE PEOPLE WITH BLOOD ON HIS HANDS

Aleksandr Yakovlev settled back in one of the leather-bound seats of the Hall of the Supreme Soviet in the Great Kremlin Palace. He was a 32-year-old Central Committee official, a young war veteran who was marked out as a high-flier. Thirty years later he would sit in the Politburo alongside Gorbachev. Arriving thirty minutes before the session, he sensed the distinctiveness and tension of the moment. Bulganin opened the proceedings. Yakovlev could see from afar that Khrushchev was nervous. He coughed uncertainly, an unfamiliar gesture. Yakovlev was an intelligent, intellectual, 'passionate', true-believing Marxist-Leninist who became a leading reformer. The Secret Speech was a life-changing moment. 'I literally went cold from Khrushchev's very first words,' he wrote later. 'Everything seemed unreal.'[20]

If Yakovlev could only gasp at the enormity of the occasion, lower-flying delegates struggled even more. Anna Karetnikova was one of them. She was thirty-nine years old. Raised by her father after her mother's death, she lost him too when he was killed in the war. She worked on the shop floor of a chemicals factory in Moscow Region for eighteen years, serving as a Party activist and rising through the ranks of the regional Party apparatus. She had recently lost her husband and become a typist and administrator. It was an unexpected honour to be elected as a delegate to the Twentieth Congress.

Karetnikova had every need to believe in the Party. She was convinced it had sheltered her during the storms of her life. During the Congress, she stayed at the Moskva Hotel – an asymmetrical Stalin-era edifice halfway between Gosplan and the Kremlin, a minute from both – before transferring to the city's Leningrad Hotel. She had an expense account of 95 rubles, and after eating where she wanted she could spend the balance on books and tickets to the Bolshoi Theatre. Karetnikova was self-consciously of the masses and resolutely serious-minded. On the day of the Congress's last, closed session, she caught the special bus for delegates and was taken straight to the Great Kremlin Palace, trundling through the Spasskaya Gate. Karetnikova was suspicious about revisiting the past. She acknowledged to herself Stalin's part in the country's achievements. But as she settled into her seat, and the revelations shook the hall like an earthquake, she held on by thinking that one way or another she believed in the Party.[21]

The speech, which lasted four hours, was recognizably a Khrushchev production. A team of writers worked on its composition, but half of it was Khrushchev's own corrections and additions, and all of it was in his tone of voice, with his condemnations, stories and asides. Khrushchev's unmistakable worldview – in a nutshell, that the revolution should be returned to the people, that they should not be sacrificed for a future generation – lent coherence to the whole performance. He described aspects of the Terror, especially the destruction of the Party, focusing above all on Stalin's personal guilt. He ripped into the cult of personality, with its unrevolutionary and un-Leninist pretensions. He revealed Lenin's own doubts about Stalin, expressed in his personal testament at the end of his life. And he condemned the prosecution of the war: the failure to prepare, the unnecessary human losses, and Stalin's theft of the glory. 'Lenin used severe methods only in the most necessary cases, when the exploiting classes were still in existence and were vigorously opposing the revolution,' Khrushchev argued. 'Stalin, on the other hand, used extreme methods and mass repressions at a time when the revolution was already victorious', displaying 'intolerance, brutality, and abuse of power.'[22]

No wonder some elderly delegates had to be carried out of the hall. Others reached for their blood-pressure pills. They feared the worst, but the calmest of them could see that Khrushchev was offering a deal. By focusing on Stalin's personal guilt, he was implying their own immunity from prosecution. And by condemning arbitrariness and state terror, he was saying that it wouldn't happen again. The NKVD (its duties split between the Ministries of the Interior and State Security after the war) had already been downgraded to a 'committee of state security', the KGB, in 1954. Khrushchev wanted to suggest that the security services were under control and that another 'meat grinder' was impossible. Their personal security and that of their families was assured. They had every reason to support Khrushchev and his project of de-Stalinization.

Above all, though, Khrushchev was offering a settlement to the entire people of the Soviet Union. The Secret Speech was an excoriation of Stalin, but it was also a partial condemnation of *Stalinism*. Khrushchev missed a lot out: the human cost of collectivization; the misery of industrialization; and many atrocities, not least the Ukrainian famine, though he did make an aside about the tragic fate of the Ukrainian people. Viewed from some of the union republics, as well as the socialist countries of the new Warsaw Pact, the speech still sounded imperial. And in focusing on the damage done to the Party, he had less to say about the devastation caused to other groups in society. Some of these omissions were hurtful, others frightening. In the end, though, the speech was epoch-making for what it *included*. After all, it made Yakovlev – always one of the most sensitive and humane of apparat officials – turn cold with shock. The speech marked the end of arbitrary power and the emergence of a stable dictatorship.

It had two great anti-Stalinist qualities. First, it heralded a shift towards a more rights-based future, in which one had the right not to be terrorized by the state, and, by extension, the right to an inviolable home and even to a version of *habeas corpus*, if only one played by the rules. The Secret Speech was of a piece with other reforms of 1956 and 1957, which began to create a version of Soviet civilization based on social and economic rights. Second, the speech made it possible to criticize Stalinist violence sharply and on the basis of evidence. Its overall picture of recent history gave people a much better chance than hitherto to understand what had happened to them, their families and their communities, and thereby to form a more independent and critical relationship to Stalinism. In order to achieve this, the Secret Speech had to be distributed among the population. The process began immediately in local Party meetings.

Anna Pankratova was a specialist in the history of the Russian working class and revolutionary movement. She had followed a turbulent career, rising up the academic ranks in the 1920s, attaining a major post in the Institute of History of the Academy of Sciences in the 1930s, but falling victim to denunciation and demotion. Yet she was not arrested and had a chance to recover. In the immediate post-Stalin era, she came back into favour as a member of the Central Committee. As co-editor of the leading academic journal *Voprosy istorii*, or *Issues in History*, she boldly oriented its scholarship in the direction of de-Stalinization.[23] Pankratova was one of many Party officials who were given the task of disseminating the speech, in the first instance to Party members, the most 'reliable' layer of society.[24] It was a purposeful and incremental process: by releasing these revelations steadily and opening up one room for debate at a time, the hope was to calm society down, not make it explode with anger. Disorders in Tbilisi that met rumours of Stalin's dethronement were a disturbing precedent.

In meeting after meeting in Leningrad in the weeks after the Twentieth Congress, the sixty-year-old Pankratova summarized the points of the Secret Speech and added her own glosses. Between 20 and 23 March 1956 alone, she spoke at nine meetings. The Party members in her audiences were generally academics, teachers and writers. Across the four days, she spoke to 5,930 people who asked 825 questions. In response to the revelations, Party members made many anti-Stalin comments, but they also expressed incredulity. People wondered why the unmasking had not come earlier, or why it focused so much on Stalin himself. Many people reflected on the extent of the suffering: that every family in Leningrad had been devastated in one way or another by atrocities or culpable neglect during the Great Terror, the wartime Blockade, or the Leningrad Affair (the political purge of 1949–50).[25]

After the Congress, Anna Karetnikova also disseminated the Secret Speech in Party meetings. She reported that young people in the Komsomol welcomed the lightening in the public mood. It was 'much more complicated' to discuss these matters with older factory workers, but former Gulag prisoners unsurprisingly supported de-Stalinization.[26] Deep in the provinces, Mikhail Gorbachev was running similar meetings. After his graduation from Moscow State University in 1955, Gorbachev returned to his home province of Stavropol in the south of the Russian republic as a Komsomol official. A rising star, he attended the regional Party meeting at which the contents of Khrushchev's speech were revealed. He spoke in favour of de-Stalinization, but the wider reaction in the room was 'mixed' and 'confused'. When he went out into the province – his task was to summarize the speech to Party and Komsomol members, many of them collective farm workers, in one particular district – he found a similar range of responses to Karetnikova's. Another common response that he noticed was a preference for silence, for reasons of personal trauma or political anxiety, or the conviction that nothing good could come from talking about the past.[27]

Knowledge of the speech rapidly diffused across the whole Soviet population, not simply among Party members. For some 'ordinary' people, it was a new chance to work through their memories of violence and even to reflect on the passing of a 'dictatorship' phase in Soviet life.[28] Sometimes people expressed de-Stalinizing sentiments but through a Stalinist discourse, of 'enemies' and 'unmasking'; the ambiguous discursive tendency was embedded in the Secret Speech itself. In the Georgian republic, where the status of Stalin was wrapped around a perception of national identity, serious pro-Stalin, student-led unrest took place almost as soon as the speech was circulated, in early March 1956; it coincided with a proposal to remove a statue of Stalin around the time of the third anniversary of his death. Troops fired on the crowds in line with an explicit directive from the Central Committee. It seemed to bear out the nagging anxiety in the Presidium that the speech risked a loss of political control, whether that meant control of the streets or of the language of revolution and Marxism-Leninism.

The revolution had a new direction, but the police state continued. Just before Stalin's death, 40,000 people a year were convicted as counter-revolutionary criminals. In 1956, the number was 623.[29] It was a dramatic fall, an extraordinary end to the mass repression of Stalinism, but the fact remained: in 1956, two people per day still became political prisoners. Even if most people lived their lives in peace, they did so in a wider context of injustice. The 'rules of the game' might have been clarified, and arbitrary government might have ceased, but dictatorship persisted; and the KGB and other coercive agencies policed the boundaries of political orthodoxy in thuggish ways.

Most destructive of all was the Soviet answer to the Hungarian Revolution. People in the Eastern bloc were soon familiar with the main points of the Secret Speech. Their responses, especially in Poland and Hungary, pushed the boundaries of the socialist order but did not go beyond it. Khrushchev had supported the Hungarian communists' decision to bring back the previously sidelined reformer Imre Nagy as a de-Stalinizing replacement for the hardline Stalinist Ernő Gerő (himself a replacement for the country's 'little Stalin', Mátyás Rákosi). But Nagy was quick to overstep the mark. In October he called for Hungarian people to be allowed to vote in multiparty elections and for Hungary to become a properly sovereign country and a neutral state. People came to the streets to defend the ideas. Khrushchev could not accept this and sent Soviet tanks to attack the protestors. As many as 2,700 were killed, and 200,000 were allowed to flee, becoming refugees on the other side of the Iron Curtain. These people had their own truths about the limits of de-Stalinization.

Yet for most people, life had changed dramatically. 'Khrushchev's speech at the Twentieth Congress was for me the first noble act of the Soviet leadership in the whole history of the USSR,' wrote Daniil Granin, decades later. 'I do not know another.' The Secret Speech was the most remarkable political achievement between the October Revolution and *perestroika*. It combined deftness and risk-taking with a vision for the revolution. Unlike anything Stalin did, Khrushchev's speech used high politics to promote the basic interests of ordinary people. It was the foundation of post-Stalin Soviet civilization, and though its values were sometimes eclipsed, its importance endured until the collapse of 1991. 'Which of them did anything of such fortitude and mercy?' Granin asked. 'Who saved or defended anyone? Who? Was there anything similar?'[30]

Months passed. De-Stalinization continued. The collective leadership was still in place. Khrushchev was first among equals. The Stalinists hated him, and so did the worried careerists. They had one big chance to bring him down.

On 18 June 1957, at a special meeting of the Presidium, they turned on him. Led by Malenkov, the chief organizer, and Molotov, the stubborn Stalinist, the rebels sought to abolish the post of Party first secretary and remove Khrushchev from political life. Together with Kaganovich, they made the case in another high-blood-pressure Kremlin moment. The careers, possibly the lives, of the men in the room were under threat; the course of de-Stalinization was in doubt; and another future for the revolution was under negotiation. Khrushchev bought time, arguing that only the Central Committee, containing top Party officials from across the whole union, had the proper powers to reorganize the Party in this way. Marshal Zhukov, the hero of Stalingrad and Berlin, and now the forthright, independent-minded minister of defence, suggested that the Presidium had the authority to rap Khrushchev over the knuckles, but not more. Looking the plotters in the eye, he said that the army would not be drawn into a coup d'état. The Presidium called a Central Committee Plenum with almost immediate effect. Zhukov made sure that enough Central Committee members could fly into Moscow on military aircraft in time; tempers rose, as Khrushchev's hard man in the KGB, Ivan Serov, squared off with Voroshilov, the ineffectual head of state; Khrushchev's years of supporting colleagues across the Party, not least in the Secret Speech itself, paid off; the vote went in Khrushchev's favour.

The plotters' intervention turned out to be one of the most counterproductive in the history of Soviet politics. They were labelled the 'Anti-Party Group' and removed from the Presidium. Malenkov, who had already exchanged the Council of Ministers for the Ministry of Power Stations, was appointed director of a hydroelectric plant on the eastern edge of the Kazakh republic. Kaganovich swapped control of the Ministry of Construction Materials for the directorship of a mine in Sverdlovsk region. Molotov was sent to the Soviet Embassy in Mongolia. Although the collective leadership formally persisted, Khrushchev was now very obviously in charge. He then cemented his position with great ruthlessness, turning on Zhukov, the man who had saved him from the Anti-Party Group. Zhukov had charisma and character, the greatest of war records and some skill in politics. Soviet leaders always feared 'Bonapartist' figures, and Khrushchev retired him while he had the chance. Zhukov arguably had the most compelling de-Stalinizing credentials of anyone in the Presidium, consistently and with clarity speaking out against Stalin – and even knowing, in his way, how to stand up to him when he was alive. In February 1958, Zhukov, the de-Stalinizer with the marshal's baton, was removed from office and later labelled – preposterously – as an Anti-Party plotter.

Khrushchev now had a clear view from the apex of Soviet power. His enemies depicted him as a buffoon. But he was not a fat bruiser with scattered words and mangled thoughts. He had something of Ernest Bevin about him. His intelligence was of a different type from Stalin's, not necessarily of a lower order. With little time for scholarship, he did not develop fine-grained critiques of ideological positions based on book-learning. What he possessed was masterly political skills, a quick brain, the ability to formulate a policy position and to spot the holes in the next person's argument. Khrushchev made a poor first impression on Sir William Hayter, the British ambassador to Moscow, who wrote back to London in 1955 that he was 'bull-headed and not very clever'. He soon thought differently. 'As soon as he applied his powerful intelligence and encyclopaedic memory to foreign affairs,' Hayter wrote in his memoirs, 'he mastered them completely.' Writing of Khrushchev's performance in talks in Downing Street in April 1956, the prime minister, Sir Anthony Eden, paid him a similar compliment: Khrushchev (and Bulganin) were as skilled as any international leaders whom he'd met in twenty years of diplomacy at the highest levels.[31] Khrushchev's KGB chairman in the 1960s, Vladimir Semichastny, later rounded on him, but he still recognized his former boss's 'inquisitive, analytical mind' which enabled him to come at complex questions from unexpected angles.[32]

Nikita Khrushchev was often a bad listener but he always had good eyes: throughout his career, however high he rose, he could see things from the perspective of ordinary people. For more than sixty years, he never stopped working. He was an organizer and a politico, an impresario and a comic turn, a visionary and a true believer. Ruthless but not cynical, he pursued the popular yearning for conscience, justice and sincerity and was prepared quite often to ignore it. Khrushchev was the man of the people with blood on his hands. The decades-long transformation of Soviet civilization after 1953 bore his ambiguous imprint more deeply than anyone else's.

Yuri Gagarin

# 3
# Gagarin's Conquest

'Mama!' shouted Zoya. 'Is your radio switched on? Why aren't you talking? The radio, I'm telling you, switch it on! Our Yura ...'

Her mother froze. She had her heart in her mouth.

Even the mother of Yuri Gagarin heard the news just like everyone else.[1]

It was 10.02 a.m. on 12 April 1961. The epoch-defining radio broadcast, a moment which all Soviet people could capture in their mind's eye and ear ever after, came from Yuri Levitan. With his instantly recognizable preface – 'Moscow speaking!' – Levitan had announced many other events, including the German invasion twenty years earlier. He was the voice of the Soviet Union. That morning, as she listened uncomprehendingly to Levitan, Anna Gagarina was in the small town of Gzhatsk, west of Moscow. Her husband was in hospital, and her daughter, Zoya, was a nurse. Anna was a peasant woman who had endured many devastations. She was stepping into a Soviet dream.

Anna was born in the village of Shakhmatovo in 1903, near Gzhatsk. As an adult, she worked in a collective farm in the region. But she was not a typical peasant woman. She spent the six pre-revolutionary years, between the ages of nine and fifteen, in St Petersburg, the Tsar's capital and the fastest-growing urban milieu in the old empire. During this time, she attended the elementary school that was attached to the Putilov armaments plant, one of the most famous factories in imperial Russia, where her father was a worker. She was literate, quick, ambitious and optimistic. It was only lack of family money that prevented her from enrolling in the grammar school to which her teachers wanted to direct her. Fleeing the hungry city as the revolution bit, the family returned to the countryside, where typhus killed her father and ravaged her relatives. She married a young villager called Aleksei Gagarin. The dream of a new life in the capital had gone. Anna reverted to her peasant roots in the village of Klushino, not far from where she was born.

If Anna's life was one of transitions, her youngest child's, Yuri's, was one of destinations: not just the cosmos, but an entirely Soviet world. He was born in 1934 into a village that was a collectivized, Soviet space. His schools were Soviet. He endured Nazi occupation. It was an extremely tough upbringing. Yet all of these experiences only seemed to expand Gagarin's Soviet patriotism. He developed interests in science, technology and engineering, and the desire to wear a Soviet uniform. After the war, the Gagarin family moved from Klushino to Gzhatsk, where Gagarin completed school. Anna Gagarina's ambitions were re-emerging. Yuri had inherited them. There was even talk about continuing his education in Moscow in a vocational college. He soon joined the Komsomol. In the end he stayed in Gzhatsk, training as a metalworker until, in 1951, aged seventeen, he moved to Saratov to study in the city's industrial college. Here he also learned to pilot aircraft at the city's local aerodrome. When he was twenty-one, he joined the air force as an officer. He became a fighter pilot. It was the elite option. Gagarin, though, could also be unassuming, fitting his manner to the occasion. He had the charisma that made an interlocutor feel like the only person in a crowded room. In 1959, he was chosen as one of twenty potential cosmonauts in the space programme.

Sergei Korolev oversaw the selection process and all other aspects of the mission to conquer the cosmos. Korolev found in Gagarin the best sort of Soviet everyman. Gagarin came from the deepest provinces; he was shaped by the collective farm, the victory against Nazism and the Soviet education system; he was honed by his encounter with Soviet science and technology; he was brave, committed to a cause, ready to enjoy himself, quick to burst into laughter and poised with a kind word for anyone. When it came to communism, he didn't have a doubt. He saw no inconsistency between enjoying a good life today and striving for utopia tomorrow. If he had any faults, it was no concern of the image that Korolev wanted to concoct. Korolev chose him as Cosmonaut Number 1.

Anna's son woke up that morning at 5.30 a.m. at the Tyura-Tam cosmodrome, later known as Baikonur, in the Kazakh republic. Thirty minutes later, he and Cosmonaut Number 2, Gherman Titov, underwent medical checks. Everything was fine. The top group set off for the launchpad in a blue bus. At 6.50 a.m., they arrived. The air was emotional and full of anticipation. People were hugging Yuri, and then he was recording a message for posterity. 'In a few minutes,' he said into a microphone, 'a mighty space ship will take me to the far expanses of the universe.' The sun was rising. It was clear and bright. Flying conditions were perfect. At 7.10, Gagarin was strapped into the *Vostok* spacecraft. Over the next hour or so, he exchanged personal and technical messages with ground staff, showing his usual good cheer. Checks continued. Take-off was timed for 9 a.m. Nerves were on open display. Gagarin was excited, but his vital signs were normal. Fifteen minutes before take-off, his mask and helmet were sealed. At 9.07 a.m., slightly delayed, the rocket switches were pushed.

The chief designer – as Sergei Korolev was universally known during his lifetime, when his name was withheld from the public – was taut, alert, completely ready. He talked Gagarin through each moment. Finally, he called out 'Take off!' as the rockets began to roar.

'*Poyekhali!*' Gagarin replied, unrestrained. 'Let's go!'[2]

Less than two minutes after take-off, Korolev and Gagarin resumed their dialogue. By then the rockets had slipped away and Vostok was in orbit. 'I can see the earth,' Gagarin said, his voice echoing round the control room at Tyura-Tam. 'What a beauty!'

The flight lasted for one hour and forty-eight minutes, which meant that Gagarin's mother, and the rest of the world, heard the newsflash while Vostok was still hurtling back towards the earth. Gagarin experienced immense vibration and sound. In the moments just before re-entry, a minor malfunction caused Gagarin's capsule to rotate rapidly, placing him and the whole enterprise in peril, yet still he remained calm. When Gagarin was 7 kilometres up in the sky, the capsule flipped open and he was ejected with his parachute. As Soviet land came into view, he could see where he was headed. It was not far from where he grew up. The Volga was there. Saratov was visible. The town of Engels was nearby. He landed just outside a village called Smelovka. As he disentangled himself and walked up the nearest hill, he saw a woman and a girl, who were understandably discomfited by the sight of a man in a space suit. And yet it made perfect sense: they had just heard the extraordinary news on the radio. Gagarin asked for the use of a phone. They guided him into the village. Moments later, a shaking, relieved Korolev knew that Gagarin was alive, and he could pass on the news to an exultant Khrushchev.[3]

Of the many personalities who together turned Yuri Gagarin into the world's first cosmonaut, his mother and father were surely the most important. But a third figure was not far behind. When Anna Gagarina was three years old, Sergei Korolev was born. It was 30 December 1906. The aeroplane had only recently been invented. Konstantin Tsiolkovsky, the father of Russian rocket science and 'cosmism', was already nearly fifty. Korolev came from a family of teachers in the south-west, in Zhitomir, in today's Ukraine. They lived in a one-storey house, whose front door opened straight onto the street, and whose wooden-shuttered windows were guarded by trees on the adjacent pavement.

Korolev became Soviet cosmonautics' chief engineer, main designer, personnel manager, planning director, bureaucratic enabler, all-round visionary and can-do boss. His amazing achievements came by a roundabout route, along which he met devastating setbacks as well as improbable luck. When he was three years old, his parents separated for good; he never saw his father again. But when he was ten, his mother remarried, and his stepfather, an engineer, not only eased the material load, but also offered a professional example. Sergei Korolev came of age during the Civil War, his adolescence stress-tested by the revolution. He went on to study at a technical college in Odesa between 1922 and 1924, where he completed a project in glider design and met his future wife, Ksenia, who was of Italian descent. Although he always warned subordinates to be respectful of all forms of technology – as if to address it with the formal 'you', or '*vy*', however close you felt to it – he himself already showed a warm familiarity with engineering, design, construction and the creation of fascinating things out of unpromising materials. In Odesa, he made a pencil holder from a discarded grenade case which perfectly combined form and utility.[4] He began an engineering degree in Kyiv and transferred to Moscow's elite Bauman Institute when he was nineteen (Malenkov was a fellow student, and they briefly overlapped). Here he worked to fund his studies, including in an aircraft factory; he piloted gliders, became absorbed in the writings of Konstantin Tsiolkovsky, paid a visit to the great man himself in 1929 and graduated in 1930. His final project was in aircraft design and construction. He also trained as an aircraft pilot.

For much of the 1930s, Korolev worked in the aeronautics industry on projects involving jet propulsion, liquid fuel and rockets. At the age of twenty-six he was already deputy head of Moscow's Jet Propulsion Research Institute. Korolev was pursuing a fine career to which he could devote a full heart. He seemed happily married and sociable among colleagues. Photographs show him laughing with co-workers, or dressed elegantly with Ksenia on holiday in Crimea.[5] By 1935, he and his wife were raising a young daughter. But in 1938, his luck turned again. On 27 June, his wife came home at the end of the afternoon and saw two men loitering outside their building, not far from Moscow's zoo. 'Probably they're coming for me,' mused Korolev, when she told him. He had bought a new gramophone record that day and he put it on the turntable. Night takes a long time to gather on June evenings in Moscow. They listened and listened to the music. The NKVD men came for him at midnight.[6]

He was sentenced to ten years' imprisonment on 27 September. It was a familiar story of fantastical, trumped-up charges of 'sabotage'. He endured the journey to the Gulag's Far East, by train and ship, through Vladivostok to Magadan, to the Kolyma gold-mining camps. 'I appeal to you to give me the chance to work again on the rockets that will strengthen the defence of the USSR,' he wrote from there to the Procuracy of the Soviet Union on 15 October 1939.[7] On 29 February 1940 he was back at Butyrka Prison in Moscow, where he languished for months, sending a densely written letter to Stalin that outlined how rocketry might save the Soviet Union. In September, he was moved to Radio Street in Moscow, to work in a specially controlled technical agency run by the NKVD, and later relocated to Omsk and Kazan. Here he worked in another *sharashka*, a research institute that was part of the Gulag, where they were developing the famous Tupolev-2 bomber as well as rocket engines. He now had much better conditions in his own 22-metre-square room in Kazan, sharing an apartment with one of his prisoner-colleagues.[8] Even so, he was not 'free'. It was still a disorienting, frightening and unjust victimization that continued for another four years and caused devastating stress to Korolev, his wife, mother and stepfather, and no doubt also to his young child. He was released early, in 1944, when his daughter was nine. The following year he was sent to Germany as part of the occupation force. His mission was to join the team that was investigating the defeated enemy's wartime achievements in rocketry.[9] Charged with determining how the Germans' V-2 missile worked, and with reconstructing operations at their base at Peenemünde, Korolev was appointed chief engineer and deputy director of the Nordhausen Institute.

By 1947, Korolev was back in the Soviet Union, helping to coordinate Soviet rocketry, which was now a major strategic priority. He spent much of his time at Kapustin Yar, near Astrakhan, in the south of the Russian republic. He complained to his wife about the extremes of weather there, not to mention the columns of dust, but there were human, even cosmic consolations: the energy of his team, the driving force of their work as an end in itself and their sense of living under 'a lucky star'.[10] In any case, the team fulfilled the mission it had set out on two years earlier. On 18 October 1947, at 10.47 in the morning, the Soviet rocket command launched its first long-distance ballistic missile, a version of the German V-2, codenamed R-2.[11] On 22 July 1951, ten years and one month after the German invasion, the Soviets constructed a rocket in which dogs could travel and survive a lengthy sub-orbital flight. The dogs that first flew were called Dezik and Tsygana; Dezik was later killed on another flight, but Tsygana enjoyed a long retirement at the dacha of one of the academicians who worked in Soviet rocketry.[12]

Following divorce, Korolev married a younger woman, Nina, in 1950. She had not endured the agony of his incarceration. His ambitions were gaining momentum. On 15 March 1953, ten days after the death of Stalin, Korolev oversaw the launch of the R-5 rocket at Kapustin Yar. It was a major breakthrough. Three weeks after that, his daughter Natasha turned eighteen. At this symbolic moment, Korolev did not express regret for what had happened to him – and indeed to her – between 1938 and 1944. 'Despite all the difficult experiences that we have lived through in recent years,' he wrote to Natasha on her birthday, 'not for one moment did the motherland give up on its care for you.'[13]

Could he really have believed that? Perhaps writing for a censor was a habit, and Stalin had only been gone for six weeks. Korolev's experiences of Stalinist rule were ambiguous to say the least. The Stalinist system had given him privileges and then set about destroying him. It had pushed him naked into the wilderness and then retrieved him. His own fate and that of his family hung in the balance for a prolonged period, prematurely ageing all of them. But Stalinism had gone. The country was de-Stalinizing. All the work for which he felt such ambition and joy held an equal priority before and after 1953. Meanwhile, his privileges endured. He enjoyed holidays and trips to sought-after sanatoria in Kislovodsk (in the north Caucasus) and Kudepsta (at Sochi, on the Black Sea). His dacha at Barvikha, in Moscow Region, which he obtained during the late Stalinist period and continued to enjoy after 1953, was a fine if unshowy place, with plenty of space for his extended family. There was a more ironic continuity, which pointed to a bigger truth about Korolev's experience of Soviet civilization, about its multiple guises and changes of priorities. He was a person who was increasingly indispensable to the Soviet state, which insisted on his public anonymity, secreted him in closed working locations, separated him off with lavish perks and protected his personal safety. Korolev liked to joke that his guards in civilian life were probably the same people as his guards in the Gulag.[14]

In September 1955, he oversaw the launch of a ballistic missile from a submarine, and in 1956, the launch of a nuclear missile. He was twice made Hero of Socialist Labour and twice received the Order of Lenin. In April 1957, he was formally rehabilitated, his arrest and sentence annulled, and his innocence proclaimed. The following year, during which he was promoted from 'candidate' to 'full' academician by the Academy of Sciences, he was awarded the Academy's Tsiolkovsky Gold Medal.

His first brush with immortality came on 4 October 1957, with the launch of Sputnik. Four months before the launch, he was intoxicated by workaholism, science and the proximity of success. 'And now we're close to our fulfilment, to the most forbidden dream of humanity,' he wrote to his wife Nina. 'In all the centuries, all the epochs, people have looked into the dark blue heavens and dreamed.'[15] The silver ball with its metallic entrails orbited the earth and caused a sensation. *Pravda* splashed the news across its 6 October issue. 'Triumph of Soviet science and technology,' it proclaimed. 'Humanity's most audacious dreams are becoming reality.'[16]

Korolev's next priority was 'the question of questions': could living organisms remain healthy during space travel?[17] The urgency of getting a man into space was palpable (and a woman could follow). The dog Laika was on board Sputnik-2 the following month and did not survive the flight. But it was becoming increasingly clear that the human conquest of space was possible. The Council of Ministers formalized the mission in 1959, and Korolev picked out his twenty cosmonauts. In 1960, the Vostok project gathered urgency. On 19 August, the dogs Belka and Strelka survived their orbital flight on Sputnik-5; so too did an accompanying zoo of different animals, plants, flies and fungi. But the technological challenges were extreme. It was a Cold-War race in which second place seemed pointless. Nerves were stretched to their limit. Korolev had his own internal battles to fight, too. His biggest test was against himself. He kept his nerve. His control of the whole enterprise, from science to people, was always precise. It was not until the week before, in April 1961, that he placed his bet on Gagarin. On the morning of 12 April, he talked the boy from Gzhatsk through his mission to the cosmos and made him a national hero, a global celebrity and the life of the communist dream. Two weeks later, Gagarin was on the cover of *Time*. His was the international face of Soviet civilization. Korolev, meanwhile, was just one inspiration behind the wider scientific renaissance of the Soviet Thaw.

Three weeks before the longest day of the year, with exams almost done and the dacha season in full swing, Boris Pasternak died. His suffering from lung cancer came to an end on 30 May 1960 in his house at Peredelkino. This village, just outside Moscow, contained the comfortable homes of many writers and musicians. It was a place of career compromises and murmurs of dissent. Pasternak's poetry expressed his own dialogue with conscience, which made him vulnerable during the Stalin period. Despite expecting it and fearing it, he was not arrested. He was a natural for de-Stalinization, but his famous novel *Doctor Zhivago*, completed during the late Stalinist era, was not published in the Soviet Union. When the Nobel Committee awarded their Prize in Literature, the Soviet authorities made him turn it down. In some ways it was a mystery why the book was banned. In *Doctor Zhivago*, Pasternak wrote an epic of life and love during the Russian Revolution. He issued a warning about how revolution created arbitrary fates and outlandish coincidences, but that was not a problem in itself. Pasternak's deeper theme was how an individual person faced intolerable trials of circumstance and retreated in desperation to a private life, but such a notion was scarcely alien to the daily reality of Soviet people. A decade later, during his enforced retirement, Khrushchev read a samizdat copy of the novel and regretted banning it. 'There's nothing anti-Soviet in it,' he concluded.[18]

As news of Pasternak's death travelled across Moscow and beyond, people made their plans to go to Peredelkino to attend his funeral. All of them were mourning the loss of a great poet; some of them were outraged that the reforms of the Thaw were not faster and deeper. Seventeen-year-old Lyudmila Ulitskaya wanted to go to Peredelkino on 2 June. She loved Pasternak's poems. They were a 'foundation' for her. It was easy enough to get there – she lived just north of the centre of Moscow – but she had a German exam that day. German was one of her strongest subjects. She needed to secure a top grade if she was to fulfil her chance of studying in the Biological Faculty of Moscow State University (the Biofak of MGU). While she stayed in Moscow to take her exam, large crowds gathered in Peredelkino. Cultural stars, such as the poet and musician Bulat Okudzhava, led the mourning. KGB agents lurked on the edge of the cemetery and took photos.

Back in Moscow, Ulitskaya fell just short of her ambition. She needed to secure 5s, or As, across the admissions tests, and she missed out in one of them. The fact that young men who had completed military service had an advantage in the competition did not help her. Instead, she went to work as a technician in a brain development laboratory at the Paediatrics Institute. She loved the work and learned essential skills with microscopes and other instruments. Her mother set the example. She was a biochemist who became head of her own laboratory at the Institute of Genetics of the Academy of Sciences. Within two years, Lyudmila's reapplication to the Biofak of MGU was successful.

For a time, after her graduation, Lyudmila Ulitskaya pursued a scientific career. Yet despite the promise of her work, she did not complete her PhD. For a start, domestic life intervened; she got married and had two sons. Divorce followed within five years, but single motherhood did not make it easier to balance a career. Her heart was no longer quite in laboratory science. She liked to write. The theatre fascinated her. Her grandmother was an actress *manquée* who had educated her in the rich world of Moscow drama. Nine years after leaving her lab, Ulitskaya embarked on a new career in theatre and had her first stories published. She went on to write plays and begin work as a director.

Later, she became one of the greatest novelists of post-Soviet Russia.[19] Her novel *Jacob's Ladder* (2015) is a family epic set in the Russian empire, the Soviet Union and Russia across the twentieth and twenty-first centuries. At the heart of the drama is Jacob, a gifted man of endless enthusiasm and constant tragedy, loosely based upon her grandfather. Throughout Jacob's life, every form of knowledge and culture that he encounters is integrated with the next: music, engineering, literature, chemistry, languages, obstetrics. It never stops. For Jacob, gaps between subjects or categories do not exist; they are morally united. 'I'm not a seeker of truth, not a fighter, a poet, a scientist,' he writes modestly in his diary as a young man in 1913. 'But I will try to be more sincere, to live justly, always to study and learn, and to respond if someone near me is crying out in pain.'[20] Writing fifty years after Pasternak's death, of a time fifty years before that took place, Ulitskaya drew on the sensibility of the Thaw. The appeal to conscience, combining and transcending the arts and sciences, was the visible centre of the *intelligentnyi* approach to life during the Thaw. It was the opposite of Bolshevism, and yet it became a part of Soviet civilization.

For all the twists of her career, Ulitskaya's interests in both Pasternak and genetics never dimmed. They were mutually dependent components of the same worldview. One was poetry, and the other was science, but they were related, not separate, forms of knowledge. For sure, most educated people had inclinations and abilities that tilted towards or away from the arts. But this was superficial, because neither made sense without the other. They were entirely intertwined, and schooling and higher education reflected that, whatever faculty one ended up a student in. Loving the structures of poems and DNA with equal intensity, Ulitskaya was not an outlier. In the age of Sputnik, it took poetry to describe the cosmos, and physics to explain the family. This fundamental lack of separation between the arts and sciences made the Soviet Union distinctive, but not unique. It was a feature of Soviet civilization, but also of the civilization of Eastern and Central Europe, of the Jewish and German traditions. And despite the challenges of operating in a closed society, it partly linked the Soviet Union with the highest achievements of Cold-War scholarship on a global level. By the late 1950s, these connections transcended the Iron Curtain in terms of geography, and the revolution of 1917 in terms of chronology. Like strands of DNA, everything was connected.

On 7 May 1959, in the Senate House of the University of Cambridge, Charles Percy Snow – Russians always allowed him his full name, not just his initials – gave one of the most famous lectures of the twentieth century. Later published under the title *The Two Cultures*, and drawing on his varied experience as a Cambridge physicist and a London novelist, he described the gulf between the arts and sciences. Britain was held back by its education system, and by the failure of the establishment to understand basic scientific principles or even to take them seriously.

Snow's works were widely available in translation across the Soviet Union. His novels were popular. During his lecture in May 1959, he drew comparisons between the two countries. He wanted to demonstrate that Soviet life integrated different forms of knowledge in a way that could unleash, not restrain, modernity's new scientific revolution. 'The Russians', as he called the Soviets, had worked out how to organize a scientific education: not just for elite scientists and high-end researchers, which even the British could manage, but also technicians and 'men' with science-based technical skills. It was the latter – possessing the equivalent of a year or so's university education in science subjects – that were so lacking in Britain, and becoming so numerous in the USSR. There was a fourth group, too: the people who took decisions and implemented them. They needed enough scientific reasoning to be able to manage and govern rationally. And they should have enough scientific knowledge to understand the case for technological investment.[21] A level of technical awareness might be specifically relevant for work in a particular ministry: not just for a sprinkling of in-house experts, but for the minister himself. As time went on, for instance, it became usual for the Soviet minister of health to have been a senior doctor.

Respect for scientific reasoning and knowledge – in the active sense of taking for granted the usefulness of even abstract scientific thought, and having some education in these subjects – was built into Soviet civilization in the post-Stalin age. Technicians were not there to be mocked as boring or detached. 'An engineer in a Soviet novel is as acceptable,' remarked Snow, 'as a psychiatrist in an American one.' This was not just a matter of the 'production' novels of the 1930s. By the 1950s and 1960s, all kinds of technical experts were heroized in wittier books and more glamorous films.[22] Perhaps this was to be expected in the age of space travel. A science professional was a typical hero in the Thaw genre of 'youth' novels. In *Ticket to the Stars* (1961), Vasily Aksenov wove a popular story about how a young medical physician in a scientific institute, researching a PhD, leads his wayward teenage brother out of disaster. The charisma of such figures was in part a consequence of their cultural breadth.

Five months after Snow's lecture in Cambridge, Boris Slutsky's famous poem 'Physicists and Lyricists' ('Fiziki i liriki') was published in the 13 October issue of *Literaturnaya gazeta*. Wittily lambasting the poets' sense of inferiority, it gave focus to an emerging debate about the arts and sciences that had recently been initiated by the author of *The Thaw*, Ilya Ehrenburg, in the pages of the newspaper *Komsomolskaya pravda*. Among the thousands of readers who wrote to the editors, many were concerned with ensuring that Soviet public culture was not merely materialistic, but was 'spiritual' and personal too, paying due attention to people's feelings.²³ In other words, science was not enough.

Bolshevism was a scientistic ideology. It partly claimed legitimacy from a kind of scientific method, and from embracing technology. One way or another, the 'science' derived from a particular way of reading Marx. The very act of *reading*, though, showed that data-driven empiricism was not enough for the Bolsheviks. Sometimes, words were everything. Bolsheviks turned words into weapons that destroyed innocent people. Some texts facilitated mass destruction. Others were sources of consolation. The early Bolsheviks were great readers. In some of their homes, Dickens, Hugo and Tolstoy were the focus of leisure time and family discussion.²⁴ It was as if these men and women played the role of the intelligentsia at home before stepping outside and using the texts of Bolshevism and Marxism to kill their neighbours.

Marxism imposed a set of 'scientific' principles on the humanities. The study of history lost its critical edge, but it gained something from the relentlessly conscientious assembly of facts (in those periods and topics which were not politically controversial). Students assumed that historical instruction could follow the same systematic step-by-step learning associated with education in mathematics and the natural sciences. This formal rigour ran through the technocratic assumptions of officials and policymakers during later Soviet civilization. During the Thaw, this technocracy facilitated major individual-facing social reforms, such as the housing programme and the expansion of welfare, while the culture of the period gave ordinary people some of the language and concepts to try, within limits, to hold this same technocracy to account. Even in political life, science and the arts could not be separated in the Soviet Union.

In 1962, Daniil Granin emerged as a literary star. His work was already popular, but his new book, *Into the Storm* (*Idu na grozu*) launched the Leningrad novelist into a more select group of bestselling authors. *Into the Storm* was a classic product of the aesthetics and preoccupations of the Thaw. Its main characters were climate scientists, and its principal setting was a research institute devoted to the geophysics of weather. As the scientists investigate storms in order better to predict the weather, the physical risks increase, the institutional tensions become acute, and conflicts between science and bureaucracy multiply. Conscience, compromise and sincerity are yet again at issue.

Daniil Granin had something in common with C. P. Snow. He embraced both arts and sciences from an early age, not seeing any contradictions between them. His favourite subjects at school were physics and Russian. Even as a student at Leningrad's Electro-Technological Institute, his studies were focused on science but incorporated an element of the humanities (in the continental fashion). Although his PhD research was interrupted by the war, he resumed a technological career in his area of specialization, electricity generation, thereafter. During the late Stalinist period, he worked in the Leningrad network of power stations and continued to spend time in his research institute. This was another zone of unity: not just arts and sciences, but science and technology, theory and practice. His first published stories emerged in this period. Within a few years, during the Thaw, as a prominent full-time author, literature became the arena in which he discussed both science and the moral world of its practitioners.

It might have seemed a bit familiar to Snow. Yet Granin and Snow had different assumptions. While they both accepted that the arts and sciences should be part of a single whole, Granin was able to claim that this unity already existed, albeit with many nuances, in his own society. His own biography embodied the Thaw's contests and synergies between the arts and the sciences (Snow's, by contrast, implied their mutual incomprehension in 1950s Britain, and the hostile coexistence of scientists and 'The Establishment').[25] With this unity assumed, Granin could explore both hard science and its human practitioners in their social context. 'In science [*nauka*], it isn't the question that's of value, but the answer, or the answer's possible existence,' Granin wrote later. 'In art [*iskusstvo*], it's not the answer that's important, but the question ... the more hopeless the question is, the greater its value.'[26] This was a universal insight and a message from the Thaw; it determined the scope of Granin's artistic investigation of science.

He offered a picture of scientific life that was richer in detail, and rehearsed at greater length, than Snow's; at times he aspired to photographic realism as a way of bridging the gap between literature and physics. Time and again, readers commented on the verisimilitude of the scientific world he conjured up. 'The life of [your] laboratory ... is very familiar to us,' wrote a group of engineers from Kursk in March 1963.[27] Nadezhda F., a teacher from Alma-Ata, suggested that 'our favourite modern writer' created 'the world of the *fiziki*' in a completely plausible way.[28] Of course, all this exposed Granin to the fact-checkers who read his novel in order to spot scientific errors, and upbraid him for being 'naive'.[29] Such a way of reading went against the spirit of the Thaw, let alone Granin's own agenda. After all, it was precisely because he was constructing a literary representation that he could describe the 'facts' with added truth. Ilya Brazhnin, Granin's fellow author and fellow Leningrader, congratulated him on his book and suggested that his fine-grained realist technique – of using 'specific material in the novel about people of science' – made it possible 'for the reader to understand as well as is possible' the inner world and the external dilemmas of the characters he created, as well as their geophysical experiments.[30]

Granin and his sympathetic readers argued that sincerity, the great Thaw virtue, explained the novel and its characters. For a scientist, sincerity was crucial to personal and work relationships, but also to professional practice and honest experimentation. Personal autonomy was the best route to being sincere. 'The head of a laboratory is his own boss,' says a scientist in *Into the Storm* who has just been promoted to this role. 'You don't have to ask anyone for anything. Freedom is a real thing.' Trying to entice the hero of the novel on board, the lab boss promises him: 'Behind my back [in the lab] you will be even freer [than me].'[31] Yet this was not the same thing as individualistic detachment. In May 1962, Granin's editors at *Znamya* sent back their comments on his draft. They liked the book but argued that the 'social and political interests' of the main characters were undeveloped.[32] This was not exactly an unwelcome, formulaic request for extra socialist depth: in the context of the Thaw, and of Soviet civilization more generally, many authors like Granin – not to mention cosmonauts like Gagarin – assumed that socialism facilitated sincerity and was not an obstacle to it. Inner life could not be separate from society and ideology. This way of reading books and poems, and watching plays and films, was as central to the Thaw as the space programme. Granin and Gagarin were part of the same continuum.

Gagarin's flight was only the start. Less than four months later, on 6 August 1961, Gherman Titov matched the feat in Vostok-2. Although the second flight lacked the utter unpredictability and sheer adventure of the first, it was longer, designed to test the durability of the human organism in extreme conditions. And Titov was even younger: 25 years, 10 months and 25 days. Cosmonaut Number 2 was famous for reciting poetry. Later, he lyrically reflected on how poets would write about the cosmos when they had the chance to visit it.[33] Titov was born in the Altai region of Siberia in 1935, his father a village schoolmaster, which gave him access to the poetry that he later liked to read aloud, as his father had done in the light of a kerosene lamp as the family gathered round the table in their village house during endless winter nights.[34]

In the team photographs of the first half-dozen young Soviet servicemen to go to space, one is a visual exception, not dressed in uniform even though she was entitled to wear the same clothes as the others. With her medals pinned to a dress instead, and her hair done up, Valentina Tereshkova embodied a different Soviet dream. She was also from a Soviet village, just like Gagarin and Titov. As a young female tractor driver, she was destined to be one of the stars of her collective farm. On 16 June 1963, Vostok-6 blasted off from Baikonur. Tereshkova was on board.

On 3 November 1964, eighteen months after her space flight, and barely three weeks after Khrushchev had been deposed from power, Valentina Tereshkova got married. There she is in Moscow, sitting next to her new husband, A. G. Nikolayev, wearing her white dress and veil, the champagne on the table, and her mentor, Sergei Korolev, on his feet.[35] Paternally, even patriarchally, he sounds forth about the joys of marriage. Radical feminism and bourgeois patriarchy locked together, apparently making the Soviet Union more secure, not less.

Throughout the Khrushchev era, the paradox of Soviet gender was sustained most famously by the country's leading female politician, Ekaterina Furtseva. She was born in 1910 in Tver *guberniya*. Sixteen years younger than Khrushchev (and twenty-four years older than Yuri Gagarin), she saw the revolution as a child, and entered adulthood just as the first five-year plan was getting underway. At the start of her career, she held a Party post in Feodosiya in Crimea, where she met Sergei Korolev. During the 1930s, she studied chemical engineering in Moscow and became a trade union activist, and then a full-time official in the USSR's central trade union administration. She entered the Party apparat during the war, taking up a senior post in the city of Kuibyshev, where many of the commissariats had decamped from Moscow during the emergency of 1941. After 1945, her Party career accelerated. Khrushchev was one of her patrons. She was elected as a deputy of the Supreme Soviet in 1950. Khrushchev steered her into the post of first secretary of the Moscow Party in 1954, and she retained this top role until 1957. When she lost this job, she gained a seat on the Presidium. In 1961, she was made minister of culture. Top Soviet politics was a masculine world: her public persona was one of cold workaholism injected with a sexual frisson. 'I am completely convinced,' argued the brilliant theatre director Oleg Yefremov, playing a straight bat to the camp but deadly seriousness that surrounded Furtseva, 'that in our time, that is to say the 1960s–70s, and in our country, the minister [of culture] ought to be a woman. In any case, a woman responds to art with more emotion.'[36] Her first husband, a pilot, left her during the war when their daughter was two years old. During the Thaw, while she was still in post in the Moscow Party, the anxiously prim apparatchik began a relationship with the ambassador to Belgrade. Her regular flights to see him escalated her sex appeal and caused ripples of scandal, but their marriage was a disappointment.

Furtseva loved Yuri Gagarin. Everyone did. He had conquered the cosmos and now his charisma was taking over the Soviet Union and even the globe. Three months after Vostok-1's launch, on 17 July 1961, Gagarin and Furtseva met at Moscow's second international film festival. Photographs show him addressing a packed room with none other than Gina Lollobrigida, film star and sex symbol. Furtseva is next to him behind a table; male and female delegates alike look up at him with rapture. Gagarin was twenty-seven; Furtseva was fifty. For a moment, it was one of the most glamorous places in the world.

Yuri Gagarin and Gina Lollobrigida were in the same room. And so was Furtseva. Gagarin was in uniform. Furtseva, with blonde crimped hair, was in a dark frock. Lollobrigida took Gagarin's hand and kissed him on the cheek. Gagarin smiled.

Not everyone was comfortable with this face of Soviet civilization. It was a long way from Lenin and the Russian Revolution. Others pointed to a much more universal lack of clarity. Evoking the image of earth described by Gagarin and Titov, the poet and 'bard' Bulat Okudzhava looked at the same 'melancholy planet' and wondered: 'what is the point?'[37] At a fluid and exciting time, the revolution still needed explaining. More than ever, it needed direction. As if to prove the point, three months later, the paths of Gagarin and Furtseva would cross again in the meeting whose aim was to set the whole future of the USSR.

Krasnoyarsk

# 4
# The Glittering Metropolis

On 17 October 1961, the Palace of Congresses was officially opened inside the Kremlin. Heavy on concrete and glass, bright and glossy, the new building was a glimpse of the communist future amid the Kremlin's eclectic ensemble of medieval domes and baroque towers. It stretched across 55,600 square metres, 400,000 cubic metres, 800 rooms, a banquet hall for 2,500 diners and a conference hall for 6,000 delegates (the Bolshoi Theatre, by comparison, had room for an audience of 2,200).[1] A vast expanse of glass walls, light marble floors and escalators faced in white plastic turned the huge two-level foyer into a box of light. 'It seemed that Vladimir Ilich was invisibly present in the conference hall,' one architect wrote of the Congress;[2] if he was, he shared the space with 7,000 loudspeakers and 4,500 lighting points, and a 'monumental' bas-relief of his own head, lit by a rising sun.[3] But for all its grandeur, the Palace of Congresses was in one sense designed for ordinary people. The Kremlin had been a closed Party-government fortress from the start of Soviet rule until 31 December 1954, when it hosted a New Year's Eve Youth Ball.[4] It was opened to the public in July 1955. In the new Palace of Congresses, gatherings of many organizations, such as the Women's International Congress, would take place, as did performances of ballet and opera, and New Year 'yolka' children's shows.[5]

On the day of its opening, the Palace of Congresses was the venue for the first session of the Twenty-second Congress of the Communist Party of the Soviet Union, which ran for the next ten days. Yuri Gagarin was one of the stars of the show. Gherman Titov was there, too. On the day the Congress opened, an article under Gagarin's byline appeared in *Red Star*, the newspaper of the armed forces. 'The great Party of Communists will take us to distant worlds and radiant heights,' he concluded.⁶ If ever such words could be taken literally, it was in 1961. Gagarin's symbolic importance in Soviet politics was confirmed the following year when he was 'elected' to the all-union parliament, the Supreme Soviet. He represented a constituency in Kaluga, the town in which Konstantin Tsiolkovsky, the muse of the space programme, had lived.

Ekaterina Furtseva was at the Congress, too. She was in her fourth year as a member of the Presidium, and had served as minister of culture since the previous May. Furtseva was the most powerful female politician in the Soviet Union. At the Congress, she and Gagarin again strode the same corridors and sat in the same meeting rooms, but they brought quite different sensibilities to the occasion. The moment was indeed historic – the Soviet Union was relaunching itself, and the metaphorical comparison with Sputnik and Vostok was unavoidable – but Furtseva did not quite grasp the nettle, while Gagarin allowed the right words to be ascribed to him. At this moment of self-consciously historic potential, Furtseva hit a plaintive note. Her set-piece speech focused on the failures of Soviet culture rather than its successes. Apparently assuming that the culture of the provinces was superior to that of the metropole, it sounded narrow-minded and tin-eared, even if a rebalancing of cultural investment across the country was essential. She ended up in a pointless war of words with the novelist Mikhail Sholokhov, who – despite his taste for the destruction of dissidents – won the Nobel Prize in Literature five years later.⁷

Gagarin's words, by contrast, summarized the agenda of the Congress and captured the mood of those who wanted to believe in the communist future. Three months earlier, the Central Committee had approved the new Party Programme after an extended discussion in the Presidium on 17 June. Major political figures were still true-believing communists. Just like their predecessors (or their younger selves) in the 1920s and 1930s, they continued to talk the language of Bolshevism in public and private.⁸ Mikhail Suslov, the country's ideology chief, guided them in precise linguistic choices – 'on page 20, instead of the words "communist ideology", let's go for "in the spirit of communism"' – but the top political establishment shared the same basic vision in 1961. Khrushchev himself was committed to the fastest and boldest journey along the road to communism. Where the draft programme promised a four-fold increase in meat production, the cautious Boris Ponomarev suggested that the data might better justify a projection of 3.5; Khrushchev countered jovially that a five-fold rise could be achieved. He thought that 'the higher the figures . . . the stronger [will be] our actions'.[9] His gigantomania echoed the madcap targets of Stalin's early five-year plans, but where Stalin's economy had caused mass death and sacrifice, Khrushchev's economy was beneficently rebalanced in favour of the individual citizen's wellbeing. But the implausible targets destabilized the economy, even in the short term.

The programme updated previous communist mission statements, the RSDLP's in 1903, and the Bolsheviks' in 1919. It also complemented the constitutions of the Soviet state, of which there had so far been three iterations, in 1918, 1924 and 1936. Discussions about a third Party programme dated back to a late Stalin-era working group, but the real leadership effort in generating such a long and complex ideological document belonged to Khrushchev.[10] He energized the project. It expressed his vision of Soviet communism. By proclaiming that 'the current generation of Soviet people will live under communism', it emphasized the point of Khrushchev's politics: that the present generation would not be sacrificed for the sake of an imagined future paradise. Its authors styled the new Party programme as a revival of the original revolutionary message, forty-four years on. No one could miss the reminder: Stalin diverted the revolution from the true Leninist path. Many of the nostrums which had seemed so extraordinary in 1919 were now part of Soviet life. The long revolution was still taking place. A socialist economy had been constructed in the 1930s; twenty years on, it was possible for a true believer to imagine the transition to communism, which, the Programme claimed, would be achieved by 1980.

Khrushchev perceived the communist future in his own way, as something with two aspects: material and moral. On the one hand, living standards, which could be statistically measured in terms of wages, benefits, housing, food and consumer goods, should be as high as possible. They should reach levels that only Marxist-Leninist economics could guarantee. On the other hand, these material improvements should be distributed equally, which implied a non-material guarantee of dignity. These two approaches underwrote each aspect of the Programme. It claimed that communism was not a fairy-tale paradise, but the logical result of very carefully calculated economic targets, and used precise data to argue that socialism would inevitably and always replace capitalism everywhere thanks to the objective laws of social development. The logic of Leninism united the global working class. Internationalism would overcome imperialism in the decolonizing 'Third World'. In the process, socialist democracy would prevail. Socialist democracy did not simply announce popular rights, like bourgeois democracy did, but guaranteed them. With this process underway, the revolution never stopped inside the Soviet Union, and its connection to the Marxist movement abroad was seamless. The revolution's next stage was the transition to communism, now on the horizon, when personal freedoms, rights, better living standards, access to culture and fuller ideological consciousness made possible a society in which crime was abolished, people could recover from their errors, society was unified in common interests, and rights and duties were fused into a single communist way of life.

At the heart of the Programme was the Moral Code of the Builders of Communism. Its twelve points sounded like a faint echo of the Ten Commandments. The passing similarity between communism and Christianity was one of form, not content. Marxism shared with Christianity its humanism, its sense of hope, faith and even love, and some of its structures of language and narrative; but it was also a system of class war that rejected the possibility of a God, and which in its Leninist variant was based on extremism and ruthlessness, not compromise and compassion. Still, there were general overlaps between communist and Christian morality. Comradeship and fraternity implied that a person was his brother's keeper; the collective was a place where one might be expected to love others as oneself; the emphasis on public ownership assumed disapproval of greed. Some even compared the Party to the Church. But the trajectory through socialism to communism that ran through the Moral Code lacked the prayerfulness and modesty towards which Christianity was supposed to tend. People were required to express devotion to the communist cause and the socialist motherland, not to God or transcendence.

Above all, work was the central virtue and was for the good of society as a whole, which meant that 'he who does not work shall not eat'. This language had a famous biblical origin (2 Thessalonians 3:10), but the contexts, purposes and aspirations were unimaginably different; the Soviet Union was the workers' state until paradise was achieved on earth.[11]

In 1961, the utopia that inspired Soviet communism was not a shining city on a hill, or a fantasy of pre-modern harmony, but a glittering metropolis that was already under construction. At the time, the glittering metropolis was a real place: the socialist city of rising living standards. In retrospect, it also seems like a metaphor for the utopia of communist progress. The Bolshevik conception of time was, like its Cold-War American counterpart, driven by progress and focused on the future. Since 1917, revolution and Marxism had given a resolutely forward march to all aspects of the Soviet way of life, from economic development to cultural production. In 1961, though, the pace of Khrushchev's reforms, the publication of the Party Programme, and Gagarin's flight in space increased the speed with which the radiant future was approaching.

Even so, Soviet people in the Khrushchev era switched between looking back over their shoulders and staring towards the horizon. The Stalinist past and the communist future were equal preoccupations. A substantial part of public culture and people's inner lives was concerned with processing the memory of Stalinist traumas. At least in theory, reflection on the past was inseparable from building the communist future, because it was only by resolving the past, and charting a clear Leninist path between 1917 and the present day, that a Leninist future became imaginable. The most important aim of the Party Programme was to create 'the person of the communist tomorrow'. Communism itself was only the entryway into the wider 'radiant future'. Just like in earlier periods of Soviet history, ideologues assumed that human matter would in some way have to be remoulded to make this possible.[12] The point was that this remoulding must not be violent. In creating the future, the Stalinist ethic itself was rejected. During the Thaw, building the future and resolving the past were the same process.

All this talk about the communist future made it only appropriate that Yuri Gagarin was a delegate at the Twenty-second Congress. The chief designer, Sergei Korolev, was there too. At the end of each day of Congress meetings and receptions, he had a longer journey home from the Kremlin than many of the dignitaries. His driver took him to a less conventional address.

In 1959, Sergei Korolev was given a house in north Moscow, in the shadows of the Exhibition of Economic Achievements. The sprawling exhibition complex was always known by its Russian initials, VDNKh (the last letter rendered by the guttural 'Kh'). In 1937, Lena Mukhina completed its symbolic centrepiece, a massive sculpture of a female collective farm labourer and a male factory worker. Arms raised, thrusting forward, she clutches a sickle, and he holds a hammer. They were moving into the future, Stalin-style.

Within sight of VDNKh was Korolev's exceptional dwelling. Not a long drive from the centre of Moscow, and surrounded by a comfortable plot of land, it was a two-storey house with large windows and spacious rooms. It had a front door, entrances at either side, and a stairway down to the basement at the back, but there was no noticeable façade; there were large windows to the right of the front door but none above it or to its left. It was painted yellow, with a flattish roof and a large terrace at the level of the first floor on the right-hand side. Korolev's house was one of a kind.[13]

On the ground floor, there was a spacious living room on the right, with a television and large sofas, the newspaper on a coffee table and views of the garden to front and rear. Coming home in the evening to his harmonious second marriage, and after hanging up his coat in the cloakroom opposite the front door, and stopping briefly to glance at the newspaper headline, he would find himself in the dining room, part of a large open space that connected to the living room, with a table that could be set for ten. Next to this was a kitchen that was well equipped by the standards of the time. Downstairs was a large basement, whose windowed rooms stretched across the house.

Upstairs was a book-lined landing with armchairs in a bay for reading. Korolev's study was at the front of the house, above the living room. His desk, piled with books, faced the door, with two armchairs and a sofa in front of it; sitting behind the desk, he had a wall of technical books to his right (the books that filled the landing had more varied subjects). He could look out of the window to his left, the view warmed by a large palm tree that leaned over the desk. Next to his study was the bedroom. The large double bed was to the left of the door. A heavy wardrobe, deep brown polished wood, was on the wall to its right. And a dressing table was in the far corner. Opposite the bedroom was a door which led out onto a terrace. Across the hall, the bathroom had a shower over the bath, a discreet flush lever on the lavatory and heavy, white-coloured fixtures. Between the bathroom and the bedroom, at the back of the house, was a sitting room, fitted with sleek, red-cushioned, angular armchairs, narrow in profile and light in weight. They were a good match for the space age. From the back of the house, from what he called his 'thinking place',[14] Korolev could stare out over VDNKh, where his fellow citizens saw the future on display and dreamed about adventures in the cosmos.

Ekaterina Furtseva, by contrast, dreamed of an elusive interior harmony. She was not a natural fit for the post of minister of culture to which she had been shifted the previous year. The times called for a more relaxed relationship between the authorities and the cultural producers whom they regulated, but Furtseva never found the right words, or a light touch, or felt like herself among the directors, conductors and writers with whom she had to schmooze. She famously blundered in, sometimes in person, when she heard that rehearsals were going off-message. Meanwhile, her marriage brought her anxiety. Nikolai Firyubin had an eye for the ladies. The gossip never ended.

The year before, they had moved from one elite apartment to another. Between 1949 and 1960, Furtseva was resident in an apartment at number 9 Gorky Street, straight up from the Kremlin. When the opportunity arose, though, she and Firyubin moved down the road and round the corner to number 3 Granovsky Street. Here you could scarcely move for Presidium apparatchiks, war-winning generals and laureates of the Lenin Prize. Her new apartment reportedly extended to seven rooms. But luxury only brought her comfort in the most superficial sense. It was no guarantee of political security. At the Twenty-second Congress, she was not re-elected to her seat in the

Presidium. She remained as Minister of Culture. Khrushchev appreciated her value, but he was realistic about her flaws and he had not forgotten her momentary stumble four years before, when Molotov, Kaganovich and Malenkov were scouting for supporters and seeking his overthrow.

After the Congress's closing session on 31 October, Furtseva's was a much shorter ride home than Korolev's. It was two minutes if the road was clear. As the chauffeurs pulled up on Granovsky Street after exiting the Kremlin, it must have already been dark. Furtseva can have had no wish to see her distinguished neighbours. She entered her apartment. Reports stated that she drew a bath. Then she attempted suicide. Her husband found her, and she was rushed to hospital. She lived for thirteen more years. Khrushchev kept her on as minister of culture. She outlasted him in office.

Korolev and Furtseva moved house at the same time as millions of their fellow citizens. Furtseva herself was still in post in the Presidium when the Central Committee and the Council of Ministers approved a major decree on housing construction in July 1957. It was one of the keynote legislative acts of the Thaw. By requiring the construction of new urban dwellings across the union, the decree redesigned every Soviet city and dramatically raised living standards. More than any other measure, it created the glittering metropolis of the Khrushchev era.

The aim of the programme was simple. One, it sought to end the country's notorious housing shortage. Two, it proposed a deadline more ambitious than anyone imagined possible, within twelve years, and possibly ten. New housing was delivered as separate family apartments. The most typical unit was an apartment of approximately forty square metres, made up of two multi-use rooms, a hallway, kitchen and a combined bathroom and lavatory. Apartments were usually arrayed in five-storey blocks that were gathered together in microdistricts, or neighbourhoods of between 10,000 and 25,000 residents, containing social facilities – schools, kindergartens, a polyclinic, a housing and welfare office – and cultural institutions such as a palace of culture. All these buildings were put together from prefabricated panels. Each genre of building was instantly recognizable to any Soviet citizen. Their format was repeated across the Soviet republics, which meant that buildings that were superficially identical were sometimes built differently, to withstand particular climatic and geographical extremes, from earthquakes to hurricanes to permafrost. A highly distinctive urban form, the socialist city proliferated beyond the Soviet space. A similar architecture and urban planning dominated the Eastern bloc and extended globally into districts of Lagos, Baghdad, Abu Dhabi and elsewhere.[15]

What changed after 1953 was not just that people had more housing space, but that they could close their own front door. They gathered in their own kitchen with relatives, friends or neighbours, in sociable 'companies' of the trusted and like-minded. A new private life emerged. In the separate apartment, domestic routines were shaped by one's own family, not by a group of neighbours in a *kommunalka*. The separate apartment became an object of aspiration but also an arena of 'normality'. Permeable membranes, created by revolutionary Leninism, separated people's public and private worlds. Khrushchev insisted on a revival of the revolution-era *domkom*, or apartment house committee, to oversee the use and upkeep of shared spaces such as stairwells. The yards between the low-rise apartment houses were open spaces where the public and private merged: where children played, women dried laundry, men tinkered with repairs, and grandmothers watched and gossiped. New voluntary brigades (*druzhiny*), wearing red armbands, patrolled neighbourhoods to keep 'hooliganism' at bay. Comrades' courts, revivified by Khrushchev, brought a popular form of revolutionary justice to the resolution of neighbourhood disputes.

Property law further complicated the public–private boundary. In the face of the overwhelming need for immediate postwar reconstruction, a decree of 1944 facilitated citizens' access to cheap state loans for the purchase of building materials. Borrowers built a small individual house, usually with their own hands, inside the city limits. The building zone looked like a shanty town, but it rehoused millions of people. Residents owned their dwelling according to the tenure of personal property. It was the loose equivalent of a medium-term leasehold (often twenty-five years). Laws defined the modest size of dwellings and outlawed the accumulation of property by a family. In

Voronezh, the share of housing owned according to this tenure grew from 37.4 per cent in 1940 to 48.4 per cent in 1950. In 1960, in Omsk, 47.1 per cent of housing stock was individual houses owned 'personally' by their residents; it was 64.8 per cent in Tashkent and 26.1 per cent in Minsk. This was a dimension of Soviet civilization that was little known in the West, where people assumed that people's ownership rights extended to little more than a toothbrush.

Khrushchev disliked the policy and put a stop to it. He thought it entrenched slum housing. But he also needed to find a way to make use of people's savings and initiative to help eradicate the housing shortage. He reintroduced cooperative apartments instead. This scheme allowed people to put down a large deposit on a good apartment, pay off the rest on easy terms and become a member of the cooperative that owned the building. It was not easy to get a cooperative apartment. Especially in the early days of the policy, certain prestigious institutions, such as the KGB, were in the best position to set them up for their employees. Even so, the concept of ownership was not alien to people who lived in apartments that were owned by local authorities – the soviets – or institutions like factory enterprises. They were on a waiting list, the notorious housing queue, often for many years; but when they eventually received the paperwork for their apartment, they had very secure rights of occupancy: so secure, that they usually thought of the apartment as theirs, that to all intents and purposes they owned it. None of this was a bourgeois compromise, but the result of particular legal values that were part of Soviet civilization.

Nikita Khrushchev's commitment to the housing programme was personal. He saw it as an expression of popular beneficence, a manifestation of living socialism and a route towards communism. It allowed living standards to be raised immediately (for those at the head of the queue) and the results to be distributed relatively equitably. People called the five-storey blocks that were built across the USSR in the 1950s and 1960s *khrushchevki*. When they didn't like them, they used the term *krushcheby* instead, playing on the Russian word for 'slum' (*trushcheba*).

His housing programme had many flaws. The rushed pace of construction affected quality. Stories of too-thin walls, leaky ceilings and narrow doorframes – of dimensions so awkward that one could not leave the apartment in a coffin – were legion. The rigid focus on targets measured in square metres of housing incentivized planners to divert resources away from local infrastructure such as roads, which not only harmed people's standards of living but short-sightedly reduced the capacity to build more housing. But the bigger picture was one of personal and economic transformations. The scale and impact of the programme made it one of the great social reforms of modern European history. It grew out of postwar reconstruction, following the mass destruction and migrations of the war (see chapter 1); in response, almost four times as much housing was constructed in the USSR in the decade after 1945 than in the decade before 1941. But the new housing programme of 1957 was of a greater scope and for a different purpose: not just to rescue the urban economy, but to give individual people more 'normal' living standards. The year-on-year rise in housing construction that followed 1957 was the biggest in Soviet history. Five years later, at a Plenum of the Central Committee in November 1962, Khrushchev declared that 50 million Soviet citizens had improved their housing conditions in the interim; 9 million apartments, with a total size of 325 million square metres, had been constructed in Soviet cities in the last four years.

The drive for housing exemplified a temporal dynamic at the heart of Soviet civilization. Housing construction, and many other aspects of Soviet experience, operated in three modes, each of which followed another. Each represented a different possible future that was embedded into the revolution of 1917. First came sacrifice, the assumption that it was completely acceptable to destroy millions of people and to reduce the living conditions of millions of others for the sake of the communist future. Very little housing was built in the 1930s, when workers were forced to endure conditions of extreme poverty. Then came beneficence, the notion that individual citizens possessed a form of rights which regulated their relationship to 'power' and made possible material improvements in their way of life. This was the assumption that lay behind the 1957 decree. More generally, it infused Khrushchev's characterization of the Soviet order as the 'All-People's State'. Last of all was paradise: the arrival of the radiant communist future, signs of which were obsessively sought in the early 1960s, and whose onset, Khrushchev promised in the Party programme of 1961, was set for 1980.[16]

Mikhail Posokhin was in two minds. Building cookie-cutter blocks of five-storey apartment houses was no fun for ambitious architects. As a professional elite, architects had enjoyed power and prestige during the Stalin era, but since the mid-1950s, their status had seeped away and that of construction engineers had risen. Engineers and builders, not architects, were the newly indispensable group. Posokhin's profession was not what it was. Yet his commission for the Palace of Congresses was another triumph in his long, successful career. And there was every sign of more to come.

In the 1950s, Posokhin moved with his family to Moscow's Pushkin Square, on the corner of Gorky Street and Tverskoi Boulevard. You could walk down the road and be at the Palace of Congresses in fifteen minutes. The windows of their home were at the front of the building, looking onto a picture postcard of Soviet Moscow. It was a creamy-white confection of an apartment block. The women's fashion shop Natasha was on the ground floor. With the famous statue of Pushkin just a few metres away, and the constructivist headquarters of the government paper *Izvestiya* directly opposite, it was a signature address. For all the space-age promise of communism, the area was also homely. Its population was a blend of *nomenklatura* and celebrities, and also intelligentsia and 'ordinary' people, many of whom lived in surviving communal apartments in nineteenth-century buildings. The pace of life there was fast and slow. Drinkers gathered on benches on the boulevard. Men in suits got into chauffeur-driven cars. Theatre culture was intense. Kids walked home from school.[17]

Posokhin became chief architect of the city of Moscow in 1960. His designs had changed dramatically over time, like those of his colleagues, reflecting the ideology of the age. By 1960 he was an exponent of international modernism. He saw the socialist city as a place whose metaphorical borders were open to the outside world. His Palace of Congresses was both a socialist and an internationalist construction. Within a few years – and despite his responsibilities for architecture in Moscow itself – he was designing the Soviet embassies in Brasilia and Washington. They shared motifs and materials with the Palace of Congresses, such as white concrete and marble, and tall, parallel columns of glass. Such buildings were the face of international architecture in Moscow, and the image of Soviet architecture in the outside world. Socialist architecture was influenced by global trends and it influenced them in turn. In 1958, Moscow hosted the Congress of the International Union of Architects, the profession's major global gathering.

By 1961, Posokhin was working on designs for Moscow's Kalinin Prospekt, which ran through the historic Arbat district and towards west Moscow. He turned it into one of the classic socialist city ensembles. It was a two-kilometre-long, six-lane, eighty-metre-wide avenue, lined by twenty-two-storey towers, including office blocks shaped like open books, high-rise residential complexes, and low-rise cultural facilities, such as the capital's new favourite bookstore, Book House, and the October Cinema, with its spectacular expanses of glass. When a substantial segment of the avenue was opened in 1967, in time for the fiftieth anniversary of the October Revolution,[18] it had wide pedestrian thoroughfares, with shops and cafés that were designed, in the spirit of the Thaw, to give people some of the things that they wanted. A shopper could call in at the Moskvichka (Muscovite, with the feminine ending) or Vesna (Spring) clothing stores, or pick up some music at the Melodiya record store, or earrings at the jeweller Malakhitovaya shkatulka (or Malachite Casket, named after a Stalin Prize-winning story collection of 1942). The flower emporium Jupiter and the perfume store Lilac were also worth a special journey or might be stop-off points on a weekend stroll.[19] Shortages and limited choice were endemic, but these were flagship shops that were open to everyone. They were not closed *nomenklatura* stores. Posokhin assumed that shopping could be exciting in 'socialist modern' surroundings. This sounds like a paradox, but it was another logically coherent aspect of the Thaw.

Posokhin and his colleagues drew on the architectural avant-garde and especially the constructivism of the 1920s. They made use of achievements, economies and aesthetic themes of mass construction technology. His design bureau deployed prefabricated parts and pre-stressed concrete and aimed for a close, streamlined relationship between form and function, but still created recognizably unique buildings. This was the so-called *tipizatsiya* style.[20] The philosophy of architecture had moved back to the freer experimentation of the 1920s and its interest in devising new ways of life. By contrast, the buildings of the Stalin period seemed heavier and more ponderous, an 'empire style' derived from neoclassicism, lacking the urgency of revolution and the dynamism of communist transition.[21]

Architecture showed that the glittering metropolis was both Soviet and international. Khrushchev's socio-economic reforms were likewise infused with the spirit of 1917 and also depended on modern technologies – such as prefabrication, social insurance and 'scientific' management practices – that were under development across the world, in capitalist democracies and socialist dictatorships alike. During the 1960s, American social scientists who were academically and ideologically averse to the dominant way of explaining the Soviet Union – totalitarianism – began to develop a new intellectual framework, the so-called convergence paradigm. Drawing on the fashionable insights of modernization theory, they posited that the Soviet Union was evolving in a modern way. They argued that the structures and practices of life in the Soviet Union and other socialist societies had much in common with those of capitalist countries. Socialist ideology made a difference, but it fitted Soviet life within the spectrum of modernity rather than making it an aberration from it.

Convergence theorists had their own way of seeing the socialist city: it was just one more example of urbanization. Some of them even conceptualized the Soviet Union as yet another type of welfare state. But if Soviet life was in some ways 'normal', its normality derived too from the revolution and from 'communism'. The glittering metropolis was the most openly ideological of places. It was of its place and time. Welfare was both so all-embracing and uneven, and founded on such a specific definition of social rights, that it simultaneously went far beyond and fell far short of a welfare state on, say, the Swedish model. And the decade that was just beginning – 'the sixties' – was most obviously taking place somewhere else: on the King's Road, at Woodstock, on the Left Bank. By contrast, the glittering metropolis incorporated many other things, including the performance of poetry, into its public spaces. Poets such as Bella Akhmadulina recited their works to massive audiences in stadiums and other venues. The performance was bound to elude control, to bring 'official' and 'unofficial' cultures into creative tension. In 1961, Andrei Voznesensky and Yevgeny Yevtushenko declaimed their epochal poems in Moscow's Mayakovsky Square, speaking into a microphone and surrounded by a crowd, while the KGB mingled and observed the audience.

Meanwhile, Soviet civilization was also being made in another urban space: welfare offices. These were allegedly a venue in which communism was constructed, but most of them were small, cramped and badly maintained. In 1961, a mere four small rooms in the basement of a public building, plus a ground-floor reception, was the headquarters of the social welfare department of Moscow's Frunzensky district. Sixteen officials worked two to a desk in 238 square metres that lacked natural light. They served 48,000 claimants – more when a re-zoning followed, one that did not coincide with improved office facilities. It made for tense exchanges with claimants.

Fraught conversations in shabby rooms determined how people really lived in the glittering metropolis, what they received and what was denied to them. From the later 1950s, welfare officials were better educated, more professional and knowledgeable, but the rooms that they occupied did not noticeably improve for another decade.[22] They were doing more complex work, dealing with a much greater volume of legislation and regulation and serving far more citizens. This was because of the introduction and implementation of two major decrees on pensions, one in 1956 and the other in 1964. The welfare system of the Thaw was much more far-reaching than before. For all its many holes and uneven application, and despite the persistence of shortages and significant poverty, this system penetrated into so many aspects of life – guaranteeing a job, organizing the housing system, offering access to sanatoria and children's summer camps, establishing sometimes intrusive prophylactic healthcare – that it had little in common with a capitalist or even social democratic welfare state. It went beyond cash transfers and care for the vulnerable or those at particular life stages, such as infancy or old age. Instead it had all-society pretensions, even claiming that it might elide the categories of state and society. The Khrushchev-era innovations of the All-People's

State and the Third Party Programme – Khrushchev's own sense of communist possibility – defined its boundaries.

Soviet people used the word 'pension' to describe most welfare payments, cash transfers and benefits. Veterans and wartime dependents had been receiving additional pensions since the late Stalinist era. In October 1956, Khrushchev sponsored the largest conceivable all-union reform to the system. The new law increased old age pensions while reducing age limits and increasing the number of eligible categories. Across the towns and cities – not villages – of the USSR, all men who had worked for twenty-five years could retire at sixty on a full pension; women needed twenty years' service and could retire at fifty-five. Those who had worked in the most arduous conditions – such as mines, or inside the Arctic Circle – could retire ten years earlier and with five fewer years of employment. There were other special cases, notably mothers of five children, each of which she had raised at least to age eight; they could retire at fifty on a full pension if they had a work record of fifteen years. The 1956 law also expanded invalidity pensions and made it easier to access them, especially by those who had never been able to work. Another type of pension was for dependents of a lost breadwinner. The law raised the number of those eligible to claim and increased the size of their benefits.

None of this applied to collective farm workers, who did not, after all, inhabit the glittering metropolis. Peasants still lived outside the full scope of the modern economy, which had consequences not only for their standard of living but also for their citizenship. Khrushchev's second major pensions decree, passed in July 1964 and brought into operation just after his ousting, on New Year's Day, 1965, brought state pensions to the countryside. A unified social fund was established from which collective farm workers received defined cash transfers. This replaced the mutual funds in each *kolkhoz* which previously made ad hoc payments to those in need. Pensions were bigger in cities, but those who lived in the countryside were plainly now enjoying more of the socio-economic benefits of citizenship than ever before.

The two pensions decrees of 1956 and 1964 enhanced living standards at major expense. The 17 billion ruble social security budget of 1950 had become 72 billion in 1960. Ten years later, in 1971, it was

171 billion rubles.[23] The change to the country's social profile was enormous. In 1940, there were only 4 million pensioners (of all categories, not just the elderly). By 1960, there were 19 million; in 1965 there were 24 million; and in 1970, 40 million.[24] Soviet society was getting older, but its access to welfare dramatically expanded across different age groups.

Thanks not least to its new pensions and apartments, the Soviet Union reached a brief high noon of equality some time around 1961. This was not inevitable. It was only one possible future of 1917. The Soviet Union was always a more equal place in social and economic terms than its capitalist contemporaries, overwhelmingly so if one disregarded the very highest echelon of political, security and cultural elites. But Soviet civilization was predicated on a sense of equality that was contingent, not constant.

For a start, the radical equality of war communism between 1918 and 1920 was a disastrous economic experiment which shook the nerves of planners for decades to come. In the 1920s, the New Economic Policy assumed that people responded positively to wage differentials and material incentives, boosting the economy. To some extent, the assumption worked. It did not last long. In 1928, the first five-year plan was a dramatic and deadly shift leftwards. This was a turn back towards Marxist class war. But it was only briefly a violent crusade for a more equal society. Stalinism stuck with violence but ditched equality. Its theorists condemned *uravnilovka*, or a tendency towards 'obsessive levelling'. After a brief dalliance with equal pay, planners understood that workers responded to differentials and incentives. Without them, there was no chance of hitting the plan's fantastical targets. Stakhanovites and shock workers got bigger rewards than their colleagues in return for norm-busting and greater productivity. The generation of promotees that rose through the ranks of industrial management and the technical professions from the humblest origins also lifted themselves out of the working class. They were a triumph for social mobility on the greatest possible scale, but they were a multiplicity of individual successes, not the raising of a whole class. The process created new hierarchies in Soviet society in the 1930s and 1940s. By the 1970s, meanwhile, the logic of those earlier developments resulted in a slowdown in social mobility as the older generation tried to pass on its privileges to its grandchildren. It was a tendency in all industrial societies, though with very particular dimensions and implications in the USSR.

The social reforms, economic management and cultural moods of the Thaw tended towards greater equality, though historians have yet to reconstruct the data comprehensively. Yet even in the 1950s and 1960s, workers responded to equality in a mixed way. Many of them deplored the equalization of access to pensions, whereby everyone who had worked at least twenty-five years received the same payments after retiring age. What was the point, they wondered, in having worked for forty-five? It was a dilemma of moral hazard to which Soviet civilization, like liberal capitalism, did not have a uniformly convincing answer, though it had a distinctive one: the invoking of rights inside the workers' state.

Pensions depended on universal rights. So did housing. Rights shaped the geography of the socialist city. As recipients of new housing, employees of the same enterprise often occupied the same building. White-collar and blue-collar workers routinely lived in the same staircase (*pod"ezd*). An accountant might live next door to a cloakroom attendant. Corruption and privilege maintained their hold during the Khrushchev era, when 'top people' still had their own apartment houses, but the housing programme fostered a kind of equality for the vast majority in theory and practice.

The same was even true at one of the USSR's most sought-after institutions of all, the Artek Pioneer camp on the Black Sea. Children could attend for an approximately two-month session, and the camp ran year-round. Its reputation was of an impossible-to-access place for the children of bosses. And yet it too was captured by the metaphor of glittering metropolis. 'The Pioneer city Artek' – insisted Anastas Mikoyan, Presidium member, when he visited during the early Thaw – 'is a city of the future communist society.'[25] Research on the sample year of 1960 shows that during off-peak seasons, the majority of children attending the camp were from children's homes, or from households where the wage-earners were from the urban working class or collective farms. In the desirable summer months, they still made up around one-third of attendees. In the January to March session, 15 per cent of children were from children's homes and 2 per cent from the very top class of Soviet life, the generals and composers; in June to August, under 4 per cent were from children's homes, and almost 13 per cent from the elites. In total, 43 per cent of attendees were from those white-collar backgrounds which could exercise influence, such as chief accountants in industrial plants. These numbers exclude foreigners, who were highly privileged, and might also exclude children from 'superstar' backgrounds who did not show up on all the paperwork. But the picture was clear. Artek was disproportionately for fancy kids, even during Khrushchev's high tide of equality. But it was not only for them.[26]

Equality rested on a legal apparatus of rights. Yet how could rights exist in a dictatorship? For some Soviet citizens, it was naive or preposterous to suggest that they possessed any rights. For others, it was axiomatic to their entire sense of self. The Soviet constitution of 1936 claimed that Soviet citizens had access to three types of rights: 'political' (such as the right to vote), 'social' (like the right to a job) and 'personal' (including a version of habeas corpus). It was an empty set of promises in a violent, arbitrary polity, but during the Thaw, some of these social and personal rights, such as the right to a pension and the right not to be arrested without due cause, gained enough viability to change the nature of the dictatorship.

The glittering metropolis was a Soviet utopia. It evoked an ideal, but one in which negotiations and compromises were constantly taking place. It was a place with permeable borders. Crossing borders of all kinds and in all ways was crucial to the Thaw. Five-and-a-half years before he gave the keynote address at the Twenty-second Party Congress, and a few weeks after his epochal speech at the Twentieth Congress, Khrushchev might have been reflecting on this very point. He was standing on the deck of a boat that was drawing into Portsmouth harbour.

World Festival of Youth, Moscow

# 5
# The Boundary Between Two Environments

Ivan Serov was also on board the *Ordzhonikidze* as it approached British waters. He was one of the most powerful men in the Soviet Union, but he was not coming to take tea with the Queen or sip whiskey in Downing Street. The previous month, he had visited the United Kingdom to check security arrangements for the forthcoming Soviet delegation. Anti-Soviet campaigners, many of whom were exiles from the USSR and other Eastern bloc countries, protested against the trip, focusing their anger on him personally. As Portsmouth hove into view, it was more diplomatic to keep his head below deck.

Serov was an obvious target. As the first ever chairman of the KGB, following the downgrading of the Ministry of State Security (MGB) to a 'Committee', he was a Chekist who had spent two decades in the business of thuggery and terror. Like so many top communists, Serov was an outsider, born in the year of the 1905 revolution in a village in Vologda *guberniya*. He joined the Party in the early 1920s as a teenager and went on to serve in the army. Rising through the officer ranks, he was one of the 'promotees' (*vydvyzhentsy*) of the Stalin era. It gave him something in common with Khrushchev, though he was a decade younger. In January 1939, he was transferred to the NKVD; in September, he moved to Ukraine. By this time, Khrushchev was already a member of the Politburo and the head of the Ukrainian republic. He became Serov's patron. In turn, the Chekist was a hard-man client who facilitated Khrushchev's rise to the top and his ability to stay in post. Their paths diverged during the war. In August 1941, Serov took charge of the forced resettlement of people of German descent from the Volga region. It earned him the Order of Lenin the following year. In March 1944, he was in Chechnya and Ingushetia, supervising the deportation of those peoples from their homes. The deportees rode in cattle wagons to Central Asia, dying and suffering in large numbers. Survivors were only allowed back home in the following decade. As the protestors in the UK pointed out, he really did have blood on his hands and all over his body.

Khrushchev controlled Serov. He used him to cement his own political position and charged him with defanging the successor agencies of the NKVD. It was yet another instance of the moral ambiguity of Thaw-era reform. Serov's status as the Chekist-reformer reflected the blurred edges and hazy moral zones of de-Stalinization. The limits of Soviet life were no longer certain. Its liminal spaces were clouded by fog and difficult to navigate, whether one was a government official, policeman, writer, doctor, accountant, factory worker – whoever one was.

Starkest of all was the boundary between East and West, the Iron Curtain. Stuck on board the Soviet naval vessel in Portsmouth harbour, Serov was lurking on a line that was no longer clearly marked, between what was interior to Soviet life and what was external to it. By the time that Khrushchev landed in Portsmouth, and Serov was patrolling the *Ordzhonikidze*'s lower decks, the Cold War had been going on for more than a decade. The Soviet Union was a closed society. And yet it was presenting a new face to the globe. The Party was inviting citizens to interact differently with the outside world, in both imaginative and practical ways. The Thaw was affecting the chemical composition of the Iron Curtain, creating spots of decay and permeability.

One can discern some of the origins of the Cold War in the Bolshevik revolution itself.[1] The capitalist powers put Bolshevik Russia in disgrace for suing for peace with the Central Powers at Brest-Litovsk, breaking the terms of international debt agreements, and above all for up-ending the laws of property and the hierarchies of class, and creating the world's first socialist society. Weimar Germany and Britain's new Labour government of 1924 were the first to recognize the USSR; the United States did not even establish a proper embassy in Soviet Moscow until the 1930s. The American distrust of Bolshevism and the USSR was particularly deep-seated. Yet the isolation of the USSR was not an inevitable consequence of the revolution. As ever, many possible futures were encoded into the events of 1917. At different times over the next seventy-four years, the revolution gave rise to a society that was partly open or completely closed, and that fluctuated on many points of the intervening spectrum.

In late November or early December 1955, Lyudmila Ulitskaya, the future scientist, theatre director and novelist, went to a performance of *Hamlet* in Moscow. Ulitskaya would soon be thirteen. Her grandmother, who had a life-long passion for the theatre, acquired the tickets and accompanied her.[2] It was a famous production by London's Tennant theatre company, directed by Peter Brook and starring Paul Scofield. They put on thirteen performances in a twelve-day period at the Moscow Arts Theatre (MKhAT), one of the most prestigious and technically proficient theatres in the capital. Sixteen thousand tickets were sold, and it was broadcast on television.[3] Brook's production did not disappoint anyone, not even the most sophisticated habitués of MKhAT. In his report to the prime minister, the British ambassador to Moscow described the play's triumphant reception.[4]

Ten months later, in October 1956, the Bolshoi Theatre came to London. It brought many of its great stars, such as Galina Ulanova, but not Maya Plisetskaya, whose father was executed during the Terror and whose mother was sent to the camps (Plisetskaya came on the next tour, in 1959). Their headline production was *Romeo and Juliet*; their TV spectacular was *Swan Lake*. Over the course of approximately one month, 55,000 spectators watched the Bolshoi at Covent Garden, with 9.5 million tuning in for the BBC programme on 21 October. Like Peter Brook's *Hamlet*, the Bolshoi tour was a high-profile breaching of the Iron Curtain, but it was special only because of its particular fame. In some ways, the Bolshoi at Covent Garden was much more important than *Hamlet* at MKhAT. The Bolshoi was a centre of excellence in world ballet, but it had been isolated from global trends and audiences for decades. Coming to London gave all the theatre's staff the chance to prove themselves on an international stage. Soviet ballet itself was being judged. It passed the test. Critics admired its novelty and pristine brilliance. Margot Fonteyn herself wrote that the Bolshoi's *Romeo and Juliet* 'burst on me as new and completely valid'.[5]

Khrushchev and Bulganin's visit to Britain fell between these two theatre tours. They arrived on 18 April and departed on 27 April. It was not an official state visit. Strictly speaking, Kliment Voroshilov, the chairman of the Presidium of the Supreme Soviet, was the ceremonial head of the Soviet state, and he was kept safely at home. This meant that they met the Queen for tea rather than a banquet, but otherwise the trip had the trappings of a top-level international visit. They had talks with the prime minister, Anthony Eden, and visited businesses, trade fairs and public facilities in different parts of the country. Everything was a great success apart from a Westminster dinner with the Labour Party. Old tensions between social democracy and communism came to the surface. Khrushchev declared that he would vote for Eden, not Gaitskell, if he had the chance. There was also a near-miss international incident when the Soviet delegation visited Oxford. Acting on last-minute intelligence, the police cancelled a visit to Eden's old college, Christ Church. In a stereotypically Oxonian moment – more show than depth – four undergraduates, all dressed as Stalin, planned to appear in the four corners of the college's main quadrangle, just as Khrushchev entered it himself from under Tom Tower.[6]

It would, of course, have been unthinkable for the real Stalin to have shown up at Christ Church. By contrast, Khrushchev's signature visit to the UK contributed to a general increase in trade and boosted the numbers of professional, scientific and cultural exchanges. Relations briefly worsened in late 1956 and early 1957 following the Soviet crushing of the Hungarian Revolution, but the gaps in the Iron Curtain continued to grow for the rest of the Khrushchev era. Notably, in January 1958, the United States and the Soviet Union concluded a treaty on educational and cultural exchanges. Three years earlier, Europe's international football federation, UEFA, came into being and brought together the countries of West and East in a single association that transcended the Iron Curtain. Despite occasional problems, this quickly matured into the sporting status quo. When Spain refused to travel to Moscow for a European Nations Cup qualifying fixture in 1958, UEFA fined the Spanish federation, and the Soviet Union went on to win the final stage of the inaugural tournament in Paris in 1960.[7]

Communities of specialist professionals in West and East exchanged technical expertise on an increasing scale. The International Social Security Association, in which ideas and policies about pensions and benefits were discussed, crossed the Iron Curtain. *Etatiste* French economic planners had been interested in the Soviet model since the 1930s. During the Thaw, they had the opportunity to travel to the USSR and meet officials from Gosplan and other agencies. Claude Gruson, who was director-general of France's National Institute of Statistics and Economic Studies between 1961 and 1967, argued throughout his time in office (and he had his opponents) that economic planning, inflected in part by Soviet models, enhanced French stability and democracy. He visited the USSR as part of a French delegation of economic planners in 1958.[8] There were thousands of similar visits from engineers, doctors and teachers. In 1955, the Soviet Union signed an agreement with Finland on scientific and technical cooperation. Nokia and other firms transferred Finnish technologies into the USSR following agreements with institutes of the Academy of Sciences in different Soviet republics, bolstered by decades-long trade deals.[9] Meanwhile, Soviet experts went on fact-finding missions to Western countries. Architects and engineers travelled to such countries as Sweden and the United States to observe mass housing developments and the use of prefabrication technologies.[10] This helped to create the Soviet-type city that was in turn partly exported to the socialist 'Third World'.

Resetting the relationship with the West was a necessary feature of de-Stalinization. It was another of the many possible futures encoded into 1917, recalling, if faintly, the working-class internationalism of the revolution but with a sharp Cold-War edge. The new cultural diplomacy was about competition and prestige as well as collaboration and exchange. The Russian language itself had a new global status thanks to the Soviet Union's superpower reach and its role at the United Nations. Foreign language instruction in the decolonizing 'Third World' became a contest between English, Russian and French. The People's Friendship University was established in Moscow in 1960 and attracted students from parts of Latin America and Asia, as well as Africa. They became specialists in their chosen fields through the medium of Russian, but were far from passive objects of Russophone indoctrination.¹¹ By the end of Khrushchev's time in office, eighty-five Russian language teachers who were Soviet citizens had been deployed across these regions, with hundreds more to follow in subsequent years. At the same time, Russian language instruction increased in capitalist countries, in response to strategic competition from the Soviet Union. The number of American high schools in which Russian was taught increased from nine to over 600 between 1957 and 1962; Soviet Russian teachers even took trips there to talk about language and culture, and to exchange pedagogical expertise.¹²

The revolution had long placed Soviet civilization on a different path from the rest of Europe. Khrushchev's claims about impending communism and Cold-War rivalries only seemed to emphasize Soviet distinctiveness in the early 1960s. Yet Ilya Ehrenburg, the author of *The Thaw* and the most cosmopolitan of Soviet writers, with long experience of Paris, argued that the revolution was an act of European culture, and that communism brought out the most European dimension of Russianness.¹³

If Soviet civilization really was a higher form of European society and culture, then the 'people of the sixties' were proud Europeans. In reality, they were anxious Europeans, full of complexes.¹⁴ How separate was their country from the West? This question assumed new layers of controversy at the time of the Cold War.

The intelligentsia was now a substantial educated public with cultural interests and an ideal claim to live according to conscience. In the USSR, it was made up of the likes of teachers, engineers, librarians, doctors, students and scientists. Varied and multifarious, it stretched across the Soviet nationalities, with dozens of republican and local iterations, linked by its foundation in Soviet civilization and its Russophone consumption of Soviet and Western culture. Its members absorbed cultural imports from the West, from Picasso to *Porgy and Bess*, from Bob Hope to Van Cliburn. Richard Nixon, then vice-president, brought the American National Exhibition of consumer items to Moscow's Sokolniki Park in 1959. He famously debated the merits of communism and capitalism with Khrushchev in an all-American kitchen. During its six-week run, 2.7 million visitors came to the exhibition. Members of the intelligentsia and working class alike left records in confidential visitors' books, expressing great interest in American life from within their Soviet worldview.[15] Soviet films such as *The Cranes Are Flying* won awards at the Cannes Film Festival. Many French, Italian, German and anglophone films were available to watch in Soviet cinemas. From the mid-1950s, more Western books were translated into Russian; many were published first in the journal *Foreign Literature*, which was so heavily in demand that its circulation was never adequate. The work of translation attracted skilled writers such as the famous children's author Samuil Marshak and became the subject of intensive training in literature institutes. Authors such as Ernest Hemingway were intensely popular. Their translated works were part of the mental furniture of educated people. In this way, foreign books transcended their own national origin, just as Soviet readers transcended theirs: the literature of the capitalist West and its Soviet audience met in a liminal space of open imaginative possibility.[16] This zone survived until the end of the Soviet Union and in a sense beyond it.

For many Soviet people, the West remained an object of fascination. Members of the intelligentsia might accrue detailed knowledge of the cultures and languages of the West, of the architecture and even street maps of cities like Paris and London, but the encounter with the West was essentially imaginary. It was almost impossible for all but the extremely privileged and extravagantly lucky – people like the author Daniil Granin – ever to travel outside the Eastern bloc. When those people did, some of them learned to act out a self-consciously correct Sovietness for their foreign hosts.[17] In a closed meeting with creative professionals in February 1963, Khrushchev told them to push forth Soviet culture while they were visiting the West as part of the 'struggle for influence' with capitalist cultures.[18] Intourist was founded in 1929 to arrange visits to the USSR by foreigners. Its aim was to accrue foreign currency for the Soviet state. In a virtuous circle that widened the zone of interaction across the Iron Curtain, the greater integration of the Soviet Union into global economic networks required more foreign currency to pay for imported machinery; one source of the money was foreign tourists' outgoings.[19] The number of foreign tourists coming to the USSR increased dramatically after 1955, though Moscow, Leningrad and the Black Sea retained the stamp of Cold War exotica; still, one million came on holiday every year between 1957 and 1965.[20] Adlai Stevenson, US presidential candidate in 1952 and 1956, travelled around the USSR on a tourist visa with friends and family in 1958, with apparently few restrictions and many opportunities to communicate spontaneously with local people. He concluded, not implausibly, that Soviet people wanted peace with America – 'and an apartment'.[21] The most evocative influx of foreign visitors during the Thaw came in July 1957, when Moscow hosted the World Festival of Youth. It was an extravaganza of uncontrolled enthusiasm, with 34,000 young people from all over the world arriving in the capital of communism to encounter each other's cultures, sports and academic learning. Friendship, romance and sex followed between Muscovites and their international guests.

Khrushchev was willing to accept the massive influx of foreigners to the World Festival of Youth partly because he trusted his subordinates to oversee the event. Ekaterina Furtseva was in charge of the city of Moscow; Ivan Serov ran the KGB. Yet Khrushchev was also temperamentally disposed to speak out in favour of the young. He trusted the judgement of his son Sergei, who had just turned twenty-two when the Festival started. Sergei Khrushchev was embarking on a technical and academic career in rocketry and ballistics and instinctively looked beyond the Iron Curtain for professional and intellectual ties. Following the Geneva summit of July 1955, Khrushchev Senior began to travel, making trips across Europe, Asia and the United States, holding meetings with statesmen but also visiting farms and factories, and engaging with civil groups and ordinary people. On 12 October 1960, during his second visit to the USA, he unwisely banged his shoe at the podium of the United Nations General Assembly, but during his first and much more successful visit to the USA the previous year, he famously befriended the Iowa farmer Roswell Garst, who fired his enthusiasm for maize (with mixed results for Soviet agriculture).

In Moscow, Khrushchev was also open to encounters from beyond the Iron Curtain. On 19 May 1959, a few months before travelling to the USA, he received a group of tourists from Florida. Stalin had eschewed foreign travel and most international contact, devising his global policy for the USSR from inside his Kremlin office and on the basis of reports that were written or filtered by the secret police.[22]

For Khrushchev, by contrast, scarcely a day went by when he did not talk to foreign dignitaries, scientists, journalists or business people. Typically, on 27 January 1958, he attended a reception at the Indian embassy in Moscow. On 28 January, he signed an agreement on economic cooperation with Egypt and hosted a reception in the Great Kremlin Palace for Aziz Sedky, the engineer who had become Nasser's minister of industry. The following day, on 29 January, he gave an interview to the publisher and editor of the West German newspaper *Die Welt*.[23]

Khrushchev was also deeply engaged in the Eastern bloc – from the crushing of the Hungarian Revolution to repeated visits and summits across the region. He combined a rhetoric of socialist friendship with strategic coercion that focused above all on the GDR and Berlin. After repeated international crises had brought him into confrontation, but also discussion, with Presidents Eisenhower and Kennedy, he approved the construction of the Berlin Wall, which began on 13 August 1961.

Yet 'Sovietization' in the bloc was a complex process, one of 'translation' rather than outright replication, with all the imperfections and unintended double-meanings that implied. Local people as well as Soviet outsiders participated. Even in the formation of secret police forces in countries like Czechoslovakia, local officials borrowed from German as well as Soviet precedents, not to mention from Scotland Yard. The security services in each country were also shaped by specific national contexts and local institutional traditions.[24] Over the next decades, despite the pressures of socialism and police states, the countries of the Eastern bloc retained their national distinctiveness. The Reichsbahn managed the railways of the GDR, and the Catholic Church sustained the religious life of Poland. Every country stayed in touch with its folk customs and national traditions, while the long-standing tensions of the region – such as the ethnic faultlines in Transylvania – continued to influence politics. But these countries were immediately recognizable as People's Democracies. They shared an urban aesthetic, consumer shortages, similar institutions and policy priorities. Knowledge and expertise circulated rather than imposed themselves. Although there were exceptions, such as the 'blood on the ice' that accompanied the Czechoslovak defeat of the USSR in the final of the 1969 World Hockey Championships, professional and personal encounters between Eastern bloc and Soviet people generally became routine and unproblematic, or amiable and trusting, or not infrequently intimate. In 1989, the 'satellites' hurriedly took the chance to claim democracy and capitalism, but until then, their presence in the socialist bloc seemed unavoidable. Soviet citizens therefore saw the classic imperial illusion: the velvet glove covered the iron fist, which allowed them to think of their civilization as fraternal and selfless in its international relations.

And so the external borders of Soviet civilization were blurred. The new Thaw architecture of the Black Sea resorts stretched across the coastlines of the USSR, Bulgaria and Romania. Artek in Crimea was a prestigious Pioneer camp for children, but there were dozens of other facilities in the region, in all these countries, for adults and families. These Black Sea resorts, sanatoria and camps were run by well-qualified medical staff; some institutions were better than others, but they looked similar – they were immediately recognizable members of a genre – with expanses of glass and light-painted concrete, pavilions, an amphitheatre with a view of the sea and a large canteen, where residents could expect meals prepared according to a specially formulated diet.[25]

The Eastern bloc was European, but the reach of postwar socialism was global. Soviet diplomacy and quasi-imperialism made inroads into the 'Third World' as the USSR supported development projects, such as the Aswan Dam in Egypt. Planners in India were sympathetic to socialist models. Communist parties governed Mongolia and China, even if relations with Moscow were difficult. Feminists from across the world, but especially those from single-party states of the Left, formed networks of cooperation that promoted women's rights in the context of 'global socialism'.[26] Cuba turned socialist after Castro's revolution. This led to the missile crisis of 1962, the most dangerous moment of the entire Cold War, though it was resolved when mutual understanding between certain individuals and interest groups in the USA and USSR prevailed. For the Soviet intelligentsia, the connection to Cuba fired the imagination and gave people from cold, tough places like the Arctic north the chance to see themselves as part of an exotic global project.[27] Soviet people could project themselves – in their intellects and imaginations, if only very occasionally in person – beyond the Iron Curtain and even into a whole-world space. Nowhere was Soviet civilization better defined than on the hazy boundaries that apparently delimited it.

The membranes of living cells suggested other grey zones and uncertain boundaries in the Soviet life of the Thaw. When Lyudmila Ulitskaya began her degree at the Biology Faculty of Moscow State University in 1962, she was immediately attracted to genetics. It was the first golden age of cell biology as a molecular science. Nine years earlier, at lunchtime on 28 February 1953, Francis Crick and James Watson, researchers at the University of Cambridge, had famously burst into the Eagle pub – they were regulars – and announced their discovery of the molecular structure of DNA, the building block of genetic material in living cells. It signalled a genetics revolution, with major consequences for the understanding of heredity and the treatment of disease.

Scientists now possessed a three-dimensional map to guide them when they crossed the boundaries of cell biology, entering the cell itself, locating the chromosomes, and observing genes. Seeing the structure of DNA made possible ever more sophisticated research into the molecular design of individual genes. But the map caused problems for Soviet scientists, who found themselves unable to use it in the way that their training and knowledge permitted. Instead, geneticists were trapped in an awkward zone, between their own institutions and those of international science, and between their instinct for scientific deduction and the ideological fantasy that surrounded them.

Genetics was an exception. Soviet science generally occupied the highest international levels. It developed the knowledge that engineers used to master space flight and nuclear weaponry; it also ranged across pure forms of knowledge. Four years before Ulitskaya started at Moscow State University's Biofak, in 1958, Pavel Cherenkov, Ilya Frank and Igor Tamm won the Nobel Prize in Physics for their work on the light-emitting qualities of particles that were travelling faster than the speed of light. In the year that Ulitskaya became an undergraduate, 1962, Lev Landau won the Nobel Prize for his theories about condensed matter in liquid helium. And two years into her degree, in 1964, she heard that Nikolai Basov and Aleksandr Prokhorov were sharing the Nobel Prize in Physics for their discoveries in quantum electronics.[28]

By contrast, DNA posed a problem for the Soviet scientific establishment. Despite the achievements of Soviet science and technology, genetics research in the USSR had been in crisis for three decades. Under pressure to increase agricultural yields at a time when food was desperately short, Stalin was drawn to the ideas of Trofim Lysenko. He promised to improve the health of crops by selective breeding. His theories, though, were based on unsubstantiated reasoning about the heritability of environmentally acquired characteristics. He refused to consider the role of genes. Yet despite his rejection of the most advanced international research, and his preference for instinct rather than experiment, Lysenko dominated agricultural science and genetic research in the USSR between the 1930s and 1960s. He was able to sideline those scientists who disagreed with him, sometimes with extreme prejudice. Nikolai Vavilov was one leading biologist who collided with Lysenko and died in the Gulag in 1943. He was rehabilitated in 1955, while Lysenko himself died of old age in 1976 in Kyiv (he was Ukrainian; he came home to die).

Khrushchev, who grew up working in the fields in Kursk *guberniya*, considered Lysenko's ideas to have a commonsensical quality and he kept him in post. Ten years after Crick and Watson's discovery, Lysenko was still, preposterously, the leading figure in Soviet genetics. But times were changing. The nature of the Thaw – liquid, hybrid, mixed – brought the boundaries of scientific debate into closer contestation. It was easier for Lysenko's rivals to stand up and make honest claims for DNA and the value of molecular research, though criticizing him personally was beyond the pale. On 11 May 1962, less than four months before Ulitskaya enrolled as an undergraduate at MGU, the Academy of Sciences held a conference on molecular biology, effectively in defiance of Lysenko. It led to the creation of a Scientific Council on Molecular Biology. The following year, Zhores Medvedev, who was both a leading biologist and a fearless anti-Stalinist voice, co-authored an article with Pyotr Kirpichnikov in the journal *Neva*, one of the most important mouthpieces of the intelligentsia. 'How did it happen that in our country the development of modern genetics was so long delayed?' they asked. 'The attempt to isolate Soviet biology from world science is a harmful remnant of the personality cult, an alienation from reality, a fear of openly and honestly admitting and correcting previous errors.'[29] In 1963 and 1964, a sequence of measures by the Academy of Sciences and even the Central Committee of the CPSU returned Soviet genetics to the international mainstream. In 1965, following Khrushchev's own fall from power, Lysenko himself was removed from office.

This was the time that Lyudmila Ulitskaya entered the third year of her degree programme in the Biological Faculty. At that point in her studies, she had the opportunity to specialize. 'This was the first year that the Lysenko department converted to a real genetics department,' she remembered many years later. Lysenkoites were removed from their posts and 'outstanding, real scientists' took their place, 'the strongest specialists in genetics', 'serious world stars'. Her teachers included Nikolai Timofeyev-Resovsky and Vladimir Efroimson.[30] Despite his great gifts, Timofeyev-Resovsky had long been a marginalized figure. He had been running a research centre at Lake Miassovo, 150 miles from Sverdlovsk in the Ural region, since 1956. Timofeyev-Resovsky was interested in the relationship between radiation and genetics; he had been imprisoned in the Gulag and, while in the 'zone', his work on radiation science had informed the Soviet nuclear programme. Ebullient and brilliant, he looked like an eternal survivor. In another indication of the pluralism that existed in post-Stalin professional life, even in unpropitious circumstances, the Academy of Sciences had permitted him this remote perch in the Urals, outside the view of Lysenko.[31] Timofeyev-Resovsky's transfer back to Moscow State University in 1965, where Ulitskaya became one of his students, was a fairy-tale coda to his career. Daniil Granin recognized that the story was a thrilling tale that revealed strange truths about Soviet civilization. He wrote a bestseller about Timofeyev-Resovsky, *The Bison*, that was published in 1987. Lysenko himself never got the point. 'I declare that we have never used and are not going to use any ideas and methods of molecular biology,' he was still announcing in 1974, nine years after he was sidelined, two years before he died.[32]

\*

The great struggle over Soviet genetics during the Thaw unfolded inside the Soviet Union's vast liminal space between the material and the spiritual. The Soviet Union was an atheist state, in which religious people were often persecuted. During the Civil War, the League of the Militant Godless had tracked down priests; many of them were killed. Yet religion was still a consolation for many, and policy was often ambiguous. In Central Asia, Soviet nationalities policy in the 1920s, tasked with establishing national identities, inadvertently worked to revive some Islamic practices which had fallen into obsolescence. Stalinism compromised with the Orthodox Church and Muslim believers during the Second World War.[33] By contrast, the logic of Khrushchev's Leninist revival demanded a renewed atheist campaign.

Khrushchev's turn against Orthodoxy was accelerated in October 1958, when the Central Committee voted in favour of a resolution 'on shortcomings in scientific-atheistic propaganda'. In 1959, the Party attacked the Church indirectly, undermining its finances by taxing the workshops that manufactured church candles, and directly, by requiring the closure of twenty-two monasteries and seven hermitages. Following discussion with the Orthodox Church, led by the Patriarch, Aleksy, the number of dioceses was reduced and restrictions were placed on the conduct of services.[34] It was a particular source of unhappiness that the status of priests was downgraded, making them more akin to salaried employees than independent men of God, no longer responsible for many of the administrative and financial duties in their parish, while circumscribing further the performance of rites and the tending of spiritual health. Between 1958 and 1965, the number of parish churches fell from 13,430 to 7,560. The most swingeing reductions were in the western part of the Russian republic, as well as Belarus and Ukraine, though in some places – such as Kamchatka, at the far eastern edge of the country – no churches remained at all.

The renewed drive against religion was couched in the language of 'scientific atheism'. For its most determined adherents, such as Presidium member Ekaterina Furtseva and leading ideologist Mikhail Suslov, atheism did not represent an awkward lacuna, a gap where God used to be, but a positive force for reshaping the Soviet person. Its precepts fitted within the Moral Code of the Builders of Communism. Atheism's material, here-and-now vision infused the tone of the new Third Party Programme, introduced at the 1961 Party Congress. It contributed to the idealism of the peak Khrushchev era. The All-Union Knowledge Society (*Znanie*) was founded in 1947; ten years later, it served as one of the vehicles for the mass atheist campaign. From 1954, it sponsored a new journal, *Science and Religion*, and launched a programme of accessible talks by lecturers who visited offices, collective farms and workers' clubs. There were 3.2 million such lectures in 1957, and 12.8 million in 1962.[35] In an offhand tone, Yuri Gagarin commented that he had not seen God during his flight in space; more earnestly, Gherman Titov, who had spent nearly twenty-four hours in the cosmos, said the same.

Orthodox believers were tormented by the risk of a godless future, but they were consoled by the past, especially the deeper past.[36] The atheistic campaign could close churches but it could not eliminate ecclesiastical expertise, destroy religious networks or extinguish faith in God. Patriarch Aleksy struggled at the hands of the bodies that supervised church–state relations, especially the shadowy Council for the Affairs of the Russian Orthodox Church, which had been run since its founding in 1943 by a secret policeman called Karpov. But the most striking evidence of resistance came from outside institutional politics. Ordinary people revealed the depth of their faith by protesting. Following orders issued on 5 June 1959 concerning the Soviet republic of Moldavia, four monasteries were closed. Attention turned to a fifth, the Rechulsky convent, which was home to 225 nuns. The nuns sent messages to their families and to nearby villages. Up to 200 people answered the call, coming to the nunnery and establishing a day-and-night protective watch upon it. KGB and Party activists arrived to face them down. A shot was fired. One of the local people died. Eleven others were arrested.[37] The nunnery was closed. Similar incidents took place in other parts of the USSR. A chain of women surrounding a church slated for demolition became a lasting image of the time.

Other leading religious groups suffered less, or in different ways. Ordinary folk raised their pitchforks against Christian 'sectarians' such as Pentecostals following invented claims of child sacrifice. Jehovah's Witnesses and Baptists also faced cruel taunting in Soviet newspapers.[38] Before 1953 and after 1964, some of traditional

Buddhist life continued in Buryatia (near Lake Baikal, in east Siberia), Kalmykia (in the Volga region north-west of the Caspian Sea) and Tuva (in outer Mongolia). Islam was the largest religion in the USSR after Orthodox Christianity. Between 1958 and 1964, it lost 22 per cent of its mosques. The impact on cities in the Russian republic, such as Kazan, was significant. But Islam was deeply embedded in the old towns and remote villages of Central Asia, where the population was growing rapidly. It was entwined in complex ways with local politics, and it was sometimes invisible to the Soviet bureaucratic gaze. Meanwhile, more synagogues were closed between 1958 and 1964 – 43 out of 135 – but the bigger threat to Jews had been during the time of the Doctors' Plot, on the eve of Stalin's death.[39] Both then and later, the Party's problem with Jews was not a matter of religion or spiritual community but of 'cosmopolitanism': the possibility of loyalty to a centre outside the USSR (perhaps 'international Jewry', or the diaspora, or Israel, or even the United States). Grafted onto older tropes of chauvinism, it ensured that everyday antisemitism and aspects of institutional prejudice continued. The particular awfulness of Soviet antisemitism was affected much less by official atheism than by the design of identity papers; it was hardly about religion at all. The fifth line of the internal passport required citizens to identify themselves as members of an ethnic group. 'Jewish' was one of them. A bureaucratic gaze was therefore immediately locked in.

In the 1960s, Lyudmila Ulitskaya was a Jew who became increasingly interested in the Christianity that derived from her culturally Russian heritage. It was another boundary. Some of the Thaw-era virtues that the intelligentsia articulated, and Soviet society more generally yearned after, had analogues in the Bible: justice, sincerity, conscience. As the 1960s went on, some Jewish members of the intelligentsia turned to Orthodoxy. Notwithstanding the genuineness of their conversion, or their mastery of a dual belief, some of them were other-thinkers – heterodox iconoclasts – by temperament and preference. They expressed their spirituality as another way of articulating dissent, as if they were speaking a new dialect of the dissident language.[40] Ulitskaya was moving into the milieu of the dissidents, but she thought that belief was a private matter. She made this clear in response to a question about her faith in a magazine interview after the collapse of the Soviet Union. 'To be honest,' she said, 'I consider that question the most inappropriate [*bestseremonnyi*] of all. The next in line is: who are you sleeping with?' For all his undoubted atheism, Khrushchev was also uncomfortable with the question, at least when he was talking to a Western journalist. 'The question of who believes in God and who does not,' Khrushchev told *Le Figaro*, 'is the personal affair of each individual. Therefore let us not discuss the subject in detail.'[41]

In the end, atheism was an unresolved question for Soviet civilization. Communism did not eliminate religion: Orthodoxy effortlessly returned to public culture during *perestroika*. Soviet atheism actually existed on the boundary between the spiritual and the material, rather than being an unambiguous example of the latter. Not believing in God was itself an expression of true belief – in Marxism-Leninism. During the Cold War, popular campaigns for peace and anti-militarism were officially couched in the rhetoric of communism, but were understood and expressed by large numbers of people in religious terms.[42] Marginal and especially poor people sublimated the idea of Soviet equality, for which they saw little evidence in the here and now, into a particular image of the afterlife (according to interviews conducted in 1964 and 1965 by social scientists working for the Institute of Scientific Atheism).[43] Thaw-era society was starkly located on the boundary between past and future, interrogating the recent history of the Stalin era while launching forth to communism; but questions of belief, in God or Lenin, which had an eternal sense about them, hovered awkwardly in the space between these temporal limits. The culture of the Thaw elevated conscience but rejected religious texts that described the sacredness of individual personhood. Renewed atheism was inspired by de-Stalinization and personal liberation, but the campaign did not offer a choice about religious belief; it demanded non-belief by all right-thinking people.

The self-fulfilling metaphor of 'thaw' created a fluid society that moved back and forth between the end of winter and the start of spring. Soviet civilization was never stuck. It always fluctuated along the boundary between environments. Other borders became more crucial as the long 1970s set in: between cultural dissent and permitted publications, or outright opposition and straightforward thinking for oneself, or central planning and the underground economy; while still others, such as the boundary between the Gulag and 'free' society, had defined the Soviet Union before 1953. No wonder that Khrushchev, with his ebullience, spontaneity and vulgarity, could not stop himself crossing a line. When he was in London in 1956, his hosts took him to the Albert Memorial and told him that the Prince Consort's first duty was to satisfy the Queen's wishes. 'And what did he do during the day?' Khrushchev shot back to the startled interpreter.[44] After years at the top, he still felt a social and intellectual insecurity. When he attended the *Thirty Years of the Moscow Artists' Union* exhibition at the Manezh Exhibition Hall, next to the Kremlin, on 1 December 1962, he could not help himself. Many genres of painting were on display, including the socialist realist canvases of Aleksandr Laktionov and the more controversial, edgy work of Robert Falk, including his *Nude in an Armchair* (1922). Choosing his words with maximum vulgarity, yelling and jabbing his fingers, Khrushchev explained what was wrong with such paintings as Falk's. He resorted to homophobic abuse, much to the fury of the sculptor Ernst Neizvestny (who loudly retorted by saying that he had fought in the war and had never had his sexuality challenged – and who later designed Khrushchev's gravestone). In putting on this unfortunate display, Khrushchev was to some extent set up by the Party ideologist Mikhail Suslov and the former KGB boss Aleksandr Shelepin, who had their own political agenda against some of these artists, but the words were pure Khrushchev. For the creative intelligentsia, and a significant number of the 100,000 viewers who had already attended the exhibition, these words crossed the wrong aesthetic line.[45]

Khrushchev was offending many reasonable people. He riled the intelligentsia and exasperated his colleagues. From 1962, the year of the Novocherkassk massacre, the public mood seemed to slip away from him. The Soviet value that he cared for most, equality, required great political dexterity to manage, but he was clumsily exposing the privileges of the provincial Party secretaries on whose support he depended. As the 1960s went on, quiet opposition to Khrushchev gathered ground in the Presidium. Leonid Brezhnev, with an easy-going manner and a flexible approach to policy, could not believe his luck.

Leonid Brezhnev and Ekaterina Furtseva

# 6

# Slush

On 27 October 1961, at the Twenty-second Party Congress, Khrushchev renewed his attack against Stalin. He reprised the Secret Speech by talking of how Stalin 'suffocated' and 'destroyed' the 'flower of the Red Army', as well as the Old Bolsheviks. Khrushchev imagined building a monument in Moscow 'to immortalize the memory of the comrades who became victims of arbitrary rule'. The only way to create a communist future was to acknowledge Stalin-era crimes, especially those that were committed against Party members, and to maintain the Marxist-Leninist line to which the Party had returned over the last few years. The redemption narrative was simplified, focusing on specific atrocities and targeting Stalin himself.[1]

On the night that Ekaterina Furtseva attempted suicide, on 31 October 1961, she survived, but Stalin was belatedly interred. Under cover of darkness, a pair of trucks drove through Moscow until they reached Red Square. They parked next to the Mausoleum. Men jumped out. They went into the constructivist red marble building and removed Stalin's body. It had lain there since his death in 1953. For eight years, the embalmed corpses of the two dictators, Lenin and Stalin, had rested next to each other, fully dressed in working clothes, protected by a glass screen, and maintained in formaldehyde. Now Stalin was buried in the ground next to the Kremlin wall, together with other heroes of the revolution. Lenin had the Mausoleum to himself. Stalin's name was removed from the front, and five large, elegant, Cyrillic letters – ЛЕНИН – were restored to single billing. Both the past and future of the revolution plainly belonged to Lenin and Leninism.

*

Khrushchev had dismantled many of the Gulag camps. He had desecrated Stalin's reputation more thoroughly than had ever seemed possible. But the process was uneven. Even the rhetoric was inconsistent. The problem went back to the start. Beria's original decree of March 1953, which began the process of emptying the camps, did not help the politicals, convicted under article 58 of the criminal code. They were the prisoners who were most spectacularly innocent of any crime. Over the next two years, 237,412 of them appealed for release, but only 4 per cent of the appeals were granted.

These numbers increased from 1956. Release was sometimes followed by rehabilitation, which meant an ex-*zek* (or former convict) was retrospectively declared innocent of the invented crimes and conspiracies of which he or she had been convicted. Many rehabilitations were posthumous, which not only cleared a dead person's reputation, but also helped surviving family members to lead more 'normal' lives. Yet most former *zeks* had a troubled transition to life beyond the wire. From November 1956, the deported nationalities, such as the Chechens and the Ingush, also began to return home. Some could only come home much later, like the Volga Germans in 1967, and others only returned in part, such as the Crimean Tatars. The manifest justice of national return created its own moral questions about practical life. Sometimes these were the same questions that all returnees faced, but in the higher concentration of a whole national community. Life had moved on since deportation. How should society balance the rights of those who had been allowed to remain with those who had been expelled? Should returnees get their old jobs and homes back, or should their successors keep them? What happened when a spouse had started a new life, and their partner returned, apparently from beyond the grave? These questions were never answered categorically. Various laws were introduced whose aim was to help returnees. In 1955, for example, district soviets in Moscow were required to give priority to former prisoners when allocating housing. The same year, the Council of Ministers passed a decree on job rights for former *zeks*. Laws that were supposed to guarantee the restitution of property and state honours were introduced in 1956. It all sounded much better in theory than it worked in practice.[2]

Aleksandr Solzhenitsyn, who soon became the Soviet Union's most famous former *zek*, faced one of the most complicated journeys home of all. He was born in December 1918 in Kislovodsk in the south of the new Soviet Russian republic. It was the height of the Civil War. There was money in his family, and plenty of religious faith. His father died during Aleksandr's infancy. He and his mother soon moved to Rostov, where Aleksandr went to school. He grew up knowing all about the loss of one civilization and the construction of another. Aleksandr's was a Soviet childhood of the 1920s and 1930s, materially impoverished, personally insecure, but with the possibility of ideological certainty. As a young man in the Komsomol, a student of mathematics, a schoolteacher, then a wartime officer, he was a normal part of Soviet civilization. He did not express doubts. Almost the same age as the revolution and saturated in its ideology, he inhabited the Soviet world. It was only natural that he supported Soviet communism.

Like most Soviet people, though, he could think for himself. He used Bolshevik words but in his own way. Called up in 1941, Solzhenitsyn was promoted to captain in 1944. His unit was engaged across the Belorusian republic and beyond, past Minsk, into Poland and east Prussia. On 9 February 1945, as fighting raged, he received a message to call on his brigadier. The men from Smersh – the military secret police – were there when he arrived. They took his gun, belt and map case, ripped off his epaulettes and removed the star from his military cap. It was all about a stray, harmless reference in a letter to his wife that the censors had chosen to read in their own way. He spent the next eight years in the Gulag.

Solzhenitsyn was incarcerated in different places. He started at the Lubyanka, then the Butyrki and Krasnaya Presnya prisons in Moscow, the New Jerusalem labour camp near the capital, where he dug wet clay out of the ground, and a facility at Moscow's Kaluga Gate. Then he was sent to a prison research institute, staffed by scientist-prisoners, at Rybinsk, on the Volga, 160 miles north-east of Moscow; this was a successor institution to the one where Korolev had been imprisoned while he developed jet engines. It was a so-called *sharashka*, a scientific-research prison; and he was imprisoned in another, at Zagorsk, an ancient town east of Moscow, where he worked as librarian, as he did in a third *sharashka*, Marfino, adjacent to Moscow's botanical gardens. Here he made friends with fellow intellectuals, including the writer Lev Kopelev. He even had the chance to see his wife, Natalia. Relatively speaking, it was a haven; his biographer speculates that his three years at Marfino 'probably saved his life'.[3] But then he was transported via a tortuous sequence of journeys to Ekibastuz, a 'special' hard-labour camp, terrifying to anyone, in the freezing Kazakh steppe. He worked various backbreaking tasks for five years, in a construction brigade, in the foundry and elsewhere.

On 13 February 1953, three weeks before Stalin died, Solzhenitsyn was released from his camp in the Kazakh republic. He was sent into exile in a desert settlement in Uzbekistan. Soon he developed cancer, and received a terminal diagnosis, but he lived (see chapter 10). It was only in 1956, after the Secret Speech, that his exile, which should have been forever, was brought to an end. Although his marriage of 1940 had ended in divorce, and his wife, Natalia Reshetovskaya, had found a new husband, they met again in 1956 and rekindled their relationship. The restored couple made their home in Ryazan, where, in September 1957, Solzhenitsyn began teaching physics and astronomy at School Number 2. He turned forty. Solzhenitsyn had never stopped writing, in his head, on scraps of paper, in battle, in camps, in exile, in hospital. He was a machine that couldn't switch off, one that endlessly tilled the fields of language, history, moralism and imagination.

The first great harvest was a short novel that recounted a single day in the life of a single Gulag prisoner. Ivan Denisovich was an everyman *zek*, a peasant, imprisoned for no comprehensible reason. He understood the world in terms of fate and personal agency rather than Marxism. His terrible experiences were part of earthly existence, no more explicable than bad weather or poor harvests. Ivan Denisovich accepts the camp as a diurnal reality, located beneath the same moon as his village, part of his life's continuum. The camp is a place of dread and lawlessness, rough, filthy and dangerous, freezing and unhealthy, run by arbitrary power, but it's also a place he endures a day at a time. Terrible as his life is, he has a lucky streak. Ivan Denisovich is a peasant, entirely rough-edged in speech and manner. As he encounters all types of people in the camp – politicals, common criminals, newly Soviet Balts, nationalist west Ukrainians, guards, gentle souls, murderous thugs, cynics, dreamers – and has to live alongside them, the camp becomes a place of universal humanity amid disgusting behaviour and conditions, where each life, however flawed or different, has an irreducible value (though not in the eyes of the authorities). By instinct and luck, he knows that there are things he can do to make his survival more possible: how to eke out a little extra sleep, where to find a few minutes of warmth, when to make a well-timed visit to the sick bay, how to collaborate with the fellow members of his work brigade to minimize work-rate while maintaining rations. He knows the value of a battered spoon, half a crust of bread, a pinch of tobacco, a friendly word, a game of cards. He knows too that an extra bowl of kasha is a happy day, an end in itself. Such knowledge and experience brings with it a kind of redemption: an existence measured in real time, not in five-year plans, Marxist schemes or professional ambitions, under the same sky as the family from whom he was severed, with the hope of rejoining them. The day that the novel records is both an account of hell on earth and a succession of small wins, a lucky day.

Perhaps the necessary factor in Solzhenitsyn's own genius was luck. He got *Ivan Denisovich* published. Against unreasonable odds, he hit on the nexus between what was possible and what was right at the most fluid moment of the Thaw. He somehow attracted the attention of the one literary figure with the moral judgement and political reach to deliver publication. *One Day* was a good book but its historic greatness went beyond the text itself and derived instead from its reception: how it was read, reflectively and quietly, and how people responded to it in what passed for the 'public sphere'. Solzhenitsyn showed that a novel about the Gulag could indeed be published and ignite a country-wide debate.

A couple of weeks after the renewed anti-Stalinist drive of the Twenty-second Party Congress, on 4 November 1961, Solzhenitsyn travelled by train from Ryazan to Moscow. He checked into a hotel in the Ostankino district. His friend Raisa Orlova, the wife of Lev Kopelev from the Marfino *sharashka*, collected the manuscript from him and delivered it to the offices of the literary journal *Novyi mir*. Both Orlova and Kopelev were already figures of moral stature in the Moscow underground of the Thaw. They were disappointed Leninists of literary and Slavic sensibility, like Solzhenitsyn himself. In the Brezhnev era, Orlova and Kopelev would both become major dissidents of international standing. Of course, dozens of unsolicited manuscripts arrived at *Novyi mir* every day, but Orlova had a connection on the staff who could get the manuscript into the hands of the editor, Aleksandr Tvardovsky.

He was not only a great literary editor but also a famous poet, the author of the very popular wartime novel in verse *Vasily Tyorkin*; and he started life in a village, where his family was victimized by collectivization and from where he escaped to find literary success in Moscow. No one apart from Tvardovsky could both appreciate *One Day in the Life of Ivan Denisovich* and work out how to get it published. He warmed instinctively to the peasant protagonist, admired the linguistic originality and respected the author's moral courage. Reading the text was like breathing the pure air of sincerity; he compared the experience to reading Tolstoy.[4] The text's direct, realist, ethical engagement was expressed in a new kind of literary language, replete with swear words, neologisms and revived archaic forms, which derived from Solzhenitsyn's reading of the classic Russian dictionary compiled by Vladimir Dal' in the library of the Marfino *sharashka*. Tvardovsky thought that Solzhenitsyn's original literary effect gave readers a chance to understand the camps in a form that transcended socialist realism and boilerplate Soviet rhetoric – useless aesthetics for addressing the Soviet tragedies of the past – while still being somehow publishable.[5] Tvardovsky knew that only Khrushchev himself could approve the publication of such a faithful work of Gulag fiction. In the early 1960s, it was only Tvardovsky who knew how to maximize the chances of such an outcome.

Tvardovsky was a longstanding anti-Stalinist. His seat on the Central Committee gave him a platform to support Khrushchev's reforms. He quietly sent the manuscript to Vladimir Lebedev, Khrushchev's private secretary, avoiding the obstacles associated with a formal approach. Although he later claimed to support the text, the 'conservative' head of the Culture Department of the Central Committee, Dmitry Polikarpov, would have killed it had he seen it blind. Tvardovsky chose well: Lebedev wanted the manuscript to see the light of day. In the summer of 1962, Lebedev and Tvardovsky discussed revisions that would make the work more agreeable to Khrushchev and better suited to publication. Lebedev bided his time. In September, while on a trip to Crimea, he read the manuscript to Khrushchev, who was absorbed by it and called for Mikoyan to join them. Khrushchev appreciated the peasant sensibility of Ivan Denisovich, the inventive earthiness of the language, and the universal realism of the portrayal of the Gulag. He understood the text's ethical urgency, its congruence with his own anti-Stalinism, and its usefulness for a wider population seeking to make sense of their experience of state violence. Plainly the consequences of anti-Stalinism fluctuated during the Thaw, but this was the right moment for such a novel. Lebedev read and read, the evening went on and on, and Khrushchev said yes, of course this must be published. Why has it not been published already? Nothing must be placed in its path.

It came out in the November issue of *Novyi mir*. People across Soviet society devoured it. Many of them read it several times before passing the issue on to friends and acquaintances. Solzhenitsyn was catapulted to the literary stratosphere. Hundreds of people wrote letters to him. The historian who has most thoroughly analysed the *Novyi mir* archive calculates that 80 per cent of these letters were favourable.[6] Some former prisoners were relieved to find a realistic depiction of the camps that gave public expression to their memories. It provided a new map with which relatives could navigate their daily grief and better see the place that had consumed their loved ones. The novel was also a source of education for the reading public generally. Many readers used it as a starting point to address the matter of who was to blame.

Tvardovsky understood that people needed some kind of public space in which shared reflection about Stalinism was possible. Justice was unlikely. But if books and films that dealt with the terrible losses of Stalinism were available, and people could talk about them, the process might reduce the psychological burden that the population carried. Even letter-writing to writers and publications served a function: the letter would be read and archived for posterity, even if there was no response and it was never published. With the exception of the Stalin period, Russian culture had long acted as a communal conscience and debating chamber about social and political problems. Following the publication of *One Day*, debates inspired by the book took place at kitchen tables across the USSR, in institutes and workplaces, at public meetings of readers in libraries and workers' clubs, and perhaps with most poignancy, in the long letters that people wrote to *Novyi mir* without expectation of a response, about their own experiences of loss and incarceration during the Stalin period and their engagement with Solzhenitsyn's text.

Aleksandr Tvardovsky himself wrote about the Terror and the return from the camps in his 1960 poem 'Distance beyond Distance'. It won him the Lenin Prize. Konstantin Simonov's war novel of 1959, *The Living and the Dead*, was inflected by socialist realism and engaged only allusively with the events of 1937, but did so sufficiently to have a powerful effect on readers long unable to place their own tragic stories in a wider national narrative. The great poets of the Thaw gave readings in enormous public venues, from city squares to football stadiums. Yevgeny Yevtushenko mused in 1963 that removing Stalin from the Mausoleum was emphatically not the same as 'rooting Stalin out of Stalin's heirs'. How to do this remained for Yevtushenko an open question, the great question of the time.

The cinema of the Thaw invited an even wider audience to share communally their memories of the Stalinist past, especially of the Great Fatherland War. Award-winning films such as *The Cranes Are Flying* (directed by Mikhail Kalatozov and released in 1960) and *Ballad of a Soldier* (Grigory Chukrai, 1959) showed how ordinary civilians shaped the war's course and were in turn shaped by its violence. Stalin was absent, and other 'great men' possessed a merely ambiguous morality. Meanwhile, public spaces created new ways for individuals to interpret their personal experience and the validity of their family memories. In Leningrad, the massive Piskarevskoye cemetery for Blockade victims opened in 1960. The following year, Stalingrad was renamed Volgograd; its vast Mamayev Kurgan memorial complex had already been under construction for two years. In the zones of wartime occupation, local investigations into collaboration with the Nazis, including by Party officials of good standing, had been a matter of public attention for some time, for example in the Belarusian republic.[7]

Publicity about Stalinist violence made it easier for individuals and families to address the traumas of the Great Terror, the Second World

War and the Gulag. But in the absence of public memorials to the state's atrocities, or a consistent public discourse, or a democratic arena in which the Party could be rigorously tested, it was much less clear whether a public consensus or moral agenda could be introduced that would make it impossible to return to Stalinism. Despite occasional interventions, such as Yevtushenko's poem of 1961 about the mass killing of Jews in Kyiv – 'Over Babyi Yar / there are no memorials' – and Anatoly Kuznetsov's documentary account of the same events, published in censored form in 1966, the Holocaust eluded proper memorialization, and many Jews emigrated from the Soviet Union in the 1970s, sometimes encouraged to do so by the authorities. Other epoch-defining atrocities, not least the Ukrainian famine of 1932–3, with its 3.9 million victims, were scarcely discussed at all. Khrushchev nodded towards the tragedies in Ukraine in his Secret Speech, but did not acknowledge them properly, just as he suggested building in Moscow a monument to the victims of Stalinism, but did not actually construct it. Other awful events, notably the deportation from and only partial return to their ancestral homelands of such national minorities as the Crimean Tatars, defied public analysis. The absence of a general and sustained public reckoning or an accepted and comprehensive narrative of events was a disaster for survivors. It also risked blunting the critical faculties of society over succeeding decades.

Even so, the Thaw created a new interface between the past, present and future of the Soviet experiment, one that, for a decade or so, remodelled the relationship between the public understanding of Stalinism, the definition of individual citizenhood and the official promise of impending communism. This interface was at least partially dependent on sincerity and truth. But it did not offer transparency or straightforward progress. This was no fairytale narrative that took the Soviet people from darkness to relative light. History and memory were aways charged and open to dispute. Aleksandr Tvardovsky and *Novyi mir* had their own sensibility, but so did other journals and publishers with more national-minded or 'conservative' dispositions. Other editors and journals were also revisiting the Soviet past, such as the national-conservative *Molodaia gvardiya*.[8] Khrushchev's own position fluctuated. In 1963, he claimed that literature focused too much on the 'dark side' of the Stalin period, citing *The White Flag*, a play by Vladimir Tendriakov and Kamil Ikramov. Debates about the cult of personality continued. At some points anti-Stalinism was emphasized; at others, it fell into shadow. But public culture maintained a general process of de-Stalinization until the crushing of the Prague Spring in 1968 (see chapter 9).[9] The Thaw was a zone of slush, not a season of discrete stretches of ice and water. It was a muddy, messy reality – and sometimes a joyous fantasy. A sudden transition to summer might have overwhelmed Soviet society by forcing a reaction from the security services. It was precisely the slush of the Thaw that allowed Soviet civilization to survive the violence of the Stalin years and to come to terms with it very imperfectly. Soviet society could not 'recover', though. And it was never clear what that could have meant.

In the spring of 1964, Vladimir Vysotsky was walking through the Moscow slush to an audition at the relaunching Taganka Theatre. The director was Yuri Lyubimov. He had just moved from a post as tutor at the Shchukin Theatre School. It was part of the Vakhtangov Theatre, in Moscow's Arbat, where Lyubimov had been an actor for many years. He'd starred in such films as *Days and Nights* (1943) and *The Kuban Cossacks* (1949), and he was married to an actress, Lyudmila Tselikovskaya. Lyubimov was also a theatre actor of major accomplishments, with more than a quarter-of-a-century's worth of roles at the Vakhtangov. Above all, he was a person of his time: the actor who had served in the NKVD's song and dance troupe during the war was also the Thaw-era teacher looking for truth.[10]

Vladimir Vysotsky was not one of Lyubimov's students at the Vakhtangov. Instead, he had trained to be an actor at the Moscow Arts Theatre and then worked at the Pushkin Theatre, which was undergoing a creative lull in the early 1960s. He was twenty-six and professionally unsettled, so he grabbed the chance to audition at the Taganka. Vysotsky showed up with his guitar. 'You have your guitar,' Lyubimov said to him. 'Perhaps you'd like to play something?' He sang one of his own songs, then another. Lyubimov asked him whose songs they were. Vysotsky told him. Lyubimov took him. The legend was, who could resist him? His first role was as the nephew in Bertolt Brecht's *The Good Person of Szechuan*, the theatre's inspirational first play that continued to run for decades. He was there from the opening night of the new theatre in September 1964.[11]

Soviet theatres belonged to the tradition of troupe and repertoire. They occupied substantial premises, employed their own company of actors, owned scenery, props and costumes, and had a large backroom staff on the permanent payroll. Actors often remained at the same theatre for many years, even their whole careers, performing alongside their colleagues in comedies and tragedies, across the range of roles and emotional registers. Tickets could be inexpensive but were sometimes in short supply. Theatres typically put on performances six nights a week and sometimes two matinées. They had a programme of plays, some of which might run for years, while others were rotated off and new ones added. Actors in the company had parts in several plays – leading in some, minor in others – and so would work a week of different roles. The new repertoire of the Taganka grew steadily. Starting with *The Good Person of Szechuan*, four further plays were added in the first year. Most striking in terms of language was *Antiworlds*, based on the verse of a major poet of the Thaw, Andrei Voznesensky.

As a visual spectacle, though, *Ten Days that Shook the World* (from John Reed's famous book about 1917) exemplified Lyubimov's project. He wanted to create total theatrical evenings that blurred the boundaries between performance and experience, and between poetry and drama. The aim was to test the membrane between actors and audience. On nights when *Ten Days* was on, theatregoers arrived at the Taganka to see actors in Civil War uniforms, complete with hats and bayonets, mingling with the crowd in the street while staying in character. Some of them were playing guitars, balalaikas or harmonicas, singing songs from 1917 or reciting revolutionary *chastushki* – brief slips of comic folk verse. Revolutionary banners hung on the walls of the theatre. As theatregoers went through the entrance, another soldier would put their bayonet to one side and check tickets with a knowing look. There were posters from 1917 and 1918 hanging around the foyer. Women in red kerchiefs sold programmes, served drinks and guided viewers to their seats. In the auditorium, a factory worker, soldier and sailor came onto the stage and shot a weapon in the air. Smoke and a smell like cordite drifted across the rows of seats. The stage was bare, but as the action proceeded, the impression was of a living space, inhabited by 250 characters, ingeniously performed by the much smaller cast.[12] The technical challenge of costume changes, understood by the audience, tested the membrane between performance and reality even further. The revolution here was high tempo, unpredictable, fragmented into individuals, but also more than the sum of its parts. Vysotsky played at least six roles, including those of Kerensky, a sailor, and an anarchist. He was immediately a distinctive face of the Taganka, with his melodious, gruff voice that seemed to summon up the force of his thorax, as well as his musicality, and his mischievous, vulnerable physiognomy.

The atrocity at Novocherkassk on 2 June 1962, when twenty-four innocent, unarmed people were massacred by the security police during a spontaneous strike (see the Prologue), symbolized the vulnerability of de-Stalinization. If the Taganka was an arena in which a limited pluralism seemed possible, and big questions of de-Stalinization could be broached in some form, Novocherkassk suggested the opposite: ice, not slush. It might have been a single violent incident, but it showed that Soviet civilization still contained a barbaric aspect. It was incapable of resolving an open clash of interests between the masses and the higher-ups. Novocherkassk was the leading example of unrest in the USSR during the Khrushchev era. Incidents of unrest were isolated and lacked leadership. Sometimes they just played themselves out. But together they hinted that a de-Stalinized Soviet Union might even be a contradiction in terms. Perhaps Soviet civilization was less varied and robust than the successes of Solzhenitsyn and Vysotsky implied. And the unrest posed a threat to Khrushchev personally, not least because he was sometimes the personal target of popular derision.

Over time, the run of small disturbances that culminated in Novocherkassk indicated to Khrushchev's senior colleagues around the Presidium table that he might have lost his common touch. Did the unrest imply that de-Stalinization was the problem, or Khrushchev personally? Protests tended to be prompted by dismal living conditions, but anger was often expressed in terms of social justice. Khrushchev was himself a target of ire. Unrest took place, for instance, in the Virgin Lands, where settlers and temporary workers encountered tough, frontier-type conditions, notably at Termitau (in the Kazakh republic) and Krivoi Rog (in the Ukrainian republic) in the summer of 1958.[13] Fishermen protested in the Far East (Primorsky krai) in May 1961. According to one disillusioned provincial, 'In the districts that border other states, everything is inexpensive, but deep inside the USSR, everyone lives in great poverty and everything is expensive.' It created a moral problem that transcended socialism. 'You can't subsist on your salary,' he went on, 'which is why everyone steals and deceives one another. You can find truth only if you pay for it.'[14] There were other protests about social conditions, for instance at Krasnodar in January 1961, Chita in December of the same year and in Sumgait in November 1963. In the army, too, conscripts expressed their anger. The historian Vladimir Kozlov isolates forty-four examples of serious unrest in the military between 1953 and 1960, including among the garrison at Perovo, then in Moscow Region (soon to be a district of the city itself) in July 1958.[15]

Perhaps this was a so-called 'crisis of rising expectations', familiar in one form or another in all modern societies. Social and economic improvements drove a reasonable hunger for more. Khrushchev's 'harebrained schemes' did not help. He was mocked for his proposals to grow maize (corn) across the USSR. His earthy manners met with a mixed reception. His ostentatious atheistic campaign went against the compromises that sustained Soviet civilization in the post-Stalin period, provoking opposition, especially among peasant women, who stood up to be counted, sometimes literally so, in human chains around their sacred spaces, for instance at the Rechulsk Convent in the Moldavian republic in June 1959. De-Stalinization caused unrest among national minorities. Georgians rose up on hearing rumours of the Secret Speech, widely imagined as a besmirching of their national son. Bitter contests followed between returnees and stayers on, or between members of different national groups, sometimes causing significant instability, at Grozny in Chechnya in August 1958, and in an Ingush 'pogrom' of July 1960. More dramatically, Chechens marched on historic foes in neighbouring Dagestan in April 1964.

Evidence was mounting of Khrushchev's unpopularity. 'How much longer will Khrushchev abuse the people and feed them promises of a bright future?' a citizen of Gorky region wrote in a dissident leaflet that was picked up by the KGB. Among his demands was the baking of unadulterated bread. 'Let Khrushchev eat that bread!' he suggested.[16] In Novocherkassk, Khrushchev's name and image were personal targets of protestors.

Khrushchev got the blame for the country's poor agricultural performance. Static output for a growing population was a problem across the union, but it created a deadly scandal in Ryazan, where Solzhenitsyn lived. The region's huge increases in meat production were fêted across the union, but they turned out to be the result of deliberately slaughtering too many animals in 1959. This caused dramatic shortages the following year. The local Party secretary lost his post – and then committed suicide. It was Khrushchev, though, who began to look ridiculous. He flailed around, searching for solutions to low production and low productivity; in 1958, for example, he abolished Machine Tractor Stations, the agencies that provided agricultural machinery to collective farms. Khrushchev was restless, fearing that food was at the heart of an emerging crisis in the USSR, just as it had been in 1917. In 1961, he travelled tirelessly and fruitlessly across the provinces, trying to get agriculture going.[17]

Between 1953 and 1962, the area under corn cultivation in the USSR increased from 3.5 million hectares to 37.2 million.[18] Thereafter the proportion of corn in the national economy fell, but the crop remained significant. The mass-planting of corn had echoes of Stalinist giantism, refracted through Khrushchevian enthusiasm, but it headlined a shift away from Stalin-era agricultural policy in a package of reforms to rural prices, wages, financial systems and welfare. Khrushchev wanted normal, modern standards of life for the countryside, and rational systems of planning and administration in the agricultural provinces, while ensuring food supplies to cities. Still, it was easy to mock. 'Why did Khrushchev become our master?' asked one citizen in a letter of 1958 to the Supreme Soviet. 'After all, he is a corn peddler, a comedian, and a swindler.'[19]

Political opponents saw the Cuban Missile Crisis of 1962 as another instance of dilettantism run amok. Some leading diplomats deplored the way that Khrushchev backed the Soviet Union into a corner by approving the deployment of Soviet nuclear arms in Cuba. They had burned with embarrassment when he banged his shoe at the podium of the United Nations General Assembly precisely two years earlier. Military hawks took a different line. Already suspicious of him for his cuts in the defence budget, and his political betrayal of Marshal Zhukov, they despised him for not humiliating the Americans, at a minimum, in Cuba. Khrushchev was eventually guided by two principles in October 1962, when the world was on a countdown to mass destruction. First, he was willing to seek compromises, to make use of 'back channels' in transatlantic diplomacy and to draw on the robustly sympathetic sense of the American president's intentions that he had taken from their Vienna summit meeting of 1961. Second, he did not want to take risks with global mass destruction. He agreed to withdraw missiles from Cuba in return for the Americans' withdrawing missiles from Turkey. It helped to save the world. Yet none of it was good internal politics for Khrushchev.

Even worse politics was Khrushchev's inconsistent attitude to the bigwigs on whose support he depended. The Secret Speech helped most of the political and administrative elites – the top dozen in the Presidium, the top 2,000 in the Central Committee, as well as the rest of them: factory directors, generals, judges, writers, composers, film stars, academicians, retail trade bosses. They wanted a promise that the KGB would not come after them as the NKVD had come after their predecessors. By describing Stalin's Terror in the first instance as an act of violence against the Party, which was a partial conclusion to say the least, and by insisting that this would never happen again, the implication being not on his watch, Khrushchev was promising them stability. And by pinning the blame on Stalin personally, he was tacitly demonstrating that the men and women in the hall need not fear the consequences of their own culpability. The Secret Speech turned the page for them, offering a new start.

But if the accommodation between Khrushchev and the top few thousand made possible reforms that transformed the Soviet Union, it also exposed the frailty of these reforms, because at the heart of some of them was a politically risky, insecure assumption about reducing the privileges of elites. And Khrushchev depended only indirectly on popular support; what really counted was the backing of the Central Committee.

Worse, he incompletely controlled the machinery of Soviet politics. Khrushchev lacked Stalin's tools and capabilities: a political system that rested on maximum control of the administrative apparatus, a keenness to unleash the secret police, a conviction that the ends justified the means and a personal capacity that was 'head and shoulders' above his colleagues.[20] Stalin was a true dictator in all senses, including as the centralizer of power in his own person. Khrushchev lacked the ability or will to do this. Stalin ensured that the men who sat in the Politburo were completely loyal to him. He personally controlled a cadre of senior managers whom he could distribute to key positions across the country. Khrushchev did not have this kind of uncontested power. Laid over this system were 'clans'. Groups of officials from the same region, informally organized as patron–client networks, and bound together by mutual understanding, local identity and a certain level of trust, helped each other up the career ladder. Khrushchev's own career was launched by his comrades from Dnepropetrovsk, especially his patron, Kaganovich. After 1953, these clans solidified and multiplied. They became competing power centres, which undermined the central authority of Khrushchev himself, even though he played the game as well: Ekaterina Furtseva was the senior figure in the Moscow clan, and she owed her promotions to him.

Khrushchev had risen to power by strengthening the Party at the expense of ministries. He could use this to grease the wheel: his former bodyguard, Valentin Pivovarov, led the Central Committee 'housekeeping' department that administered the provisioning of goods and perks to senior Party figures.[21] The problem was systemic, though, because he had fewer of 'his people' working for government agencies than Party organizations. On a formal level, Khrushchev launched major administrative reforms whose aim was to strengthen the Party, in sharp distinction to the way it was weakened catastrophically during the Terror. Above all, Khrushchev wanted the small units of Party life in apartment houses and workplaces to mobilize the population and thereby facilitate the everyday implementation of the new Third Party Programme of 1961, and its promised drive towards communism in the foreseeable future. These were not the instincts of a machine politician, husbanding power and capable of keeping hold of it indefinitely.

He loved power and politics, and he enjoyed the material comforts of success, but he had an awkward relationship with privilege and luxury. This placed him in a tricky position with many senior figures, who wanted better access to the good things in life. In both Moscow and Kyiv, the older generation of the family joined the Khrushchev household, bringing to it an uncompromising peasant ambience. Khrushchev's wife recalled her father-in-law catching the tram from the House of Government in Moscow to collect rationed potatoes and carrying them home 'on his back'. Khrushchev was reputed not to like the grand apartment on Granovsky Street, preferring country walks and socializing with local deer and foxes at the rural Moscow Region dacha to which he was also entitled. According to his son Sergei, Khrushchev put off as long as possible the use of an armour-plated ZIS limousine after he became entitled to it in 1950 and immediately relinquished it when Stalin died. He was also indifferent to Malenkov's plan to house the post-Stalin Presidium in a newly constructed compound of mansions in the south-west of the city, not far from the university, but he was also quite willing to go along with it.

When Sergei matriculated at the Moscow Power Engineering Institute, the Malenkov family bought him a Faber case of instruments for technical drawing that looked so 'genuinely valuable' that he 'never risked using it'. On another occasion they bought him an expensive set of magnifying glasses, whose usefulness and elegance seemed striking to him. They were just what he wanted, and few people had such things, but they were not obscenely lavish gifts. Khrushchev's children married into an elite of apparent princelings, but they did not enjoy the same trappings as their peers. Sergei Khrushchev got married in June 1957. After his wedding, he and his wife went straight to work at a precision engineering plant at Zagorsk, one of the medieval towns near Moscow.[22] Partly thanks to Khrushchev's example, this second generation did not follow their fathers into power.

The tension between elites and equality with which Khrushchev struggled was exemplified in his education law of 1958. It was a modernizing measure that extended compulsory schooling by one year. But it was also a step towards communism. By requiring pupils to spend time working on the factory shop floor or in a collective farm, it sought to emphasize the value of manual labour, to remind everyone that this was the workers' state, and to prevent a privileged caste from forming.[23] This drove top people round the bend. The prospect of cherished offspring delaying matriculation into higher education was almost heretical for many parents in the intelligentsia and the senior management cadres. Also unpopular was the law's shift towards making schooling in republican languages, such as Armenian or Estonian, non-compulsory. All-union officials claimed that the curriculum in the republics was overburdened with three sets of language lessons – Russian language, the local language, a foreign language – and that only two out of three were manageable. Khrushchev most likely wanted to streamline the curriculum, to make it modern and technologically minded and to equip the younger generation for the construction of impending communism. The senior administration of local republics, as well as many ordinary people, preferred to keep all three languages at the cost of an extra year of schooling compared to peers in the Russian republic. In practice, most of the time, the republics pursued their own path despite the letter of the law, but the impression of Khrushchev's high-handedness remained.[24]

Meanwhile, other changes discombobulated privileged officials. There were plans to decentralize the functions of economic ministries and Gosplan agencies, creating 105 province-wide units of economic management (*sovnarkhozy*, or councils of national economy) that combined the functions of different economic branches. Some leading officials would therefore have to move out of Moscow: a fearsome prospect. The *sovnarkhozy* were dismantled a year after Khrushchev fell from power, though some aspects of their decentralizing agenda survived.[25] Another proposal was for term limits. Party secretaries would only be able to serve in top jobs for less than a decade. Khrushchev was even experimenting with ideas about multi-candidate, though of course single-party, elections. More concretely, he reduced spending on the army, redirecting resources to welfare services and consumer goods production.[26] But this did nothing for his relationship with senior officers.

On 12 October 1964, Brezhnev put a call through to Khrushchev, who was on holiday at Pitsunda on Georgia's Black Sea coast. Khrushchev had been on the go for months; he was seventy years old and he needed a holiday. The dacha there was large, the grounds extensive, and the location spectacular. He was there with Anastas Mikoyan. Brezhnev requested that the Party first secretary come back to Moscow immediately for an emergency meeting of the Presidium.

It was an inappropriate request, against the norms and hierarchies of political life, but Khrushchev had to go. On 13 October, his plane touched down at Vnukovo airport. He was driven straight to the Kremlin. The Presidium meeting began at 4 p.m. One by one, its members launched personal attacks on Khrushchev. After more than three hours, they adjourned, due to reconvene in the morning, and Khrushchev went home. Back in the Kremlin on 14 October, Khrushchev briefly defended his record but accepted the verdict of his colleagues. He would be given a pension and required to retire to a dacha outside Moscow. It was a far more modest residence than Pitsunda. He would have no place in public life. On his last night as first secretary, between the two emergency meetings of the Presidium, he had spoken to Mikoyan on the phone. His words are some of the most suggestive in Soviet history. 'Could anyone have dreamed of telling Stalin that he didn't suit us any more and suggesting he retire?' Khrushchev said. 'Now everything is different. The fear is gone and we can talk as equals. That's my contribution.'[27]

It was reported only allusively in the newspapers. As news of his enforced retirement filtered out across the Soviet Union, people waited to see what would happen next.

Newspapers were one thing. Paper itself was another. Aleksandr Solzhenitsyn did not have any paper during his decade of incarceration. His irresistible creativity only had a mental outlet. He composed stories and poems inside his head and stored them up for the time when he could write them down. One of these became the long narrative poem *Prussian Nights*. It drew on Solzhenitsyn's military experience shortly before his arrest, when he was serving in eastern Germany as a Red Army captain. The contrast with life back home, and with the Poland they had just come through, was everywhere obvious: 'They lived, these devils, well!' Arriving in an emptying town, the soldiers consume its booze and look for plunder. Solzhenitsyn's narrator finds that even the stationery is better than back home. 'If I had paper like this,' he says, 'I'd never leave my desk.'[28]

Paper was a valuable commodity. It represented the difference between 'freedom' and confinement. The evidence for Solzhenitsyn's arrest was confected by the authorities' twisting out of shape comments that he had made on paper, in his recent letters. No part of the dictatorship was built out of more paper than the Gulag administration, with its enormous working archives. The deprivation of paper was a form of punishment, which it took a special kind of intelligence to overcome.

After Stalin, paper and the page took on new meaning. In a society that was obsessed with reading and writing, it offered new possibilities and compromises, new ways of communicating. Bella Akhmadulina was one of the great poets of the Thaw, a famous cultural figure whose verse was set to music and whose interests extended to song and film. In one of her first published poems, she wrote that she was 'shy and hesitant' when faced with an untouched piece of paper, and compared it to how a pilgrim might feel 'at the church door'.[29]

During the Thaw, the people of the Soviet Union turned the page and began a new story about Soviet civilization. But in October 1964, they stood poised, unsure of what was coming next. They were again 'hesitant before the page'. Soviet life was all about the future, and nobody knew what the future might hold, but people at least were not afraid. Khrushchev had retired. It was nothing like the death of Stalin.

PART TWO

# Eternal Red Star (1965–74)

New Year Ball, Palace of Congresses, the Kremlin

# 7
# New Year with Brezhnev

When the people of the Soviet Union celebrated New Year, the great popular festival of the Soviet calendar, the occasion transcended communism. Like New Year, communism pointed forwards and made promises about the future. 'With still more friendship / Will our people live' ran one New Year verse called *Green Pine Needles*.[1] But New Year comes round every twelve months. Soviet time was not simply a unidirectional force, pushing ever faster forwards towards communism, like a rocket launched out of the dry earth of the Kazakh wilderness. Time in the Soviet Union also moved in regular cycles, marked by recognizable and comforting signposts on the calendar. The Stalin period was arbitrary and unstable; the Khrushchev era was constantly dynamic. Developed socialism, as the ideology of the Brezhnev years would become known, offered steadiness, even permanence. It was the latest time signature at the core of Soviet civilization. As Brezhnev raised his first New Year glass as leader of the Communist Party, the Soviet Union was settling in for eternity. During the years that followed, the Party introduced policies that seemed to offer not only a new stage of revolutionary historical time, but even a different sort of winter, imagining climatic changes that would create a gentler environment for Soviet civilization.

At the turn of midnight on 1 January 1970, Brezhnev invented a New Year tradition. He delivered his first New Year broadcast on all-union television. It was by necessity pre-recorded, rolling out across the country's eleven time zones. It was not much more than a dull economic report with a routine revolutionary flourish: 1970 was the centenary of Lenin's birth. On the surface, the language was the opposite of Khrushchev's dramatic, unpredictable rhetoric. But Brezhnev was not boring. Or not yet.

He was another outsider, born on 19 December 1906 in Kamenskoye (known as Dneproderzhinsk between 1936 and 2016, when it reverted to a Ukrainian version of its former name). It was a small iron-making town in Dnepropetrovsk province, close to the Donbass and to Yuzovka (later, Donetsk), the big steel and coal town to which a teenaged Khrushchev would migrate two years after Brezhnev's birth. Leonid Ilich Brezhnev's family was ethnically Russian, but he was born and raised in the Ukrainian lands of the Russian empire. As Brezhnev advanced his career through the Party and government institutions of Ukraine and the USSR, he worked closely with colleagues who were also associated with the region of his birth. The 'Dnepropetrovsk clan' became one of the principal competing power centres of Soviet politics.

From birth, Brezhnev had a head start on Khrushchev, who spent his first fourteen years in rural poverty. Brezhnev's father worked in the higher reaches of the skilled urban working class. His mother stayed at home with the children. Leonid attended a grammar school, though he was far from a star pupil. He was about to turn eleven when the Bolsheviks came to power in Petrograd. Political chaos, Red Guard atrocities, German occupation and civil war swept past the family's front door. They kept their heads down. By contrast, Khrushchev was old enough to become an organic part of the revolution. Brezhnev was too young, and he was in no rush to get involved.

In 1921, his family retreated back towards its place of origin in Kursk province. Two years later, Brezhnev enrolled at the city's agricultural technical college. He studied there for four years, more interested in amateur dramatics than ideology, becoming a candidate member of the Party only later, in 1929. The year after graduation, he married Viktoriya Denisova, who had been a student in a medical college nearby and then worked as a midwife. They had two children: Galina, who was famous for ostentatious greed in the 1970s, and Yuri, less well known, who eventually resigned from ministerial office because of allegations about economic crimes. Brezhnev facilitated the grasping inequality which his children came to signify, and he himself enjoyed the perks of office, not least hunting at a *nomenklatura* lodge. Yet his own approach to power and politics was not always unattractive. He was a socialist on a summer beach.

Brezhnev began his itinerant career during the first five-year plan. He was allocated a job as a surveyor of agricultural land, tasked with checking and registering the progress of collectivization in the Urals. Brezhnev pursued the opportunity readily, even as it opened his eyes to the violent disorders of collectivization. He went out of his way to make the lives of the dekulakized more bearable, but his job facilitated their immiseration. He was soon promoted to head of his department. His success gave him a way out. The family moved to Moscow, where he took courses at the Kalinin Institute for Agricultural Machinery, before moving back to Ukraine and taking metalworking jobs and metallurgy courses in Zaporozh'e and his native Kamenskoye. At the age of thirty, he undertook military service in the Far East.

On his return to Ukraine, his career took off. He was good company, smartly dressed and hardworking, a natural networker who looked and sounded the part. He had an interest in people, even a concern for them, which was the basis of his practical approach to socialism. In 1936, he was appointed to the Party apparatus of his renamed hometown, Dneproderzhinsk. The following year he moved to a senior role in the regional centre, Dnepropetrovsk. When the Germans invaded, he joined the army as a political commissar. He spent the war in uniform, mostly attached to units fighting in the south and in the Ukrainian republic, ending the war as the head of the political administration of the Fourth Ukrainian Front.

The sky was now the limit. First of all he ran the city and region of Zaporozh'e, then Dnepropetrovsk, then he had a job in the Central Committee in Moscow, then he ran the republics of first Moldavia and then Kazakhstan. His leading biographer argues that in Kishinev he focused his energy on raising ordinary people's living standards, increasing the supply of food and the provision of education. Yet Brezhnev was also responsible for collectivizing agriculture in the newly annexed republic. In Kazakhstan, in the early years of the post-Stalin period, Brezhnev worked so hard, constantly on the move across the republic's vast territory, overseeing much of the Virgin Lands campaign, that he had his first heart attack at the age of forty-six. It was early, even for a communist boss. He was a baron who succeeded under Stalin and Khrushchev alike – and he had the premature heart attack to prove it.

Brezhnev was back in Moscow at the Twentieth Party Congress in February 1956, where he was elected as a candidate member of the Presidium. He stood by Khrushchev during the 'Anti-Party plot' of 1957, after which he was promoted and given responsibility for a wide range of industries. In 1960, he began a four-year stint as chairman of the Presidium of the Supreme Soviet. The post carried the ceremonial status of head of state. He travelled widely. At home, he managed a project on constitutional reform that came to fruition fifteen years later. It was an ideal seat from which to chair the removal of Khrushchev in October 1964. He was the natural successor. No wonder his colleagues toasted him with such abandon when New Year came round a few weeks later.

The Bolsheviks transferred Christmas celebrations to New Year. Yet it was only during the Thaw, with its opportunities for openness and consumption, that the party got going. The Kremlin itself was opened up to the public to mark the new year of 1955. In the 1950s, New Year trees were commonly set up in public settings, such as schools and government buildings, not just in people's homes.[2]

Children had their own festivities, gathering at a *yolka* (the same word as fir tree). This was a variety performance, with singing, dancing, verse, skits and a visit from Grandfather Frost and the Snow Maiden (*snegurochka*). The most sought-after tickets were for the Kremlin's *yolka*. After its opening in 1961, the Palace of Congresses hosted the *yolka* twice daily in late December and early January to an audience of 2,000 a time. Children brought home a Kremlin-shaped packet of sweets, with an orange and nuts. Others attended smaller-scale but no less captivating events at their parents' workplace, or at theatres, Pioneer palaces, schools and workers' clubs. Teachers and youth workers organized familiar activities in the run-up to New Year: concerts, games, fancy-dress parties and competitions for best-decorated classrooms. They rehearsed classic songs which recalled New Year, such as the repertoire from the Soviet *Puss in Boots* or *Pinocchio*, and practised scenes from such plays as Nikonov's *Telepathy*.[3]

## NEW YEAR WITH BREZHNEV

On New Year's Eve, a family might have 'champagne' – *shampanskoye* – a sparkling mix of wines that had been available on a mass scale since the 1930s. Caviar, red or even black, was especially desirable, though its acquisition depended on whether one lived near a suitable port, had the right contacts, or if it just happened to be available. Cod liver – or a tin of ham – were also popular if sometimes unobtainable. Wives, sisters, mothers or grandmothers spent hours preparing large bowls of different salads. New Year was a gendered festival. *Vinagret*, a popular imitation of French cuisine, contained chopped-up beetroot, potatoes, salted cucumber and pickled cabbage, laced with sunflower oil. *Olivier*, the true New Year favourite, was a mayonnaise-doused mix of chicken and peas, finely chopped carrots and potatoes, as well as onion and salted cucumber. Meat or fish set in aspic with a mixture of vegetables and garlic, whose classic version was known as 'herring under a fur coat', was a common dish. There might be carefully prepared Turkish coffee and there was always leaf tea, and sweets from confectionery plants such as Moscow's Red October factory. Their blue-riband *Stolichnaya* liqueur chocolates were an accessible luxury. White-whipped *zefir* and chocolate-coated oranges – *marmeladka* – were universal. The woman of the house might make a *Napoleon*, a layered cake filled with custard.[4]

Certain gifts were irresistibly of the Brezhnev era, such as French perfume for one's wife or fiancée. Other family members might get an attractive shirt, a loved book with a beautiful design, or a game from a toy shop such as Moscow's Detsky Mir (Children's World). For a photography enthusiast, an East German Leica might be the most memorable gift of one's childhood. Soviet people shopped carefully. A child might expect one or two presents rather than a stocking-full from Grandfather Frost. When the gifts were opened and the table was cleared, and midnight approached, someone might pull out a guitar or accordion and start singing 'Oi moroz, moroz', evoking the frost of the season.[5]

As movies migrated from the cinema to the television, and as more people owned a TV set, it became possible to create an all-union New Year celebration. Eldar Ryazanov directed the New Year favourite *Carnival Night*, released in cinemas to meet the New Year of 1957. It joyfully satirized the last-minute preparations of a House of Culture to put on a New Year ball, poking fun at the stuffy director and the ways that his ideological nervousness interfered with even the most trivial aspects of the spectacle. The film made the transition to New Year TV screens during the 1960s. Then came Ryazanov's New Year blockbuster *The Irony of Fate or Congratulations on a Light Steam!* The second half of the title (*s legkim parom!*) was the salutation offered to someone who is leaving the bathhouse, or *banya*. It was released in the New Year of 1976. Filmed largely in domestic interiors, it was a natural for the small screen and replicated the material setting in which many viewers were themselves seeing in the New Year. Its story was preposterous but everlastingly touching: a Moscow doctor, unaccustomed to alcohol, gets hopelessly drunk on a New-Year visit to the *banya* with his friends, mistakenly boards a Leningrad flight in the place of one of them, takes a taxi to his home address which turns out to be physically identical to the new apartment block in Moscow where he lives with his mother, lets himself in via the identical lock, and ends up falling for the schoolteacher who lives there. Complete with star actors and an equally star-studded soundtrack, it was impossible for Soviet people not to love, or love to hate, *The Irony of Fate* as it became the early-evening centrepiece of New Year programming in the second half of the Brezhnev era.

Back in the 1960s, and for decades thereafter, *Little Blue Flame* (*Goluboi ogonek*) counted viewers down to midnight. The show replicated a café-style setting where celebrities socialized, were interviewed to camera and joined the viewer in watching a succession of lounge entertainments.[6] From New Year's Day of 1971, *Song of the Year* became a fixture in the TV calendar. The show had a competition format and blended new music with old favourites. It tried to appeal to different generations in every family so that they might watch it together, though in the second half of the 1970s it became more focused on youth culture.[7] Still, it was a shared New Year experience for millions. Deracinated Christianity, limited consumerism, light entertainment, family ties and friendship were the most common components of this secular and barely socialist celebration. It was the lowest common denominator of recognizably Soviet practices. For many it was a cherished all-union holiday. An illusion persisted that across time zones and republics, Soviet civilization was ringing in a single new year.

Winter and the cold were unyielding signifiers of Soviet civilization. The political overtones were blunt – cold war, deep freeze, ice-bound – but the reality was more subtle, shaping life and identity in diverse ways. Large parts of the Soviet Union across the European and Central Asian republics experienced very cold winters; it was only in a few south-western locations, notably the lowlands of the Caucasus, that winters were milder. The Russian republic itself contained vast stretches of land that were synonymous with temperatures so low that they were hardly bearable: Siberia, the Far North, the Arctic Circle. The Gulag, which remained a component of Soviet civilization though no longer its core, was shaped by the cold.[8]

In the Brezhnev era, the camps were only a terrible fringe on society, but a harsh coldness still formed the central life experience of many Soviet people. For instance, the naval shipbuilding town of Severodvinsk, near Arkhangelsk, was founded in 1936 and became the closed site of the massive Northern Machine-Building Enterprise (Sevmash), a military plant, in the 1970s. In seventeen years, between 1962 and 1979, the city's population doubled, to 197,232. As Severodvinsk was filled with migrants who were born in at least slightly warmer climes, they naturally enough made much of the town's isolation and coldness, defining it in terms of extreme 'harshness' in a way that born-and-raised locals did not think to do.[9]

Planners promised would-be migrants that the climatic extremes might ultimately be ameliorated. All modern societies in the 1960s and 1970s dreamed of 'taming nature', with devastating results. Most notoriously, in hot Central Asia, the Aral Sea largely disappeared after decades of aggressive irrigation policies.[10] To take one example from the Soviet cold zone: acid-rain-causing sulphur dioxide emissions from the Severonickel combine in Monchegorsk grew from 99,000 tons in 1966 to 274,000 in 1975.[11] One reason for environmental degradation was the prioritization of human needs at all costs, which in the Khrushchev and Brezhnev years meant the urgent need to make its freezing hinterlands slightly more habitable for individuals (by contrast, under Stalin, taming nature meant extracting resources from freezing places for the sake of future paradise, at a catastrophic cost to the workers and prisoners who were doing the taming). In *A New Year's Fable*, published in 1960, Vladimir Dudintsev wrote of a young scientist who works in a research group devoted to the study of sunlight. Even in Moscow, days are short in the weeks around New Year. Productivity and health are at risk. The group's aim is to transform everyday life in the sunless Far North, though this project turns into a fairy tale.[12] In real life, planners in Leningrad in the late 1960s were exploring other fantastical options for Far Northern settlements by creating artificially mild microclimates inside what would later be called biospheres.[13] More realistically, architects and engineers went to great lengths to adapt the standardized apartment block designs of the post-Stalin decades to conditions of extreme cold.[14] Although there was a senior research group working in Leningrad, local collectives of construction experts in places such as Murmansk, Yakutsk and Magadan devised innovative solutions for making buildings habitable in the extreme cold.[15]

These experts in urban development had to face a phenomenon that was becoming better understood in the post-Stalin period: *vechnaya merzlota*, or 'permafrost'. This was the 'permanently frozen earth' on which major industrial cities in the Far North had been constructed since the 1930s. Soviet scientists began to argue that permafrost, or ground that has been at zero degrees Celsius or lower for at least two years, was not actually a fixed organic structure but one that would change over time as temperatures fluctuated. They came to describe the cryolithozone, a space of heat exchange in which permafrost was connected to the rest of the earth in a single 'system'.[16] The insight helped to make further growth and construction in the region possible, for better or worse. Olenogorsk – Reindeer Mountain – was such a place. First built in the tip of the Murmansk region as an iron-ore settlement, its population more than doubled between 1959 and 1979, from 12,100 to 27,369.[17] This was the improbable reality of life north of the Arctic Circle long after Stalin-era breakneck industrialization. The development was economically indispensable, scientifically impressive and technologically complex, but it was too cold and distant to comprehend. Karelia and other wooded northern places were the mysterious taiga. Further north was the desolate tundra, where trees could not grow. Metropolitan types looked at these places with wonder and sometimes with contempt.

The conquest of cold was a modern project. It had imperial overtones. It was Soviet civilization in action, an example of the Communist Party's drive to colonize its resource-rich 'periphery'. 'Internal colonization' gambled on ecology and made racist assumptions about the indigenous populations of the Far North.[18] This allowed the state to dispossess and move these people in the name of modernization; it also gave material for ordinary people to make constant jokes about the dimwitted, stereotyped Chukchi (the Soviet equivalent of Eskimos). But it could only ever have partial success. Climate was changed by humanity but would ultimately have a life of its own.

Ordinary Soviet people often seemed to understand this instinctively. Living with the cold and seeking positive and personal meanings in it was central to Soviet civilization from the bottom up. After all, five months of snow was a place to bury the past, discard the unmentionable and enjoy the present. Winter could be a white blank page. On a good day – with a blue sky and crisp air – it even offered new beginnings. In Nikolai Moskalenko's 1971 film *Young People*, the heroine follows her heart when winter sets in, turning her back on a life of privilege in one of Moscow's elite apartment houses for dour conditions with her fiancé, an engineer tasked with building prefabricated apartment buildings, who lives in a hostel. Moscow was cold enough in winter, but at least it had proper seasons; large tracts of the Soviet Union were only defined by their wintry climate. A poet from Yakutia, Aleksei Mikhailov, wrote in a collection entitled *Snow* that was published in 1971 about 'silent snows', swooning deer, and the way that the Taiga and other rivers 'sparkled'.[19] The Ukrainian painter Tatyana Yablonskaya (Tetiana Yablonska) featured snow and ice in many of her canvases. Snow was like a solvent in which different elements of Soviet civilization dissolved, from socialist realism to folklore to mystical nationhood: from the straightforwardly wintry Soviet scene of *Wedding* (1964) to the Soviet reds and timeless peasant mood of *Paper Flowers* (1967) to the uncertain atmosphere of *Winter in Old Kyiv* (1976).

Winter shaped much of the material culture of the Soviet Union. It explained the thick, peeling radiators of city apartments (switched on and off externally on a given day of the year, so that temperature regulation in one's own home was a matter of opening a small upper pane, or *fortochka*), the massive Slavic stoves of village houses and the insulating rugs with elaborate weaving that often hung on the walls of rooms across the union, in town and country alike. In the long 1970s, when they were better able to afford it, and if they could circumvent shortages, people spent more money on better-quality fur coats and hats. Brezhnev referred to the supply and quality of fur coats in his report to the 1972 Central Committee Plenum. In the early 1970s, a proper fur coat (or *shuba*) remained a luxury item; an overcoat with a fur collar was much more common. Synthetic, fur-like fibres were a cheaper option compared to mink, sable or polar fox. A hierarchy of coats emerged, and the most desirable of them were a perfect example of the paradox of 'socialist luxury'. Even the academic intelligentsia, at once self-conscious about ideological contradictions and more used to focusing its limited resources on necessities and culture, became increasingly interested in acquiring furs in the 1970s.[20]

More democratic, though, was knitting, of polo-necked jumpers, socks, hats and gloves. The vastness of virgin snow in the countryside was a symbol of ideal beauty and 'democratic' accessibility. City-dwellers thirsted to visit it, in their ancestral village, where elderly relatives might still live, or at their exurban dacha if it was built for winter habitation. Cross-country skiing in urban and exurban parks, and the countryside proper, was more popular than skating; it was a common sight to see polo-necked, bobble-hatted couples holding their skis on badly heated suburban trains. Artificial slopes were constructed in Moscow itself, for example near the university in the Lenin Hills. Winter cross-country skiing holidays were also available. In 1980, fifteen days spent skiing around Monchegorsk in the Murmansk region cost 98 rubles, bookable between January and May. It was considered extremely beneficial for health.[21] All of these winter habits were obviously Soviet, the look deriving instantly from materials and shortages, but they were also normal, beyond ideology, not very different from life across most of Central and Eastern Europe.

*

In October 1952, between the end of his job in Moldavia and the start of his post in Kazakhstan, Brezhnev had been in Moscow, embarking on a brief spell working as a Central Committee secretary and then a top official in the Ministry of Defence. He was provided with a three-room apartment on a wide avenue in the west of Moscow that was soon renamed Kutuzovsky Prospekt. It became his permanent home when he returned from Alma-Ata to Moscow. Later, his wayward daughter Galina was given the apartment next door.[22] Brezhnev never lived in the Kremlin. In house number 26, his neighbours included Suslov and Andropov. It was Boss Row. Kutuzovsky Prospekt, with its forbidding apartment houses built in the Stalin period, was one of the most desirable locations for the *nomenklatura* during the Brezhnev era. Further on, near Kuntsevskaya metro station, two impressive apartment blocks were built for Central Committee officials during the Brezhnev era. Brezhnev also had the use of State Dacha Number 1, known as Glitsiniya (Wisteria Lodge), on the Crimean coast. It was a short drive from hunting grounds and only sixty footsteps from the sea. Brezhnev loved to spend his spare time clad in swimming trunks or carrying a gun. The house had actually been built in 1955 for Khrushchev, but his much shorter holidays were spent in the less grand house at nearby Pitsunda.[23]

On the surface, this was a deceleration of social mobility. It looked like the corruption and stasis that were consistent with the motif of stagnation. But Brezhnev's political order – developed socialism – was actually another future of 1917. It was the latest instalment of the revolution, guided by revolutionary texts and teachings: a revolutionary iteration in which equality remained hardwired into mentalities if not practices, and where stability, private life and *nomenklatura* corruption played a growing part. Soviet civilization, ever malleable, accommodated these characteristics, each of which was traceable to 1917. The elite that ran the Soviet Union in the long 1970s wanted more for themselves than their predecessors had. Brezhnev enjoyed the use of property and possessions that were much superior to those available to Khrushchev.

It was not only material goods: viewed from the capitalist West, the rewards were puny. Equally important were psychological benefits: staying indefinitely in one's job and passing on privileges to one's offspring. Although these benefits went against the spirit of the revolution, the *nomenklatura* continued to institute social and economic policies that were inspired by 1917, and maintained coercive institutions that also derived from the earliest days of the revolution. Mikhail Suslov was an example of this inextricable link at the heart of Soviet civilization. His office was served by a well-organized, stable bureaucracy and by well-educated officials who remained in post for years.[24] He kept his role as the country's propaganda chief and exercised powerful influence as a member of the Politburo and a Central Committee secretary, dying in office only a few months before Brezhnev.

After the terrible anti-Party violence of the Stalin era, and Khrushchev's disruptive but peaceful and equality-inspired attempts to control the privileges of elites, Brezhnev set about an institutional politics that aimed at 'stability of cadres' and 'trust in cadres'. First of all, Khrushchev's *sovnarkhozy* were abolished. These were the 'councils of the regional economy' that decentralized the administration of whole economic sectors to the regions. They had been unpopular with Moscow-based officials. In 1966, after a fourteen-year spell, the Presidium was returned to its original name, the Politburo, and Brezhnev took the older title of general secretary rather than first secretary. In symbol and practice, Brezhnev deliberately attempted to rule as part of a collective and to establish a relationship of steady predictability with senior officials in Moscow and across the union.

The principal justification for Khrushchev's ousting had been to end his alleged tendency for dictatorial decision-making and vulgar treatment of colleagues. Power would now be divided up within the Presidium (and then the Politburo) and exercised collegially. Brezhnev headed the Party and chaired the political system as a whole. Anastas Mikoyan, the great survivor of Soviet politics, stayed on as chairman of the Presidium of the Supreme Soviet, or head of state, for another year, after which Nikolai Podgorny assumed the role until 1977. Aleksei Kosygin was 'prime minister', chairman of the Council of Ministers, or head of government, through to 1980. This greater clarity and stability was supposed to go up and down: a 'power vertical'. The aim was to cement in place local Party secretaries across the republics and the provinces who enjoyed local legitimacy while being clearly responsible to Moscow.[25]

\*

As the Kremlin bells rang in the year of 1965, a mild optimism existed among reformers and many members of the intelligentsia. With the festive season not yet over, on 5 January, the Procuracy of the USSR even began the process of scaling back the sentence that had been passed against the Leningrad poet Joseph Brodsky earlier in 1964.[26] Implausibly accused of 'idleness' and 'hooliganism' – terms used in legislation usually designed to outlaw absenteeism and anti-social drinking – Brodsky was convicted and exiled to the province of Arkhangelsk. His verse was far from an all-out attack on Soviet power; it simply fell outside the parameters of Soviet culture. The perception of the threat he posed depended on the shifting politics of the Thaw.

In the following years, the days around New Year were emblematic of such political fluctuations. Sympathetic contemporaries tried to believe that the Thaw continued until 1968, when tanks crushed the Prague Spring. In January 1968, Alexander Dubček took over as first secretary of the Communist Party in Czechoslovakia and set about economic and cultural reforms that he called 'socialism with a human face'. When it went too far, and crowds gathered to protect it, Warsaw Pact tanks entered the country in August, ending the lives of as many as 137 demonstrators, exiling Dubček to Moscow, and requiring the replacement of his reforms with a less politicized version of post-Stalinism, 'normalization'. In the Soviet Union, the three New Years that preceded the Prague Spring were a time to observe the Thaw under strain, when de-Stalinization was under pressure.

On 4 January 1966, the KGB chairman, Vladimir Semichastny, and the head of the Procuracy, Roman Rudenko, wrote to the Central Committee to update them on the case of Aleksandr Solzhenitsyn. After the success of *One Day in the Life of Ivan Denisovich*, he had become on object of suspicion for the security services and judicial authorities. Semichastny and Rudenko announced to the Central Committee that Solzhenitsyn's works were hostile to Soviet power and could not be published inside the USSR. To avoid the risk of foreign publication, they arranged the confiscation of the author's archive. The following day, on 5 January, with the ice still crisp, Brezhnev held personal talks with the first secretary of the Union of Writers,

Konstantin Fedin, about how to deal with the dissident writers Andrei Sinyavsky and Yuly Daniel.[27]

A New Year later, in 1967, the most independent and Thaw-spirited of the literary journals, *Novyi mir* – Solzhenitsyn's publisher – was under pressure from the authorities. Its editorial staff, headed by the legendary Aleksandr Tvardovsky, began the working year on 5 January with a visit from the Union of Writers. The purpose of the three-day talks was to make *Novyi mir* 'admit their errors', restore discipline, get with it.[28] Tvardovsky made a career out of publishing different-thinking works that steered a millimetre inside the permissible. This latest situation derailed even his capacity for compromise. With the snow beating softly on the windows of *Novyi mir*'s offices in early January 1967, it felt to those inside that an individual author might still be able to carve out a position of 'permitted dissent', but a whole journal could no longer maintain a progressive position.

One New Year on, on 4 January 1968, Tvardovsky was again in meetings with the hierarchy of the Union of Writers. This time they were discussing Aleksandr Solzhenitsyn's extraordinary epic *Cancer Ward*. Tvardovsky wanted to publish it. He had no doubt: it represented 'an unarguable good for Soviet letters'.[29] Given Semichastny's edict of two years earlier concerning the 'arrest' of Solzhenitsyn's papers, it was interesting in itself, regardless of the outcome, that the literary establishment was discussing *Cancer Ward*. But the snowy cityscape outside the window remained pristine, untroubled by Solzhenitsyn's novel. It was unpublished in the USSR until *perestroika*.

The New Year smash-hit film of the late 1960s was the comedy *Zigzag of Fortune*, yet another festive success for its director, Eldar Ryazanov. Its celebration of snowy winter scenes and unintended comic consequences hit the Soviet big screen on 30 December 1968. Yevgeny Leonov played an aspiring photographer in a provincial town, caught up in a moral dilemma that threatened his personal and work relationships. Near the end of the drama, the characters see in New Year and Leonov appears before his colleagues disguised as Grandfather Frost.

When the film came out, Leonov was forty-two. Balding and rotund, his expression poised between vulnerability and geniality,

Leonov was instantly recognizable across the USSR. He was born in Moscow during the time of the New Economic Policy and raised in a communal apartment; people loved him because he had the face and the sympathies of a Soviet everyman. Leonov could have followed his father into a life of engineering, but instead started his professional acting career when he was twenty-one. While the country was enduring postwar devastation, he joined the company of Moscow's Stanislavsky Theatre and was soon enjoying success on stage and in the cinema. Twenty years later, in 1968, he transferred to the city's Mayakovsky Theatre and completed work on *Zigzag of Fortune* with Ryazanov.

At the heart of the film is the strange truth that money talked in Soviet civilization. A comic story set in and around a local photography studio, *Zigzag of Fortune* relates what happens when the studio's hard-pressed co-workers form a mutual savings fund to support each other. Leonov's character takes charge. With his hands on the cash box, he succumbs to temptation, surreptitiously taking out the reserve of twenty rubles. At the nearest branch of the state bank, he purchases a prize-bearing savings bond. When the number comes up, and he wins 10,000 rubles, he first becomes arrogant, then regretful, as chaos is unleashed on the working *kollektiv* and the friendships that surround it. After all, to whom did the winnings really belong? The message was clear enough. Money might be necessary in the socialist age, but in excess it did not bring happiness.

When Brezhnev came to power, it was already clear that money was no longer doing enough to make the economy work. As ever in the Soviet economy, agriculture was the principal problem. In 1962, agricultural shortages, rises in food prices and consequent unrest led to the import of grain from abroad. In time this was paid for with foreign currency from oil exports, as the ruble itself remained nonconvertible. This 'deal' would become central to the Brezhnev-era economy, following the discovery and exploitation of energy reserves in western Siberia in the second half of the 1960s. At a micro level, inside the countryside itself, money was also a problem. Collective farms, as opposed to state farms, had long been in the habit of paying agricultural workers only partly in cash, which led to the widespread use of eggs as a substitute currency in the 1960s.[30] The government was aware that injecting money into the lives of rural-dwellers was essential for the modernization of their economic life.

Even worse was the absence of normal incentives, especially in the operations of enterprises. In Hungary, economic reforms had followed 1956. The reforms allowed greater autonomy for factories, construction 'firms' and other institutions, and a kind of mixed economy, nicknamed 'goulash communism', emerged. This seemed to offer the promise of greater efficiency, higher productivity and better standards of living. It might be a promising model for the Soviet Union itself to pursue.

What followed was the last great attempt to reform the Soviet economy until Gorbachev came to power twenty years later. It was forever associated with Brezhnev's partner at the top of the collective that ran Soviet politics. Kosygin, who had long experience in running economic ministries, was now the knowledgeable supremo of the Soviet economy. He tried to use that authority and expertise in a one-off attempt to make a revolutionary economy that was fit for the 1960s.

During revolutions, time accelerates, creating a greater number of distinctive generational cohorts. The generation born a mere decade after Khrushchev enjoyed some of the benefits of the revolution while experiencing fewer of its sacrifices. They were the 'Brezhnev generation'. Too young to risk all during the revolution or to fight in the civil war, but sometimes old enough, if they were orphaned by those terrible events, to survive alone, they were the cohort that benefited most conspicuously from the policy of positive class discrimination. In the 1920s and 1930s, promotion through the workplace was accelerated for those with the right proletarian origins, creating a new social layer of 'promotees' or 'advancers'. Some of them took over the high offices of victims of the Great Terror. These people came to power in the 1960s, across the regions and in Moscow.[31] Then, having risen from nothing, they tried to pass on privileges to their own children. It happened in one form or another in all modern economies. But dramatic social mobility was central to Soviet civilization from the start, so this seemed a paradigm shift in the Brezhnev era.

Aleksei Kosygin was the second-most famous member of the Brezhnev generation. Born to a proletarian family in St Petersburg two years before Brezhnev, he had a gold-star promotee's career, ending up as people's commissar of textiles by the age of thirty-five. By 1964, he had accumulated almost thirty years at the top of government, many of them in economic management, with a focus on light industry.

Inspired by his long-standing bird's-eye view of the Soviet economy, interactions with the Eastern bloc and readings in socialist economic theory, especially the work of Yevsei Liberman, Kosygin now had the power to act on his analysis of the weaknesses of the Soviet economy. Growth was low. Productivity was weak. Central planning was not working effectively; fixed prices were disrupting efficiency. He saw systemic deficiencies in the way that enterprises worked. An 'enterprise' was the socialist equivalent of a corporation or firm, dozens of which clustered in big-city factory districts, but a single one of which dominated a monotown, or socialist 'company town'. In any case, they provided not just work but also welfare. These enterprises enjoyed substantial investment, had plenty of workers, were privileged in comparison to collective farms and were part of a society in which industry was valued. But this was no longer the 1930s. The country was not in the throes of an industrial revolution. Growth had slowed dramatically. Kosygin argued that boosting growth to revolutionary levels required enterprises to embrace technological and organizational innovation. These changes were much more difficult for a centrally planned economy to achieve than building heavy industrial plant, but Kosygin seized the moment and designed a set of economic reforms.

He presented the proposals at the September 1965 Plenum of the Central Committee in a matter-of-fact, flourish-free analysis.[32] He was a low-key performer, lacking the easy manner of Brezhnev. Kosygin wanted to re-imagine the Soviet enterprise so that it was more incentive-driven and autonomous – controlled more from within by managers and workers, and less subject to heavy-handed external direction by planners – and therefore more productive, even able to reinvest a small profit. Central planning would become more flexible. For an individual enterprise, the interests of Moscow-based planners and local managers should be brought into closer alignment. The reform, which was approved soon after Khrushchev's fall, drew on open debates among economists and managers that had taken place during the Khrushchev era.³³ It aimed to bring Soviet practices closer into line with the more dynamic examples of reform in the Eastern bloc, though did not go as far as the 'market socialism' being developed in Hungary, and really sought to strengthen rather than undermine the concept of a planned economy. Even at this moment, the chance was missed to go further and deeper. Some changes were immediately obvious. For instance, newspaper editors commissioned sociologists to run social surveys to help them work out what readers wanted.³⁴ This seemed a new and promising route for matching supply and demand, creating new things, serving individuals and improving quality. It was a plausible potential future of 1917. The policies were proposed in 1965 and rolled out with the start of the eighth five-year plan in 1966. They were limited first to a few dozen enterprises and then, as the plan went on, to a few hundred.

A few months later, in the New Year of 1967, Kosygin the workaholic was focused not, for once, on the economy, but on his wife, Klavdiya. He called her Klavochka. She had endured treatment for cancer the previous autumn, often as an inpatient in one of the best hospitals in the country. At New Year, the family surprised her by bringing her a favourite dress and a hairdresser, then taking her home to their apartment at Granovsky Street for a celebration and a party on the night of 31 December. In the way of the 1960s, not least in the Soviet Union, they did not talk about the cancer. She died on 1 May.³⁵

They had been married since his early twenties. This personal disaster was now matched by the failure of his signature reform. When data from the eighth five-year plan did not show dramatic results, the programme was shelved. Yet Kosygin remained in charge of economic policy until 1980. He signed off proposals to reform the organizational structure of some large enterprises in 1973; his regulations on adjusting planning systems were approved in 1979. But none of these laws seemed to reverse the falls in production and productivity that had marked the Soviet economy since the middle of the Khrushchev era. Nobody could say what would have happened had Kosygin's 1965 reform been pursued to its conclusion.³⁶ Some liked to claim that the reform might have saved the Soviet economy. For later critics of the Soviet Union, any substantial reform by its nature destabilized the Stalinist core of the Soviet system and made systemic collapse more likely.[37] Andropov and then Gorbachev, like Khrushchev, thought the reverse. But sidelining the Kosygin reform meant that the crucial issue of prices could be avoided. An implication of the reform was that a more rational connection between price, supply and demand must in time emerge; but such a connection, even if it created efficiencies, might actually have been a risk to Soviet civilization. One of the consolations of life during the Brezhnev era was that prices of basic foodstuffs, housing, public transport and other necessities were very low, in a stable and predictable way. As we saw in the Prologue, the demonstrators at Novocherkassk in 1962 were protesting about a rise in food prices that seemed to undermine the legitimacy of the Party. After the massacre, prices were held steady for a considerable time; this was possible because central planners, unencumbered by Kosygin-style reforms or concerns about hidden inflation, could set prices in line with political priorities. The popular assumption that Party and government were in control of prices and could still provide basic goods was an important feature of Soviet civilization. When people could no longer make such an assumption at the turn of the 1990s – though that leaps ahead of the story – Soviet civilization quickly lost all content and meaning.

Meanwhile, in December 1965, with New Year approaching, Sergei Korolev was working at the cosmodrome on a spacecraft that could fly to the moon. There was still time to beat the Americans in this particular leg of the space race; Neil Armstrong would not reach the moon until 1969. Korolev and his team could not make the Luna-8 land safely. There was every chance that its next iteration, the Luna-9, would work better. It was all-consuming work, just as he liked it.

Back home in Moscow, Korolev collapsed. He tried to put his wife Nina's mind at ease, but did not seek medical help. He was anyway scheduled for admission to hospital in early January. Before then, work was too pressing. On 23 December, he was a delegate at a plenary meeting of the Party committee of Moscow Region (its *obkom*), held in the Marble Hall of the Moscow Soviet. Such commitments did not detract from his real work at the cosmodrome, but energized it. He took strength and inspiration from human contact, gaining accumulated energy from being always on the move. These commitments also increased his strength, not depleted it, because they exposed him to the workings of Soviet power at multiple levels, replenishing his knowledge of its moving parts and consolidating and expanding his unique collection of contacts. On Christmas Day, which fell on a Saturday – not celebrated of course, as the festivities took place at New Year, and Orthodox Christmas anyway fell on 7 January – Korolev went to the Kremlin. The meeting was about the eighth five-year plan, in which Korolev had to justify and secure the space budget.

The next day, Nina and Sergei went to Star City to socialize with the cosmonauts, some of whom, including Gagarin and Tereshkova, had recently moved into new apartments. Their party had the air of a house-warming about it, the promise of a new beginning. Together, they all enjoyed the facilities of the place, including a swimming pool. It was Soviet and yet it was exceptional: there was high privilege here. Perhaps reminded of this, Sergei acted on a promise to Nina when they got back home: he wrote to a contact of his at the Ministry of Foreign Affairs requesting he facilitate the purchase by the Korolevs of a two-seater Mercedes sports car.

Yet even as he met people, talked and sorted through his domestic affairs, Korolev never stopped thinking about his real work. Back in his office, as well as in his study at home, he worked over the next few days on an article for *Pravda* and an official report. But he was unwell. He had pain around his heart, though medication allowed him to keep working.

The date of his birth fell on 30 December. He was the exact contemporary of Brezhnev, and two years younger than Kosygin. This 'birthday' was thirteen days before the anniversary of his actual birth, as he was born under the old Julian calendar that was scrapped in favour of the Gregorian calendar when the Bolsheviks came to power. The change pushed the Russian date into the future by almost two weeks towards what was already an international standard. It was the most effortless of the communists' modernizations. It moved Korolev's birth and birthday into the following year, apparently making him a year younger. Even in marking his birthday, Korolev was in the vanguard of Soviet civilization.

Family and friends gathered at the Korolevs' house to see in the New Year, but in the end they did it in the absence of Sergei and Nina, who were invited at the last minute to a party hosted by Boris Ponomarev, the long-time head of the International Department of the Central Committee. They understood: it was a party that one could not turn down.

As 1966 got underway, Nina noted an unusual 'pensiveness', even 'sadness' about her husband as he tried to relax by listening to Tchaikovsky in the living room. On 4 January he was preoccupied as he went to work. He was uneasy when he and Nina visited relatives that evening. The following day, as planned, he was in the Kremlin hospital, the best there was, where he would be operated on by two of the country's best-known surgeons. A biopsy was conducted on the 11th, on the basis of which an operation was arranged for three days hence. While he was waiting, on the 12th, he marked his fifty-ninth birthday (according to the new calendar).[38] Perhaps he was no age. During his life he had known great stress and joy, prolonged exhaustion and sustained excitement. His heart gave out during the operation.

Twenty days later, the unmanned Luna-9 spacecraft made the first 'soft' landing on the surface of the Moon. Stuck there for all time, Ozymandias-style, it was a monument to the chief designer.[39] The Soviet space programme was already rolling on without him.

Marshals Voroshilov and Budyonny

# 8
# People in Uniform

Korolev went first; Gagarin went second.

By early 1968, two years after the chief designer's death, the first cosmonaut had spent almost seven years as the ultimate Soviet celebrity. Gagarin was the face of the Soviet Union when he went abroad. He was the object of joy in public encounters across the union. From all corners they bestowed honours upon him: Hero of the Soviet Union, Order of Lenin, Honoured Master of Sport; he was president of the Soviet–Cuban Friendship Society and honorary citizen of Athens. He had a large four-room apartment in Star City. He drove fast cars, enjoyed women, went fishing with his friends. It wasn't enough. He craved respect, not plaudits. These feelings energized him to complete an engineering degree at the Zhukovsky Academy. Above all, he wanted to be a pilot again.

Getting to fly was not automatic. Others made decisions about what he did and how his life was protected. He was in the armed forces, part of a hierarchy, serving as notional 'commander' of the cosmonauts and, more usefully, as deputy commander of their training centre. His seniors placed limits on what he could and could not do. They allowed him to return to the cockpit.

On 13 March, he began a two-week sequence of training flights near Moscow with a co-pilot, Vladimir Seregin, in a MiG-15. After this he would be allowed to fly MiG-17s by himself. These training flights were short. Their last one was scheduled for 27 March. The plane disappeared from radar screens and smashed into trees at 10.48 a.m. They found Seregin's jaw, but there were no remains of Gagarin: just his wallet, which contained a photo of Korolev.[1]

*

They made the announcement on the radio the next day, after the air force inspected the scene and confirmed the pilots' deaths. Newspaper obituarists wrote with unrestrained sadness. The journalist Pavel Barashev, who was a good friend of Gagarin, used images that had shades of communism and the Bible. 'Loving life, believing in people,' Barashev wrote, 'he always was and remained A PERSON, and today the earth with unending grief drops flowers on the grave of its Son.'[2] As if unsure how to manage the public response, the authorities were cautious about displays of grief and did not respond to swirling conspiracy theories. As the Brezhnev era went on, though, they permitted and then encouraged a 'cult' of Gagarin, which consisted of statues, portraits, sculptures, friezes, museums and public rhetoric across the Soviet Union.[3]

As the statues often showed, Yuri Gagarin was a man who wore a uniform. Between the ages of twenty-one, when he joined the army, and thirty-four, when he was killed, he served in uniform, moving through air force units and up through promotions, becoming a cosmonaut, and wearing a variety of military dress. As the 1960s wore on, he seemed to revel in the increasingly elaborate costumes and medals in which his image was captured. One famous photograph showed him wearing a white dress uniform and standing alongside Fidel Castro.[4] Gagarin was wildly popular, dead and alive, though people came to see these pictures with a view not untinged by irony.

It was just one example of how in the early Brezhnev era uniforms displayed top-down coercive power while also hinting at the limits of that power. Looked at in one light, a uniform fosters conformity, unease and fear. In another, it looks very silly. Images from the late 1960s and early 1970s – street scenes, the interiors of public buildings – show a significant proportion of people in uniform. There's the policeman on guard at the children's library, mingling with the fur-collared young mothers; the army officer picking up his dry cleaning, making jokes to the women with hair-dos behind the counter; the group of conscripts lolling in front of the bus station; the women from Aeroflot, all crisp whites and blues, eating dumplings in a city canteen; the potbellied officer exchanging small talk with a smart train attendant in green serge uniform, holding her hat under her arm, in the middle of the concourse; the men from one or other of the security services waiting to go inside a football stadium; the female border guards sitting on a bench while passengers stream past.

Many KGB operatives dressed in plain clothes, but others wore uniforms, some of which were made distinctive by blue flashes and caps. They were the latest incarnation of the Cheka, the Extraordinary Commission for the Struggle with Counter-revolution and Espionage, whose title was derived from the initials of its first two words, ChK, or *che ka*, which were weighted equally in pronunciation, as if with a monotonous insistence, and set up days after the Bolsheviks seized power. Feliks Dzerzhinsky, a Pole, was the Chekists' boss. In 1922, following the end of the Civil War, when the Bolsheviks' hold on power seemed more secure, the Cheka was reinvented as the State Political Administration, or GPU. When the Soviet Union was founded and given constitutional shape the following year, the GPU gained the prefix 'Unified' and thus became the OGPU to reflect its all-union coverage. It was an 'administration' (sometimes translated as 'directorate', *upravlenie*) that fell under the auspices of the People's Commissariat of Internal Affairs, or NKVD. Between 1934 and 1943, the secret police were known simply as the NKVD, such was the Commissariat's focus on internal security, and the massive resources it devoted to the prosecution of the Great Terror and the expansion of the Gulag. Monstrous *chekisty* such as Nikolai Yezhhov were in charge.

Even as the Terror ended, the security apparatus grew and became a bureaucratic empire within the state. During the Second World War, the Gulag was integrated into the war effort in economic and penal terms. In 1941, a new People's Commissariat of State Security, NKGB, came into being. Standing alongside the NKVD, and, like all other commissariats, relabelled as a ministry in 1946, it cast an enormous shadow over Soviet society. The dismal empire was run by the most dreaded Chekist of all, the rapist, bringer of misery and incarcerator-in-chief, Lavrenty Beria, first as head of the NKVD, then as a deputy chairman of the Council of Ministers during the late Stalinist period, when he competed for power with other security ministers while accumulating resources and *kompromat*. He wore some of the most frightening uniforms of all, the stars, stripes and boards set off by his rimless circular spectacles.

In 1954, after Beria had been deposed and killed, the Ministry of State Security (the MGB, the relabelled NKGB) was administratively downgraded. It became the Committee of State Security, or KGB. The more autonomous and powerful ministry that it had been before (the MGB) was now abolished. As a committee of the Council of Ministers, the KGB was still placed very high in the political hierarchy, directly answerable to the Presidium (the Politburo again from 1966) – but it was precisely this direct, straight-line accountability that was supposed to bring the secret police under control. No longer would they be encased in an impenetrable, unanswerable ministerial labyrinth that generated its own imperial reach, devastation and chaos. Khrushchev was determined that a re-run of the Great Terror should forever be impossible, and the establishment of the KGB was one way to achieve this.

Its first chairmen were therefore clients of Khrushchev: Ivan Serov, who served from 1954 to 1958, Aleksandr Shelepin (1958–61) and Vladimir Semichastny (1961–7), though Shelepin and Semichastny later turned against him. Serov was unmistakably a person in uniform. He had served in uniform for decades, working his way upwards through the organs of power (see chapter 5), accumulating blood on his hands in every uniformed post. Shelepin and Semichastny were, by contrast, operatives who wore suits. They were what passed for politicians in the USSR. Shelepin had run the Komsomol and then been a deputy chairman of the Council of Ministers. Semichastny succeeded him as head of the Komsomol and then went to Baku to serve as second secretary of the Party in Azerbaijan. They were hard-nosed, educated men – Shelepin was nicknamed 'Iron Shurik' – entirely ruthless, willing to stamp on rivals and destroy nonconformists, comfortable with the details of ideology and the intricacies of committee-based government; they were adept practitioners of the 'neopatrimonialism' of Soviet administrative politics in this period of stability, *au fait* with both its patron–client ties and its complex, modern, institutional systems.[5] They were revolutionaries for a new age.

But the ultimate machine politician to run the KGB was Yuri Andropov. He succeeded to its chair in 1967 and retained it until the death of Brezhnev in 1982, at which point he himself became the general secretary. Born in 1914, he was forty-four years younger than

Lenin, thirty-six years younger than Stalin, and twenty years younger than Khrushchev. He was Brezhnev's junior by eight years and Gorbachev's senior by seventeen. Andropov was another outsider, born in a remote part of Stavropol region to a working-class father and a schoolteacher mother. In time, he used this class biography as best he could to gain some of the benefits of the 'Brezhnev generation', but he blurred the facts of his background, perhaps because of his disputed Jewish ancestry, not least concerning his grandfather, a jeweller from Karelia. Andropov was a shadowy man from the start.

He graduated from a technical college that specialized in water transportation in the small town of Rybinsk, on the Volga, before starting an itinerant administrative career in the Komsomol. He went with his young family to pursue work assignments in Yaroslavl and Karelia. Following the invasion of Finland proper and the onset of the Winter War, he served as the head of the Komsomol in the new Karelian-Finnish republic, partly annexed from Finland, between 1940 and 1944. This was a union republic in its own right, just like Russia or Armenia; it existed for fourteen years until 1956, when it was downgraded into an autonomous republic inside the RSFSR. It seemed the slightest of all the union republics in which to strike up a career. His critics pointed this out, together with the fact that he had never run a ministry or a major territory, that he had no experience of industry or agriculture,[6] that he had never worked in a financial institution, and that they were never quite sure about his background. He stayed in the north-west after the war until 1951, attending evening classes at university in the union capital, Petrozavodsk, graduating with a degree in history and ascending the career ladder in the Party. It was then that he achieved a breakthrough in his career, when he was appointed to a post in the Central Committee apparatus in Moscow. Shortly after Stalin's death, he transferred to a senior role in Molotov's Ministry of Foreign Affairs, and within two years he was made ambassador to Hungary at the age of thirty-nine. His tour there lasted four years. When he came back to Moscow, he enjoyed a decade of senior Central Committee jobs, dealing with the Communist Parties of the 'fraternal' republics behind the Iron Curtain. He became a big player in the party-government buildings of Old Square.

It was the profile of a man in a suit, not a person in a uniform.

Like every other apparatchik, he walked a tightrope during the Stalin period, living a high-stress life in the atmosphere of fear, ever vulnerable to arrest, but he was not a large-scale perpetrator, with direct experience of organizing or administering violence, of choosing victims or signing death warrants. He did not wear a uniform, tout a pistol, oversee camps or command killing fields. Between 1953 and 1967, his Party and government roles focused outwards, working at the highest political level with the countries of the Eastern bloc; it was imperial work, but it also had elements of diplomacy about it, and it fostered a broader view of the world than purely domestic Party administration might have brought. Legend had it that when he was in post at the Lubyanka, he would go home in the evenings to his comfortable apartment on Kutuzovsky Prospekt, where his neighbours were Brezhnev and Suslov, and read banned books from the archive of the KGB, one of the most cosmopolitan of literary depositories. It was certainly true that he campaigned against corruption, aspired to economic reform and was the patron of Mikhail Gorbachev. The two men shared origins in Stavropol; Andropov liked to visit the region, with its clement weather and health resorts. They became acquainted in April 1969, when Gorbachev was the second Party secretary of the Stavropol region, and met frequently thereafter. On 27 November 1978, Gorbachev was in Moscow, just elected as a secretary of the Central Committee. He paid court to the top Politburo men. Andropov seemed to tease him: was Gorbachev getting too close to Kosygin? This flustered the younger man. 'Yuri Vladimirovich,' he said to Andropov, 'are we still friends?' Andropov put him at ease and assured him that they were. 'And' – Gorbachev recalled, years later – 'Andropov was a man of his word.'[7]

Yet Andropov was still the Chekist-in-chief who chose career over conscience, and coercion not kindness. He demanded orthodoxy and feared dialogue: he might have liked books, but he was the reverse of a literary-leaning *intelligent*. In a report for the Central Committee that he signed off on 3 July 1967, less than two months after he became chairman, Andropov revealed his priorities for the KGB. He gave examples of political crimes and suspicious activity against the state: in 1965–6, for example, he claimed that the security organs had uncovered fifty nationalist groups with more than 500 members, not to mention an uncounted number of 'anti-Soviet groups' with 'restorationist' agendas in Moscow, Leningrad and other cities. Andropov therefore called for more people in uniform, with an immediate bonus of 1,750 new KGB officers, 500 sergeants and civilian employees and 250 cars (he seems to have got more). Any police chief asks for more money; more revealing was that Andropov immediately seemed to question the judicial direction that the country had followed for a decade and a half. After listing some of the types of Gulag inmate whose sentences were cancelled after 1953, he went on with macabre suggestiveness: 'Some of these categories once again embarked on the path of anti-Soviet activity [after their release].'[8] The implication was that the post-Stalin amnesties were reckless; anti-Soviet behaviour should always be stamped out. In the course of 1967, the KGB discovered 11,856 pamphlets or flyers that carried anti-Soviet messages. They brought 738 persons to 'justice' for political crimes.[9]

This was the period when the KGB made use of psychiatric hospitals on a significant scale. They incarcerated dissidents, sometimes for a few days, sometimes for a long period, in a large number of 'regular' psychiatric clinics. In the early 1970s, the KGB also ran two psychiatric clinics of its own, one of which was located in Rybinsk, the obscure town near Yaroslavl where Andropov had gone to college and which was briefly renamed after him following his death. Block 12 of Mordovian camp number 3 was the other. Smaller KGB psychiatric facilities were located in some other prison camps. The dissidents did not need the treatment. Instead they were physically intimidated by staff, surrounded by distressed and sometimes violent patients and given dangerously inappropriate drugs. The subtext – that disagreeing with the Party was a symptom of mental illness – was almost incidental. 'Apart from the extraordinary filth of the conditions,' wrote a contemporary chronicler, describing Block 12, 'the orderlies are reported as exercising a reign of terror. Though common criminals serving their terms, they even have the right to administer injections as punishment.' Meanwhile, in 'regular' psychiatric wards, dissident prisoners reported 'bedlam' and extreme overcrowding in the late 1960s.[10] Up to 1,000 dissidents were placed in psychiatric facilities and threatened with the use of psychotropic drugs over an approximately twenty-year period.[11]

It was also the time of 'prophylactic measures' – a conspicuously medical metaphor – which targeted 12,115 citizens in 1967, according to Andropov himself, in a letter he wrote to Brezhnev.[12] Subsequent research suggests 70,000 citizens were subjected to prophylactic measures between 1967 and 1970.[13] The KGB might telephone a person, write them a letter or call in at their home, and require them to attend an 'informal chat' at local headquarters. Such a person might have witnessed an incident, or made an off-hand comment, or even played a bit part in opposition activity. At HQ, they would endure an intimidating interview – sometimes played in a friendly key, and perhaps all the more sinister for that – sign a 'confession' and be given a warning. The aim was to forestall unrest and to keep would-be 'other-thinkers' in their place. Frightened and inoculated against potentially dissident activity, they might keep themselves to themselves, and opposition might not spread further. That was the theory. In public, Andropov even called this 'the most important method of solving problems assigned to the organs of state security'.[14]

Later, during *perestroika*, the then KGB chairman, Vladimir Kryuchkov, revealed that the secret police secured 7,250 convictions between 1960 and 1980 for 'anti-Soviet agitation', a specific crime designed to target dissidents.[15] This was one political prisoner every day for twenty years, which extended to the moral and personal destruction of perhaps hundreds of thousands of their fellow countrymen – the convicted, their families, those who were forced to emigrate, those who were not convicted but were subjected to intolerable pressure, those who were caught up by other legislation. This was a low-key civil war by the police and the Party against those who too openly expressed a different view of the world, or who happened to be overheard, or who crossed the wrong road at the wrong time and got caught up in the machinations of authority. For these people at least, there was no useful rule of law to protect them.

Perhaps it is a moral question that historians cannot judge, but there seems to be a gap between Stalinism and this type of dictatorship. Andropov was not a re-Stalinizer. His activity in office was not Stalinist in scale, context or even in its basic principles. Yet he plainly sidelined de-Stalinization and promoted the police state. The end of the Thaw is often dated to the year after he took over at the Lubyanka.

As ambassador to Budapest in 1956, he played a significant role in the crushing of the Hungarian Revolution. He gained a reputation for barbarism among the Hungarians. The 'clean-up' that followed the destruction of the revolutionaries was frightening: 10,000 arrests, 200,000 refugees. Andropov's role was to represent Soviet interests, not to oversee secret police operations.[16] He also learned a lesson for himself about the risks to Soviet power associated with political reform and easing off police control. For almost the whole of the Brezhnev era, Andropov was the boss of hundreds of thousands of people who wore uniforms. This was his life. He was the most visible and famous representative of the organs of state repression, the inheritor of the crown of Dzerzhinsky, Yezhov and Beria. 'Andropov', like 'the Lubyanka', was a synecdoche for the KGB. But despite the organization's addiction to symbols – its sword and shield – he did not wear a uniform himself.

The fact that he preferred a blackish suit, white shirt and dark-grey patterned tie, like a deputy headmaster ready to torment his pupils, told its own truth about the period. This truth had two sides. Andropov did not create a Chekist cult around himself – one dressed up in uniforms, weapons and symbols – but he understood the workings of power with a craftsman's intimacy and deployed them to the limit. He was an uncompromising disciplinarian who was obsessively committed to the Party's power, and yet he was also a modernizer, possessed of a certain intelligence that gave him a particular view of the intelligentsia that he considered such a threat.[17] His tenure at the Lubyanka coincided with the outright end of the Thaw, but he retained some of its principles: that the secret police should be under control and that they should not egregiously break the law on a mass scale. The KGB was the largest secret police force in the world, with as many as 750,000 employees, a quarter of whom were uniformed enforcers. Perhaps 65,000 KGB personnel were stationed in Moscow itself.[18] The time of Andropov's accession was crucial for the KGB. In 1967, 24,952 agents were recruited, a 15 per cent rise in total uniformed personnel.[19] The Stasi in East Germany was proportionately much bigger, though; in 1990, it had around four times as many agents per head of population as Soviet Lithuania had had in 1971, admittedly a suggestive rather than a precise comparison.[20]

KGB people insinuated themselves into society, painting lines that Soviet people knew they could not cross. Some of the lines were laws; others were so-called rules of the game. Agents thuggishly went after the line-crossers, from dissidents to the parents of recalcitrant teenagers, and also pursued 'real' criminals. They policed borders with the outside world – physical borders with barbed wire, imaginative ones in banned books and songs, and personal ones in encounters between Soviet people and foreigners inside the USSR. Agents listened in, engaged in surveillance, evaluated public opinion and destroyed public displays of 'other-thinking'. Economic enterprises above a certain size had a KGB office, whose staff were tasked with making sure that the enterprise was working in line with the requirements of the command economy; it had the incidental advantages, for the Party, of further suppressing the risk of industrial unrest or employee whistle-blowing.[21] KGB agents even occasionally went after corrupt officials and underground entrepreneurs, at least those who had lost the support of the patron higher up the chain who protected them.

The KGB was an indispensable element of Soviet civilization, truly 'organs' that were necessary for the USSR to function in a recognizable way. But it seems likely that the KGB lacked the sheer number of personnel per thousand head of population, the efficiency, or the sense of how to control society that was possessed by the East German Stasi; there is no evidence that it administered or aspired to create an enormous network of routine informers, extending into almost every group of acquaintances, even every extended family, of the type that the Stasi apparently achieved. One estimate, based on research about the Lithuanian republic, is that 0.2 per cent of the population informed on colleagues or acquaintances, with the numbers tilted towards sectors on which the KGB were particularly focused, such as cultural production, sensitive scientific research and elite administration, and much smaller in others.[22] Following the social catastrophe of the 1930s, the level of trust was again relatively high in the 'small communities' of Soviet life: groups of neighbours, networks of acquaintances, workplace collectives and friendship groups (*kompaniia*).[23]

Andropov did not seek a security empire like the one that Beria famously ran. True, the KGB turned up in all sorts of places: together with the Ministry of Internal Affairs, it had an association with Dinamo Moscow that went back to the 1930s, facilitating the player transfers and investments that allowed the famous football club to become Soviet champions in 1976 and finalists in the European Cup Winners' Cup in 1972. But Andropov preferred a clearly defined 'state within the state' to the amorphous and uncontrollable tentacles of an empire. His state within a state was characterized by bureaucratic orderliness. Andropov oversaw the KGB's four 'main administrations' (often translated as 'chief directorates'): foreign intelligence, internal security, communications and cryptography, and the border guards. Alongside this were nine other administrations that were of lesser importance. It was a tidy structure which the chairman aspired to 'see' from his office desk. He made it more effective still by treating his people well. Compared with the extreme uncertainties that their Stalin-era predecessors had endured, Andropov's employees enjoyed lives of stability and privilege. *Kegebeshniki*, KGB people, famously had good salaries and easy access to sanatoria and housing. The KGB was one of the first organizations to help its employees into cooperative apartments when the scheme was introduced in the 1960s.[24] KGB people liked to think of themselves as the best of the best, but the agency was riddled with nepotism, partly because senior Party officials were looking for opportunities for their offspring to spend some time in the West, and the KGB was one of the best options available.[25]

Not all security personnel worked in the KGB. The Ministry of Internal Affairs (MVD), long stripped of its secret police, employed more than half-a-million people in uniform. Most obvious were the police (the *militsiya*, or militia), who wore a different uniform, grey jackets and red caps. These 'militiamen' patrolled streets across the union and worked in many different security departments. The MVD also controlled an 'Interior Army'. Its ranks included prison guards, who ranged from the sadists who used to work in the worst hellholes of the Gulag to the listless dead-enders, such as Sergei Dovlatov, an improbable disciplinarian, who happened to be drafted to a camp and later managed to leave the country and became a major novelist. Among others, the Interior Army also incorporated the thick-armed riot police, eyes glistening with the anticipation of inflicting pain on fellow citizens who could not fight back. There were separate Ministries of Internal Affairs for the union as a whole and for every republic, and an elaborate network of departments across every region. The MVD ran its own higher education establishments and had links to certain schools.[26]

One regional leader, Nikolai Zakharov, ended up in a spectacular uniform: gold shoulder boards, bejewelled stars, a chestful of ribbons and medals. A product of the Brezhnev generation, he made his way out of the Novgorod countryside, where he was apprenticed to a cobbler, then worked and studied in Leningrad, moved to Khabarovsk and ended up joining the NKVD in Moscow in 1940, serving in the secret police during and after the war. He was one of the 'promotees' who quickly moved up the ladder. He became the MVD's deputy minister in Latvia, the minister itself in the Chuvash ASSR in the Russian republic, and then head of all MVD operations in Kemerovo region, which covered a substantial part of Siberia. When the KGB was formed in 1954, and Zakharov was only forty-five, he was promoted into its higher reaches rather than remaining in the ministry; he was head of the KGB's Ninth Administration, responsible for internal security, and was already first deputy chairman of the entire organization when Andropov assumed the chair. By then he was almost sixty, and Andropov soon shunted him aside. He worked as deputy minister of mechanical engineering for most of the 1970s. During his last four decades, his apartment was in the House on the Embankment, the building where Khrushchev's family had lived for a time in the 1930s. Formally called the 'House of Government', it had become notorious during the Terror, so many of its residents were arrested by Zakharov's predecessors.[27]

Although 'politicals' were now only a small minority of the prison population, and the total number of camps shrank considerably after 1953, the MVD continued to run a substantial penal network in the form of scattered camps rather than local prisons. Urban jails, such as Lefortovo in Moscow, were typically either holding facilities run by the KGB or 'isolators' for prisoners on remand. People who were convicted of regular criminal offences moved into the main penal system. They usually ended up in MVD camps, in barracks rather than cells, which were often located far from their homes in a kind of penal 'periphery'.[28] Some of the brutality previously experienced by political prisoners in the Gulag was exported to camps for regular criminal convicts in the decades after 1953. The different nationalities that populated the camps experienced a relative equality in their experience of brutal incarceration; the penal system was arguably a space in which ethnic difference was less acutely experienced in the Soviet Union.[29] Even after they were released, former prisoners faced constraints on where they could settle through the application of the *propiska* system, the stamp in the internal passport which was a kind of residence permit. Famously, there was a 100-kilometre limit, excluding them from residence in Moscow and its environs. Former prisoners clustered around the '101st kilometre', both a geographical designation and a cultural symbol. Still, for all its misery, the prison system was no longer associated with the mass incarceration and premature deaths of innocent people. De-Stalinization had a long-lasting effect. Khrushchev's personal interest in downgrading the Gulag paid off. In 1969, a new statute for regulating prison camps was introduced at the all-union level and in each of the republics. It entrenched the reforms of the Khrushchev era, but did not extend them. According to the most careful historian of the post-Stalin camps, there was no return to the extreme harshness of the Stalin period, and Stalinist principles did not return to the penal network after 1953.[30]

Other agencies also secured the state. Most notable was the GRU, the main organ of military intelligence. It was concerned with foreign operations, like the First (later redesignated the Second) Main Administration of the KGB. After the KGB, the GRU was the second-largest secret police force in the world. The two agencies were the Foreign Ministry's so-called 'near and distant neighbours'. The phrase was a reference to the topography of Moscow. Yet by the first decade of the Brezhnev era, the KGB and GRU were both so big that they required new headquarters in new locations. The KGB retained the Lubyanka, but from 1972 its foreign operations were directed from a Langley-style complex in the forested southern edge of Moscow, in the Yasenevo district. Pyotr Ivashutin, Andropov's opposite number in the GRU, pushed for the expansion of his existing HQ in Moscow's Arbat district, but had to accept instead a converted but brand new hospital building in north-west Moscow. It was sometimes referred to as the Glass House or the Aquarium, such was its design, but most people who worked there called it after its nearest metro station, Polezhaevskaya.³¹ During the seventies, municipal facilities in the surrounding north-west districts noticeably improved, as stand-offish people in GRU uniforms gained special access to the tall new apartment blocks in the area.

On special occasions, Brezhnev dusted off his ever more illustrious military uniform. His career during the war, as a commissar rather than a fighter, had been a distinguished one, but he was now, without further noticeable service, promoted to the military stratosphere. On 21 March 1974, he became a general. Two years later, on 7 May 1976, he was elevated to marshal of the Soviet Union. With braggadocious underlinings meant for his own eyes only, he reported in his notebook that the senior official Aleksei Kopyonkin had come to his office on 10 May and 'said that he had heard the voice of an officer, he had heard the voice of a general, and now he was pleased that he'll hear the voice of a marshal'.³² By now, however, the general public tended to respond with derision to this inflation in Brezhnev's uniforms and medals.

The Soviet army was the largest in the world. Following postwar demobilizations and then Khrushchev's spending reductions, the armed forces reached a consistent size of around 3.6 million men in 1958.³³ Conscription was deeply embedded in Soviet civilization. In 1939, a new law revised military service. It was applied with revolutionary ferocity during the Second World War. After the victory, demobilization was soon followed by remobilization, as the Cold War deepened. It was enabled by conscription. A law of 1954 further expanded the scope of conscription in response to the Korean War. Khrushchev made military cuts for the sake of the welfare and housing budgets, and to consolidate his own power in the face of the perceived political threat from Marshal Zhukov, but the army pushed back. Conscription continued.

A new conscription law was passed in 1967 and came into effect on 1 January 1968. It required boys to serve from the age of eighteen, younger than before, but for a shorter term of two years. Each year, they entered the ranks for the first time either in the early summer or early winter. Enthusiasts among them undertook some voluntary military training when they were at school, organized by the Volunteer

Society for the Army, Air Force and Navy (DOSAAF). Some children, often those from military families, attended a school linked to the armed forces. The army took the most recruits, but young men were also drafted into other armed forces, including the internal security troops of the MVD. Military service was usually derided as a waste of time, to be deferred for as long as possible, for instance by spinning out one's time as a student. It was also feared because of the intense bullying and hazing – the so-called *dedovshchina*, the rule of the 'grandfathers', or NCOs and other regulars – that it sometimes entailed; and later for the chance of death in the Afghan War. For some it was the start of a military career. Officers undertook military education in special academies. The career in military uniform was supposed to confer a privileged lifestyle for one's family. It was supposed to lock people in uniform into support for the Party, make them willing users of coercion, if necessary, to defend the ruling order and their place inside it, but the advantages of service dwindled.[34] As the 1970s went on, living conditions in some garrison towns and ports declined. There were reports of poor medical care for military families. Up to 100,000 officers were left to find their own apartments.[35]

The uniformed security state reinforced gender norms. Gagarin's fancy uniforms projected masculine glamour.[36] Voluntary school-age training in the DOSAAF segregated boys and girls, and promoted conservative habits.[37] The conscription law of 1967 defined military service as male, though women could be drafted during wartime. In the 1970s, women tended to work in the armed forces (and GRU) only in administrative and technical support roles,[38] though their participation in the MVD and KGB was broader.

Uniforms hinted at a psychology of violence. Some in the Brezhnev generation, which was running the country after 1964, avoided the call-up for military conflict, but the age cohort before Brezhnev's – their elder brothers and fathers – served repeatedly in uniform, in the First World War and then the Civil War. Some had been in the Imperial Army for years, victims of hazing and isolated from their families; a significant number had fought in the Russo-Japanese War of 1904–5. In or out of uniform, they participated in revolutions, endured coercion and lived through famine, atrocities and epidemics between 1905 and 1921. Historians have sometimes argued that they were brutalized, willing to participate in the violence of the 1930s. Yet many young veterans of the Civil War fought, two decades later, in the Great Fatherland War, having endured the 1930s as victim or perpetrator, and went on to lead a 'normal' life in society and family after 1945. Post-traumatic stress disorder was widespread, but its effects can be traced on individual lives rather than on a whole-society scale.[39] Violence was embedded in Soviet civilization. So was uniformed coercion. But the uniforms alone did not make their wearers lifelong perpetrators of violence. A much deeper and more personal psychology was at stake, one that was human rather than merely Soviet.

The human touch was emphasized in public culture. Representations of the men and women in uniform were common in film, TV and novels during the 1960s and 1970s. This illuminated their ubiquity, softened their dreadful edges and gave them a touch of glamour. Even military service looked better when it was depicted in the context of a romantic drama. In *Spring Call-Up* (1976), conscription did not seem too bad; a wayward, lovelorn conscript, played by heartthrob Igor Kostolevsky, mopes around, breaks rules, and still his sergeant smiles benignly on. The barracks are clean and bright, cleaning duty gives a chance to phone home surreptitiously, and the conscripts' uniforms are not uncomfortable. Eleven years earlier, Vadim Kozhevnikov, who was one of the most establishment of Soviet writers, published the bestseller *The Sword and the Shield*, about Soviet intelligence agents during the Second World War. It was filmed as a major four-part TV series and shown in 1968. The first two parts were broadcast in August, while Warsaw Pact forces were crushing the Prague Spring. There was a connection. Viewers watched it because it was compelling entertainment, but it helped to legitimize, even celebrate, the place of the people in uniform in Soviet civilization.

Kozhevnikov's success inspired Yulian Semyonov, the author of popular detective and spy novels, to write a wittier and more characterful sequence of novels about wartime intelligence, headlined by the classic *Seventeen Moments of Spring*. The novel was published in 1968. A twelve-part TV series, directed by Tatyana Lioznova at the Gorky Studio, followed five years later. Shot in atmospheric black-and-white, with an all-star cast including Vyacheslav Tikhonov and

Oleg Tabakov, it was the most popular and influential of all Soviet television programmes. Here the uniforms were all German, because the programme followed a long-term Soviet infiltrator into the Nazi intelligence agency, the SD, in the final days of the war. The spy was Standartenführer Max Otto von Stirlitz. Soon the name was universally known in Soviet society, loved and revered, the object of affectionate irony, the subject of countless jokes. *Seventeen Moments* was extremely exciting. It was difficult not to sympathize with Stirlitz's emotions and personality. The effect was patriotic: Stirlitz was homesick after many years outside the motherland; viewers felt pride in his achievements. Once again, popular culture lent the secret police some unearned lustre. *Seventeen Moments* was repeated three times in the year following its initial release; Gorky Studio estimated that 200 million Soviet people saw it, effectively the entire TV-viewing population.[40] Confident and long, its format emphasized the permanence of Soviet civilization.[41] It implied that the population owed something to the people in uniform who had defended it.

Yulian Semyonov, the creator of Stirlitz, helped to build the cultural foundations that underpinned this sense of Soviet eternity. He was born in 1931: the same year as John le Carré. Unlike le Carré, Semyonov did not work as an intelligence officer, but, like him, his life was intertwined with the secret agencies. When he was a student, during the late Stalinist period, his father – a Jewish editor – was arrested. (Semyonov was a pseudonym; he was born Yulian Liandres.) Yulian ended up excluded from the Moscow Institute of Oriental Studies with only one year of five left on his degree. But his father was released, and Yulian completed his studies at Moscow State University. He already knew Yevgeny Primakov, a graduate of the Oriental Institute and another habitué of the secret world, who later ran the secret services and served as one of Boris Yeltsin's prime ministers. The two men became friends, and their lives were always connected. Semyonov learned Pashtun and other languages and served on the staff of *Pravda* in Asia and elsewhere. Primakov did the same. For Primakov, it was an almost open cover; *Pravda* foreign correspondent was a typical day job for a KGB agent.

In the 1960s, Semyonov began a writer's life in Moscow. He soon had a comfortable apartment and dacha. His royalties were extremely handsome. He travelled all over the world, meeting Ted Kennedy in Washington, Ernest Hemingway in Cuba, Georges Simenon in Paris.[42] He stayed in touch with Yevgeny Primakov. Starting in 1963, with *Petrovka, 38*, Semyonov wrote a sequence of detective novels that spanned the Brezhnev era. The hero was Major Vladislav Kostenko; number 38 Petrovka Street was the MVD police HQ in Moscow. Readers related to Kostenko's worries at work and home; they recognized his circle of friends, acquaintances and neighbours; they admired his lovely wife, his empathy for sympathetic victims, his capacity for charm and friendship. He was what a Soviet citizen might want of a person in uniform. These novels were full of insider information about police procedure. Semyonov invented memorable villains – wartime turncoats, vicious murderers, high-class thieves – and described the subcultures and marginals, the greed and bad judgement, the corruption and injustice that Kostenko encountered every day. The plots were intricate and fast-moving. There were very occasional references to Brezhnev's scientific-technical revolution,[43] but the reader almost had to look for them. But that only made Kostenko more natural, more normal. He was one brick in the uniformed wall of eternal Soviet rule. And, for readers, he was also one of them, or within their grasp. Fans felt better for spending time with Kostenko. Fictional or not, he made Soviet rule a little more secure.

The sum of these men and women in uniform made it impossible to challenge the power of the Communist Party. Most people passed their days not much noticing the organs of coercion, even making jokes about their silly uniforms and, in the case of regular policemen (*militsionery*), their general foolishness and stupidity. A joke recorded from 1969 described a potential policeman being positively evaluated by an MVD selection board. 'What's three times three?' the selectors ask. 'Ten,' the applicant replies. 'And if you think about it again?' 'Ten.' 'And if you really think about it?' 'Ten.' 'Ignorant,' goes their evaluation, 'but principled.'[44] For all the changes in Soviet life since 1953, these uniformed officers were still the personnel of a police state. This sinister designation meant something different after 1953 than it did before. It no longer meant that the apparatus of coercion was overwhelming in its scope. No longer was it intimately tied to every aspect of life. No more did the apparatus arrest and execute innocent people randomly and arbitrarily. It did not run the country; it was not out of control; it did not define the core ethic of Soviet civilization as much as it had done in the past.

Still, it was not unreasonable to call the Soviet Union a police state when Andropov took over at the Lubyanka and in the years that followed. For one thing, the sheer number of uniforms showed just how much the security apparatus was swollen to an unnatural size. For another, the KGB and its partners made a nonsense of the idea of the rule of law. If a person is completely innocent, went a joke from the 1970s, the court will *reduce* his sentence.[45] Against all possible odds, one small group of citizens stood up against this darkness in Soviet life. They had a light within them; it left them sharply silhouetted against the curtain.

Elena Bonner and Andrei Sakharov

# 9
# To the Square

Three women, a baby and five men converged on Red Square at noon on 25 August 1968. It was five months after Gagarin's terrible final flight and four days after the crushing of the Prague Spring. Larisa Bogoraz, Tatyana Bayeva, Viktor Fainberg, Pavel Litvinov, Konstantin Babitsky, Vadim Delonye, Vladimir Dremliuga and Natalya Gorbanevskaya, who was pushing the pram that contained her infant son, made their way separately to the far end of the Square, near the Moscow River. The big, sloping area around St Basil's Cathedral, Lobnoye mesto, was often the site of historic events. It was here that Peter the Great had gathered the supporters of his dynastic rivals and executed them. When people talked about going 'to the square' to protest, this was one of the places that history conjured up for them.

They were members of the intelligentsia: philologist, physicist, poet. Some of them knew each other and some did not. They had responded individually to a notice that came out through the underground dissident network. None of them was quite sure who would turn up. They sat down on the steps of St Basil's Cathedral. It was the global era of sit-in protests. Few were as dangerous as this one. The danger was the point. None of the eight expected that they would end the day in their own homes. They imagined prison, labour camps, even worse. But their consciences pointed them in the direction of Red Square. Pavel Litvinov later said that on that morning, as he made his way to the square, he felt calm, even joyful.

They took out banners. The slogans expressed solidarity with the people of Czechoslovakia and shame of their own government. Within moments, KGB officers in plain clothes came towards them. The secret policemen yelled an antisemitic phrase, grabbed the banners and assaulted at least two of the protesters. They smashed into Litvinov with a heavy bag filled with books. Viktor Fainberg was punched in the face and lost his front teeth. Although the KGB people ordered the protestors to move on, none of them did. The sit-down protest continued until seven of the eight were manhandled into KGB vehicles and driven away. Some bystanders who had sympathetically observed the protest were also arrested.

For ten minutes, they left Natalya Gorbanevskaya, the protestor with the baby, on the steps. Then they worked out what to do: they came for her as well. In the car, they beat her, but they released her that evening. It was assumed that this was because she was the mother of two young children.[1] Twenty-one-year-old Tatyana Bayeva, who was arrested, was soon released, and though she was repeatedly interrogated and troubled by the police, the case against her was not pursued. The other six faced a joint trial in September and were given sentences ranging from two to four years, which they served in prison, mental hospital or remote exile.[2] Gorbanevskaya was dealt with separately. She was rearrested, held in remand in a mental hospital from September 1968 and tried later, alone, in July 1970; she was sentenced to indefinite incarceration in a psychiatric ward. Police confined her in very frightening living conditions. Doctors tormented her with endless drugs and treatments. Lawyers harassed her in a legal labyrinth.

Gorbanevskaya was one of the dissidents that the authorities seemed to hate with a special venom, revealing a particular feeling of disgust and inadequacy on their own part. She was not one of them. Instead, she seemed the incarnation of another part of Soviet civilization that they distrusted but could not destroy, one which focused on a liberating version of socialism that secured individual rights, required one to read and ask questions and yearned for cultural pluralism. Born in a Jewish family in Moscow in 1936, when the city was on the cusp of the Great Terror, she was escaping Stalin ever after. When she was still a small child, her father was killed at the front. She began studying in the Philology Faculty at Moscow State University in the year of Stalin's death. By the third year of her degree, when Khrushchev was giving the Secret Speech, she was already friendly with opposition-minded students. At that point of the Thaw, Soviet students were expressing a wide range of views, and some of them aspired to hold government to account, including in public meetings,³ but Gorbanevskaya was friends with those who went too far, distributing material about the invasion of Hungary and the suppression of the Hungarian uprising. In 1957, a few weeks after her generation had mixed with thousands of foreign visitors at the World Festival of Youth, she was excluded from the university. It was as if she was out of tune with the times, or the times were out of tune with her. She restarted her life by travelling to Leningrad and enrolling as an evening-class candidate at Leningrad State University, where she again studied philology – Russian language and literature – and then returned to Moscow to work as a librarian and translator. She had been writing poetry since she was a teenager and some of it was published in samizdat from 1961.

Gorbanevskaya was temperamentally and intellectually drawn to the dissidents. She became part of a milieu of like-minded men and women, defined by friendship, solidarity, an anti-totalitarian mentality, an uncompromising sense of conscience and a willingness to take very considerable risks. She found a significant number of other Jews among the dissidents. Gorbanevskaya was a supporter of Aleksandr Ginzburg and worked with him to defend and publicize the cases of those who had been arrested for 'political crimes'. When the high-risk samizdat periodical *The Chronicle of Current Events* was launched in April 1968, she put herself forward as editor, organizer, typist and visionary. She had just emerged from a fearful encounter with the security services. In February 1968, when she was heavily pregnant, she was transferred from a maternity hospital to a psychiatric ward under KGB direction. The physical and mental abuse of her by policemen, KGB officers, lawyers, doctors, nurses and medical orderlies continued after the August demonstration. An April 1970 commission chaired by a corresponding member of the Academy of Sciences (one step short of the august rank of academician) signed her off as schizophrenic and required her to 'be sent for compulsory treatment to a psychiatric hospital of the special type'.⁴ (Subsequent analysis of the diagnosis and, still later, examination of her by international psychiatrists revealed no sign of mental illness.) She was only released in February 1972, after enduring incarceration in a succession of institutions, including the Kazan specialized psychiatric hospital, the Kashchenko psychiatric hospital and the Serbsky Institute, not to mention the Butyrka jail in Moscow. She could breathe free air after that, but the KGB were on her tail.

One of the banners on 25 August read 'For your freedom and ours'. It was a distinguished reference. Its heritage in the Polish national and dissident movements would have been well known to certain passers-by. Gorbanevskaya loved the slogan, partly because she loved Poland, and partly too because of the words' inclusive resonance. She pointed out that Russian democrats of the previous century had also adopted the slogan to show that freedom in Russia was inseparable from freedom across the empire.[5] The slogan linked the struggles of the demonstrators in Czechoslovakia to those of the men and women on Red Square. At the centre of a sit-down, peaceful demonstration, the slogan joined the Soviet Union to the discourse and repertoire of protest that marked the 'global 1968'. The slogan also connected the mighty handful of 25 August with 250 million of their fellow countrymen. Some of these were national dissidents in western Ukraine and the Baltic republics, who acknowledged the power of the gesture.[6] One of Litvinov's inspirations was Martin Luther King; another was Gandhi. For the dissident Lyudmila Alexeyeva, the slogan proved that freedom in Poland or Czechoslovakia was indissoluble from freedom in the Soviet Union. The dissidents were creations of Soviet civilization, and precisely for that reason their cause transcended Soviet borders and wove their moral code onto an international tapestry of protest, community and human rights. They were heirs of the international socialism of 1917 and successors of the cosmopolitan intelligentsia that had become entwined with the revolution. 'The Moscow thaw was inseparable from the Prague Spring; the Moscow trials were inseparable from the invasion of Czechoslovakia,' wrote Lyudmila Alexeyeva. 'Freedom, like slavery, recognizes no national boundaries.'[7]

History, though, was inclined to make an opposite assumption. Rather than seeing the dissidents as Soviet people with outward-looking intellects and transnational perspectives, outside observers tended to assume that dissidents must be inspired by causes that originated from abroad. The claim was that they were mouthpieces for Western values: that human rights and democracy had no connection at all to

Soviet civilization, not least, the argument went, because the USSR had changed so little since the 1930s.

The history of the dissident movement showed something different: that the dissidents were Soviet people, an organic part of Soviet life, and not an unnatural, foreign body within it. It was difficult to call them liberals, as their contemporaries in the West often wanted to do, and as historians have sometimes implied, even imposing an ahistorical 'liberal subjectivity' on them, as if they were Western people who happened to have Soviet citizenship and live in the Soviet Union.[8] The ideas about political and personal rights that dissidents supported were liberal, completely recognizable to their Western counterparts and plainly the result of a very long interaction between Russian and other European lines of political development, ultimately expressed in meretricious form in the Soviet constitution; but many dissidents seemed to retain socialist assumptions about the economy rather than liberal preferences for private property and free markets.[9] Benjamin Nathans, the leading historian of the dissident movement from outside the former Soviet countries, points out that dissidents never spoke out against the Soviet social settlement and simply accepted the egalitarian and emancipatory dimensions of its welfare institutions and ideology.[10]

This mentality was the basis of the dissident critique of Soviet power. Dissidents typically criticized the authorities from within Soviet civilization, using Soviet categories, and not from outside, using Western ones. The truth was that socialism and rights and the wider international language of human rights had common sources, and that the Soviet experience was one offshoot of a shared modernity. Aleksandr Vol'pin was one of the first heterodox intellectuals during the Thaw and after to argue that the Party's core doctrine of 'socialist legality' should not be contemptuously dismissed, but should be the benchmark from which to hold the authorities to account. The Soviet constitution listed many rights. The dissidents argued that people should live as if they really did have the right to hold public meetings, exercise free speech or have access to a proper trial. They should challenge the authorities to respect their own laws.[11]

Nowhere was this challenge more heartbreaking than in the treatment of certain national groups. These were people who seemed at least doubly vulnerable. Some of them had been deported from their historic homelands during the Stalin era. Although many of them had returned during the Thaw, they still endured discrimination. Dissident communities in Moscow formed links with members of some of these nationalities, such as the Crimean Tatars, and tried to offer support, though the authorities had little interest in observing their own laws about equal rights based on nationality. In fact, the Crimean Tatars created their own lines of dissent and other-thinking in a parallel track to other Soviet dissident communities, privileging literature and samizdat in the process, working within a recognizably Soviet set of discourses and practices.[12]

Dissidence was embedded into Soviet civilization in another way. Like all other features of Soviet life, it was the product of chronology, of turning points. The dissidents were creatures of the Thaw – they were children, or even grandchildren, of the Twentieth Party Congress – who used the insights of the Thaw to deal with the challenges of the two decades that came between Khrushchev and Gorbachev. Dissidence could not have existed without the transformation (and improvement) in Soviet life that had taken place since 1953. Many dissidents were in their twenties and thirties while Khrushchev was in power. Gorbanvskaya was twenty and Larisa Bogoraz was thirty when Khrushchev gave the Secret Speech; Pavel Litvinov was twenty and Viktor Fainberg was thirty when Gagarin flew in space. In the fast-moving world of Stalinism and post-Stalinism, there were older cohorts with noticeably different life stories. Litvinov's parents-in-law were Lev Kopelev and Raisa Orlova (forty-three and thirty-seven respectively in 1956). Orlova had delivered Solzhenitsyn's manuscript to *Novyi mir* in 1962. Both she and Kopelev came of age during the 1930s and subsequently underwent profound processes of personal de-Stalinization. On the night of 24 August, the day before the Red Square demonstration, Litvinov spent the evening with a gathering of sympathizers at the apartment of Kopelev and Orlova. Aleksandr Galich – dissident poet and bard by night, screenwriter for blockbuster films by day – was there. Galich was the same age as Orlova: thirty-seven at the time of the Secret Speech, forty-nine in August 1968. In one of his verses he sang, 'Can you come to the square? / Dare you come to the square?' This was an intoxicating moment for Litvinov, who seems not to have been afraid. He revelled in the atmosphere. In order to protect the older generation, which the younger dissidents assumed were physically less likely to survive imprisonment, Litvinov kept his mouth shut and went to the square without them.[13]

Late-1960s and early-1970s dissidence was one of many afterlives of the Thaw. Lyudmila Ulitskaya, the great post-Soviet novelist, inhabited this world: personally and intellectually liberated when she turned twenty-one in 1964, ever after seeking nooks and crannies – the kitchens of the like-minded in Moscow's Arbat and Dinamo districts, the poems of Brodsky, the Jewish Drama Theatre – where the oxygen of the Thaw remained trapped. Others who, like Ulitskaya, were children when Khrushchev gave the Secret Speech, also carried the legacies of the Thaw with them. Tatyana Bayeva celebrated her ninth birthday shortly before the Twentieth Congress, but its agenda of de-Stalinization shaped her attraction to the protest movement of 1968, and carried her, aged twenty-one, to the August demonstration on Red Square. Valeria Novodvorskaia, born in 1950 and a bookish fourteen-year-old when Khrushchev fell from power, seemed to develop her critique of Soviet power in whole form out of the literary sensibility of the Thaw. She began her studies at Moscow's Pedagogical Institute of Foreign Languages, which was named in honour of Maurice Thorèze, but was expelled in 1969 for organizing an underground opposition group with some fellow students.

The Thaw, of course, had its own uneven chronology, its refreezes and new springs. Its legacies for the long 1970s were bound to be complex. And while the end of the Thaw is conventionally dated to 1968, with the crushing of the Prague Spring, the four years that lay between those events and the fall of Khrushchev in 1964 were not a straight path away from de-Stalinization. The authorities' approach to Joseph Brodsky, for example, was an uneven, meandering, horrible sequence, in which the secret police targeted him, left him alone, and went for him again throughout the 1960s. His treatment defied easy periodization. And the start of dissidence as a movement is often traced to 1965, even though other aspects of the Thaw, in the production of films, for example, were at that point still operating in a relatively open environment. On 6 September, for example, a great classic of Thaw cinema, *I Am Twenty* (also known as *Ilyich's Gate*), was celebrated with the Special Jury Prize at the Venice International

Film Festival. Marlen Khutsiev's movie had been subject to substantial cuts and remained controversial for its depiction of free-wheeling, free-thinking, anti-Stalinist young people in Moscow. But even in its reduced form it was still a major statement of the intricacies and even heterodoxies of Soviet civilization, and was a point of connection between Soviet pluralism, however limited, and Western culture.[14]

Two days later, on 8 September 1965, Andrei Sinyavksy was arrested in Moscow. He left his apartment and walked to the trolleybus stop at Nikitskie vorota, a stone's throw from the Arbat, from where he had to make his way to give a lecture to the company of trainee actors at the Moscow Arts Theatre. Four days later, on 12 September, Yuli Daniel, who had been in the painful process of separating from his wife, Larisa Bogoraz, was arrested at Moscow's Vnukovo airport. Bogoraz, who would later be one of the Red Square protestors of August 1968, had recently been appointed to a university lectureship in Novosibirsk. Sinyavsky and Daniel were literary people who occupied overlapping worlds – members of the Moscow intelligentsia, possessors of socialist heritage, inheritors of family culture, practitioners of literature and theatre, regulars in the cultural hinterland adjacent to the semi-legal underground. Perhaps the Thaw had made them complacent. They were both forty, so they knew the risks. Both of them had written controversial works, critical of Soviet power, and agreed for their books to be published in Paris, Sinyavsky using the pseudonym Abram Tertz, while Daniel called himself Nikolai Arzhak. As news of their arrests became widespread, disquiet spread among their friends and sympathizers. On 5 December, Constitution Day, at six o'clock in the evening, around sixty of them gathered at the great poet's eponymous monument on Pushkin Square, on Gorky Street in central Moscow. Many though not all of them were students. It was not yet clear what fate would befall them – three years later, the Red Square Eight had no illusions – but what they had in common was a conviction about individual rights and socialism, and an ability to suppress fear and live with very high risks. The KGB were waiting and arrested twenty-two of them, though they released them again later that day. The basic outlines of the dissident argument and their tactics were becoming clear. So too was the approach of the authorities: aggression and surveillance that stopped short of open warfare on the dissidents.

The KGB built their case against Sinyavsky and Daniel, and the trial took place over three days in February 1966. For Lyudmila Alexeyeva, this was a new kind of repression. 'Even Stalin' – she suggested – 'had never prosecuted writers for writing.'[15] Alexeyeva and other friends of Sinyavsky and Daniel waited outside the court. The trial was formulaic. Sinyavsky was sentenced to seven years and Daniel to five. Daniel benefited from the fact that he was injured while serving in the war. Western journalists in Moscow followed the case closely. It was widely reported abroad. This formed the mythology of Soviet dissidence as it was constructed in the West. It also informed the network of transnational support that sympathizers in the United States and Western Europe, such as the conscientious and loyal Peter Reddaway of the London School of Economics, tried to keep up.[16]

In November of that year, the twenty-eight-year-old Anatoly Marchenko was released from custody and moved to internal exile. Unlike Sinyavsky and Daniel, he was a true outsider, born in a place and among people who were unimaginably distant from the Moscow intelligentsia. He came from the small town of Babarinsk, deep in Novosibirsk oblast. Although he was a one-off, he developed similar arguments to other dissidents about the gap between the actions of the Soviet authorities and their own laws. He combined intellect and courage with passion and impulsiveness; he hated the KGB with his whole being. He believed that Stalinism had come back to the Soviet Union, and that the awful camps to which he was confined were a straightforward continuation of the Gulag. Many historians disagree,[17] but his arguments were not merely historical. Instead they were born of a suffering, vision and ethics that came out of the camps. Even if the experiences of society as a whole were no longer Stalinist, his own were. Persecuted by the secret police, incarcerated by the state, unprotected by law or rights, his 1970s were every bit as terrifying as the 1930s and were therefore accessible to similar frames of moral analysis. Yet even among the diverse outliers who were starting to make up dissident communities and networks, Marchenko's was an unusual case. He had tough-minded working-class credentials. For the next few years he was in and out of jail, camps or exile. His health declined. Larisa Bogoraz wanted to save him. She married him.

*

Other opposition-minded individuals and groups existed who did not belong to the dissident milieu or have links to it. Some of them protested more or less spontaneously in ways that drew on Soviet language and traditions. The uprising in Novocherkassk in 1962 was a famous example. It was a landmark of Soviet history for good reason: it was an exceptional event. There were few moments of social unrest on any scale until Gorbachev's era of reform. One possible reason was that the authorities had learned their lesson and did not try to raise food prices again, or make any other move that had a sudden impact on living standards. Another was that the police state continued to target anyone who publicly voiced opposition. The scope of police action in the Baltic republics has been easier to study than in many other republics because of the availability of their KGB records for the 1970s. These show that spontaneous unrest had little chance of ever getting going.[18] The rare instances of mass protest in the USSR in this period, moreover, did not seem to operate within a Marxist framework as was at least sometimes the case during the Thaw. In May and June 1967, the largest riots of the first half of the Brezhnev era gripped Chimkent and Frunze in the Kazakh and Kirgiz republics respectively. The cases were similar, and there was a dynamic between them. Out-of-control crowds targeted police stations, prompted by rumours of a death in custody – a murder by policemen – of a driver in Chimkent called Ostrukhov and a soldier in Frunze called Ismailov. The authorities estimated that 1,000 people were involved, seven were shot dead, fifty were injured, and forty-three were put on trial.[19] These people were neither more angry nor less fearless than the dissidents, or worth less than them. They simply had a different agenda, one that could never gain the mythic edges of the dissident enterprise.

Solzhenitsyn, the Soviet Union's most challenging voice, was not really a dissident either. He was a giant, but he was self-absorbed rather than community-minded; he believed that his own literary work transcended the dissident cause. Solzhenitsyn accepted at face value the yearning of the Russian and Soviet intelligentsias to believe that a book could change the world – but he assumed it was his book that would do so. He was extremely courageous, but it would have been counter-productive to sacrifice himself, because he had to write the masterpieces. The only figure of comparable global stature to Solzhenitsyn was Andrei Sakharov. He was a very different person, an archetype of dissidence.

Sakharov was born in May 1921 a stone's throw from the Kremlin and at the heart of the old intelligentsia. It was two months after the Bolsheviks had presented their programme for dictatorship at their Tenth Party Congress, and two-and-a-half years after Solzhenitsyn was born in the provinces. It was a household which observed the behaviours and moral outlooks of the intelligentsia. His father was an academic and science writer who gently guided him towards a career in physics. Sakharov enrolled at Moscow State University (MGU) during the Great Terror in 1938. He showed no interest in politics though he guardedly spoke out against antisemitism. He joined the evacuation from Moscow in 1941 and continued his studies at a relocated MGU, in Ashkhabad. He graduated early with an abbreviated degree, worked in armaments engineering and got married to Klavdia. They started a family and went back to Moscow so that he could attend graduate school. He quickly completed a higher doctorate in nuclear physics. His mentor, Igor Tamm, guided him towards the Soviet weapons programme. No longer could he lead an intelligentsia life in a place where the authorities did not interfere too closely; he had to take responsibility for the lethal potential of his research. He and his family moved to the closed town of Arzamas-16, a kind of Soviet Los Alamos, where they enjoyed a privileged lifestyle. Sakharov could not enjoy it fully. His work turned him into one of the fathers of the Soviet thermonuclear bomb.

When they were long back in Moscow, at the height of the Thaw, he had enough perspective to observe the cracks in Soviet life between his own understanding and the reality of the world. Sakharov was especially worried about the fallout from nuclear weapons testing. He even contacted Khrushchev to express his concerns. He remained in post at his Academy of Sciences institute, with a formidable array of privileges, but he had deep doubts about his own profession and the conduct of the government. His crisis derived from his understanding of socialism. He worried about ecological devastation, the consequences for human health, the dangers of nuclear war with the United States, the implications that his own lifestyle had for the promise of

Soviet equality, the living conditions of ordinary people, the arbitrary aspects of government, the unmistakable lurking of the police state and the incapacity of the current leadership to deliver human rights. Sakharov was not a charismatic public performer. But he started to speak up. He was not involved in the Sinyavsky-Daniel trial, but he began to support people who were targeted by the secret police.[20]

The course of Sakharov's life switched to a high-risk trajectory. But he still had the option of quietly reversing from his dissident cul de sac and returning to the Soviet highway; for him, at least, 'forgiveness' was possible in the post-Thaw years. His prestige was such that his missteps might be disregarded and he might still peacefully return to academic life and enjoy his old privileges. Instead, he reached his point of no return in July 1968 and kept on going. A month before the Red Square demonstration, Sakharov finished writing his *Reflections on Progress, Peaceful Coexistence and Intellectual Freedom*. It was the length of a short book when filled out with other texts, but also reproducible in a newspaper. He had worked hard on it, sitting at his desk through long evenings at the top-secret 'installation' where he was employed. Sakharov argued that the crisis facing humanity could only be resolved by a convergence between the United States and the Soviet Union, in which capitalism adopted the moral advantages of socialism in terms of economic equality and cultural conditions, and the socialist system incorporated all kinds of personal and political rights. The quality of life in both societies would improve. This would be the basis for global interventions: tackling poverty in the developing world, halting military adventurism, slowing down environmental degradation, and securing the planet from the threat of nuclear war.

Sakharov's tone and argument were plainly the products of post-Thaw Soviet civilization. In fact, Sakharov sent a copy of the text to Brezhnev. The polemic made uncomfortable claims for the Party – and Sakharov was denounced by many in the provincial and central leaderships as 'counter-revolutionary' – but the analysis was cool-headed. Sakharov offered an alternative path for the Russian Revolution: one that was anti-Stalinist, internationalist, committed to peace and ecological sustainability, and founded on rights. His was an independently Soviet critique of Soviet power. For all its power and accessibility, it was not a text that could have been written abroad or imagined in the West. In one of its most revealing passages, Sakharov condemned Stalinism out of hand. He stated that it had 'many common features' with Nazism. But he emphasized that it was *periodization* that determined Soviet reality: that it was the *Stalin* period that was equivalent to Nazism – a period that in the USSR was twice the length that it was in Germany – and that Stalinism was in 1953 replaced by de-Stalinization. And despite their shared violence and destructiveness, there was a fundamental and rhetorical difference between Stalinism and Nazism, even at the height of their equal barbarism and ferocity. 'Stalinism' – he wrote – 'exhibited a much more subtle kind of hypocrisy and demagogy, with reliance not on an openly cannibalistic programme like Hitler's but on a progressive, scientific and popular socialist ideology'. Sakharov unblinkingly wrote that the cynical appropriation of this ideology for violent political purposes had destroyed millions of lives, and made fools out of others. Khrushchev had begun the process of de-Stalinization but 'it still has a long way to go'. Exposure and discussion of Stalinist atrocities needed to continue indefinitely. As the Thaw came to a close, Soviet society was in a vulnerable position. Neo-Stalinists, where they existed, should be removed from government. Sakharov boldly mentioned one by name: Sergei Trapeznikov, head of the Science Department of the Central Committee.

The alternative to Stalinists like Trapeznikov was not American capitalism, or any other 'Western' system. What was needed instead was to develop the humane inheritances from 1917. Sakharov saw the Prague Spring as a potential display of these. They offered 'socialism with a human face'. Sakharov's parents had raised him in a humanistic milieu, where learning was valued and the works of Russian culture, and European culture more generally, had been constantly available. None of these was inconsistent with Bolshevism, though in Bolshevism they coexisted with the potential for extremely violent politics. Sakharov renewed the Thaw's rejection of such an approach. The socialism that Sakharov came to espouse derived instead from plural voices, as well as the revolution of 1917, his perspective onto Europe – and his experience of the catastrophe of Stalinism. He described his views as 'profoundly socialist'.[21] 'Most of us evolved in a similar pattern,' wrote the leading dissident Lyudmila Alexeyeva, in a memoir of her generation. 'We were socialists in 1953; we were still socialists in 1956; we had few thoughts about socialism for the twelve glorious years of the thaw; then, in 1968, we believed again.'[22]

Alexeyeva and her 'company' (*kompaniia*) of friends formed a nucleus of sociability, intellectual exchange and mutual support. They stare out of photographs taken at parties with immense comfort in the presence of each other. Each possessed their own vision of Soviet civilization and the value of the person, and they talked about it endlessly; but they also helped each other – and others too – with all the practical resourcefulness that networks of friends and relatives developed in Soviet society. The KGB knew who they were. Sometimes they harassed or arrested them. Like other such groups, they were merely unarmed civilians standing exposed against a police state staffed by empty-eyed men who did not hesitate to deploy targeted violence and disregard the law. All that protected them was the flimsy front door of their apartments.

Such a company of friends might be compared to an intellectual or literary 'circle' (*kruzhok*) from the earlier days of the nineteenth-century intelligentsia. But the decades of revolution and Stalinism had changed everything. Alexeyeva and her friends were much more exposed. They required greater commitment from each other and developed much stronger bonds of trust.[23]

They sought to defend human rights in general and to stand up for their fellow citizens who had been arrested or were on trial for political reasons. Although they wanted to show that such rights as free speech were not abstract, but had as concrete an effect on people's lives as the right to a pension, they could come across as supercilious or preoccupied with abstracts. Many of them were members of the intelligentsia, and those who were not were interested in intellectual matters. Dissidents and the intelligentsia occupied connected circles in Soviet life.

In the late 1960s, the intelligentsia comprised a large section of the Soviet population. It had an official, sociological status. Marxism-Leninism theorized that it was a 'layer' of society whose members might belong to different classes. More concretely, the creation of a new social identity, the engineering-technical intelligentsia, became increasingly important in Soviet society during the postwar decades.

Technical specialists – the holders of degrees in scientific and technological subjects – had undergone, like all graduates, a five-year degree programme which was not entirely focused on a single subject. They were used to reading more widely. Marxism-Leninism and the history of the Party were compulsory subject matter, but a certain level of literary culture was expected of all students. The gap between sciences and arts as fields of intellectual inquiry was relatively narrow, as we have seen, and it was plausible for graduates of all subjects to be members of a capacious intelligentsia.

Institutions of higher education (known by the acronym *vuz*) were entry points to the intelligentsia, while the people who worked in them, the academic intelligentsia, were a major sub-section of the intelligentsia as a whole. Much higher education took place in so-called institutes, which focused on a particular area of knowledge (such as aeronautics or foreign languages). These could be high-prestige places; the Moscow State Institute of International Relations, which trained diplomats, was probably the most famous, and was subject to nepotistic claims on its admissions process. Many cities also had a university. The Academy of Sciences oversaw a large network of research institutes. By the late 1960s and early 1970s, the universities that shaped earlier incarnations of Soviet civilization were established in their basic professional function, of producing and disseminating knowledge. They were also arenas of relative freedom of speech, in which student discussion clubs, for instance, proliferated even after the Thaw.[24] Yet when students from Moscow State University spoke out for an open trial for Sinyavsky and Daniel, and then some of them attended the protest on Pushkin Square, the university's Komsomol sections gathered information about the students' activity and sent the details further up the chain for a decision.[25] Whether professors, lecturers and researchers made up a high intelligentsia together with novelists and theatre directors, or shaded into the 'mass intelligentsia' that was also the preserve of schoolteachers,[26] they helped to create a hinterland, even a fuzzy and indefinable one, in which the dissidents were located.

'Intelligentsia' transcended a merely sociological category. In everyday encounters, it was instantly clear whether a person was a member of the intelligentsia. Membership required a certain commitment to the life of the mind – expressed in reading fiction, being curious about the outside world, appreciating the continuum of knowledge between the natural sciences and the arts, enjoying theatre or cinema. It was a matter of enlightenment and civilization, but also refinement and culturedness, and above all empathy, kindness and decency. Members of the intelligentsia should be *intelligentnye*, moving out of themselves to offer help to others, though a person did not have to be in the intelligentsia to behave in an *intelligentnyi* way. Intelligentsia was a moral category. If you were a careerist your membership of the intelligentsia had become formulaic; if you worked for the *apparat*, you were of the *apparatchiki*, not the intelligentsia.

The moral qualities of the intelligentsia were a set of attitudes and behaviours that shaded into the dissident mindset. Dissidents wanted to hold the authorities to account by using Soviet institutions. Their thinking drew on the heritage of the nineteenth-century intelligentsia, transposed now to an all-union level and drawing on cultural traditions of nationhood and resistance among intelligentsias from other parts of the Russian empire. By the 1970s, while the intelligentsia as a whole – academic, cultural, 'mass' – became more conformist, the dissidents represented a 'heroic form of exodus from the Soviet communist project'.[27] The dissidents were a very specific corner of the Soviet intelligentsia. Historians have wondered if they have paid the dissidents too much attention: they were small in number and did not obviously have major effects on the society of which they were a part. But their significance far outweighed this mechanistic way of looking at the past. Their moral and cultural characteristics make them overwhelmingly interesting in their own right.

It was not immediately obvious why one person became a dissident and another did not. Some of it was a matter of chance, of being born into a particular family, or finding oneself in a particular educational institute, workplace or apartment building. It was easier to locate the dissident milieu in big metropolitan cities or academic centres than it was in remote, smaller places. Dissidents seemed to have one thing in common: an instinct to examine, without fear or favour, what was right and wrong in Soviet society, and a personal need to intervene accordingly. It required a predisposition for danger or a capacity to overcome fear by sublimating it in the pursuit of conscience.

For such people, conscience was embedded into Soviet civilization from the start. Political consciousness (*soznatel'nost'*) – an explicit and informed engagement with communist teaching, leading inevitably to acceptance of society's consensus position – was one thing. Conscience (*sovest'*) was another. How could one be sure that the exercise of individual conscience would lead one to support the Party? The Party encouraged honesty and self-sacrifice, but only for the sake of a totalized greater good. In practice, people made sense of these qualities in their relationships with others. Dissidents elevated conscience to a political level, assuming that conscience required them to make political demands of the state.[28] Sincerity was another virtue that socialism was supposed to encourage but that in reality came from within. Like conscience, it had cultural origins in Russian traditions, with parallels for other nationalities, but in practice it was an attribute, sometimes manifested in disarming and naive ways, that a person simply possessed. Living with such virtues did not make a dissident a 'nice' person, sometimes the reverse. The historian Roi Medvedev, brother of biologist Zhores, wrote major works that criticized Stalin, but he spoke with discomfiting positivity of Andropov for the liking of some of his fellow other-thinkers.[29] Dissidents were made of the same human material as the rest of their fellow citizens. They sometimes did great things for the wrong reasons and allowed pettiness to limit the scope of their achievements.

There was no outright 'psychic' explanation for dissidence.[30] Demanding that the Communist Party and government of the Soviet Union observe its own laws was an approach that emerged from a constellation of historical events. An active interest in human rights derived from a particular strand of Soviet civilization. These were external, 'real' historical forces, not simply the internal consequence of a disembodied individual character. Of course, it was the combination of these external and personal factors that created dissidents. Dissidents in general did not approve of the label. For a start, it was an English word with Latin roots. The KGB, with its antisemitic heritage and distrust of 'cosmopolitanism', deployed the foreign-sounding label like a weapon. It gave the dissidents an air of otherness, of something to be distrusted. They often described themselves as heterodox 'other-thinkers', using a Slavic word, *inakomysliashchye*.

The influence of the dissidents seeped into the rest of the

intelligentsia, even towards those who knew almost nothing of them. Reading was at the heart of it. Networks of samizdat readers extended widely in the post-Thaw period. Sometimes they began with a trusted colleague, neighbour or fellow student passing across a banned, typed text, something like the poems of Joseph Brodsky, who was finally expelled in 1972, or an older, innocent classic that was banned for unfathomable reasons, as if by accident. Readers might be 'occasional' consumers of samizdat, interested in a particular book, or involved merely by chance. Others were more deeply committed. Exposure to *The Gulag Archipelago* or *The Chronicle of Current Events*, even if it was fleeting, was most often remembered as the experience that shaped a reader's understanding of the world of samizdat. But reading samizdat was only vaguely seen as an act of resistance. It created a loose community of readers that linked the dissidents and, in its broadest sense, the intelligentsia.

The intelligentsia temperament – the desire to read widely, to talk in groups about one's reading, to push back, at least notionally, against censorship – was a condition of reading samizdat. Producing samizdat required much more, though – it also needed an appetite for extreme risk-taking and a more coherent, convinced oppositionism. The typists were indispensable. Most of them were women, and they usually worked for free. Their activity was conspiratorial, but it was also an extension of the working day; it was an intelligentsia scene, but it also rested on very practical and entrepreneurial questions of supplies and distribution. Even getting hold of paper was not always easy, and typists might have to search their city for enough foolscap and carbon paper if there was a fluctuation in the deficit. In other words, it helped if they brought the practical resourcefulness, not simply the mental furniture, of Soviet civilization to their task. Typists might try to hoodwink the authorities by having a 'clean' and a 'dirty' typewriter, the latter used for underground work. The KGB could make out traces of a text on the ribbon and hardware of the typewriter. Typists were ready for interrogation. And yet of course they were often invisible. The editors of *Samizdat Leningrada*, Arseny Roginsky and Aleksandr Dobkin, were ever after part of dissident lore, but the typists who worked with them – Elena Rusakova, Tatyana Pritykina, and Natalia Dobkina – were almost never mentioned.[31]

Despite the opposition between its practitioners and the KGB, samizdat was not antithetical to Soviet civilization. Instead, samizdat depended on a set of practices that, as literary historian Josephine von Zitzewitz writes, were 'perfectly Soviet'. It provided items that the state chose not to provide, or banned; it required networks that depended on the high levels of trust that existed in certain social milieux and between certain categories of strangers; it was obsessed with texts, by definition it was focused on literature, and it was subsumed with 'bibliophilia'.[32] All of these were Soviet characteristics. To an extent, the networks of readers formed unofficial publics whose existence and beyond-closed-doors debates were tolerated by the authorities.[33] The scholar Serguei Oushakine calls this the 'mimesis' of samizdat. 'Instead of juxtaposing their discourse against official discourse, instead of distancing themselves from the sources of this discourse,' he writes, 'the dissidents chose a strategy of identification with the dominant symbolic regime.'[34] And yet, from the outside, the dissidents seemed to be Western sympathizers adopting a Western strategy. The story of dissidence was the story of continuum: from the texts of Soviet laws to the typescripts of samizdat, from empty vocalizing about rights to its sincere expression, from one side of the Iron Curtain to the other.

In the five years or so after they had sat down on Red Square, the eight protestors endured periods of imprisonment and internal exile in remote locations in Siberia. Larisa Bogoraz then returned to Moscow, where she remained active in the dissident community. Her husband, the dissident Anatoly Marchenko, died in a prison camp, aged forty-eight, in 1986. Between 1974 and 1976, five of the eight were stripped of their citizenship and forced to emigrate. They settled in Paris or New York, but they did not have easy lives. Natalia Gorbanevskaya, for example, remained stateless for decades. In the summer of 1983, Vadim Delonye, a poet who came from an academic family, who was barely yet a man when he went to the square, died in his sleep in Paris at the age of thirty-five. By then – and this takes us ahead of the story – the man who had overseen their beating, exile and expulsion, Yuri Andropov, had been promoted into the highest office in the land and was living out a natural lifespan.

Lermontov Sanatorium, Odesa

# 10
# Socialist Bodies

While the dissidents gathered fleetingly on Red Square, and Czechoslovakia was locked into Soviet-style socialism 'for ever', Aleksandr Solzhenitsyn hid himself away. He was carrying out profoundly subversive work. The KGB were watching. He feared time was running out. And so he wrote quickly, with merciless self-discipline, at his dacha. He was revising chapter 96 of his great novel about scientists in the late Stalinist Gulag, *The First Circle*, when he saw long columns of military vehicles rolling down the road that was 100 metres from his desk. They were going south. He knew the destination: Prague.[1]

Writing and all forms of public expression were becoming more difficult, even dangerous. The Thaw's spaces for debate were narrowing. Hostile elements in the KGB showed a more open interest in Solzhenitsyn. In September 1965, they confiscated some of the papers that he secretly stored at the home of his friends Veniamin and Suzanna Teush. Seniavsky and Daniel were arrested at about the same time (see chapter 9). Solzhenitsyn did not work at the family home in Ryazan for fear that it would be raided. He was scarcely undercover, but he did move around, and he avoided putting all his eggs in one basket. In the years that followed, Solzhenitsyn did some of his most concentrated work sitting in wooden houses, or outdoors, at wooden tables, surrounded by trees and open land, within earshot of running water. Sometimes a friend or ally brought him to their dacha to lie low. Tvardovsky invited Solzhenitsyn to his place at Pakhra; the family of Lydia Chukovskaya opened their dacha up for his use; he frequented Rostropovich's dacha at Peredelkino. He went to Estonia, where he wrote sections of *The Gulag Archipelago* in remote rural seclusion, and his supporters hid copies of the drafts. Sometimes he went out to the countryside near Ryazan, to a village he and Natalia adored: Solotcha. Above all, he loved to work at his dacha near Obninsk. If he was alone, as he was for stretches of time, he slept in a narrow single bed, peeled his own potatoes and vegetables, sorted his own buckwheat, prepared his own porridge and soup, made use of a simple stove and worked ferociously. It was not simply an ascetic lifestyle; it was how he was. 'He felt positively uncomfortable,' wrote his biographer, 'without a hair shirt of some kind.'[2] Solzhenitsyn was physically hardened, his fit Soviet body first wrecked by the Gulag and then honed by literature.

In the second half of the 1960s, he created more major works that did not yet see the light of day, especially the great novel *Cancer Ward*, which Tvardovsky had hoped to shepherd past the censors. Solzhenitsyn endured the gaze of the KGB and the disappointment of non-publication. He was an ambitious man in personal and moral terms. It was unthinkable for him to write merely for himself, for a permanent lower drawer. His mission required him to protect his papers and his person: to preserve that which was material and of the mind.

Yet he took risks. The moral stature that came with physically standing up and metaphorically putting one's head above the parapet was in itself a statement of ambition; it might even, for all its danger, facilitate publication of one's work, at least in the West. Solzhenitsyn was aware too that a Soviet writer lived corporeally inside the Soviet Union, was physically part of a Soviet community of one kind or another: a member of a group of persons who gathered in private rooms or public places, whose bodies felt pain and endured incarceration and were in all ways vulnerable to the long arm of the KGB. This meant that total retreat into writerly solitude was neither possible nor desirable. 'Underground is where you expect to find revolutionaries,' he wrote. 'But not writers.'[3]

In October 1969, he turned up at a meeting of the Ryazan Union of Writers, only to be expelled from membership of their branch. The following month, the union secretariat in Moscow approved the decision. Of the secretariat's members, only Daniil Granin supported Solzhenitsyn, at some risk to himself.[4] Some members of the wider union in Moscow also tried to put their weight behind Solzhenitsyn.

They included Vladimir Voinovich, who later emigrated and effectively became a dissident, but also authors who found ways to critique the system from within, such as Yuri Trifonov, the great writer whose principal subject was the moral dilemmas of contemporary urban life, and Vladimir Tendriakov, one of the major exponents of the village prose movement. Solzhenitsyn responded with an open letter to the literary establishment which was circulated in samizdat among bold and interested readers. 'OPENNESS, honest and complete OPENNESS – that is the first condition of health in all societies, including our own,' he wrote, chiding his colleagues. The following year he was awarded the Nobel Prize in Literature but not allowed to collect it in person.[5]

His struggle went on. Often isolated in rugged settings, Solzhenitsyn fused mental and physical exertion into a single, extraordinary literary output. His working regime required his whole body, not simply his mind, to be supple and engaged. As a toiling writer, he was aware of his physicality. This mind–body wholeness explained his writing: his extraordinary productivity, his unwavering belief in himself and his ideas, and his literary interest in certain themes, including physical health.

As a teenager, at school and university, Aleksandr Solzhenitsyn knew that his body belonged to the Soviet Union. At the peak of the Stalin era, it was natural enough to accept this, even on occasion to celebrate it. Solzhenitsyn had a robust physicality in his youth. He loved the cold, so his schoolmates called him 'Walrus'. From the age of eighteen, he spent long summer holidays on cycling trips. One of Solzhenitsyn's trips was a month-long tour of the Caucasus, travelling up the Georgian military highway, climbing mountains and dipping across passes.[6] It was no easy feat. No doubt he benefited from the compulsory fitness lessons and health checks that were a part of higher education. He might have seen that on May Day 1936, men and women in revealing sportswear took part in the parade on Red Square. Their muscles and curves showed what the ideal Soviet body was supposed to resemble: the parade itself, let alone photos or paintings of it, was a work of socialist realism. This physicality was an erotic charge in Stalinist public culture.

Solzhenitsyn showed that the physical survival of their body was a *zek*'s first aim in the camps. Ivan Denisovich mused constantly about cold, tiredness, pain and hunger. At the start of the single day that is the subject of his story, he feels sufficiently unwell to go to the camp sick bay. Sick days have to be registered the evening before, but Ivan Denisovich takes a chance. The medical orderly on duty records a temperature of 37.2 Celsius. It's high enough to keep him in the sick bay until the doctor arrives, but if the doctor thinks that the patient is fit – that he's tried to shirk – he'll be locked up in the cells. This is a worse fate than going out to work. It's a gamble; while he nestles behind his desk, the orderly advises him to go to work instead. Ivan Denisovich agrees and does not take the risk. He looks at the orderly. 'How can you expect a man who's warm to understand one who's cold?' he wonders.[7] No wonder that health and hospitals were a crucial arena in which Soviet civilization was shaped.

Between the mid-1960s and mid-1970s, the Soviet health system reached its maximum effectiveness. According to published data, the number of doctors per 10,000 population, which had doubled between 1940 and 1950, doubled again by 1970, from 14.6 to 27.4. Although most indicators suggested that the healthcare system was running into trouble in the late 1970s, central planning could at least train and deploy personnel. The number of doctors almost doubled in the twenty years following a major healthcare decree of 1960, from 20.0 to 37.4 per 10,000.[8] As a point of contrast, there were 18.3 doctors per 10,000 population in the United Kingdom in 1977 and 25.7 in the United States in 1983.[9] Notwithstanding differences in definitions (some dental surgeons were included in Soviet numbers) and in the reliability of published Soviet statistics – a complex problem, as the science of Soviet statistics was highly developed but also politicized – the overall pattern was clear. One common claim was that a quarter of the world's doctors worked in the Soviet Union.

There was another way of looking at this. From the mid-1970s, the health of the Soviet population seemed to stall and even decline. On the one hand, infant mortality fell and women's lifespans increased into the seventy-plus range, in a way that was familiar in the West. On the other, male life expectancy was stuck in the mid-sixties, making the USSR an outlier among countries that claimed to be developed. Depending on how one calculated it – evaluating published statistics or the stray comments of ministers – the proportion of the budget devoted to healthcare was stalled at between 3 and 4 per cent in the 1970s, and probably closer to 3 per cent, at a time when growth rates in the economy overall were decelerating.[10] There were ecological harms – air and water pollution, as well as radiation leaks from power stations and armaments tests – and issues over diet, tobacco and alcohol.[11] Stress, with its devastating impact on middle-aged health, was incubated in Soviet housing, which even in the new apartment blocks remained overcrowded by European standards. Health suffered too because of the general anxieties that derived from urban life, with its shortage economy, and from rural decline, with its emptying villages. Alcohol-based diseases proliferated. Sometimes the Soviet state or the Communist Party of the Soviet Union actively spoiled particular lives, dividing families, blocking careers, denying access to better housing, and in other ways too damaging a person's health. People complained about the quality of dental care. Shortages of anaesthesia caused great suffering later in the decade. The quality of healthcare was very varied across the USSR, with especially little on offer in the countryside, not least because of poor roads and the distance to bigger hospitals; the ethical choices this demanded of physicians were scarcely consistent with the vision that Soviet civilization asserted.[12]

Ingrained into healthcare was the principle of all-round treatment marked by regular check-ups. 'Prophylaxis,' insisted the USSR's first commissar of health, Nikolai Semashko, in 1925, 'is a complete system.'[13] It was the distinctive core of the Soviet approach. Facilitated by an overbearing state in a way that capitalist countries were ill-equipped to match, prophylaxis nevertheless required and cultivated a level of individual citizen autonomy. In a glossy volume dedicated to 'sixty years of Soviet healthcare', published in 1977 and co-authored by sixty prominent physicians, nine leading doctor-politicians wrote the chapter on prophylaxis. Boris Petrovsky, minister of health from 1965 to 1980, claimed in his celebratory chapter that prophylaxis was coded into the institutional organization of the health system, that it served society and the economy as a whole as well as the well-being of individual persons, and was even the 'leading principle' of Soviet medicine.[14] Semashko had earlier sensed this potential. Like his successors, he was himself a doctor. He helped to develop the characteristically socialist and Bolshevik principles that shaped the healthcare system: central planning; universality; and preventive, ongoing care alongside treatment for specific conditions. Prophylaxis was expensive and included a range of innovative concepts, such as so-called 'prophylactoria' centres for sex workers to receive medical care and vocational retraining, which were not developed at any scale.[15] More typically, prophlyaxis ranged across the welfare and medical systems – from social insurance to paediatrician-designed outdoor regimens at Pioneer camps to anticipatory blood tests and self-designed herbal treatments initiated by the run-down middle-aged – and effectively became part of the Soviet lifestyle.

Prophylactic care was not cheap. Some people had better access to it than others. For instance, members of the Union of Writers were entitled to an extensive annual check-up at a union-funded clinic. Each writer set aside a complete day and went for tests and examinations in the various departments of the clinic, from ENT to ECG and from eye checks to scans. If they didn't go, they would not receive an up-to-date medical certificate and would not be admitted to one of the union's sanatoria.[16] Acquiring the right piece of paper – the relevant *spravka* – was an exhausting and interminable element in Soviet people's lives. It also became a medicalized aspect of everyday bureaucratic routine. Somebody beginning a catering job – working in the kitchen of a canteen, say, or as a waitress in a restaurant – needed to present a medical certificate before they could start work; the same was true for people who wanted to go to a public swimming pool, or a Pioneer camp, or indeed any sanatorium or rest house. It was not simply a formality; it was a basic principle of public hygiene and social life.

Since shortly after the end of the Civil War, 'physical culture' had been celebrated and encouraged, a sign of *kul'turnost'*.[17] Thereafter, people were taught how to do exercises at school with the view that this should be a lifelong skill and habit; *fizkul'tura* was also embedded in university curricula and radio broadcasts. Across the population, it was common (though scarcely universal) to do exercises after getting up, if only a few stretches, and there was a moment on the radio every morning when they were encouraged. Eastern and Central European norms of physical culture thus combined with Soviet planning.

Meanwhile, central planning determined the life chances of the disabled. For instance, the Leningrad Institute for Prosthetic Research developed not only artificial limbs but also blueprints for accessible apartments and public buildings.[18] Work placements were distributed to people with particular disabilities. Blind people often worked as masseurs in sanatoria, for example, and certain factory roles were made accessible to those with mobility constraints. Medical-Labour Expert Commissions evaluated the capacity of disabled people to work and made recommendations about the allocation of jobs and value of welfare payments on a defined ranking system. Miserable prejudices remained, especially against those with severe disabilities that required round-the-clock care. Such people were often confined to small apartments while their mothers heroically cared for them for decades. Not only family but a version of 'civil society' stepped in for the disabled when the state neglected them. But this was sporadic. The All-Russian Society for the Deaf (VOG) was an autonomous organization which effectively and ambitiously advanced their interests. It turned them into a community of disabled people.[19]

Such fluidity in social organizations also existed in hospitals, where it created a tension. On the one hand, management and investment were centralized, planned and hierarchical. And yet, on the other, the routine operations of institutions and the decision-making of individual citizens were based on a striking level of autonomy. This tension was inherent to Soviet civilization. It was manifest too in prophylaxis. The preventive approach to medicine accustomed Soviet people to having check-ups, requesting tests and seeking attention. It expanded everyday medical knowledge, especially among women. Soviet citizens in need of treatment therefore acted as if they had options. One port of call was the *terapevt*, a loose equivalent of a general practitioner. Another was the polyclinic, where it was possible to have a same-day appointment with a gynaecologist, paediatrician or ear-nose-and-throat specialist, without a referral from a more general physician. When the worst threatened to happen, some patients responded by looking for the best specialist or drugs that were in short supply. In Yuri Trifonov's novel of 1969, *The Exchange*, the middle-aged son of a woman stricken by cancer borrows money, has his colleagues at work cover for him, and crosses the city to find the medication of choice. Fifteen years earlier, Aleksandr Solzhenitsyn also discovered the web of personal autonomy, professional hierarchy and economic planning that determined his own access to cancer treatment.

Just over a year before his sentence came to an end, in early 1952, Solzhenitsyn underwent an operation inside the camp medical unit. The surgeon was a German prisoner. It was cancer. The operation was a success, and so they made him go out and work in the dark and cold as soon as it was physically possible. Following his release from the camp and his instalment in exile in the small Uzbek settlement of Kok-Terek, he experienced a spring and summer of fresh air. He had much more 'freedom'. By the autumn, though, the cancer was back, and a new torment and unfreedom had replaced the old. He had stomach problems and was losing weight. His MVD monitors, who tightly circumscribed the boundaries of his exile, allowed him to seek medical attention in the nearby town of Dzhambul. The doctors found a large tumour and referred him to the major cancer hospital in Tashkent. He needed official permission for this journey too, so he had to go back to Kok-Terek and seek the relevant paperwork from the MVD office. It was not immediately forthcoming. In pain, feeling nauseous and gravely discomforted by a swollen abdomen, he was given three weeks to live by the local doctors.

Eventually, at the turn of 1954, he was allowed to set off, on public transport and by himself, for the oncology centre at Tashkent. On arrival, he was immediately admitted and treated. Two female doctors took charge of his care. Lidia Dunayeva, who ran the radiology department, possessed an intuitive expertise that sped up his diagnosis. A leading American specialist on precisely Solzhenitsyn's type of cancer later concluded that his treatment regimen was the same as it would have been at a major cancer hospital in the United States in 1954. Over the six weeks that he was a patient in Tashkent, Solzhenitsyn had around fifty X-ray treatment sessions. The same American physician suggested that a patient with Solzhenitsyn's disease had around a one-third chance of living five years. Solzhenitsyn's recovery seemed like a miracle; he left the hospital and went back to Kok-Terek.[20]

A decade later, he was in very good health. Not only had he

recovered; he was cured. He started to write about his illness. By the end of the 1960s, he had completed the manuscript of the novel *Cancer Ward*. The team at *Novyi mir* loved it. Aleksandr Tvardovsky himself thought that he could find a way to publish it. But as the political and cultural climate cooled, this proved impossible.

Kostoglotov, the hero of the novel, has spent years in the camps and gone on to develop a cancer like Solzhenitsyn's. In a specialist oncology hospital in Uzbekistan, he waits to die. In the hierarchy of the hospital, the status of patients is flattened. Cancer makes 'equals' of them all. One of Kostoglotov's fellow patients is a Party official, whose pretensions, denials and phone calls cannot save him from cancer: just when he needs them most, the scientific structures of Marxism and the infallibilities of the Party are completely useless. It is a workaholic female doctor, plugged into American research, who saves Kostoglotov, helped by other female medical staff whom he loves and respects. An intensive X-ray programme turns out to cure him, like it did Solzhenitsyn, but that only becomes clear with time; he is desperate to take control of his own treatment, to find out more about it and to calculate his odds. He has a small stock of a particular birch fungus that he got from a well-known village herbalist a few weeks earlier, by travelling 150 kilometres in contravention of his exile sentence, when he felt his disease returning. When ground to a powder and added to liquid, it was supposed to have anti-cancer properties.

On her rounds, Vera Kornilevna, the doctor who is especially kind to him, spots the complementary medicine at his bedside and expresses alarm. 'Oh, I know all about your sacred science,' Kostoglotov replies. 'If it were all so categorical, it wouldn't be disproved every ten years! What is there for me to believe in?' He feels an overwhelming need to have some control over his treatment, to complement, not replace, the X-rays, in a way that also replenishes his self-worth.[21] The British journalist Michael Binyon, who spent 1967–8 working for the British Council in Minsk and a decade later represented *The Times* in Moscow, pointed out that 'Russians ... have a strong and tested belief in the efficacy of herbal and folk medicine,' but put this down to a mixture of culture, climate and quackery,[22] rather than a generally existing desire to seek out personal autonomy and dignity. The apparent paradox was that Soviet civilization was not only capable of accommodating this expression of initiative, but actively depended on it, not only in the realm of healthcare but in the operations of society more generally.

This was also true for the Sakharov family. Klavdiya Sakharova had shown worrying signs of ill health since September 1964, when she collapsed with gastric bleeding. Sakharov took her to the Kremlin Hospital. Located on the western side of Moscow, it was the most prestigious medical institution in the country. Neither the doctors there nor those at the Petrovsky Clinic, where she went the following April when she collapsed again with the same symptoms, detected (or looked for) cancer. She was checked over again in October 1968. Although this examination took place three months after the publication of his *Reflections* in the *New York Times*, Sakharov was not yet beyond the pale. (Or perhaps it was an oversight; he somehow kept his medical privileges for another two years.) He and Klavdiya were planning a visit to a sanatorium in the southern town of Zheleznovodsk that belonged to the Council of Ministers. As regulations dictated, they had to have a check-up before they could receive the voucher for the sanatorium. Klavdiya was losing weight. She felt pain all the time in her abdomen. The doctors did their usual tests, including an X-ray of the intestines. They found nothing wrong and sent her off to the sanatorium, entirely relaxed about her condition.

Within a couple of weeks she felt worse. Her circulation was weakening. In December, she was admitted to the Kremlin Hospital. In January, she was belatedly diagnosed with cancer. There was little time left. She spent a few weeks at home. At the end of February, she returned in agony to the Kremlin Hospital, in the hope that her pain might be better managed there. Sakharov was willing to try anything that might give his wife the faintest chance. He rushed off to Kaluga, near Moscow, where a retired doctor had been independently developing an anti-cancer vaccine. It was an unproven treatment. They tried one ampoule, but it made no difference. Klava, as the family called her, died on 8 March, International Women's Day.[23]

Soviet doctors were large in number and high in prestige. Like medics in all modern societies, they were tough-minded gatekeepers to their difficult-to-enter profession; they earned good money; they possessed authority and mystique. In a prizewinning three-part TV film from 1976, *The Days of Surgeon Mishkin*, the title role was played by Oleg Yefremov, an actor who possessed authority and mystique in abundance. The casting was perfect. As a founder member of the Sovremennik – the famous Thaw-era theatre – and then director of the influential Moscow Arts Theatre, Yefremov was completely convincing as a charismatic original to whom everyone looked up. The doctor that Yefremov played was a senior surgeon in a provincial district centre. He was dedicated to his patients and his vocation; he could find the words for recalcitrant patients and difficult colleagues; he felt the tragic losses that were inherent to medical practice while possessing the capacity for carrying on. He had high ideals, a human touch, and a modest lifestyle, not to mention an assured, good-natured, masculine superiority.

In a moment which self-consciously makes light of the confusing status of doctors in Soviet society – members of a privileged caste in a relatively flattened wage structure – Dr Mishkin and a colleague watch a workman in the hospital who is trying and failing to drill a wall and hang a picture. Mishkin takes over. But you are intelligentsia people, the workman says, not the working class. No, Mishkin replies to his baffled interlocutor: you are the lumpenproletariat. It is doctors who are the true working class. Mishkin might live simply, be dedicated to his working collective, talk naturally to his uneducated patients and never stop working, but the working class could hardly confuse him for one of their own: he was paid an unusually high premium for moving to a remote location, more for rising through the hospital ranks, and most doctors in his position were also happy to accept 'gifts' from their patients. Soviet people instinctively recognized this sociological complexity – it was on the surface of Soviet civilization, a normal feature of it, not shamefully hidden away – as Yefremov's natural performance in a middlebrow TV drama seemed effortlessly to reveal.

Senior doctors tended to be men. They performed their masculinity. Overall, though, the medical professions were dominated by women. Even before 1917, 10 per cent of doctors and dentists in the Russian empire were female, the highest proportion in Europe. According to published data, women became the majority of doctors and dentists in 1937. Their proportion increased as a consequence of the Great Fatherland War. By 1950, 77 per cent of doctors were women. The percentage fell slightly over the next three decades, to 69 per cent in 1980. It varied from republic to republic: in 1983, it was more than 70 per cent in the Russian, Kazakh, Estonian, Latvian and Lithuanian republics, and the lowest rate was in Tajikistan, where 52 per cent of doctors were women.[24] When Vladimir Soloukhin, a well-known writer belonging to the 'village prose' literary movement, was admitted for surgery in the early 1970s at the Herzen Institute in Moscow, a prestigious centre for oncological medicine, his doctors were mostly women, from junior medics to top surgeons and legendary old-timers. His account of his experiences, published in the journal *Moskva* in 1975, saw the hospital as a hierarchy, with the patient at the bottom and the most distinguished doctors at the top. Hospitals were managed in a centralized way by a 'chief doctor' who had the authority to make operational decisions, while clinical judgements were the preserve of a meeting of specialists. The style of 'one-person' management across the economy was a feature of Soviet civilization that dated back to the end of the Civil War. In a hospital setting, a leading female doctor might have to play on a masculine language. 'The patients look upon the arrival of the doctor in charge as a great event, a gift of grace,' Soloukhin wrote, describing the surgeon's daily round in a way that is familiar in any modern hospital, 'but when Agnessa Petrovna's voice boomed out in the corridor, a reverential whisper passed along the wards: "The General has come. The General . . . Agnessa Petrovna."'[25]

Unlike the matter-of-fact and authoritative female doctors whom Soloukhin encountered, male doctors were prone to act out their masculinity. In *Morning Round*, Aida Manasarova's film of 1979, a senior cardiologist, played by the popular star Andrei Miagkov, brooks no challenge, shouts down a patient's anxious relative and cannot bear the slightest questioning of his expertise, workload or personal sense of order, almost having a fistfight in the process of turning down a bribe. (By contrast, Miagkov's most famous film role, the male lead in *The Irony of Fate or Congratulations on a Light Steam!*, was as a mild-mannered polyclinic doctor, though the viewer never sees him at work.) Very senior medics were disproportionately male. They overwhelmingly dominated the Academy of Medical Sciences and the top ranks of the Ministry of Health. And yet there were crucial examples of female leadership. If the gender balance of the medical professions as a whole told a particular story about Soviet civilization, the male predominance among the top bosses told a more universal one, bringing the USSR into line with its Western European and American rivals.

The minister of health, who in the Soviet system was a doctor, was usually a man. But not always. At the age of thirty-two, fifteen months after the German invasion of the Soviet Union, Maria Kovrigina was appointed as one of the deputy commissars of health in the all-union Commissariat of Healthcare. She was an outsider, born to a peasant family in the Urals. In 1950, when she was forty, she became minister of health, but in the more junior government of the Russian republic rather than the USSR. In the weeks before Stalin's death, at the hysterical height of the Doctors' Plot, she was moved back to the central all-union government as the first deputy minister of health. The following year, she was promoted again, becoming the USSR minister of health. She was forty-four. Kovrigina's stellar career had at last delivered her, while still a relatively young woman, into one of the peaks of the male world of Soviet politics. She remained in office for almost five years. Kovrigina's politics were a mixed bag. She was, alas, a good fit to oversee medics during the campaign against the Doctors' Plot. Yet, as a Thaw-era minister, she was a determined supporter of the restoration of legal abortion in 1955. Not quite trusted, she left office in 1959, and was appointed rector of the Central Institute for the Continuing Education of Doctors in Moscow, where she remained until 1986, by which time she was seventy-six.[26] She was a true 'doctor-organizer'. Kovrigina was the only female among the eight Soviet ministers of health in the post-Stalin period; two others served for almost exactly the same terms as hers, four for less, and one, Boris Petrovsky, for substantially more.

The Bolsheviks' sex revolution marched on in the 1970s. Over its *longue durée*, the revolution changed understandings of sexuality and the circumstances in which people had sex. It expanded a person's sexual autonomy in some ways but created new patriarchal controls in others. Women's sex lives were still shaped by the legacies of 1917, though by the 1970s, many of these legacies had been internationalized. Abortion was permitted from 1920, banned in 1936 and legalized again in 1955. Even this belated restoration took place eighteen years before abortion was permitted in the United States. Yet the pill was only sporadically available. It was mainly used as a fertility or menopause treatment. In 1974, guidance about the risks associated with the pill from the Ministry of Health disqualified up to 90 per cent of women from requesting it. Planners did not allow for the mass production of the drug. Contraception was often limited to condoms, which were not always available, though doctors began to offer inter-uterine devices in the 1970s. Production of condoms and IUDs was set at approximately 20 per cent of demand.[27] Although abortion was freely available, the overall system of reproductive health was tilted towards male control. It opened the gaze of the state onto women's intimate experiences without expanding their options; a 1971 article in the popular health journal *Zdorov'e* provided a detailed overview of the practicalities of the calendar method of birth control (the assumption was that this was the best approach that was available).[28] It was not surprising that women frequently had to resort to abortions. One historian calls the Soviet Union the 'abortion empire'. During the 1970s, legal abortions averaged a steady 7.5 million per year, or 20,000 per day.[29] Western experts speculated whether abortion rates were higher in the Soviet Union than anywhere else in the world.[30]

A new campaign was launched against the spread of sexually transmitted diseases in the first half of the Brezhnev era, with toughened legislation dating from 1971. The Ministry of Internal Affairs worked with the Ministry of Health to locate, examine and treat people who were suspected of deliberately infecting others with venereal diseases such as syphilis and also those who rejected medical care. Policemen brought suspects in; the medical authorities tested and treated them; the results might be the basis of criminal proceedings. In the Latvian republic, for example, convictions peaked in 1973 at over 100 cases.[31] Meanwhile, men still paid for sex. Decrees by the Council of Ministers; municipal checks on residence requirements; police patrols; the comrades courts; activists on *druzhiny* patrols; 'prophylactic chats' by the KGB; let alone the more straitlaced interpretations of Bolshevik dogma by administrators: none of it could eradicate prostitution. Brothels conducted their profitable business deep in the shadow economy. Freelance sex workers made use of well-known pick-up zones, the backs of taxis, and rented rooms. Fines were worth the risk: the extra income allowed some women to survive or do quite well – notwithstanding the brutality they often endured.[32]

The divorce rate grew rapidly following a law of 1965 that simplified the legal process of divorce and another of 1967 that came down harder on divorced fathers who did not support their children. In the 1970s, only the United States outstripped the USSR in the number of divorces.[33] Perhaps this gave women more control over their bodies, though the housing shortage forced significant numbers of divorced couples to continue to cohabit. Meanwhile, the spaces in which it took place gave Soviet sex a distinctive aspect. Even in separate apartments, family members competed for privacy, and effort had to be expended to mask intimacy from the older or the younger generation.

Plenty of sex was going on during the Brezhnev era, notwithstanding the Soviet Union's reputation of being a prudish dictatorship where repression was also sexual and double standards were the norm. Despite its prevalence, getting divorced, or even being subject to a denunciatory claim of adultery, could be a serious hindrance to a Party career. The codified Family Law of 1968 made it more difficult for single mothers to support their children and fostered a morally exculpatory discourse towards them.[34] And yet, women's sexual experiences seem to have changed more quickly after the Thaw than before. Existing personal practice eventually migrated to public discourse, especially during *perestroika*, rather than the other way around.[35] The lack of a public sphere in which sex could be discussed in detail, and even subversively – in, for example, women's magazines – most likely left some women less able to express their sexuality in an active and informed way.[36]

In the 1960s, the medical study of sexuality – 'sexopathology' – became established in the USSR. In 1963, the first all-union sexopathology training conference was convened in Gorky.[37] Soviet publishing witnessed a wave of sex-education manuals in the post-Stalin period. The aim of these manuals was to highlight apparently problematic sexual practices, and to advise parents and teachers about how to prevent them. It was a new type of public information. People might support it or react against it, they might appropriate it or reshape it, and there is no way of knowing how it influenced sexuality in thought and practice, but the authorities could not contain this discourse and use it to control people's sex lives. By 1960, books by Czech and East German sexologists were published in the USSR. They had large print runs, as many as 200,000, and their content and tone were more explicit, even discussing homosexuality, though using the language of predation, abnormality and treatment.[38] Meanwhile, in the long 1970s, some legal scholars debated in public the arguments for the decriminalization of homosexuality. Others, notably in Latvia, made the case for adding female homosexuality to the statute book. The first practical moves to decriminalize homosexual sex dated from reforms to republican criminal codes in 1959, though the putative measures came to nothing.[39] The Gulag was partly responsible for the widespread if unspoken knowledge of homosexual sex in the Soviet Union after 1953; twelve million people had spent time behind the wire in the Stalin period, where same-sex relationships and rape alike were common.[40]

Sex between men had been decriminalized in 1922, forty-five years before similar laws were passed in London and Bonn. But in 1934, these acts were again illegal. The anti-sodomy law demanded sentences of between three and five years. It remained in force until the Soviet collapse. During this period, at least 25,688 men were convicted under this statute, though according to one of its leading historians, the total number was likely to be nearer 60,000. Between 1961 and 1981, there were 14,695 convictions in the Russian republic, with 7,468 in the other union republics. Circumstantial evidence suggests that there were fewer of these in Moscow and Leningrad than in smaller towns, and that the police turned a blind eye to cruising grounds in Tallinn and Tartu in Estonia. But in some other major centres, including in Latvia and Ukraine, the KGB stepped in during the long 1970s, maintaining files on known homosexuals and using blackmail to extend their knowledge of networks of gay men. The police gathered data from sexual health clinics in Latvia. They also targeted prominent cultural figures such as the film director Sergei Paradzhanov, who was incarcerated between 1974 and 1977 for homosexual activity.[41]

Like the police and the Procuracy, the medical profession pursued sexual minorities. A gay man risked very serious punishment at the hands of the Soviet state, but he could also be treated, even 'cured', as could lesbians. Medical treatment was sometimes a complement of a penal sentence and sometimes an alternative to it. For some, it involved admission to a psychiatric facility, even in the 1970s or 1980s. For others, a more complex range of treatments was invoked thanks to the development of 'sexopathology' from the 1960s. The aim was to restore gay people to full productive capacity at work and in the heterosexual family by bringing together the insights of sexology with the practicalities of medical treatment. Medicalizing sexuality was a way of controlling it; homosexuality was a disorder which the authorities could prevent from getting worse.[42] Sometimes homosexual men and women themselves wanted to be 'cured', and sometimes they welcomed 'treatment' as a way to avoid incarceration. Sympathetic doctors might sign off a course of treatment of whose value they themselves were sceptical precisely to help a gay man avoid the penal system.[43] If homosexuality was a sickness, it must by definition not be a moral failure; such were the mental contortions that a parent might perform in satisfying themselves that they were acting for the best in admitting their son or daughter to a clinic. But while psychiatric clinics were usually separate from the penal system, they were still places where doors were locked and pain was administered, for example with electric-shock therapy. (There was of course another contradiction, too. If sexopathology described homosexuality as a medical condition, why was there a law against it?)[44] Women who were caught having sexual relations with other women – for instance, in a hostel attached to a higher educational institute or industrial enterprise where privacy was at a premium – or who were exposed as lesbians through gossip and misplaced confidences, sometimes faced moral scrutiny rather than medical attention. They could even face a comrades' court, where their transgression was discussed without ever being spelled out, and the language of sexuality might be omitted entirely; it was a public humiliation and might even lead to a social 'boycott', which could have its desired effect of breaking up relationships.[45] It was a kind of mob rule that was familiar in many societies.

Physicians and sexologists examined the bodies of developed socialism from their own professional angles. Geneticists adopted the most penetrating perspective of all. A decade on, aftershocks still rang out from the revelatory debates that had smashed Soviet genetics in the early 1960s (see chapter 5). Most of the leading positions in the new and reformed genetics institutes were occupied by scientists who accepted the internationally established standards of research into cell biology, not the version promoted by Lysenko. Nikolai Timofeyev-Resovsky, a world leader in genetics, continued to run his own genetics department in Obninsk until 1969, when he took on a retirement job at Moscow State University. For all such scientists, the socialist body worked and malfunctioned according to the almost unimaginably complex mechanisms of cell biology, and therefore genetic heredity, that were steadily being uncovered by research groups across the world. But Lysenko cast a shadow, even in the long 1970s. This gave the 'nature versus nurture' debate a particular and sometimes disabling piquancy in the Soviet Union. At the end of the 1960s, a murky collection of his opponents prevented Timofeyev-Resovsky from obtaining the country's highest scholarly distinction, blocking his election as an academician. The KGB targeted the biologist Zhores Medvedev, who had been the most distinctive anti-Lysenko voice during the Thaw; his dissident activity had diversified, but he continued to speak up for a rational attitude to genetics and in 1970 he was for a short time incarcerated in a psychiatric ward. Nikolai Dubinin, who was widely published in the 1970s, was the best-known Soviet researcher to raise unfounded questions about the international genetics orthodoxy.[46]

Meanwhile, in the 1970s, biologists at the Institute of Cytology and Genetics at Akademgorodok, near Novosibirsk, explored the ways in which environment might determine one's genes through the science of epigenetics. Their ingenious experiments on the domestication of silver foxes were conducted according to international standards, not Lysenko-like speculation.[47] Although the socialist body was subject to a specific ideological and social context, one that affected a person's sex life, diet and even their physical shape, the scientific establishment accepted during the long 1970s that a socialist body was genetically the same as a capitalist body. Such was Cold War convergence.

A loose speculation about nature and nurture swirled around the writings of Solzhenitsyn. The imputation of national characteristics to inmates in the Gulag might have derived from a person's social learning or genetic inheritance, depending on how you read it, but his descriptions of Russian and Ukrainian identity increasingly had a Slavic primordialism about them. More compelling was the moral position on which *The Gulag Archipelago* was founded. Solzhenitsyn famously argued that 'the line separating good and evil passes ... through every human heart.' He himself was subject to an especially wide range of Soviet bodily experiences, from hunger to cancer to the physical ecstasy of working with a full heart. As he raced to finish *The First Circle*, his body was in better condition and less subject to extreme stress than earlier in his life. There would be more shocks to it soon enough.

Tolyatti

## 11
# A String Bag

The room was about fifteen square metres, or one-and-a-half times the 'sanitary norm', the formal – though often unmet – allocation of housing space per person. It was on a corner. Large windows covered two of the walls. One faced a veranda; the other had a view of the garden. A bed jutted out from the third wall. The bedside table was oval in shape; a peacock design was on its surface. It was a gift from Jawaharlal Nehru, prime minister of India for seventeen years following independence from the British Empire. There was a tape recorder on the table. It was slick and West German, manufactured by Uher. Next to the tape recorder was a record player. It came from the UK and was a gift from Kwame Nkrumah, the first prime minister of the Gold Coast and then Ghana after the British left. By the door that led out of the room, onto a terrace, was a radio. This was made in Minsk, one of the Soviet Union's centres for the production of radios and televisions. On the dresser was a Braun shaver, straight from West Germany. An armchair faced the big window. It was Finnish, with a reclinable back and a raisable footrest, a gift of President Kekkonen, the architect of postwar politics in Finland. The room also contained books and records, medicines and an old safe. Among the paintings on the wall was one by Boris Zhutovsky, of a bear and a ladybird.[1]

This was Khrushchev's room in the dacha that the family had occupied since January 1965. It was allocated to them after his ousting from office. Perhaps it contained only modest accoutrements. After all, the tape recorder of first choice for top Soviet people in the know was a Sony. Khrushchev and his family had never shown much interest in luxuries, but everything was a matter of comparison, and there were signs here of significant comfort: not just the gifts from international contemporaries, but also the size and privacy of the room. Some of the items he possessed, like the Western-branded electric shaver, were sought-after but realistic acquisitions for a fairly wide group in the population. In Ryazanov's classic New Year film *The Irony of Fate* (1975), the female lead (a teacher) and her responsible-looking fiancé exchange items that are famously desirable, partly because they might just be within reach: she gives him a foreign electric razor, and he gives her French perfume.

Khrushchev's emphasis on individual personhood made possible his invention of Soviet mass consumerism. Brezhnev and his colleagues did not change direction after 1964, but they followed their own distinctive path towards consumer socialism. Two factors throw light on the continuities and contrasts that followed that year.

One was economic. Khrushchev oversaw increased availability of certain consumer goods. Production of washing machines, which were at this time rudimentary, semi-automatic devices, rose from 83,000 in 1955 to just over 2.5 million in 1964. Vacuum-cleaner production went up from 121,000 in 1955 to 535,000 in 1964.[2] But economic growth slowed in the early 1960s. The industrial sector grew at an annualized rate of 8.9 per cent between 1953 and 1960, but 6.6 per cent between 1960 and 1964.[3] Under Khrushchev and Brezhnev alike, the government did not know how to manage a mass-scale shift to intensive-growth sectors like electronics, but they worsened their chances by not developing major economic reforms. Kosygin's reform of 1965 did not become a durable economic policy. And yet planning became more stable, and economic growth was steadily maintained at late Khrushchev-era levels in the first nine years of Brezhnev's term. Investment in agriculture was more systematic. In time, oil exports paid for grain imports. Food prices did not go up, and planners maintained other prices until the later 1970s, when there were selected and controlled rises. Inflation was hidden inside the economy. People tended to accumulate savings while they waited for the chance to spend their money on major purchases, such as a car, for which they were being held in a queue. In these circumstances, the production of consumer items expanded, choice increased, and expectations rose. Thanks to this Brezhnevian economic driver, consumer socialism took on a greatly more recognizable quality in the later 1960s and 1970s than during the Thaw.

The other factor was the routinization of Soviet modernity in a way that required a more obvious convergence with the West than in earlier periods of Soviet history. Certain categories of everyday modern life became less contested – 'individualization, privatization, commercialization', according to the historian Natalia Chernyshova, who also highlights a growing 'fluency in modern technology' among Soviet people.[4] What resulted was the spaces of the Soviet city of developed socialism and the world of things that shaped the everyday experiences of Soviet people from the late 1960s onwards. All of the categories that Chernyshova mentions were certainly necessary for the speedy acceleration of consumer socialism. But they continued to draw conspicuously on Marxism-Leninism, an ideology that combined German and Russian socialist theories. They were shaped by the shortages that were all the Soviet economy was capable of delivering. And they drew on the ethical charge that was central to the Thaw.

Some of the toughest debates that shaped Soviet civilization were about the supply of goods to ordinary people. In Estonia, geographical proximity to Western Europe facilitated the appearance of certain items in shops for the local *nomenklatura* and, more generally, in the underground economy. Unquantifiable, unslakable, mysterious desire increased the cost of Western goods, inflated by a label, a seam, a colour or zip. Symbolic qualities – the dream of abroad – combined with production and quality shortfalls in the planned economy to generate a familiar consumer lure.[5]

Despite the major changes associated with de-Stalinization, the Soviet Union remained an economy of shortages in which consumption was always suppressed. Deficits were a systemic feature, caused by the absence of normal markets; they were also the consequence of malfunctions of the centrally planned economy; they resulted too from particular decisions of planners, which rested on ministerial-level judgements about which goods to prioritize. It was easier to get desirable goods in Moscow, Leningrad and certain republican capitals, such as Riga and Kyiv. Closed nuclear cities, such as Arzamas-16, where Andrei Sakharov was posted, were a niche location which had the best of everything. Smaller metropolitan centres had certain good things and not others. People in mid-sized provincial towns asked relatives in bigger centres to send them better clothes and dreamed of the salami that was available in Moscow. A 1970s joke had Brezhnev describing the central planning of consumer supplies. 'Centralization means bringing everything into Moscow,' he says, 'and letting the population sort it out.'[6] People travelled to Moscow specifically to get things they wanted, or returned from family or work trips laden with bursting canvas bags. 'What's long and green and smells of salami?' went another joke of the time. 'The train out of Moscow.'[7]

Consumer socialism turned cities into the urban centres of a visually striking Iron Curtain universe. It was all there: the food shops that lacked sausages, the overcrowded bookstores, the thirsted-after jeans, the home-made skirts in bright colours, the Sony tape recorders and bootlegged records made out of X-ray plates, the women's magazines with shots of Eastern bloc bikinis, the ever-higher apartment blocks with their still-cosier homes, the planned urban space with its concrete monoliths, red flags and open squares. At least four mutually dependent principles underlay the Soviet consumer experience: an ideological approach in which the integrity of individual needs was acknowledged; a political approach which recognized that suppressing consumption to the barest minimum was no longer prudent; a practical approach which assumed the interdependence of the planned and informal economies; and a jurisprudential approach which incorporated the consumer into a wider understanding of citizenship.

Being a successful consumer in the USSR required savviness and flexibility: knowing where to shop, creating time to queue, forming the personal connections and exchanging the favours that were as important as cash. Practically minded people who could navigate the informal economy were much more likely to get what they wanted. The verb *dostat'* became ubiquitous. It meant 'get', 'acquire', 'find', 'source'. The usual assumption was that the transaction required luck or ingenuity, that it was unexpected or serendipitous. *Blat* was the capacity to get things in the absence of normal purchases, drawing on 'pull' or chains of acquaintanceship. Some people really did carry a rolled-up string bag (*avos'ka*) just in case a queue formed for an unforeseen item.

Always a shaper of Soviet experience, the queue was a signature of developed socialism in particular, when there was more shopping to be done than before. The queue might form fairly spontaneously as a line outside a store, perhaps when people suddenly heard that a shipment of Czech boots or Turkish jackets had arrived. Goods from abroad had a special status in Soviet life that was only sometimes justified by a difference in quality. The queue might snake down the street as the day went on. Sometimes queues were 'virtual', when people showed up and were given a slip of paper with their number in the line. People might join a queue when they saw one, even for an unforeseen item, in a loose equivalent of an impulse purchase, on the basis that they might not see whatever it was for a long time and it would come in useful one way or another, possibly as currency in the economy of non-cash exchanges.

One man recalled a characteristic incident from circa 1970. As a student in a morning lecture, he heard that a shipment of jeans had arrived at a local department store. He and his friends abandoned the lecture and rushed to the shop. It was packed. He handed his money to someone else, better placed, who darted through the crowd, bought any pair that was available, and handed them back. They were too long and too tight, with a poorly stitched label that fell off after washing, and at thirty rubles cost his month's student stipend.[8]

Consumer socialism was an elaborate set of informal economic practices and rituals. It was also the consequence of a centrally planned economy with new priorities, and it rested on a particular form of rights. These rights derived from consumers' citizenship rather than their purchasing power. At the centre of consumer socialism was a new understanding of citizenship. Soviet consumers had a rough economic deal but they also had rights. Shops and cafés were legally required to keep complaints books and to present their contents to government. Aggrieved consumers also wrote directly to the authorities, for instance to the city soviet, but also to the semi-autonomous People's Oversight department, and to the Workers' Bureau of Complaints and Feedback.[9] Customers complained about the availability or quality of goods and sometimes the level of service. Newspapers, magazines and broadcast media also gathered stories about consumer dissatisfaction by featuring letters from disappointed customers. Local and central TV stations helped to elevate consumer rights into a familiar discourse. Shows about consumer experiences that drew on viewers' letters were interspersed into a schedule that included programmes on other aspects of consumption, hobbies and everyday law.[10] It seemed to presuppose a rights-backed entitlement to buy things and then enjoy their use in one's free time – though the reality of shortages and lack of choice undermined the usefulness that this discourse presented, even at times rendered it ridiculous.

After all, shop assistants did not usually assume that the customer was always right. The plan devised substantial incentives – cash bonuses, workplace childcare – and cultural pressures whose aim was to make service workers feel valued enough to develop the relaxed and engaged demeanour that boosted sales. But often the incentives did not materialize, while rising expectations among customers increased the popular perception of a general culture of poor service.[11] The development of consumer socialism had inevitably expanded the number of people who worked in the service economy. Between 1959 and 1970, the number employed in the retail sector increased from 1.1 to 2.1 million. By 1970, 91 per cent of them were women; the vast majority of restaurant employees were also women and were often held in low esteem. Jobs in cafés and shops raised specific problems for Soviet civilization. A 1969 article about tipping in the weekly *Literaturnaya gazeta* led to a storm of debate, prompting hundreds of readers' letters about whether a socialist employee should receive extra payments for doing their job.[12]

Shops did not have colour and visual variety. Visitors who were used to the multicolour shop fronts and advertising hoardings of New York or Tokyo, with their constant reinvention of consumer space and experience, thought Soviet cities were grey. They had merely functional shop fronts, not much neon, basic cars and a narrow range of fashions. Planning created some expansive consumer spaces while shutting down others, the convenience and vibrancy of which had in some cases evolved over centuries.

Soviet people went shopping in stores with separate functions – bookshops, furniture shops, stationers, stores that stocked electric goods such as TVs and radios. A department store – the *univermag* – was also a feature of every town. It was one of the most popular places to buy clothes. There were shops that specialized in fur – *mekha* – and fur coats became increasingly sought after during the long 1970s, in the sense that they became a more affordable luxury, within the reach of more people. More urgent was underwear. Like other goods, it was subject to the dictates of central planning, the caprices of the underground economy, the boosts of trade with the countries of the socialist bloc, and the exotic and erotic charge of the West, in this case tantalizing glimpses of French or Italian lingerie in a magazine or film. During the 1970s, designers worked with materials and publications from those countries to produce better-quality underwear that was easier to obtain. Planners directed investment towards necessary items, opening a vast new plant in Liepāja in Latvia in the middle of the decade that specialized in such things as elastics.[13] Even so, the best way of finding desired underwear was from a lucky chance on the black market, or from an acquaintance who had visited East Germany or Yugoslavia and shopped wisely while there.

People bought newspapers and other printed matter at kiosks, which were located in places with a constant footfall, such as next to stations, rows of shops or park gates. Thirsty urbanites bought beer or *kvas* at special drinks dispensers, filling up a glass, rinsing it out and then replacing it for the next customer. Most popular of all were the stalls – the mobile freezers – that sold ice cream throughout the year. The salesperson, usually a woman, wore a white coat and hat as hygiene regulations dictated. She dispensed one of the signature consumption items in all of Soviet civilization. Like cigarettes, Eskimo ice creams were mass produced but individually consumed; they were a unifying element in Soviet civilization but created personal stories and memories. Strikingly, the municipal ice-cream carts represented an unusual business model in the planned economy. They were owned by the ice-cream manufacturers, and so the manufacturer sold its product direct to the consumer. In almost all other official consumer sales transactions, there were intermediaries, owned by other institutions – delivery vans and shops – that created the appearance of cooperation and careful planning. Planners feared that the direct-sale model encouraged corruption, even profit.[14]

The money that was essential for organizing the planned economy – those currency units that were transmitted from a ministry to an enterprise and thence to another enterprise – were in a sense a notional unit of accounting. And access to the most desirable things for the most well-to-do – the best apartment in central Moscow, the posting in Paris for one's child – required non-cash transactions: favours and promises made by knowing the right phone numbers. But cash was central to the lives of ordinary Soviet people, as well as to the operations of the underground economy. Soviet people had accounts at the state savings bank (Sberbank). They were paid in rubles and went to shops and markets where they bought things with these rubles. Khrushchev had one eye on the communist future, when money would be otiose, but he still made sure that, before then, his economic team were committed to the 'full-value ruble'. Wage increases and pensions reforms ensured that people had more money to spend. Financial measures sought to maintain the value of this money. In 1957, officials stopped 'voluntary' payments for savings bonds (the enforced savings programme of the Stalin period, whereby the state 'borrowed' funds from the population). Income tax was abolished in 1960. The currency reform of 1961 redenominated the ruble, knocking a zero off every banknote.[15]

Consumer socialism was a cash economy. Cash remained an incentive for labour; differentiated wages had been policy for decades. In the 1960s and 1970s people had the expectation of spending some of their income on a wider range of consumer goods. Cash was necessary in all kinds of transactions, including 'presents' for doctors or nurses and payments for moonlighting plumbers. Vouchers for holiday resorts and Pioneer camps might not be free but require a partial cash payment, while transport tickets were subsidized but paid for in rubles. Deficits and almost-enforced saving hid inflation. Stable prices for consumer goods were not always useful if the goods themselves were not available.

Capitalism was much better at consumerism, but central planning still delivered significantly more goods, greater choice and better quality by the 1970s compared with the 1950s. Consumers had become more discerning. For example, significant numbers of washing machines and fridges were now going unsold; before, everything was snapped up as soon as it hit the shops. Many potential customers already had basic models and were willing to wait a bit longer for a more substantial upgrade, knowing that more advanced and larger versions were already being manufactured somewhere and there was hope of getting one eventually.[16]

Socialists looked at the fashion industry and pondered the conceptual and practical challenges that it posed for Soviet civilization. Soviet people, like people elsewhere, found the styles of 'the sixties' appealing. The impresarios of the Soviet fashion industry joined the excitement of the age and ignored, where they could, the culturally conservative voices that decried bright colours and bold hemlines as louche capitalist imports. But the Thaw itself opened up the fashion industry and gave it confidence. New creative agencies were founded. One of the biggest was VIALegrpom, the All-Union Institute of Product Assortment and the Culture of Dress (within the Ministry of Light Industry). It oversaw design laboratories and fashion houses, looked for catwalk models, ran fashion shows, and brought miniskirts and bikinis to the Soviet market, with alternative products for Central Asia.[17] The All-Union House of Design (ODMO), which was founded in 1949, worked intensively in the Central Asian and Caucasian republics in the 1970s to create women's clothes which followed the grain of national motifs. Designers took advantage of Uzbek cotton and sometimes silks and made original use of existing forms such as the embroidered gown (*khalat*).[18]

There was, of course, a gap between the higher reaches of the fashion industry and the reality of shops. In Leningrad, between January and June 1962, 70 per cent of the supply of clothes in shops came from old designs. Customers complained about the lack of availability of particular sizes and the seasonal non-availability of important items (no sandals in summer, for example).[19] The situation improved during the Brezhnev era. Not only did Soviet fashion attract more international interest than before, especially in the seven years that followed 1964, but the designs filtered into the shops, the volume of clothes there increased, and checks showed that the level of quality was higher. Between 1971 and 1975 – the years of the ninth five-year plan – the Soviet consumer economy attained its uncertain apogee. This was the first of the five-year plans that set growth targets at a higher level for consumer goods than for capital goods; in the second half of the 1970s, heavy industry would again be emphasized over light industry. The immediate consequence was that production of clothes doubled in the decade through to 1975. The work of ODMO expanded during those years in terms of activity and personnel. Most positions in women's fashion were held by women.[20]

The Eastern bloc had its own understandings of luxury. It was a marker of inequality, visible, for instance, when a very top person got hold of a fancy foreign car. Or luxuries were things that were broadly available but expensive, like a special fur coat. Luxuries could be small items of occasional pleasure. And luxury goods occupied a place in people's imagination, comparable in cultural power to the way that others tried to visualize Paris or Rome.[21] Desirable Soviet aesthetics depended on individual tastes. People created their own material universe inside their homes and dachas.[22] A modernist aesthetic became more fashionable in the 1960s. It could be observed in new furniture designs that were produced in sufficient numbers to be widely purchased – armchairs crafted out of slim pieces of wood, conjuring a sleek and dynamic profile, for example – and which were also pictured in such periodicals as *Dekurativnoe isskustvo* (*Decorative Art*), showcased at exhibitions and filmed in exciting, brightly lit night-time urban interiors in the movies of the time. Proponents of this style celebrated a stripped-down, conspicuously modern spareness. Even a frying pan was an object that could have narrow lines and pared-back originality, in, say, the angle of its handle.[23] Yet there were, of course, people who cultivated a completely different aesthetic, one of clutter, sometimes with a preference for antique objects, and a love for religious art, born of nostalgia or spirituality.

A smaller number of things, in scale and variety, existed in Soviet homes than in American ones, a so-called 'economy of storage' rather than of shortage. Supply was unpredictable. Consumers might overbuy when possible and build up stocks of particular items (say, razor blades). People invested their own subjective worth into goods that they purchased for a fixed number of rubles, using them to store a value, passing them on in other transactions, repurposing them and ascribing new values to them, as well as using them for their original purpose.[24] People found ways of adapting existing spaces – a sealed balcony, a walk-in cupboard, a garage – to make use of consumer items in their own way, creating a dark room for photography, a gym to lift weights or a tiny workshop in which to make and repair clothes.[25] Soviet people often developed high-end skills in sewing, knitting, interior decoration or DIY, ingeniously turning generally available products into unique things (that were nevertheless unmistakably Soviet).[26]

Shopping for food also required resourcefulness in distinctively Soviet locales. In 1963, the Moscow Soviet reconstituted the Danilovsky market, south of the centre of Moscow, as a large open-air space in which collective farm workers could sell their produce.[27] It was a roaring success. Planners and local people alike in the 1970s imagined something better: a vast covered market at Danilovsky. The vision was eventually realized in 1986. The structure recalled the space age, with its vast crenellated cupola, vented at the top to allow in sunlight and air. It was a bold, socialist modern structure in which to house a market, an optimistic vision of consumer socialism on the eve of *perestroika*. Yet food shopping often took place in tattered surroundings. Markets might be erected in a broad space between apartment houses. Grocery shops, with the plain sign *Produkty*, were the equivalent of convenience stores, selling basic foodstuffs. A very small grocer's, of the type that might be found in a village, had a row of shelves behind a single counter. Tall-ceilinged urban food stores, with more than one counter, sometimes around three of the walls, were a classic milieu of developed socialism. Items were on the shelves. There might be many gaps. With the help of a shop assistant, a customer totted up the total cost of their purchases, paid at a cash desk, and went back to the counter to collect their goods. No wonder those who caught a glimpse of an American supermarket thought they were hallucinating.

There was, though, a bigger food store – the *gastronom* – some modern versions of which experimented with self-service formats. The most famous food store was Gastronom Number 1 on Moscow's Gorky Street, which inherited the premises of the grand imperial grocer, the Yeliseevsky emporium. Even though it was open to ordinary customers, it was a byword for corruption. Managers kept the best goods out of sight and sold them to the higher-ups. The management of Gastronom Number 1 was targeted by the KGB in the early 1980s as part of Andropov's anti-corruption drive.

One of the least accessible institutions of all was the *beryozka* shop. These foreign-currency emporia, named picturesquely after a silver birch tree, came into existence on a small scale in 1961 to allow foreign tourists to spend their own currency on high-level souvenirs in specially designated shops. The first ones opened at airports and hotels in Moscow, Leningrad, Arkhangelsk and Sochi. In 1963 a *beryozka* opened in the heart of Moscow, on Gorky Street. As the 1960s gave way to the 1970s, the network continued to grow, with increasing numbers of shops in more cities, and a greater range of deficit goods on offer. A foreign sailor in Khabarovsk might find his beer of choice there. Soviet citizens who happened to have convertible currency could walk in and spend it on a sought-after item (and receive foreign-currency change) until the regulations became more complex in 1969. From the mid-1950s, it was also possible to receive cash remittances from family abroad. Soviet professionals with hard-currency earnings ranged from cultural professionals, who might have gone on tour and saved their expenses, or had a book translated by a foreign publisher, to teachers, doctors or engineers seconded to long-term projects in the developing world. Some of these people could soon buy a car, washing machine and fridge without dipping in to their regular salary. Two hundred such foreign-currency shops existed in the USSR by the end of 1973.

Even though the numbers of potential *beryozka* customers increased from year to year – by the early 1980s, as many as three million people per year made some kind of foreign trip, accruing currency in the process – the shops' ambience was still one to envy.[28] By then, the *beryozka* had become a symbol of aggressive inequalities, a window on the West that was inaccessible to almost everyone. A joke that was current in 1984 described a Chukcha – a native inhabitant of the far north-east – who flees to Moscow, aiming to get to the West. He happens to go into a *beryozka* shop. Thinking he has already made it to the West, he asks for political asylum.[29]

It took the authorities a few weeks to allocate 'permanent' accommodation to the Khrushchev family after the patriarch's enforced retirement in October 1964. The Central Committee signed over a dacha, the one where the former first secretary would sit in his Finnish armchair. It was located at the village of Petrovo-Danyle, in the countryside to the west of Moscow. It was a low-slung wooden house where it was possible to live comfortably in the depth of winter. Built on a raised platform, and edged with a veranda, it had views down to the river and across the fields. There were other dachas and pensions nearby. The Khrushchevs' plot was surrounded by a green fence; the entrance was guarded by the KGB. Nikita and Nina Khrushchev lived at the dacha with their daughter Lena and her husband, Viktor. The young couple had one of the dacha's rooms, off the hallway. There was a bright room at the heart of the dacha, with a big table and a wide, whole-wall window, from which Nina ran the house. With six rooms in all, it was very comfortable by any reasonable Soviet standard.[30]

Although the dacha became the centre of Khrushchev's life, he was not exiled from Moscow. He was also presented with an apartment in the city. It was at number 19, Starokonyushenny Lane, in the Arbat district. This was a famous zone of medieval Moscow, north of the river and barely a kilometre from Khrushchev's old office in the Kremlin. Not all the members of the high intelligentsia for which the Arbat was famous welcomed the growing number of residences for Party functionaries in the district,[31] though Khrushchev's was a special case. His family's new apartment had four substantial rooms with high ceilings and comfortable dimensions. Like at the dacha, the spouses slept separately. Khrushchev took a large and quiet but dimly lit room; Nina's room was smaller, down a corridor that led off the hallway. There was a living room and also a dining room, as well as an office which was filled with books. His son Sergei wrote that Khrushchev read a lot in retirement, novels as well as works on politics and economics. He went to the theatre very occasionally. Slightly beyond the Arbat was the Soveremmenik, a progressive new theatre that opened during the Thaw. Khrushchev was acquainted with the screenwriter and playwright Mikhail Shatrov. He admired his film about the revolution, *July 18*, and accepted the invitation to watch his play *The Bolsheviks*.[32] This was not the conduct of a man under house arrest.

These arrangements reflected Khrushchev's complicated status in the eyes of his successors. They wanted him to disappear but they lacked the will to make this happen properly. In official communications they referred to him namelessly. But he was not sent into exile far from Moscow: quite the reverse. Petrovo-Danyle was a step down from Gorki-2, where the real bigwigs had dachas, or the summer homes at Pitsunda or Livadia, but he still had neighbours from the Central Committee, including the minister of finance, Arseny Zverev.[33] His apartment in Moscow was not on Kutuzovsky Prospekt, where he would have rubbed shoulders with Brezhnev and Andropov, or on Granovsky Street, where he and Molotov, back from 'exile' as ambassador to Mongolia, would have had to avoid each other. But political movers-and-shakers lived in the neighbourhood, a brisk walk from the Kremlin. Ordinary people saw him and stopped for conversation, just as they did at Petrovo-Danyle. The move was a downgrading from his residence in the Lenin Hills but only as far as a five-room apartment in a fine central Moscow building, which seemed impossibly grand to almost all of his fellow countrymen.

Even though the housing programme was ever after associated with Khrushchev, it continued at a high tempo through to the end of Soviet rule. Apartment houses grew in height from five to eight or twelve storeys, later to eighteen or more. The prefabricated panels on their façades were shaped as large rectangular blocks, sometimes in different pastel shades. Apartments of the 1970s were bigger than in the 1950s. Walk-through rooms were now rare. Nearly all apartments were one-, two- or three-room designs, quite often with a kitchen big enough for a small sofa, and also a substantial balcony, even a so-called *loggia*, and a claustrophobic walk-in cupboard. Others were smaller and shabbier. Although the range of housing for the bottom 99 per cent was much more restricted in choice than in capitalist countries, the socialist city was in some ways diversifying, as inequality became more noticeable.

Welfare professionals tried and often failed to deliver more equal outcomes in these urban spaces. Soviet welfare was originally conceived as a mostly urban project. Even though Khrushchev's second major pensions reform extended state benefits into the countryside, and the income gap between city and countryside narrowed during the Brezhnev era, urban space developed as a kind of 'welfare city' in the Khrushchev and especially Brezhnev years. Microdistricts were conceived as integrated neighbourhood units with between 5,000 and 20,000 residents, more as time went on, in which people lived and had access to everyday welfare services: notably kindergartens, schools and polyclinics, but also welfare offices, cultural centres ('clubs') and libraries, and some kind of sports facilities. The architecture of most of these local public buildings was familiar: up to three storeys and block-like in appearance, though when new microdistricts were carved out of older urban zones, the buildings might be historic. Paths and roads connected up different parts of the microdistrict. Not all families owned cars. Residential zones were not overrun with traffic or parked vehicles.

In the 'Ukrainian' microdistrict in Tashkent, proposed as part of the response to the earthquake of 1966, planners positioned eight nine-storey housing blocks along four of the microdistrict's boundaries and thirty blocks of four storeys in its interior. There were also three kindergartens and a variety of other buildings. The nine-storey apartment houses were long, modular and futuristic. Plans for a microdistrict in Baku named Akhmedly consisted of a long, wedge-shaped area, with a ribbon of tall blocks along the short edge and a combination of public buildings, semi-circular housing blocks and green space in the interior.[34] There were common elements with capitalist urbanization, but property relations, state investment, the economic activity of residents and the ideological imprint of Marxism-Leninism ensured that the microdistrict contributed to the 'intensification and increased effectiveness of the development of the socialist city'.[35]

Trams, buses and trolleybuses, with metros in major centres, connected up a city's different zones. In 1966, the new metro was opened in Tbilisi. The following year, a metro system opened in Baku. Efficient public transport had been a selling point of Soviet civilization's self-presentation since work began on the Moscow metro in 1936. It was idealized in the culture of the Thaw, for example in the attractive tram journeys that punctuate the film *I Walk Around Moscow*. Now, though, a new set of urban spaces emerged that were associated with the crowded commute to or from work. These included the extremely packed bus, in which people passed tickets back and forth over strangers' heads to get them validated; the electric suburban train, with the vague hint of risk on their hard wooden seats – the abusive middle-aged drunk coming home, the teenager with a knife in his bag– which brought satellite towns on the edge of metropolises into commutable range; and the metro, through whose teaming but elegant stations passengers shuffled at peak time, moving at a pace that did not interrupt their reading. The discomfort of these spaces at rush hour was self-reflexively acknowledged in Soviet culture. This was true of samizdat, not least in Venedikt Erofeyev's novel *Moscow-Petushki*, an extended riff on alcoholism, much of whose action takes place on suburban train journeys. More revealing was the way these spaces were realistically depicted in mass culture, such as in the opening sequence of Eldar Ryazanov's popular 1977 melodrama *An Office Romance*, which shows the main characters' hectic but mundane journeys into work. Automobile manufacture increased considerably between 1965 and 1975, from 201,000 cars per year to 1.201 million, though people queued for years to obtain one.[36]

Nothing exemplified the design and layout of socialist urbanity better than the new cities developed between the 1950s and the 1970s. They revealed Soviet modernity: its self-conscious focus on technology, its ideological prescriptions applied to everyday life, its use of culture as an enveloping and participatory process, in which architecture and urban form themselves were part of the socialist performance.[37] Even so, life there was rough-and-ready and sometimes transient. Between 1966 and 1970, 30,000 workers left their jobs at the hydro-electric plant at the new town of Bratsk to restart their lives in other places. One-third of them gave the reasons of poor housing and inadequate childcare.[38]

The most famous of the 1960s new towns was Tolyatti, founded in 1964 in the Stavropol region – Gorbachev's territory – and named after the long-time Italian communist leader. The plant that gave the town its purpose, the Volga Automobile Factory (VAZ), was a collaboration with Fiat. The Italian motor giant worked with VAZ in the mass-production of Zhiguli cars, the standard family vehicle, named after the nearby Zhiguli sea, and traded in the West as the Lada. By 1970, 660,000 vehicles equivalent to Fiat-124s were being manufactured every year.[39] The city that grew up around the car plant was designed according to the 'most progressive' urban planning, including 'strict geometry', 'original silhouettes of public buildings', 'wide avenues' and 'huge green lawns', which allowed 'one to see to the very horizon and the steppe', wrote one Soviet author, 'and the hills, and the forest, and the huge sky'. The first apartment blocks had five and nine storeys, but planners soon signed off others of twelve and sixteen storeys.[40] Boris Rubanenko, chief architect, designed the boulevards and apartment blocks, an ensemble that was beyond the human scale, in the district immediately around the car plant.[41]

Tolyatti was subject to other principles of the socialist city, not least participation in culture and sport. In 1972, for instance, several members of the Union of Artists of the RSFSR were invited to the new city to run workshops for young artists. In the 1980s, the authorities claimed that the city had 130 sports halls, more than 500 sports grounds, courts and pitches, two ice-hockey rinks, three covered swimming pools, six stadiums and a palace of sport, with 8,000 children enrolled at afternoon sports 'schools'. Not long after construction began on the plant, 350,000 people lived in the city. On the edge of the Gorbachev period, it was still possible to write of the city that 'in recent years it has become its own particular laboratory for all of the country'.[42]

Yet individuals lived in this 'laboratory' in their own personal way. More pets, for example, lived in these urban spaces than ever before. One historian speaks of their 'rehabilitation' after Stalin.[43] The population of domestic animals increased because pet-owners had more discretionary income than before. And the domestic realm was expanding; the mentality of devoting more of one's personal resources to domestic happiness was normalizing. The relationship between the animal and human worlds in the Soviet Union had always been close, in villagers' everyday lives, and in urbanites' leisure in forests, lakes and dachas. But the chance for urban dwellers to keep indoor pets, sometimes unsuitably large dogs, was mostly a feature of the Thaw's individualization of the domestic realm combined with the consumer opportunities of the 1970s.[44]

The Khrushchev family always kept pets. In retirement, Khrushchev spent a lot of time with the family's German shepherd, Arbat. This dog was really his daughter's, but when Lena came to live with her parents at the dacha, Arbat followed the former Party boss around.

Khrushchev had grown up around animals, and worked as a shepherd before moving to the city. There is a well-known photograph of him taken in 1966, sitting outside, talking to Arbat, who looks up attentively; Khrushchev has a rook sitting on his arm. Arbat would sometimes carry Khrushchev's portable metal chair in his teeth when they went for a walk.[45] Earlier, when the family was back in Kyiv after the war, they kept two German dogs at home, brought back from conquered territory and given to Khrushchev as a gift. Sergei Khrushchev described how his father liked to collect all kinds of animals – wild, part-tame, domestic – at the dacha. Back in the Stalin period, an Arctic aviator brought a polar bear cub home. After it outgrew his Moscow apartment, he gave it to Khrushchev's head of security, who brought it to live at his boss's dacha to the delight of Khrushchev and his children. Soon enough, the animal got out of hand and went to live in the zoo.[46]

The man for whom equality was indispensable to Soviet civilization died in the best hospital in the country. In 1971 he suffered a period of declining health and increasing despair. He had grown to dislike the coming of autumn. With its faded colours and accelerating darkness, it was the opposite of spring. In spring, he liked to work in the dacha's plot, tilling soil and tending vegetables, until he was tired. It recalled his peasant childhood.

On Monday 6 September, after a couple of days of chest pains and breathing problems, Khrushchev was taken by his security detail to the Kremlin Hospital in Moscow's Kuntsevo district. His doctor accompanied them. Khrushchev did not want the fuss of an ambulance journey; he feared its implications. The doctors made Khrushchev comfortable, but he had a heart attack during the night. His wife and children shuffled round the ward to try to help. He died on Saturday, 11 September.

Brezhnev followed events. On the day that Khrushchev died, Brezhnev had an appointment at the Kremlin Polyclinic Number 1 at Granovsky Street and then, at his dacha, took calls from Suslov, Andropov, Podgorny, Grishin, Kosygin, Shelepin, and other members of the Politburo.[47] It was not a typical Saturday afternoon schedule at the dacha. In line with tradition, the funeral took place on the third day, the following Monday, at the Novodevichy cemetery. There would, of course, be no state funeral or burial at the Kremlin wall. They gave out inaccurate information about the time of the funeral to avoid a 'pilgrimage'. Troops entered the district.[48] The Central Committee paid for the funeral and sent one of its members as a representative. Mourners gathered at Kuntsevo and then went to Novodevichy, which was closed to the public for the day. Brezhnev spent the morning holding meetings in his office in the Kremlin, only a few kilometres from the cemetery. Khrushchev's son Sergei spoke at the graveside, though he had to ask permission to do so on the morning of the funeral, lest his eulogy be misrepresented as a political speech at an unauthorized gathering. Sergei was relieved that *Pravda* had at least announced the death on their front page that morning, albeit in a small typeface and without an obituary.

Even while the family was attending at the hospital and then dealing with the awful aftermath, the KGB moved in. From the day of the death, they searched the dacha and the apartment, going through his papers and looking for materials that might compromise the current leadership. All they found were the most anodyne documents, but they took some of these with them. Meanwhile, KGB officers were at the funeral.[49] It felt a long way from the Thaw. A new iteration of the Bolshevik revolution was underway. Mature socialism, developed socialism, the Brezhnev era, the long 1970s: the era might have any of these names. De-Stalinization was in abeyance. The times had a sinister side. But this was not neo-Stalinism, or even stagnation. Khrushchev was dead, but his legacy was everywhere – buildings, streets, things, shops and even the socio-economic rights that existed alongside the post-Stalin police state.

Vladimir Vysotsky (right) in Hamlet, Taganka Theatre (premiered in 1971)

# 12
# On Stage, Off Stage

Khrushchev had left the stage. But just before he did – and then just after – he restored his connection to the intelligentsia, who admired and reviled him in turn. Back in 1962, Khrushchev had made a fool of himself at the Manezh exhibition with his comments about contemporary art, to the disgust of the intelligentsia in its broadest sense and to his own later regret. The decoupling of Khrushchev from the 'cultured' public was a symbolic moment. De-Stalinization was a project that brought together sections of Party, intelligentsia, and the wider population. It could not have made the progress that it did had any of these three elements been missing. Now, in the early 1970s, the Party had turned its back on active de-Stalinization in favour of a softer-focused promotion of the revolution. The public was decreasingly well informed about the Terror and the camps. Writers struggled to find a way to speak in public about the Stalinist past. All this raised uncomfortable questions for the former first secretary at the end of his life. He was unsettled and depressed.

The last visitor at Khrushchev's dacha, in late August 1971, was Yevgeny Yevtushenko. His verse, declaimed by the author himself in stadiums and read by his fans in bestselling editions, was a marker of de-Stalinization. For a time, his was a political voice that originated outside the Party but was openly celebrated on a wide scale. His poem 'The Heirs of Stalin' had warned back in 1962 that de-Stalinization should not simply be venerated as a fact but needed constant vigilance and further work if it were ever to be meaningfully achieved. Yevtushenko's verse was both permitted and dissenting; and yet, in the comfortable celebrity it brought him, his work locked Yevtushenko more deeply into the 'system'. Soon enough, the dissidents despised him. He missed his chance to support Sinyavsky and Daniel during their trial and, as Lyudmila Alexeyeva pointed out, he went on to write a poem about the Bratsk hydroelectric power station instead.[1] In the garden, Khrushchev talked to him about the politics of Stalin's death and the struggle with Beria. They stayed outside for hours, and then came into the house. Yevtushenko spoke of a recent trip to Lake Baikal and his conversations there with local people about Stalinism. 'People haven't the faintest idea what happened back then,' he concluded.[2] Had de-Stalinization succeeded by creating a kind of normal life in which people were no longer preoccupied with the past, or had it failed because culture was much less capable of generating critical discussion that engaged a wide public? It was wishful thinking to believe the first. This was one of the questions that haunted Khrushchev in his retirement.

At the Manezh exhibition in 1962 he had famously had words with Ernst Neizvestny, crudely insulting the sculptor and his work. Still, Neizvestny's studio near Moscow's Prospekt Mira – Peace Avenue – continued to operate over the next decade. Neizvestny turned out bronze figures, centaurs and crucifixion scenes shaped by abstractionism, with nothing to do with socialist realism at all. He also received important commissions for monumental public art, which bolted socialist subjects onto his own aesthetic. These included *To the Children of the World*, installed at the Artek Pioneer camp in 1966, and the sprawling façade of the Central Committee headquarters in Ashkhabad, entitled *Faces of Turkmenia*.[3] Nobody's sculpture was more original and more widely shown. If this was a paradox, it was explained by inner qualities of his work that the authorities could perceive as Soviet, or which they believed were not a threat; and it was explained too by his entrepreneurial gifts and his ability to deal successfully with the many branches of bureaucracy concerned with artistic commissions, censorship, the supply of materials, the manufacture of artworks, urban planning and exhibitions. Like Yevtushenko's earlier poetry, Neizvestny's sculpture developed in its Soviet context while being *sui generis*.

After Khrushchev's death, the family turned almost immediately to Neizvestny to design the memorial stone. He quickly agreed. It was an unconventional and risky choice on both sides. Neizvestny knew he would attract extra attention from the KGB, who gave him a talking-to at the Lubyanka and warned him of foregone commissions and lost prizes.[4] He wilfully took on the challenge, though he ended up emigrating to the United States in 1976, when the KGB eventually opened the door for him.

Neizvestny said that he took the commission because of his admiration for Khrushchev and his fascination for the paradoxes that defined him. Khrushchev had removed fear from Soviet society, Neizvestny argued, but he could not manage the governing apparat because of the absence of that fear. Political higher-ups were on tenterhooks because of Khrushchev's unpredictable behaviour – his so-called 'voluntarism' – but the policies and speeches were, Neizvestny thought, part of a consistent political logic directed at improving individual lives and reducing corruption. As for Khrushchev's personal character, he admired the dynamism and the predisposition to reform while being 'dumbfounded' by his 'unique *nekulturnost*", or complete absence of civilized culture and good manners.[5] For Neizvestny, Khrushchev was a bifurcated politician.

Khrushchev's memorial consisted of two tall interlocking slabs of stone, one of black granite and the other, which was slightly in the foreground, of white marble. A bronze head of Khrushchev was inlaid on the white side. The completed memorial was placed over his grave at the Novodevichyi cemetery. In conversation with Sergei Khrushchev, Neizvestny claimed that this represented Khrushchev leading the Soviet Union out of the darkness of Stalinism and into a better place.[6] But the two sides of Khrushchev's political personality, not to mention the conflicts in his conscience, also seemed to be represented by the juxtaposition of darkness and light. He was, after all, the man of the people with blood on his hands. The monument was unveiled on a rainy day in the third year after his death. They closed the cemetery that day and only allowed in family members, a few guests, including Neizvestny himself and Yevtushenko, who said a few words, some journalists and a battery of security men. Later, though, it became a place for people to visit and reflect upon what had happened in their country's recent history, though public gatherings of any size were, of course, impossible.

Before all this, one afternoon in 1970, Vladimir Vysotsky came to

Khrushchev's dacha. The visit was not planned. Vysotsky had long wanted to meet Khrushchev. The opportunity spontaneously emerged. Khrushchev's granddaughter Yulia, whom Vysotsky knew, got him to the dacha and past the security guard, and as far as Nina Petrovna, who let him in. Khrushchev and Vysotsky had a light meal together. Vysotsky – not Khrushchev – had some vodka. They talked about the theatre. Vysotsky might have sung for Khrushchev, though he did not have his guitar. The atmosphere was friendly. There is a very limited record of the meeting from Khrushchev's side, but Vysotsky talked at length about it to his close friend Viktor Turov, the Belarusian film director. According to Turov, Vysotsky opened up to Khrushchev about his inner fears: that he was famous but insecure, sometimes part of society, sometimes not, and while his songs were very widely known, they were not 'legalized'. What was the point of all this for himself and his fans? Vysotsky lived at top speed, fuelled by alcohol and, later, drugs. He asked Khrushchev, who, seven years before, had been one of the two most powerful men in the world, but was now beyond the pale in a way that he was not, for advice about which member of the government might deal sympathetically with his case. 'Have you *seen* their portraits?' Khrushchev shot back.[7]

In these three encounters, either side of the grave, the warmer relationship between Khrushchev and the intelligentsia showed how far away the Thaw seemed at the turn of the 1970s. And yet its legacy was set. Contemporary art was a good example. What is remembered about the Manezh exhibition of 1962 is not the fact that a show featuring diverse modern artists was put on in the very centre of Moscow; it is that Khrushchev himself showed up and ridiculed it. By September 1974, contemporary artists were reduced to exhibiting their work in a vacant plot in south-west Moscow; thugs sent by the KGB wrecked it with bulldozers. Yet Khrushchev's three encounters also showed that the cultural practices of the post-Thaw years themselves were unpredictable. The poet, sculptor and renaissance man in question were not dissidents but they were true originals. They were not excluded like the artists of the 'Bulldozer exhibition'; they added unique components to Soviet civilization but they had an awkward relationship to the Soviet order. Many others were in the same position. For some of them, the tension could not be sustained indefinitely. Neizvestny emigrated; Vysotsky died young. For others, like Yevtushenko, a more durable sequence of compromises became possible. Some artists left the stage, others stayed on it, pushing against unpredictable force fields that gave Soviet civilization a protean form rather than a constant, 'stagnant' shape.[8] After all, only two weeks after the culturally and psychologically ruinous 'Bulldozer exhibition', the authorities permitted many of the same artists to put on a show of their work in Moscow's Izmailovsky Park.

A decade on from the foundation of the new Taganka, on Wednesday, 6 March 1974, at 5.30 in the afternoon, members of the theatre began a special show at the Ministry of Civil Aviation in Moscow. It was winter, but forty minutes of gloomy daylight remained. Yuri Lyubimov, the director, told stories about the theatre. Vladimir Vysotsky, the great celebrity, came on last and sang his own songs about fighter pilots, planes and flying. Alla Demidova, Vysotsky's close friend, and an actress from the troupe, wrote in her diary that his performance was 'a crazy success'.[9] Of course, it always was.

Vysotsky summed up the strangeness of cultural celebrity in the Soviet dictatorship. He was a massive hit, but he was also a one-off. He was not even conventionally handsome. Vysotsky did not have any of the trappings of an earlier age of Soviet celebrity, of a Stakhanovite, cosmonaut or film star. Nor did he have much in common with his celebrity peers in the 1970s: he wasn't an anodyne singer, a reliable comic or a platitudinous sportsman. Still, since the late 1960s, Vysotsky had been a Soviet celebrity, fêted and adored. Even at the heart of the apparat, they loved him, at least in 1974. The Party could never have invented anyone like him in a century of meetings of the Cultural Department; nor could the men of the KGB have thought up an enemy with his words or his voice. He was sincere but, at that time, also acceptable, radiant but not Party-minded. Vysotsky's originality was mercurial, but it existed inside the system.

His film roles – often defined by his guitar playing and singing – took standard parts into edgy territory. In *Vertical*, directed by Stanislav Govorukhin and Boris Durov, and released in 1967, Vysotsky plays a guitar-wielding radio technician on a mountain-climbing trip. He finds himself in uneasy liminal spaces that stretch beyond comfortable

Sovietness – on the edge of physical danger, personal sincerity and, in his songs, lyrical ambiguity. Mountaineering was a fashionable and faintly glamorous Soviet activity which here was rendered uncertain and uneasy. In Kira Muratova's *Brief Encounters* (also 1967), Vysotsky plays a geologist who has had relationships with both a senior official and her housekeeper. Geologists were attractive figures during and after the Thaw, educated, well-travelled and romantic. But Vysotsky's character does not form straightforward relationships, and his singing and guitar-playing make him magnetic but not wholesome. The film is decentred, digressive and with an uncharacteristic narrative and morality, but Odesa Film Studios pushed it though Goskino, the state cinema administration. Vysotsky's beauty, as his admirers perceived it, came from within and could not be shaped or defined by others. KGB people feared this, but they did not ban him: in 1974, quite the reverse.

The puzzle of Vysotsky's celebrity was partly explained by the wider paradox of Soviet censorship. Soviet censors were destroyers and stranglers in that they broke some artists and denied oxygen to many great works, but they did not usually operate a blunt instrument. Censors sometimes had a productive effect; artists thought round the problem of how to coexist with them, and they in turn chose when to avoid exercising the full weight of their powers. In the 1970s, censorship could sometimes be evaded, and its impact could yield unanticipated outcomes, contributing to the particular forms that a star like Vysotsky assumed.

Nowhere was this truer than in the Taganka, and not least in the unexpected choices that Yuri Lyubimov made about its repertoire. On Tuesday, 16 April 1974, a month after the show at the Ministry, the Taganka's new play, *Wooden Horses*, opened. The second half of April was the rainy prelude to spring. Cheeringly, one could wear a light jacket and carry an umbrella, and arrive at the theatre for a 6.30 start in sharp daylight. *Wooden Horses* was based on Fyodor Abramov's eponymous novel. Abramov was one of the leading exponents of the 'village prose' movement. The movement's writers were loosely united by a subject and a sensibility. They hailed from the deepest rural provinces of the Russian republic, including from Siberia, and aimed to describe the life of the world from which they came – its personalities, relationships, ecology, landscape, even its politics – with an unvarnished, precise realism. Many of the stories and novels resembled tough, unhappy exposés. They did not fall back on clichéd tropes or use a socialist realist structure, in which a character moved from interior darkness and social malignity towards socialist consciousness and commitment to the Party. Instead, they often showed that the Soviet government benefited rural-dwellers only in the very long term through its clumsy modernizations, which so often went against the grain of local culture and the deeply held desires of local people. There was a violence and misery in some of these texts that did not have much in common with the radiant future. Yet the stories and novels were published, despite the strictures of Soviet censorship, and in perverse ways because of them. In 1974, an extra censor's hurdle was cleared, when the Taganka was allowed to put on *Wooden Horses*.

Soviet culture in the 1970s contained multiple permitted discourses that derived from a limited and sometimes unspoken negotiation between cultural producers and censors. Getting challenging work published or produced on stage or screen was not impossible, but it required entrepreneurialism, flexibility and skill. An author, editor, filmmaker or theatre director had to operate inside the interstices of the censorship administration. They had to know the expectations of particular censors, and even cultivate personal relationships with some of them. When a film studio decided to go ahead with a new movie, it had to submit the script to Glavlit, the censorship authority that was responsible for literary materials. Once Glavlit had approved or modified the script, Goskino took over the censorship of the movie and discussed the results with the studio. The director then re-edited the final production to satisfy Goskino's demands. Given the wide range of films that were produced in the USSR in this period, many of which had nothing to do with socialism and some of which formed the basis of informed criticism of it, the censorship process cannot have been blunt. Films produced in the Ukrainian republic during the Thaw and the early Brezhnev era animated discussion about the diversity of Ukrainian national identity and its relationship to Sovietness.[10] It seems even to have been the case that censors, many of whom were themselves graduates of film schools, sometimes worked with studios to improve productions and to protect them from interventions higher up the bureaucratic ladder. In any case, assumptions about diametric opposition between 'creator' and 'controller' bore little relationship to the shifting realities of the 1970s.[11]

An integral part of Soviet civilization from the very start, the censorship system had taken on a formal shape in 1922 with the creation of the Main Administration of Literature and Publishing (Glavlit). By 1955, Glavlit employed 6,708 staff. Only about 300 of these worked at the head office in Moscow. The rest were scattered across regional offices, ranging from a whole territory or province (*krai* or *oblast*) to a city or district. But censorship was more diffuse. Writers subjected their work to self-censorship; the work of publishers, editors and even translators edged into censorship, at least at the edges.[12] And the whole infrastructure of censorship extended into other areas, too: libraries, bookshops, palaces of culture.

Soviet people considered themselves the best read in the world. Texts and reading always formed Soviet civilization. A sociological study based in a town in the Voronezh region between 1969 and 1971 indicated that 58 per cent of the population read fiction very regularly.[13] Readers borrowed books from libraries and subscribed to magazines and 'thick' journals, but many of them also built up substantial collections in their own homes, which they stored behind glass in the period's ubiquitous dark-wood shelving units. In Moscow, a major new bookshop, Book House, was built into the concrete of the new thoroughfare, Kalinin Prospekt, which from the late 1960s ran through the city's Arbat district in the direction of the Kremlin; some of the avenue's tower blocks were designed in the shape of open books (see chapter 4). On the street outside Book House were stalls selling second-hand books. Second-hand bookshops had an especially difficult relationship with the censorship authorities. With their constantly changing and unpredictable stock, often including titles that had not been on the horizon of officialdom for some time, they struggled to comply with every detail of Glavlit's guidance. A new set of guidelines for second-hand bookshops was introduced in 1977: another complex regulation that might or might not be complied with.[14]

At the Taganka in 1974, Alla Demidova played one of the peasant women in *Wooden Horses*. According to a leading critic, her performance was triumphant not because she mimicked the woman's accent but because she found a natural sound that combined her own voice, as a member of the metropolitan intelligentsia, with the cadences of northern Russia in 'an organic intonation'.[15] Another critic later pointed out that in focusing on a specifically 'national problem', the remote Far North countryside, the Taganka revealed again its European ambitions, showing 'Russian history through a prism of national self-criticism'.[16] Demidova did not talk down to her character. Focusing on the conversation between two village women, staying close to their accents and language, the production brought the village to the city. It described the moral crisis and threat that Soviet power posed to an older way of life, no longer from dekulakization and famine, but instead from unfettered modernization and urbanization.

Vysotsky's rival as the most famous off-beat celebrity and top cultural all-rounder in the USSR was one of the village prose writers. Vysotsky the Muscovite was the ultimate metropolitan star, but Vasily Shukshin had traded a village in the Altai for the celebrity stratosphere. He found his way to Moscow and enrolled at the Gerasimov Film Institute (VGIK) at the age of twenty-five. Earthy and wiry, with an ebullient on-screen persona that was apparently ever ready for sex, Shukshin performed in some blockbuster roles. He was a heroic, impudent, everyman soldier in the 1975 epic *They Fought for the Motherland*. But he also wrote important works of fiction, including *Red Berry* (*Kalina krasnaia*, 1973), the story of a doomed criminal who is released from jail and cannot escape his old ways. Shukshin revealed a textured rural world, though not one that had anything to do with socialist realism; there was no redemption in *Red Berry*. He took *Kalina krasnaia* to the big screen as both director and leading man. Shukshin mastered multiple creative professions and different modes of presenting Soviet life; like Vysotsky, he was a 1970s renaissance man. And like Vysotsky he died young, in 1974 at the age of forty-five; a number of his films came out posthumously. Suggestive of the subtlety of his work, and the strange workings of the censorship apparatus that permitted it, was his role as a provincial playwright in the 1975 two-part film *Can I Speak?* Here he starred opposite the equally charismatic and sexually taut Inna Churikova, who leads the administration of a local town. The two meet at a party. On his lead, she relaxes into a conversation about what should and should not be performed, and agrees to reconsider for official approval a play of his which has previously been rejected. She takes the script and reads it.

Yet across the range of Soviet cultural production, the Soviet censorship machine was powerful and extensive. For all the successes of the Taganka in keeping a rich repertoire going in the 1970s, Lyubimov and his colleagues faced many setbacks. The Taganka's staging of another rural play that came out of the Thaw, *The Tough*, was banned in 1968, despite repeated attempts over several years and talks with Ekaterina Furtseva and her successor as Moscow's boss, Viktor Grishin. There was no way round its depiction of despair in village life. Their inventive and personal production of Molière's *Tartuffe*, which premièred three months after the crushing of the Prague Spring, was permitted, but the theatre then endured an intimidating and apparently coordinated press campaign against it. Lyubimov's adaptation of Gorky's *Mother*, which opened in May 1969, was malformed by the censors to the extent that it ended up satisfying neither the theatre not the authorities.[17]

Even so, it was not easy to get a ticket. Theatre tickets were often deficit items: demand outstripped supply. Later, by 1983, Moscow itself contained thirty-five professional theatres. It was not unusual for a theatre to have more than one auditorium – a main stage and a minor stage – and some had 'filial' branches, too. Overall, the number of seats was around 40,000, or around five seats per 1,000 inhabitants of the city. This meant that if every seat was taken every night by a Muscovite, then every Muscovite could theoretically go to the theatre twice a year. According to one calculation, one-third of places were taken each night by people visiting the capital, reducing capacity for Muscovites. But many of them had no interest in the theatre anyway – though there were plenty who would go every week if they could.[18]

Ellendea Proffer Teasley first caught sight of Joseph Brodsky when she was twenty-five and on an extended visit to the Soviet Union with her husband, the Slavist professor, Carl Proffer. She was a graduate student; Brodsky looked like one. They entered his room in central Leningrad on 22 April 1969. It was Lenin's birthday. The old revolutionary would have been turning ninety-nine. 'The most remarkable thing about Joseph Brodsky is his determination to live as if he were free in the eleven time zone prison that is the Soviet Union,' she wrote. 'His code of behaviour is based on his experience under totalitarian rule: a man who does not think for himself, a man who goes along with the group, is part of the evil structure itself.'[19]

The Proffers were right that Brodsky could not live as a free man in the Soviet Union. His poetry and his conscience could not allow him to live a normal life there. There was no compromise, no way of keeping him on the stage of Soviet life and culture. Yet Brodsky was nothing if not a creature of Soviet civilization. He became a person by occupying the physical spaces that the revolution had brought into being. Most famous among these was the communal apartment in central Leningrad where he was brought up. In one of his best-known prose writings, he described the 'room and a half' which he shared with his parents, carved out of a once-grand pre-revolutionary dwelling. Here he sought privacy from his parents behind stacks of books, makeshift curtains, cupboards and wardrobes.[20] Unable to fit in to Soviet society, he was labelled a 'parasite' and then ejected, but not before he had accrued a substantial following of those who admired his poetry. By contrast, he flourished in the United States and won the Nobel Prize fifteen years after his expulsion.

Like Brodsky, Aleksei Amalrik was charged with being a parasite. He also spent time in internal exile, in his case in a Siberian village, and endured a frustrated, unfinished career. Amalrik might not have had Brodsky's genius, but he shared his constitutional incapacity for creative and intellectual compromise. Aspiring to be a historian, he did not complete his undergraduate studies after courting controversy by arguing about the Viking origins of early Rus. It was a wilful act of self-destruction. Even then, he believed that the truth was not divisible and that the moral cost of compromising with authority was never worth it.

Amalrik argued that Soviet writers had the option of remaining in the USSR and standing up to the KGB, neither collaborating with them nor publishing anything on the Party's terms.[21] In exile, Anatoly Kuznetsov, whose book on the Nazi massacre of Jews at Babyi Yar in Kyiv had been published in censored form in the USSR in

1966 before his emigration, took a different view. He pushed back against American journalists' questions about why the Soviet people did not overthrow the government. Kuznetsov thought the journalists were 'naive': the KGB had enormous repressive power at its disposal, and the people had no way of organizing effective opposition to the government. Amalrik excoriated Kuznetsov. He thought Kuznetsov overestimated the repressive power of the Soviet machine and cast the moral question wrongly. It was possible to remain in the USSR and struggle from within.

Amalrik was inviting his fellow citizens to take a big risk. This risk was manageable for dissidents but incompatible with a normal life. Dissidents' attempts to lead lives strictly according to conscience were pivoted on calculations about extreme risk. For them, the risk was not only acceptable, but was the only way to live. Most cultural figures were much less bold. Some of them were only interested in fortune and celebrity. Many writers and artists did seek to work according to their conscience but also did not want to take the risk of ending up in prison or in a manual job in a Siberian village. Others wanted to keep living with their families inside the country of their birth while writing or performing in useful and attractive ways for their fellow countrymen. Their only option was to create works that pushed boundaries without crossing them, that were 'permitted dissent' rather than dissidence.[22] But as an officially approved writer or artist, they also enjoyed the perks of the creative union dining room, the deluxe sanatorium, the foreign-currency store and even foreign trips. It could be difficult to distinguish them from the *nomenklatura* whom they liked to think that they were holding to account. Some of them, like Yuri Trifonov, who never joined the Party, retained their credibility. Others did not. 'In Russia, a poet is held to higher standards than anyone else,' wrote the dissident Lyudmila Alexeyeva in her memoirs. 'When he loses courage, he loses his talent.' She wrote of the great Thaw poet Andrei Voznesensky, who in 1968, the year of the heroic demonstration on Red Square and of the slogan 'for your freedom and ours', was devastated – but only to be denied permission to make a trip to the United States. 'While the intelligentsia was fighting to keep its brethren out of prison,' she wrote, 'Voznesensky was trying to salvage his plans for foreign travel.'[23]

There were individuals among these groups who provided a transcendent moral example, such as the Red Square demonstrators of August 1968 (see chapter 9). But there were others who succeeded in offering intellectual or emotional tools for interpreting the moral dilemmas of Soviet life precisely because they were not capable of reaching this standard or did not aim for it. Instead, they occupied a 'grey zone'. The joke was that the authors who occupied this place came in two types: the rural writers and the Trifonovites.[24] It was Yuri Trifonov who made the urban prose of the 1970s so original that it attracted the interest of the Nobel Prize-awarding committee. Trifonov was born into a revolutionary family in Moscow in 1925 and endured the arrest of his parents during the Great Terror when he was still a child; his father was shot, and his grandmother thereafter raised him. His bottle-top spectacles prevented him from fighting at the front, and he instead worked in an armaments factory in Moscow during the war. Remarkably, given that his life chances were inevitably reduced by the arrests of his parents, he ended up attending the Gorky Institute for World Literature and writing a Stalin Prize-winning novel while he was still in his twenties, but he really found his voice in the late 1960s. Trifonov's great contribution was a cycle of novels that described the moral dilemmas of Muscovites in the long 1970s. The books analysed family relationships, affairs, workplace rivalry, memories of terror, squabbles over housing space, urban encroachment on the countryside, inter-generational tensions and many other situations. His style was realistic, though he often ranged back and forth in time. In fact he also wrote historical fiction. Characters, time, situations, settings: all spoke of connections to 1917 and of an ongoing revolutionary imperative. Trifonov did all this while abandoning socialist realism and writing in a way that was also interesting to readers who knew nothing of the Soviet Union. He never joined the Party, and some of his envious colleagues in the Union of Writers sometimes tried to traduce him. But Mikhail Suslov, perhaps strangely, respected his unconventionality.

Readers of Trifonov's historical fiction appreciated his deep research and psychological penetration.[25] Trifonov's contemporary-set work was bound to elicit a more emotional response. His novel *The Exchange*, which was soon turned into a play at the Taganka and was published in 1969, concerned the moral and family anguish that arose when a middle-aged woman sought to ensure that she, her husband and her daughter would be able to make use of her dying mother-in-law's allocation of housing space after her death by arranging a timely exchange of dwellings through an agent. It was a particularly Soviet setting – one way of moving house in the absence of a market – but a universal dilemma. 'I am also the mother of a married son,' wrote one reader, Vera Kh., to the offices of *Novyi mir*, where Trifonov's work was published, 'and "the exchange" in your sense has been completed in our family very often and very painfully. We all live together, and you should have seen with what heat we read your novel.'[26]

Other cultural forms and institutions struggled less effectively than Trifonov to produce works of pure conscience in an environment of cultural compromise. In the Bolshoi Theatre, the repertoire was increasingly filled with classics, including new productions of *Spartacus* and *Swan Lake*. The artistic director, Yuri Grigorovich, teased out some experimental lines, but from around 1970, his interpretations seemed increasingly routine, much to the chagrin of the Bolshoi's great star, Maya Plisetskaya. But this might not have been censorship in action, more a way of working out how to deal with Ekaterina Furtseva, the tense minister of culture who also subjected the Taganka to endless shredded nerves.[27]

Meanwhile, in 1969, Dmitry Shostakovich completed his Fourteenth Symphony. Unlike some of his more accessible pieces, it was an uncompromising work, musically complex and suffused with a bleak, fearful and unresolved moral vision. Even so, the symphony was permitted and was performed. The ambiguity of music gave composers, especially those of international fame, more flexibility in the face of the censors than writers. No wonder Shostakovich admired great writers who could get round the authorities. He expressed awe for the way that Yevtushenko delivered such 'honest and truthful' poems as 'Stalin's Heirs' and 'Babyi Yar' to millions of people who read them 'peacefully, legally, without looking round, without fear'.[28] Shostakovich believed that the themes of death and absence of redemption in the Fourteenth Symphony were obvious, and it seems that listeners at the time agreed.[29] And yet this was an uncertain achievement for 'permitted dissent'. The authorities could make their own claims for the music. Following his death in 1975, a celebratory volume of 1980 attributed the following words to him concerning the Fourteenth. 'Shostakovich' urged the audience to reflect, while listening to the symphony, on 'the best, progressive ideas put forward by our socialist society'. He was supposed to have concluded: 'Such were my thoughts as I composed this symphony.'[30]

The most conventional culture could avoid these ambiguities. Its creators sometimes made quiet fortunes. Writers were not employees of the state, but if they were to make a living, they were members of the Writers' Union. A very small number of them, like Mikhail Sholokhov, who lived off the reputation of his 1920s novel *Virgin Soil Upturned* until his death in 1984, grew rich by any standard. Meanwhile, spectator sport was built into Soviet culture, like it was in all modern societies. Football was the most popular sport, but never with the same depth as in Spain or Italy. The number of supporters turning out at grounds more than halved in 1970–74 compared to 1965–9, partly because of the rise of television. Average attendance figures dropped from more than 30,000 to 13,000. It was also a time when the champions diversified away from Moscow: Zarya Voroshilovgrad in 1972, Ararat Yerevan in 1973 and Dinamo Tbilisi in 1978.[31] Pop music aligned more closely with Western European sounds in the 1970s. No pop star was more popular than Alla Pugacheva. Typically – for the USSR expected its stars to have the right training – she was well educated in music and had shown an early interest in conducting. She was picked off the radio and given a part in children's TV. By 1975, when she was twenty-six, her celebrity, which would last decades, was beginning. It was then that she performed several of the songs in Eldar Ryazanov's huge New Year hit film *The Irony of Fate*. Following that, one door after another opened.[32] Perhaps the most popular entertainer across the whole of the USSR was the stand-up comic Arkady Raikin. He performed across media but really struck enormous fame with his eponymous TV show in the mid-1970s. Raikin's was a slapstick world of pulled faces, fake noses, wigs, props and women's clothes, something that could appeal to varied audiences in different republics, and which just occasionally got near the knuckle of Soviet life.[33]

Radio helped to shape Soviet civilization. It delivered public information and entertainment – the whole range of revolutionary messaging, direct and indirect – into factories, communal apartments and collective farms from the start. The voice of Yuri Levitan, the great establishment announcer and newsreader, was universally known. He had told the people about major events for decades, most famously the Nazi invasion. But by the late 1960s, television was taking radio's place. One survey of 1968 indicated that almost everybody watched television every day, but that radio audiences had fallen to around three out of four workers. It was now attracting listeners in certain niches, especially among the intelligentsia.[34] Planners had decided that televisions should be owned by families and located in their own homes rather than in 'red corners' of apartment buildings or workers' clubs. In the age of mass escapism new TV shows became very popular. *KVN – The Happy and Witty Club* – was a game show launched in the 1960s that caught the all-union imagination. On a given day in 1975, the scheduling on the First Channel opened with morning exercises at 9.10 a.m., and went on to include communist ceremonial broadcasts, a nature programme, shows for children, two films, a drama series, the news at 9 p.m., and a sports round-up at 10.55.[35]

Vysotsky's on-stage and onscreen charisma made the audience sense a connection to him, feeling that he was on their side. Among friends, he often kept open house long into the small hours, not turning people away. His capacious imagination and mercurial personality gave him a light touch. The authorities kept an eye on him, and at times he became a person of concern (above all, in the year after his death). But he knew exactly how to steer within the boundaries of acceptability. He could have been the most glamorous exponent of permitted dissent, but his work did not really sound like dissent. It was not a critique of Soviet civilization. It just took its readers, listeners and viewers outside its boundaries while making them think that they were still within its limits. In taking people to places that Soviet civilization usually could not reach, Vysotsky was a confidence trickster of the utmost sincerity.

Aleksandr Solzhenitsyn never met Vysotsky, or at least there is no record of it. Vysotsky's wife stated that he had read *The Gulag Archipelago* with her during a trip to Paris; Solzhenitsyn, it was said, sometimes liked to listen to Vysotsky's songs. In 1974, they were two of the biggest stars in Soviet culture. In the biggest sense, they were fighting on the same side: theirs was the team playing for conscience, integrity and the sacred values of the individual person. But there were many political differences between the two men, including on big questions of race and nationality. It was partly a result of their difference in age. Vysotsky was far too young to have fought in the war, let alone to have been incarcerated in the Stalin-era Gulag. Instead, he had played his guitar in Western cities. He liked to relax in a milieu of bohemian excess. Vysotsky lacked the earnestness of Solzhenitsyn. He took risks but not like Solzhenitsyn did.

They had a different sense of nationality. A feeling of Russianness, expressed through language, landscape, characters and references to history and culture, ran through Vysotsky's work. It had a diffuse Russophone inclusiveness to it and was not a political vision. Solzhenitsyn had a national purpose that grew more focused over time. *Cancer Ward* was set in Uzbekistan. It meticulously described its Uzbek characters, how they talked and behaved. Solzhenitsyn himself had not only lived in exile in Central Asia after his release from the Gulag, but he had survived cancer there. He had a serious aim in cataloguing the republic's landscape and institutions and in making an argument about their Soviet reality. Solzhenitsyn did not exoticize Central Asia. He just assumed that Russia (and Ukraine) possessed a higher civilization. In September 1973, with the KGB on his tail and a return to a labour camp a real possibility, he wrote an open letter to the Central Committee. In it he spoke of 'our people', the east Slavs – presumably speaking Russian – who needed greater protection than any other group in the USSR. 'I wish all peoples well,' he wrote, 'and the closer to us and the more dependent upon us, the more fervent is my wish.' Solzhenitsyn was not an imperialist. He regretted Moscow's original expansion outside its Slavic core. He was absorbed in Russian culture and disliked what he saw as the trivial obsessions of the West, the challenge from an 'asiatic' China, and the devastating damage that Bolshevik modernity had wrought on the ecology as well as the culture of Russia. He excoriated communism and the KGB. Marxism was 'a primitive, superficial economic theory'. As much as he deplored Soviet rule over all parts of the USSR, he could not escape looking at the 'periphery' with the eyes of the imperial centre. He pointed to 'the incomparable sufferings of our people', meaning the Russians and Ukrainians, between whom he could not draw a precise political distinction. The real resources that Russia had to draw upon could be found in its history, not in an abstract Soviet future.[36]

Aleksandr Solzhenitsyn sent his letter one week after Andrei Sakharov was nominated for the Nobel Peace Prize. He was in touch with English-language publishers and translators about the future appearance of *The Gulag Archipelago*. His routine remained precise. Worried about causing trouble for his second wife, Natalia, he was staying at Lydia Chukovskaya's dacha in Peredelkino. He lived and wrote in a single room, keeping a pitchfork handy behind the bed for the moments when he wanted to stretch his muscles and reconnect with nature (and to defend himself if necessary). His main project was the completion of his literary memoir, later published as *The Oak and the Calf*, but he was absorbed by several writing tasks. One day a week, he went to Moscow, carrying a rucksack and stocking up on tins and other essentials.

What he was storing up for himself was trouble. The BBC Russian service broadcast a programme at 1.45pm on 28 December 1973 that announced the publication of the first volume of *The Gulag Archipelago* in Paris. Solzhenitsyn was listening in the kitchen while he was eating his lunch. It was the first he heard about it; he thought it would be released on the Orthodox Christmas, ten days later. It was a solemn moment, an overwhelming triumph. He had the chance to celebrate, but the KGB was closing in. Ever since his release from the Gulag two decades before, his relationship to the organs of coercion had been uncertain. Now they had every reason to go for him. On 14 January 1974, *Pravda* attacked. They called him a 'traitor'. He became a global *cause célèbre*, with writers in Washington, DC, protesting on his behalf, and writers in the Soviet Union divided in their response. He was followed and faintly harassed. On 12 February, he was in his new wife's apartment in Moscow, late in the afternoon. They were working when there was a knock at the door. He was not expecting them. Eight secret policemen arrested him and took him to Lefortovo prison. It was dark. Inside, they humiliated him, like any convict, putting him in a cell with a pair of currency speculators. Within an hour, the deputy chief prosecutor of the Soviet Union, Mikhail Malyarov, was interrogating him. The charge was treason, article 64 of the penal code. It was worse than he feared. He slept fitfully overnight. When he got up, his blood pressure was rocketing. The guards brought clothes suitable for outside and told him to dress. Solzhenitsyn believed that his case was the biggest in the Soviet Union. He wondered if they would take him to the heart of Soviet power, to the Council of Ministers in Old Square or to the Politburo in the Kremlin.

Instead, he had to sit in his cell and wait. Eventually they brought him to another room in Lefortovo. Malyarov was there. He told him of his fate. Solzhenitsyn was to lose his Soviet citizenship with immediate effect and be expelled from the country. The prisoner insisted in return that his family be allowed to join him. All he could extract from Malyarov was a promise, in writing, that they could follow.

They drove him straight to Sheremetyevo. He was wearing another man's clothes and his own crucifix and watch. He sat in the empty forward cabin of an Aeroflot flight to Frankfurt. The other passengers were behind, out of view. He was with eight Chekists, one of whom was a doctor. They gave him 500 marks when they landed, and he walked down the steps and into the hands of the West German authorities. Heinrich Böll, who won the Nobel Prize in Literature two years after him, in 1972, had offered him sanctuary in his village home near the capital. Solzhenitsyn was thinking about his family and about his work. Most essential of all, his wife would have to smuggle out his 'whole enormous archive ... every single page of importance (and I had few that were unimportant)'.[37]

It broke his heart to leave his native soil. Like other dissidents in exile, he thought that it was the communist bosses who should have to leave the country, not himself. Still, Solzhenitsyn had won. No writer more decisively shaped the world's view of Soviet civilization. He found the truth, told the truth and unforgettably described the fundamental basis of the Soviet experience. But he did not tell its complete story, or account for its durability, or explain the 'legitimacy' of Soviet civilization. He lacked the anguished subtlety of writers like Yuri Trifonov or performers like Vysotsky. With his heart in the past and his distrust of the future, Solzhenitsyn was not looking at the present. He had left the stage of Soviet life and was no longer an active player in its everyday dramas. As the car took him through the darkness towards Bonn, 200 million of his fellow countrymen were still living through Soviet eternity. Or so it seemed. A major international treaty would be signed the following year which, some would later claim, hit Soviet civilization like a cannonball below the waterline.

PART THREE

# Faded Paradise (1975–84)

Svaneti region, Georgia

# 13
# Oil Fields and Silver Birches

On 1 August 1975 the great statesmen of Europe and North America gathered in Helsinki. Brezhnev was there. Gerald Ford was there. So were Harold Wilson, Helmut Schmidt and Valéry Giscard d'Estaing. There were thirty-five heads of state or government, and they were all men. A thirty-sixth man joined them. He was the secretary-general of the United Nations, who was there in an honorary capacity and so did not sign the international agreement that was the subject of the meeting in the modernist fantasia of Helsinki's Finlandia Hall. After two years of negotiations, firstly in Helsinki and then in Geneva, the thirty-five governments on either side of the Iron Curtain were finally signing an agreement whose stated aim was to secure good relations and proper cooperation between their countries and to establish meaningful rights within them. It was a storied moment in post-1945 world history.

Thirty years earlier, the Second World War had ended without a peace treaty. Helsinki was a kind of substitute. Two years in the making, and thirty years overdue, the Helsinki Accords were the culmination of the Conference on Security and Cooperation in Europe. Some historians later came to see this as the turning point in postwar affairs that led to the end of the Cold War and the collapse of the Soviet Union a decade-and-a-half later. But what the Helsinki Accords really did was calcify the status quo. Meanwhile, inside the Soviet Union, Brezhnev's physical and mental decline was apparent from the mid-1970s. A few years later, living standards began noticeably to fall. The bright visions of paradise were becoming faded. For a moment, from Helsinki all the way to Khabarovsk, it was if time had stopped: as if developed socialism had something of eternity about it.

*

As the 1970s hit their mid-point, did it really make any sense to say that the revolution was continuing? In 1977, when the new constitution was eventually unveiled, it was fully six decades since 1917. At a time when advances in mortality had briefly been reversed in the Soviet Union, sixty was the average length of a man's life (women lived longer). A man born in 1917 – a twin of the revolution – had statistically run his lifespan. If he had lived a revolutionary life, had his twin, the revolution itself, somehow died of old age?

Some people assumed this. In 1986, Gorbachev used the word 'stagnation' to describe the late 1970s and early 1980s; he wanted to show that the previous version of socialism to his own had run the revolution into the ground, and that his reinterpretation of Leninism, and sheer energy, would give the revolution another chance. But late-1970s ideology, rhetoric and aesthetics, and to some extent public policy, everyday life and popular mentalities, told a different story: that the revolution did possess signs of life.

At the time the Helsinki Accords were signed, the Soviet Union's revolutionary *eminence grise* was a tall man in a business suit. He had a full head of off-white hair. He wore rectangular spectacles with curved edges. He might have been a professor or a senior manager. He was something of both. In 1975, Mikhail Suslov had been a member of the Politburo for twenty-three years (with a two-year break following Stalin's death). He was the Party's ideology supremo. This meant he oversaw phalanxes of civil servants with doctorates in philosophy, whose well-paid job was to tease out fine shades of meaning in the texts of Marx, Engels and Lenin. Suslov also looked after the propagandists charged with popularizing these ideas and explaining their importance to the wider population. He himself was an interface between text and power. The Talmudic traditions of the revolution survived in Suslov. He championed an obsessive textualism and a Marxism-based approach to all questions of policy. Unsurprisingly, he was yet another outsider. He was born into a family of peasants in Saratov *guberniya*. The Bolsheviks had come to power two weeks before his fifteenth birthday. He owed everything to the revolution, joining the Komsomol in the midst of the Civil War, getting his Party card when he was barely on the cusp of adulthood, making his life in Moscow, enjoying an elite education at the Plekhanov Economics

Institute and then the Red Professor Economics Institute. In his late twenties, he was set for a high-flying Party career, and he dodged the bullets that hit many of his contemporaries between 1936 and 1938.

Instead, Suslov never stopped talking about the revolution. In the Brezhnev era he lived in a handsome apartment on Kutuzovsky Prospekt and glided through a capital city that was marked by political stability and, for the most part, economic steadiness. But he was forever dreaming about October. In a speech in January 1973, he commended the Institute of Marxism-Leninism – the country's powerhouse of ideological explanations, which had just been awarded the Order of Lenin – for its role in the development of scientific communism as a theory and potential future. 'Their works' – he insisted – 'were and remain a life-giving source of strength for the Party, the working class and workers of all countries, a reliable guide in the struggle for the revolutionary transformation of society, for communism.'[1] In September 1976, he made a celebratory speech at the Kirov engineering plant in Leningrad. 'Throughout all the history of their factory,' Suslov claimed, 'the Kirov workers have carried with honour their faithfulness to the ideals of socialist revolution.'[2]

In 1977, a major TV series, *Our Biography*, was launched. It devoted one episode to every Soviet year since the revolution of 1917. Each episode lasted approximately one hour, and together they made up a biography of the Russian Revolution played out over sixty years and connected by a forward-facing revolutionary dynamic. 'Revolutionary pathos and revolutionary teleology,' writes the scholar Serguei Oushakine in an analysis of the series, 'were used as a form of emplotment.'[3] The opening sequence of the 1976 episode, for instance, began with a montage of images from the mid-1970s whose light, placement and sequence recalled the earliest Soviet cinema. The images in the next scene, of life in Yakutia, emphasized the interplay of rapid movement and northern light, focusing on animals, machinery and trucks, and then the construction of the Baikal-Amur railway, one of the Party's signature projects in the 1970s.[4] Continuity and forward movement took place simultaneously in this revolutionary production.

Meanwhile, dissidents and others who did not voice the Party line were expressing 'counter-revolutionary propaganda'. This was the widespread complaint made against Sakharov in 1968 from leading local Party figures across the USSR: conformists knew that the way to express total loyalty was to invoke the revolution as an ongoing process.[5] Molotov expressed revolutionary enthusiasm from the opposite perspective. On 1 November 1977, he was engaged in a conversation with the journalist Feliks Chuev that would be published much later. The old Stalinist, who had sat in the Politburo while his wife was sent to the camps, and who had approved the 'judicial' murders of so very many, was eighty-seven. He had another quiet nine years of life left to live. He expressed contempt for 'poor old Brezhnev' and for his version of socialism. Molotov's assumption was that revolution should be the index for judging the dynamics of socialist society, just as it had been in the 1930s. 'They have taken the soul, the revolutionary essence, out of Marxism,' he lamented.[6] The post-Khrushchev period was often described as the 'scientific-technological revolution (STR)'. Its texts were an update of Marxism-Leninism that sought technical advances and a shift to intensive growth and innovation in the era of developed socialism. Analysts were understandably worried about the illusions of the STR, notably the gap in computing technology with the United States that was increasingly apparent as the 1970s went on.[7]

The durability of revolution required a focus on the future. The ideology of the 1970s was future-focused, but no longer like during the Thaw, when ideology, technology, foreign affairs, urban space and policymaking – from sputnik to *khrushchevki* – all suggested that the 'radiant future' was almost close enough to touch.[8] Even so, a Soviet sense of historical time had always been predicated on the future, on the building of a new society, on the creation of utopia, on advancing historical stages, and on a cultural system – socialist realism – whose aim was to create a version of reality in its revolutionary development. To bring the future within reach, time had to be conquered, just like the rest of nature. At the start of Valentin Kataev's classic novel *Time, Forward!*, published in 1932, the hero wakes up before his alarm clock goes off. 'He always rose at six,' Kataev wrote, 'and was always ahead of time.'[9]

In the 1970s, the Strugatsky brothers, Arkady and Boris, were the most famous sci-fi writers in the Soviet Union. They wrote unsettling, decentring narratives which combined the familiar with the sinister, the ordered with the wild, the recognizably present-day with the unimaginable future. *Roadside Picnic*, which came out in 1972, describes a post-apocalyptic 'Zone', a future in which there is no obvious governing ideology or international borders, let alone a Soviet civilization. This was a futurism that transcended the revolution but positioned the future at the centre of popular culture. Soviet science fiction was a conduit with the West; the worlds that it conjured up were not clarified by Soviet references or made comprehensible by an engagement, however tangential, with Soviet ideology. Possible futures crossed borders, even worlds.[10]

A few years after the publication of *Roadside Picnic*, the celebrated director Andrei Tarkovsky used the novel as the basis of his film *Stalker*. Released in 1979, it sold millions of tickets and was praised by the general director of its studio, Mosfilm, precisely for its tendency to provoke discussion.[11] It was not his first sci-fi production. In 1972, Tarkovsky released *Solaris*, an anxiety-inducing space-travel film about the crises and hallucinations of its protagonists. Andrei Tarkovsky looked back as well as forward; he had a sense of history as well as of the future. Another of his great films, *Andrei Rublev*, was released in 1966. Telling the story of the great fourteenth-century icon painter, it depicted an uneasy medieval world whose sensibility was not obviously accessible to its modern audience. It was almost as if the time signatures – past or future – did not quite matter. In both cases, stretching over hundreds of years with the present-day as an uncertain focal point, Tarkovsky's films made 1970s audiences sense a world that was more complicated and less certain – and certainly less eternal – than Brezhnev's speeches implied. In a less self-conscious way, time-travel blockbusters did some of the same work. Like in the United States, this genre was one of the staples of popular culture. *Ivan Vasilevich Changes Professions*, which opened in cinemas in 1973, was a madcap farce about an inventor working on the prototype of a time machine who accidentally sends a local communist busybody and a burglar back to the time of Ivan the Terrible. In 1985, a children's serial, *Guests from the Future*, came to TV screens. Filmed in Gorky Studios the year before, and based on a novel of eight years earlier, it was an exciting tale of accidentally discovered time travel: a Soviet boy from the present, a science-mad girl from the future and pirates from another dimension who want the time machine for themselves.

From the Soviet perspective, the 1975 Helsinki Accords and the milestone that would follow, the 1977 Constitution, were both the product of a particular understanding of historical time, of forward movement and revolutionary change. Even the 1970s Soviet countryside was the site of the ongoing revolution. It was a place of massive projects, in which the BAM railway and new cities were built. Six years before Helsinki, the great West German historian Reinhart Koselleck, whose writings were beginning to form an influential set of theories about the historicity of time, published a scholarly article about the meaning of 'revolution'. Plainly it concerned the movement of time in a way that was not normal. He pointed to the word's original sense of 'circularity'. Koselleck's counterposing of two meanings of revolution – a sudden rupture, and an ongoing period of self-conscious change, linked by the possibility of permanent, enduring transformation until the revolution's aims have been achieved – was a model that could be applied to the Soviet Union, though he himself did not do that. It helped to explain the sense of historical time in the long 1970s.[12]

Obviously there was a conceptual tension between the 'normal' qualities of the 1970s, which people so often remembered with nostalgia, and the decade's status as the latest instalment of the revolution. The Thaw also embodied a dual historical time. It looked forward towards the communist future, and specifically the year 1980, by which point communism was supposed to be achieved. Simultaneously, the Thaw looked backwards. Its source for the communist future was a historical one, the texts of Leninism and the inspirations of 1917. And a good part of the period's cultural work was focused on the immediate past: providing people with a limited means for coming to terms with the horrors of Stalinism while not calling into question the goodwill of the Party or its monopoly on power. Under Brezhnev, by contrast, talk of communism was only formulaic. Instead, the focus was more directly on the present: reasonable living standards, a sense of normality, the whole deriving from a permanent and unquestioned acknowledgement of the beneficence of the Party. Western scholars began to conceptualize this as the result of a social contract, according to which Party and government provided adequate living conditions, stability and the promise of private life, in exchange for permanent tacit support and occasional public endorsements, for example by voting, taking part in a parade or not standing in the way of one's children joining the Komsomol.[13] But this social contract was a static formulation, based on uncertain empirical foundations and outside of the dynamism of historical time.

It was also problematic when later scholars conceptualized 1970s normality as late socialist eternity. The anthropologist Alexei Yurchak described the 'eternal state' (*vechnoe gosudarstvo*) of the USSR. It was not that the Soviet Union was stuck, like a broken record, or that it was experiencing stagnation. Eternity was a different matter. People were living through a civilizational epoch in which historical rupture was unimaginable: an eternal present whose point of terminus was only theoretical. This was not a unique way of interpreting the world around one. It was familiar to many in Western Europe and the United States. Despite social and economic turbulence, capitalism and democracy in the 1970s also seemed likely to last 'forever'.

But 'eternal present' was an insufficient metaphor. Yurchak showed that many Soviet people remained committed to certain Soviet values. These values were the products of a specific historical context, the post-Stalin reinterpretation of a revolutionary way of life. The revolution continued to exert a destructive as well as a creative influence. For Yurchak, 'late socialist' normality was an arena in which 'control, coercion, alienation, fear and moral quandaries were irreducibly mixed with ideals, communal ethics, dignity, creativity and care for the future'. In the 1990s, Yurchak pursued a major interview project with subjects who were Komsomol members in Leningrad in the early 1980s. He described how the landscape of 'ideological representations' – 'documents, speeches, ritualized practices, slogans, posters, monuments, and urban visual propaganda' – became normalized in the decades after 1953 as an 'authoritative discourse'. The majority of people operated within this discourse, for example by participating in May Day parades, without paying much attention to the precise forms of words that were used.

They were not 'brainwashed'. But perhaps they tended to value the things that lay behind the words: the welfare system, the emphasis on education, the access to culture and the status accorded to working-class jobs, as well as the sense of stability. Yurchak disagreed with the liberal assumption that Soviet people who did not 'believe' in the slogans of Soviet power acted in public 'as if' they did, while they talked quite differently in the privacy of their own kitchens. This was the notion that drove Václav Havel's argument about 'the power of the powerless' and, in a different form, Stephen Kotkin's argument about 'speaking Bolshevik'. Instead, they operated within the prevailing authoritative discourse and chose to accept some of its conclusions.[14]

Thinking about the future required one to reflect on alternative possibilities. The revolution always contained multiple futures. The most uncompromising dissidents thought that the Soviet Union might eventually collapse; Andrei Amalrik had wondered whether the Soviet Union would survive until 1984. In other words, they imagined a future fundamentally different from the present. American policymakers and academics also analysed different possible Soviet futures. The scholar George W. Breslauer wrote a short book in 1978 entitled *Five Images of the Soviet Future*, in which he discussed such possible futures as 'socialist democracy' and 'elitist liberalism' and speculated on their relative likelihood and possible implications.[15] Such voices articulated dramatically different possible futures precisely because they perceived an unnaturalness in the Soviet Union, a departure from historic normality, an ongoing revolution that had lasted six decades already.

Even the 1970s socialist city, imagined later as a landscape of timelessness, of endless queues and eternally prefabricated architecture, had ubiquitous references to the future encoded into it. The intense association between the period that historians later called 'late socialism' and its spaces and objects evoked a fixed link between the chronological and the material – things were vividly of their time and place – but this link was only obvious after the event. Nostalgia for the 'lost world' of the Soviet domestic realm and its material traces became a widely felt emotion in the immediate post-Soviet years, though not, of course, in the 1970s.[16] Yet some buildings and things seemed to exist outside of the time references of the Brezhnev years. For instance, Stalin-era architecture was still widespread and extant in nearly all Soviet cities. The historian Anatoly Kalashnikov argues that monumental buildings from that period sought to evoke the future rather than a thousand-year timelessness or an anchor in 'history'. In their materials, locations, motifs and functions they were not simply neoclassical simulacra of imperial buildings in Paris, Washington, Fascist Italy or Nazi Germany.[17] Instead, they came to offer a particular vision of the socialist future. The most dramatic example was the seven late-Stalinist skyscrapers (*vysotki*) that were built in Moscow from 1947. Perhaps the most distinctive was the main building of Moscow State University, a massive academic complex in the Lenin Hills whose construction was decreed in 1948. The chief architect, Lev Rudnev, put together a futuristic design that combined a thrusting central tower with elegant wings, or 'zones', studded with smaller towers, socialist sculptures of students and books, and large, metallic clocks. By April 1950, builders had got as far as the sixteenth floor from where Rudnev could gauge their progress and look down upon the city. The historian Katherine Zubovich describes the sky-high view of the metropolis that unfurled before him, including older barracks for workers and the rough-and-tumble of part-completed postwar reconstruction projects.[18] Not only was the new main building of Moscow State University, and the other grandiloquent skyscrapers, a sign, by contrast, of the future, it would also remain so: with its Gotham City strangeness and technological self-consciousness, it still looked like the revolutionary future in the 1970s.

Soviet time, then, had more than one mode – past, present, future – each of which was revolutionary in its own way and emerged at particular moments. Even while they were still taking place, the February and October revolutions were instantly historicized. Participants felt themselves to be taking part in a sequence of historic moments. And from the start, these moments were deliberately re-created and re-enacted, for example in the mass-participation crowd scenes of Eisenstein's movies. In the 1970s, this process of re-enactment continued: not in the sense of dressing-up, but in the sense of a constant cultural replication and reimagining of events that had taken place almost six decades before. The anniversaries were constant. On 13 July 1973, Mikhail Suslov gave a speech at a meeting to mark the seventieth anniversary of the Second Congress of the RSDLP. A tiny political sideshow at the time, featuring émigré revolutionaries to whom very few people back home were listening, this was actually the historic gathering at which the party split and the Bolsheviks and Mensheviks were formed. The 1973 event showed that the historical congress continued to exist in the imagination of the Soviet present; Suslov argued that it would continue to shape the future.[19] The connecting point was Lenin. 'Lenin lived, Lenin lives, Lenin will live' was a universally known slogan of the time. At a major event in the Kremlin Palace of Congresses on 22 April 1970 to mark the centenary of Lenin's birth, Aleksei Kosygin, head of government, described Leninism as a form of teaching that was everlastingly organic: 'creative, developing, always alive'. 'The life-affirming strength of Leninist doctrine is manifested in its orientation towards the future, its calling forwards, arming the people with an historical perspective,' he went on. 'All our life, our present and future, is bathed in the light of Leninist ideas. And precisely because of this, the image of Lenin and his ideas is immortal.'[20] Yet another anniversary took place on 18 January 1974: the fiftieth anniversary of Lenin's death. Mikhail Suslov was a star turn that day at a conference on theoretical matters at the Hall of Columns, where Lenin and Stalin had both lain in state. He argued that Lenin's 'theory and practice are eternal'.[21] Such invoking of Lenin as the consistent ideological focus perhaps made for a more stable sense of historical time,[22] but in yet another paradox that strengthened Soviet civilization, developed socialism meant that stability and revolution were indistinguishable.

Two months before the 1973 anniversary conference, the French photographer Henri Cartier-Bresson made a trip to the Soviet Union. He photographed Palace Square in Leningrad while it was decorated for the celebrations and parades of early May. A famous image showed a vast, building-size cut-out of Lenin, which seemed to be walking out of the wall and striding in pursuit of a man and his child, tiny by comparison with Lenin. Oblivious, they were walking quietly towards the camera. There was no getting away from the Leninist past.

Or the past more generally. Culture-makers nurtured an interest in the past.[23] This could be lyrical and non-specific – an interplay of light, fabric, words and landscape – in, for example, the director Andrei Kochalovsky's 1969 film of Turgenev's *Nest of the Gentry* and his brother Nikita Mikhailkov's version of *Oblomov* ten years later. It could be about identity and place, in cities and rural landscapes. From 1965 onwards, the All-Russian Society for the Preservation of Historical Monuments and Culture (VOOPIiK) was a loosely civil-society-equivalent pressure group inside the Russian republic whose campaigns reflected the historical interests of 'ordinary' people and a concern for the historical integrity of their environment.

Immersing oneself in the past was also a scholarly and literary activity. Historians such as Evgenia Gutnova spent whole careers, beginning in the resolutely future-focused 1930s and continuing through the multiple time zones of the 1970s and 1980s, reconstructing the medieval world while coming to terms with their own Terror-wrecked family histories.[24] Marxism was an essential methodological element, but the subject matter – in Gutnova's case, England in the middle ages – was primarily of interest for the sense of the past it evoked. Others, such as Pyotr Zaionchkovsky, wrote as critically and carefully as they could about the nineteenth-century hinterland of the Russian Revolution. They were joined by Yuri Trifonov, whose precise, evocative and carefully researched novel about the revolutionary-terrorist People's Will movement, *Impatience*, was published in 1973. Trifonov's self-conscious fascination with the process of historical research, and its relationship to literary presentation and a person's sense of historical time in the present day, ran through *Fireglow*, his book about the revolutionary experiences and tragic fate of his father (published in 1966), and his novel about a woman's grief for the loss of her middle-aged historian husband, *The Long Goodbye*. This book, which ranged back and forth in time and partly concerned a need to put the record straight, was set in contemporary Moscow and published in 1973. Meanwhile, scrupulous biographies of recent historical figures turned into a publishing phenomenon in the 1970s.[25]

Dissidents also needed to get the past right. Trifonov wrote about the past with sincerity but in a way that could be published. Dissident historians like Aleksandr Nekrich and Roi Medvedev were focused on revealing the factual 'truth' about the Soviet Union's own history of terror, war and deportations. They wrote for samizdat. Aleksandr Solzhenitsyn was engaged in the same enterprise, but with a literary sensibility rather than a historian's technique.[26]

By the 1970s, everyone – 'ordinary' people, literary writers, historians, officials, dissidents, even architects – was increasingly interested in one particular historical event: the Great Fatherland War. The decade began with Andrei Smirnov's classic film, *Belorussky Station*, in which four members of a military unit, now pursuing quite different walks of life, meet again, more than two decades on. In the emotional climax of the film, they visit the nurse who served alongside them. She takes her guitar and they sing their old verse together (in words written by Bulat Okudzhava), beginning softly – 'Here the birds are not singing / And the trees have stopped growing'[27] – before reaching lyrical heights of nostalgia and togetherness. There was not a dry eye in the house.

The process of memory management was not tightly controlled; it could not be, since these were raw memories, and veterans were not only ubiquitous and relatively young, they also had a powerful, semi-autonomous association to represent them. The construction of memorials was chaotic and took decades. In Moscow, the memorial complex at Victory Park was not even finished when the Soviet Union collapsed, though the understated eternal flame and stars for hero cities that were fashioned into the space beneath the Kremlin walls was an evocative site of remembrance. But it was not enough for some. 'Thanks to the creation of memorial complexes . . . (Volgograd, Novorossiisk, Kyiv, etc.), the great feat of the people materializes in the memory of generations,' wrote one resident of Kostroma to Brezhnev in October 1982. 'But in this memorial chain the central link is missing.'[28] He meant Moscow. 'Conservative' networks in the publishing and security establishments, for instance associated with the *Molodaia gvardia* literary journal, tried to reconfigure the Soviet victory in narrowly Russocentric terms. They were only inconsistently influential.[29] Local 'pathfinders' searched out and preserved memorial sites for the sake of local identities; they were organized activists, but they were not controlled by Party or government.[30]

At the same time, there were officially endorsed *decentralizations* of memory production (one more of Soviet civilization's sustaining paradoxes). The novelist Daniil Granin and Belarusian journalist Ales Adamovich collaborated during the 1970s on an oral history of the siege of Leningrad in which they gathered testimony from more than 200 survivors and published it in an influential and admired book.[31] It was a sincere project, the result of Granin and Adamovich visiting the homes of those who gave testimony, then writing up their words in the form of a documentary account, and investing the whole presentation with their own literary worldview. Such a project could not be managed by an imposed agenda. A few years later, Adamovich co-wrote the screenplay for the Belarusian film *Come and See*, a violent and terrifying account of childhood during the war, in which nightmares and reality bleed into each other, creating real events of unimaginable savagery on the screen. 'It's not easy to watch this film,' wrote the *Cinema Art* reviewer in 1985, shortly after it was released, praising its 'open' and 'uncompromising' qualities, and its capacity to present 'the most bitter truth'.[32]

The illusion of eternity reflected across the countryside. Here the landscape stretched to the horizon in the way it had always done and the urban visitor had the impression that time moved much more slowly than in the cities. Yet the revolution had wrought full-scale, fast-paced destruction and created the Soviet village precisely by upending time. This process continued as Soviet managers sought to tame new corners of nature. By the 1970s, socialist progress in the countryside was predicated on the assumptions of ongoing and unyielding – even merciless – modernization.

By the Brezhnev era, the countryside seemed to be leaking people unstoppably. People felt that they were living through the end of an era. Mobility was a central experience in Soviet life from start to end. It defined the lives of Civil War refugees, migrants rushing to Stalin's industrializing cities, deported populations and evacuated civilians fleeing the Nazi invasion. Migration was always an anxious process in which two different electric charges were brought into proximity, government control and personal autonomy; very often what resulted was an official willingness to look the other way in millions of individual cases precisely in order to achieve the Party's overall goals.[33]

Officially speaking, the process of movement was modulated by residence laws and identity papers. One scholar describes the Soviet Union as 'the passport society', referring to the 'internal passport' which since 1932 had been necessary for all official transactions and contained the residence stamp, or *propiska*. This listed one's address: the place where one was supposed to live.[34]

Yet while these identity papers were essential to the surveillance society and the police state, they also contributed to a sense of citizenship, right and even pride.[35] People took 'ownership' of the document because without it they could not navigate any major or minor changes in their relationship with agencies of the state. It did not exactly stand in the way of the relative freedom of movement that existed in the USSR: it was checked and stamped when its carrier changed jobs or address, moved to a new town or republic, or went on a trip and stayed in a hotel. Farm workers celebrated when they were brought fully into the internal passport system in 1974.

In the 1974 film *Hello Doctor*, the chairman of a collective farm makes a toast. 'Let our children not forget the land of their fathers,' he says, 'and let there be more celebrations in our homes like the one we're having today.' It is a poignant moment. His own son has made his home in the city and rarely comes back to the ancestral village. The 'land' of the toast is the Russian *zemlya*, which means 'earth', with all the literal and figurative connotations of 'the soil'. The film is cast in the light of a desperate optimism and implausible realism. Many of the village houses are new, two-storey, detached buildings, painted white, with deep-set balconies, large windows and flat roofs. It looked like a feature in the journal *Arkhitektura SSSR*. Plenty of young people remain in the village; the balance between the generations looks normal, the community somehow natural and safe, if self-consciously so. The local doctor is kindly and Chekhovian; the *kolkhoz* chairman wears a smart suit. In fact the premise of the film is that migration from city to countryside is quite possible. The main character is a friend of the *kolkhoz* chairman's son, a high-flying city doctor who opts to spend some down time in the countryside before accepting that his destiny consists in making the move permanent. He persuades the chairman to have a necessary operation; he finds his own natural way of talking to all the local people. His character embodies the ideal that city and countryside were two naturally connected halves of the same civilization.

The fact was that the countryside was in trouble. Valentin Rasputin wrote elegies not just to a disappearing Siberian civilization, but also to a fading rural world. He began his major novel of 1976, *Farewell to Matyora*, with one of the most evocative opening sentences in Soviet literature. 'Once more spring had come,' Rasputin wrote, 'one more in the never-ending cycle, but for Matyora this spring would be the last, the last for both the island and the village that bore the same name.' The island was due to be artificially flooded, so it would disappear below the surface of the Angara River. Soviet modernization was responsible. The Bratsk hydroelectric plant, with its massive dam, was upstream. Its construction necessitated rising water levels in other parts of the river. Lenin had claimed in 1920 that communism was equivalent to Soviet power plus 'the electrification of the whole country'. Fifty years later, the authorities were still following up on his agenda. Yet ordinary people hit back. In *Farewell to Matyora*, some old peasants choose to defy the authorities as the artificial flooding caused by the hydroelectric plant gets under way. They opt to become one with their island and river, and with the remains of their ancestors, rather than to resettle in urban high rises. In real life, others organized peacefully and in limited ways against such developments. Rasputin himself was involved in the opposition to the proposed cellulose plant at Lake Baikal. In both fiction and real life, the 'dissent' was a natural part of Marxism-Leninism. People found an alternative voice because the post-Stalin system accommodated a certain discordance, and even relied on the dialectics of a very limited pluralism beneath the surface of official unanimity. Rasputin's book was published and turned into a film, and he remained one of the country's grandest authors. The opposition to the cellulose plant at Baikal was in effect planned by an officially permitted interest group, which spoke out in print and at Party meetings, though ultimately to no avail.

The Soviet countryside was also under threat because of the government's full-steam-ahead extraction of fossil fuels. In 1976, the total depth of oil and gas drilling in the Soviet Union exceeded fifteen million metres for the first time. It had more than doubled again by 1983.[36] Soviet observers claimed that boreholes had never been drilled faster than they were in the Tyumen oil field. They claimed too that productivity was escalating: that between 1973 and 1976 the number of workers per brigade fell from 363 to 214. They could complete the same amount of work, constructing roads to drilling sites, installing equipment and undertaking the range of geophysical operations. For *Pravda*, this was a kind of miracle, and socialism was responsible.[37] The real miracle was the foreign currency it generated. Planners used the petrodollars to buy foreign grain.[38]

On 30 April 1976, Brezhnev went to the massive Likhachev car plant in Moscow to award the working collective there the Order of the October Revolution. The Party's aim, he said, was to generate policies which offered 'the best life for Soviet people'. 'People' (*narod*) was not just an abstract whole-union collectivity; it was, Brezhnev said in gendered terms to his audience of car workers, 'you, your wives and children, and veterans of labour who have already retired to their deserved leisure'.[39] The 'new person' was central to the theories of developed socialism. He or she possessed individually human qualities, the best of which, Brezhnev maintained at the Twenty-fifth Party Congress in February 1976, were 'being principled and honest, and having depth of feeling', but for Brezhnev these characteristics owed a great deal to the revolution and the care of the Party.[40] It was twenty years, almost to the very day, since Khrushchev had delivered the Secret Speech elsewhere in the Kremlin. Brezhnev did not acknowledge his debts to Khrushchev. He did not mention the Thaw's emphasis on the significance of individual personhood. But the lineage of his arguments was obvious, and anyone, if they wanted, could see their connection to the rights that had taken limited but concrete form in the USSR over the last twenty years.

The Twenty-fifth Congress took place six months after Brezhnev had signed the Helsinki Accords. It was a short leap from claims about the status of the Soviet person to arguments about human rights – at least in theory.

Even so, commentators and then historians made the argument that 'rights talk' in the Soviet Union must have been imported from outside, especially via the Helsinki Accords, and that this infectious discourse might even have destabilized the USSR and contributed to its collapse sixteen years later. The agreements at Helsinki were predicated on the assumption that international and domestic 'legitimacy' were determined by a common set of principles that countries on either side of the Iron Curtain could sign up to. After more than two years of negotiations in the Conference on Security and Cooperation in Europe, the thirty-five parties agreed on the Final Act. It consisted of three 'baskets'. The first, on international security, formalized the borders between states in Europe. This was the overdue peace settlement that was never signed in the 1940s, because it effectively approved the postwar borders of the Soviet Union. But the Accords also referred to self-determination as a principle. This was a double-edged message for a Kremlin that had sent tanks to Prague seven years earlier and whose policy for the Warsaw Pact was driven by the so-called 'Brezhnev Doctrine', that no socialist state could leave the Bloc.

The second basket defined economic and cultural connections between the signatories: not just trade, but also professional exchanges and cultural delegations. This web of ties across the Iron Curtain had grown ever thicker since Stalin's death. In that sense the Accords described a pre-existing situation that had already come about thanks to numerous bilateral agreements between the Soviet Union and other states. The Accords made a headline and a virtue out of this reality, added legitimacy to the process, and assumed that the USSR was a constant partner in international exchanges. Yet this was not enough to convince the Americans to grant their 'Most Favoured Nation' trading partnership to the USSR; cross-Curtain connections had their limits, and the Soviet Union did not determine them on their own terms. The third basket made statements about human rights, humanitarian aid and the reuniting of families divided by border controls: things which were superficially inimical to the socialist dictatorships.

Why did the Soviet Union sign up to the third element in this deal? From one perspective, the Accords look like a trade-off between baskets. Perhaps, if the Soviet negotiators wanted above all to secure international recognition of their borders, they were willing to make statements that they did not mean about human rights. But the concept of sovereignty that defined international borders was informed by assumptions about the rights of individual citizens, for example to cross those borders. One reading of the Accords, therefore, is that they represented, overall, an interpretation of rights and sovereignty that had much more in common with Western European and North American values than with those of the Soviet Union and its satellites.[41] As a result of the Accords, the argument goes, a discourse of human rights and democratic sovereignties entered the Soviet space. One vector was the dissidents, and in particular the Helsinki Watch movement that was inspired by the Accords; another was Mikhail Gorbachev himself, who learned to talk the language of human rights and to put it on show in his conversations with President Bush.[42] It might even have been the case, goes the maximal version of the argument, that Helsinki contributed to and even caused the end of the Cold War and the collapse of the Soviet Union.[43]

If this is true, 1975 really was a turning point in the history of the Soviet Union. But 'rights talk' had flowed through Soviet discourse for decades before 1975. Even though their use was often cynical, the words themselves and the concepts they described were familiar. By the time of Helsinki, Soviet dissidents had already been framing their critique of the Soviet authorities in the same way for ten years: by appealing to the government to observe its own laws and to respect the rights that people legally and constitutionally possessed.[44] This was a version of dissent that was not invented in the West but in the USSR. And a limited version of rights had governed some aspects of Soviet life for the last twenty years – rights to social welfare, for example, and even a sense among many of a restored right to an inviolable home – providing Soviet citizens with a new, post-Stalin benchmark for interpreting rights and, by implication, sovereignty.

What was more, by the time that the Helsinki Accords were finalized, preparations for the new Soviet Constitution were also underway. It was already forty years since the introduction of the Constitution of 1936. Ideologues argued that the constitution of the USSR needed to be updated. Brezhnev himself launched a draft of the proposed constitution at the Plenum of the Party's Central Committee that began on 24 May 1977. The document was inevitably complex and wide-ranging, a mix of useful constitutional jurisprudence and artful socialist realist legalism. At the heart of the country's new constitution was a recognizable regime of rights. These rights were supposed in theory to be wide-ranging and secure. At the May Plenum, it was social and economic rights that were given centre stage, but so-called 'civil rights and freedoms' were also mentioned. Plainly the latter – if they were to have the merest iota of plausibility – needed substantially more interpretation and explanation than official speeches at a Party Plenum were able to provide. Meanwhile, another kind of relationship was also described: not just what the state owed to the people, but also the duties of citizens to the state and to the people as a whole.[45]

The Plenum launched a four-month cycle of public meetings, often at workplaces, in which the draft constitution was discussed by, they claimed, 140 million people. Employees who were Party members or trade union activists – or who were susceptible to the pull of semi-compulsory voluntarism – asked questions about particular clauses of the proposed document and also raised gripes that were only tangentially connected to the main matter under discussion. Newspapers presented these meetings in a ritualistic way that belied their variety.[46] The process came to an end when the Supreme Soviet voted in favour of accepting the new constitution on 7 October.

The eternity of developed socialism might also be a form of hell. Another vision of changeless time was of being trapped in a waking nightmare. In 1967, the poet-dissident Natalya Gorbanevskaya asked her readers about the meaning of 'forever'. Her alarm clock, next to her head, was not like the one in Kataev's socialist realist *Time Forward!* that we encountered earlier in this chapter; it 'wakes me – this time forever – / for eternity, for new everlasting pains'.[47]

Gorbanevskaya highlighted a debilitating, tormenting paradox: the waking nightmare. Soviet paradoxes were multiple and apparently sustainable. They had a life of their own, one that might threaten the system's logic, but not its viability. Ordinary folk possessed brains sufficiently capacious to accommodate divergent thoughts. 'Unlike philosophers,' writes a historian of Britain after 1945, 'most people happily live with contradictions.'[48] And so the Soviet Union was a dictatorship of 'rights'. Eternity was transient. Paradise was faded. And this was an empire at war with imperialism.

Cotton farming, Uzbekistan

# 14
# Hammer and Sickle as Far as the Eye Can See

Natalya Gorbanevskaya had one sense of eternity; Aleksei Leonov had another. Although he was not related to the great actor Yevgeny Leonov, with whom he shared a surname, Aleksei was no stranger to the satisfactions of creativity: he was an accomplished artist and in his youth had wondered if he could make a career out of his talent. But in the 1970s he was famous for a different reason. The eternity he briefly stepped into was not the timelessness of art, but the universe itself. Leonov was one of the best-known and most charismatic of the cosmonauts who came after Gagarin. He had once shared a room with Cosmonaut Number 1. They were contemporaries, born within ten weeks of each other in 1934. The two men shared childhood experiences of poverty as well as the push of youthful ambition. They were both talent-spotted during service in the air force and entered the space programme as very young men. Gagarin was the first person to fly in space; Leonov was the first human being to walk outside in the cosmos. On 18 March 1965, he exited from Voskhod-2 while three other crew remained on board. Leonov stayed out there, in open space, for twelve minutes and nine seconds. He called it 'free gliding and floating'. The exit into space and re-entry into the spacecraft required Leonov to spend an additional twenty-three minutes and forty-one seconds outside the main cabin in the same deep vacuum that existed in the open cosmos.[1]

It was a triumph of technical skill, professional competence and personal courage. Leonov was exposed to the most unpredictable conditions and extreme physical and psychological strain. He could only accomplish his mission thanks to the ingenuity of scientists and his colleagues' nerveless mastery of technology. Exposed in the heavens, the Soviet Union was on display. Walking in space, where time conformed to different rules, Leonov exemplified the unshakability of Soviet power. The Soviet Union was there for the long haul. As the great socialist multinational federation, it had superseded capitalist empires, with their in-built obsolescence.

Leonov's experiences surpassed Soviet borders, not only literally, in that they took place in the cosmos, but also in a general professional sense: he belonged to the very tiny group of space travellers, and their status transcended nationality. Some of them were Soviet; some of them were American. They occupied the stratosphere, a place of alpha achievement and convinced careerism without state boundaries. (In 1967, the United States and Soviet Union had both signed up to a UN charter that declared space to be demilitarized.) Leonov had characteristics that all the spacemen shared, regardless of nationality, and recognized in each other. One was a performative, conformist masculinity. All the American astronauts who went to space in the 1970s were men; the first woman was in 1983. Although the Soviet Union announced a new cadre of female cosmonauts in 1978, there was a gap between Valentina Tereshkova, whose mission was in 1963, and Svetlana Savitskaya, who went to space in 1982. Leonov was a man's man whose identity was shaped by masculine pride in the prestigious institutions within which he excelled. He was an individualist, in the sense that he was driven to fulfil a unique set of career achievements. Like his peers in the USA, though, he could only personally succeed in tandem with the institutions he inhabited and by instinctively joining in and leading the group. Years later, when he no longer had to say it, Leonov wrote of the Komsomol in his memoirs: 'I am still proud today that I was a member of this organization, and that three times I was voted in as a member of its central committee.'[2] He might have been talking about an Ivy League university and its wrestling club.

No wonder that Leonov got on so well with his American colleagues. They were friends and rivals who understood each other better than most of their fellow countrymen understood them. Ten years after his space walk, he blasted off again (he had also been part of an aborted mission in 1971). Leonov and Valery Kubasov manned the Soyuz spacecraft that was launched in Baikonur on 15 July 1975. On the same day, at Cape Canaveral in Florida, the latest Apollo spacecraft also counted down to take-off. Three Americans were on board: Thomas Stafford, Vance Brand, and Donald Slayton. Two days after launch, the Apollo and Soyuz met in space and docked on. The crews mingled, communicated and worked together on both spacecraft, overseeing experiments and tests, and posing for TV audiences back home. Aleksei Leonov's closest American colleague was Thomas Stafford. At one point they worked together in the Soyuz while the other three were in the Apollo. The two men had a rapport which Leonov even characterized as 'tender'. As if to prove the fact that these elite spacemen had a mutual comprehension that transcended international boundaries, Stafford's wife told Leonov that he understood her husband better than she did. Later, as a mutual honour to which Leonov's daughter-in-law and Stafford's daughter mercifully did not object, Leonov's grandson was named Tomas and Stafford's was called Aleksi.[3]

The Apollo-Soyuz mission was one of the most spectacular results of détente, the warming in Soviet–American relations that took place during the 1970s. Ever since the death of Stalin, the dialogue between Washington and Moscow had moved generally towards peaceful coexistence, interrupted by explosive moments, worst of all the Cuban Missile Crisis in October 1962. Brezhnev had a cooler head. This made him responsive to Nixon and Kissinger, with their counter-intuitive strategy of making overtures to China and the USSR. Risk could be reduced and efficiencies made by negotiating for smaller nuclear arsenals. The 'Nixon to China' summit took place in February 1972. He then went to Moscow in May, where he and Brezhnev signed the Strategic Arms Limitation Treaty (SALT). This imposed limits on both sides' capacity to use intercontinental ballistic missiles. The treaty acknowledged an 'equality' between both sides based on 'a spirit of reciprocity, mutual accommodation and mutual benefit'. Neither side should therefore seek 'unilateral advantage at the expense of the other'.[4] Cooperation in space was a breathtaking accomplishment.[5] Engineers from both sides had already begun to meet in 1971, in Houston and Moscow, preparing the technical ground for the docking mission.

Of course, they had to overcome a long background of mutual hostility. Capitalist and socialist countries remained distinct from each other in almost all ways. Crossing the Iron Curtain was a major experience, taking a person to a very different place. And yet, the Iron Curtain was now a slightly less impenetrable barrier. It did not exactly go with the grain of détente when the chess grandmaster Bobby Fischer said in 1972 of his upcoming cycle of twenty-four games with Boris Spassky: 'It is really the free world against the lying, cheating hypocritical Russians.' By the end, though, open reporting about the match led to support and admiration for Fischer in the USSR and for Spassky in the USA.[6]

One of the densest and most repeated cross-Curtain transmissions was between the Soviet Union and Finland in the realm of technology exchange. By 1978, Finland exported more to the Soviet Union than to anywhere else, while Helsinki was Moscow's third-largest export market. This was the product of deep and repeated technical co-operation that began in the mid-1950s. It was institutionalized through close links between ministries, as well as between the Academy of Finland and the Soviet Academy of Sciences, which arranged meetings of technical experts. Nokia was a crucial point of contact. Finland's massive international conglomerate helped the USSR to import, for example, the electronics components that were essential for computing in the 1970s, sometimes from third parties such as the West German giant, Siemens.[7]

Soviet cities became very distinctive in the 1960s and 1970s, with their housing blocks, wide avenues and concrete-and-glass public buildings. This was partly because of the long and uninterrupted gaze of Soviet architects and engineers beyond their borders, as delegations travelled to the West, and their counterparts came to the USSR, and major international conferences were held in Moscow and Leningrad.[8] The socialist city, with its display of statues, slogans and posters, and the assumptions about equality and welfare that drove the design of its open spaces and institutions, was partly constructed in the form of a conversation with socialist-inspired architects in cities as distant as Lagos, Accra and Baghdad.[9] Meanwhile, Soviet actuaries compared notes with Italian experts on social insurance in the meetings of the International Social Security Association (ISSA), and American and Soviet delegations of doctors repeatedly travelled to each other's hospitals. Certain groups of Soviet academics – even an extremely select number of historians, though they were carefully vetted by the KGB – got the chance to spend time in American universities.[10]

In some of the same universities, a school of American social scientists posited the theory of a universal modernization process. The idea was that most countries, capitalist or not, shared certain features of development. Scholars who analysed an apparent social convergence between the Soviet Union and the United States used these cross-Curtain encounters as evidence for their hypothesis.[11]

The long gaze to the West gave many Soviet professionals and cultural figures a deep if narrow and inconsistent understanding of the outside world. Both the USSR and USA had the range of modern institutions. They shared many modern technologies and basic experiences of modern life. And both countries were progressive, focused on the future. Paradoxically, both countries had a sense of their own exceptionalism. Their messianic destiny manifested itself in the imperial development of their hinterlands. By the 1970s, both countries were anti-empires that looked suspiciously like empires, spreading their message as far as the eye could see, and much further, even into space.

That issue of whether or not the Soviet Union was an empire – or, better, in what ways it was an empire – was a matter of life and death for Soviet civilization. Debating the empire question blew life into the theoretical body of the new Soviet Union in 1922. Sixty-nine years later, the fragmentation of the 'empire' into constituent nations was the way that the Soviet Union collapsed, though perhaps not the reason why it did so.

The USSR was the anti-imperialist successor state of the Russian empire. It still took up approximately one-sixth of the earth's land surface. This fraction was often repeated in newspapers and books and added to the country's mystery and prestige.[12] The long river-based border with China, Mongolia and North Korea was just one example of the seemingly unlimited geographical and human diversity that the Soviet Union contained. This border, running along the Argun, Amur and Ussuri rivers – an immense space, but, even so, not one of the great river systems of the USSR – was also just one more border zone of troubling geopolitical complexity that the Soviet

Union had to manage. Its Asian neighbours were also closed communist societies, yet the relationship with China in particular was a high-risk one, based on imperial tensions rather than ideological sympathies. On 2 March 1969, Chinese troops on the border attacked a detachment of their Soviet counterparts on Damansky Island in the Ussuri River. The flashpoint extended into repeated small battles over the next months, which only ended with a meeting between Aleksei Kosygin and Zhou Enlai in September.[13]

Such geopolitical considerations – defending extremely long borders, projecting power into the 'near abroad' – looked imperial. The RSFSR was much the largest republic, and Russians were the biggest ethnic group. In time the Russian language became increasingly dominant in the USSR. This affected certain all-union institutions, not least the army. By the postwar period, the USSR was made up of fifteen union republics. Opponents of the USSR in the Baltic republics and west Ukraine described the system as an empire from which they sought national independence; elsewhere, for instance in Armenia, local people talked more inchoately about 'the Russians' when they wanted to express disaffection with the centre. Moscow was the capital of the Soviet Union and the Russian republic. It had the look and feel of an imperial centre with its grand socialist architecture, relatively high standard of living, cultural critical mass and large, diverse population. St Petersburg had been the capital of the Russian empire for 200 years before the revolution, but the Kremlin and Red Square conjured up pretensions of an older metropole. The conversion of the east Slavs to Orthodoxy had made Moscow into the 'third Rome' of Christendom, while the Bolshevik revolution, by turning Moscow into the centre of world revolutionary socialism, led to the label of the 'fourth Rome'.[14]

This was a good example of how a set of imperial symbols and mentalities seemed to survive the great break of 1917, but in reality were constituted on completely new ground as an element in Soviet civilization. In one way or another from the start, and distinctively so in the Brezhnev era, an imperial worldview was encoded into some of the political and administrative structures of the USSR. This did not mean that there was an obvious historical line between the old Russian empire and the Soviet Union; in some ways, just the reverse, because of the depth of the historical rupture that accompanied the Bolshevik revolution. Instead, imperial mechanisms and mentalities of one kind or another were re-created at different times after 1917, sometimes changing shape, sometimes vanishing and then reappearing, as the method for governing an extremely large and diverse territory in the absence of democratic elections and representative government that could properly be held to account. Some of the appalling, endemic violence deployed by Stalin, and the much more sporadic political violence that occurred after 1953, had an imperial dimension.

Brezhnev sought a rapprochement or narrowing of gaps (*sblizhenie*) between national groups; he seemed to step back from Khrushchev's dream of an ultimate post-national unity (*sliianie*). But the structures of Soviet rule centralized power in Moscow and were predicated on the assumption that a central authority was exercising control over a periphery. This control could not be questioned; it was in certain ways repressive; and it was at the very least based on a clearly understood hierarchy. For instance, in every republic in the 1970s, the Party's first secretary was a member of the titular nationality: an Armenian in Armenia or a Kazakh in Kazakhstan. But the power behind this throne was very often invested in the second secretary, who was always either Russian or Ukrainian and was appointed directly from Moscow. This was a tacitly accepted way of governing rather than a formal set of rules. These second secretaries were serious functionaries, often with industrial and then Party experience. They typically spent five years in their appointment, sometimes significantly longer; they developed a level of expertise related to local republican affairs before their arrival and had plenty of time to develop this further once they were in post. Sometimes they exercised a proconsular sensibility, for instance acting as the arbiter in policy and personnel conflicts in the republican apparat, before returning to a promotion back in Moscow.[15]

Party bosses continued to use the language of 'friendship' and 'fraternity' to describe the connections between the republics. There was a self-referential quality to this, as if it became true when one said it. On 28 November 1973, the Lithuanian republic was awarded the Order of Friendship of Peoples. According to Mikhail Suslov, the award recognized 'friendship between peoples, which is dear to the heart of every Soviet person'.¹⁶ Even on a good day, such sentiments sounded disingenuous when it came to the Baltic republics. But the situation in other parts of the union was more complex. In the mid-1970s, the authorities promoted the display of national motifs in the public cultures of the titular nationalities of the union republics and autonomous republics, as well as among smaller ethnic minorities, though not in cases where this risked political controversy.

It was a short step from taming minority nationhood to appropriating it. Cuisine was an accessible and enjoyable vector for the transmission of national experiences. More national-themed restaurants and deli-style food shops opened. There were crazes for national cookbooks. Karim Makhmudov wrote many such books. *Uzbek Dishes* was his most successful; it was published in 1958 and republished a further five times through to 1982. Other similar books enjoyed increasingly large print runs, often in the hundreds of thousands, in the long 1970s.¹⁷ In this way, elements of Central Asian cuisine found their way onto Russian dining tables in Leningrad or Belorusian kitchens in Minsk.

Elements of empire were present in even these apparently harmless transactions. They bolstered ties between peoples and spread knowledge and experience among Soviet nations, but they did so on the terms of the imperial centre and exoticized the periphery. But the Soviet Union was not a typical empire. It was an empire that acted as a multinational socialist metropole, rather than the protector of a nationally Russian core.¹⁸ The centre was cosmopolitan, even if Russians had ultimate control over it in the decades after Stalin. People from different nationalities were very visible in Moscow in all areas of all-union accomplishment – from politics to TV, from science to literature. Russians themselves lacked some of the institutions of other republics and were poorer than people in the Baltic republics. Lines of equality tended to cross republican borders. The Russian republic was a geographically and demographically awkward zone; it was massive, but in some ways it was a weak imperial centre. The RSFSR was much less clearly defined than, say, the Georgian republic, which was much more recognizably 'Georgia' than the RSFSR was 'Russia', a place that had never existed as the territorial embodiment of a nation. In Yuri Slezkine's well-known formulation, the Soviet Union was like a communal apartment in which each of the other republics had its own room but 'Russia' controlled all the common areas, a zone which was not cohesive but brought great power with it.[19]

As Geoffrey Hosking has argued, Russians were both 'rulers' and 'victims' in the Soviet Union.[20] At the top, the balance tilted towards Russians-as-rulers in the 1970s much more than before. Between 1971 and 1982, eight men were promoted to become full members of the Politburo. Seven of them were Russian, and one was Ukrainian.[21] This directly contrasted with the 1920s and 1930s, when the Politburo, headed by the Georgian Stalin, was much more diverse, and nationalities policy incalculably more violent. (Six of the twelve full members of the Politburo elected in 1934 were Russian, as were four of the nine more junior 'candidate' members.) For a time, the Central Committee's Department of Propaganda, which Suslov headed, had corners that were nostalgic for the Stalin period. Especially in the department's RSFSR section, Russian national-sympathizers, who were generally antisemites, held some influential positions. Their impact waxed and waned: mostly removed during 1973 and 1974, they enjoyed a revival in 1976.[22] During the 1970s, aspects of cultural Russianness that had been previously marginalized from public culture were given freer rein. The Russian rural folk and their way of life were treated with new respect by village prose writers; landscape and its protection were fought over by environmental campaigners whose civil-society-type organizations were permitted; it became respectable for ambitious people to show an interest in Russian history and heritage in specific ways, for instance in antiques, even icons, and the discoveries of local historians (practitioners of *kraevedenie*). It seemed that both of the historic elements of Russian nationhood – those defined by the adjective *rossiisky*, which refers to anything associated with the Russian state, and *russky*, which describes ethnic, cultural and linguistic Russian things – were enjoying a revival.[23]

At its clumsiest, this revival in Russian nationhood promoted an unhistorical and patronizing attitude to the Ukrainian and Belarusian republics, according to which Russian nationhood seemed mainly to consist of unresolved complexes about its east Slavic neighbours.[24] Yet Ukraine and Russia coexisted in many Soviet families. Khrushchev and Brezhnev were ethnic Russians who were substantially from

Ukraine; Gorbachev's mother was Ukrainian, and his wife, with two Ukrainian parents, was brought up in Siberia. In the long 1970s, the most common way for members of all nationalities to interpret their national identity was from within the Soviet frame of reference. Other national groups in other republics grew in consciousness during the 1970s. In Georgia, where the titular nationality had a very long history and an especially distinctive language and culture, around sixty films were produced per year during the Brezhnev era. Facilitated by central planners in Moscow, the Georgian film industry fostered Georgian national identity while being a source of interest and entertainment across the USSR as a whole.[25]

Moscow's relationship with the other countries of the Warsaw Pact – Poland, East Germany, Czechoslovakia, Hungary, Bulgaria, Romania – was at once more imperial and more permissive than its connection to the republics of the USSR. As the superpower in the Eastern bloc, the Soviet Union was alliance leader and economic linchpin. But if America ran a loose 'empire by invitation' in NATO, the Soviet Union dictated to a bloc of satellites which had not chosen their compulsory orbit and were not allowed to divert from it. Even though the term 'satellite' has fallen out of favour among historians, who tend to emphasize the unique features, capacity for agency and national integrity of each of those countries, none of these concepts is inconsistent with the imperial politics of the region. Yet the new empire in Central and Eastern Europe was not pre-programmed into Soviet civilization. 'The Eastern bloc' came about because of the international circumstances of the early Cold War and the devastating opportunism of the Nazi–Soviet pact. It was the pact's secret clauses – not the revolution – that were the original sin of Soviet empire in the region.

Yet in the 1970s, almost no Soviet people thought about that; they did not know about the secret clauses of the pact, and many of them had forgotten about the pact itself. Instead, they shared in the proliferating popular interest in metropolitan Soviet eateries that specialized in Bulgarian, German, Polish, Romanian or Hungarian cooking, or Czech coffee and cakes, as an opportunity to experience the 'near abroad'.[26] More and more people had the chance to go there – on visits to Dresden and Berlin, or Prague and Karlovy Vary, or Budapest and Lake Balaton. Especially enticing was the prospect of visiting the department stores of Yugoslavia, not a member of the Warsaw Pact, but the socialist country that was most open to the West. In 1967, the passport laws were adjusted so that Soviet tourists did not need a foreign passport to travel to the Eastern bloc. The internal passport – a person's identity papers – were sufficient.

Meanwhile, the USSR received cultural imports from its partners in the developing world. Cuba, with its promise of exotica, exercised a particular hold on the Soviet imagination. Exchanges between Cuban and Soviet dance troupes created what one historian describes as 'spectacular embraces' between leading dancers from both sides. One high point was the production of the ballet *Carmen* in Moscow in 1967, which dripped with a sensual Cuban aesthetic. Ekaterina Furtseva, Moscow Party boss turned culturally insecure minister of culture, banned it after a single performance, until it was toned down and relaunched in 1969.[27] Furtseva was as usual speaking to her own anxieties, but the fascination that Cuba had in the eyes of Soviet people, tired in the middle of winter, derived not only from joy in Cuban culture, satisfaction in their revolution, and yearning for their sunshine, but also from racialized stereotypes about Cuban sexuality.[28]

The revolution still dominated the Soviet gaze on the wider world. In the 1970s, anti-imperialism was a revolutionary understanding of sovereignty that was paradoxically equivalent to the projection of Moscow's geopolitical interests. In July 1975, Mikhail Suslov, the country's ideology chief, described the range of liberation and anti-imperialist movements on which the Soviet Union was keeping an eye: the success of the Vietnamese communists, the development of 'anti-fascist revolution' in Portugal, the downfall of the Greek junta, leftist successes in France, Italy and Japan, mass strikes in the UK and the USA.[29] The KGB secretly funded a range of sympathizers, such as foreign communist parties, as well as partners of convenience, like the Irish Republican Army (IRA). This was global Realpolitik. But at a rhetorical level, it was the revolution in action.

During the 1970s and early 1980s, the KGB and GRU were notorious for their overseas operations, including in NATO countries. This was Soviet sovereignty writ large, the projection beyond borders of the global interests of the revolution and the needs of the international working class.³⁰ According to the KGB mentality, it was precisely this vision of sovereignty that was required to keep imperialism under control. 'Imperialism,' Andropov declared at the Central Committee's Plenum of April 1973, 'despite all its predatory nature, is forced to reckon with the growing defence and economic might of our country and of the whole socialist fraternity.'³¹

These were strange anti-imperial credentials. Not less tarnished was the USSR's claim to be the great anti-racist state.

No aspect of Soviet life was performed on a bigger stage than race: it stretched across the whole of the Soviet Union, incorporated a dazzlingly diverse cast, required people to assume complex multi-role identities, and even adopted global scenery with an even bigger company of actors in the 1960s and 1970s.

By the mid-1970s, students from sub-Saharan Africa had been coming to the USSR to complete degree programmes for fifteen years. Thousands were enrolled at any one time. They focused on scientific and technological subjects. Significant numbers stayed in the USSR thereafter, but the aim was to train specialists who would take their skills back to their country of origin and set about building a society that owed something to Soviet examples, and to deepen links between Moscow and sympathetic 'Third World' governments. But starting on 16 October 1975, Nigerians studying at Lviv's medical institute began a sit-in. Protests spread to Kyiv and included Black Africans from many countries. Students excoriated racist rumours, offensive slurs and inflexible bureaucracy. The protest was 'resolved' at the highest levels of republican government in Kyiv, with interventions from African embassies.³²

Soviet anti-racist rhetoric was underscored by the reality of racism. Convictions about racial equality were given their form by a set of racially charged assumptions: that the route to improvement for Black Africans led through the European model of Marxism-Leninism. (The same principles applied to race-based attitudes towards Soviet citizens such as Uzbeks and Tatars.) In 1975–6, when anti-racist protests took place in Lviv and Kyiv, there were 6,331 Black African students in the USSR; in 1979–80, the number had doubled.³³ While students came from dozens of countries (and not just in Africa, but from across Asia and the Eastern bloc, too), and studied alongside their Soviet peers at all kinds of institutions across the republics of the USSR, including the most prestigious, one was particularly associated with them. The foundation of Moscow's Peoples' Friendship University, soon named in honour of Patrice Lumumba, the assassinated Congolese revolutionary, was announced in February 1960. Opened to students that autumn, it began with a cohort of 597. They came from fifty-four countries. The institution was never closed off to Soviet students, who made up 10 per cent of the initial enrolment. Foreign students were given intensive instruction in the Russian language and the opportunity to take preparatory courses; in exchange, they did not have to take compulsory classes in Marxism-Leninism. Otherwise they faced exactly the same requirements as students at other institutions, but completed their studies in one fewer year, thanks to an exceptionally intensive programme of instruction.[34] Attempts to make 'Third World' students express gratitude for the international education programme they enjoyed, and especially the high stipends they received, only increased their vulnerability. In fact, differential financing in favour of African or Asian students, though designed with anti-racist intentions, might have reified racial identities and inadvertently inspired racism.[35]

This was empire as a development project.[36] Central Asia was the primary site of the USSR's internal 'Third World'-style development. Development was an inherently racialized process, implying progress by a non-white periphery towards the achievements of the white metropole. It was a much calmer process than such violent modern interventions as the Kazakh famine of the 1930s or the building of the Karaganda Gulag complex. In the 1950s Central Asian economies were developed more 'normally' with the aim of rationalizing agriculture, expanding industry and bringing ever more people to live in bigger cities, where they would abandon the remnants of the traditional way of life. In Uzbekistan, the capital city of Tashkent was redesigned in modern shape after the devastating earthquake of 1966. The design of the Tajik capital, Dushanbe – formerly known as Stalinabad – was unrecognizable in the 1980s when compared with its humble shape in the 1950s. Avenues were wide, green spaces were common, and the characteristics of Soviet urban form – squares surrounded by government buildings, microdistricts, palaces of culture and workers' clubs – were in place. The major development project in the Tajik republic was the Nurek dam. A new city was built in its shadow. Nurek was publicized as a centre of Soviet internationalism: foreign workers were invited there, including graduates from the Peoples' Friendship University, and so were other visitors from outside.[37]

Yet development policy was implemented flexibly, determining hierarchies as well as giving rise to many positive interracial relationships. Many Central Asians got on with their lives by ignoring those aspects of Soviet development that did not suit them. Large numbers remained in their villages or in small urban settlements. In the 1970s, the population of the region was growing much more quickly than in European Russia. Families were large. Extensive kinship networks were indispensable to the functioning of the informal and formal economies. Islam remained a powerful influence. Women wore the veil much more often than Soviet norms preferred. Modernization was partial. In 1980, for example, mechanical cotton harvesting in Tajikistan was at a peak, but still only accounted for 36 per cent of the total harvest. Policymakers aspired to bring more social services deeper into the provinces. The construction budget devoted to the Tajik countryside tripled between 1964 and 1967, but over the long run this investment seemed to encourage people to stay where they were.[38] Meanwhile, the vertical structures of Soviet power brought ethnic Russians into the republics, both as urban migrants and as senior officials; harmonious relations with local people often followed, with many marriages.

Even so, Soviet people could not avoid looking at the world as part of a racial hierarchy. Antisemitism was a complex and upsetting case. Even during the Stalin period, Jews occupied an ambivalent position. The phenomenally successful Jewish contribution to the revolution and to the building of revolutionary society gave way to a period of Terror, when many leading Jews were targeted.[39] It reached its awful peak with the Doctors' Plot. During the 1970s, informal limits on the admission of Jews to certain institutes of higher education, and roadblocks on their political ambitions, coexisted with the flourishing of Jewish talent across the professions and culture of the USSR.

For instance, de facto quotas limited Jewish numbers at the highly prestigious Mechanics and Mathematics Faculty of Moscow State University. They took their entrance exams in a separate room and were given extremely difficult problems to solve. Yet a significant number of Jewish students passed the test and entered the programme. Many of them went on to extremely successful careers.[40]

By the 1970s, mixed marriages were very common in the Soviet Union and had been for twenty years. The children of these biracial unions – Russian and Kazakh, say, or Ukrainian and Georgian, or the offspring of almost unlimited possible combinations – did not face any particular stigma. But they often struggled with an interior discomfort. At the age of sixteen, they were obliged to select a nationality on their internal passports. If their parents had retained different surnames, some children compromised by keeping, say, an Armenian surname while opting for Russian nationality.[41]

In the long Soviet 1970s, the number of migrants who came to Moscow and Leningrad from the Caucasus and Central Asia increased. Migrants imbibed the discourse of 'friendship of peoples', relied on it in fashioning their new lives, and accepted its terms in their relations with others. Racism was still potent. Despite appearances, people from the Caucasus were 'blacks'. Even members of the intelligentsia faced the micro-aggressions of superiority complexes and social exclusion. Market traders faced rougher language and sometimes violence (but not as much as African students). By the 1970s, assumptions that Caucasians were the mainstay of the second economy – comments abounded that the black market as a whole was coordinated inside the Aragvi, the biggest Georgian restaurant in the capital – racialized informal economic transactions to an improbable degree. But even though migrants might gather in temporary accommodation, socialize together and rely on ethnic networks, there were no race-based ghettos, and the structures of administration and welfare were open to all.[42]

Soviet diasporas extended the reach of the Hammer and Sickle. The socialist dictatorship was a closed society but, over seventy years, three main waves of emigration broke out from the deceased Russian empire and then the Soviet Union: following the Bolshevik seizure of power and during the Civil War; during the Second World War; and in the long 1970s.

Between 1971 and 1980, emigration took on a more textured quality than before. More than 300,000 people were permitted to leave. Most of them were Jewish. Some of them were denied exit visas or had to apply multiple times; they were the so-called refuseniks. Between 1968 and 1987, 270,000 Jews emigrated from the USSR, as much as one-eighth of the total Soviet Jewish population, with a peak of 51,000 Jewish emigrants in 1979. Two-thirds of the emigrating Jews went to live in Israel: all of them at the start of the 1970s, less than half at the end.[43] They flew out of Moscow to Vienna and then headed towards New York, in a journey of sometimes overwhelming sensory burdens, practical anxieties and poignancy. The next largest group were German; this generally meant that they were descendants of people from the German lands who had settled in the Volga region in the eighteenth century. Otherwise indistinguishable from their twentieth-century Russian neighbours, they had been made to pay for their German roots, which sometimes extended to their religious choices, when Stalin targeted and deported them. Now they were given the chance to resettle in West Germany. America was the destination of nearly all of the estimated 10,000 Armenians who formed the third nationality to emigrate in significant numbers in the 1970s.

Even these Armenians, who joined earlier generations of exiles from their Caucasian homeland in a substantial diaspora, and who were members of a small nation with a long history, a distinctive culture and a sociable ethic that valued networks deriving first of all from family ties, struggled to maintain a coherent sense of national identity in emigration. By the time the Soviet Union collapsed, nine out of ten Armenian-Americans had married outside the diaspora, and acquisition of the language among their children was very low. Although it was easier to maintain links with the 'old country' than it had been during the Stalin era, when it was almost impossible to do so, the connection between Armenians living in America and those in Armenia was nevertheless loosening. Yet there were still mobilizing and unifying themes that animated the Armenian diaspora internationally. Most important was memory of the Armenian genocide, committed by the Ottoman Turks in 1915–16. In 1975, a small nucleus of violent activists founded the Armenian Secret Army for the Liberation of Armenia. Others founded the Justice Commandos and the Armenian Revolutionary Party. In the furnace of 'Asia Minor', assassins successfully targeted Turkish government officials. In the United States, despite the tendency of assimilation, new attempts were made to create Armenian schools, to endow university chairs in Armenian studies and to raise the profile of Armenians in national affairs, even if the Armenian language itself sometimes lapsed, and the framework of organization owed its form more to American civic culture.[44]

Soviet diasporas also existed within the USSR itself. The mobility of national groups inside the USSR significantly shaped Soviet civilization through a familiar process of destruction and creation. The deportations of national minorities, for example the removal of the Chechens and Crimean Tatars from their historic homelands during the Second World War, were terrible crimes and caused unbearable suffering. But voluntary mobility led to creative dynamism and melting pots. According to official data, 14.9 per cent of marriages in 1979 were between citizens from different groups (as marked on 'paragraph 5' of their internal passport), say between a Ukrainian and a Kazakh. Many interpenetrations of ethnicity, language and family life followed in countless personal formulations of Sovietness.[45] Citizens in blended families had to decide whether their version of Soviet internationalism privileged the Russian language, which might not only be the family's lingua franca but also confer advantages in schooling and career for their offspring. Parents of mixed children might opt for an official identity of Russian or Ukrainian if their other nationality, such as Jewish or Crimean Tatar, could expose them to discrimination. Some cities, such as Baku or Moscow, were historically cosmopolitan. But people moved to all kinds of places across the USSR – Nurek in Tajikistan, say, or Akademgorodok near Novosibirsk – to take advantage of attractive jobs in development projects or appealing institutions. In the Kazakh republic, the titular ethnicity was always in a minority – still below 40 per cent in the 1980s – and families from very many Soviet nationalities made their homes there, with all kinds of mixed marriages resulting.

Ethnic mobility blended Soviet people, but it also transplanted national micro-communities, with their own languages, traditions and webs of personal connections, from outside their republic of origin to other parts of the USSR. The historian Erik Scott analyses 'internal diasporas' and argues that the Soviet Union was an 'empire of diasporas'. True, these communities had not crossed international borders, or found themselves lacking citizenship in a new land with an alien bureaucracy. Some nationalities, such as Ukrainians who lived in Russia, or Russians who lived in Ukraine, often scattered, assimilated, and less obviously formed diasporic communities. Other groups also had deep ties but were more distinctive. For example, Georgians dispersed into many parts of the USSR and played a major role in Moscow, including in Party administration, intellectual life, entertainment, cuisine, the underground economy, in fact in almost all areas of Soviet life. Stalin and Beria were Georgians, as were other leading politicians and secret policemen, but the Georgians' significance was so deep and widespread that Stalin was far from a decisive cause in their success. While they helped to shape whatever part of Soviet society they found themselves in, Georgians also identified with each other, not least through their language, which was incomprehensible to the uninitiated, folk tales, song, literature and Georgian Orthodox Christianity, which offered elements of a shared hinterland even in the era of atheism.

Georgians and other national minorities were both members of ethnic peripheries and influential elements in the imperial metropole. The Soviet empire was run not by a phalanx of Russians in the interests of Russians, but by Russians plus a congeries of diasporas in the interests of the Soviet Union. These interests were ideological, material and geopolitical, pushing forward a particular vision of socialism that ranged across communitarian welfare and technological development; it maximized economic advantages for a multi-ethnic elite in an economy of shortages; and it projected Soviet power into its geographical hinterlands and its zones of rivalry with the United States. None of these projects particularly favoured Russians. In fact, they created opportunities for and were executed by people from many Soviet nationalities. And Russians were also exploited by the empire, thanks to KGB surveillance and the 'internal colonization' by the Soviet empire of Russian territory, which demanded adherence to modernity – as in other countries – but also suppressed consumption and stifled dissent.[46]

Notwithstanding, or even because of, the rumours about his own Jewish heritage, Andropov's principal concern was with Jews. Even thousands of miles from their original homes, the men and women who lived in Brighton Beach and Tel Aviv were Soviet people. They retained many of the practices of Soviet life and some of its attitudes. There were communities of former Soviet people, which were foci of socializing and mutual support. But they did not form a legitimate Soviet constituency in their adopted homeland. Nobody talked about 'Soviet Americans'. Their experience pointed towards the scope of Soviet civilization but also its shallowness. It could be exported as a revolutionary movement to other, quite different societies, like Cuba. It was also exported in the habits and worldviews of individuals, some of whom struggled to adapt to their new home societies. But it was not exported to whole Soviet communities.

Unlike the condition of, say, Armenian heritage, Soviet civilization could not exist without the institutions of the state. It could not generate a widespread attachment to socialism or national identity that was independent of a person's relationship to the state and sometimes the Party. With the benefit of hindsight, this hinted at a problem that the Soviet Union was never able to overcome. But this vulnerability in 'Sovietness' and identification with the state was not defined in national terms. The national question was not a hairline crack in the skeleton of Soviet life, dooming it one day to break, but a liveable condition that generated high energy and chronic fatigue in turn, depending on variations in internal and external conditions. In the end, the Soviet Union fragmented along national lines like any modern empire, but it did not seem to collapse *because* of the inbuilt contradictions of empire. These contradictions might even have contributed to the sustainability of the USSR. It was when the people who ran the state gave up and walked away that the USSR no longer had a chance.

Party meeting in a car factory

# 15
## *Homo Sovieticus*

Brezhnev made a trip to Tashkent eight months before his death. It was March 1982. While he was there, he visited an aircraft factory. It should have generated a typical item on the news: the elderly leader was staying in touch with all branches of the economy in all republics of the union. But what happened that day did not make it on to TV. Brezhnev was walking past a balustrade inside the factory when the railing collapsed. A crowd of workers were leaning against it and the whole structure gave way. His bodyguards leapt to protect him. But masonry and metal rained down from above. Perhaps Brezhnev was lucky to get away with a broken collarbone and mild concussion. It could have been worse, but these were serious issues for an elderly man who was already sick and over-medicated.[1]

As had been the case since the mid-1970s, Brezhnev was shuffling rather than walking. His speech was very slow. He sometimes forgot basic information. The white dust of old age seemed to have been sprinkled all over his face and hair. He still had some of his old conviviality, but it was suppressed by exhaustion.

Sixteen years earlier, on a previous visit to Tashkent, it all looked so very different. It was still the middle of the night in Moscow when news of the terrible earthquake of 26 April 1966 was called through to the capital. Brezhnev went straight there. He toured the scenes of catastrophic damage, feeling the aftershocks and hearing the screams, and promised urgent reconstruction. It was an assured political performance, even an empathetic one.

The two trips bookend the Brezhnev era, revealing the gap between leadership and its absence. Shambling Brezhnev became a synecdoche for a country which was also slowing down. He lost interest in work and sought escape. Some of the people around him, especially his corrupt and ill daughter, exemplified the consequences of a lack of ideological commitment. Only a few years earlier, Brezhnev had walked around the world stage and seemed to be rewriting the course of the Cold War. But now, Brezhnev's lack of dynamism and even passivity were among the qualities that a few authors, deploying the biological language of a different species, were assigning to the despised *Homo sovieticus*.

Four years before the incident at the Tashkent aircraft factory, in August 1978, Aleksandr Zinoviev, with his wife and daughter, boarded a flight out of Moscow. They took just one suitcase with them, filled with books for the daughter.[2] Zinoviev had been a successful academic philosopher with a post at Moscow State University. He was also a sociologist and novelist – even a 'sociological novelist' – whose satirical and contemptuous writings about Soviet society could only be published in samizdat and then in the West, where the appearance of *The Yawning Heights*, an important book whose reckless originality went far beyond the limits of permitted dissent, led to his removal from the USSR. Zinoviev was expelled with his wife and daughter, ejected as a misfit who could not be accommodated or remade. Expulsion was, for Zinoviev, better than incarceration, but it led to a life of unhappiness and isolation.

In 1982, the year of Brezhnev's Tashkent accident and later his death, Zinoviev published *Homo Sovieticus*, a philosophical-sociological-novelistic pastiche that claimed to describe Soviet people, to whom he gave a fake species name, which he abbreviated to Homosos. 'The Homosos is a fairly disgusting creature,' he wrote. 'I know that because I know myself.'[3] It was not always easy to see how much of the text was knowing satire and how much was psychological self-revelation, but he certainly wanted to show that *Homo sovieticus* displayed psychological self-abasement, or at least psychological damage. This made Soviet people passive in the face of authority. He pointed out that nobody kneels before the authorities under communism. Quite the reverse: 'under Communism,' Zinoviev wryly posits, 'the human being is obliged to stand to attention.'[4] Soviet people, he observed ironically, did not collaborate with the authorities; they participated in power.⁵ Zinoviev saw moral decay in the inner lives of Soviet people, which, he argued in a more directly sociological work, *The Reality of Communism*, derived from the communalism of their existence. This had many consequences, among which was 'a tendency to make everyone mediocre'. According to Zinoviev, mediocrity extended not just to economic performance, cultural output and general living, but also to moral conduct. 'If an individual can get away with breaching the moral code in his relationship with other individuals and needs to, then he will breach it,' Zinoviev wrote.⁶

Zinoviev's shift from abstruse philosophical reasoning to concrete sociological concerns was a personal one, and the writings that resulted were idiosyncratic. Yet academic sociology in the USSR also provided a route towards the same destination: the strange explication of the mythical *Homo sovieticus*. It was during the Thaw that sociology became established as an academic discipline in the Soviet Union; in the first half of the Brezhnev era, it prospered. In 1958, sociology was institutionally embedded in the Academy of Sciences for the first time. After this, sociology departments or research units were opened in various major universities. The aim was to use methodologies inspired by Marxism and draw, where appropriate, on international scholarship, to research more 'scientifically' than hitherto topics of essential interest for policymakers and academics, such as the family, work, leisure and industrial life. Igor Kon and his students in Leningrad were responsible for innovative research into sexuality – a new and suspicious field – that was widely translated. Major research centres, far from Moscow, generated substantial work of international interest. The Tartu school in Estonia worked on mass communication; its inter-disciplinary agendas were pushed forward by the famous linguist Yuri Lotman. Most significant of all was the department at Novosibirsk, where such figures as Tatyana Zaslavskaya and Rozalina Ryvkina worked. For a time, the academic centres at and near Novosibirsk (in the famous Akademgorodok) seemed to revivify the Thaw, even if it was in a very limited academic setting; they fearlessly critiqued existing orthodoxies and sought out, where they could, intellectual connections and ideas from beyond Soviet borders.⁷ It was possible to go too far. Zaslavskaya's colleague,

Yuri Levada, gave a sequence of lectures in 1968 that sought to decentre the basis of sociology away from Marxism and to explore 'structural functionalism' as an additional theoretical paradigm. In 1972, he lost his job, and his writings were banned.[8]

But he had the last laugh. His work was permitted again from 1985, and during *perestroika* he was back in post at Novosibirsk. What he did next takes us ahead of the story: in the Gorbachev era he founded the most respected public-opinion research centre in the Soviet Union; it continued to work in post-Soviet Russia. What is important here is an image and a phrase that his work established in the minds of his fellow countrymen, as well as outsiders. For all his scholarship, he, as much as Zinoviev, helped to create a stereotype that defined the long 1970s in the minds of a later generation: *Homo sovieticus*.

At root, the assumption was that decades of dictatorship – even of totalitarianism – had modified the mentality and behaviour of Soviet people to the extent that they were, as the biological term suggested, a species apart. *Homo sovieticus* did not have the qualities of a person who had spent their life in a liberal democracy, a capitalist economy and a state governed by the rule of law. Characteristics which *Homo sovieticus* lacked included a coherent sense of personhood and individual autonomy; the capacity to form beliefs, as they had spent their lives being 'brainwashed' by communist power while not sincerely believing in it or anything else; and the range of normal moral commitments to other people.[9] Hence Mikhail Gellner, an exiled dissident living in Paris in the early 1980s, argued in a book that was heavily influenced by George Orwell's *Ninety Eight-Four* that Soviet power had created a new type of 'infantilized' person with little personal agency or initiative. Borrowing a phrase from Stalin's toast at the victory celebrations on 24 June 1945, and taking out of context phrases from Khrushchev, Brezhnev and Suslov, he argued that the Party had successfully reduced ordinary people to 'cogs in the machine'.[10] It was possible for a literary scholar, writing in the UK in the 1990s, to describe *Homo sovieticus* as a mere 'receptacle' to be filled up with cultural products as the authorities decided.[11] And Vladimir Bukovsky, a dissident who endured several spells in labour camps before being expelled from the Soviet Union in 1976, lamented the fact that those who stood up to the secret police apparently occupied an opposite moral pole to those who did not: 'Soviet man,' he wrote, 'created a countless multitude of self-justifications to facilitate his collusion with total violence.'[12]

The slang word *sovok* emerged during these years to describe a lazy, morally questionable, conformist person who had few good qualities but whose litany of weaknesses was a product of Soviet society. A *sovok* was the opposite of a true member of the intelligentsia or a decent, kindly worker. There was snobbery and unkindness in the word, and there was sometimes a hint of eugenics: what could one expect of the population in the second half of the twentieth century if tens of millions of the best people had been killed in its first half? *Homo sovieticus* was not a much more generous phrase. Later, when historians tried to reconstruct the inner lives of Soviet 'subjects', traces of *Homo sovieticus* persisted in some of their studies. In an influential scholarly article of 2000, Anna Krylova argued that a tendency among observers to counterpose the pre-1917 'liberal subject', who possessed an individual conscience and was morally autonomous, against the Soviet individual that came into being afterwards had created a false set of assumptions about Soviet personhood. Totalitarian theorists in the United States assumed the destruction of this liberal subject, and claimed that Soviet people had been deformed by 'violence and propaganda'. Even when it became possible to imagine individuality again during the Thaw, it was described in liberal terms; the assumption was that individual tendencies must originate – chronologically or geographically – from outside the revolutionary paradigm of the USSR. Later hisorians, Krylova points out, tended to assume that a person's expressions of individuality or moral reasonableness were forms of resistance to their Soviet surroundings.[13] The analytical risk associated with all this historical scholarship – despite its weight of interpretive sophistication and empirical evidence – was, therefore, that it incidentally revisited the categories of *Homo sovieticus*.

Two screens onto which the inner lives of Soviet people were projected, according to the founding authors of *Homo sovieticus*, were the worlds of work and democracy. By the 1970s, the great cliché about Soviet workers was that they pretended to work and their employers pretended to pay them. And people queued up to vote, year after year, for the only option on the ballot paper. What was more passive, indolent and morally disengaged than all that?

The Soviet Union was the workers' state. In other words, work was the cardinal virtue in the USSR. It was the basis of material value and the source of moral worth. The revolution was celebrated as the triumph of the workers. Out of it came the dictatorship of the proletariat. Mass-scale industrialization, the great achievement of early Soviet civilization, took place thanks to the labour of the workers. The workers' state was incarnated in industrial plant, family history, film, photographs and the socialist realist factory novels that remained popular among a section of the national readership.

By the mid-1970s, those grandiose images of industrial construction in the 1930s belonged to the mythologies of Soviet civilization. The Soviet industrial economy was of course no longer growing at such a rapid tempo. But tens of millions of Soviet citizens continued to work in large industrial plants, mills and mines. Massive new industrial projects were getting underway, such as the construction of the VAZ car plant and the new city of Tolyatti that surrounded it. This was also the era of the BAM railway, which was to run from Lake Baikal to the Amur River. Industrial work was one of the themes of cinema in this period, so citizens continued to see a cultural presentation of how workers lived and laboured. But films tended to be driven by the moral dilemmas of the characters rather than the socialist realist aesthetic which had lionized labour. Sometimes they presented tensions between workforce and management. *The Bonus* (*Premiya*), released in 1974 and starring Yegneny Leonov in the leading role, was a claustrophobic drama that largely took place in a single room in a construction trust, with an industrial landscape visible through the windows. Leonov plays a brigade leader who rejects the bonus that management want to pay his team. The bonus is so small that it offends his dignity. Leonov's character, whose strength comes from within, is a more substantial figure than the management. You don't get a medal just by not being a capitalist, he tells them.

As *The Bonus* reminded its audience, this was still the workers' state. Or at least it was in the sense that heavy industry and the workers who staffed it were at the heart of Soviet life. They were periodically in a struggle or at least a dialogue with men in ties and women in skirts: with managers and administrators, as well as with trade union officials. And they were part of a society that constantly praised them and rewarded them fairly well, but continued, as Marx might have explained, to extract a surplus from their labour and distribute it not to those who owned industrial plant, but to those who oversaw the state.

*Homo sovieticus* was supposed to be unduly obsessed with equality, which critics perceived as mediocrity. Party ideologists and policy-makers also came to deplore an obsessive focus on levelling, so-called *uravnilovka*, all the way back in the early years of the revolution. This referred to equal wages and conditions at the expense of reasonable incentives and differentials. Bonuses, as Leonov's character showed, were built into the system of Soviet wage scales and they contributed to working-class wages. For decades there had been a tension in the Soviet wage structure between two imperatives of Marxist-Leninist revolution. There was the romantic, liberationist drive which tended towards an insistence on equality. And there was the modernist, 'technicist' push towards rationality, which was the ideological basis of planning and incentivized wage structures.[14] The combination of these two countervailing pressures helped to keep the workers' state going, determining conditions, career rewards and a certain sense of the moral value of work that derived from the revolution. The workers' state continued to present industrial jobs as heroic and to dispense significant wage and welfare advantages to certain categories of manual worker, especially those employed in dangerous sectors such as coalmining or in the toughest climatic zones, in particular the Far North. Surveys, comments in trade union and workplace meetings, and letters to management show that workers were preoccupied with a moral economy of labour, associated with the link between wages and the quality of work.

By the 1970s, social mobility had apparently slowed down. The *nomenklatura* sought to protect its privileges. These included being paid for thirteen months of a year, having access to cheap but excellent produce and being able to use the best sanatoria and hospitals.[15] They worked hard to pass on privileges where they could to their children. The son or daughter of a member of the boss class was derisively known as a *mazhor* (deriving from the French *majeur*) in popular slang. For most people, the *beryozka* shops were 'another world' from which they were cut off. Remembering them after the Soviet collapse, one Muscovite suggested that if a person was conspicuously well dressed, one assumed that they had been shopping in a *beryozka*. 'Such was the stratification of society,' the respondent concluded.[16]

With the benefit of hindsight, Soviet society was described as 'stagnating', one feature of which was reduced social mobility. But Soviet sociologists looked to educational data to reveal a more fluid society. In 1950, 3.2 per cent of the population had attended a higher education institute, but in 1976, 24.6 had. They also found evidence of a narrowing of wage ranges. In 1956, the ratio between the top 10 per cent of incomes and the bottom 10 per cent of incomes was 4.4:1, but in 1975, it was 3:1.[17] Wage differentials between urban and rural areas also narrowed, while cities became more accessible for rural migrants.[18]

Honours and awards undermined the principle of equality, but they nevertheless tended to reward long service in a way that cut across 'class' identities. The old imperial honours system was dismantled in 1917. Civilian honours in the USSR praised the working class. This reinforced the economy of the five-year plans. The Order of Labour was established in 1927 and renamed the Order of Socialist Labour in 1938. At the top end, Heroes of Socialist Labour found themselves the recipients of an epic prize, equivalent in status to that other major bauble, Hero of the Soviet Union, and one notch behind the highest prize, the Order of Lenin. A famous scientist, say, or a senior Party figure might win this award, sometimes more than once. But the Stalin Constitution of 1936 gave the Presidium of the Supreme Soviet the authority to create new orders, and in the decades that followed, a total of nineteen were established. Some of these had a special political function, such as the Order of Maternal Glory, introduced to encourage Stalinist pro-natalist policy in the 1930s. As time went on, many more people found themselves the recipients of honours, largely – as was perhaps appropriate in the workers' state – for doing their jobs. In 1974, the Order of Labour Glory was introduced. It had three levels. Hundreds of thousands of people were inducted yearly into the third group. They were given this award for a certain distinction in their working record, marked by length of service, qualifications and achievements. Like others who received grander honours, they were given a range of privileges, including pensions that were upgraded to the highest rate, reduced domestic bills, free use of public transport and the possibility of making a claim for better housing space.[19]

Meanwhile, the full social wage, including income from work, as well as the range of social benefits and subsidies, had gone up by enough to create a better standard of living than before. People felt economically more secure. One could work fewer hours, thanks to legislation that reduced the working week to five days. The shift started in Azerbaijan, where, in October 1967, 1,958 enterprises, employing 362,000 people, moved to the five-day week. Substantial practical problems inevitably followed, but the change remained in place.[20]

People had more time to themselves. Increases in leisure between the 1950s and 1980s consolidated a socialist private realm. Here people used their free time as they wished. Opportunities for relaxed friendship increased with extra leisure and occupancy of separate family apartments. Surveys indicated that people tended to socialize with others from the same or similar workplaces and jobs, and that strong ties with neighbours and friends accounted for almost as much socializing as with relatives.[21] This private space of personal warmth was far from the stereotype of instrumental relationships in communal settings that was the apparent world of *Homo sovieticus*.

Increased free time also expanded a particular kind of public sphere, one dependent on private space, personal time and individual decision-making. Hobbies and activities were enabled through special-interest magazines, public facilities or the blind eye of the planning authorities. The economy of shortages forced hobbyists to develop the creative and practical skills to make versions of the things that they would have liked to buy. There was a gendered aspect to this. Some women were highly skilled in the making and repair of clothes, for example, while some men had an aptitude for car maintenance or DIY. Plainly, a certain proportion of this 'leisure' time was disguised labour, sometimes all of it; but it could also be a source of enjoyment and the bridge to an associated hobby. The magazine *Modelist-konstruktor* had an annual circulation of 850,000 in 1982; this had more than doubled by 1989. Other prominent publications which were devoted to making things rather than buying things, sometimes out of scarce materials that one might locate in unconventional ways, included *Motorboats and Yachts*.[22] The former publication was launched in 1966 and was devoted to practical engineering and technology for people who wanted to create new possessions or repair them; the latter journal dated from 1963. There was also a popular TV programme called *You Can Do It* that was devoted to the same leisure pursuit. These were hobbies that emerged on a large scale during the Thaw and were enabled by a Thaw-era public sphere and modern media industry, but in both cases they grew more significant in the 1970s and 1980s. Dachas, owned by a larger segment of the population every year, operated in multiple pairs of zones: both private and public, male and female, consumption and production, leisure and labour. They were the place where Soviet people worked hardest during their leisure hours.

As Alexandra Oberländer points out, it was a paradox that people often worked so hard during their time off – at the dacha, sourcing consumer items, queuing up, doing DIY, exchanging favours and, above all, enduring the double burden if one was a woman – while their formal job was becoming less productive. One did not have to go along with the insulting joke about 'pretending to work and pretending to be paid' to see that a range of pathologies had infected the workplaces of developed socialism. A 1982 survey suggested that 10 per cent of workers always left early. Work time was lost for administrative checks, voluntary service, personal moonlighting and cigarette breaks. There were many reports of alcohol abuse at work. In other words: people worked very hard, but not always at the workplace.[23] Even so, certain workplaces (for instance, relating to the defence industry) were much more rigorous, while certain professions (such as schoolteaching) offered fewer options for leaving early.

Trade unions also occupied a superficially paradoxical position. After all, they never organized strikes. This might suit *Homo sovieticus*, who, according to the stereotypes, lacked the instinct for solidarity. Trade unions existed so that a person with a grievance did not have to head 'to the square'. Soviet civilization accepted that citizens could have complaints, though never with the system itself, only with the system's malfunctions. Trade unions were designed to make the planned economy work better, not to bring it into question. They enhanced, in theory, workers' sense of belonging to their enterprise and to the whole Soviet project by facilitating their access to sanatoria, sports clubs and many other institutions of Soviet civilization. Trade union representatives and enterprise managers together oversaw the push to meet planned targets as the quarterly deadline approached. Unions helped when a worker had a specific grievance against the employer – an apparent error in enterprise-owned housing allocation, say, or a miscalculated wage packet. But they emphatically did not organize strikes, or counterpose themselves in any way against authority. By definition, this would not make sense: they were *part* of institutional authority.

It was assumed that it was worthwhile for a worker to join a union. White-collar employees and blue-collar workers alike joined trade ('professional') unions, or *profsoiuzy*, and the claim was that 98 per cent of them did so. They paid 1 per cent of their wage packet and received in exchange access to a range of social and welfare benefits in addition to those provided directly by the state. Industrial workers who were employed in enterprises made up around two-thirds of trade union membership in the 1970s as part of thirty-one different trade unions.[24] These unions had local branches run by volunteers and activists. Even in the 1930s, representatives were chosen by their peers in competitive elections.[25] In the 1970s, a worker who stood up at a meeting and made a speech about poor working and living conditions, as one Valery Vecherenko did in Norilsk in 1976, might find themselves, as he was, representing his colleagues in a local committee and successfully bringing to light management practices that were substantially negligent of worker safety; the newspapers made much of these cases.[26] Different trade unions were interconnected in a single powerful bureaucracy, the All-Union Central Soviet of Trade Unions (VSTsSPS). Its head was a major player in all-union politics. Nikolai Shvernik held the post between 1930 and 1944 and again between 1953 and 1956; in between, he occupied the most senior of all the country's ceremonial seats, chair of the Presidium of the

Supreme Soviet. Viktor Grishin ran the All-Union Central Soviet of Trade Unions between 1956 and 1967, for much of this time as a candidate member of the Politburo; after 1967, he ran the city of Moscow and from 1971 sat around the Politburo table in the Kremlin. Grishin's successor for the next eight years was Aleksandr Shelepin, who had served as the second KGB Chairman after Ivan Serov, and who combined the chairmanship of VSTsSPS with membership of the Politburo.

Trade unions, therefore, played a very significant role in all-union politics and in the everyday lives of ordinary workers. But unions did not act in the way that they had done before 1917, or even in the 1920s. They no longer formed a collective of working-class people and protected their interests in opposition to anyone who would encroach on them, employers or government alike. They were no longer incubators of working-class solidarity and identity. Instead, they were one of the mechanisms by which 'state' and 'society' – not discrete categories in the USSR – maintained their relationship to each other. The conventional descriptions of totalitarianism that were developed in the United States by political theorists in the immediate postwar years were not of much use by themselves in describing Soviet life in the 1970s. But the continuum between trade unions and management hinted at a totality in the Soviet order. Soviet trade union personnel coexisted with workplace management as part of a combined team whose aim was to keep the enterprise on track to meet its targets. Managers, trade unionists and foremen worked together during 'socialist competitions' to increase productivity and output.

In 1917, the working classes of the Russian empire had been the most powerful and determined in the world, capable of pushing forth a socialist revolution. Even during the 1920s, when it was impossible to challenge Soviet power but the economy had some 'mixed' and decentred features, the working classes were already losing the character of an autonomous group. The social mobility on which the Stalin-era five-year plans depended did not elevate the working class as a whole, only individual members of that class, 'promotees' who got on in life by advancing out of the working class and into management and the technical intelligentsia. There were moments of spontaneous protest, such as at Teikovo in 1932, but strikers were easily crushed. Three decades later, the protest and strike at Novocherkassk in 1962 was also spontaneous. The language and actions of those days suggested the existence of a working-class identity incubated by decades of public culture; workers were still revolutionary. Trade unions contributed to a sense of working-class identity through facilitating access to social services. Having access to the full range of these services – the components of the social wage – generated a basic sense of Sovietness, of belonging to Soviet civilization. Trade union representatives of particular character, when faced with a fortunate alignment of circumstances, chose to expose the transgressions of management and to defend individual workers in workplace disputes.

When the unions were passive, sometimes courts filled the gap. Numerous court decisions in the long 1970s found in favour of the worker against management in cases of unfair dismissal. For example, in 1971, the management at the Kostroma Vodka Factory tried to move a worker called Viktorov to another part of the plant that he could not properly access because he was disabled. When he missed work too often, they fired him for absenteeism. His trade union representatives accepted the verdict. But when he appealed to the courts, they protected him, and he kept his job. Numerous other similar cases were heard in the Brezhnev era, and later in the decade more legislation in this area was passed. This tendency culminated in an RSFSR decree of 1979 that laid down the conditions that management had to meet and unions had to observe before a worker could be dismissed. It was so rigorous that it became very difficult to dismiss someone from their job, effectively providing further legal teeth to the constitutional right to employment.[27] Some argued that this exacerbated the low productivity of *Homo sovieticus*, but it was emblematic of a complex legal relationship between workers and the authorities, as well as, among many workers, sincere but selective ideological attachments.

Aleksandr Zinoviev argued that *Homo sovieticus* was incompatible with democracy. 'We are against democracy,' he maintained absurdly, 'because it prevents us from struggling for democracy honestly and without the use of lies and play-acting. And so, down with democracy!' Zinoviev was right: 'Soviet democracy' was certainly a paradox, and quite possibly an oxymoron. The absence of meaningful democracy in the USSR created a range of political, administrative and moral challenges which contributed to keeping Soviet citizens in their place. There was no shortage of elections in the Soviet Union. People were forever voting: there were all-union and republic-level elections for the Supreme Soviet, as well as local elections, trade union elections and shows of hands at workplace meetings. But as most of these votes were rubber-stamping decisions which had been made higher up the chain of authority, they had almost no democratic value. Zinoviev described people who were not active agents but were told what to think, required to vote in elections without choice and called upon to hold banners whose slogans they had never really thought about.

But as Zinoviev's absurdist line indicated, 'Soviet democracy' was not an absent phenomenon, but rather one that required decoding. For a start, why bother with elections at all if they presented no choice and one could not vote out the Party or change the government? One answer was that the Soviet Union was a modern state. Modern states were democracies. Therefore the Soviet Union was a democracy. Soviet leaders could not talk to their Western counterparts without making this claim – it was the basic lingua franca of international legitimacy – but of course none of them fell for it.

Another reason was to surveil, inform and mobilize the population. The election campaign was much more important than the election. Party activists knocked on doors to inform people about the campaign issues, and also to make sure that all residents of a dwelling were listed on electoral registers. For a month or so before Supreme Soviet elections, which took place approximately every four years, the campaign dominated the national and local press and, from the 1960s, the TV news. 'Top' people were often candidates. They included Politburo members. Brezhnev himself was a Supreme Soviet deputy between 1950 and 1982, first for a seat in Dnepropetrovsk oblast, then in Kazakhstan, then in Kuibyshev, and finally in Moscow. Candidates gave a few set-piece speeches in their constituency during the campaign. In a campaign speech in Tolyatti before the RSFSR Supreme Soviet elections of June 1975 (the all-union and republican Supreme Soviets had their own elections) Mikhail Suslov described the range of socio-economic institutions, not least the 'mass community' (*massovye obshchestvennye*) membership-based organizations such as trade unions and the Komsomol, which were essential for the educational and participatory functions of Soviet 'democracy'. They were led by the Party, the avant-garde of the communist movement, just as it had been in October 1917. Together, people expressed their unity and unanimity through their membership of these groups. Likewise, Party members and the rest were unified; Party and the people could not be disentangled.[28] Soviet democracy was a display of unanimity.

Most of the campaigning activity was conducted by proxies. Campaign meetings were held in workplaces. Party and trade union officials gave speeches to outline Party policy, Soviet achievements, the international situation and local issues. Members of the audience asked questions, sometimes expressing spirited opinions within the context of what was permitted. And that was precisely the function of the public information that was presented during the campaign: to clarify to the population the words to use and the range of ideas to express when talking about policy. During the Stalin period, this could be a matter of life and death, but it provided useful pointers even in the 1970s. Election day itself had festive qualities. Public buildings such as schools turned into ballot stations, bedecked with banners. A holiday atmosphere prevailed in the centre of towns. Activists ran about, chiding people to come out and vote. People did. The aim was to secure the highest possible turnout, which meant the closest possible expression of unanimity. Of course, such an expression said nothing about the inner life of *Homo sovieticus*. Or if it did, it implied the possibility of scepticism, the awareness that unanimity was a performance.

There were two other main claims for Soviet democracy: accountability and participation. Soviet 'democracy' offered a very limited measure of accountability. The Communist Party of the Soviet Union was on one level accountable to the ongoing revolution and, even more mystically, to Marx, Engels and Lenin, but on a more practical level, each element of the Party – factory 'cells', regional committees and so forth – was answerable to the committee above in the Party hierarchy. Khrushchev had imagined a decentralized future for the Party as it moved towards the communism of 1980, but in reality the country only became more bureaucratic as time went on. The Party itself contributed massively to this process of administrative thickening by multiplying personnel, making processes more complex, devising new regulatory frameworks, using more paper and accumulating files. After he became general secretary, Brezhnev aimed to 'increase trust in cadres' by removing the threat of term limits from regional Party secretaries. Even if this made the relationship between the Politburo and the localities less arbitrary, it did little to make local Party organizations more accountable to their memberships and to the wider population.

Policymakers became more aware of this deficit in the 1970s and of the risk it posed to Party legitimacy. For example, in a decree of 1976, approved by the all-union Central Committee, the city Party apparatus in Tbilisi was called upon to carry out its core functions properly, implementing central directives as well as punctiliously observing its own decisions. But it should also educate Party members and regular citizens about current economic and political issues, and 'develop supervision procedures' so that the city Party committee's interactions with local people were properly monitored. Such measures were examples of how 'intraparty democracy' in the city was expected to increase.[29] Another approximation of accountability was the consultation exercises that were launched before the introduction of major legislation. For example, the development and drafting of the 1977 Constitution was a very long process. It included many consultative meetings for ordinary members of the public. Such meetings were scrupulously written up in stenograms. Nobody spoke in opposition to the Party. Instead, many of them expressed a range of acceptable but independent-minded views that reflected their own personal and sometimes idiosyncratic understanding of the moral universe that the ongoing revolution had created.

Nevertheless, these views were shaped and to some extent stunted by the absence of accurate public information. Although the information space as a whole was a flexible and complex arena that could not be understood only as the result of hardline censorship, Party and government were still by far the most powerful players within it. People lacked the sources of information to challenge their claims. Restrictions on travel abroad dramatically reduced the inflow of knowledge. The state itself was one of the most secretive in the world. Officials understood that this made the economy less efficient, but it was seen as a way of ensuring political stability.[30] As de-Stalinization became entrenched, officials seem to have become more relaxed about confidential information, circumventing secrecy protocols more often by resolving issues in phone conversations, and to have come to trust each other more.[31] But this was a problem, too: greater trust among the boss class only excluded everyone else. Secrecy undermined trust between the population and the authorities. It made it even more difficult to suspend one's disbelief and talk of 'Soviet democracy'. People learned to navigate a 'map of knowledge' in social, political, cultural and scientific life that was partly obscured by epistemological and geographical zones of secrecy.[32] From this map it was only a short leap to urban legends and conspiracy theories. Spending too much time on these only further undermined any residual capacity an ordinary citizen had for holding power to account.[33]

According to Party theorists, developed socialism offered the most promising territory yet for the development of Soviet democracy. 'More and more working people are drawn into administering the country,' claimed a standard text, 'managing public and state affairs and creating the necessary conditions for the all-round harmonious development of the individual and for strengthening the unity of the Soviet people.'[34] Outsiders rightly expressed extreme scepticism about what democracy could possibly amount to in the Soviet Union. After all, elections usually had a single candidate, and when there were nomination meetings for which several candidates could stand, they were either all Party members or featured a token candidate who was notionally non-Party but was warmly expressive of the Party's virtues.

Representation was therefore not a function of so-called Soviet democracy. There was zero chance of changing the government. Instead, participation trumped representation and lent some very loosely democratic characteristics to Soviet civilization. In Western Europe after 1945, 'moderate' democracy delivered effective government and stability in part by restraining popular involvement in electoral politics – keeping it as the preserve of cautious, centre-ground, white, largely male and often technocratic 'elites' – and rediverting much of this associational and communitarian energy to clubs, trade unions, school boards, local pressure groups and, later, single-issue organizations linked to, for example, anti-nuclear and environmental campaigns. These groups added to the democratic quality of Western European life not through augmenting mass involvement in elections, but by increasing the sum of people who were actively engaged in political issues and who were therefore indirectly holding their government to account.[35]

The Soviet Union did not possess the rich associational culture of Western Europe. But by the 1970s, it did have elements of a civil society. These included large autonomous organizations such as the All-Russian Society for the Deaf, the Soviet Committee of War Veterans and the All-Russian Society for the Preservation of the Monuments of History and Culture. There were also ad hoc campaigning groups such as that which sought to protect the pristine qualities of Lake Baikal in the face of the proposed cellulose plant there. In each case, these groups had a long lineage in Soviet history, or powerful backers, or an agenda that fitted with the revolutionary project. They did not hold government to account. But they did tilt the dial in favour of a particular popular interest and help to protect it. Participation in them made a loose contribution to 'Soviet democracy'.

In a paradoxical way, so did membership of the Party. Of course, the Party defined the absence of democratic choice in the USSR. For some, membership was merely a matter of career necessity. At senior levels, both centrally and locally, the Party was another branch of administration, albeit a separate one, concerned with such matters as ideology, oversight, compliance and personnel development. For a certain type of ordinary member, the Party offered opportunities to sit on committees at factory and neighbourhood level, to speak in public meetings and to express either ideological enthusiasm or busy-body tendencies, or both. It contributed to the making of particular decisions, for instance about the siting of a minor road, and organized voting drives and other forms of 'voluntary' involvement in the local community. Denunciation still existed in attenuated form. Low-level Party committees, run by 'activists', followed up on reports about members' bad behaviour. Volunteer-activists also contributed to the running of trade unions, for example as representatives in a particular workplace. There were other forms of voluntary participation in the official institutions of community life, such as in neighbourhood patrols, or *druzhiny*, and in the comrades' courts, which also depended on volunteers.

Soviet people gathered in communities, known as collectives, such as groups of colleagues or neighbours, or fellow enthusiasts for a particular hobby. Collectives sometimes had very generally democratic values within them: values of collaboration, mutual support and the absence of obvious hierarchies. Others were larger networks that were based on patron–client ties. Zinoviev argued that the *kollektiv* derived from a toxic application of communal values. And yet collectives could not exist without their members trusting each other, or knowing whom in the group to trust.[36] They depended on people in the group watching out for each other. Members might cover someone's back when he left work early on an errand for a shortage good, or form an ad hoc fund to lend money to someone who was running short. There was a mutual responsibility about this – *krugovaya poruka* in Russian – which in part derived from a long social and cultural tradition in the east Slavic lands, of groups finding ways to manage themselves in difficult economic circumstances without the intervention of the official authorities. The conceptual artist Ilya Kabakov, working out of a studio he had fashioned on an upper floor in central Moscow and collaborating with collectives of other-thinking artists under the gaze of the authorities, produced various disturbing or strange images of 'communality' and communal life in the 1970s, while acknowledging his own position inside the Soviet communal heritage.[37] Such complexity was Soviet normality. It was a long way from *Homo sovieticus*.

Aeroflot ticket counter, Tashkent

# 16

# The Danger Society

On 27 March 1978, it was already a decade since the crash in which Yuri Gagarin had died. He was still an uncomplicated hero. The songwriters Aleksandra Pakhmutova and Nikolai Dobronravov, who were friends of Gagarin, captured aspects of him in song. They saw his death as the high point of the revolution, defined by the fearless risks that had launched him into space. 'What a lad he was!' they wrote. 'How he could sing, and he was cheerful and brave, he lived the life of a risk-taker!'[1]

Depicting Gagarin as the last romantic swashbuckler of the revolution was an attractive conceit that superficially captured one of the major transitions between the Thaw and the era of developed socialism. The Thaw possessed the romance and optimism that the later period lacked. A structural explanation was the shift in how society calculated risks. One of the participants in an oral history project that was researched thirty years later illustrated 1970s attitudes to risk. A research scientist, speaking in 2002, he remembered the 1970s as a predictable time of low social risks connected with the operation of the economy and welfare system; personal risks – cancer, divorce, accidents – were, of course, another matter. 'I wouldn't want to continue living as we had in the 1970s,' he said, 'although everything was planned out like nowhere else, perhaps, on earth. I knew, for instance, that when I turned forty I'd be given a table clock, at fifty a crystal vase, at sixty a twenty-ruble raise, and that my pension would be 140 rubles. I knew exactly what to expect until I died!' Yet *perestroika* and the 1990s changed everything, recalibrating all the indexes of social risk. 'Now I'm not certain about anything and that's just fine! [laughing]. That's life!'[2]

People remembered the long 1970s as low-risk and eternal-seeming. In real time, people's experience of the 1970s and early 1980s was of interruptions, false starts, decisions, dilemmas and personal crises. Risk crowded into people's lives in uncontrollable ways. But the inevitability of personal risk coincided with very significant reductions in social risk. For some, not least the likes of Vladimir Vysotsky, it was an uneasy juxtaposition. The sense of reduced risk required a personal cognitive dissonance about the greatest risk of all – nuclear weapons and nuclear power – and depended on total censorship about the industry's accidents and weaknesses. An explosion and radioactive leak in 1957 at the closed city of Ozyorsk was just one disaster invisible to the population. The people who worked in the nuclear industry enjoyed the best salaries and living conditions but knowingly took risks whose end point they could not see.[3] And the decline in economic growth forced the Politburo to gamble on people's lives – actually it condemned millions to a premature death, as the age of mortality fell – by reducing public spending on health from its Khrushchev-era peak of 6 per cent to between 1 and 2 per cent.[4]

Before Stalin's death, social risks were extremely high. In what might be conceptualized as a 'danger society', people endured the possibility of arrest, execution, extreme poverty, famine and industrial accidents. Under Khrushchev, many of these risks were dramatically reduced, but the very excitement and drama of the Thaw created other senses of uncertainty. By the 1970s, not only had the danger society dissipated, but the state was doing the opposite of what Marx had promised and Khrushchev had tried to legislate for: it was not 'withering away' but was growing denser and more regularized. In so doing, it further reduced the incidence of social risk inside the Soviet dictatorship. Economic regulations, welfare decrees, constitutionally backed rights and legislated entitlements reduced some risks to a minimum.

Social insurance expanded in the Soviet Union after 1953. The total social-insurance budget increased from 17.9 billion rubles in 1950 to 352.96 billion rubles in 1980.[5] In Voronezh oblast, spending on pensions and benefits went up from 178.6 million rubles in 1971 to 204.6 million in 1973 to 238.4 million in 1975.[6] For all its radical scope, the mechanism – and language – of 'social insurance' was actually the most conventional aspect of the Soviet welfare system. The term 'social insurance' (*sotsial'noe strakhovanie*) had been used in Soviet legal and regulatory documents for decades and it was common in popular speech. The USSR had joined the International Social Security Association (ISSA) in 1947. ISSA's aim was to promote social-security schemes, of which social insurance was the longstanding archetype. Soviet specialists in the field met their peers from capitalist as well as socialist countries at international conferences.

Like in some other countries, social insurance was a metaphor. Britain, for example, set up a system of National Insurance (NI) after the Second World War, with taxpayers making NI contributions alongside their income-tax payments, but in reality benefits came out of general taxation. The metaphor of social insurance existed for historical reasons – it continued the familiar vocabulary of the nineteenth and early twentieth centuries, when workers really had paid into a fund from which they could draw in times of unemployment or sickness – but it provided an additional consolation, too. People in both capitalist and socialist countries became greatly exercised when they thought that the connection between paying in and paying out was broken. These feelings were at least as acute in the Soviet Union as they were in capitalist countries. After all, in the workers' state, labour was the cardinal virtue. A perception emerged that freeloaders benefited from the extra risk that longer-serving or more conscientious colleagues had taken on through greater salary sacrifice. Social insurance was prone to charges of moral hazard. 'Why do they want me to be on the same footing as him?' asked a sixty-year-old during the lengthy consultation exercises that preceded the pensions legislation of 1956. He had worked for forty-five years while his resented co-worker also stood on the cusp of retirement after accumulating only twenty-six years' service. Policymakers resolved the issue by persisting with the metaphor of social insurance, but people had to suspend their disbelief. A Moscow academic wrote to the Central Committee about the proposed pensions legislation in 1956: 'Explaining to a worker who earned, let's say, 930 rubles [per month, pre-ruble re-denomination] why he receives an identical pension to his comrade who earned 800 rubles and who worked in the same conditions and in the same factory shop will be impossible.'[7]

Planners therefore had to manage perceptions and realities of risk alike. Socialism and would-be communism had not engineered risk out of existence, despite eliminating, for instance, the risk of unemployment. Insurance was necessary not only for the welfare system but for industrial enterprises and other economic actors. This was especially important in the more rational planning environment that accompanied de-Stalinization. The Main Administration of State Insurance (Gosstrakh), which traced its origins to 1921, was reformed.[8] Enterprises were legal personalities. This gave them a formal responsibility for their actions. Soviet managerial culture placed plenty of authority in the hands of the director. In the absence of statutory decentralization, much of their autonomy was merely informal. But they had to honour their contractual obligations to other enterprises. Managers took out insurance at the local Gosstrakh office in order to diffuse the burden of risk that the enterprise faced. Citizens could also purchase insurance policies for the things they owned as personal property, which could, for example, include a dacha. They could also take out life insurance and insurance against disability.[9]

The historian Paul Josephson detects cultural traits in Soviet mentalities – a certain fatalism, a willingness to disregard personal hazards, a kind of 'unsafety'.[10] Even so, the transition to managed risk was a structural element in the post-Stalin transformation of Soviet civilization. A small example was the massive upswing in the production of good-quality respiratory equipment for the likes of coal miners in the long 1970s. In 1977, 150 million devices were manufactured, costing sixty million rubles. It spoke to a new biopolitics in the USSR that was based on a different understanding of risk and a post-Stalin conception of individual wellbeing, even rights.[11]

In some parts of the Soviet Union, natural disasters were a foreseeable risk. Tashkent's inhabitants were used to earthquakes, most of which were fairly minor. People in the city therefore had a general sense of the risk of earthquakes, but they depended on accurate information from the authorities in order to gauge risks on each specific occasion. Here the Soviet authorities conspicuously failed to help the population manage its sense of risk. In April 1966, Tashkent was hit by an earthquake that caused mass damage across the city. Old parts of the town became uninhabitable: as many as 95,000 dwellings were severely damaged but often not in a way that made survival impossible; infrastructure was dislocated, and schools and other institutions became unusable. The number of dead was disputed, but it seems unlikely that it was above the low hundreds. This was a terrible cost in itself, but was a smaller death toll than in some similar disasters. It did not stop daily life from resuming. Wholesale reconstruction soon began. Even so, there was a disconnect between the enormous damage to property and the number of victims; the authorities at one point claimed that only eight people had been killed.[12] Public information seemed unreliable, which increased suspicion; the absence of public trust made it even more difficult for people to gauge risks. The most trusted source was the republic's chief seismologist, Valentin Ulomov. He went on television and told people what was safe and what wasn't, what to expect and what not to fear.[13]

Even in the realm of natural disasters, risk was more difficult to manage after developed socialism had ended and *perestroika* begun. Around midday on 7 December 1988, an earthquake of 6.9 on the Richter scale – Tashkent was 5.2 – hit 50 kilometres north-west of Armenia's second city, Leninakan. Even though the Soviet Union was now a considerably more open place, and welcomed the arrival of foreign aid, at least 25,000 people were killed; quite possibly 50,000 were.[14] The coexistence of Soviet life and considerable risk was exemplified by the proximity of a nuclear power plant to the zone of mass destruction. The risk was disproportionately borne by minorities. *Perestroika* had brought longstanding tensions between Armenians and Azerbaijanis to the surface of political life. Violence followed. Azerbaijani villages inside the Armenian earthquake zone were cut off from receiving help.[15]

Risk management was based on actuarial sciences, substantial mathematical expertise, and an established science of forecasting. Soviet mathematicians won the Fields Medal in 1970 and 1978; six later Fields Medal winners were educated in Soviet schools during the period. Soviet schools were good at teaching maths. As a subject, it suited the rigorous pedagogical research and training that teaching institutes developed. Textbook authors introduced even young pupils to problem-solving and fluid mathematical thinking. Specialized physics and maths schools flourished during the 1960s and early 1970s.

Older pupils who were outstanding prospects had the chance to compete in mathematics Olympiads. As many as 80 per cent of the later Soviet Union's leading mathematicians were educated in such schools, including four of their Fields Medal winners, like Efim Zelmanov, who attended Novosibirsk School No. 10 in the late 1960s and early 1970s. This schooling facilitated applications to the intensive and challenging degree programmes offered by leading institutions such as the Mathematics and Mechanics Faculty of Moscow State University. It turned out to be a 'golden age of mathematics education'. Many of the specialized maths schools became havens of intellectual autonomy, in which teachers encouraged their pupils to use maths to think critically about the world and then to develop a sense of 'truth' as an absolute concept.[16] Later in the 1970s, though, the peak of maths education was reached. The KGB were suspicious that specialized maths schools employed and enrolled above-average numbers of Jewish teachers and pupils. And pedagogical missteps followed. A controversial mathematics pedagogical reform, associated with the leading mathematician Andrei Kolmogorov, ineffectively attempted to transfer methods that worked with Olympiad-level pupils to all pupils.[17] But Soviet maths education remained world-competitive.

Thanks in part to the quality and number of mathematics graduates, planners became more acutely focused on likely future trends and scientific forecasting after 1953. A new Economics Research Institute was founded in the Academy of Sciences in 1955. One of its briefs was 'perspective planning'. In 1964, the Kyiv-based scientist Gennady Dobrov published groundbreaking work on models of scientific forecasting. Aleksei Kosygin, the country's economic boss from 1964, repeatedly praised forecasting and referred to its incorporation in central planning. In 1968, the Society for Scientific Forecasting was founded with support from luminaries in the Academy of Sciences, but it remained an unofficial, if approved-of, organization.[18] Leonid Kantorovich, a leading mathematician and economist, began work in the 1960s on computer models for economic planning, in an almost post-ideological, post-Marxist spirit.[19]

Cybernetics and information technology, which emerged in the USSR after Stalin's death, gave policymakers additional tools for understanding risk. Clemens Günther points out that cybernetics elevated 'information, feedback and rationality' into a new way of looking at the world, one that offered variety and engagement with the West, and implicitly demanded pluralism.[20] In other words, computer science offered an alternative epistemology that gave its practitioners the ability to imagine possible risks in modern terms. Applied mathematicians and computer scientists like Andrei Ershov made a brilliant contribution towards computing technology in the USSR. Ershov was a visionary with a dream of incorporating information technology into the Soviet curriculum.[21] He was invited to address the leading conference of American computer programmers in 1972 and spoke of the need to connect technical coding with the logical abstractions of mathematics and the mission of opening programming to a wider public.[22] Computing experts began to see the potential of networking, the basis of a putative internet. But central planning failed for once to create a nationally integrated network, of the type that was on the cards in the United States, and ended up with a fragmented entity of weak potential.[23]

The most spectacular 'safe' risk that many people took was air travel. Aeroflot, founded in 1923 and celebrated as 'the mighty wings of the motherland', enjoyed a ceremonial day from 1979 every 9 February. By the mid-1960s, Aeroflot was a large-scale international operation, flying from Moscow to fifty countries.[24] In 1981, the Ministry of Civil Aviation declared that Aeroflot flew to 105 major cities in 85 countries.[25] By 1990, it was claimed that Aeroflot flew 777 internal kilometres for every inhabitant of the USSR in a dense all-union network (though this was one-third of the corresponding figure for airlines in the USA).[26] Aeroflot liked to think that it was the global rival of PanAm but morally superior to it because it promoted equal social chances among passengers rather than profits for shareholders.[27] In the long 1970s, the most widely reproduced advertisement in the streets of Moscow was for Aeroflot. It showed a slim aircraft at the top of the poster and the airline's insignia at the bottom, and in between a flight attendant, who was smiling and offering a tray of fruit and a glass of juice. The slogan was 'use the services of Aeroflot!'[28] At the turn of the 1980s, new airliners were coming into operation to satisfy burgeoning passenger numbers (as much as a

33 per cent increase over the course of the last five-year plan). The new Ilyushin-86 was an 'airbus' that could carry 350 people.[29] On Aeroflot's sixtieth anniversary in February 1983, the Minister of Civil Aviation claimed that in a single summer's working day, Aeroflot carried 600,000 people.[30] In May 1977, the Ministry of Civil Aviation announced plans for a new airport at Tallinn that was capable of serving 700 passengers per hour. It was necessary for the increasing numbers of tourists to the city's Old Town. The plan also anticipated the needs of the 1980 Moscow Olympic Games; the sailing events were held on the Baltic.[31]

Of course, the air routes into and out of the Soviet Union were open to very few Soviet citizens. They were as heavily policed as any Iron Curtain border. A Soviet person needed an exit visa to leave the country, an entry visa for their international destination and the right paperwork for their return. None of this was easy to acquire in the offices and waiting rooms of bureaucratic Moscow. It was an even more dismal prospect if one lived in a distant province. Despite the many connections that crossed the Iron Curtain, the Soviet Union remained a society that its citizens could seldom leave.

Frustrated other-thinkers, instinctive emigrants and members of certain minority groups were among those who wanted to travel by any means necessary. Mark Dymshits and Eduard Kuznetsov, a Jewish refusenik and a dissident, tried in desperation to exit the USSR by hijacking a plane. They were sentenced to death on Christmas Day, 1970. Six months earlier, they were arrested together with ten accomplices at Smolny Airport in Leningrad. They were booked on to an internal flight to Priozersk and got as far as the boarding area. Their plan was to seize the plane when it landed, collect four further comrades and fly to Sweden. Dymshits was a pilot, and the plane was a small Antonov, just the right size for their group. Their ultimate destination was Israel. But the KGB came for them. Andrei Sakharov's future second wife Elena Bonner was one of the dissidents observing the trial of Dymshits and Kuzetsov. When the death sentence was announced, and the KGB officers in the room celebrated, Bonner turned on them. 'Fascists!' she shouted. 'Only fascists would applaud a death sentence!' Twenty-five years after victory over the Nazis, 'fascist' was still the ultimate insult in the Soviet Union, and the men shut up. Soviet dissidents and international dignitaries followed Bonner's courageous lead and called for a reduction in the sentences. Sakharov himself tried to speak to Brezhnev using a Kremlin telephone line from the Institute of Atomic Energy. For six days, the men's fate hung in the balance. On New Year's Eve, the death sentences were commuted, and the convicted men were given fifteen years instead.[32]

This awful case showed the special pathology of Soviet civilization. But hijacking and air disasters were familiar fears and common subjects of 1970s popular culture in capitalist countries as well as in the USSR. In Yulian Seyonov's 1979 thriller *Stand-off* (*Protivostoyanie*), a Brezhnev-era murderer and wartime traitor plots his escape from justice by attempting to seize an airborne plane on an internal route and diverting it to a foreign destination. Semyonov's heroic detective Kostenko, a staple of seventies popular culture, saves the day. As the action reaches its culmination, happier experiences of air travel and holidays in Abkhazia come into his mind. 'Kostenko remembered how he once flew to Gulripsh ... it was a long time ago, so long ago that it was frightening to imagine it, and they spent two days lying on the beach, keeping quiet, skimming stones and, in the evening, drinking wine.'[33] Despite its frightening potential, air travel retains its happy associations by the end of the book, as a version of normality, and the deep nostalgia of endless socialist time, are restored.

It was an illusion. On 15 February 1977, an Ilyushin 18V, flying from Tashkent via Nukus, missed the runway at Mineralnye Vody in the south of the Russian republic. Seventy-seven people were killed. Two years later, on 29 August 1979, a Tupolev-124 broke up in the air near Tambov, en route from Odesa to Kazan (via Kyiv). All fifty-eight passengers and five crew were killed. And two years after that, on 7 February 1981, a Tupolev-104 bound for Khabarovsk in the Far East crashed shortly after take-off from Leningrad. It was a navy plane. Fifty passengers and six crew, including more than two dozen senior officers, were on board.[34] Throughout the Brezhnev era, more than one such tragedy took place on average per year. Aeroflot retained a safe record for international travel; it was internal flights that were risky. The causes were a mixture of mechanical failures, weather problems, human error and systemic negligence.

*Pravda* did not report the Mineralnye Vody, Tambov and Leningrad disasters. Most jarringly of all, Aeroflot's annual foundation day was celebrated the day after the 1981 Leningrad crash, with the press ritualistically headlining the airline's achievements rather than reporting the previous day's disaster. It was impossible for passengers to compute risk using proper information. The movies offered still more speculative data about the risks of flying. In 1980, Mosfilm released the blockbuster *Air Crew (Ekipazh)*. Following the Hollywood disaster movie formula, it told the personal stories of the crew of the Tupolev-154 aircraft, raised tension, exploded into big action scenes and offered the consolations of resolution and recovery. Yet the authorities insisted that *Air Crew* represented a uniquely Soviet sensibility. Goskino, the state agency that regulated the film industry, pointed out in an internal note of November 1980 that viewers found the film appealing and accessible, 'convincingly convey[ing] the features of the Soviet way of life, its moral principles, and the optimistic atmosphere of socialist society'.[35]

The themes ran through many other productions. *Wingspan*, released by Odesa Studios in 1986, was a claustrophobic story about a flight from Khabarovsk to Sverdlovsk via Irkutsk on an Ilyushin-18, which faces mechanical failures, bad weather and closed airports. *Three Per Cent Risk*, a Lenfilm production of 1984, concerned the decisions made by test pilots. It overlaid masculine identities onto the process of risk calculation. The 1969 film *Not Under Jurisdiction* interlaced the risks faced by a test pilot in two contexts, the decisions he makes while flying and in his personal life.

In the early days of the Cold War, the Soviet Union signed bilateral agreements with such states as Norway in order to permit overflights of each other's territory.[36] This made international flying safer and more efficient. Eventually, in 1970, the Soviet Union became a signatory of the Convention on Civil Aviation. It came late to the organization, which dated from 1944 and already had 119 other members. But in the context of détente it was possible to work more closely across the Iron Curtain to expand aviation lines and improve safety. And yet on 1 September 1983, Korean Airlines flight 007, en route from New York to Seoul, veered off course into closed Soviet airspace after stopping in Alaska. Soviet defence systems could not distinguish between this civilian jet and a hostile intruder or an American surveillance plane. They sent a warning; and then they shot the Boeing 747 out of the sky, killing 269 people. The following month, in his regular *Sovieticus* column in *The Nation*, the historian Stephen Cohen described the events in terms of global risk. 'After all,' he wrote, 'if Soviet radar cannot tell a jumbo jet from an RC-135 in two-and-a-half hours, will it be able to distinguish between a Pershing missile launched from West Germany and a large errant seagull in six minutes?'[37]

Cohen drew attention to the most modern and total of risks. And yet Soviet cities were still vulnerable to the age-old urban risk: fire.

An architectural classic of the 1970s city was Moscow's Hotel Rossiya. Constructed between 1964 and 1968 on the south-eastern corner of Red Square, adjacent to the Moscow River, the hotel was a vast rectangle of white concrete and glass, with a central tower topped off in gold. It was made up of several interconnected blocks and had 3,000 rooms. The hotel's name was interesting, too. How could 'Rossiya' – 'Russia' – fit into the USSR? Once the question had been asked, it kept coming back. As if to add architectural confusion to historical complexity, the Politburo itself stepped in to position a row of twelve medieval churches, including the Church of the Conception of St Anne, next to the modern monumentalism of the new hotel.[38]

On the night of 25 February 1977, fire caught hold of part of the hotel. There had been whispers about safety protocols. Forty-two guests were killed. Viktor Grishin, the first secretary of the city of Moscow (the de facto mayor with a seat on the Politburo), came down from his home in the nearby Arbat district while the nighttime blaze was at its height. He was stricken – or he panicked, given that a familiar pathology of the Soviet bureaucrat was the fear of having no one left to whom one could pass the buck – and made a forlorn attempt to direct operations on the ground. Grishin was a tough operator who did not hesitate to skim off the considerable advantages of his position for his family's good. Even so, the disaster seemed to knock him sideways. He offered Brezhnev his resignation. 'Get back to work,' Brezhnev is reported to have said, apparently with some sympathy for his colleague.[39]

The Rossiya was important to the people who ran the Soviet Union.

It was not the best hotel in the city. Visiting functionaries above a certain rank stayed elsewhere, at the Hotel Moskva, just beyond the northern edge of Red Square. The National Hotel also had a certain cachet. Diagonally across 'Fifty Years of October' Square from the Moskva, at the bottom of Gorky Street, it had a sought-after restaurant that looked towards the Kremlin. Old communist romantics still talked of the Metropole, five minutes' walk behind the Moskva, across Revolution Square, beyond the Bolshoi Theatre, where revolutionaries had lived during the Civil War and the 1920s. The Rossiya, though, was a big, new, Brezhnev-era project, and it had many devotees.

One of them was a rising star from Stavropol called Mikhail Gorbachev. He stayed at the Rossiya whenever he was called to Moscow, even though he was formally entitled to use the facilities of the Moskva. Like Khrushchev half a century earlier, Gorbachev visited Moscow ready for the thrill of proximity to the sport of high politics. When he was in town, Gorbachev liked to take a room on the tenth floor of the Hotel Rossiya, on the side that overlooked the Kremlin.

On 25 November 1978, Gorbachev arrived in Moscow on a flight from the new airport at Stavropol, whose construction he had overseen. He went to the Rossiya and took room 1098. The occasion was a Plenum of the Central Committee. He spent the afternoon socializing with friends and acquaintances from his region before receiving a call direct from Brezhnev's office. They had been trying to reach him since his arrival. He didn't lose another moment. The party he was enjoying was only a few minutes' walk from Red Square.

In the Kremlin, it was already early evening. Konstantin Chernenko received him. Chernenko held a senior post in the Central Committee with some responsibility for personnel. He had good news. Brezhnev wanted to put Gorbachev forward for election as a secretary of the Central Committee at the Plenum on the following day. It was a sign that he was in line for the Politburo. If the politics worked out, it would mean leaving Stavropol and taking up a post in Moscow. Gorbachev tried to make a joke and lighten the atmosphere. Chernenko was inscrutable. Gorbachev thanked him and left. Later that night, perhaps anticipating the politician's self-mythologizing, he looked down on the Kremlin from his room in the Rossiya.[40]

*

Mikhail Gorbachev was born on 2 March 1931 in the village of Privolnoe in Stavropol region. It was almost 100 miles from the provincial capital, in the south-western extremity of the Russian republic, on the edge of the north Caucasus. His grandfathers were substantial peasants. Both of them were arrested and imprisoned relatively briefly in the late 1930s. Mikhail was too young to remember those events but they shaped his understanding of Stalinism. The other early trauma was the war. Privolnoe was occupied by the Germans.

Mikhail's father, Sergei, was the great influence on his early life. They worked together in the fields, handling machinery and bringing in the harvest, even when Mikhail was home for university vacations. Their extraordinary combined efforts brought recognition to them both. Sergei won the Order of Lenin. Mikhail, at the age of seventeen, was presented with the Red Banner of Labour. He distrusted the ethics and practices of collectivization, though he kept his doubts to himself until he was in a position to propose reforms in the 1960s. At school, he was an excellent pupil, graduating with a silver medal (German was his weakest subject, preventing him from achieving all 5s or straight As, and hence a gold). He was sociable and loved amateur dramatics. A conscientious member of the Komsomol, he even became a candidate member of the Party proper when he was nineteen. He was the ultimate provincial go-getter, headed for the most famous university in the country.

In 1950, Moscow State University contained many outstanding students from a variety of backgrounds. But the southern Russian accent was unfashionable. A peasant's hands lacked sophistication. It took Gorbachev time to adopt the manners of the intelligentsia and the poise of the careerist. Later, he rolled these two qualities together, so far as one could, into the outlook of the enlightened Thaw functionary. His choice of subject, Law, in some ways helped. It suggested an open mind and gave him a fairly broad view of other legal systems.

What really changed his world was his relationship with Raisa Maksimovna Titarenko. She also came from a village background and was the first in her family to attend a higher-education institute. More than Gorbachev, she had a gentle, cultivated manner and was more instinctively 'cultured', interested in things and people for their own sake. She was his better half. They married in September 1953 and completed the last two years of their studies as spouses.

Gorbachev's first extended job on graduation was in the Komsomol in Stavropol, back in his home region. He set up home and Raisa joined him. Their daughter Irina, their only child, was born two years later. Gorbachev began by working as an 'agitator', an activist and organizer charged with communicating the Party line. Within a few months, Khrushchev gave the Secret Speech. Gorbachev travelled around the province to outline its contents to rank-and-file Komsomol and Party members. It required the capacity to listen. The speech changed the lives of everyone in the Soviet Union, and set the course of Gorbachev's career.

He segued into the position of a natural de-Stalinizer, combining political nous with moral conviction. De-Stalinization was in any case a more obvious fit than Stalinism with the values of his childhood and the atmosphere that Raisa was trying to develop at home. It responded better to his own tough-minded intellectualism and practical good sense. As his career progressed, it became the heart of his political approach.

Soon he headed the city Komsomol organization. In the year that Gagarin flew in space, 1961, Gorbachev began running the Komsomol apparat for the entire region (oblast). He was thirty. The following year, he moved into the main Party apparatus and started to accumulate specific policy experience in agriculture. Between 1961 and 1967, he completed demanding part-time courses at the city's Agriculture Institute, graduating with another bachelor's degree, in agronomy. His was a politics of policy knowledge and ideological expertise, things which required disciplined reading and structured instruction. He was an instinctive life-long learner. There was no sense in describing an *apparatchik* as a member of the intelligentsia, because the *raison d'être* of the latter was, in theory, to use morality and culture to hold the authorities to account. But Gorbachev had the interests and range of an *intelligent*.

Twice he was considered for senior posts in the KGB, both in the Stavropol region and in Moscow. He did not express any interest in these jobs, and the fact that he was vetoed for one and sidetracked for the other confirms that he was never a potential *silovik*, or man from the security ministries, and lacked the 'qualities' of a KGB man. In 1966, instead, he became Party boss of Stavropol city, and in 1970, of Stavropol Region. At thirty-nine, he was one of the barons of the Soviet Union. He stayed in post for eight years and played the roles in Moscow that were commensurate with his status, on the Party Central Committee from 1971 and as a deputy in the Supreme Soviet from 1974. Stavropol was one of the union's giant agricultural provinces, with nearly 500 collective farms. He seems not to have resorted to fiddling and corruption. Instead he learned ever more about the science and practice of farming, turned himself into a top-class athlete of bureaucratic politics and continued to steep himself in Lenin's writings. He pushed major projects which were backed by agronomists, such as the Great Stavropol Canal, but also decentralized local production, improved access to machinery, and incentivized rural workers, leading to dramatic accelerations in harvesting in some districts.[41] It meant that in 1978 he could say, among other things, that Stavropol's output of wool was the highest in the Russian republic: its ten million sheep accounted for 27 per cent of republican wool production.[42]

Gorbachev's success derived from his mastery of patronage politics. In Stavropol, Gorbachev depended on his close relationship with Fyodor Kulakov, his predecessor-but-one as the boss of the oblast. The name Kulakov derives from *kulak*, or 'fist', and he was a tough operator who liked women and vodka, and once – fruitlessly – called up Raisa when Gorbachev was away on a trip. He was a ruthless player, bringing enterprises and institutions from neighbouring territorial jurisdictions under his own control, boosting Stavropol oblast output in national data sets.[43] It made him a classic provincial 'dictator', a dynamo of self-propulsion, determined to win. When Kulakov went to Moscow in 1964 to take charge of agriculture for the Party, Gorbachev had an ally in the capital, and Kulakov had his own eyes on the highest of prizes. Back then, in 1964, it was too soon yet for Gorbachev to take over as chair of Stavropol Region – it was Leonid Yefremov's turn, but he was not far off retirement. When Yefremov left the post, Kulakov spoke up for Gorbachev, and he was appointed to the post of Stavropol oblast boss. Kulakov was a senior figure in the Central Committee; the following year he was elevated to the

Politburo. His support counted for a lot. Gorbachev would not have gained promotion without it.

His other patron was Yuri Andropov. The KGB boss came to take the waters from time to time in Gorbachev's bailiwick. They became close acquaintances. The famous moment that Gorbachev always liked to remember took place in September 1978. Andropov had called him the previous month to say that he was coming to a spa in Kislovodsk. Gorbachev was sure to plan his own vacation for the same time. A few weeks later, a train carrying Brezhnev to Azerbaijan passed through Kislovodsk. The occasion was significant: the city of Baku was gaining the Order of Lenin. Local leaders came out to greet the train at major stops. Chernenko, Brezhnev's leading lieutenant, was travelling with him. When the train pulled into Kislovodsk, it was a starry evening. The platform was surrounded by the distant beauty of the Caucasus mountains. Brezhnev came down the steps. Chernenko, who was wearing a tracksuit, like many Soviet people on long-distance train journeys, followed. Andropov and Gorbachev greeted them: four present and future general secretaries.[44]

Fyodor Kulakov, still a possible successor to Brezhnev, had died a few weeks before. He was barely sixty, felled by a heart attack after a night's drinking. His patron's death created a gap in Moscow for a top official with an interest in agriculture and the potential to sit in the Politburo. It was Gorbachev's big chance. Less than two months later, half a world away from the railway platform at Kislovodsk, Gorbachev was on the tenth floor of the Hotel Rossiya, looking down on the Kremlin, and pondering his family's move to Moscow. It was a risk, but there was no other way.

They were there before New Year. Gorbachev found that one of his first ceremonial duties in the capital was attending a gala conference at the Hall of Columns to mark the inaugural Aeroflot Day on 9 February 1979.[45] No doubt that was a straightforward occasion. The wider changes at work and home were more complicated.

It was bound to be a difficult transition. Mikhail and Raisa Gorbachev had been prominent people in Stavropol for twenty years. They knew how to live there. For all their dash of cosmopolitan experience – MGU graduates who had travelled abroad, subscribed to literary journals and consumed Moscow's culture on their regular visits to the capital – their lives had mostly been spent in the 'deep' provinces. They did not have the effortless insolence of big-city people. Mikhail in particular spoke with a flat southern accent that drew attention to his origins. Raisa now had to give up her job as a teacher at the local institute. Moscow was attractive, but it was unfriendly. They loved its theatres, but Mikhail had little spare time. Their accommodation was impressive, but it was unfamiliar. They were young enough and looked the part, but their high-flown neighbours weren't much interested. Gorbachev threw himself into his work. He was looking for the chance to apply his practical and theoretical knowledge and adapt his policy innovations to an all-union agricultural scale. Less than a year after starting work as the Central Committee secretary devoted to agriculture, he was elected as a candidate member of the Politburo. He was a full member eleven months later, while he was still getting used to his Zil limousine. It gave him great power but in defined areas. He had no say over the two most consequential decisions of the next few months, to invade Afghanistan and to send Andrei Sakharov into exile in Gorky.

The Politburo was not a cabinet based on collective responsibility, let alone a committee open to scrutiny by a legislature. It had lost accountability to the institution of which it was the head, the Party. Instead, it was a mechanism for delivering dictatorship. Gorbachev even had to request routine information about the budget, which was neither publicly available nor circulated among the Politburo. Decisions about foreign policy were made by a small inside group that focused on Andropov, Dmitry Ustinov, the defence minister, and Anatoly Gromyko, the foreign minister. Boris Ponomarev, the Central Committee supremo for foreign affairs, was also involved. Brezhnev was formally in charge. In the absence of Ponomarev, but with Chernenko in tow, this group approved the invasion of Afghanistan in a meeting at Brezhnev's dacha, near Moscow.[46]

Soviet forces launched operations on 24 December 1979, less than a month after Gorbachev's promotion. The aim was to defend the Marxist government of a neighbouring country with close ethnic, linguistic and cultural ties to Tajikistan. In Washington, the invasion looked like reckless Cold-War flailing that imperilled world peace. President Carter expressed outrage.

A few months earlier, in March 1979, the Tajik-majority city of Herat, in the west of Afghanistan, had been convulsed by a violent rising. Soviet advisers were among those targeted by the crowd. The Afghan government asked for airborne and ground-based military support from the Soviets in their desperate attempt to restore control over the city. The new communist government in the country was under threat from its own incompetence, the balkanization of the Marxist movement, its political violence, the brutality of its collectivization programme and the rise of Islamist sympathies in the wake of the Iranian revolution. By December, not intervening was the bigger risk. One hundred thousand troops crossed the border, and around that number remained at any one time over the course of the 1980s.

It came at a terrible price, above all for Afghans, but also for young Soviet men and women and their families. One million people died. The great majority of them were local men, women and children, who had neither asked for the Soviet presence nor elected the Marxist government. It was the Soviet Union's Vietnam. Military service was more feared than ever before. For young men and the families who loved them, it had become a deadly risk.

Andrei Sakharov took the risk in his own way, the last in his long sequence of political gambles on his own life chances. As expected, he had immediately spoken out against the war. This time, the authorities shut him up decisively: not by imprisoning him, but by removing him from Moscow. On 22 January 1980 he was pulled over by KGB officers while he was travelling to a research seminar in an Academy of Sciences car. They took him to the prosecutor's office, where he was told that his state honours, such as Hero of Socialist Labour, had been withdrawn. He and his beloved second wife, Elena Bonner, would be forced to live indefinitely in the closed city of Gorky to the east of Moscow. They were taken straight there on a KGB flight. Their apartment was on the first floor of a twelve-storey building on Gagarin Prospekt. They were stuck, unable to travel around or communicate in ways that most Soviet citizens took for granted. Dissidents lived very risky lives, and Sakharov's luck had run out. The most famous dissident in the Soviet Union had finally been silenced.

*

International risks abounded. The Solidarity movement briefly challenged socialist power in Poland and the integrity of the Warsaw Pact. Growing out of strikes in the Gdansk shipyard, and led by the charismatic electrician Lech Wałęsa, it was the greatest independent movement in the history of the Eastern bloc. The first Polish Pope, John Paul II, formerly archbishop of Krakow, drew massive crowds on his visit home in 1979, which seemed to exacerbate the risk to Soviet power. Andropov made it clear that Warsaw Pact tanks would not be sent over the border in a risky venture to restore the status quo.[47] Instead, General Jaruzelski became first secretary and declared martial law. It kept the socialists in power and Polish 'sovereignty' intact, but still further discredited Soviet control.

The crisis in Poland coincided with the election of Ronald Reagan to the White House. Reagan looked at the Cold War with a new clarity, aiming for peace while expressing boldness. The Americans were talking about the Strategic Defense Initiative, which the Western media referred to as 'Star Wars' after the blockbuster movie of the time. It amounted to the militarization of the cosmos. Star Wars was a half-baked plan, but the Soviet defence establishment panicked. If the Americans pulled this off, the Soviet armed forces would not be able to defend the country.

In November 1983, a few weeks after the Soviet air force had shot down Korean Airlines flight 007, NATO began its massive Able Archer military exercise on West German territory. The Warsaw Pact knew what to expect. But in the context of Reagan's challenges to the Soviet Union, the Politburo chose to think that Able Archer was a cover for nuclear mobilization. There had already been a false reading on Soviet early-warning systems in September. Only a cool-headed reaction by the officer on duty had prevented a nuclear response. Soviet generals were tetchy in part because of a widening gap in technology: microchips in ballistic missiles were significantly more advanced in American weapons than Soviet ones. In a first strike, the Americans now had a theoretically high chance of destroying the great majority of the Soviet arsenal before it could be launched; the Soviet side did not have the capacity to do this. 'Nukes were supposed to be the ultimate insurance policy,' writes the leading historian of microchip technology – but the Soviet premium, already extremely burdensome, was now a much worse investment than before.[48]

For some in the KGB, the game seemed to be up: but even if this meant that the Soviet Union was going to 'lose' the Cold War, there was still no plausible connection between diplomatic 'defeat' and domestic collapse. Technology and expertise allowed planners to manage risks and to run the economy in a stable way. But choices about technological development, and the constraints that planning placed on innovation, also contributed to slowdown, dead ends and a deteriorating position for the Soviet Union in its rivalry with the United States. Andropov knew it. Gorbachev knew it. They talked about reform.

Hippies in Latvia

# 17
# Misfits

By the time that the Olympic torch arrived in Moscow in July 1980, the city had been the capital of half the world for decades. Now, the International Olympic Committee promised, it was to be the capital of the entire globe for the next two weeks. The Communist Party wanted to showcase developed socialism in its greatest city by celebrating great sporting victories. But the Americans got in the way – or the Soviet Army did. The *siloviki* in the Politburo underestimated American fury about the invasion of Afghanistan. President Carter was already uncomfortable with the shades of grey inherent in détente. Afghanistan seemed the ultimate black-and-white case, the moral wrong that set the USSR apart. Carter wanted to marginalize the Soviet establishment, to make them the misfits of the international system. By April 1980, he had built a coalition of sixty-five countries that agreed to boycott the Games. It was part of a package of measures, including trade embargoes, notably on grain.

Brezhnev claimed throughout his career, at least until the invasion of Afghanistan, that he was committed to international peace and cooperation.[1] What might have been his legacy was now at risk. Yet the Olympic boycott was far from total. Despite the British government's support for the American initiative, many British athletes competed in the 1980 Games. Before the opening ceremony, police carted off the city's most conspicuous misfits: the drunks who clustered at railway stations, the currency speculators outside hotels, the wrong sort of prostitutes, the tramps and their dogs. Citizens who worked in the city but without the right papers were suddenly liable to be caught up in a document check. The city limits were more tightly policed than before, creating inconveniences for commuters from Moscow Region or those who wanted to enter the capital from a neighbouring town.

The Soviet Union was the superpower that did not fit with international norms; Soviet society was tightly regulated but contained many people who did not fit in. These 'misfits' were the marginals and deviants subsequently recorded by historians.[2] More generally, they were everyone who tried to be themselves in ways that did not quite seem normal. The *Stalinist* order could quickly dispose of such people when its administrators chose to, but after 1953, Soviet civilization changed shape and for the most part accommodated its misfits, though often without respecting or even acknowledging them, in an ever-changing and unstable process. This process did not expand the parameters of what was 'normal'. Instead, it shared some of the general characteristics of how modern urban societies became diverse. It was another version too of the Leninist dynamism which dated back to 1917, according to which certain people were included in and others excluded from full participation in revolutionary society.

Inclusion was the other side of exclusion: sixty-three years on, the Russian Revolution was proceeding according to the same dialectic. And so at the Olympic Games, the authorities opened the city up to an unprecedented volume of direct telephone communications, with 1,600 new 'channels' routed through an exchange station on Butlerova Street in the south-west of the city. The KGB did not like this but later made use of it in the monitoring of early computer networks.[3] Ordinary Muscovites were encouraged to get involved in the Games. On the opening day, a secret report by the Moscow City Committee of the Communist Party noted the Olympic-themed lectures, discussions and 'political information programmes' that were taking place in workplace and neighbourhood collectives. Intelligence suggested that people welcomed the Olympics, not least because of the noticeable fall in urban crime and the better service that was offered in shops and public transport.[4] It was the biggest influx of foreign visitors since the World Youth Festival of 1957. Even though the Thaw-era festival was from another age, when optimism and international idealism were easier to kindle, the Olympics of eternal socialism were still a touchstone memory for the people who experienced them: a moment of cosmopolitan excitement. Yet 45,000 people in uniform, from the

KGB and the Ministry of Internal Affairs, were brought into the city.[5] The beautification of Moscow was rushed and skin-deep. It paid no attention to the interests of local people. A solitary Italian protested on Red Square about the treatment of gay Soviet citizens. Nobody joined him.[6]

Staging the tournament was an awkward fit for Soviet civilization. After twenty-five years of raised investment in the consumer and welfare sectors, during which urban development and architecture were much more focused on the practical needs of citizens than before, the Games were an ostentatious reversion to different construction priorities. The works cost 610 million rubles.[7] A new indoor stadium was built at Prospekt Mira, and the vast Olympic Village, which later became a hotel complex, was erected at Izmailovsky Park in the west of the city. And yet the tenth five-year plan did not necessarily prioritize the Games. The Olympic Stadium was not a new structure but an existing one: the Lenin Stadium of 1955, a massive ensemble with 103,000 seats in the south-west of the city, overlooking a bluff in the river and not far from Moscow State University.

Planners and officials made routine decisions about the Olympics from inside the worldview of Soviet civilization. In 1978, 9,330 skilled workers from the union republics were assigned to work on Olympic construction projects in the capital, but only half had arrived on site by December. Construction enterprises, republican governments and the central authorities in Moscow had other priorities. Estonia was to host the sailing and rowing competitions of the Games. In May 1978, the highest ranks of the Estonian Communist Party wrote to the Central Committee in Moscow to request the allocation of an extra 600 workers. They ended up with 200. In making their appeal to the authorities in Moscow, the Estonians did not invoke a warning about international humiliation if the USSR failed to complete its Olympic construction on time. Instead, their trump negotiating card was the threat of diverting their own permanent construction workers to make up the shortfall. Without new migrant labour, construction of housing, kindergartens, hospitals and schools in the Estonian republic would slow down and even stop.[8] The point was that welfare was an even higher consideration than international prestige in the mental apparatus of decision-makers. This did not mean that the social system was working well. It simply meant that it was indispensable to Soviet civilization in a way that the Olympics were not.

Brezhnev was present at the Olympic opening ceremony. In the stadium, he began his speech of welcome with a sequence of vowel sounds – 'O-o-o-o-o' – before one of his advisers took him by the elbow. 'Leonid Ilich,' he said, 'those are the Olympic rings. This here is your text.'[9] The joke gained currency because enough people felt a reflexive contempt towards Brezhnev, not to mention towards the political system that kept him in office. Brezhnev was in no condition to be running the Soviet Union, and people could see it. He still appeared on the news, walking and stumbling, talking and slurring. His symptoms could not be kept out of view in the way that American journalists agreed to keep President Roosevelt's wheelchair out of shot four decades before. It was a different time, and TV was king, even in the Soviet Union. From about 1973, Brezhnev became increasingly dependent on sedatives. First they helped him sleep. Then they got him through the day. His emerging addiction was an open secret in the Politburo. Medical support allowed him to cope. He had a nurse on call. Sometimes he retreated to a sanatorium or to Crimea. But the condition affected his ability to make decisions and run a full day of meetings, and caused him to struggle with his weight. His speech slowed and dulled. Other health problems crowded in. One complaint after another weakened his heart. He had problems with his stomach. After 1975 it was increasingly obvious that he could not govern normally.[10] Party bosses speculated about the politics of it. The Politburo kept one eye on the succession. Ordinary people, some of whom had once quite liked him, shrugged their shoulders and made jokes.

He had grown increasingly fond of medals and honours. It was a cult of personality reduced to the absurd, an inert theatre of mild vanity. Nobody fell for it or feared it. Brezhnev took it seriously, partly out of self-regard, and partly because of an interest in political display. By the end of the 1970s, he struggled to stay standing for long periods on top of Lenin's Mausoleum on 1 May and 7 November.[11] By contrast to this uninvolving ceremonial, the politics of the Thaw were dynamic and unpredictable. Then there had been great political and cultural contests with unknown outcomes. Dramatically different visions of the revolution were placed in conflict. History was at stake and public culture was sometimes cast in moral shades of grey, not just bright – or faded – red. When Khrushchev became a political problem, his opponents described his dismissal as removing a nefarious cult of personality. Yet, as Khrushchev liked to say (in different words), nothing became his leadership like his leaving of it. They could get rid of him precisely because Khrushchev's 'cult of personality' was nothing more than an overbearing political posture, rehearsed, for the most part, behind closed doors. It made him a difficult colleague who was past his sell-by date; it did not make him unremoveable. The Presidium had enough middle-aged politicos to challenge and replace him. Back in 1964, at the point of succession, Brezhnev himself was an attractive figure. His most recent major biographer draws a warm portrait of him in those years.[12] The 'cult of personality' politics of the second half of the Brezhnev era seemed a much-diminished arena by comparison with the first half.

And yet Soviet politics were not finished in the second half of the 1970s and the early 1980s. This was not only a gerontocracy headed by a man with a record-breaking yield of ribbons. The revolution continued to exert its passion. Mikhail Suslov, the Politburo's ideology supremo, put forward Marxist-Leninist solutions for late 1970s problems that were precise and sincere, despite their lack of efficacy and his own deficit of warmth. He headed an ideology apparatus filled with educated and intelligent officials, who sought to graft philosophy onto politics, even if economic reforms, not ideological contortions, were urgently necessary. Yuri Andropov had an alternative vision of the revolution that was grounded in a practical approach to politics and policy. And Mikhail Gorbachev was using his Politburo seat to develop – quietly for now – another Lenin-inspired attitude to reform.

On 10 November 1982, three days after public celebrations to mark the sixty-fifth anniversary of the Bolshevik revolution, Brezhnev died in his sleep at his dacha just outside Moscow. He was buried at the Kremlin wall five days later, two days longer than the usual custom, but the funeral was an international occasion. George Bush, Reagan's vice-president, spoke to Andropov and commented wryly on the similar trajectories of their careers. Bush, among other appointments, had been an ambassador who then ran the CIA. It was said that Brezhnev supported Vladimir Shcherbitsky, who was head of the Ukrainian republic, as the next general secretary. Chernenko's seniority placed him in line. But Andropov was head of the KGB, possessed a clear 'vision' of how the Soviet Union should develop and had the ambition to lead, even though he was already ill with kidney disease. He chaired Brezhnev's funeral committee and followed him as general secretary.

Andropov was no Beria. They were both Chekists, but Andropov wanted to make the Soviet Union run efficiently, so that society's misfits did a normal day's work rather than faced arbitrary arrest quotas. Yet he was ruthless. He brought the sensibility of his Lubyanka office to his room in the Kremlin. He hounded dissidents and sent them to jail. As the country's security boss, he navigated the USSR's purposeful drift away from the relative pluralism and openness of the Thaw. He targeted Solzhenitsyn. And yet, somehow, he was the acceptable face of coercion. The complicated, important figure of Roi Medvedev – dissident, socialist, author of anti-Stalin works, but faithful to the Soviet Union and distrusted by Andrei Sakharov – wrote a not unsympathetic biography of him.[13] Andropov seems not to have been personally violent or venal. He was rumoured to relax by reading the banned literature that his fellow citizens could not access. He had a comfortable apartment on Kutuzovsky Prospekt, a very fine official residence, but it was not the more ostentatious *nomenklatura* accommodation preferred by his colleagues on Granovsky Street and other locations adjacent to Gorky Street. When he got the top job, he did not move into the Kremlin. While he had access to all the perks, and took holidays at the very best resorts and sanatoria, he does not seem to have abused his privileges or been ostentatiously corrupt. On the one hand, his closest allies were the tough *siloviki* in the Politburo, and he had a careful grip on the organs of coercion. On the other, he was close to Mikhail Gorbachev, whose company he enjoyed, with whom he had open and spirited exchanges, and who was his protégé. All of this gave him a certain ambivalence, but perhaps not much. After all, he had been the KGB boss for fifteen years.

Gorbachev's success in developing incentives and boosting agricultural production in Stavropol fascinated Andropov. He came to power in 1982 with a reformist agenda. Once again, his approach combined coercion and progressiveness, shaped and justified by Leninism. It was yet another manifestation of the destruction–creation dialectic of the revolution. He therefore maintained the level of spending on consumer goods production for the direct benefit of the population, but introduced measures to clamp down on infractions of workplace discipline. Revealingly, his approach drew on a productive debate among sociologists, legal scholars and other interested professionals and members of the intelligentsia during and after the Thaw.[14]

The impact was immediate and obvious. Policemen walked into daytime cinema viewings to check that the audience was not bunking off work; they patrolled the streets in greater numbers and asked passers-by why they were not at the factory. In June 1983, a new Law on Workers' Collectives was approved. The aim was to require workers to participate in workplace meetings and to demonstrate their commitment to labour. This could in theory have a democratizing tendency and at a stretch might therefore improve morale, but its oppressive potential was plain. It was more likely to lengthen working hours and to tighten horizontal ties of surveillance by one colleague of another. It had a hint of totalitarianism about it, updated for 1983.

And yet it was matched by another instinct: to decentralize the economy and boost incentives for workers and managers to increase output and quality. Following a reclassification of certain goods by central planners, enterprises that produced the best and most innovatory items were permitted to make small profits on them. Bonuses for workers followed. The administrative burden placed by ministries on enterprises was reduced. Wages were calculated more on the basis of productivity than before. The steps were small, and were limited to certain places and industries, but they were the link between Kosygin's sidetracked reforms and Gorbachev's fundamental transformations.[15]

Andropov's vision was yet another development of Soviet civilization. It was the USSR's lost Chinese future: increased discipline, economic decentralization and political uniformity. But this was a dead end for the revolution. The policies did not obviously respond to popular needs or aspirations, though given time they might have raised living standards. Gorbachev's reforms, by contrast, were more plausible. They ran closer to the grain of Soviet consciousness and

Russian sensibility because of their deliberate Leninist revivalism and explicitly European approach. Andropov wanted to limit pluralism, to maintain social and cultural conformity. He wanted to retain the coercive power of the KGB and the monopoly of the Communist Party on power. Andropov was Gorbachev's enabler, but he was not his inspiration.

The discipline drive exposed one of the core questions of late Soviet life. If paradise was faded, did anyone really still strive towards it with true communist enthusiasm? Typically, *Pravda* published a letter in early 1977 in the name of an electrician from the Minsk region. He was a communist activist in his factory's party apparatus. Keen to emphasize the link between ideological initiatives and economic output, he was worrying away about one of his fellow activists in the factory. 'I remember,' he wrote, 'how he was always rooting for the honour of the collective, how he never walked past even the smallest imperfection in the workplace.' But he had changed. He had even lost interest in Party business. It turned out that he had been offended in a Party meeting, when his view had not been taken seriously.[16] The gap between an enthusiast and a would-be misfit was relatively narrow; the Party's historic role, at times of mass mobilization, was to bridge this gap, but this no longer seemed possible.

Reformers recognized the need to work with the grain of certain human instincts – the desire for recognition and community, not to mention for a nice life and the ownership of things. Soviet civilization was flexible enough to accommodate these instincts, but only up to a point. Go too far, as one very quickly could, and a person no longer fitted in. Family prosperity quickly became a social pathology when it rose above a fairly modest level. Two years before he directed *Zigzag of Fortune*, his comedy about the lottery win of a workplace collective (see chapter 7), Eldar Ryazanov made another blockbuster, *Watch Out for the Car!*, which was also about the problems of money and greed. The comedy revolves around an insurance agent called Yuri who takes regular leave from the office to steal fancy cars from corrupt officials, drive to other parts of the country, sell them clandestinely and then donate the money to children's homes. Thus Robin Hood came to Soviet civilization. He almost meets his match in Dima, the manager of a consignment store, a middleman enterprise through which people could sell unwanted goods and buy a range of consumer items. These shops were legitimate, but they were havens for mark-ups and kick-backs. Dima specializes in under-the-counter sales of especially desirable electronic goods like imported tape decks. He accrues enough cash to build a dacha, much bigger than the rules allowed, and to fit it out with imported goods. Dima also drives a particularly splendid Volga, which Yuri eventually succeeds in stealing, selling and donating the proceeds thereof.

The film hinted at a parallel Soviet world: organized crime. Hard men, some of whom had nurtured illegal enterprises while in the Gulag and even gained the 'honoured' title of thief-in-law (*vor-v-zakonye*), made illicit fortunes. Gennady Karkov, known as 'the Mongol', was a major underground entrepreneur who helped create the gangster sector in the Soviet economy. He was arrested in 1972. This sector complemented the planned economy as the 1970s went on. Veniko Shengelaya ran an underground fabric business in the Chechen-Ingush Republic that he had split off from an official institution. It seemed to be precisely that: an *enterprise* that employed many people who worked in reasonable conditions and helped to generate a certain amount of wealth which filtered into the Soviet economy, while providing goods that complemented those manufactured in enterprises that worked officially and were accounted according to the plan. Shengelaya even sold the business on. He was publicly exposed in 1981 and sentenced to a lengthy jail term.

These underground entrepreneurs had a certain position in Soviet civilization. A slice of the population knew directly of their work. Others came across them incidentally. And others read about them in popular novels or saw them in films. Yulian Semyonov wrote about an underground jewellery business in *Ogaryovo, 6*, a 1972 novel that was subsequently filmed and which featured the charismatic detective Vladislav Kostenko. It was not a harmless enterprise, but rooted in violence and murder and extraordinary enrichment. Mercifully Kostenko restored order where there was chaos.

Organized crime was an example of the misfit problem in Soviet society. It was an analytical question: whether misfits were marginals who were extraneous to mainstream Soviet life, or whether they were more directly integrated, perhaps through symbiotic relationships with official society and the planned economy. Otari Lazishvili ran a vast underground business in Georgia and was very close to Vasily Mzhavanadze, boss of the republic for the two decades through to 1972. They were both brought down after Eduard Shevadnardze, later Gorbachev's foreign minister but at the time chair of the Georgian MVD, went after them.[17] During the 1970s, the hierarchy of the Communist Party in the Uzbek republic helped to oversee perhaps the most financially corrupt scheme – infesting the cotton trade – in the whole of Soviet history. Again, it was exposed. Most awkward of all was Galina Brezhneva, the 'first daughter' of the Soviet Union, who famously lived a venal life, which her father periodically tried and failed to deal with.

Organized crime, with its violent core, was only the pinnacle. There were all sorts of criminals in the USSR. Wars and famines in the thirty years after 1917 inevitably led to localized explosions of crime. Mass amnesties after Stalin's death prioritized those who had been convicted of non-political crimes such as rape or armed robbery, leading to panics in many communities and after-effects across society that persisted for years. Many stories of crime in the USSR were universal ones. Crime harmed the lives of Soviet citizens just as it did those of people who lived in capitalist countries, thanks to the same pathologies, not least male aggression against women, child abuse and alcohol-fuelled violence. But there were differences. Cities contained down-at-heel neighbourhoods but not 'ghettoes' or zones that were difficult to police. Universal employment also cut off one source of petty criminals and their tendency to turn to violence. Meanwhile, the high numbers of police and the scope of the security state as a whole made crime a riskier activity than it was in some places.

Crime affected ordinary people; it was a fact of life. But it was also a deeper societal challenge. The word 'crime' recurred in reference to Soviet civilization. For its critics, the Soviet Union itself was a criminal enterprise run by gangsters and murderers from its very beginning. Emigrés and Cold Warriors claimed that the country was run by an illegitimate 'regime' that had imposed itself on the country in a coup d'état and stolen the property of the population as well as that of foreign investors. From exile, Solzhenitsyn argued that the murderous essence of Bolshevik rule revealed itself at the start, that there was an organic and unbreakable link between Lenin and Stalin, and that the criminal imprint of the Gulag Archipelago on all aspects of Soviet life was thereafter ineradicable. In the Baltic republics – to take the most irreconcilable example – large parts of the local population viewed the annexation of their countries as a criminal affront to international law, a view that was widely shared by the United States and its allies.

Meanwhile, the Bolsheviks used allegations about crime, especially the so-called counter-revolutionary crimes defined by article 58 of the criminal code, to drive forward the revolution. Labelling all sorts of people as counter-revolutionary criminals allowed the Party and government to commit the enormous state-run atrocities that were intrinsic to collectivization and industrialization in the Stalin era. Putting people on trial for such 'crimes', and then executing or imprisoning them, was a vicious response that required one to make a set of assumptions about the individual's own culpability. By definition, the people's state and its ideology could not be responsible for the failures or malfunctions that caused shortfalls in the plan or 'abnormalities' in community life. Only the 'conspirators' against socialism and the Soviet Union could be blamed. Yet before 1917, socialists argued that crime could only be explained by taking into account the social context – poverty and social dislocation – alongside the perpetrator's personal responsibility. In the swirling chaos and misery of the 1930s, it was a retreat from progressivism to claim that the context did not clarify the crime. And yet the purpose of incarceration in the Gulag was not simply punishment; it was also reform. The aim was that an inmate would return to society as a true believer and a loyal participant. Carceral redemption was perhaps the purest expression of Stalinist totalitarianism: it was the voluntary reshaping of the self in the surroundings of official unanimity, police violence and licensed brutality at the hands of non-political criminal prisoners.

No wonder that criminologists struggled to adapt these principles to the demands of the late 1970s and early 1980s. Stalinism's balance of punishment and redemption, and its rejection of explaining crime in social terms in favour of attributing exclusively personal responsibility for it, together with its decoupling of crime from justice according to any reasonable understandings of those words, was of little use for the quite different world of the Brezhnev era. During the Thaw, the process of reinterpreting Soviet crime began. Khrushchev's unmasking of Stalin's cult of personality and his description of some of the atrocities that accompanied it made possible a limited range of public and private discussions about the place of state crimes in Soviet life. The re-emphasis on 1917 as the source of ideological legitimacy and inspiration, and the attribution of a different status and set of rights to the individual person, facilitated a more rounded understanding of the contexts and causes of crime. The revitalized discipline of sociology offered an academic framework that drew on an international scholarship and pointed towards evidence-based explanations for crime. More generally, in culture and the professional press alike, experts and ordinary people debated how punishment should fit the crime, and how justice and socialism were supposed to align.[18]

It was a more promising way of analysing crime than inventing fictitious conspiracies and targeting innocent people with deadly prejudice. Yet the accused person in the 1970s faced a quick trial sitting in a 'cage' inside the courtroom, no jury, and, if guilty – and guilty verdicts were the norm – a lengthy sentence in a prison camp. Stalinism was over, but the Ministry of Internal Affairs and all the other organs had never been cleansed. The death penalty remained integral to the judicial system and was extended beyond treason and related crimes to murder in 1954. More than 16,000 murder trials between 1954 and 1964 led to death sentences, even though these sentences were in direct contravention of the original revolutionary promise that had outlawed capital punishment in 1917.[19] There were other parts of the justice system that told different stories about Soviet civilization. The comrades' courts, an early Bolshevik innovation reintroduced by Khrushchev, brought some community-minded people, activists and busybodies into the administration of justice as lay officials at a very local level, trying low-level offences, often those that transgressed neighbourhood social norms. In the early 1980s, 300,000 such courts were in operation across the USSR.[20] During the Thaw, Khrushchev insisted that he was returning to principles of socialist legality that derived directly from 1917. The rhetoric remained long after the Thaw and continued to guide a generation of legal theorists.

Crime was more likely when cities became less habitable. Signs of urban anomie were becoming obvious by the early 1980s. Shabbiness was common in public buildings and housing developments. Architects were designing microdistricts with twenty-storey apartment blocks in configurations that were practical and sometimes comfortable but which created a windswept, impersonal ambience. Drug abuse was getting worse, as supply routes out of Afghanistan opened up. Misfits multiplied.

Fifteen years before the death of Brezhnev, the famous actor Yevgeny Leonov played two minor roles in quick succession. Both films were about distinctively individual persons who made their own decisions about how to live. *The Magician*, released in 1967, recalled the culture of the Thaw, with its emphasis on vibrant socializing, personal relationships unfolding without the interference of institutions and its charismatic backdrop of Moscow's Arbat district under reconstruction. Much of the magician's work takes place at private parties in people's apartments. His 'tricks' really do seem magical – and the moral lesson he draws from his failed relationship with his fiancée is that happiness lies within himself, and might be released by doing a magic trick for a child. None of this could be explained by Marxism-Leninism, and none of it obviously lay within the formalities of Soviet life. The following year, *Literature Lesson* was released. It also starred Leonov as a secondary character, and the action takes place in the same part of Moscow as *The Magician*. The film is about a new teacher, a recent graduate, who is late for lessons every day. He takes his pupils on their own terms and talks to them naturally, as if they are on the same level. His pleasant eccentricity and natural credulity shades into a disarming tendency not to hide his doubts and scepticism. As the film goes on, his desire to pursue his real vocation, literature, increases. In the end he quits his job and leaves the school. Unable to flourish inside the prototypical Soviet institution, a school, he sets out to make his own way. And that is OK.

Schools were like they are everywhere: they cultivated a sufficient conformity; they established hierarchies; they made claims about the needs of the majority; they created spaces for exploiters. But some of them contained pockets of free-thinking or even other-thinking, creating communities of potential misfits. The specialized maths and physics schools that reached their heyday in the 1960s and 1970s became well known for developing strong ties between independent-minded teachers and intelligent – impressionable – young people, who were taken far beyond the curriculum. It helped to form some of the best mathematicians in the country, even in the world, but also equipped some with a worldview that effectively ejected them from Soviet civilization.[21]

It was a self-reinforcing cultural trope: the teacher who, possibly at risk to themselves and their career, nurtured a class or a select group, cultivating a sceptical worldview or idealistic mentality and a feel for poetry and music. *The Key That Can't be Transferred to Others*, directed by Dinara Asanova and released in 1976, takes place in a Leningrad school, where Marina Maksimovna, the form tutor of class 10B, spends free time with her pupils, talks critically and expansively with them on weekend excursions and seems to encourage a sense of communication and group solidarity that incidentally but perhaps inevitably excludes other teachers and the children's parents. It certainly has nothing to do with Soviet power or conventional ideology. In the end they get their revenge on her. Marina Maksimovna's group risks turning into a collective of misfits, rejected by the rest of the school and excluded from normal family relationships. Even worse, they risk failing to conform to the standards of inclusion that are necessary for a decent trajectory after leaving school. This was fundamentally what worried parents. Marina crossed a line and lacked the power to protect herself. She had to leave, but it was not too late for the children. Viewers could find Marina sympathetic or naive; such room for speculating about what a Soviet misfit might be was now built into the cultural space of Soviet civilization.

Lyudmila Ulitskaya had a darker view. In her historical novel about misfits during the Thaw and its aftermath, *The Big Green Tent*, she describes the same risky line that the charismatic pedagogue and the clever kids who loved him walked. In her novel, the extra-curricular talk is for a small group of apostles, exploring hidden historical sites in Moscow and learning about literature with the clever teacher whom they worship. Like in *The Key That Can't be Transferred to Others*, it is impossible to separate emotion from intellect in these formative conversations. But Ulitskaya describes a more claustrophobic, higher-stakes world. Her characters take greater risks. When the young teacher falls in love with one of his chosen ones, a female pupil about to graduate from school – and it is a love match – they all cross irretrievably into the domain of the misfit. It wrecks their lives. Ulitskaya was writing forty years later, but she was describing the milieu that shaped her own life as a Soviet person. She had enjoyed the outlook of the misfit and some of the lifestyle, but she couldn't commit to the worldview as a whole: it was too risky, it would damage her family, and it would put a stop to her career, first in science, then in theatre. Ulitskaya was not yet writing novels, but Dinara Asanova was a major director playing at the top of her game. She was a one-off who found a way to fit in so that she could express her uniqueness. When she was forty-two, in 1985, she died suddenly in Murmansk. She was there to direct another film. 'There was no other director of her generation,' writes Catriona Kelly, richly describing the subtle paradox of the successful Soviet misfit, 'who had the vulnerability, the self-belief, and indeed the managerial leeway to work in her high-risk, creative, yet apparently "unprofessional" manner.'[22]

Dinara Asanova managed to make a bohemian career at Lenfilm, combining unique individuality with insider expertise. Yet most Soviet misfits were only looking for a way to be themselves. That was what the characters in *The Magician* and *Literature Lesson* really wanted. Other misfits were more outrageous, superficially beyond the Soviet pale, but they too were trying to be themselves rather than to make a dissident case. They also needed a space to occupy within society. The authorities had either to find them a space, however liminal or vulnerable, or to imprison or destroy them. They were reluctant to use extreme prejudice to exclude people – Stalinism was over – though this was still a police state in which members of a sub-culture were routinely hated and bullied. But they could be hurt or made afraid while simultaneously being given some space to exist. Accommodating misfits was a necessary part of mature Soviet civilization. This even applied to what seemed an outlandish oxymoron: Soviet hippies, whose world has been researched by Juliane Fürst.

They wore bright clothes, painted flowers on their skin, smoked pot and joined an underground of parties and music; the men had long hair and strings of beads, and the women wore elaborate, swirling dresses of many patterns, and they were all inspired by a way of life that they traced to San Francisco. They seemed antithetical to Soviet society but many of their values were the same as the revolution's, especially those that aligned with personal liberation, gender, international peace and a commitment to the communal. When they gathered in open spaces, the police went for them. In October 1970, hippies from across the USSR travelled to a 'congress' at Tallinn. The KGB arrested leading hippies while they were arriving by train; the event was called off at the last moment. Sometimes the police went for individual hippies too, and they ended up in psychiatric hospitals, diagnosed with schizophrenia – even accepting the fake diagnosis as the only way to reconcile their inner life, their personal choices, and the recalcitrant environment in which they found themselves. Soviet hippies talked about being part of a *sistema*, a group of the like-minded, a network that hung out together and socialized communally. Yet *sistema* was also a scientific word for complex and ordered 'systems', and in time 'Soviet system' as well became a standard phrase among social scientists and historians for their entire object of study. The truth was that one *sistema* was buried in another. The KGB would plainly have preferred the hippies never to have existed. Even though a significant number of hippies were from the families of senior Party members, they were disgusting to the law-enforcing mind. But their habits and worldview, their material culture and economic reality – all these things were as much Soviet as they were from the global hippie movement.[23] Hippies were part of Soviet civilization just as the KGB were. The police state had a lot of control and still used a lot of force, but they did not own Soviet civilization; the USSR was a more complex *sistema* than that.

Hippies were not dissidents. They were people being themselves. Normality in the Soviet 1970s partly consisted in that aspect of modernity: of people trying to be themselves. The hippies were eccentric and marginal, but they were 'normal' in this sense. They were part of Soviet civilization rather than a threat to it, and they did not present themselves as critics of it. Similarly, rock music had elements of the underground and the marginal, as well as the official and mainstream. It came out of the West, sometimes in an official and licensed way, such as during Elton John's visit of 1979, sometimes in bootlegged records made out of X-ray plates. *Jesus Christ Superstar* was first performed in Vilnius in 1971. It was extremely popular, not least among Party officials.[24] Crazes for such bands as The Beatles and Deep Purple made their music impossible to suppress. They were not played on the radio, but it was easy enough to find copies of their music and at times difficult to escape them. And this music was scarcely subversive in any real sense. In his anthropological study of 'the last Soviet generation', Alexei Yurchak showed that it was common to be an enthusiastic consumer of Western rock and a supporter of whichever pillars of Soviet rule one found most useful.[25] There was no contradiction: or it was another self-sustaining paradox. Such bands as Akvarium emerged in an underground milieu, occupying that familiar halfway house that was tolerated but not given official exposure. *Roksi* was launched in 1977 as a samizdat journal – not an over-the-counter magazine – dedicated to rock music. By showing that rock was a Soviet form, not simply a Western import, and that rock musicians aspired to professional status, it implied that rock music's marginality was only temporary.[26] In Moscow, bands such as Arsenal and Mashina vremeni (Time Machine) played to hundreds of fans at a time, but they remained 'unofficial'. By the early 1980s, the lead singer of Mashina vremeni, Andrei Makarevich, was 'an officially recognized superstar', who lived in a fine apartment on Leninsky Prospekt in Moscow and insisted in an interview with the gold-standard rock journalist Artemy Troitsky that he really was not 'a bourgeois sell-out'.[27]

It was a capitalist-equivalent journey from misfit to celebrity, and it showed again the elasticity of Soviet civilization. Yet sometimes misfits could only be ejected. Some hippies found themselves on one-way flights out of Sheremetyevo after being granted exit visas, heading for new lives in the United States. Many of the Jewish emigrants who left the USSR in the 1970s, bound for New York or Tel Aviv, were not misfits at all, but were conventional people, often well educated, with professional qualifications, and deeply immersed in Russian culture, but who had been pushed to leave and who were worried about their children's prospects. Other Jewish émigrés were indeed misfits, including some irreconcilable intellectuals who found themselves unable to operate in Soviet society. Meanwhile, significant numbers of people in the Baltic republics and the western edge of Ukraine were still misfit populations, trying to lead normal lives but not accepting the terms of their citizenship. There were too many of them to be given exit visas. Volodomyr Ivasiuk, a celebrity composer of Ukrainian pop music, troubled by mental health problems and an unreconciled sense of self and identity, was found dead in May 1979 in a forest near Lviv.[28]

Spirituality was not a bar to being part of Soviet civlization but it undermined the prospects of an easy life. Society was as materialist as ever, with its five-year plans, fact-based risk management, focus on technology and manufacturing of consumer items. The atheist drive of the Khrushchev period had come to an end. Effectively, another compromise was reached with the leading religions. Religious practices in the villages of the Central Asian and Caucasian republics now took place largely out of view of the authorities. Urban planners now more often accepted the position of VOOPIiK and many other sympathizers from across Soviet society who sought to protect Orthodox churches, such as the Kazan church at the New Maiden convent in Leningrad (redesignated as 'the Mausoleum' in the 1920s), which had been considered vulnerable in 1972.[29] The attraction of icons was revived. Many were transported from villages to city apartments, where they were family owned or privately sold. It also informed the spiritually charged sculptures of Ernst Neizvestny in the early 1970s and the actual icon painting of Ivan Glazunov in the later 1970s and early 1980s. But these were only the external and material manifestations of spiritual possibility. It was the immaterial that really animated those who professed a connection to spiritualism and lived by what was spiritual, and it was those sentiments that were difficult to fit within Soviet civilization. This went beyond conventional religion. Hippies looked for a spiritual outlook. Occult circles and groups devoted to the 'esoteric' and paranormal became more common in the 1970s. Mystical texts circulated in samizdat. This sense of the world shaded into experimental psychology, spiritual healing, yoga, cosmism, Siberian shamanism, Indian teachings and Tibetan texts. All of this was misfit territory. But it was also the subject of academic learning. In Leningrad, the walls between the Academy and these other worlds turned out to be thin and even porous. Scholars from various disciplines met in Leningrad offices, often with foreign visitors, to discuss the academic basis of the paranormal, not to mention their own 'psychic experiences . . . and esoteric correspondences'.[30]

Gay people were at-risk misfits but were not a misfit group as such. After taking a more progressive approach to gay rights in the 1920s, the Soviet Union had fallen behind other modern societies by the long 1970s. The gay communities that were emerging in the United States and other Western countries, where informal networks and formal institutions alike facilitated mutual support, resistance, culture and representation, were absent in the Soviet Union. Gay sub-cultures were deeply submerged in Soviet society. There were established meeting places for gay men in certain public toilets, even one in an underpass at the Alexander Gardens, next to the Kremlin. A short walk away was the small, enclosed garden around the famous statue of Karl Marx, across the road from the Bolshoi Theatre. It had been a cruising ground since the 1930s. The fact that it was almost within sight of the Lubyanka only increased the fear that it was a site of surveillance as much as of sociability. Its strange durability prompted rumours by the 1970s of a moratorium on investigations, though later research showed that the numbers of prosecutions for sex between men did not decline. But the 'salons' of homosexual men and women persisted and might even have increased in number.[31] If homosexuality was thus excluded as far as possible from Soviet civilization, a wide range of heterosexual relationships were included. Couples without a marriage stamp in their internal passports often described themselves as 'husband' and 'wife' in everyday life, though they might have trouble checking into a hotel. Parents, of course, hoped for the best match for their children – 'associative mating' rose with ever-increasing enrolment in higher education while traditional unions persisted in parts of the Caucasus and Central Asia – but a diversity of acceptable marriages existed in the USSR. This was partly a reflection of the mixed marriages that proliferated across Soviet society, as well as the relatively young age of marriage compared to many other modern societies. There was also the sheer diversity of urbanites' decision-making about relationships. *In Love by Choice*, a 1982 film that starred the heartthrob Oleg Yankovsky, was based on the conceit that one person could wilfully take the decision to fall in love with another (a librarian and former footballer prove the point).

The spectrum of inclusion in Soviet civilization was complex. There were those who rejected a conventional Soviet life in the spirit of 1960s counter-culture but were not in turn excluded by Soviet society, or at least not completely. The Kaza café in Riga's Old Town had a bohemian, intellectual atmosphere. It was a place of free talk and laughter where women, youths, hippies, and a rainbow of diverse people gathered. A few were dissidents, or near-dissidents, or married to dissidents.[32] Many did not express opposition. They were permitted to live on the margins, trading security for autonomy. But the café itself was centrally located, and some of its habitués combined their nonconformist sensibility with a regular job and a more comfortable life.

On 1 September 1964, on the corner of Nevsky Prospekt and Vladimirsky Prospekt in the centre of old Leningrad, a new café opened its doors for the first time. It was soon named the 'Saigon' by its habitués. The naming was an example of local people appropriating institutions such as cafés by giving them names that stood adjacent to or in distinction to the values of the 'system', sometimes ones which evoked a dreamed-after West. The Saigon apparently got its name when a policeman came inside and tried to enforce the no-smoking rule within, saying the place looked like a bombed-out Saigon (the Vietnam War was underway). Cafés were part of the planned economy, but that was no barrier to their becoming their own places. Many of them cultivated their own particular interior style, clientele and specialities. The Saigon consisted of three connected rooms, where customers queued at the counter to get their order. One little-used room was for alcoholic drinks, another was a cafeteria that served hot food, but the main room served famously good coffee from espresso machines. It was this area that became a crowded bohemian hangout, attracting artists and poets, marginal university types, under-the-counter traders, especially in books, and a group of deaf-mutes. Open between 9 a.m. and 3 p.m., and then 4 p.m. and 9 p.m., it was the site of long, convivial, caffeine-fuelled conversations and unexpected encounters between people who did not work many conventional hours. Some regular customers brought their own wine and were charged a cover of 70 kopecks for the privilege. Drugs were sometimes exchanged. After it closed its doors for the last time in 1991, sociologists even came to describe it as an example of an 'informal public sphere', whose members were marginals – and, for primmer Soviet observers, an 'underclass' in an 'indecent place' – but they were still part of Soviet society.[33]

On 9 February 1984 at 4.50 in the afternoon, Andropov died as a result of the isolation that he had helped to impose on the people of the Soviet Union. His kidney disease would have been treated with better dialysis equipment in a hospital in West Germany or the United States, and he would probably have lived longer. Not only did he not seek treatment abroad, but he lived 'modestly' within the rules until the end,[34] which allowed him access to the best conditions the Kremlin Hospital offered. The succession was a quick affair. Konstantin Chernenko, a Politburo veteran and already number two in the Party, was an elderly and perhaps unprepossessing successor but he respected Andropov and knew how to sidestep Gorbachev's potential candidacy. The promotion of the Party operative from rural Siberia was uncontested on the day after Andropov's death.[35]

Andropov and Chernenko were outsiders, like all the top Soviet politicians. They came from the geographical and social margins and migrated to the political heights. Thanks to the revolution, many other politicians took similar journeys over seven decades. The two old men were the opposite of misfits, but they could never have once imagined fitting in where they ended up. Remnants of a misfit mentality survived even in the Kremlin. It was the paradox of post-Stalin normality: misfits were intrinsic to Soviet civilization.

Natalia Gundareva (and Oleg Basilashvili) in *Autumn Marathon*

# 18
# The Life Cycle of Eternal Socialism

By the end of the 1970s, Yevgeny Leonov, the star of Aleksandr Vampilov's *The Elder Son*, had become a national treasure. His fans loved him. The establishment honoured him. He was elevated to the stratosphere in 1978, appointed a People's Artist of the USSR in a ceremony at the Kremlin. On stage and screen, Leonov's crumpled face expressed every emotion. He helped to define and explain Soviet life to the people who were living it. His many roles captured the sense of a socialist life cycle, of reproduction from one generation to the next, during the brief age of Soviet eternity. Leonov's films hinted that a sense of permanent civilization was fixed at the level of every Soviet family.

Even so, economists were already seeing by the early 1980s that eternity was a mirage. A few began to look for sources of possible reform. Aleksei Kosygin, the author of the failed economic reforms of 1965, remained in the Politburo until his death in December 1980. He was never shunted upstairs or into a merely ceremonial post. He retained substantial control over light industry and domestic economic life. Some would-be reformers still admired his sidelined programme. Two months after his death, in February 1981, the Politburo renamed a range of facilities in his honour: a cotton mill in the Volgograd region, the Moscow Textiles Institute (which already bore the honour of the Red Banner) and a secondary school in the Moscow region. They placed a memorial board on the wall of Leningrad's October Spinning and Weaving Factory, where he had served as director many years before, on Leningrad's Kirov Institute of Textiles and Light Industry, where he had studied, and outside his elite apartment house at 3 Granovsky Street in Moscow.[1] Meanwhile, an outlying cadre of Soviet sinologists were looking with interest at Deng Xiaoping's market reforms in China.[2]

So 'eternity' did not shape the mentalities of all Soviet officials, some of whom imagined a quite different economic trajectory, but assumptions about the durability of Soviet civilization were a given in Soviet everyday life and culture. This sense of durability defined the external framework within which many human relationships were formed. This was the habitus in which Yevgeny Leonov's best work was developed. The complexity of being a parent was at the heart of Leonov's repertoire. In *The Elder Son*, his physiognomy expressed the deep furrows of fatherhood, manifesting aches that turned acutely painful while his character stood on the precipice of middle-aged terrors. Three years earlier, in the 1972 comedy *School Break*, he played a driver who dutifully attends evening school with his grown-up daughter. Leonov's sympathetic countenance made him a natural for dealing with young children, too. In the 1970 classic *Belorussia Station*, in which four veterans from the same platoon meet up at a comrade's funeral after more than twenty years of separation, Leonov plays the one with young children, whose domestic life was one of charming disorder. Even better known was his role in a film of the following year, where his gentle authority and twinkly smile made him entirely believable as the head of a pre-school nursery.

That film was created by one of Leonov's many admirers, the director and screenwriter Georgy Daneliya, a Georgian who influenced the blockbuster tendency of 1970s cinema. Daneliya cast or wrote several of Leonov's leading roles: the kindergarten director who was a doppelgänger for a murderer in *Gentleman of Fortune* (1971), the down-on-his luck plasterer who ends up lodging with a womanizing plumber in *Afonya* (1975) and the irresponsible workman on the lookout for a drinking partner in *Autumn Marathon* (1979). The actress Ninel Ismailova wrote that 'a democratic essence' (*demokratichnost'*) was Leonov's 'core quality', partly because he took on so many working-class roles.[3] Leonov himself played this up in an interview with *Socialist Industry* in 1976. 'The psychology of the worker,' he said, 'is my psychology.'[4] In *Autumn Marathon*, a melancholy Leningrad comedy, a university teacher, Buzykin, played by the Leningrad great Oleg Basilashvili, is being slowly destroyed by his own personality. He spends his days remorselessly pushing himself from one compartment of his life to another. At one point, Buzykin even misplaces a visiting Scandinavian Slavist, whom Yevgeny Leonov's character then takes on a drinking spree. Nobody is driven further to distraction than Buzykin's long-suffering wife, played by one of the most beloved of Soviet female leads, Natalya Gundareva. She is worried and irritable, unsure of how to deal with her grown-up daughter's own transition towards motherhood.

If Leonov (born 1925) was the socialist everyman-dad, Gundareva (born 1948) was the Soviet Union's mum. *Autumn Marathon* was not their first experience of working together. They had known each other since the start of the decade, when Gundareva began her theatrical career. She joined the company of Moscow's Mayakovsky Theatre straight out of theatre school. Leonov was also part of the company. He had spent twenty years at the city's Stanislavsky Theatre and would shortly move on to Lenkom (a self-consciously grand venue named after Lenin's Komsomol, and just off Moscow's Pushkin Square), but his few years at the Mayakovsky overlapped with Gundareva's launch.

Such performers as Leonov and Gundareva had imaginations big enough to conjure up the joys and terrors of parenthood for their audience. Leonov's performances drew on experience, too; his own son turned seventeen in 1975, when *The Elder Son* was in production. On 30 September 1974, Leonov sent a letter to the boy from Leningrad; they corresponded very regularly when he was working on location. 'It's a long time since I felt such joy from a play or a film script,' he wrote, describing Aleksandr Vampilov's text and especially his creation of Sarafanov, the father in *The Elder Son*. Leonov was already inhabiting the character, drawing partly on his own family life. 'I say to myself: "I am Sarafanov",' he wrote to his son, 'and an absolute clarity comes to me, as if everything is being sincerely performed in front of me: the people, their actions, the facts.' Leonov reflected on Sarafanov's predicaments of fatherhood, before seamlessly moving to their own father–son relationship as if it was part of a whole. 'You have to read Chekhov, he'll help. Andrei, take down the little green volume, and we'll read it together. Don't annoy your mother, Andrei: you won't pass your exams without algebra. Call me after twelve at night or before nine in the morning.'[5]

Gundareva, though, had to make it up. She had no children of her own and never would. Her direct experience of maternity was as a daughter, not a mother. When she was working out how to play her signature role, as the mother of ten children in the 1980 classic *One Day Twenty Years Later*, she reimagined her early family life and drew on the personal characteristics of her own mother, Elena, a senior engineer.[6] Gundareva was born in 1948 and brought up in a communal apartment in the Taganka district of old central Moscow. There were forty-three residents; they competed for the use of one bathroom. Gundareva was an only child. Natalya's grandmother helped to bring her up, carrying her soup out to the yard if the child refused to come in to eat. Round the corner from the yard where she played as a child was what would become the great Taganka Theatre of the Thaw, the one that Yuri Lyubimov built and Vladimir Vysotsky breathed life into. It came into its own when she was sixteen years old, but by then the family was living in modest accommodation a stone's throw from Red Square. They could look out of the window and check the time on the famous clock on the Kremlin's Saviour Tower.

In the late 1970s and 1980s, Gundareva was an indeterminate age on screen, sometimes looking like a very young woman, but often playing roles that cast her as significantly older than her own age. It made her a mother-figure for all seasons. In *A Sweet Woman* (1976), she played Anna, a young single mother who ages as the film goes on. Her child is the result of a teenage liaison with a medical student. But Anna's sweetness is ambiguous. She is a confectionery factory worker who resourcefully makes the best of her job. She leaves her son with his father's parents, gentle souls from the intelligentsia, throughout his infancy, but shows them no kindness in return. Later, she marries a war veteran and makes him trade on his privilege to move quickly through the housing queue for a better apartment, while neglecting her son. It suggested that *meshchanstvo*, or vulgar bourgeois selfishness, is contrary to good Soviet motherhood. Six years later, in 1982, Gundareva played Lyulya in *Children's World*. The character was an anxious thirty-something single mother of an infant boy. This made her an outlier; the Soviet Union was still a country where many couples started their family when they were very young. Her older friend, Misha, comes to visit at New Year. While Lyulya dotes on the boy as he succumbs to a temperature, Misha scours the city for the specific gift that the boy believes Grandfather Frost has promised him. Misha does it because his own mother somehow contrived to preserve his childhood illusions during the siege of Leningrad, and because he wants to be a father to the child. Likewise, Gundareva's leading role in *One Day Twenty Years Later* idealized motherhood. Her character, Nadya, sits in a school reunion and looks back on the last two decades of her life. Her former classmates are bored, embarrassed or insensitively sympathetic when they hear she is a mum who works at home. At the end, her ten children show up and she becomes the centre of attention. Everyone else's lives suddenly seem similar, even monochrome.

Giving birth ten times defied all kinds of odds. One was statistical. Fewer children were being born in some of the republics. The Soviet Union was growing older, but at different rates in different places. This altered the demographic profile of the European parts of the USSR, and the demographic balance between republics. By the 1970s and 1980s, under pressure from the housing shortage, many families outside the Central Asian and Caucasian republics opted to limit family size. A disproportionate number of family units in the western zones of the USSR now contained a single child. In the Russian republic, the population grew by 4.9 per cent between 1969 and 1979, but by 3.9 per cent between 1980 and 1989; in the Ukrainian republic, the corresponding numbers were 3.5 and 1.7. But in Uzbekistan, population increase was 26.4 per cent in the 1970s and 27 per cent in the 1980s, while in Tajikistan it was even higher: 28.9 and 32.3.[7] Even more than in other countries, medical statistics and demographic data were a contested field between scientific practitioners and government, but Soviet demographers held their ground in the face of the censors and published accurate data;[8] Soviet civilization pondered its growing demographic maturity.

In 1977, when the new Soviet constitution was approved, the Soviet Union turned sixty. The rituals of the Soviet life-cycle contributed to the 'maturing' revolution. 'Octobering', an alternative to ceremonies such as christening, was introduced during early Bolshevik rule. It met with a mixed response. By the 1960s, though, a synthesis between Bolshevik discourse and everyday ceremonial had emerged. The so-called 'Solemn Registration of the New-Born Child' combined the social modernization and communist promise that marked the Khrushchev era. At one of the local soviet's public buildings – perhaps at one of the new 'Baby Palaces' – parents received the birth certificate, could celebrate in a banquet hall, make purchases from a shop, see the on-call doctor or nurse and receive information booklets. A secular analogue of godparents participated.[9] But traditional birth rituals persisted. They had always been ineradicable in the small towns and villages of the Central Asian and Caucasian republics. Across the Slavic republics of the USSR, even conformist communist parents might look away and allow a grandparent to take the child to their ancestral village to be christened by an Orthodox priest.

One complex zone was the *obshchezhitie*, a residential block or hall of residence, with single or shared rooms and communal facilities located off corridors. These places were owned by institutions such as universities or factories and maintained for the use of their staff, who were usually waiting in the queue for their own apartment. Single people were often trapped there. The sanitary norm allocated a defined number of square metres, rather than rooms or entire apartments, per person; single people were never quite entitled to all the square metres that made up even the smallest apartment. In *The Residence is for Single People*, released in 1983, Natalia Gundareva's character Vera lives in an *obshchezhitie* for the use of female workers in the textile factory where she is employed. Vera also operates an unofficial dating agency for her friends and acquaintances, sending personal adverts to magazines, distributing photographs, working out likely matches, arranging the rendezvous, offering advice about hair and make-up and issuing her judgement on the male suitor. From time to time the match ends in marriage – ultimately her own, to the new 'commandant' of the *obshchezhitie*, a grizzled former sailor – and a succession of weddings therefore punctuates the drama.

Weddings combined long-standing traditions with state atheism: the white dress, the smart suits, the registry office (the largest of which were styled as 'Wedding Palaces'), the legalistic jargon of the office clerks and the rubric of 'registering the marriage', stamping one's internal passport, and the banquet where guests called out 'bitter!' so that the newly married couple could kiss and create sweetness. Yet Soviet civilization incorporated a variety of wedding rituals. For instance, in Buryatia (near Irkutsk and not far from Mongolia), there was a revival of traditional Buryat ceremonies after 1953, or at least a tendency to inflect modern Soviet-style weddings with older forms, such as ritualized gift-giving.[10] Across the union, one characteristic mark of Soviet civilization was the consistent tendency to marry young – before twenty – and to have children soon after. This did not change in the 1970s, in part because of the unreliability of contraception. High marriage rates at young ages might also have led to family structures that allowed almost all women to work outside the home. In 1971, women were again a majority of the workforce, at 51 per cent (the figure had been as high as 56 per cent in 1945, when so many men were in the army or were prematurely dead, but had fallen to 46 per cent ten years later).[11] It might have been that the availability of abortion as contraception of last resort, together with the more stable extended family households that resulted from long-term urbanization (56 per cent of Soviet people lived in towns and cities in 1970), as well as the availability of kindergartens for some families, and above all the economic inducements of paid work, all combined to make it plausible to raise a child in young adulthood. On top of this, many families in the Slavic republics now limited themselves to one child. Plenty of people in young middle age were already grandparents, regardless of education or profession.

Women usually gave birth in a hospital or maternity home (*rod dom*). Rules were strict. Women were admitted for a significant period around childbirth. Visiting was tightly regulated for sanitary reasons. When the father came, he removed his jacket and shoes and donned a white coat and special slippers, but most maternity homes did not allow them through the door at all. Instead, a familiar scene was of new fathers pacing outside, shouting up to the windows for updates. Extremely few were present at the birth, which was also true in much of Western Europe at the time, though attitudes were changing there more quickly. All of this increased the authority of the medics and reduced that of the woman who was giving birth. It was their institution; she was isolated. Their tendency to talk down cruelly to new mothers – to express *khamstvo*, or merciless rudeness, based on a complete imbalance in power relations – became a stereotype.[12] For decades, society had encouraged the active and well-informed patient, conditioned not to wait for a problem to develop, and to have basic medical knowledge. Yet the expectant mother's choices narrowed in the maternity hospital. During the postwar Stalinist period, Soviet experts pioneered the principles of the Lamaze childbirth method, which soon became popular among some groups of women in the United States, France and elsewhere. It emphasized 'psychoprophylaxis', seeking to control pain with mental techniques and breathing exercises, not with epidural medication. Lamaze derived from a commitment to women's autonomy as equal marriage partners and independent-minded expectant mothers. In the US, one of the consequences was that husbands should play a role during childbirth. The paradox was that Lamaze was not a matter of choice in the Soviet Union, let alone by the late 1970s. It helped to close off women's options and to isolate them within a system that denied them anaesthetics. By then, the popularity of Lamaze was in decline in other parts of the world. Epidural anaesthesia was improving in effectiveness and safety, and women had greater agency. But pain-relief drugs were not on offer in the Soviet maternity ward. 'I pity the women of my generation, the poor girls of the 1970s, who could not even imagine that such [maternity care] happens,' wrote an émigré to Israel, comparing her own experiences with those of her daughter many years later.[13] The tough, brilliant journalist Yevgenia Albats gave birth to her daughter in Moscow in 1988. Albats found the maternity home intolerable. She had to ask, cap in hand, to use a shower. For Albats, an opponent of the Soviet system, this was further proof that the Soviet Union was institutionally sexist. She argued that powerful men, from the Politburo to the hospital, were incapable of understanding the needs of women, of seeing them as equals, or providing adequately for their specific needs.[14]

In 1984, Natalia Gundareva starred in the title role of a two-part TV series called *Children's Home Boss*. In this workplace drama, Gundareva's days switch between resolving children's conflicts and giving speeches in local Party committees. Gundareva's children's home, like similar Soviet institutions, was both an orphanage and a residence for children with different needs, from the disabled to those affected by family breakdown. Soviet parents could 'renounce their rights' to a child, and the plot of *Children's Home Boss* in part revolves around such a case. Generally speaking, such children were institutionalized. So too, as a rule, were those who spent their entire childhoods in state care, yearning for a mother and a father. Law and culture alike tended against fostering and adoption, which only really became properly established, with at least reasonable financial provisions, in the early to mid-1980s, at the time that Gundareva's film was released.[15] The institutionalization of children also extended to boarding schools, which proliferated after Khrushchev's education reform of 1958. In 1974, the total population of children's homes and boarding schools was 886,000.[16]

The characteristics of fatherhood seemed to change in the 1970s. Large numbers of young people came of age during the Thaw never having known their fathers, who were killed during the war. By contrast, fathers were more present during the Brezhnev era, which contributed to a 'softened' form of masculinity in the period, though generational conflicts remained common.[17] The stereotype was that the mother was in charge, and there was an underlying assumption, especially in working-class families, that the father was a weaker figure, more susceptible to temptation and foolishness.[18] Policymakers and commentators criticized the fathers of the Brezhnev era for 'covert absence' and 'paternal passivity'.[19]

The father in *One Day Twenty Years Later* was nothing like this, and neither were many other fathers; but this film still wanted to show that the relationship between a person and their mother was at the centre of the Soviet experience. The large cohort of only children in the USSR gave the mother–child relationship a focused intensity that was easy to idealize. Certainly in the Russian republic, but in others too, a kind of 'extended mothering' took place, a multi-generational sequence of sometimes invasive matriarchal relationships. Patterns of upbringing might have an authoritarian streak; the writings of Benjamin Spock on child-centred family life only penetrated into Soviet discourses in the early 1980s. Consumer shortages of toys and children's clothes also moderated the codes and practicalities of motherhood, creating a domestic economy of hand-me-downs, small treats, few but highly prized presents and of a mother sporadically and deeply preoccupied by getting necessities and waiting in queues.[20] Still, mothers and grandmothers helped to define Soviet civilization.

During the long 1970s (and after), tens of millions of children were forever singing a 1962 favourite by Arkady Ostrovsky and Lev Oshanin. They asked for everlasting sunshine and sky, ending: 'Let there always be Mummy, / Let there always be I.' Nowhere was the eternal sense of late Soviet time more illusory than in this ubiquitous song.

There were gaps between the generations. Tensions festered. It was the same in all societies. In one of the most hilarious scenes in all of Soviet cinema, in the film *The Courier* (released in 1986 and set in the last gasps of the pre-*perestroika* era), the actor Vladimir Menshov attends a polite soirée in an intelligentsia household. Apropos of very little, he launches into a diatribe against the way that his grown-up son – otherwise an entirely respectable youth – drinks condensed milk straight from the tin. Completely losing his sense of propriety, getting red in the face and gasping, Menshov is yet another middle-aged man melting down, and the professor host, played by another star, Oleg Basilashvili from *Autumn Marathon*, has to console him. These were the gripes and frustrations of modern life. They happened everywhere, not just in the USSR. Near the end of the film *Valentin and Valentina*, about the love between two students, the two young protagonists run towards each other across a cityscape of central Moscow. When they come together and embrace, the viewer can see that the roof of the industrial building in the distance behind them is topped with tall letters spelling out the second half of Lenin's famous slogan – 'electrification of the whole country'. In a melodrama which focuses on whether two students can really make a life together, and in which a suffocating mother, played by the star Tatyana Doronina, steals the show, the glimpse of Lenin's words seems entirely ironic. The film is really about the loosening controls of an anxious, fearful mother unable to come to terms with generational change.

'The old guy was tough,' says one architect to another. 'He lived through all the epochs.' It is the closing scene of a two-part film of 1979, *In Faith and Truth*, about the housing construction drive and the architects who worked on it. Yevgeny Leonov was one of them, but for once he only had a minor role. They are gathered at their mentor's funeral, in a cemetery next to a church on the edge of Moscow. Snow and ice are everywhere. It is a 1970s moment: big hats, fur collars, suede coats, magnificent sideburns and superfluous shades. The old man that they have come to bury was born at the end of the nineteenth century. His was the cohort that was coming to adulthood at the time of the revolution. They were old enough to fight in the Civil War and made their entire careers as Soviet people, navigating – or sinking into – the country's successive tragedies and triumphs. The old architect's generation died in droves during the Terror, and if they lived, often lost their sons in the war; if, like him, they were lucky, they lived to enjoy stability, a decent salary, their own home and a reasonable pension. They were the old people of developed socialism, the wrinkled face of Soviet eternity. As a leading architect and a holder of the Order of Lenin, this man in particular enjoyed all the privileges. At the end, he was blessed. 'He died beautifully,' one mourner says, looking back to the old man's sudden death, where he was surrounded by friendly faces. 'Everyone should die like that,' says another.

Retirees made up a growing proportion of the population: 13 per cent of Soviet people were over sixty in 1975, double the proportion of fifty years before. Some republics, especially in Central Asia, had a significantly younger profile than others.[21] These demographic developments broadly matched those of other industrial societies. If an ageing population was a familiar element of modernization's later stages, so was the Soviet Union's medical response. Soviet gerontology developed in tandem with that of other modern health systems on the other side of the Iron Curtain.[22]

This made the elderly into a more distinctive cohort, with greater legal entitlements, material advantages and cultural capital than in earlier periods of Soviet history. Even so, it was only after 1991 that the elderly became more clearly defined as a separate group of the population, members of the 'third age'. 'In Soviet times, everything was simple,' said one interviewee in a much later sociological project about the subjectivity of old age. 'Everybody were "comrades" ... whatever their age.'[23] Even so, the Brezhnev generation were becoming a distinctive cohort of elderly Soviet people. As they grew into old age, they benefited from Khrushchev's pensions reform, as well as the complementary material advantages of being a veteran of the war or a holder of a labour honour. During the Thaw and the long 1970s, Soviet physicians worked intensively on the sub-discipline of gerohygiene, a branch of medical knowledge devoted to maintaining the health of the elderly through prophylaxis, exercise and attention to psychological factors, allowing them to support their children and grandchildren and sometimes to continue working outside the home.[24] The elderly also played a disproportionate role as volunteers and 'activists' in social organizations like neighbourhood patrols.[25] Older people naturally enough felt the range of melancholic emotions and anxieties associated with ageing. The pull of politics and push of ideology scarcely made any difference to this fundamental, chemical interiority.[26] Old people's personal subjectivity in the post-Stalin decades was therefore a variable combination of one's relationship with the state, involvement in the neighbourhood, sense of being indispensable for one's family – above all, of one's individual temperament and experience.

The mass housing programme made it possible for the generations to live apart, though multi-generational households were more common, especially when a grandmother lived with her children. In Central Asia and the Caucasus, the cohabitation of extended families was more common than in other parts of the USSR, though the possibility of migration and mobility – the Armenian settling in Irkutsk, the Uzbek studying in Kyiv – was shared across the republics. In fact, by 1979, 43.9 per cent of old people lived apart from their families, up from 30.9 per cent twenty years earlier.[27] Overall, though, economic realities and social norms combined with family ties to encourage grown-up children to tend to their parents in old age. Youngish grandmothers and great-grandmothers famously played an outsize role in bringing up children while mothers were at work. This tended to create an idealized memory of grandmothers – *babushki* – among those living through developed socialism.[28] Even so, nursing homes for the elderly grew in number and sophistication over time, with architects working carefully on rational and appropriate designs of interior and outside space alike; they had 200,000 beds in 1980, double the number compared to 1960.[29]

'Gerontocracy' became a description of high politics, but it was also a powerful metaphor for certain aspects of Soviet society. By the late 1970s and early 1980s, growth was noticeably slowing down in some socio-economic sectors; there was a sense of systemic ageing in two areas whose perceived success was intrinsic to post-Stalin Soviet civilization, healthcare and social welfare. Crucially, a declining proportion of national income was devoted to expenditure on health. In the tenth five-year plan (1976–80), spending on healthcare grew annually at 6 per cent. Growth per annum fell to 4 per cent in the next five-year plan (1981–5), but nobody really believed that the social system was growing; some estimates indicated that only 1.5 per cent of GDP was devoted to healthcare by this point. Indispensable drugs and other items were in deficit. By Chernenko's period in office, the main hospital in Yerevan reported shortages in 126 out of 825 standard medications. Substantial and serious medical research continued, but as the 1970s wore on, it suffered from familiar problems associated with institutional hierarchies, poor career development, inflexible planning and shortages of laboratory items. Reports emerged of dismal conditions. Most worrying were rises in infant mortality in 1984 and 1985.[30] More widely, life expectancy fell in the 1970s after decades of rises, by approximately 2.1 years for men and 1 year for women. It then stabilized and rose slightly by the mid-1980s (falling again in the 1990s).[31] In retrospect, it looked like the harbinger of the end of an empire and a way of life. But it was hardly the demographic crisis of the late Roman Empire. And the even more striking crisis in male health of the 1990s did not lead to a further political collapse.

On 13 July 1980, the company of the Taganka Theatre performed *Hamlet* for the 217th time. It was almost the summer break. Everyone was exhausted. They had recently got back from Poland, where they'd performed *Hamlet* among other plays in their repertoire. Vysotsky was especially tired. Only a person with an iron constitution could have endured his way of life. But he had heart trouble and had been in and out of hospital for years. Alcohol, drugs and tobacco made it all worse. He became an alcoholic in the 1960s and a user of different narcotics, including heroin, in the 1970s. In 1980, he was forty-two. His personal life brought joy and strain; his first marriage, which gave him two sons, ended in divorce, and his second wife, the film star Marina Vlady, a French actress born of Russian parents, lived far away in Paris. Vysotsky travelled to France regularly, and also visited other capitalist countries, including the United States, but endured a series of stressful encounters at the local passport office to make sure his exit and entry visas were in order. Aside from his work at the Taganka and on tour, he gave solo concerts, singing and playing his guitar, and made movies. His concerts were held across the Soviet Union, from clubs in Moscow to stadiums in Central Asia. It earned him extra money. Without this top-up, he got 150 rubles a month, like the other actors at the Taganka: a merely ordinary wage in return for rehearsing and performing an all-consuming set of roles. But he went from a demanding schedule to a total one not only for more cash, but also because he was convinced that song and verse could lift a person; and he was worried about his reputation and beset by ambition, fired by a nagging doubt that he had something to prove: that he was too much of a jack-of-all-trades, and not a proper poet like Yevtushenko or as polished a performer as Okhudzhava. Shortly before his death, he was giving five concerts a day in Bukhara. Every song and speech was an exposition of his emotional energy. His friends feared for him. Yet they still burned the midnight oil with him, night after night, in the salon in his Moscow flat, while he finished off his third pack of Winstons of the day, poured more drinks and took another tablet. He listened to whoever called in, laughed with them, recited his verse for them until somebody cried and he never turned away a friend. Then he sat writing poetry at his desk until the sun came up.[32]

An on-call doctor sat in the wings on that night of 13 July, waiting for something to happen. It was stuffy in the theatre, and Vysotsky could not keep up; he took a tablet when he needed it. As ever, Alla Demidova was playing Gertrude. Vysotsky struggled to remember his lines. Demidova prompted him. Before the interval, something went wrong with the curtain, and it suddenly fell, striking the coffin on the stage. Demidova was sitting on the coffin and she was wheeled round, so that she came face to face with the ghost of Hamlet's father, whom she, as Gertrude, was not supposed to see.[33] Everything looks like an omen in retrospect. In verse and song, Vysotsky embraced the proximity of death, as he had been doing for years. Many of his songs expressed a wilful melancholia, such as 'Save our Souls' (1967), about a doomed submarine crew, and his fans seemed instinctively ready to associate him with a Christ-like mythology when he died.[34]

Vysotsky's schedule went remorselessly on. The following day he put on a concert at Moscow's Institute of Epidemiology and Microbiology. On 16 July, he gave another in Kaliningrad. Two days later, he played for the last time at the Taganka. It was the day before the opening ceremony of the Olympic Games. He was noticeably ill, gasping and muttering to himself in the wings. Over the next few days he felt worse and thought he was dying. He lay down at home. People came and went. He died on 25 July.[35]

Vysotsky knew that he was dying both in the long term and the short term: that the combination of his work rate, lifestyle and heart problems meant that sooner rather than later his heart would give way. For cancer patients in particular, though, the usual practice was not to know for sure: doctors revealed the truth of a terminal diagnosis only to relatives but not to the patient. In the mid-1970s, Vladimir Soloukhin, the writer of village prose, toured the Sklifosovsky Hospital in Moscow with his very good acquaintance, the hospital's distinguished head of surgery, Boris Petrov. The doctor was already seventy; he was immensely distinguished and had been honoured by universities across the world. He still did his rounds of the hospital and conducted difficult operations. They saw one woman on the wards who had difficulty swallowing. She was exhausted and blotchy. She manifested an 'indifference touched with an inner cynical bitterness' and 'in the depths of her eyes ... the faint light of hope'. It was the same paradox and ultimate truth that so often attended death, anywhere and everywhere, especially among those due to be taken before their time: knowing the worst and yet never quite losing hope. Petrov told her she would soon be feeling better. The illness was taking its normal course. When they left the room, Petrov turned to Soloukhin and told him that the woman was suffering from the final stages of oesophageal cancer. Why, then, Soloukhin asked, did you tell her that things would get better? 'In the first place, as a doctor,' Petrov answered, 'in no circumstances do I have the moral right to tell a patient that he will get worse and die soon. And, in the second place, she cannot get any worse. Anything now is better for her, including death...'[36]

Keeping knowledge of terminal cancer from the patient was sufficiently embedded into everyday life to become a cultural trope; it was, for example, the device upon which the plot hinged in Yuri Trifonov's novel *The Exchange*, which was published in 1969 and entered the repertoire of the Taganka in 1976. This happened in many countries, but it was a formalized practice in Soviet medicine. The premise was that knowledge of a terminal diagnosis harmed the standard of life of a patient and reduced their lifespan further. It revealed a conflict in Soviet civilization between the ideal of liberated personhood associated with revolution and the exclusive hierarchies created by modern institutions and expertise. Yet, patients could see, if they looked, the implications of being discharged from hospital without a treatment plan for a cure. Or they could come to an agreement with their relatives about exactly how much knowledge was most helpful to have. Treatment at home was a common part of Soviet medicine; in many contexts, across one's lifespan, it was not unusual for doctors to visit or for emergency care to be provided at home for conditions that were fairly routine. End-of-life care at home was something else, though. Management of pain, in an economy where painkillers and anaesthetics were in relatively short supply by the early 1980s, was sometimes barely possible. The impact could be devastating.[37] Hospices were absent until 1990 and there were few after that, though at that point the hospice movement in the United Kingdom was only two decades old and its facilities were difficult to access.

'How does one die after Vysotsky?' asked Yuri Trifonov, poetically but with a poignant irony, as he himself died young the following year during an operation.[38] Forget the run of general secretaries that was about to follow – Brezhnev in 1982, Andropov in 1984, Chernenko in 1985; it was the most famous funeral in the Soviet Union since Pasternak's in 1960. Vysotsky lay in his casket on the stage of the Taganka, and numberless mourners shuffled past. They brought the open coffin out of the theatre and into the square outside. There were thousands of people. Flowers were everywhere. Police cars revved. KGB people blended in. Crowds gathered at the cemetery.

The Soviet way of death had Orthodox features: the calling of a priest, the removal (*vynos*) of the body from its first resting place, the open casket, interment three days after death, the special significance of forty days in the calendar of mourning. There was a jostling and wailing, even a 'DIY' strain to the culture of death – the crowd in the apartment courtyard, the truck used to carry the coffin. It bore the imprint of super-fast modernization, peasant migration and the ethnic and religious heterogeneity of the USSR. New efforts were made to establish a durable, secular, socialist funeral rite from the mid-1960s, as the epoch of eternal socialism got underway. A state official pronounced a forward-looking liturgy at the House of Civic Funerals or the person's home. The open coffin was often accompanied by a black-framed photograph of the deceased; the mourners might wear black armbands. Another ceremony took place at the graveside. The rite seemed again to exemplify a compromise between communist atheism and comprehensible tradition, between Party power and popular practice, embedded now forever in the modern socialist order.[39] In 1977 and 1979, decrees were introduced that sought more effectively to regulate cemeteries. Large socialist-modernist crematoria, set amid comfortable gardens, were built in the 1970s and 1980s in major metropolitan centres: Tbilisi in 1974, Kyiv in 1975 and Sverdlovsk in 1982, among many others.[40] The flip side of development was the tarmacing of disused cemeteries, a harsh process of Soviet modernization that was still embedded in urban planning in the 1970s.[41]

1931 was not the worst year in Soviet history. It was probably not even in the ten worst years – unless 1931 was the year when your own number came up, if you were a dekulakized peasant, or a worker killed by industrial negligence, or the child of an incarcerated parent. Children born in 1931 were members of an ambivalent Soviet generation. Many of them had young parents, who could barely remember life before the Russian Revolution. Others had slightly older parents, who might have participated in the days of October and then fought in the Civil War. Either way, the homes into which these children were born were Soviet homes. If they were from the countryside, their family probably lived on a collective farm. If their origins were urban, the view from the window was probably of a Soviet industrial cityscape.

But there were many places and experiences that were intermediate and transitional, part of a shifting and incomplete Sovietness. A birth year of 1931 meant that a baby emerged into a world that was being turned upside down during the first five-year plan.

This child would turn five in 1936, when a brief improvement in people's economic fortunes, the so-called 'three good years' of 1934, 1935 and 1936, were coming to a close. The child's first clear memories might have coincided with the introduction of the country's new Constitution in 1936, when the Party claimed that socialism had been attained and universal civil rights existed. What that meant in practice became clear the following year, in 1937, when the child turned six. During this most notorious year in Soviet history, the peak of the Great Terror, it was possible that a grandfather or a cousin might randomly be arrested and shot. If that happened, it would be a formative experience for any six-year-old.

In 1941, when the Germans invaded, a 1931 birth turned ten; in 1945, he or she was fourteen. Tens of millions of those children experienced occupation or displacement, open warfare, bombing, or evacuation, bereavement, hunger, poverty and orphanhood. Many of them died before reaching adolescence. Neither builders of 1930s socialism nor veterans of the war, this cohort became adults during the postwar Stalinist period and were already twenty-two when Stalin died. Some of them benefited from the dramatic social mobility of this period – more so than the next generation. Theirs was a cohort that still had a good chance of taking advantage of manic social transformation and affirmative action. Significant numbers who were born in very poor conditions in the most obscure parts of the USSR found routes to highly credentialled educations, accelerating through their professions and becoming leading figures.

The 1931 generation was twenty-five when Khrushchev gave the Secret Speech. Its members spent the Thaw establishing themselves in careers and family life. This was a young adulthood of dramatically new cultural opportunities, as well as social improvements. They had a much better chance than their parents of obtaining adequate housing while their children were still young, not to mention having a choice of reading matter and discussing it openly with friends behind their own front door. When Khrushchev fell from power, they were thirty-three. Eighteen years later, when Brezhnev died, they were fifty-one. These people were among the most dynamic and imaginative citizens who populated the developed socialist era. But most of them only knew about the outside world not from travel but from what they could read, watch and listen to. Plenty of them lived tough, hard-scrabble lives. They were true creations of the Soviet system.

Among the people born in 1931 were the prize-winning – and blind – mathematician Anatoly Vitushkin, the Olympic gold-medal-winning shot putter Galina Zybina, not to mention the two men who would bring the country to its end, Boris Yeltsin and Mikhail Gorbachev. By 1985, this complicated, ambivalent generation – the Gorbachev generation – was reaching its mid-fifties, and it was taking over.

PART FOUR

# The Country That Committed Suicide by Accident (1985–91)

Raisa Gorbacheva and Mikhail Gorbachev

# 19

# The Last Revolutionary

On the cusp of power, out walking in the garden, Mikhail Gorbachev turned to his wife Raisa. She was his first adviser, his trusted companion, his love match. It was the night before the Politburo confirmed his appointment as general secretary. They were out of range of KGB recording devices. 'We can't go on living like this,' he said.

Gorbachev liked this memory. He described it in his autobiography and referred to it in interviews. Raisa did too, making much of it in her memoirs.[1] It contains a rich, historic sentence, almost too good to be true, and open to unending interpretation: *we can't go on living like this*. In part, Gorbachev meant that the ongoing revolution, underway now for sixty-eight years, was blocked by economic inefficiency and ideological compromise. He wanted the revolution to relaunch, more effectively and humanely. Meanwhile, new developments in the arms race heightened the obstacles in the revolution's path. President Reagan's attempts to militarize the cosmos with the Strategic Defense Initiative – the Star Wars project – threatened a new level of financial and technological challenges. Yet the arms race was not an existential threat to the Soviet Union so much as to the whole planet. Gorbachev was worried about the risk of either superpower launching a first nuclear strike by accident. Living like this was just too dangerous, and it turned out that Reagan had similar worries.

Years later, Gorbachev had his own reason to emphasize his conversation with Raisa. It lent a retrospective coherence to his narrative of *perestroika*, suggesting he had a clear sense of the problem from the start. For posterity, the conversation had a different value. It offered a window onto the range of possible futures that were visible to contemporaries at the moment of Gorbachev's appointment. Assuming he really did say those words to Raisa, and that their memories had not created them, the sentence revealed a moment when the imagination of Soviet politics suddenly broadened, and Gorbachev could at least conceive of a turning point towards reform. He had not yet made a decision or devised a plan. But his words to Raisa suggest that a choice existed at that moment. 'Thus I heard these words for the first time,' she said later. 'Today millions of people have repeated them, whole legends have arisen around them. That night, you could say, a new stage began, sharply changing our life and mine.'[2] Some historians would later claim that *perestroika* – the term Gorbachev himself deployed for his political and economic reforms, a word for 'rebuilding' that was usually associated with the refashioning of an existing structure rather than the reconstruction of a whole society – was waiting inside him, and that once he was in power, he had the chance to deliver it.[3] Gorbachev agreed.

Everything about Gorbachev's politics and career was a product of Soviet civilization. Gorbachev became a tragic figure – his ideology crashed, his politics failed, his beloved wife died – but that was unknown in 1985. The least-worst analytical tool that we can use to interpret his career at that point remains the one he used himself – that he was a child of the Twentieth Congress. He was also a workaholic, a person of duty and an alpha competitor, possessed of a ruthlessness that had a cruel as well as a benevolent edge. When he arrived in Moscow in 1978, he was forty-seven years old, and many fellow politicos saw him as the man to watch. The following year he was a candidate member of the Politburo. The year after he was a full member. He was a green-fingered politician who knew when to keep quiet – he did nothing to block the invasion of Afghanistan in December 1979 or the exile of Andrei Sakharov to the city of Gorky the month after – precisely because it would not have occurred to him to do otherwise.[4] To have spoken out against decisions that had already been made could only have been quixotic, which was not a recognized feature of Soviet high politics.

When Andropov became general secretary in 1982, Gorbachev retained the agriculture portfolio, but his authority increased. He occasionally stood in for the boss, who was often in hospital. Everybody knew that Andropov wanted Gorbachev eventually to succeed to the leadership (perhaps after the head of the Ukrainian republic, Vladimir Shcherbytsky). Andropov knew that the nature of Soviet politics required him to die before the matter could be settled. By that point, the question of succession would be beyond even him.

Following Andropov's death, the old men of the Politburo had enough power left to block Gorbachev's promotion. Konstantin Chernenko got the nod. Chernenko was another outsider, born in a Siberian village six years before the revolution. He died thirteen months after assuming power at the age of seventy-three. In the interim, Gorbachev had strengthened his grip on Politburo politics. He had rivals for the top job. Grigory Romanov was the period's great orchestrator of Leningrad politics. Heydar Aliyev was Azerbaijan's boss for thirteen years before coming to the Politburo in 1982. Vladimir Shcherbytsky, approaching seventy, ran Ukraine for a similar period. Yegor Ligachev was a clever and effective Central Committee man, a sprightly sixty-five with almost a quarter of a century at the top of Party politics behind him. Nikolai Ryzhkov knew all the levers of the planned economy and was the technocratic option. The Politburo unanimously lined up behind Gorbachev.

The last Soviet revolutionary was also the last great outsider, the boy from beyond Stavropol whose accent Muscovites laughed at. But in the sixty-eight years of socialist revolution, the meaning of 'outsider' had inevitably changed. Gorbachev was not an insider like the men born in Moscow of Moscow parents, the slick professionals with smooth promotions and secure lives. He had the chip on his shoulder that came from his village origins, and the electric energy of extreme ambition. Gorbachev was an historic figure, but not because he was an aberration, or because he could look at the USSR like an outsider, or because his eventual reform plan derived from external, Western sources. He was a creature of Soviet civilization. After thirty years of hand-to-hand conflict in committees, he was bound to pursue reforms that were Soviet in design and inspiration. Completely accidentally, they caused the end of the USSR.

The economy was in decline. According to data from the CIA, GNP growth had fallen from a postwar high of 8.9 per cent per annum, during the most rapid stage of late Stalinist reconstruction, to a new low of 1.7 per cent between 1981 and 1985. Such was the change between the fourth five-year plan and the eleventh five-year plan. By the early 1980s, CIA numbers on the Soviet economy were noticeably lower than official Soviet ones. They suggested that growth in GNP between 1984 and 1985 was 0.9 per cent.[5] Ordinary people saw longer queues and under-pressure welfare and health systems.

Even so, the Soviet economy was not in a tailspin. Some sectors performed better than others. Textiles, for instance, were in a relatively strong position. Between 1945 and 1985, the area under cotton cultivation grew by 60 per cent. Even between 1965 and 1985 alone – the Brezhnev era and its immediate aftermath – the increase remained robust at 36 per cent (the average increase of all crops was 9 per cent). This was the basis of continuing increases in the output of fabric, rising from 6,152 million square metres in 1970 to 7,677 in 1985. In 1986, the Soviet Union accounted for 17 per cent of world cotton production (in third place behind China and the United States).[6] Meanwhile, pre-*perestroika* reforms hinted at the promise of a mixed economy. For example, before Gorbachev, twenty polyclinics in Moscow were permitted to charge a fee. A total of 570 fee-charging medical institutions, mostly in dentistry, existed across the USSR by the mid-1980s. At the start of 1986, measures were proposed to permit this form of budgeting more generally.[7]

Soviet society was more urban, diverse, complicated and in some ways more plural than two decades before; it was more modern, with a greater range of interests and insecurities. There were crowds of educated young professionals, multitudes of old-age pensioners, streams of ethnically diverse migrants and many other still more varied groups: they all needed to access the advantages of modern life at a revolutionary tempo, but often could not. Soviet civilization was in this sense 'stuck'; the Party and government needed to be more responsive and open-minded.[8] Meanwhile, popular values, which combined a 'vernacular' Marxism-Leninism with common morality, were under threat. By the mid-1980s, this 'everyday socialism' was undermined by corruption, which damaged social justice, and by hierarchy, which hampered equality, and by the unresponsive state, which made individuals and collectives (self-supporting groups of co-workers or neighbours) further detached from the Soviet project.

At the same time, HIV and AIDS were beginning their transmission across the USSR. Three months after Gorbachev was appointed as general secretary, the Ministry of Health began urgently to look for possible cases of the disease. Medical debates and public discourse were framed in homophobic terms from the start. Yet the first reported case of HIV was of a young teenage girl who was diagnosed in 1984 following a blood transfusion in the previous decade.[9] Narcotics created another public-health crisis. During the 1970s, the authorities periodically clamped down on the cultivation and sale of substances grown or manufactured inside the USSR, from opium poppies to LSD; the Caucasus and Central Asia were international entry points for heroin and other drugs. The drugs trade was given momentum by the chaos of the Afghan War. Increased deaths from drug use, the transmission of HIV through dirty needles, the cheap deaths of sex workers as the AIDS epidemic began: all these were signs of the moral distress that accompanied the onset of *perestroika*.

Gorbachev thought that 'the system' needed to be reformed. But he operated within policy frameworks that would have been recognizable to Andropov. Pointing to low growth rates and the urgent necessity of increasing national income, he fruitlessly increased investment. The tagline for the policy was 'acceleration' (*uskorenie*). More money was channelled into technological research as well as into the military, but in the absence of energizing systemic reforms, which came slightly later, the effect was transient. Growth improved briefly in 1986 but fell back again in 1987. A related issue was workplace discipline. Gorbachev carefully read Andropov-era workplace surveys. One of these investigated 800 enterprises in Moscow and claimed that only around 10 per cent of workers were still on duty in the final sixty minutes before clocking-off time.[10] There were many reasons for this, including the flexibility of a workplace *kollektiv* in which co-workers helped each other deal with the exigences of Soviet life by standing in for them when they needed to be elsewhere – queuing for a deficit item, searching for medical treatment for a family member, dealing with a childcare crisis. But alcohol abuse was another cause of absenteeism. This was a concrete problem that government could target.

The new general secretary might have been a Soviet man, but he had a unique style. If the novelty of his appearance and manner was obvious from the outside – Margaret Thatcher famously called him a man she could do business with, even before he became general secretary – it was apparent too inside the Soviet Union. He was smart and bright, sober and dynamic, well educated and full of ideas. Metropolitan types might parade their prejudices when they heard his provincial southern accent, but they could not match him. He could wade into a crowd, talk to ordinary people and occasionally stop talking and *listen*. He shone with the prospect of a better politics. It was a complete contrast to his predecessors. Power had skipped a generation. The gerontocracy was vanishing. Typically, on 16 and 17 April, a month after assuming the leadership, he had meetings with Party members in Moscow's historic Proletarsky district (*raion*), a cradle of the revolution, before touring its signature car plant, where Zil limousines were manufactured, speaking to workers, designers and managers. Khrushchev had found energy in similar interactions, though as a talker not a listener. Then Gorbachev went to the Nagatino district, talked to pupils and teachers in School Number 514, conversed with shoppers in a department store, and doctors, nurses and patients in the City Hospital Number 53. It might have been a bit more stylized, rehearsed and awkward, but Gorbachev also paid a call on Tamara and Vyacheslav Nikishin, a 'typical' young couple who lived in the district. What was especially interesting was how the media constructed these interactions, how much the newspapers made of them.[11]

Lenin supported temperance. Andropov pondered alcohol controls. Gorbachev swallowed the measure whole. He had the abstemious temperament, the political capital and the momentary lack of self-awareness to go for a maximal anti-alcohol policy. Prohibition – at least in partial form – was bound to be unpopular and even ridiculous, but he introduced it all the same. They called him the 'mineral water secretary' (*mineral'nyi sekretar'*, a play on *general'nyi sekretar'*). The reform had support across key members of the Politburo, not least Yegor Ligachev, who would play a leading role in the drama of *perestroika*. Much of the policy work had been developed before 1985. There were, of course, parts of the USSR where no problem existed, especially in those regions and republics dominated by Islam, but the drinking cultures of the Slavic republics in particular flowed through many factories. Three times as much vodka and other spirits were produced in 1980 compared with 1940. Health suffered, though the exact impact in a society where consumption of tobacco and saturated fats had also been rising, while other indicators of diet and lifestyle were improving, was difficult to quantify.[12] Still, by the late 1970s, life expectancy of men and women had diverged, falling to 62.5 for men but rising to 72.6 for women. Alcohol was likely a major cause. Petty and violent crime alike – domestic violence above all – were fuelled by alcohol. Between the eighth five-year plan (1966–70) and the eleventh (1981–5), state income from the sale of alcoholic drinks almost tripled, reaching 169 billion rubles. Gorbachev argued that this revenue's very indispensability for investment in social and consumer sectors created a destructive dynamic at the heart of the Soviet economy.

The proximate aim was to stop people drinking on the job and prevent them showing up hungover in the factory, but the policy went much further than this. Gorbachev's campaign began shortly after his assumption of power. In May 1985, the All-Union Voluntary Society for the Struggle for Temperance was established. This association occupied the grey zone between voluntary activity and state initiative, the territory of Soviet civil society. Alcohol could now only be purchased in certain shops between 2 p.m. and 7 p.m. Drinking was banned near schools, hospitals, stadiums and some other public institutions. Tighter laws on underage drinking were introduced. The legal limit was now twenty-one.[13] Estimates vary, but according to Gorbachev's leading economist, Abel Aganbegyan, sales of pure alcohol fell from 8.4 litres per capita in 1984 to 4.3 in 1986. Tax revenue fell by as much as ten billion rubles per year. Sales of sugar skyrocketed as people made moonshine, leading to shortages and rationing.[14]

At least in theory, the reform criminalized ordinary people, who were really just going about their lives and not doing anything 'abnormal'. After all, moderate drinking with sociable meals was as much a part of Soviet habits as drunkenness. For most people, 'going out' at the weekend meant a perambulation round the park, a trip to the cinema or a visit to friends rather than a binge. Drinking was not sexualized by advertising. Town centres were not gridlocked by a 'Friday night' culture. And there were taboos. University teachers drank tea with their students, not sherry or wine. Meanwhile, by 1986, various indexes associated with alcohol abuse had fallen: car accidents by one-fifth, crime by one-quarter, and absence from work by one-third. In 1980, 26.4 deaths per 100,000 were attributed to alcohol; in 1987, it was 9.1. The life expectancy of women rose by one year between 1984 and 1987, but it rose a full three years for men. All the statistics can be critiqued on archival and epidemiological grounds, but the tendency was clear. Gorbachev claimed in 1988 that the reform had saved one million people from premature death.[15]

At 1.23 a.m. on 26 April 1986, the power plant at Chernobyl's reactor number 4 exploded during a planned shutdown. Preternaturally, in this Soviet territory reclaimed from the Pripat marshes, it sounded 'like a human moan', according to one of the men in the control room. Firefighters rushed to the inferno. Gorbachev received the news a few hours later, at 5 a.m. He was wakened specially; Nikolai Ryzhkov, the head of government, had been formally overseeing operations since 2.40 a.m. In the hours and days that followed, Gorbachev had a short fuse, an exposed nerve and a limited sense of the problem.

Different methods were used to bring the situation under control and to confine the dispersal of deadly radiation. Dropping sand onto the reactor from helicopters, burying it from above, was one; channelling liquids through newly built tunnels was another; sending lead-clad soldiers onto the roof with shovels for a few seconds apiece was a third.

They were flying blind. But leadership – or perhaps its absence – made everything worse. From the management of the reactor through the regional and republican Party apparatuses, and all the way up to the Politburo, major figures refused to take responsibility. This had a dreadful consequence. It delayed a public announcement by several days, denying people the chance to protect themselves against radiation poisoning. Among many egregious omissions, evacuations were postponed and major public events, notably May Day celebrations in Kyiv and elsewhere, were not cancelled.[16]

Only on 14 May did Gorbachev address the country about the Chernobyl disaster. He came on television and his speech was published the next day as a splash across the front page of *Pravda*. His comments were a masterclass in the ambivalences of Soviet civilization on the eve of its radical reform. He was, on the one hand, nineteen days late. He assumed that people already knew what was going on. He claimed that the Politburo was working round the clock. His stock of Cold War clichés about the Americans and West Germans was a familiar distraction from the issue at hand. In his discussion of the causes of the disaster, he was verbose yet lacking detail. Sitting behind a desk, papers in hand, he looked like a Party boss, not a revolutionary on equal terms with the people, or even a dictator pleading for their help in the face of destruction.

And yet, on the other hand, he did give the speech. He did not have to. This was not like previous tragedies, including the Ozyorsk nuclear leak of 1957, which were not acknowledged, let alone publicized. It was a release of public information. Gorbachev didn't only talk in ideological abstracts, and he avoided a description of heroic or villainous types, but instead mentioned real individual persons, emphasizing personal wellbeing and the value of single lives. He named particular victims and heroes and spoke of 'the deep compassion' that the Party and government expressed for them. 'Providing aid for people, I repeat,' he underlined, 'will remain our foremost task.' The point was not quite cynical. He praised the objectivity and assistance of the International Atomic Energy Agency under the leadership of Hans Blix, hinting at future international cooperation in the protection of the planet.[17] The speech went on and on – that was a feature of the Soviet genre, and one which suited Gorbachev – but it contained a note of novelty.

A week later, construction of a 'sarcophagus' to encase the buckled, emitting reactor got underway. The tide was turned, but the deaths, sickness, trauma, bereavement and ecological defilement went on. With the benefit of hindsight, it was common to argue that Chernobyl exposed all the flaws of the Soviet system, setting the USSR on a direct line to collapse. The case rested on the claim that the last remnants of trust in the Party and government now evaporated, and also that Ukrainians now began to turn against the union more decisively, prefiguring the fragmentation into national republics of 1991.[18] And the case emphasized the USSR's international humiliation. 'Chernobyl in 1986,' wrote one historian three decades later, 'spelled the end of Soviet civilization.'[19]

All of this was impossible to prove. The Soviet Union had survived much worse. Other countries long outlasted nuclear disasters. In any modern society, people's long-term responses to a single event, even one that nearly everyone agreed was tragic and disastrous, are bound to vary. Their levels of understanding and their assessment of risk and significance differ; the lasting imprint on their consciousness is particular for every person. The sheer improbability of Soviet collapse in 1991 suggests that immediate causes might have special significance. Even the popular feeling and expression of Ukrainian nationhood seemed to change quickly during a few months in 1991, making Ukraine a proximate cause of collapse rather than a design flaw in the Soviet project overall.

The argument that Chernobyl broke the USSR was associated with another claim, that the explosion only exposed existing failures of Soviet technology that were already dooming the USSR to breakdown. Understandably enough, the RBMK reactor had a terrible press after April 1986. But this was not the case before. Sonja D. Schmid argues in her analysis of the technological, managerial, planning and personnel elements of the Chernobyl catastrophe that it was a Soviet event in a Soviet place where Soviet technology was used, but it is impossible to isolate 'a singular, inherently Soviet' cause for what happened. The very complex interconnection of processes, practices and even ideology led to disaster, but in the end the disaster at Fukishima twenty-five years later showed that the nuclear sector in Japan was also subject to ultimately similar vulnerabilities.[20]

Even the claim that Chernobyl opened Gorbachev's eyes to the necessity of *glasnost* (the core principle that the reformers paired with *perestroika*, usually translated as 'openness', suggesting free speech and transparency, and deriving from the Russian word for 'voice') bears the marks of narrative convenience, imposed by observers after the event or by Gorbachev's own memory. For sure, ecological apocalypse convinced him that his fellow citizens deserved accurate public information. He now accepted the desperate need to communicate in more modern and effective ways with the population, and by extension to create a more open relationship with the outside world. But while the vision of openness became increasingly vivid, the role of Chernobyl as a cause in its creation was not always easy to make out. For a start, international access to the site of the Chernobyl power plant was curtailed soon after it had initially been permitted. In July 1987, a semi-open trial of six local officials began in the semi-closed city. In lieu of a transparent public inquiry and an honest holding of the negligent to account, it looked like a whitewash of the higher-ups and an attempt to keep the blame within the plant itself. Although it was not a Stalinist show trial, it was an uncomfortable reminder of the failures of Soviet justice. The defendants included Viktor Briukhanov, director of the plant at the time of the explosion, and Nikolai Fomin, the chief engineer. They were useful scapegoats.

But more important was the record of the 410,000 'liquidators', inadequately remembered and rewarded, the men who stopped the disaster with gloveless hands, shovelling burning graphite and digging tunnels under the reactor. A true *glasnost* of Chernobyl might have had more to say about them. They sacrificed their health and ensured that the deadly radioactivity did not spread further into the USSR or other parts of Europe.[21]

Two months before the tragedy of Chernobyl, on 25 February 1986, Gorbachev described his vision of society and politics. It was far from *perestroika* fully formed. Many possible futures still lay open, but it showed the mental world – one of 1980s Leninism – in which *perestroika* was being incubated. Gorbachev talked for several hours on that cold Tuesday in the Kremlin's Palace of Congresses, where the Twenty-eighth Congress of the Communist Party of the Soviet Union was opening. As the exhausted audience listened to his peroration, he declared that 'fulfilling the testament of the great Lenin' was their task. Gorbachev meant what he said. He was a sincere, educated Leninist who knew his way around the many volumes of Lenin's complete works. Like a rabbi or a philosopher, he repeatedly read the foundational texts, interpreted them and agonized over them, and sought within them the justifications for the positions he wanted to adopt. What he chose to emphasize was acceleration, democracy and social (or socialist) justice.

'What we need,' Gorbachev told a group of workers in Budapest the month after the Chernobyl meltdown, 'is more dynamism, more social justice, more democracy – in a word, more socialism.'[22] It was imperative that growth rates be boosted, that corruption be reduced, and that individuals had more say even in political life, but Gorbachev saw all of these things as natural results of 1917, if only ideology was properly interpreted. All of the core policies of *perestroika* and *glasnost* that he and his colleagues formulated over the next two years sprang from this formula. 'A decisive acceleration of the socio-economic and cultural development of Soviet society which involves radical changes on the way to a qualitatively new state is undoubtedly a revolutionary task,' Gorbachev wrote the following year. It was 'not merely a sequel, but an extension and development of the main ideas of the revolution'. The revolution needed kickstarting again. '*Perestroika* is a revolutionary process for it is a jump forward in the development of socialism, in the realization that we had no time to lose,' he wrote. 'It is very important not to stay too long on the starting line, to overcome the lag, to get out of the quagmire of conservatism, and to break the inertia of stagnation [*zastoi*].'[23] By definition, the latest update of the Marxist-Leninist revolution was focused on the future. On 25 February 1986, at the Twenty-seventh Party Congress, Gorbachev talked of how the delegates had to reflect on the Soviet Union in the twenty-first century and, more generally, 'humanity's tomorrow'. By the end of his very long speech, he was still talking about the future construction of communism.[24] Acceleration was precisely about speeding up progress towards the future. It was a revolutionary concept.

Economists such as Abel Aganbegyan and Leonid Abalkin designed an economic programme to match these principles. Aganbegyan became especially well known. An Armenian, born in Georgia and educated in Moscow, he spent his career in the higher reaches of Soviet academic research, immersed in its culture and testing its limits. A year younger than Gorbachev, he came of age during the late Stalinist era and completed his education during the Thaw. In the 1960s, he effectively argued that Kosygin's reforms did not go far enough. He claimed that excessively centralized planning put too much pressure on the circulatory system of the economy, so goods and money could not move around freely, inhibited by the lack of finance and credit. Firms and individuals could not get hold of the cash that they needed. Shortages of goods were one result. Hidden inflation was another. A third was a breakdown in incentives. This distorted the 'normal' relationship between waged work and material reward. Instead, people got the extra things they needed by 'speculating' on the black market, engaging in corruption and criminality and falling back on their perks and privileges, which were dispensed in kind or via alternative currency mechanisms.[25]

Gorbachev's first loosening of central planning came in November 1986. The Law on Individual Labour Activity was a tentative experiment in legalized entrepreneurialism. It permitted pensioners to work full time, and others to work part time, in self-employed roles. The law aimed to increase the sum of productive work in the economy, boost incomes and make it easier for people to take on second jobs. To some extent it formalized existing practices, but that very formalization marked a change in the way that the economy was officially imagined. It was confined to only a few sectors of the economy and also introduced some constraining regulations. In January 1987, joint ventures with foreign businesses were permitted, provided that the foreign ownership did not exceed 49 per cent. A few months later, in June, the Law on State Enterprises gave more autonomy to management, especially in their financial operations. Enterprises took substantial control over securely fixed five-year budgets. Having received their allocation, managers devised production targets, attracted sales, and decided on purchases. Enterprises had to fulfil state orders and stick within guidelines administered by industrial ministries, but they were allowed to take their parent ministry to court if their interests diverged.

Momentum was gathering. Twelve months on, in June 1988, the Law on Cooperatives allowed citizens to set up a business – a cooperative – and officially register it, maintaining a proper set of books and paying tax. Cooperatives could be large or small, and they could employ workers who were not cooperative members. For those Party members still committed to an undiluted Marxism, this sounded like an exploitative relationship between capital and labour. For them, it was a crack in the ideological edifice of Soviet civilization.

Yet for others it only proved the elasticity of the Russian Revolution, updating Lenin for a new generation, and drawing on the best lessons of the New Economic Policy, Kosygin's 1960s programme, and even the mixed economy of Hungary. Cooperatives caught on, especially in the form of small service-sector businesses such as hairdressers and cafés. Within six months, the authorities had more than 13,921 cooperative businesses in their records, and almost twenty times this figure at the start of 1991.[26] Cooperatives also formalized existing underground ventures. Dozens of funeral cooperatives were founded in Soviet cities; they were newly legitimate 'businesses' that had been providing funerary objects and services for decades.[27] Many doctors always had an entrepreneurial energy, working on the side and taking cash payments; some now set up medical cooperatives, making out-of-hours use of state facilities, sometimes officially. An opinion survey suggested this was an awkward transition in the medical economy: 69 per cent of cooperatives did not have enough equipment, while 34 per cent of patients thought that 'private' doctors were 'more attentive'.[28]

The 'cooperative' concept went with the grain of Gorbachev's expansive Leninism. *Perestroika* was based on a neo-Leninist version of democracy which united economy and politics into a single whole. Abel Aganbegyan formulated a coherent critique of Marxist-Leninist economics as a Soviet insider, not a liberal outsider. This meant that democracy extended to the workplace as much as the debating chamber, or such was the revolutionary theory.

The June 1987 Law on State Enterprises gave workers the right to vote in elections for enterprise director (subject to ministerial confirmation). Had Soviet democracy been confined to the workplace, it might have begun to work effectively. But Gorbachev proposed fundamental reforms to the political system as well. Political pluralism was by definition beyond constitutional law, which stated that the Party was the leading force in Soviet life. What Gorbachev the democrat had to prove was that Soviet civilization was flexible enough to accommodate truly competitive elections and even multiple parties. This meant learning from the lessons of the more politically vibrant years of the 1920s, but also going beyond them, back to the first days of the Bolshevik revolution and onward to a completely different political future.

*

Gorbachev was an Olympic-class machine politician who longed for a more interesting and prestigious politics in which to compete. He performed the entire high-political repertoire, from smooth-talking patronage to policy wonkery, from Leninist fluency to workaholism, from total understanding of the *apparat* to alpha-boss behaviour. Good decisions about top personnel were crucial for any practitioner of Soviet politics. He replaced one generation with another. They knew policy and the Party. Some were charismatic. All were men. And they were all outsiders, born in villages or factory districts, like their outsider-predecessors, who built Soviet civilization from the outside in. Gorbachev brought in Nikolai Ryzhkov, a top economic administrator, as chairman of the Council of Ministers. Gorbachev's new foreign minister was Eduard Shevardnadze, soon to become a global star. Yegor Ligachev entered the Politburo with responsibilities for Party management and ideological development. Gorbachev kept in post Andropov's successor as KGB chairman, Viktor Chebrikov, and cemented their bond by installing him in the Politburo. For Gorbachev, the KGB was not *ipso facto* a driver of repression. It was also a simple fact of life, the provider, for example, of the domestic staff who looked after his family. Assuming part of the perspective of Andropov, who was his much-admired patron, Gorbachev looked at the KGB as an organization of effective people who could be harnessed for the implementation of reform.[29] He was a child of the Thaw, assuming that Khrushchev had brought the secret police under control. And so Chebrikov was an ally.

Gorbachev admired the Party intellectual Aleksandr Yakovlev (whom we last met at the Twentieth Party Congress in chapter 2). He was enjoying a brilliant Party career when Kosygin and Brezhnev decided that he had expressed his reformist ideas too boldly in print. They exiled him to a gilded cage: he took up the post of ambassador to Canada in 1973. Gorbachev had known him over the years and brought him back to Moscow: in 1985 Yakovlev served as his adviser with special interests in foreign affairs; in 1986 he was promoted to a Central Committee secretaryship; and in 1987 he joined the Politburo.[30]

Even Gorbachev made a fatal error, though. Viktor Grishin, the long-time Moscow boss, was a symbol of the Brezhnev era. He was

Mister Moscow, speaking up for the interests of the capital, and was not without a popular appeal. But he danced a very fine line between corrupt practices and adequate administration. His family famously had access to the best things that were available. He was loosely associated with the corrupt retail outlets that Andropov targeted in the early 1980s. Running Moscow was also an all-union appointment. Khrushchev and Furtseva were two previous holders of the job. Gorbachev needed a new broom if the capital was to be a cleaned-up showcase for *perestroika*. He chose Boris Yeltsin as Grishin's successor.

Yeltsin was born one month earlier than him in 1931. He was another outsider, hailing from a village in Sverdlovsk oblast, in the Ural region of the country. Smashed to pieces by collectivization, the family moved to a nearby township and lived in a dugout (a *zemlyanka*, a dwelling dug out of the earth and reinforced by timber), before his innocent father was arrested when Yeltsin junior was three years old. After his father's release, they moved to Perm oblast (renamed after Molotov for much of the 1940s). It was the gateway to Siberia. His father started work at the North Urals Heavy Industry Construction Trust. When Yeltsin turned eighteen he moved to Sverdlovsk to study at the Urals Polytechnic Institute, a major regional centre for the training of technical specialists. His marks were good. He attended the long days of lectures, but was incapable of studying in anything other than long spells of inactivity followed by intense bursts of work. Living in the institute's communal hostels without a spare kopek and spending rambunctious vacations living off the land in the surrounding pristine countryside were everyday Soviet experiences. It was a different life from Gorbachev's, stuffily reading law at Moscow State University and busting harvest records with his father at the tail-end of summer vacations.

He graduated as a construction engineer. When Khrushchev was giving the Secret Speech, Yeltsin was working in junior hands-on roles for a construction trust (a large local 'firm'), learning the ropes in Sverdlovsk. They were building apartment blocks. He saw the implementation of Khrushchev's signature programme at first hand during the 1950s and 1960s. Yeltsin married Naina in 1956 and they had two daughters, one of whom, Tatyana, worked closely with him in 'the family' that ran Russia in the 1990s. In early adulthood, he already liked vodka very much. Meanwhile, he joined the Party and stood for local office while being promoted through the construction sector. In 1968, he switched to a full-time career in the Sverdlovsk *apparat*. His patron was Yakov Ryabov, Party first secretary in the city, who admired Yeltsin's dynamism. By 1976 Yeltsin had overtaken his mentor, appointed first secretary of the whole Sverdlovsk region, a true Soviet baron.

He was a natural for the boss class. He was ebullient and good at delegating and had clear ideas about policy. At six foot two and eighteen stone, with a shock of hair and a loose tie, he physically dominated a field or a building site, let alone a conference room. He screamed and banged the table, but was also thin-skinned. And he had inside knowledge of a major sector of the planned economy, understood the wheels of patronage and had the gift of being underestimated. He knew how his fellow citizens were trying to survive in an economy that suppressed consumption. Yeltsin had the narcissism of the careerist but he tempered it with useful empathy.

His term of office began when he was forty-five, and he was the leading politician in the region of Sverdlovsk for the next nine years. He and Gorbachev overlapped as province-level first secretaries – very loosely comparable to state governors in the USA – but Gorbachev was several years ahead of him. Both men had to manage the economy, improve lives, balance interests, distract Moscow, use the KGB, appease the cultured, mollify the scandalized, appeal to patrons, disarm clients and promote themselves. But where Gorbachev liked wonkery, read Lenin and nudged towards a vision of reform, Yeltsin enjoyed the crowd. No doubt already lubricated, he reached out to ordinary people at official events, handing out flowers to construction workers when the city's metro was opened in 1980, or singing with peasants during visits to remote collective farms.[31] Yeltsin engaged with ordinary people. They enjoyed talking to him. But he had the vulnerability of the showman.

In April 1985, he got his chance. Gorbachev brought him to Moscow as a Central Committee secretary with responsibility for construction. He had an office on Old Square and an apartment in an elite Party building on Tverskaya-Yamskaya Street, the continuation of Gorky Street, further up from the Kremlin. The family were also provided with a dacha. It was the one that Gorbachev had used before his elevation to the Kremlin. Yeltsin travelled across the country to major construction projects. In his first volume of memoirs, published in 1990 when he was devising a persona for election campaigns, he described a trip to Uzbekistan soon after his move to Moscow. When a crowd gathered outside his hotel, his KGB guards did not let them near him, but he demanded that they allow anyone up who wanted to talk to him. Later, he was in a restaurant when the staff told him that the bill had already been settled by the republic's Central Committee. 'Unable to restrain myself, almost shouting,' he dictated to his ghost-writer, 'I demanded to have my bill.'[32]

Yeltsin, the would-be man of the people, enjoyed his real elevation eight months later. Gorbachev called on him to replace Grishin as first secretary of the city. The post came with promotion to the Politburo. It was Yeltsin's moment. Yet he was uneasy. By now Yeltsin was well known and well regarded, with a reputation for popularity and competence; Gorbachev had known him since they dealt with each other as regional bosses in the 1970s, though they never liked each other or communicated at quite the same register. Still, Yeltsin was fifty-four, energetic and original, ready for reform.

From the start, even before the first political reforms were introduced, Yeltsin brought a new style to Moscow city politics. He talked more frankly and accessibly in Party meetings and in visits to factories. Grishin had overseen a complex patronage network in the city *apparat*, which Yeltsin now wilfully disrupted. For a time he caught the bus to work, to the disquiet of his chauffeur and KGB detail. Television cameras were often on hand as he clambered up, ran his hand through his hair and conversed with fellow passengers. Gorbachev could not match his common touch. For all his alcoholism and sporadic haughtiness, Yeltsin could talk to ordinary people on their own terms and even listen to them, whereas in his walkabouts in Soviet crowds, itself a dramatic departure from the conduct of his predecessors, Gorbachev enjoyed what he thought was adulation.

In the evenings, in his comfortable home, Gorbachev returned time and again to his reading of Lenin and Marx. It was through Lenin that he developed his ideas about grass-roots and workplace democracy. Even in early 1987, though, this did not seem to satisfy him. He was already interested in Western policy and in relationships with Western leaders. It was personal; he cared what they thought about him. Gorbachev's breakthrough as an international statesman came at the summit with the United States that was held at Reykjavik in October 1986. Here he displayed a relaxed rapport with the American president that was a revelation for many observers. In his talks with Reagan, Gorbachev pushed for reductions in nuclear stockpiles. Both men were open to the dream of a nuclear-free world. In the end they could not agree on a treaty – they would later – but they had laid the temperamental basis for the agreements that would effectively bring about the end of the Cold War.

Gorbachev met Reagan and then Bush at regular set-piece summits and shared many telephone calls with them. He took hundreds of meetings with other international leaders. The American and Soviet leaders met in Geneva eleven months before the Reykjavik summit, and then in Washington at the end of the following year. Human rights were on the agenda at that summit's first session, in the Oval Office on the morning of 8 December 1987. It was precisely one year since the death of Anatoly Marchenko in custody (see chapter 20). Gorbachev learned to talk the language of human rights with Reagan and other Western leaders, though he was no soft touch: interlocutors on Capitol Hill noticed that he spoke robustly and defended Soviet interests. He also brought to Washington, in his Homburg and overcoat, his occasional habit of plunging into a crowd. On the third day of the summit, he ordered his motorcade suddenly to stop on Connecticut Avenue so that he could meet the people who lined the route.

He pushed for more radical political reform. At the January 1987 Plenum of the Communist Party, Gorbachev proposed competitive elections for senior Party posts at local, republican and all-union level. This did not yet mean general elections in which the entire population had a vote: in 1987, twenty million people were members of the Party (out of an adult population of approximately 200 million). Gorbachev even hinted that the Politburo should not be spared democratic exposure. His reasoning went back to Lenin. At the Tenth Party Congress in March 1921, at the end of the Civil War, Lenin had pushed the concept of democratic centralism and a ban on factions. The latter measure did not mean the complete end of debate. In a semantic ploy that was pregnant with a different future, Lenin discussed the possibility of different Party 'platforms'. Factions were out, but platforms might be in, and could even be the basis of competitive elections to Party congresses. This idea was revisited at the end of the 1980s as a way of squaring the circle of Gorbachev-era Soviet democracy. One indivisible Party: and yet a choice.[33]

As these positions became the subject of determined debate among politicians and public alike, Gorbachev found himself in charge of a turbulent and almost unimaginably complex political environment that was subject to unpredictable change. His biggest problem was Boris Yeltsin. They traded blows in a fierce, personal and sometimes disturbing sequence of encounters across 1987 and 1988. At the Nineteenth Party Conference in June 1988, an ad hoc meeting (not a full Party Congress) to discuss *perestroika*, the two men argued in public, with Yeltsin making a barnstorming populist pitch; people watched on television. Meanwhile, the conference approved a new parliament, the Congress of People's Deputies, which would convene after democratic elections the following year. Beyond the conference stage, the arguments were about the direction of the revolution. Three months before the Nineteenth Conference, a letter was published in the newspaper *Sovetskaya Rossiya* from Nina Andreyeva, a lecturer from Leningrad. She criticized *perestroika* in terms that were sympathetic to the Stalinist past. Behind the scenes, 'conservatives' and radicals at the top of the Party seemed to be lining up on opposite sides, arguing about the legacies of Lenin and Stalin.

Gorbachev was indeed the last revolutionary. He had unleashed an unprecedented pluralism and a new struggle for the past, present and future of the long Bolshevik revolution. *Perestroika* and *glasnost* were not a transition to liberalism, but the final incarnation of the many-sided revolution. As the last revolutionary, Gorbachev ranged across the vanguard of Soviet civilization during its final advance into the radiant future. It was a second Soviet renaissance, and it was a Soviet disaster.

Andrei Sakharov: parliamentarian

# 20

# Phone Call to Gorky

The morning of 25 January 1987 in Moscow was very cold but crisp and dry and bright. Pushkin loved days like these. They had a clarity about them. The atmosphere was full of energy. The snow looked beautiful. Anyone might yearn to wrap up and get outdoors. To a person whose mood tracked the brightness or dimness of the sky, these were optimistic conditions, moments in which *perestroika* might be made to work, in which Soviet civilization could be stripped down and relaunched.

It was Vladimir Vysotsky's birthday. He would have turned forty-nine that day. It was six-and-a-half years since his death. A substantial crowd gathered in the Vagankovskoe cemetery, where he was buried. They were the intelligentsia, broadly conceived, in all its variety, from a modest, private lover of verse to a grandee of the cinema, a complex group portrait in fur hats, caps, berets, padded suede jackets and glittering fur coats. Among them, milling around, was Eldar Ryazanov, the movie director, one of the most famous men in the Soviet Union. He was responsible for such films as the New Year classic *The Irony of Fate*. An American journalist approached him. Why, he asked, have so many of you come out to the cemetery on such a cold day? 'Because people come to Vysotsky regardless of the weather,' Ryazanov replied. 'You see, conscience does not depend on the weather. And he was the conscience of our people and spoke the truth at any time no matter what.'[1]

Ryazanov, the alpha career man, could not be at such a place for one reason alone. Of course he was there to mourn Vysotsky's passing and to commune on its significance with a crowd of the like-minded. But he also had a camera crew in tow. He was making a four-part documentary about the artist they all loved. His talk of conscience was relevant, a connector between the desperate sincerity of the old Russian intelligentsia, the nervous positioning of the Soviet intelligentsia and the uncertain moment – January 1987 – in which they all found themselves on that morning in the cemetery.

Conscience was a lesson that could be learned from Vysotsky's work and life. Yet Ryazanov's comment to the American journalist about Vysotsky and the value of conscience was a performance. He was performing the role of a Soviet *intelligent* for a foreign correspondent who came from the West. He was performing the role of great director, as sincere as he was accomplished, for his own cameramen and for the people overhearing in the cemetery. And he was performing his best self for posterity, for the television audience which would eventually watch his documentary and even the readers who would later buy the book that tied in with the film. But it was most likely a sincere performance; the words were familiar and the speechifying was characteristic, but the feeling, at such an uncertain moment, must have been instinctive and deeply experienced by many people in the cemetery, including Ryazanov. Why else would they go there?

The moment seemed uncertain in comparison with just a few years before. When Vysotsky was being buried in the cemetery in 1980, there were KGB everywhere. Afterwards, when the Taganka tried to put on a show to celebrate his life in 1981, the KGB and the Ministry of Culture struck back. The ghost of Vysotsky was unbearable to them. For many years, the conflict between Yuri Lyubimov, director of the Taganka, and the authorities had been creatively productive if personally nerve-racking, but at that point it took on a sinister edge. Lyubimov's Taganka was on the point of evisceration. He ended up on a plane to America. But the mood at the cemetery seemed different in January 1987: unafraid, optimistic in a prickly way. The charge of *glasnost* fizzed in the cold morning air. When they were broadcast later in the year, Ryazanov's films about Vysotsky seemed unforced and even free. They assumed that Vysotsky was almost bigger than the KGB. They danced on the edge of open political talk. In the first episode, one of Vysotsky's friends, the actor Vsevolod Abdulov, said spikily: 'Nowadays you read every day in the paper and listen on the television and radio – they say what a real Soviet person should be.

For God's sake! Such a person lived among us.'[2] Abdulov was talking about the man of whom the cultural authorities and secret police had become afraid at the end of the 1970s and the early 1980s, regardless of whether he was dead or alive. The point was that 'power' had in the end rejected Vysotsky, but Abdulov thought that Vysotsky's characteristics and work were a great achievement of Soviet civilization, much greater than anything that derived from convention or authority. Andropov's people removed Vysotsky from television, and yet Gorbachev's were showing him from every angle and using his life to talk directly and indirectly, on TV, about contemporary politics.

Six weeks before the gathering at the cemetery, Anatoly Marchenko, long weakened by hunger strike, died in confinement in a labour camp at Chistopol in Moldavia. He was the most stubborn of working-class dissidents who had spent years in prison camps (see chapter 9). Marchenko's was a more inflexible voice of conscience than Vysotsky's. He could not compromise with Soviet power at all. For Marchenko, it was absurd to talk of rights in the Soviet Union or of genuine changes since the Stalin era. He had not been allowed to see his family for three years. His guards beat him; on at least one occasion during his current incarceration, in 1983, they repeatedly smashed his head against a cement floor. He believed that nothing protected him: that nothing stood between his unarmed self and a weaponized, brutal power. The same principle applied to everyone else, too. It was just that he was a marked man and was in prison, so he was especially vulnerable. He started a hunger strike on 4 August 1986. He wrote to delegates at a conference in Vienna that was monitoring compliance with the Helsinki Accords and explained that the purpose of his hunger strike was to encourage the Soviet government to honour its obligations – something the delegates themselves were signally failing to do. George Shulz, the American secretary of state, himself drew public attention to Marchenko at the conference. But Marchenko's suffering went on, punctuated by force-feeding and made worse by illness. In November 1986, the authorities offered his wife Larisa Bogoraz and their son a theoretical opportunity to emigrate with Marchenko, but it was far from clear whether his conscience would allow him to do this. And Larisa could not see him in time to ask. An amnesty for political prisoners had been announced. Marchenko was set to be freed. It was too late. He died on 8 December.[3]

Exactly one week later, Andrei Sakharov and Elena Bonner were at home in Gorky when somebody knocked at their door. It was ten o'clock in the evening. They looked askance at each other. Two telephone engineers stood on the threshold. A KGB man followed them in. Like a significant number of their fellow countrymen, Bonner and Sakharov did not have a phone, but unlike most of them, who were waiting in a queue, the two exiles were deliberately excluded to make their ostracism even tighter. The engineers installed the phone and left. Weirdly, the KGB man told them to expect a phone call at ten on the following morning. Perhaps, they wondered, a high-up journalist had been given permission to interview them.

The next morning they waited. It was not until three o'clock that it finally rang. A woman told Sakharov to hold the line for Mikhail Sergeevich. That, of course, meant Gorbachev. In the transcript that Sakharov made straight after the call and then inserted in his memoirs, Gorbachev adopts a rapid, slightly awkward air: the statesman part-way through an afternoon of calls. He puts the wrong stress on Elena Bonner's surname. But the message was extraordinary. 'You can return to Moscow,' Gorbachev said. 'Go back to your patriotic work.'

Decades on, one can sense a tension on the line. It seemed that Gorbachev was openly redefining Soviet civilization while Sakharov listened in. The work of a human-rights campaigner was no longer antithetical to Soviet power but a celebrated part of the same project. But the two men came from contrasting worlds. Gorbachev was the village boy turned workaholic careerist. Sakharov was the metropolitan *intelligent*, born and raised, who broke off his stellar career in science for a higher calling. Gorbachev was sympathetic to the intelligentsia, and his wife was even more so, but he lacked their temperamental preference for sincerity and doubt over power and certainty. They were born exactly a decade apart, but Gorbachev seemed much younger. Sakharov looked threadbare and stooped after a few years of exile. It made for an awkward juxtaposition, even in a few surviving lines of dialogue.

Sakharov did not mumble his gratitude and wait for the general secretary to end the call, as Gorbachev perhaps expected. Instead he reminded Gorbachev that Marchenko was recently 'killed in prison'. 'We've released many,' Gorbachev replied, 'and improved the lives of others.' Sakharov had recently written to Gorbachev appealing for the release of a list of political prisoners. Gorbachev told him that he had read the letter but disputed that all the prisoners were, as Sakharov put it, 'sentenced illegally, unjustly' and 'ought to be freed'. Against the odds, wearing his tatty clothes, holed up in the shabby flat in Gorky while his dear wife looked on, Sakharov had taken control of the call from the Kremlin. 'I urge you to look one more time at the question of releasing persons convicted for their beliefs,' he said. 'It's a matter of justice.' Now it was his turn to align the cause of dissidence and the primacy of human rights with the new reformist phase of Soviet civilization. 'It's vitally important for our country,' Sakharov said, 'for international trust, for peace, and for you and the success of your programme.' Gorbachev had little to say in response. Sakharov thanked him and said goodbye, ending the exchange, as if he were the one in charge.[4]

It was one of those extraordinary phone calls – like Stalin's calls to Pasternak and Shostakovitch – that somehow pulled back the curtain on the drama of Soviet life. Sakharov's release was a statement of a revised Soviet approach to human rights. Gorbachev's phone call was a harbinger of a new Soviet politics. The encounter between the two men would recur on political prime time in 1989 and would define the brief promise of Soviet pluralism.

Meanwhile, the ghosts of Vysotsky and Marchenko stayed put in the new political arena. Vysotsky's friends and admirers, men like Stanislav Govorukhin, entered union-wide political debate, while Yuri Lyubimov came back to the Taganka in 1989 after five stateless years in America. They all constantly invoked him. In December 1988, the names of Sakharov and Marchenko were linked again. The European Parliament introduced its new Sakharov Prize for human rights. Nelson Mandela, still in jail, and Anatoly Marchenko were jointly awarded the first Sakharov Prize. At that moment, almost any future was on the table for South Africa and the Soviet Union. But Marchenko was dead; Sakharov, shockingly, had only a year left; Mandela would live for another quarter-of-a-century. Perhaps the Soviet Union and its successor states needed Andrei Sakharov as much as South

Africa needed Nelson Mandela. With the benefit of hindsight, the ceremony at Strasbourg in December 1988 looks almost unbearably poignant.

The evolution of Gorbachev's democratization – from worker participation in factory management to contested national elections – marked his shift away from Soviet civilization. It did not have to be this way. Gorbachev could have chosen a form of democratization that was consistent with Soviet civilization rather than one which undermined it. *Perestroika* in general was just one more incarnation of the revolution. It had features of the New Economic Policy and the Thaw and was driven forward by Leninism. The Soviet Union had periods of relative pluralism in specifically defined areas of social, cultural and institutional life; it introduced limited versions of rights; it described itself as a democracy. But outside of some very narrow contexts, it could not tolerate contested elections. The fundamental reason for this was mandated in the Constitution: the leading role of the Communist Party in the life of the Soviet Union. By definition, the USSR was a Party dictatorship. The Party defined and staffed all the executive bodies of the USSR, from city soviets to the Kremlin. Elections could not change any of these bodies, let alone the government of the Soviet Union as a whole. Instead, Soviet elections, of which there were many, had a contrary function. Rather than encourage pluralism, they required unanimity, by communicating messages about acceptable political conduct and discourse, and by achieving 99 per cent turnouts in single-candidate votes. And rather than existing as a mechanism for occasionally changing the government, they helped to ensure that the government never changed.

Grass-roots participation in economic management and in very local administration, such as neighbourhood committees, trade unions and Party cells, sometimes had a culturally democratic element and was embedded in Soviet civilization. Developing this feature, even quickly and intensively, might have been a more obvious way of introducing political reform into the Soviet Union in potentially productive ways that aligned with Gorbachev's vision. Instead, Gorbachev went for broke.

On 9 April 1989, elections were held for the Congress of People's

Deputies, following a competitive process of nomination. It was the country's new parliament, replacing the old Supreme Soviet. Most people had the chance to vote in a genuinely contested election. Sometimes 'power' was held to account. For example, in the Khabarovsk region, the Party first secretary lost to the chairman of a local state farm. He admitted the core problem in attempting to move from *apparatchik* to politician. 'None of us has learned how to win the general public's political or ordinary human sympathy, and there has been no need for it,' he said. 'Look at how we Party officials frequently appear to people – pompous, sullen, unsmiling. But the campaign struggle – yes, struggle! – for victory requires not only competence and a clear-cut political position but also tactical know-how, oratorical skills, delicate diplomacy and, finally, human charm.'[5] In Kyiv, electoral arguments were sharp and were likewise focused on issues of accountability of unelected administrators versus emerging politicians.[6] This was not yet the time and place for debating nationality.

Almost 173 million people voted, or 89.8 per cent of the electorate. In other words, the system no longer generated unanimity but it was encouraging high levels of engagement. There were three categories of deputy. One third – 750 – were elected in territorial constituencies; 554 of these held contested elections, with the rest only having a single candidate. Another 750 seats were elected by different nationalities, at the level of union republic, autonomous republics (within union republics), autonomous regions (equivalent to provinces but governed by a titular national group) and so on. Slightly more of these seats – 203 – only ended up with one candidate, but the rest (547) were the subject of competitive election. The final group of 750 deputies was chosen by public organizations like trade unions. Fewer of these were contested on election day, though like all the other seats, they had been subject to competitive nomination proceedings, a little like American primaries. The typical deputy was a man from a white-collar profession. In total, 17.1 per cent of the deputies were women and 18.6 per cent were from the industrial working class.[7] The most interesting candidate of all was Andrei Sakharov, who was eventually nominated for one of the thirty seats that were allocated to the Academy of Sciences. That meant that his own election was uncontested, but he took a full part in the noisy campaign. One of his speeches was in front of a crowd of 200,000 at Moscow's Luzhniki sports complex.

Meanwhile, the violent potential of the revolution was not finished. The organs of coercion still retained their Andropov-era power. When a mass demonstration gathered in Tbilisi on the night of 8 April, the authorities struck back. The peaceful protestors wanted greater autonomy for the Georgian republic and also to ensure that Abkhazia remained part of their republic and was not itself granted autonomy. On 8 April, the protests had already been going on for several days. Tensions were high. The security forces went for the demonstrators. They killed nineteen of them. Hundreds more were injured. They used spades rather than guns and released poison gas. Gorbachev himself insisted that the situation must be resolved peacefully. Evidence collected by a commission of the new Congress suggested this was true. The orders came from elsewhere.[8]

Six weeks after polling, the Congress of People's Deputies convened for its first session. At the time, it looked like one act in a global struggle for democracy. Four days earlier, students in Beijing had started the Tiananmen Square demonstration. A summer and autumn of liberation was beginning in the satellite states of the Eastern bloc. Poland had already convened a national round table to instigate democratic reform. But for the most part, the USSR was a trailblazer in the spring of 1989 and earlier. At stake were the biggest questions about Soviet democracy. In the first session of the Congress in May and June, Sakharov's quiet voice, inflected with a speech impediment, was broadcast throughout the massive hall of the Palace of Congresses. He spoke repeatedly to the hall about the most neuralgic issues, calling, for example, the Afghan War 'a crime against the Fatherland'. On the last day of the Congress, Gorbachev, in the chair, gave Sakharov only five minutes of the fifteen he had requested to sum up his opposition to the general secretary's closing statement. He overran. Gorbachev switched off his microphone. Sakharov carried on talking – and everyone could hear him. Gorbachev's switch didn't work. This moment was captured live on TV with millions tuning in. Once again, just like in the phone call to Gorky, the professor gained the upper hand in conversation with the general secretary.[9]

For Gorbachev, there was nothing inconsistent about an element of choice coexisting with the perpetuation of Soviet power. A year earlier, *perestroika* had seemed briefly to hang in the balance when hardliners hit back during the so-called Andreyeva affair. In response, the forces of democratization naturally conflated Soviet rule with the emergence of pluralism. 'We can and must revive the Leninist practice of socialist society – the most humane, the most just,' opined *Pravda* in April 1988. 'We will follow the revolutionary principles of *perestroika* firmly and undeviatingly: more *glasnost*, more democracy, more socialism.'[10] Democracy in the hands of the Communist Party remained Gorbachev's position, even as his democratizing reforms gathered pace.

Anatoly Sobchak disagreed. He was a law professor at Leningrad State University who had sought a trade union nomination for the Congress of People's Deputies. Seeking to detach the Party from its monopoly hold on power, he became concerned about another question: the powers of the presidency. In 1990, Gorbachev stood for the newly created post of president of the Soviet Union. For Gorbachev, whose power derived, as it had for his predecessors, from his position as general secretary of the Communist Party of the Soviet Union, being called president would burnish his international prestige while solidifying the power of the Party in the organs of government at a time of political flux. Sobchak agreed with the introduction of a presidency, but for the opposite reason. He argued that the Soviet Union could only become a democracy if presidential power was not only strengthened, but rooted in the authority of the state rather than the Party. Then the Party might atrophy. Pluralism might replace it.[11] It was clear that Gorbachev's democratization was already having unintended consequences, notably the rise of Boris Yeltsin in the rival powerbase in the USSR's Russian republic, but Sobchak imagined a still more dramatic Soviet pluralism.

Gorbachev's problem was not only that he embarked on political reform at the same time as other reforms; he also got his politics the wrong way round. He held elections without parties. The existence of multiple parties had not yet been legalized. There was now a choice, but there was still only one Party. Gorbachev intended to democratize the Soviet Union, and the Congress of People's Deputies offered debate but not structured, sustainable pluralism.

Sobchak, the popular but professorial Leningrad deputy, argued for the urgency of pluralism. The new Soviet Union that he wanted to build required not just a diversity of opinion and the freedom to express it but also the eradication of the Party's monopoly. For all its raw energy and brilliance, captured by a proliferation of small groups and platformed in a cacophony of meetings, campaigning lacked sustained focus, discipline and organization.[12] Gorbachev could not see beyond the Party. As M. Steven Fish, an American political scientist who observed all this first-hand, put it: 'The electoral openings of 1989 and 1990 were at once too sudden and too partial.'[13]

With hindsight, the question became how revolutionary Gorbachev's democratization really was. Observers sometimes called this another Russian Revolution.[14] They meant that it was a dramatic departure from Soviet precedent, and that its consequences were transformative. They were right. But there was another way of looking at the question. Was Gorbachev's democratization the next chapter in the ongoing Bolshevik revolution? The version of democratization that Gorbachev pushed through was idiosyncratic – like all versions of democracy. But it was a dramatic decentring away from the principles of Soviet democracy. The combination of *glasnost* plus a form of democracy which, for all its faults, seemed to offer a route towards two principles antithetical to Soviet democracy – representation and accountability – plainly posed a risk for the Party. Gorbachev was the last revolutionary, but his commitment was waning, even if he did not yet admit it, even to himself. As it became more transformative, *perestroika* was turning counter-revolutionary.

During the second session of the Congress of People's Deputies, which opened on 12 December 1989, everything was still possible. At Gorbachev's request, Sakharov had recently been working in a team that was designing a new draft constitution for the USSR. Just as in the text that initially brought him to the world's attention, *Thoughts on Progress, Peaceful Coexistence and Intellectual Freedom*, Sakharov combined Soviet socialism with competitive democracy, human rights and the rule of law. The constitutional programme he helped to develop was practical and focused on the specific wellbeing of Soviet citizens. As Soviet civilization was coming to an end, this was a plausible vision for its replacement – one that could potentially unite a majority of the population in most of the republics. Heading into the second session of the Congress, it needed a sincere, trustworthy and powerful voice to press its case. This was Sakharov's moment: his historic role. He would give his major speech to the Congress on 15 December.

On the night of 14 December, after days of meetings and interviews, he had dinner with his wife. He then had a rest before finishing his text for the next day. When Bonner found him, a couple of hours later, his heart had already given way.[15]

It is impossible to look back at images of Andrei Sakharov in 1989 without a sense of inexpressible sadness. In Czechoslovakia, Václav Havel, the playwright who was the country's leading dissident, became president of the country at the end of December. Two months later, Nelson Mandela was released from jail; four years after that, in the country's first post-apartheid election, he was voted in as president. In the Soviet Union, the only comparable figure to Havel or Mandela was Sakharov. He lacked their charisma or sense of retail politics. His speech defect and gangly, crumpled, professorial bearing made him unlikely to command a crowd. He was charismatic in small groups but did not have a presidential manner. Sakharov could grasp a problem, see it from all angles and make fruitful and surprising connections between different branches of knowledge. But he was less equipped to knock the heads of hardened political operatives together or schmooze deals out of people who hated each other. And yet in a world where these other fairy tales came to pass – where the playwright who was denied a stage for decades and the freedom fighter jailed for twenty-seven years reached their country's presidencies – why could it not also happen to the exiled human-rights campaigner who never flinched in the face of power?

*Perestroika* was no fairy tale. Even the mildest of economic reforms caused despair among many ordinary Soviet citizens, who feared losing the advantages of socialism as they perceived them. After 1953, the Party's legitimacy rested on its abandonment of the principle that the ends justified the means. The revolution was no longer a zero-sum game. Everyone should perceive some personal gain, now or in the near future, from each new measure that was introduced. But as *perestroika* began, people immediately expected each new reform to create losers as well as winners. The Law on Individual Labour Activity of November 1986 was a modest deregulation of the labour market. It extended freelance work opportunities to certain groups, allowing them legally to work two jobs. Officials acknowledged that it caused anxiety. A senior official in the State Labour Commission tried to reassure people, saying the law expanded 'participation in socially useful work for a wide circle of citizens' and increased wages, but did not create capitalist-style hiring practices or the chance for a new generation of bosses to live off unearned income.[16]

The Law on Cooperatives, introduced the following year, brought these risks into the open because of its chaotic consequences, which Gorbachev and his principal policymakers did not anticipate. Understandably enough, there was a group of Soviet citizens, risk-taking and entrepreneurial by temperament, who were desperate to take whatever chance came their way in order to make a fast buck. The new law gave them the licence to do so, but at the cost of social instability. Holes in the legislation allowed cooperatives to operate in conjunction with state enterprises, the financial regulations unwittingly making it easy for state bosses to strip assets from the enterprises they managed. Or they could engineer shortages in the market, inflating prices and making a killing, which happened, for example, at the Yava cigarette factory in Moscow.[17] The underground enterprises and corruption that paradoxically helped to sustain socialism, precisely because they gave 'entrepreneurs' a stake in the Soviet economy, now exploded into a combination of legal business and mafia operations whose practitioners would only benefit from the demise of the USSR.

Meanwhile, the banking system was unexpectedly deregulated. For years, it had consisted of a central bank (Gosbank, the State Bank) and five institutions which worked in various sectors of the economy, from savings (Sberbank) to agriculture (Agroprombank). Now the number of banks proliferated as a side-effect of the economic reforms. The Law on Cooperatives facilitated the establishment of twenty-four new banks by December 1988, while the joint-stock company legislation was the basis of a further seventeen. The new Soviet banks did not accumulate savings and issue credit on an adequate scale, or unblock flows of money around the economy to everyone's benefit. There was no time to set up the proper financial framework. Instead they were foci for get-rich-quick schemes and organized crime.[18] They were an unnecessary innovation, perhaps an early indicator that policymakers lacked confidence in Soviet civilization; they could easily have been banned for a time and designed out of the reform programme until the Soviet Union was ready for them. Other 'transition' economies were much more cautious about the banking sector and were more stable as a result.

Under the weight of Gorbachev's economic reforms, some of the hidden strengths of Soviet civilization now transmuted into disadvantages. The first was the flexibility of central planning, and the power that skilful managers – of industrial enterprises or other institutions – could exert within it. This flexibility had allowed the five-year plans to work. It was a major reason why the Soviet Union reproduced itself over several generations and why the revolution kept going for so long. Informal practices were the oil that greased the machine, making it possible for enterprise bosses to buy or barter additional raw materials from their contacts, negotiate direct with ministries by phone, glad-hand local Party secretaries and make deals with neighbouring institutions over such things as housing stock and food supply for workers. None of this was visible in the formal plan. The details were only clear to the initiated. Networks emerged which were exclusive, based on trust and impenetrable from the outside.[19] The 'system' depended on a vast stock of information about how the economy really worked that was only available to senior managers, all of whom saw it only from particular angles. Gorbachev's reformed enterprises and cooperatives created a fast-moving current in which these information gaps widened further. Managers had a unique opportunity to exploit the 'information asymmetry' for their own personal gain. It allowed them to cash in, monetizing their Soviet-era privileges, sometimes on an epic scale. For most citizens it meant the removal of a whole range of certainties and their replacement with something opaque and threatening.

The beneficiaries of reform took advantage of another unexpected linchpin of Soviet civilization, quickly loosening it until it fell out. Property relations, like information gaps, lay at the centre of Soviet economic and social life. If the theory of communism had yielded its expected result, or the expectations of the 'totalitarian' school of observers of the Soviet Union had been borne out, then property would have been a very simple matter in the USSR. The state would have owned everything until both it and the concept of ownership withered away. In reality, Soviet property law allowed for a diversity of forms of tenure. Rights of ownership and of use were not clearly demarcated, and even shaded into each other. This was true of the relationship between ordinary citizens and their housing and had a much more general resonance, in the way that managers and workers perceived 'socialist', or public, property. It was within these paradoxes that Soviet civilization found its surprising coherence and sustainability. These were not the Marxist contradictions that were supposed to cause a state to collapse.

In 'normal' times, the nuances and compromises of property relations made the Soviet Union stronger. They expanded a sense of ownership among citizens and of identification with the state. For example, a citizen who lived in an apartment owned by the local soviet, or council, enjoyed rights of occupancy that were so secure that he or she often considered themselves the rightful owner.[20] The tools, spare parts and contacts of a local authority plumber might by rights belong to the soviet, but he had access to them after the end of the working day and used them to moonlight and boost his income. Perhaps nobody lost from those transactions. True enough, it was a low-level erosion of law, but there is no evidence that this eroded in turn the legitimacy of Soviet power, if anything the reverse. Law structured a large part of social life, but the Soviet Union was not governed by the rule of law; it was a dictatorship. Other transactions edged further into criminality. In the workers' state, did that timber warehouse really belong to one's employer, or might one help oneself to a few extra planks for the dacha one was building? The discipline drives of the 1980s targeted thefts of 'socialist property' – things like these that were formally owned by the agencies of the state – but the grey zones of ownership perhaps expanded the economy, increased people's identification with socialism and the state, improved living standards and plugged gaps in supply and provision.

But the Law on Enterprises and the Law on Cooperatives started to undermine the sustaining paradox of property relations. By distorting the Sovietized worldview of ordinary urban people and fracturing their existing relationship with the economic and political authorities, the laws contributed to the hollowing-out of Soviet civilization that accompanied the later part of *perestroika*. The Soviet state perhaps did not depend on the existence of its accompanying civilization, but the state could not survive the impact of policies that broke the incentives that had hitherto connected 'elites' to it in an unshakeable bond. Yet these two laws inadvertently contributed to precisely that process. Soviet managers in all walks of life had long taken advantage of their rights of use rather than of ownership to enjoy access to many good things in life. Now they saw the opportunity to enjoy a much richer future if they could turn rights of use into outright ownership, and perks into cash. This was even true in the Komsomol, where Mikhail Khodorkovsky, a young official, used his position to begin dealing in computer equipment. He quickly made a fortune.

The reforms rewarded opportunism, incentivizing economic greed as well as promoting ideological malleability.[21] If these bosses no longer needed 'communism' or the Party to do well in life, and could instead live much better off the fat of economic reform, then they had every incentive to abandon the long revolution in favour of 'capitalism'. They learned to talk about democracy while dropping off their profits at Capital Bank.[22]

Gangsters took advantage. The underground entrepreneurs of the 1970s and 1980s were already rich, having spent years buying and selling, building and storing, quietly working with crooked officials and dodging the KGB. They were in prime position to use their power to threaten more legitimate businesses and profitable small companies that might soon have become 'normal'.

The cost was unimaginable. Access to affordable food items in the USSR seems to have peaked in the late 1970s. By 1990, it had dropped considerably, as supplies fell and prices rose. Shelves were empty. Toilet paper, soap, sausage: the shortages robbed people of dignity. Even worse, many of them sensed that they were standing on the edge of an abyss, that the ground was about to be cut from beneath them, that it was all about to get dramatically worse. Soviet civilization was emptying visibly and in real time. Its welfare system might no longer be there to protect Soviet people at the time that they needed it most.

By 1989, per capita consumption of meat had fallen 6.8 per cent over the preceding fourteen years. Over the next two years, it fell a further 11 per cent. Over the course of the next twelve months, it fell by 14 per cent, declining to the level of 1965. Between 1980 and 1989, per capita consumption of milk and dairy products fell by 4.8 per cent. Yet between 1989 and 1991 it dropped by an extra 11.8 per cent, and between 1991 and 1992, by a further 19 per cent, to amounts last seen in the 1950s.[23] By the end of 1991, a skilled steel worker in Perm, beyond the Urals, spent 70 per cent of their wage packet on food, and a new pair of children's boots cost a full week's earnings.[24] Understandably enough, the economic reforms were desperately unpopular. The All-Union monitoring survey recorded 15 per cent approval of the reforms among factory workers in 1988, and 12 per cent in 1990.[25] This was the difference between the steady decline of the late 1970s and early 1980s, which well-designed reforms might at least have arrested, and the precipitous freefall of *perestroika* and then collapse.

In 1990, Gorbachev pushed on rapidly and much more deeply. These were days of the highest pressure. He was a workaholic and a tough decision-maker, apparently made from an uncrackable substance, but even he could hardly have managed without the unconditional support that Raisa offered when he came home in the evening. Soviet civilization was coming apart at the seams. Gorbachev could no longer claim that he was following a Leninist agenda. Unmoored from the past, he was pressing forward into the future through the most hazardous and unpredictable waters.

Politics reached a point of no return. This did not mean that the Soviet Union was going to collapse. State failure still seemed unlikely. It required the disintegration of the republican system on nationalist lines, a process whose form was still scarcely possible to conceive. Yet the Soviet Union was no longer shaped by a generally understood 'civilization'. In March, the Congress of People's Deputies approved the ending of the Party's monopoly on power. A new position of USSR president was introduced, which became Gorbachev's. The same month, the Russian republic of the USSR held elections for its parliament, the Supreme Soviet of the RSFSR, which convened in the so-called White House. This broad building, a lattice of windows and white-faced concrete, was constructed between 1965 and 1981 as the House of Soviets. In May, the deputies elected Boris Yeltsin to the newly enhanced position of chairman. This gave him a substantial position from which to challenge Gorbachev, to push the case for reform, to strain relations between the Kremlin and the republics and to increase his own power.

Economics too reached a tipping point. In the summer of 1990, Gorbachev put in place a team led by the economists Stanislav Shatalin and Grigory Yavlinsky. Their proposals were called the Five Hundred Days Programme. Gorbachev welcomed their ideas. So did Yeltsin. What they proposed was effectively a transition to a market economy. Central planning and social rights were to be confined to the ash heap of history. Gorbachev, no longer acting like a Leninist or a revolutionary, accepted this. Economic crisis left him in despair, while the social democracy he had witnessed in parts of Western Europe offered a new political vision.

Gorbachev's *perestroika* was often compared with Deng Xiaoping's reforms in China. Both reform programmes led to the end of socialist economics and the creation of a kind of free market. The contrast was the scope of reform, and its dramatically different results. Where *perestroika* ranged across many areas of life, Chinese reforms were largely limited to the economy. The Soviet Union collapsed, but free-market China was still ruled by the Communist Party decades later. One common observation was that Gorbachev did too much and too quickly, that he should have stuck, like the Chinese, to the economy, and not interfered with politics: that there was an authoritarian path he could have followed instead, preserving the union and avoiding economic immiseration. But this was to misunderstand how Soviet civilization worked by the 1980s, and how Gorbachev perceived it. Economic reform was impossible without political reform, or at least economic reform required a democratic aim that transcended mere economic growth. Gorbachev's vision was too self-consciously European, and too focused on rights, for the Chinese model to work in the USSR. Abel Agenbegyan, one of Gorbachev's top economists, had insisted that only democracy could drive *perestroika*. Democratization was intrinsic to economic reform, because people power meant nothing if it was a mere vote once every five years. It had to extend into all parts of life, not least the factory and its management.[26]

Aganbegyan pointed out that political decisions guided economic reforms. For Soviet civilization to work in the late 1980s, ordinary workers had to be involved in that decision-making process. Economic reform required decisions about the distribution of investment and the setting of priorities. This in turn demanded a new managerial structure in which workers had a role.[27] *Perestroika* had to combine economic and political change, otherwise it was not *perestroika*.

When Chinese officials critiqued *perestroika*, they were struck by the practical failures inherent in the design of Gorbachev's economic measures. His economic reforms did not offer a coherent strategy to rectify long-term falls in productivity, for instance by focusing on computerization. Neither did they do anything for people's standards of living, to keep the workers on side.[28] This critique was reasonable, and it was different from saying that Gorbachev could have reformed the economy without changing the politics, and by being more like Deng Xiaoping. The imaginary Chinese path also underestimated the extent of the crisis by 1990 and overestimated the room for manoeuvre that Gorbachev enjoyed.

On 15 October 1990, the Nobel Foundation announced that Mikhail Gorbachev was the laureate of that year's Peace Prize. It was fifteen years since Andrei Sakharov had been awarded the same honour. Sakharov had not been allowed to travel to Oslo to take up the prize. Gorbachev – for a quite different reason – was also unable to collect the award in person. He sent the deputy foreign minister to speak in his absence. 'I would like to assure you,' said Andrei Kovalev on Gorbachev's behalf, 'that the leadership of the USSR is doing and will continue to do everything in its power to ensure that future developments in Europe and the world as a whole are based on openness, mutual trust, international law and universal values.'[29]

Lazar Kaganovich, the iron communist who was Khrushchev's patron in the decade after the revolution, and whom Khrushchev had expelled from the Party after his attempt to bring the government down in 1957, told the journalist Feliks Chuev in January 1991 that the Soviet Union had been humiliated, reduced to living off aid from Luxembourg. Kaganovich was ninety-seven but he was still sharp enough to mock Gorbachev's Nobel Prize. 'He has more prizes than Brezhnev,' Kaganovich said sardonically. And he could not come to terms with *perestroika's* apparent rejection of violence in its repertoire of governance. Socialism, he argued, was humane and democratic, but talk of this was mere 'sweet sugar' without acknowledging that the only route towards it was 'through blood and violence'.[30] Such were the ethics on which Khrushchev had tried to turn his back and which Gorbachev more completely rejected.

Yet Kaganovich's dream of death and socialism received a brief fulfilment. In the small hours of 13 January 1991, a twenty-three-year-old Lithuanian woman, Loreta Asanavičiūtė, was mown down by a military vehicle outside the television station in Vilnius. She stares out smiling and dark-haired, head tilted slightly to her left, from one of the surviving photographs that is publicly available. Asanavičiūtė had post-school accounting qualifications and worked as a seamstress and knitter. She played folk music in a band associated with her local House of Culture. Perhaps this fostered her view that Lithuania should be independent. She held hands with fellow protestors on the Baltic Way of August 1989. On the night of 12–13 January, she was at the TV station with her family.[31]

She died in hospital four days later. Twelve other Lithuanians were killed as a result of the events of 12–13 January. They were participants in a large pro-independence demonstration. The killings were ordered not by Gorbachev but by the security services. Gorbachev immediately condemned them, and a spontaneous protest march flowed through Moscow. There were at least 100,000 protestors who were trying to speak in favour of the rights of Baltic citizens. It was a rerun of Tbilisi in 1989. Other localized cases of state violence in the Baltics followed. Gorbachev might not have been in control of it, but he had responsibility for an apparatus that wanted to use episodes of violence to bring the situation back under control. The new riot police, the OMON, would cause trouble in Riga in the early summer.

As the Soviet Union ran out of money, Gorbachev spent more time trying to cash in the goodwill he had developed with Western leaders over the last few years. It was easier to get warm words out of them than dollars or Deutschmarks. The Chinese were more enthusiastically forthcoming, quickly agreeing to 'commodity loans' of certain foodstuffs and consumer items, amounting to $333 million in 1990 and $730 million in 1991, though they of course had their own agenda, and their support had obvious limits.[32] After the fall of the Berlin Wall in November 1989, and American 'victory' in the Cold War, there was no chance of support comparable to the Marshall Plan. Congress eventually passed an aid package, and Helmut Kohl offered support, but Gorbachev's authority and status were shrinking. On 10 July 1991, Yeltsin was elected as president of the Russian republic – a new post. And his election was by popular, direct vote – a new method. There had been nothing like this in Soviet history. Gorbachev was also a president, but an unelected one, and his popular legitimacy was now a shadow of Yeltsin's. Now the tectonic plates under the Soviet Union really were shifting, and the possibility of national disintegration was becoming more real. Even now, it was not inevitable. In March, an all-union referendum offered support for a new union treaty whose aim was to make the connections between the republics fairer and more durable. Six republics did not participate, but nine did, including Ukraine.

In July 1991, Soviet civilization had already been irreversibly dissolving for months, but the Soviet state remained in place. The state was not yet decolonizing itself, and it was still possible that it would not do so, or do so only in part. Most people were dependent on it and could not conceive of the disappearance of their country, the USSR. Soviet civilization needed the state in order to exist, but the state, in the way of states, did not need its animating civilization for it to endure. The end of a state is a rare event; more likely is its adaptation. Yet the Soviet state came to an end six months later. Short of invasion, the only way that the Soviet Union could collapse even on national lines was if its government committed suicide. Gorbachev never had any intention of doing that. His reforms turned out to be suicidal, but it was suicide by accident.

The Baltic Way

## 21
# The End of Soviet Civilization

The revolution was coming full circle – it really was a revolution in the proper sense of the word, and one that had been going on for more than seventy years. It began at a time of anguish about the price of food, and its demise took place amid related suffering. In both 1917 and 1991, people were driven to despair by low levels of consumption, but what really pushed them over the edge was a jagged sense of injustice. 1989 was Russia's freest year since 1917. Politics spilled far beyond the rooms of politicians. The media became a public square. Debate between ordinary people broke out in streets, offices, kitchens, canteens, in the yards between apartment blocks and in front of televisions broadcasting the sessions of the Congress of People's Deputies. Students dozed off on the metro clutching the political leaflets they planned to hand out at the next station. The popular understanding of what *glasnost* was had little in common with a liberal 'freedom of speech',[1] and it derived instead from its Soviet context, including a stubbornly surviving socialist commitment to 'truth'. Assumed to be a fact-based requirement of Marxism, this commitment was pursued by the most enlightened journalists even in the 1970s, though only across a limited range of non-political subjects.[2] *Glasnost* was therefore the basis of a dynamic, vulnerable, tumultuous pluralism that came from within Soviet civilization.

Between February and October 1917, Russia was governed by the 'dual power' of the Provisional Government and the Soviet of Workers, Peasants and Soldiers. They were located at opposite ends of the centre of Petrograd. The Soviet enjoyed power without responsibility while the Provisional Government faced the thankless task of keeping the reformed Russian empire united and on a constitutional trajectory.

In 1991, with two presidents in Moscow, dual power was back. The parallels were irresistible. Talk of 1917 could anyway be heard everywhere. Gorbachev was weighed down, exhausted and wounded by the burdens of office. Yeltsin was waiting for his moment. He enjoyed the perks of office, not least the booze and debauchery of foreign trips. Only Gorbachev really had responsibility, but the institutional power of Yeltsin was growing. It was dual power updated for a new failed state, seventy-four years on.

And then Yeltsin stepped up, and the arc of history changed.

At 4 a.m. on 19 August 1991, troops from the Sevastopol regiment of the KGB surrounded Mikhail Gorbachev's government dacha in Foros, in Crimea, where he was taking a holiday. His plane and helicopter were blockaded on the runway. Two hours later, the minister of defence sent out a warning to commanders of military districts across the country to prepare themselves (the question was: for what?). By 9.30 a.m., military vehicles were rolling through Moscow. Normal TV and radio programming was disrupted. At 11.34, the plotters – the deputy president and the heads of the security ministries, the organs of coercion – made their declaration to the country. Gorbachev was unwell. The bosses were back.

This was the August coup whose failure led to the unstoppable rise of Boris Yeltsin and the humiliation of Mikhail Gorbachev. But this failure was not preordained. The plotters made stupid errors of judgement and lacked a strongly united front. How could they, for example, not have arrested the president of the Russian republic of the USSR, Boris Yeltsin, who succeeded in turning the situation to his advantage and gaining political momentum as a result? Yeltsin called for calm, remained in the capital and became a focus for opposition to the coup. He clambered up on a tank outside the White House and spoke out for democracy and against violence. Perhaps it was made for TV, but it also offered courage and leadership. The plotters, by contrast, were unappealing and hit many wrong notes. With retrospect, the coup never had a chance.

But their message was comprehensible. Performed attractively, it could have been a counter-case to *perestroika*. 'We favour,' they insisted, 'truly democratic processes and a consistent policy of reform leading to the renewal of our homeland and to its social and economic prosperity, which will enable it to take a worthy place in the world community of nations.[3] For what it was worth – and 'democracy' meant nothing to them – it sounded like a comforting return to developed socialism, not the painful and confusing rupture that *perestroika* had come to offer.

At 10.20 p.m., Elena Bonner, the widow of Andrei Sakharov, responded. She asked Muscovites 'to defend the Russian government and the Russian president', as well as the president of the USSR. 'Today we must prove that we deserve the name of the people of the capital,' she called out, 'that we are more than just a mob concerned with buying sausage.'[4]

Bonner had spoken out on other occasions in a pitch-perfect way and with astonishing courage, such as when she had called KGB men death-cheering 'fascists' in a dissident trial of 1970. But she spoke on 19 August without the more nuanced vision of her husband, a vision which was capable of accommodating an apparent paradox within the comprehensible terms of Soviet civilization. Sakharov would have found a way to say that freedom and sausage were both essential, and it was time to go to the square to defend them both. But he wasn't there, and the values underpinning Soviet civilization were anyway being knocked completely out of shape.

At the start of this book, I argued that six categories shaped Soviet civilization: periodization, revolution, personhood, normality, culture and decolonization. In 1990 and 1991, these categories became so blurred and weakened that Soviet civilization effectively came to an end. This means that in the last fifteen months of the Soviet Union, but before the total disintegration of the final weeks, the way of life, the mentalities, material world and imaginative universe that sustained the Soviet Union irretrievably decayed. The end of Soviet civilization came before the political collapse but did not cause it – or rather, we have no way of saying exactly how it could have caused such an enormous and chaotic sequence of breakdowns in the operations of the state. It seems likely – though not possible to prove – that empires generally collapse because of external shocks, economic crises and geopolitical challenges rather than because of a terminal crisis in civilizational confidence. A different political settlement and calmer approach to the economy might have kept a reduced USSR going indefinitely,[5] and even allowed it to evolve into a democracy and a European partner. Events, contingencies and personalities were at least the immediate cause of the collapse. But without its fundamental civilization, such a Soviet Union would have been a different country anyway.

There were several Soviet Unions. Chronology marked out the end of one and the beginning of the next. The history of the Soviet Union was ultimately defined by a debate about its periodization. Stalin's death in 1953 and the Secret Speech of 1956 were the crucial dates in the transformation of the USSR. This book has argued that they marked a fundamental and irrevocable exit from Stalinism and were the basis of a stable civilization and functioning state, neither of which was bound to collapse in the short or medium term.[6] But 1985 was also crucial. The elevation of Mikhail Gorbachev to the position of general secretary put in train a sequence of events that led to the possibility of civilizational and state collapse. Periodization shapes explanations of these events. When did *perestroika* become a truly radical reordering of the way of life and politics? When did it turn into the driver of Soviet collapse rather than the inspiration for a Soviet renaissance? From the start of his term of office, Gorbachev had ideas about reform and a willingness to experiment with new policies. His approach quite quickly assumed the contours of a programme, defined not only by the crucial concepts of *perestroika* and *glasnost*, but also by a range of others, such as acceleration and democratization. Yet *perestroika* did not emerge in whole cloth; it was never imagined in advance as a coherent project, and its consequences were not foreseen. Gorbachev's reforms quickly collided with the exigencies of real-world economics, political complexity, human motivations and global diplomacy. They created a momentum that outpaced their origins in Marxism-Leninism.

The sub-periodization of the *perestroika* period provides a framework for interpreting how the Soviet Union collapsed and throws suggestive light on the causes. By 1988–9, the consequences of reform on the lives of ordinary people were already undermining Soviet civilization: a Soviet ideological and cultural worldview could no longer be coherent; the gulf in interests between ordinary people and their bosses could not be hidden; and the shock of economic dislocation was overwhelming. In 1990, new free-market policies were introduced whose aim was to overcome the economic crisis. Gorbachev was plainly transforming himself into a social democrat. Marxism-Leninism was no longer the guiding force of policy development. Soviet civilization now had no obvious content or meaning. By 1991, further unintended consequences of these policies were encouraging economic managers to abandon their support for the Soviet state, while a 'perfect storm' of events led to the disintegration of the USSR into nation states.

But periodization was also an active agent in these processes as well as a retrospective explanation for them. As Soviet civilization became an empty vessel, the whole concept of periodization itself lost meaning. Soviet people had long been trained in the Marxist fashion to think of their civilization as something that progressed in defined periods or stages, and which was moving forward into a comprehensible and better future. Such a vision was now replaced by an outlook on chaos; any sense of revolutionary time was scrambled. The end of Soviet civilization must have had some relationship to the collapse of the Soviet state, though historical explanation can only really attribute the causes of collapse to the particular events of 1991. But one thing seems clear. Soviet civilization came to an end before the collapse of the state and thereafter it ceased to exist. Of course, many practices, objects and thought-processes associated with 'Soviet life' continued to influence people's ways of living after 1991 in all the republics, though with diminishing significance over time,[7] while elements of Soviet civilization were still manipulated and propagandized in the post-Soviet states, sometimes with lethal effect.

Gorbachev was the last revolutionary. *Perestroika*, *glasnost* and democratization were all inspired by his interpretation of Leninism. His reform programme was supposed to return to revolutionary first principles – admittedly only the ones associated with creation and liberation rather than destruction and elimination – and the people who surrounded him crafted revolutionary ideological frameworks in which to explain his policies. The reforms of the late 1980s were about creating a new path for the revolution to develop. Gorbachev was interested in the New Economic Policy, and the political ethics of Leninism, especially what he saw as their potential for pluralism. One of the most striking revolutionary developments that followed was the dream of decentralizing management and creating a democratic spirit in enterprises. The aim was to raise economic productivity. But pluralism and political choice, and their relationship to the economy, exploded out of the constraints that Soviet revolutionism or Bolshevik legacies could place upon them. By 1990, economic policy was no longer determined by revolutionary planning but by promises about free markets.

*Glasnost* created an endlessly polyphonic, beguiling, chaotic and enriching array of debates.[8] Interpreting the Bolshevik revolution of 1917, and its relationship to Stalinism and usefulness for *perestroika*, was crucial. These discussions took place in long-standing publications like *Literaturnaya gazeta* and *Ogonek*, which were now unbound from tight censorship, on TV programmes, in public meetings, leaflets and public forums like the Congress of People's Deputies. Often the focus of debate was the first two decades or so of Soviet rule. Truth-telling and revelations, which were often historical, proliferated.[9] The facts about the secret clauses of the Nazi–Soviet pact were finally announced, prompting anguished discussions about the comparability of Stalinism and Nazism. Books that before were only published abroad or in samizdat – such as *The Gulag Archipelago*, *Doctor Zhivago* and *Life and Fate* – were now for sale in bookshops and available for public debate. Each of these held up a magnifying glass to the devastation that flowed out of 1917, and the connection between Leninism and Stalinism. In 1987, Tengiz Abuladze's film *Repentance*, which was made and banned in 1984, was finally released. Moving back and forth in time, and combining devastating imagery and allusive dialogue, it depicted the Terror in a Georgian town and the destructive memories and effects it still produced decades later.

The fact that one of the leaders of the reform movement in the Congress of People's Deputies, Yuri Afanasiev, was a historian was symbolic of the wider truth that recent history and contemporary politics were now joined together in a further collapsing of revolutionary time. The Memorial organization was founded in 1989 as a publicly approved pressure group devoted to rescuing the horrors of Stalinism from obscurity. It offered accurate, people's history – a combination of scholarly precision and public participation – to help the population actively understand the past and begin to adapt to its reality. Local activists and scholars worked together to uncover killing fields and burial grounds and to prevent abandoned camps from disappearing. They provided material and psychological assistance to victims and their families and created monuments, museums, public events and books. Archivists worked with historians to persuade officials to bring crucial documents to public attention. In 1990, the USSR Association of History Teachers was founded. Some of its members now tried to apply the new knowledge and sensibility of the times to an outdated school curriculum. At the radical edge was the innovative and charismatic young pedagogue Tamara Edelman, who taught in an esteemed school in central Moscow.[10] And yet schools across the USSR were in desperate trouble as funds dried up and soon even teachers' salaries were a fraction of a living wage.

Everybody in the Soviet Union had been reckoning with the past in one way or another, deliberately or subconsciously, all their lives. Stalinism had touched every family. For some, it was the cause of bereavement, orphanhood and ruptured relationships. For others it was a matter of massive practical disruption and unresolved misunderstandings between generations that might never be articulated. This was true in every region and republic and among all kinds of people.

It was true too inside the Politburo. Yegor Ligachev came to Moscow in 1983 as secretary of the Central Committee, a stepping stone to the Politburo. He was an Andropov protégé. Before this, he had headed the Party apparatus in Tomsk region in Siberia for eighteen years. Tomsk was a landscape with many physical as well as emotional scars from the Stalinist period. In 1979, when he was in office there, mass graves from the era of the Great Terror were bulldozed at the township of Kolpashevo on the river Ob. The option of giving the victims a decent burial was rejected. Instead they and their resting place were simply obliterated. It was a monstrous violation which reopened old wounds and became a flashpoint during *perestroika* and after. Ligachev was the Party boss, the baron of Tomsk, but he denied any knowledge or participation.[11]

And Stalinism had its defenders, people like Nina Andreyeva, whose letter had challenged the reformers in the run-up to the Nineteenth Party Conference in 1988. Lazar Kaganovich's views had changed little since his ousting from the Presidium thirty-two years before. Even Molotov, who was also still alive, and whose capacity for endless hours sitting in committee meetings in support of Stalin had given him the nickname 'Stone Arse', thought that Kaganovich was an 'extreme Stalinist'. Kaganovich complained to the journalist Feliks Chuev that *perestroika* was founded on a mistaken understanding of history. Gorbachev and his supporters ignored the 'mighty strengths' of the Stalin period 'which drove us forward' and instead saw only 'the disadvantages and the dark stains'.[12] But what was really striking for any observer of late Soviet public culture was the unrestrained way in which the past was debated, and the willingness to see the logical connections between Stalinism and 1917.

The Thaw and *perestroika* were dramatic and compelling periods of historical reflection and debate, in which history became a matter of public interest with the purpose of helping individual people lead their lives in less anxious, more 'normal' ways. But the Thaw reinforced the legitimacy of the revolution. Khrushchev condemned Stalinism by arguing that it was an error and therefore a tragedy: a departure from Leninism, not one of Leninism's possible futures. Now, thirty years later, many citizens concluded the opposite, that the revolution of 1917 was the ultimate source of destruction. 1917 became a harbinger of 1937. At the same time, Gorbachev's last policies in 1990 and 1991 were plainly unrelated to socialism. Gorbachev was the last revolutionary, but by 1990 the revolution was over. This emptied Soviet civilization of its most important content, and placed the Soviet state on shifting ground.

For several years, *perestroika* placed the individual person at the centre of reform. It emphasized a language of dignity. Policies were designed with the aim of improving individual lives. Personal freedom became a virtue worth fighting for. The end of the Cold War took place because the Eastern bloc disintegrated, and that happened because Gorbachev did not send troops to kill protestors in crowds (though men in uniform, acting without Gorbachev's prior knowledge, attacked unarmed civilians inside the USSR, in Tbilisi and Vilnius). The reduction in nuclear stockpiles accompanied Gorbachev's turn outwards. Denuclearization was a fraught and complex process in political, strategic and industrial terms; starting to carry it out showed the extent of Gorbachev's commitment to peace and the power of his vision. His rhetoric of a 'common European home' and his willingness to use a universal language of human rights was an extension, as he saw it, of the person-centred elements of a Soviet perspective. Yet it did not feel like this for many people, who began to experience *perestroika* as a violation of their perceived social and economic rights.

When Khrushchev condemned the revolutionary ethic that the ends justified the means, and instead looked for other revolutionary legacies to form the ideological basis of post-Stalinism, he was creating a new phase of Soviet civilization. Stalinism had imposed an ethic of sacrifice on the population. Other ethical modes – those of beneficence and paradise – which also had a revolutionary heritage now determined the course of the Thaw. Policies such as the housing programme began as straightforward welfare measures designed to improve the living standards of as many people as possible. When Khrushchev began to emphasize Leninist idealism more strongly at the end of the 1950s, and then promised the achievement of communism by 1980, the housing programme assumed its own paradisiacal dimension: it emphasized not only much better material conditions and accelerated construction targets, but also equal provision, a joined-up (even total) social welfare system and communal, communitarian ways of living outside of the home itself.

In a way it was the familiar Marxist tension between, on the one hand, the rational, technical and scientific, and, on the other, the romantic, mobilizing and utopian. Under Brezhnev, the promise of impending communism was dropped as a workable programme, though a scaled-down version of its language remained. But social policy continued in a substantial way to benefit the whole population through the multi-sided programme that made up the 'social wage': guaranteed work, cash transfers, housing, holidays, prophylactic healthcare, children's extracurricular activities, sports facilities and subsidized cultural opportunities, as well as the more conventional elements of pensions, hospitals and schools. Provision declined as investment fell from the late 1970s, but the principles remained. This was the most fundamental way in which state and Party acknowledged the quality of individual personhood. There were many other ways in which they did precisely the opposite.

When Gorbachev signalled his approval of the Five Hundred Days Programme, he was turning his back on socialism and the revolution for good. The proposals that Yavlinsky and Shatalin put forward were for the transition to a market economy and the end of Soviet planned economics. The consequences of this were seen more clearly in 1992, after the Soviet collapse, when shock therapy – the breakneck introduction of market economics – got underway. Written into this approach to economic reform was a return to an ethic of sacrifice. Living standards were dramatically suppressed in the short term for the sake of sustainable improvements in the medium term. Of course there was no comparison with the sacrifice of the Stalin period, but the ends were again invoked to justify the means, as government no longer even pretended to offer beneficent policies to help individuals experiencing crisis; while paradise was again proclaimed, this time as the ideal world of advertising. In 1990–91, the precipitous decline of the broadly conceived welfare system amounted to the sudden removal of a major element of Soviet civilization; and it destabilized the state to the extent that people could no longer trust the welfare system or the value of their wages.

The political scientist Vladimir Shlapentokh called the Soviet Union 'a normal totalitarian society' and sought reasons for its collapse in the way that normal life worked in the USSR.[13] Yet normality was suspended throughout the period of *perestroika*. The late 1980s and early 1990s were part carnival, part horror movie. They were exciting, frightening, miserable and exhilarating. What they were not was normal. All areas of life, and all forms of social relationships, were destabilized. This ranged from the operation of the workplace, where the value of wages was imperilled, to the conduct of politics, where the exclusive power of the Party was ended. The few saw the one-off opportunity of exhilarating enrichment. Socialist normality was suspended overnight. Time telescoped dramatically. As Alexei Yurchak suggested, 'everything was for ever until it was no more'.

Regardless of the reforms, living conditions and economic life were anyway becoming more shabby and sometimes squalid as the 1980s went on. The relative decline in spending on healthcare since the late 1970s created shortages of anaesthetics and other essential drugs. It reduced investment in new medical technologies and stalled the upkeep of buildings and infrastructure. Hospitals became dirtier: paint flaked; concrete crumbled; pockmarks accumulated. Housing construction continued, but conditions faded. The great housing breakthrough of thirty years before was a folk memory, a touchstone moment in family histories. Khrushchev's reform was still working in practice – even in the late 1980s, every day thousands of citizens were given the keys to a new apartment, though now these sought-after apartment houses were twenty storeys high and set amid massive geometrical arrangements in bigger microdistricts. The apartments from the 1950s and 1960s were long past their best. Despite the promise, the housing problem had not been solved. Apartments were often overcrowded. Conditions which back in the 1960s seemed like a big improvement on what had gone before, and which could be imagined as a waystation on the track to a better life in the era of impending communism, were now simply ordinary.

The shabbiness of urban space directly challenged Soviet normality. In an *Arkhitektura SSSR* discussion of autumn 1987 about what had become of the socialist city, which included the contributions of several architects, B. Neliubin wrote of the problems of 'drug addicts, drunkenness, social passivity', which he thought derived from the fact that 'our cities are primitively functional', and that they had lost their 'philosophical' and 'spiritual' life.[14]

By the late 1980s, as a direct consequence of *glasnost*, sex was much more openly on display. Some people, some of the time, welcomed this. It was a source of knowledge and excitement, adding shades of colour to late Soviet life. Sex education for children was made easier in 1989 with a translation of the *Encyclopaedia of Sexual Life*, published in

France in 1973. Sex and nudity were now on television and film. Gay people made extremely tentative steps into the public sphere. Pornography was available, sometimes next to the stands that sold newspapers. Video clubs offered more explicit content. Prostitution was more widespread and publicly obvious.[15] Graffiti had long been part of urban life, but its messages were now particularly nihilistic. Slogans observed and recorded by scholar John Bushnell in prominent parts of central Moscow in 1988 included 'All we need is beer, anarchy and dirt', 'All the world is made of shit' (in massive letters), and, in English, 'FUCK OFF'.[16] The TV programme *Culture, Traditions, Morality* expressed anxieties about the disintegration of normal relationships between generations and social groups. In 1991, Vera Alyontova, the famous actress who had played the lead in *Moscow Doesn't Believe in Tears* a decade earlier, used a regular TV appearance to broadcast such a message, seeking proper moral connections between people. Her smart suit and perfect hair-do offered a fixed point that viewers could briefly keep in focus while the world seemed to be disintegrating around them.

Like in any modern society, normality was a condition of long-term legitimacy. Soviet civilization could not survive the end of Soviet normality.

For a time, the cultural life inspired by *perestroika* and *glasnost* was driven by enthusiasm and even joy. The instinct to engage with the outside world, to read about foreign countries and see new truths about them on TV could partly be satisfied. Many people viewed the West not only with fascination but also with hope. The 'TV bridge' broadcasts run by the American journalist Phil Donahue and his Soviet opposite number Vladimir Pozner brought audiences from both countries into dialogue, alignment, misunderstanding and controversy – and were a remarkable sign of the times.[17] Soviet cultural production itself rose to the challenge of openness. 'Our hearts demand change! Our eyes demand change!' sang the charismatic rock star Viktor Tsoi to massive crowds during *perestroika*. His best-known song featured images of sunset over a Soviet kitchen and encouraged people to see within themselves the capacity to live differently, not to accept just the 'simple scheme' of 'cigarettes and tea at the table'. Tsoi had been part of the underground rock scene for more than a decade, though now he found his moment with philosophically charged music that came out of Sovietism but conspicuously transcended it. His fans began to find greater strength in his lyrics than in the increasingly empty, brittle and vulnerable forms of Soviet civilization. There were connections to Vysotsky, not least early death and the legends that followed; Tsoi died in a car crash in 1990, at the age of thirty-eight, while on tour in Latvia.

The cultures of developed socialism had been created in a relatively flexible, large and varied space. If one includes samizdat and other examples of unofficial or banned work then this space becomes even larger. But legally available culture stretched from recognizable propaganda to variety entertainment to 'permitted dissent'. It could accommodate debates in original and unexpected forms, from the novels of Yuri Trifonov to the films of Kira Muratova to the sculptures of Ernst Neizvestny. But even when it stretched the boundaries of what it meant to be Soviet, permitted culture remained Soviet. It invited people to ask questions and challenged their moral outlook. But it did not defy the normality or reasonableness of society or aim to create profound uneasiness about social life. Yet this is precisely what happened during *perestroika*.

For two decades, the comedies of Eldar Ryazanov made knowing jokes and mildly subversive asides, but they were familiar, reassuring depictions of Soviet life. Even *The Garage*, from 1979, a sometimes darkly claustrophobic film about material one-upmanship, corruption and lack of trust in a garage cooperative at the Academy of Sciences – one of those forms of property in which elements of individual and collective, workplace and neighbourhood, but not state, cohered – offers a reasonable resolution within the boundaries of normal Soviet expectations. But everything was different in his 1988 movie *Dear Elena Sergeyevna*. Four high-school students, about to take their final exams, turn up at their teacher's apartment, apparently to thank her and celebrate their time at school. Inside, the mood soon darkens. The pupils offer her an apparently irresistible inducement to help one of them get through the exams. Soviet life – the manners of the teacher, the sacredness of learning, the classic domestic interior – has been broken from within by the sudden changes of *perestroika*. Each character's pathologies are revealed in turn, until attention turns to the ringleader. Inside this claustrophobic, dangerous interior space, a young psychopath has the opportunity to pursue his desire to control and humiliate others. The rooms are entirely Soviet; his mental illness is completely human. Not only has Soviet normality been shattered before the eyes of the viewer, but human pathologies turn out to have little to do with Soviet life. And there is nothing about Soviet civilization that offers any means of redemption. Viewers found the film compelling and alienating.

The same year, Vasily Pichul's *Little Vera* was released. It shows the lives of young people of student age in a crumbling port city, socializing and hanging around, waiting for something to happen. Vera, aged around twenty, starts a sexual relationship with a male student which is depicted more graphically and with greater nudity than in any other Soviet film hitherto. Vera has wit, charm and hope, but she is a bright light in a dim landscape. She occupies spaces packed with implied violence which occasionally bursts out. The family has its own separate apartment, but it is small and uncomfortably intimate. We see Vera in her working-class home, with her mother preparing chickens and serving salads while her truck-driver father drinks vodka. At the end of one evening, the national anthem plays from the radio in the family's kitchen, while the camera pans round the constrained space: an untidy jumble of possessions, a line of salted fish, scuffed pans, a rack of plates dripping above the sink, a poor paint job on the wall and her mother coming home, exhausted, carrying a heavy bag of shopping. Worse happens later. Culture was depicting and reinforcing a world that had moved on from Soviet life. There was moral equivalence that no longer seemed to be modulated by Soviet expectations. The focus on everyday squalor was merciless. In another classic *perestroika* film, Petr Todorovsky's *Interdevochka*, about a Leningrad nurse who doubles as a sex worker with foreign clients, the protagonist enjoys good luck before her life completely fragments. Dreamily and nostalgically she looks back to Soviet civilization as a route back to normality. But it has gone – together with the people she loves.

People could not watch these movies and think that they were part of a settled and comprehensible civilization: just the reverse. Culture showed that normality had disappeared. Its depiction of material things, moral dilemmas, social formations and personal relationships was suddenly outside the boundaries of a reasonable, comprehensible way of living. Unlike even a few months earlier, a culturally constructed and represented vision of Sovietness could no longer show people resolving interpersonal problems or offer them a fresh start. Soviet civilization had become irrelevant. Then it disappeared.

Decolonization and its contestations had always been part of Soviet civilization; but the Soviet Union was an empire, and it could only tolerate decolonization to a certain level. This meant that national identity was extremely complex in the USSR. The historian Krista A. Goff, for example, writes of 'nested nationalisms', an evocative image for the way that one form of national expression lay inside another, like the parts of a matryoshka doll.[18] Beneath the overarching identity of 'being Soviet', which for some was a pseudo-national identity as well as an attachment to a set of all-union mentalities and practices, was the titular nationality of each republic, such as Azerbaijanis in Azerbaijan. Members of the titular nationalities had certain rights that were constitutionally backed and derived from the relationship between the all-union centre and the republic. But there were also hundreds of non-titular nationalities, which were considered by their actual members to be their primary national identity. The titular nationality in a republic might benefit from devolved powers but then use them to reinforce its prejudice against smaller national groups in that republic. In the Azerbaijani republic, minorities included Lezgins and Armenians.

Some non-titular national groups were still formally recognized, notably as Autonomous Soviet Socialist Republics. Abkhazia was a famous one, the home of many Abkhazians who lived in Georgia. There was the Karelian ASSR, which resulted from the annexation of territory from Finland during the Second World War. And yet many other nationalities had no formal status or territorial connection. The Finnish Ingrians for years lived an exposed existence in the western parts of the Russian republic. Jews were from time to time targeted in part because there was no republican infrastructure to support them.

The Soviet Union was de facto an empire but this distribution of rights, together with other factors, made it a complex and contradictory empire. There was the way that republics, even in Central Asia, did not really feel like colonies on the Western European model. There was a shift from affirmative action to development investment in some republics. And there were instances of real emancipation that accompanied the rhetoric of postcolonialism. It is perfectly reasonable to argue that these paradoxes of empire made it possible to manage national identity and nationalism in an indefinitely sustainable way. Soviet civilization could accommodate 'nested nationalism' in very diverse forms. Even in summer 1991, when the mood in several republics was plainly moving away from Moscow, nationalism did not seem an imminent threat to the integrity of the Soviet Union. The shifting, variable balances of decolonization and imperial control, which somehow supported the Soviet state, persisted. Soviet civilization was already on the ash heap of history in 1991, even as the power structures of the Soviet Union scrambled to seek ways to outlast it, as a would-be democratic and free-market state, and a geopolitical bloc. But the rise of nationalism that year served to discredit whatever aspects of Soviet civilization remained.

And then, in a dramatic final act, the Soviet Union, its state and apparatus of republics, decolonized itself out of existence in the last weeks of 1991.

Gorbachev returned from Foros to Moscow at two o'clock in the morning on 22 August. TV cameras were trained on the aircraft stairs as he and his family descended. In a light jacket and trousers, he looked washed out. He had noticeably aged. Raisa looked disoriented. He made a speech and came up with many of the right words, graciously thanking Yeltsin, appealing to all the nationalities. William Taubman, Gorbachev's biographer, argues that this was yet another contingency, another moment that Gorbachev might have seized to strengthen his own position and even that of the Soviet Union as a whole. It was a missed chance. He could have travelled to the White House and enjoyed the adulation of the crowd. It was his moment of maximum popularity. He went home with his unhappy and ailing wife instead.[19]

Like water flowing downhill, power now moved towards Boris Yeltsin. For perhaps a year, the Communist Party had not been acting as the custodian of Soviet civilization, but had been reduced to discharging one of its other functions: managing its property, or rather adjusting its paperwork and hiding the ownership of its assets.[20] Yeltsin now consolidated his power in the absence of Soviet civilization by banning the Communist Party on 6 November in the territory of the Russian republic. He was deep in the process of a much more consequential task, of rapidly accruing political prospects by appealing to a national cause that he largely invented: raising the often dormant spirit of Russian nationhood, seeking liberation of the White House from the Kremlin, of Russia from the USSR, as if it was England claiming independence from the United Kingdom. Nationalism was now accelerating across the USSR. It recalled the revolutions of 1848, when nationalism swept like a bush fire across Europe. 'Nationalism was the most dispersed, emotionally intense and contagious experience of the revolutions,' writes Christopher Clark, author of an epic history of those events. 'It flared up with extraordinary speed. It abolished or reversed the hierarchy between centre and periphery.'[21]

Nationalism was most deeply rooted in the Baltic states, which had only been added to the USSR in 1940 and had a previous history as independent countries. On 23 August 1989, on the fiftieth anniversary of the Molotov–Ribbentrop Pact, two million Baltic people across the three republics joined hands in a massive human chain. This was not only a striking and even beautiful tableau; it was also a courageous action by the organizers and participants. They took the risk because Gorbachev's commitment to non-violence was now a durable matter of international record. It was no longer likely that the security services would open fire on the crowd. It was an inspiring example that suddenly became infectious in the summer and autumn of 1991. A fortnight after its two-year anniversary, on 6 September, the Soviet Union recognized the independence of the Baltic states.

As Soviet civilization dissolved, nationalism became an alternative mentality, or source of loyalty, or understanding of politics, or a tactical route towards money and power for the ruthless. The pandemic of activist national feeling broke out first because certain politicians, like Yeltsin in Russia, used it as an anti-Soviet vehicle to power, and then because it was a language of protest that was at once familiar and exciting for crowds who had lost the reassurance of Soviet civilization and needed a new political, social, economic and cultural start.

Nationalism offered a coherent and plausible message in all these dimensions and rapidly gained momentum in places with very long national traditions, such as Georgia's, and those with a newer sense of nationalism, such as Ukraine's. In some other republics, especially in Central Asia, national feeling was more limited and support for the Soviet state more pronounced. In Tajikistan, there was no plan for true secession, and the republic found itself only 'slouching towards independence'.[22] Yet the cultural roots of Central Asian national identities were better defined than ever. Campaigners for the Turkmen language, for instance, had been gaining popularity and confidence during 1990 and 1991.[23]

On 10 September, Armenia declared independence, though the centre did not yet recognize it. The other two republics that had already crossed the psychological Rubicon away from Soviet power were Georgia and Moldavia (Moldova). In foreign governments, it was clear that Gorbachev possessed only a shadow of his former power as national sentiment and power swept across the USSR. 'There was a pop-up quality to the nationalist wave of 1848,' Clark goes on. 'Mass meetings saturated with the sounds, colours and symbols of the nation had a deep impact on those who experienced them, partly because they were so new.'[24]

Nowhere was this truer than in Ukraine. Ukrainian nationalism had developed over the last hundred years but was rarely understood as the basis for statehood. Even in the first half of 1991, when Ukrainian national feeling was becoming noticeably stronger, it still did not generate a conspicuous independence movement. In the March 1991 referendum, the Ukrainians voted for the all-union treaty, at a time when expressions of national independence in the Baltic republics were already unstoppable. National feeling in Georgia, Moldova and Armenia had also caught fire and created independence movements. All six of these republics boycotted the referendum. Among Ukrainians, though, almost exactly the same percentage voted in favour as in the Russian republic (71 and 73 per cent respectively). Support was higher in the Belarusian republic (84 per cent) and in the different political cultures of the other six – Azerbaijan plus the five Central Asian republics – the figure was in the mid-90s.

The key change that doomed the Soviet Union in the autumn of 1991 was the efflorescence of nationalism in Ukraine. Everybody knew that Ukraine effectively cast the decisive vote in the future of the USSR. There could be no Soviet Union without Ukraine. Even more, there could be no Soviet Union without Russia. But the best way for Yeltsin to remove Russia from the union was by getting Ukraine to vote leave. In the Ukrainian republic, September, October and November were months of high political engagement and emerging national fervour. An independence referendum was set for 1 December, the same day as the republic's presidential election. What happened was the same as in other republics: when elites sensed that their interests were best served by jumping ship away from the Soviet Union by backing independence, and rolling the dice seemed less risky than the misery of the status quo, a popular national movement coalesced. Leonid Kravchuk had a stellar Party career and wound up as chairman of the Supreme Soviet of the Ukrainian republic, renamed the Supreme Rada following the August coup. He now shifted towards the independence agenda. This was the centre of his presidential and referendum campaigns. It ended in a triumph. Apparently against all odds, and certainly against Kravchuk's expectations, more than 90 per cent of citizens, on an 84 per cent turnout, voted for independence. Kravchuk was voted in as president with 61 per cent support; his nearest rival gained 23 per cent.[25]

The men and women who ran the innermost elements of the Soviet state apparatus sought to keep their roles in the new world of sovereign nationhood, sometimes adopting its language and values, sometimes simply inhabiting its structures of power and wealth. On the morning of 26 August, four days after Gorbachev landed in Moscow after the failure of the coup, the body of Nikolai Kruchina was found on the ground underneath his seventh-floor window. The KGB said it was suicide. Kruchina ran the privileges and perquisites operations of the Party's Central Committee, distributing the good things in life to his colleagues and managing the Party's property empire. The following month, his successor also fell out of his apartment window. They and at least one other senior official in the same department died while the KGB tried to maintain a veil over the financial operations that accompanied the formal liquidation of the Party, which was about to be banned. Large amounts of money had been funnelled out of the USSR and through 'friendly firms' into investments abroad. Some of the money was supposed to go to foreign Communist parties and other influence operations; some of it was rainy-day money in the event of systemic collapse in the USSR. This complex web of financial operations told a number of stories. One was about the disappearance of the Party's vast wealth just as the Party was about to be signed out of existence, and the role of the KGB in that operation. Another story was that elements in the KGB had a back-up plan and were ready to move on to the successor state if the Soviet Union came to an end.[26]

It was an example of Max Weber's argument about the durability of bureaucracies, and their capacity to reposition themselves and survive even during a crisis of state failure. The KGB found a way to reinvent itself by abandoning the Soviet Union. It was a paradox – how could the KGB exist without the USSR – but it was a way for individual secret policemen to retain some power and privileges. For those who were interested, it could be done under the guise of nationalism. The 'Russian Party' was influential in the KGB. There were analogous situations in other republics. In Belarus, the KGB even continued to call itself the KGB. But it was in the Russian republic that it had the most deadly consequences thirty years later.

In other branches of administration, officials jumped ship, sometimes acquiring state assets. Enterprise managers positioned themselves so that they could take advantage of the privatizations that followed the collapse. At the top end, the oligarchs came up with extraordinary ways of capitalizing on the situation and made spectacular fortunes. This was a general process of the elites rushing for the exits and grabbing what they could.[27] It was the hidden wiring behind the surface of national independence movements. Popular nationalism, after all, emerged because aspects of the state were collapsing; it did not in itself make the state collapse.

Neither did 'the West', however powerful it was. President George Bush telephoned Kravchuk the day after his triumph in order to congratulate him. Bush told him that the United States was getting ready to discuss with his government the issues that worried it most, not least nuclear weapons. If such thorny problems could be resolved, then Bush would be able to retrofit the result as a triumph for his agenda of national sovereignty and human rights as he entered re-election year.

But these were indeed retrospective positions for Bush. In August, before the coup, Bush had come to Ukraine and made his famous 'Chicken Kyiv' speech, in which he spoke out against 'suicidal nationalism' and described the virtues of Gorbachev and the advantages of union with the other republics. He had in mind the civil war that was developing in the former Yugoslavia. Such an outcome – and one made unimaginably worse by the possible use of nuclear weapons as well as their spontaneous and uncontrolled proliferation – seemed a plausible nightmare scenario in the summer and autumn of 1991. Bush was opposed to the break-up of the Soviet Union until the moment before it happened. Leonid Kravchuk came to Washington on 25 September 1991 and spent more than ninety minutes in sometimes awkward dialogue with Bush in the White House. It was not a meeting of minds. Kravchuk was now talking firmly about the advantages of Ukrainian independence in the context of the de facto disintegration of the union centre. Bush constantly rowed back against Kravchuk's progressive feints. He wanted to preserve what he could of the status quo. Bush was in wider conversations with other NATO leaders about the diplomatic configurations that might keep the Soviet Union intact as long as possible.[28]

In other words, Bush did everything he could to slow down the spread of nationalism and promote institutional continuity in the USSR. Western leaders and Western powers did not cause the collapse of the Soviet Union: just the reverse. There is a case that they accelerated Gorbachev's reformist thinking a few years earlier: Gorbachev and Reagan found a modus vivendi in their shared commitment to peace; Gorbachev was fascinated by the West and keen to find evidence to improve the design of his reforms; he was committed to the nostrums of human rights, but also wanted to talk about democracy and universal rights in a way that sounded like his Western peers; Gorbachev helped bring the Cold War to an end and allowed the Eastern bloc to go its own way in 1989 in part because he trusted Bush not to take advantage. Reagan and his government had a substantial part in ending the Cold War. But none of this was the same as causing the collapse of the Soviet Union.

Instead, that was the result of the unimaginable forces unleashed by *perestroika* and *glasnost*, which during 1991 finally attacked the Soviet state from within the interstices of Soviet institutions and society. The precipitate cause of collapse was the rise and noise of titular nationalisms, and their capacity to win over local populations in the quest for national sovereignty. It worked because the major politicians in the republics, led by Yeltsin, found a way to equate national sovereignty with their own wealth and power, and to use popular national feeling as the vehicle for steering the political and financial interests of their governing cliques through the extreme turbulence of 1991, which is not to say that some of them did not come to believe in nationalism themselves. The process reached its peak on 8 December. Yeltsin, Kravchuk and Stanislav Shushkevich of the Belarusian republic met in the Belovezh forest in Belarus as representatives of the three surviving republics that had constituted the original USSR (the fourth, Transcaucasia, had long been split into republics with titular nationalities, while the Central Asian republics had originally been part of the RSFSR itself). They signed the accords to end the Soviet Union. It now had to be ratified by the sovereign parliamentary bodies of each republic. The Central Asian republics, which supported the continuation of the USSR, were left in the lurch, though their leaders naturally enough found a way of taking advantage.

On Christmas Day, power switched from the Soviet Union to the new Russian Federation and the other republics. 'Russia' became the largest and most substantial successor state of the USSR, taking its seat at the Security Council of the United Nations. That day, *Pravda* speculated on its front page about whether the new Russia was going to join NATO. It was a moment when anything could happen, and some people pushed into the future with exhilaration. In the Kremlin, though, the mood was nervous, even fearful. Yeltsin reached for alcohol. The transition from Gorbachev to Yeltsin was a graceless one. The two men could not bear to be in the same room. It grew dark in Moscow, and the red flag came down from the Kremlin.

People started arriving at the Taganka Theatre for that evening's performance. It was *The Master and Margarita*. The première had taken place more than fourteen years earlier, on 6 April 1977. Bulgakov's novel had only recently been made legally available, and only then in an incomplete form. Its route to the stage of the Taganka was unsurprisingly a complicated one. Yuri Lyubimov remembered that they tried 'every possible and impossible' way of dealing with the censors.[29] It required innovative staging to accommodate the material and spiritual worlds that the novel conjured up. The novel strained at the boundaries of Soviet civilization, but Lyubimov worked out how to put it on and make sure the audience saw it.

On 25 December 1991, with Soviet civilization gone for good, the Taganka's *Master and Margarita* no longer existed as the product of a dance with the censorship authorities. It had to be appreciated in a different way. Layers of meaning associated with one's relationship to the dictatorship were no longer relevant. The play could be enjoyed for its own sake.

And yet it was a troubled and anxious night. Gotlib Roninson had spent a large part of his career in the company of the Taganka. He performed in many of its plays, including *The Master and Margarita*. Born in 1916, Roninson was not quite a twin of the revolution. He was a film actor too, well known for taking on character roles in comedies. Roninson often worked with Eldar Ryazanov. He had a small but perfect role in *The Irony of Fate*, where he talks about air travel with the drunk protagonist who is about accidentally to get on a plane to Leningrad. The classic new year film would be on TV yet again in a few days' time. In December 1991, Roninson was fast approaching seventy-six, and still performing.

He did not show up at the theatre that night and so an understudy went on for him. His friends at the Taganka were worried and went to find him. He had died suddenly that afternoon following a stroke.

From the age of one, Roninson lived his whole life under Communist rule. He outlived Soviet civilization, which had already gone, and he just about lived up to the expiration of the Soviet state. Roninson spent his life playing roles that helped to stretch and define the edges of Soviet normality. Late that night, as his friends gathered in his apartment on Krymsky val, they saw his body laid out. He was yet another lost component from the experience of Sovietness. The curtain had gone down on Soviet civilization and now on the USSR too. At the Taganka, the show went on.

Circa 1991, in the USSR

# Afterword

A wide gulf – in historical interpretation, current events, and personal experience – separated the planning and completion of this book. In the summer of 2018 I designed it in outline. I started work straight away, making rapid progress on the easy bits.

Then, in 2020, the Covid pandemic interrupted and redefined the project, not least because it stopped me from travelling to Moscow, where I'd expected to spend many months. The pandemic also adjusted the perspective of the argument, as I will explain below.

But what really delayed *Exit Stalin* and forced me to re-evaluate my understanding of the Soviet past were the catastrophes of early 2022. In the bleak new year, my wife died of cancer. It was three days after our twentieth wedding anniversary. In our reduced family, my daughter and I faced a devastated world. A few weeks later, Russia invaded Ukraine. Now the world outside turned pitch black too. I was completely at a loss.

During the last nine months of my wife's illness I stopped even cursory work on this book. After she died, I could hardly read or write a sentence for another nine months. I still tried to do the other parts of my job, but grief relentlessly eviscerated my ability to concentrate on any task that was not immediately due.

When I slowly came back to scholarly work, my confidence in historical explanation had dissolved and reassembled itself in a different form. I accepted that no single book, including mine, could adequately serve as an overarching explanation for the Soviet collapse (Vladislav Zubok's *Collapse* perhaps gets the closest, in part by eschewing an easy verdict).

# AFTERWORD

The process of collapse, with so many moving parts, was impossible to capture with a snapshot. It was more like a massive, roiling, expanding, shrinking weather system chaotically pushing through the atmosphere than a defined political event. Instead, I stuck close to another question which I thought was more plausibly historical: 'how did the Russian Revolution over the long run generate a society that was, for a time, simultaneously revolutionary and long-lasting?' It was a question which could deal with the monumental effects of Stalin's death; which would be principally focused on the period before civilizational breakdown and state collapse set in; and which acknowledged that collapse, when it came, was apparently unexpected and driven by contingent events and personalities. This approach detached two independent phenomena from each other: the practices and mentalities of the Thaw and late socialism, which might be called Soviet civilization, from the collapse and end of the Soviet Union; and perhaps too it assumed that the Soviet Union could survive for a time after its 'civilization' had disappeared.

After the pandemic was underway, I would learn three lessons that adjusted my argument and the shape of the book. First: state collapse really is a very unlikely event. It was in the summer of 2020, well into my work on the book, that my understanding of Soviet history began to change. My wife was born in the Soviet Union, and we retained close links to Moscow. In England, she and I watched with growing excitement the progress of the election campaign in Belarus. Aleksandr Lukashenko had been in office since 1994 and won every 'election' since then. He was an outright dictator. Living standards in Belarus had atrophied. There was no free air. In the run-up to the presidential election of summer 2020, Lukashenko arrested his opponents or forced them into exile. Sergei Tikhanovsky used his popular YouTube channel to make level-headed criticism of the government. It was a platform for a serious presidential bid. They threw him in jail at the end of May. Valery Tsepkalo, who had long experience in politics and business, and was a major opposition figure, put his name forward. Under enormous pressure, he fled the country in early July. Viktar Babaryka, a leading businessman, began his campaign, but his candidacy was deregistered. He was arrested and given a long sentence on trumped-up bribery charges.

## AFTERWORD

Astonishingly, the wives of the first two, Svetlana Tikhanovskaya (Sviatlana Tsikhanouskaya in Belorusian) and Veronika Tsepkalo joined with the campaign manager of the third, Maria Kolesnikova, in organizing the opposition to Lukashenko. They appeared in public as a triumvirate, but Tsikhanouskaya was the candidate. Perhaps because she was a woman, perhaps because she was a political novice, Lukashenko underestimated her and permitted her candidacy.

The three women were young, modern, coherent, bright, elegant and optimistic. They offered a mesmerizing message about love, honesty and unity. Tsikhanouskaya was a political natural, delivering positive, clear responses on TV, never getting rattled and almost always looking presidential. It was as if a Danish alloy was being mixed into an east Slavic amalgam. It was impossible to listen to her and not to weep for a completely different future. Kolesnikova, Tsepkalo and Tsikhanouskaya took the public by storm. They travelled the country and addressed great crowds. When election day came, on 9 August, it was obvious that Tsikhanouskaya had won by a landslide.

Crowds packed Minsk to protect the election result, but Lukashenko refused to concede. Insisting he had won, he sent in armour-clad riot police to beat up unarmed protestors. Many were arrested and crammed into holding cells. Lukashenko flew over Minsk in a helicopter together with his teenage son. He clutched a sub-machine gun. Tsikhanouskaya was not prepared to take risks with the protestors and asked them to go home. It was the difference between a politics of love and a politics of death. Her politics lost. She and Tsepkalo were given no choice but to flee abroad. Kolesnikova refused to leave and was soon serving a long prison sentence.

The elites did not abandon ship. There were no lifeboats. They stayed loyal to the president and to the system that had rewarded them with privileges. The *siloviki* – the armed men and women in uniform, above all the paramilitary OMON – had themselves been rewarded with very good salaries and nice apartments for years. With every protestor's leg that they broke, they more deeply implicated themselves in the dictatorship. They had nowhere else to go and could only double down on their role in the system.

I watched all this and understood just how improbable state failure really is. Everything seemed stacked against Lukashenko's political order. It looked like the enormous crowds only had to push a little harder. A history of the Belarusian revolution of 2020 would have analysed the demise of an unproductive economy still stuck to Soviet practices, run by a president who used to be a collective farm chairman; the collapse of a political system that had become inflexible, unresponsive and illegitimate; and the triumph of people power and the unstoppable momentum of the crowd. It would have seemed inevitable, but of course it didn't happen. As a comparator phenomenon to 1991, the Belarusian non-collapse added weight to the interpretation that the end of the USSR was an improbable event that could not have happened had administrative and economic elites not switched sides. What modulated a situation of extreme instability seemed to be contingency, personalities and violence (deployed or withheld). It could not be captured by a grand one-sentence summary of the reason for collapse.

The second lesson I learned was that Soviet civilization was indeed defined by its multivalency, but that I had underestimated one set of voices: the dissidents. That summer, Alexei Navalny and his team at the Foundation to Combat Corruption were still working in their Moscow office, gathering evidence for their investigations and putting out their YouTube shows to expose venality and discuss politics. Navalny riffed and joked but also talked with authority and seriousness. It was always a charismatic performance. In August he set off on a trip to Tomsk to make a film about his latest corruption investigation. His allies in branches of the Foundation were preparing for local elections in September. Navalny was campaigning for 'intelligent voting', encouraging people to cast their ballot tactically for the party most likely locally to defeat United Russia, the establishment party that controlled all the organs of elective office. There was still a public square featuring Ekho Moskvy, the radio station; *Novaya gazeta*, the independent newspaper famed for its investigative journalism; the YouTube channels of independent journalists; Navalny's Foundation; and a broadly 'free' atmosphere in bookstores and at certain public events. Navalny's team acted as if they had a chance. They had carefully calculated that their plan for tactical voting might give the opposition a toehold in the Duma.

## AFTERWORD

On 20 August, with his work in Tomsk complete, Navalny boarded a flight back to Moscow. A few minutes after take-off, he experienced severe pain and collapsed. He would have died if the flight had continued on its route, but the pilot landed at nearby Omsk. News of Navalny's life hanging in the balance was flashed around the world. My wife and I waited in a hospital car park – she would shortly have surgery – peering at his colleagues' tweets for news of his fate. Amid high drama, the Kremlin permitted his evacuation to Germany, where he recovered at a specialist toxins department. That autumn, Navalny and his colleagues worked with the Bellingcat organization of investigative journalists to piece together what had happened. Using data from airlines, mobile phone networks, CCTV cameras and other sources, they worked out exactly which secret policemen were guilty of poisoning him. The *coup de grâce* came when Navalny prank-called them from his new base in Germany, posing as a senior official, and got one of them to admit to exactly what had happened. Then they posted it on YouTube.

When he was well enough, Navalny returned to Moscow in January 2021. It was hard to imagine a more courageous action. He was arrested as soon as he arrived at the airport. There were significant protests in major cities, which the authorities crushed. Moscow contained hundreds of thousands of armed paramilitaries who were clad in armour and were perfectly willing to attack disabled people and old ladies. They now beat up thousands of protestors and hurled them into the buses that took them to the cells. During the Covid pandemic, the authorities had multiplied their surveillance technologies: closed-circuit cameras, facial recognition, public transport cards, and access portals for public services. They now reaped the machines' potential.

For seven years I ran a blog called *Beyond the Kremlin*. I posted short pieces which offered historical contexts of current events. But now I could not think of any historical explication that clarified the terrible immediacy of Navalny's fate and the apparently impossible predicament of the opposition. Clarity, such as it was, came from those journalists and sociologists who were capable of combining on-the-ground knowledge with skilled analysis.[1] There was no reason why historical context or chronology was even remotely as useful. It was time for historians to cede the ground to expert witnesses. The blog had run its course.

Later in 2021, my wife was becoming more ill, suffering from a fourth round of her cancer and undergoing painful and arduous treatments aimed only at alleviating her symptoms. She was courageous, passionate, clever, witty, sincere, open and constantly engaged with the feelings of other people. The policemen and the politicians were precisely the opposite, though they would long outlive her – and get worse. Perhaps I was bound to translate my overwhelming sense of moral chaos to my understanding of historical explanation.

Although she was not a historian, my wife taught me more about the Soviet past than anyone else. We met one winter morning at the end of the 1990s. I had already been living in Moscow for a year; Boris Yeltsin was still president; any future seemed available. It was long before I imagined writing about Soviet history, but she immediately introduced me to her Soviet hinterland: in her friends' homes with their Soviet layouts, in Moscow's last Soviet cafeterias, on streets that evoked Soviet-era stories she wanted to tell me. We watched Soviet movies together; I read Soviet novels she thought were important. We often went to the theatre three times a week – she was a proper Moscow theatre-person – but even as the audience wept and laughed together, I listened for the Soviet echo that she instinctively heard in the performances. In the process I sensed how actively she valued individual personhood and distrusted abstract collectives. It became crucial to how I thought about Soviet history, but that was a second-order matter: these things were really ways of learning about her. We were still doing them all twenty years later, and our daughter was an integral part of this lived cultural continuum between family and work, past and present, here and there, and it was only getting more interesting, but then – mid-way through writing this book – the continuum snapped.

Two days before my wife died, in her room at the hospice, we talked about the Russian armies that were massing on the Ukrainian border. It was seven weeks before the invasion. Nobody knew whether they would invade; I could not imagine it.

'Of course they'll invade,' she said.

## AFTERWORD

The unlimited futures that had existed twenty-three years before had narrowed to a single point. Her life was about to end. The space in which we had lived for all those years, the big open zone shared by Russia and 'the West', was about to be evacuated and boarded up.

Russia's armed forces launched their full-scale invasion of Ukraine. The Russian government now finally decapitated the already enfeebled opposition. Any surviving independent media were banned. The number of those declared as 'foreign agents' increased. Honest voices were silenced. Brave figures such as Vladimir Kara-Murza and Ilya Yashin were arrested and given very long sentences. Navalny, already in a maximum-security prison camp and wasting away, was hit with one further trumped-up charge after another.

Opposition in Russia was effectively impossible. The few individuals who were fearless enough to take on the government combined sincerity, conscience, self-sacrifice and tolerance for risk and pain, as well as ambition and vision. Every day, thinking about my wife, I constructed the conversations we would have had about what was happening to these people. It was impossible to look back on the Soviet past without reflecting on what Navalny and the others, whom I never met but so often thought about, told me about it through the example of their actions.

The third lesson was that the collapse of the Soviet Union was no longer an historical question. Historians of the Soviet Union in Ukraine now endured an unimaginable torment. They conducted their teaching in bomb shelters in what must have been the highest levels of dread and stress. Their colleagues in the Russian Federation faced a different torment. A sharp reduction of their professional scope coincided with the spectre of military service and the closure of their country. Every person's response was different, but waves of personal crisis, moral anxiety, shame and fear broke endlessly through the intelligentsia. Historians of Russia, Ukraine and the Soviet Union who were from other countries stood outside these overwhelming pressures but were often heartbroken nonetheless. Cut off from their libraries, archives, collaborators and imaginative source, their sense of their subject and their method of conducting it were transformed. It was a professional crisis with unpredictable consequences. For some individuals, it raised personal and intellectual dilemmas that defied resolution.

The war forced every historian of the USSR to return to first principles. After February 2022, assumptions about centre–periphery relations, the status of subalterns, the relative significance of national identities, the importance of place, space and symbols: all of these things had to be built into the foundation of analysis rather than merely connected at the edge. *Exit Stalin* aimed to describe an all-union civilization while drawing primarily on years of research and personal connections in Moscow, not the provinces or republics. I could not change my experience. Halfway through the book, I could not alter the fundamental scholarship on which it was based. A primary but far from exclusive focus on the union centre was not an unreasonable approach to such a project. But it was not enough. I wanted to engage sympathetically with the mentalities of more Soviet people from more places. This could not be a comprehensive approach. The 'history in fragments' structure of the book, instantiating its argument about ongoing revolution, contingency and multiplicity in Soviet civilization, now looked even more like a montage than I had imagined it would when I started.

I looked again at place names in the book's early chapters that before had meant nothing to me but now carried a terrifying charge. Zhdanov was from Mariupol. Khrushchev once took part in revolutionary politics in Bakhmut. Every day I wondered whether my historical conclusions were appropriate in the world that came after the massacre at Bucha. I did not literally begin the book again, but in a looser sense I did.

Past and present were now in open dialogue. Somebody who was twenty when the USSR collapsed was only fifty when the full-scale invasion began thirty years later. Before, it had been easy to overcome the challenge of studying recent history. The Soviet Union was recognizably over. Historians did not necessarily find a more reliable perspective on the more distant past. But what had been complete was suddenly unfinished. Before, most writers who analysed the Soviet collapse agreed that it was surprisingly peaceful. Although there were conflicts in Nagorno-Karabakh and Tajikistan, there was no post-Soviet nuclear civil war, which was the nightmare scenario debated by George Bush's White House. But an account written after 2022 could not take such a position. The facts had changed. And until this war and any other connected wars are concluded, the facts will change again.

This can only affect our understanding of the end of the USSR. It is as if investigators have reopened a cold case or someone has written an historical novel with multiple endings. We thought we knew the end – the Soviet Union is over, Soviet civilization is long gone. But did the Soviet past cause the war in Ukraine or make it unlikely? Did the Russian president invent an historical narrative that might justify his war – despite years of peace and the densest web of close interpersonal connections between Russians and Ukrainians – or had history really accumulated fundamental ruptures of which he merely took advantage? The answer not only alters how we look at current events; it makes Soviet history look different.

For an outsider like me, who has inhabited the Soviet past for more than twenty years, the only way to move from an absent answer to a better set of questions was by using imagination as much as intellect to catch glimpses, through a glass darkly, of Soviet civilization.

Instead of a conclusion, I imagine a young man in a shabby overcoat and a striking fur hat, perhaps borrowed from his father, riding the escalator up from the shiny week-old metro station at Moscow's Pushkin Square. It's a Tuesday: 23 December 1975. He looks about twenty years old. The boy might even have been born on the day that Khrushchev gave his Secret Speech. Perhaps he's the son of an orphan whose father was killed at the front. Classes at the institute will have finished for the day. He's grasping half-a-dozen tickets – Vysotsky is playing in *The Cherry Orchard* at the Taganka that night, perhaps the tickets are for that – and he looks full of a story about how he acquired them. At the exit, kindergarten children, wrapped layer on layer, looking like spheres, are waiting with their teacher. Outside, snow settles on cars and buses in the last of the late-afternoon light. A weatherbeaten woman with intelligent eyes is selling ice cream from a cart near the metro. Three policemen pause and walk on. A few young friends are gathered at Pushkin's statue on Gorky Street. They're stamping their feet against the cold, their faces glistening with snowflakes. The student with the tickets breaks into a loping run when he sees them. He skids on the ice. They laugh and touch each other's arms. Come on, one of the young women says, taking his hand, let's all walk down the boulevard.

# Notes

In the main text, I have transliterated Russian words (usually places and names) in the way that seems most familiar and accessible for English-language readers. With such an aim, it is impossible to adopt a consistent transliteration system. In the endnotes, I have used such a consistent system (a modified version of the Library of Congress system) while also reproducing the precise spellings of names and titles as they appear in the publications I cite. This follows scholarly convention, and occasionally means that the same name might be spelled in two different ways in the same endnote.

## PROLOGUE: 2 JUNE 1962

1 Samuel H. Baron, *Bloody Saturday in the Soviet Union: Novocherkassk, 1962*, Stanford, 2001, 64. The outline of events that follows can be found in this essential book.
2 David Mandel, *Novocherkassk 1–3 iiunia 1962g: zabastovka i rasstrel (na osnove svidetel'stv ochevidtsev i interv'iu s P.P. Siudoi)*, Moscow, 1992, 38.
3 V. A. Kozlov, *Neizvestnyi SSSR: Protivostoianie naroda i vlasti 1953–1985gg*, Moscow, 2006, 383–4.
4 Joshua Andy, 'The Soviet Military at Novocherkassk: The Apex of Military Professionalism in the Khrushchev Era?' in Melanie Ilic and Jeremy Smith (eds.), *Soviet State and Society under Nikita Khrushchev*, London, 2009, 181–96 (esp. 189, 193).
5 Vasily Grossman, *Everything Flows*, trans. Robert Chandler, London, 2011, 122.
6 Cf. the sympathetic accounts in Sidney and Beatrice Webb, *Soviet Communism: A New Civilization?*, London, 1935; Corliss Lamont, *Soviet*

*Civilization*, New York, 1952. The Webbs' question mark was famously dropped in subsequent editions.

7 For discussions of the early emergence of Soviet modernity and its long-range effects in the 1970s, see Stefan Plaggenborg, *Experiment Moderne; Der sowjetische Weg*, Frankfurt, 2006; and Marie-Janine Calic, Dietmar Neutatz and Julia Obertreis (eds.), *The Crisis of Socialist Modernity: The Soviet Union and Yugoslavia in the 1970s*, Göttingen, 2011.

8 Stephen Kotkin, *Magnetic Mountain: Stalinism as a Civilization*, Berkeley, 1995 (quotation on 364).

9 Books by scholars, popular historians and broadcasters excavate the material 'archaeology' of Soviet civilization. See Karl Schlögel, *The Soviet Century: Archaeology of a New World*, Princeton, 2023; Aleksandr Vas'kin, *Povsednevnaia zhizn' sovetskoi stolitsy pri Khrushcheve i Brezhneve*, Moscow, 2017; *Namedni: Nasha era*, broadcast on NTV and narrated by Leonid Parfenov (1997–2001), and subsequently issued as a series of books on later Soviet decades under his authorship. While some of this work, e.g. Parfenov's, can prompt post-Soviet nostalgia, other uses of the 'Soviet civilization' term are polemical, e.g. S. G. Kara-Murza, *Sovetskaia tsivilizatsiia*, 2 vols., Moscow, 2001. Soviet civilization also existed in a wider international context during the Cold War. The post-1945 ideologues of the Soviet Union appropriated the same rhetoric of 'civilization' that came into vogue in other parts of Europe and the United States after the Second World War in order to describe the process of post-empire, post-genocide rebuilding. See Paul Betts, *Ruin and Renewal: Civilising Europe after the Second World War*, London, 2020.

10 Svetlana Alexievich, *Second-Hand Time*, trans. Bela Shayevich, London, 2016 [2013], 28–9.

11 Dissidents could appropriate and explore the term 'civilization' for their own uses: Andrei Sinyavsky, *Soviet Civilization: A Cultural History*, New York, 1988.

12 See, e.g., James Mark and Paul Betts et al., *Socialism Goes Global: The Soviet Union and Eastern Europe in the Age of Decolonization*, Oxford, 2022.

13 Jörg Baberowski, *Scorched Earth: Stalin's Reign of Terror*, New Haven, 2016, 429.

14 Interview with Serguei Oushakine on 'Scholarly Zeit Guest' YouTube channel, 13 October 2022.

15 Benjamin Tromly, *Making the Soviet Intelligentsia: Universities and Intellectual Life under Stalin and Khrushchev*, Cambridge, 2014, 8.

16 Cf. Richard Vinen, *A History in Fragments: Europe in the Twentieth Century*, London, 2000.

17 Cf. Stephen Lovell, *The Shadow of War: Russia and the USSR, 1941 to the Present*, Oxford, 2010; Rudol'f Pikhoia, *Moskva, Kreml', vlast'*, 2 vols., Moscow, 2007; Alexandre Sumpf, *De Lénine à Gagarine: Une histoire sociale de l'Union soviétique*, Paris, 2013.

## CHAPTER 1: NIKITA KHRUSHCHEV'S REVOLUTION OF MULTIPLE FUTURES (1917–53)

1 N. G. Tomilina, *Nikita Sergeevich Khrushchev: Dva tsveta vremeni, dokumenty iz lichnogo fonda N. S. Khrushcheva v 2-kh tomakh*, Moscow, 2009, vol. 2 of 2, p. 446 (razdel 7, doc. 2).

2 Discussion of Yuzovka in this section is largely informed by Theodore H. Friedgut, *Iuzovka and Revolution*, vol. 2 of 2: *Politics and Revolution in Russia's Donbass, 1869–1924*, Princeton, 1989, ch. 6.

3 Nikita Sergeevich Khrushchev, *Vospominaniia*, vol. 1 of 2, Moscow, 2016, 692.

4 Yuri Slezkine, *The House of Government: A Saga of the Russian Revolution*, Princeton, 2017, book 1 and *passim*.

5 William Taubman, *Khrushchev: The Man and His Era*, New York, 2003, 44–5.

6 Friedgut, *Iuzovka*, vol. 2, 237–9.

7 Friedgut, *Iuzovka*, vol. 2, 293.

8 Adam Tooze, *The Deluge: The Great War and the Remaking of the Global Order 1916–1931*, London, 2014, ch. 5.

9 Khrushchev, *Vospominaniia*, vol. 1, 29.

10 Taubman, *Khrushchev*, 48–51.

11 Andy Willimott, *Living the Revolution: Urban Communes and Soviet Socialism, 1917–1932*, Oxford, 2017.

12 Douglas Smith, *Former People: The Last Days of the Russian Aristocracy*, London, 2012.

13 Igal Halfin, *From Darkness to Light: Class, Consciousness and Salvation in Revolutionary Russia*, Pittsburgh, 2000.

14 Terry Martin, *The Affirmative Action Empire: Nations and Nationalism in the Soviet Union, 1923–1939*, Ithaca, 2001.

15 Khrushchev, *Vospominaniia*, vol. 1, 26.

16 Khrushchev, *Vospominaniia*, vol. 1, 27.

17 Ronald Grigor Suny, *Stalin: Passage to Revolution*, Princeton, 2020.

18 Leon Trotsky, *The Revolution Betrayed*, New York, 1937, 103.

19 Lewis H. Siegelbaum, *Stakhanovism and the Politics of Productivity in the USSR 1935–1941*, Cambridge, 1988.
20 Donald A. Filtzer, *Soviet Workers and Stalinist Industrialization: The Formation of Modern Soviet Production Relations, 1928–1941*, London, 1986.
21 Moshe Lewin, *The Making of the Soviet System: Essays in the Social History of Interwar Russia*, New York, 1985, 220–21.
22 Nicholas S. Timasheff, *The Great Retreat: The Growth and Decline of Communism in Russia*, New York, 1946.
23 Lynne Viola et al., *The War Against the Peasantry, 1927–1930: The Tragedy of the Soviet Countryside*, New Haven, 2005.
24 E. A. Rees, *Iron Lazar: A Political Biography of Lazar Kaganovich*, London, 2012, 104.
25 Lynne Viola, *The Unknown Gulag: The Lost World of Stalin's Special Settlements*, New York, 2007.
26 J. Arch Getty and Oleg V. Naumov, *The Road to Terror: Stalin and the Self-Destruction of the Bolsheviks, 1932–1939*, New Haven, 1999, 588.
27 R. W. Davies et al. (eds.), *The Stalin–Kaganovich Correspondence, 1931–36*, New Haven, 2003, 52: ch. 1, doc. 1, Kaganovich to Stalin, 11 August 1931.
28 Khrushchev, *Vospominaniia*, vol. 1, 40.
29 Sheila Fitzpatrick, *Education and Social Mobility in the Soviet Union*, Cambridge, 1979.
30 Slezkine, *House of Government*, 409.
31 Kirill Abramian, *1937 god: N. S. Khrushchev i moskovskaia partorganizatsiia*, Moscow, 2018, 176.
32 Khrushchev, *Vospominaniia*, vol. 1, 102, 106–7.
33 Khrushchev, *Vospominaniia*, vol. 1, 343.
34 Mark Edele, Sheila Fitzpatrick and Atina Grossmann (eds.), *Shelter from the Holocaust: Rethinking Jewish Survival in the Soviet Union*, Detroit, 2017, esp. 1–8 and ch. 2 (Edele and Wanda Warlik, 'Saved by Stalin?').
35 Oleg Budnitskii, 'The Great Terror of 1941: Toward a History of Wartime Stalinist Criminal Justice', *Kritika* 20:3 (2019): 447–80 (448, 453).
36 Oleg V. Khlevniuk, 'Deserters from the Labor Front: The Limits of Coercion in the Soviet War Economy', *Kritika* 20:3 (2019): 481–504 (483–4, 490, 494, 499).
37 Rebecca Manley, *To the Tashkent Station: Evacuation and Survival in the Soviet Union at War*, Ithaca, 2009, 1.
38 Valerie A. Kivelson and Ronald Grigor Suny, *Russia's Empires*, New York, 2017, 303.

39 M. I. Semiriaga, *Kollaboratsionizm: priroda, tipologiia i proiavleniia v godu Vtroroi mirovoi voiny*, Moscow, 2000.

40 Franziska Exeler, 'The Ambivalent State: Determining Guilt in the Post-World War II Soviet Union', *Slavic Review* 75:3 (2016): 606–29.

41 Seth Bernstein, 'Rural Russia on the Edges of Authority: *Bezvlastie* in Wartime Riazan', November–December 1941', *Slavic Review* 75:3 (2016): 560–82 (561–3).

42 Mark Edele, *Stalin's Defectors: How Red Army Soldiers Became Hitler's Collaborators*, Oxford, 2017, 35, 85–7; on Vlasov, see Catherine Andreyev, *Vlasov and the Russian Liberation Movement: Soviet Reality and Emigré Theories*, Cambridge, 1987.

43 Christian Gerlach and Nicolas Werth, 'State Violence – Violent Societies', in Michael Geyer and Sheila Fitzpatrick (eds.), *Beyond Totalitarianism: Stalinism and Nazism Compared*, Cambridge, 2009, 133–79 (175–6).

44 Vasily Grossman, *Life and Fate*, trans. Robert Chandler, London, 1995, 395–7.

45 Christopher Clark, *Time and Power: Visions of History in German Politics, from the Thirty Years War to the Third Reich*, Princeton, 2019, ch. 4.

46 Taubman, *Khrushchev*, 188.

47 Tomilina (ed.), *Dva tsveta vremeni*, vol. 1, 104 (razdel 2, doc. 5: stenogram of speech of 22 December 1944).

48 Tomilina (ed.), *Dva tsveta vremeni*, vol. 1, 155 (razdel 2, doc. 11, speech of October 1945).

49 N. S. Khrushchev, *Mobilizovat' vse sily na vypolnenie i perevypolnenie plana dobychi i otgruzki uglia*, Stalino, 1946, 5.

50 Robert Dale, *Demobilized Veterans in Late Stalinist Leningrad: Soldiers to Civilians*, London, 2015, 16, 19, 22, 37–8. On the robustness of veteran identity and networks, see, e.g., Amir Weiner, *Making Sense of War: The Second World War and the Fate of the Bolshevik Revolution*, Princeton, 2000.

51 Mark B. Smith, *Property of Communists: The Urban Housing Program from Stalin to Khrushchev*, DeKalb, 2010, 37.

52 Donald Filtzer, *The Hazards of Urban Life in Late Stalinist Russia: Health, Hygiene and Living Standards, 1943–1953*, Cambridge, 2010, ch. 1.

53 Juliane Fürst, *Stalin's Last Generation: Soviet Postwar Youth and the Emergence of Mature Socialism*, Oxford, 2010.

54 Smith, *Property of Communists*, 31, 37.

55 Wilson T. Bell, *Stalin's Gulag at War: Forced Labour, Mass Death, and Soviet Victory in the Second World War*, Toronto, 2018, 9, 14, 150, 153.

56 Golfo Alexopoulos, 'Amnesty 1945: The Revolving Door of Stalin's Gulag', *Slavic Review* 64:2 (2005): 274–306.
57 Steven A. Barnes, *Death and Redemption: The Gulag and the Shaping of Soviet Society*, Princeton, 2011, ch. 5.
58 Joshua Rubenstein, *The Last Days of Stalin*, New Haven, 2016, 66.
59 Elena Zubkova, *Obshchestvo i reformy, 1945–1964*, Moscow, 1993.
60 Dmitrii Shepilov, *The Kremlin's Scholar: A Memoir of Soviet Politics under Stalin and Khrushchev*, ed. Stephen V. Bittner, trans. Anthony Austin, New Haven, 2007, 87. The conversation was with Shepilov, a powerful ideologist in his own right, who reconstructed it twenty years later.
61 E. Iu. Zubkova et al. (eds.), *Sovetskaia zhizn' 1945–1953*, Moscow, 2003, 135 (doc. 2.2/35: report to chairman of VTsSPS, V. V. Kuznetsov concerning the reaction of the population to increased prices for rationed goods, 20 September 1946).
62 O. V. Khlevniuk et al. (eds.), *Politbiuro TsK VKP(b) i Sovet Ministrov SSSR 1945–1953*, Moscow, 2002, 398 (doc. 300: Zhdanov to Stalin, 5 January 1947).
63 Kees Boterbloem, *Life and Times of Andrei Zhdanov 1896–1948*, Montreal, 2004, 239.

CHAPTER 2: THE MAN OF THE PEOPLE WITH BLOOD ON HIS HANDS

1 Gosudarstvennyi arkhiv Rossiiskoi Federatsii (State Archive of the Russian Federation, hereafter GARF), fond (collection, f.) 5446, opis' (inventory, op.) 54, delo (file, d.) 153, list (folio, l.) 28 (letter to Voroshilov, 9 March 1953).
2 Mikhail Gorbachev, *Memoirs*, London, 1995, 59.
3 Andrei Sakharov, *Memoirs*, New York, 1990, 164.
4 V. A. Kozlov et al. (eds.), *Kramola: Inakomyslie v SSSR pri Khrushcheve i Brezhneve 1953–1982gg*, Moscow, 2005, 75–7 (documents for 6 March 1953).
5 Barnes, *Death and Redemption*, 204.
6 GARF, f. 5446, op. 54, d. 154, l. 11 (letter to Voroshilov, c. 9 March 1953).
7 GARF, f. 5446, op. 54, d. 154, l. 4 (letter to Voroshilov, 11 March 1953).
8 Semen Ekshtut, *Iurii Trifonov: Velikaia sila nedoskazannogo*, Moscow, 2014, 65–6.
9 Jeffrey Brooks, *Thank You Comrade Stalin! Soviet Public Culture from Revolution to Cold War*, Princeton, 2000, ch. 8.

10 Jan Plamper, *The Stalin Cult: A Study in the Alchemy of Power*, New Haven, 2012, 14–15, 279.
11 Simon Sebag Montefiore, *Stalin: The Court of the Red Tsar*, London, 2003, 4.
12 Elena Zubkova, *Russia after the War: Hopes, Illusions and Disappointments*, Armonk, 1998, 154.
13 Miriam Dobson, *Khrushchev's Cold Summer: Gulag Returnees, Crime, and the Fate of Reform After Stalin*, Ithaca, 2009, 41, 48. On the variety and confusion of Thaw discourses among the population, see Iurii Aksiutin, *Khrushchevskaia ottepel' i obshchestvennye nastroeniia v SSSR v 1953–1964gg*, Moscow, 2004.
14 Stephen V. Bittner, *The Many Lives of Khrushchev's Thaw: Experience and Memory in Moscow's Arbat*, Ithaca, 2008, 48–50.
15 Denis Kozlov and Eleonory Gilburd, 'The Thaw as an Event in Russian History', in Kozlov and Gilburd (eds.), *The Thaw: Soviet Society and Culture during the 1950s and 1960s*, Toronto, 2013, 18–81.
16 Daniil Granin, *Prichudy pamiati*, Moscow, 2019, 16.
17 Tsentral'nyi gosudarstvennyi arkhiv literatury i uskusstva Sankt-Peterburga (Central State Archive of Literature and Art in St Petersburg, hereafter TsGALI SPb), f. R-107, op. 1, d. 30, ll. 3, 4, 45; f. R-107, op. 1, d. 34, l. 23.
18 TsGALI SPb, f. R-107, op. 1, d. 30, ll. 124–7 (from Galina F. to Granin's editors, 8.10.55).
19 K. Aimermakher et al. (eds.), *Doklad N. S. Khrushcheva o kul'te lichnosti Stalina na XX s"ezde KPSS: Dokumenty*, Moscow, 2002, 185ff.
20 Aleksandr Iakovlev, *Omut pamiati: ot Stolypina do Putina*, vol. 1, Moscow, 2001, 176–7.
21 Lev Lur'e and Irina Maliarova (eds.), *1956 god: seredina veka*, St Petersburg, 2007, 99–101: testimony of Anna Karetnikova.
22 Aimermakher et al. (eds.), *Doklad N.S. Khrushcheva*.
23 Roger D. Markwick, *Rewriting History in Soviet Russia: The Politics of Revisionist Historiography, 1956–1974*, Basingstoke, 2001, 50–53.
24 A. V. Savel'ev, *Neobychnaia kar'era Akademika A. M. Pankratovoi*, Moscow, 2012, chs. 7–9.
25 A. V. Novikov, 'Pervaia reaktsiia na kritiku "kul'ta lichnosti" I. V. Stalina', *Voprosy istorii* 8 (2006): 3–21 (5–6).
26 Karetnikova testimony in Lur'e and Maliarova (eds.), *1956 god*, 101.
27 Gorbachev, *Memoirs*, 76–7.
28 Polly Jones, *Myth, Memory, Trauma: Rethinking the Stalinist Past in the*

Soviet Union, 1953–1970, New Haven, 2013, ch. 1; Dobson, *Khrushchev's Cold Summer*, ch. 3.

29 Robert Hornsby, *Protest, Reform and Repression in Khrushchev's Soviet Union*, Cambridge, 2013, 57.

30 Granin, *Prichudy pamiati*, 50.

31 Cited in Mark B. Smith, 'Peaceful Coexistence at All Costs: Cold War Exchanges Between Britain and the Soviet Union in 1956', *Cold War History* 12:3 (2012): 537–58 (544).

32 V. E. Semichastnyi, *Bespokoinoe serdtse*, Moscow, 2002, 52.

## CHAPTER 3: GAGARIN'S CONQUEST

1 A. T. Gagarina and T. A. Kopylova, *Iurii Gagarin: glazami materi*, Moscow, 2011, 154. Note 'Yura' is an affectionate form of Yuri.

2 V. A. Mitroshenkov and N. A. Tsymbal, *Pervyi kosmonavt planety Zemlia*, Moscow, 1981 (for timings on the day).

3 Asif A. Siddiqi, *Challenge to Apollo: The Soviet Union and the Space Race*, Washington, DC, 2000, 279–81.

4 Photo in Nataliia Koroleva, *Zhit' nado s uvlecheniem! Sergei Pavlovich Korolev*, Moscow, 2017, 54.

5 E.g. Koroleva, *Zhit' nado*, 88, 91.

6 His daughter recounts the story of his arrest in an interview with Iurii Dud' on his YouTube channel: 'Kolyma: rodina nashego strakha', 23 April 2019.

7 Koroleva, *Zhit' nado*, 119.

8 Koroleva, *Zhit' nado*, 102–41.

9 Much of the information in this paragraph comes from a brief autobiographical statement that Korolev wrote in February 1952. L. A. Filina, '... *Byl veku nuzhen Korolev*': *po stranitsam arkhiva Memorial'nogo doma-muzeia akademika S. P. Koroleva*, Moscow, 2002, 10–11.

10 Letter of 12 October 1947, Sergei to Nina, Filina, '... *Byl veku nuzhen Korolev*', 19.

11 Anton Pervushin, *Pervye v kosmose: shag v neizvestnost'*, Moscow, 2017, 49.

12 Pervushin, *Pervye v kosmose*, 64–8.

13 Koroleva, *Zhit' nado*, 194.

14 Asif Siddiqi, 'Scientists and Specialists in the Gulag: Life and Death in Stalin's *Sharashka*', *Kritika*, 16:3 (2015): 557–88 (588).

15 Sergei to Nina, 8 June 1957, Filina, '... *Byl veku nuzhen Korolev*', 78.

16 *Pravda*, 6 October 1957, 1.

17 Aleksandr Romanov, *Korolev*, Moscow, 1996, 306.
18 Peter Finn and Petra Couvée, *The Zhivago Affair: The Kremlin, the CIA, and the Battle Over a Forbidden Book*, London, 2014, 112, 256.
19 Interview with Nikolai Solodnikov, 'Eshchenepozner' YouTube channel, posted on 3 October 2018; interview with Grigorii Mastrider, 'Knizhnyi chel' YouTube channel, posted on 31 July 2019.
20 Liudmila Ulitskaia, *Lestnitsa Iakoba*, Moscow, 2015 (translation above by Mary Catherine Gannon, in Ulitskaya, *Jacob's Ladder*, New York, 2019, 253).
21 C. P. Snow, *The Two Cultures*, Cambridge, 1998, 37–8.
22 Petr Vail' and Aleksandr Genis, *60-e: mir Sovetskogo cheloveka*, Moscow, 2013 (first published 1988), 117–26.
23 Susan Costanzo, 'The 1959 *Liriki-Fiziki* Debate: Going Public with the Private?', in Lewis H. Siegelbaum (ed.), *Borders of Socialism: Private Spheres of Soviet Russia*, New York, 2006, 251–68 (257).
24 Slezkine, *House of Government*, ch. 15 and passim.
25 A. G. Waring, 'Science, Love and the Establishment in the Novels of D. A. Granin and C. P. Snow', *Forum for Modern Language Studies* 4:1 (1978): 1–15 (7–8).
26 Granin, *Prichudy pamiati*, 126.
27 TsGALI SPb, f. R-107, op. 1, d. 35, l. 68 (letter of 8 March 1963).
28 TsGALI SPb, f. R-107, op. 1, d. 35, l. 74 (letter to editors from Nadezhda F.).
29 TsGALI SPb, f. R-107, op. 1, d. 36, l. 1 (Ivan N. B. of Moscow to Granin, 3 August 1964).
30 TsGALI SPb, f. R-107, op. 1, d. 35, l. 85 (Il'ia Yakovlevich Brazhnin to Granin, 30 March 1963).
31 Daniil Granin, *Idu na grozu*, St Petersburg, 2019 (first published 1963), 30.
32 TsGALI SPb, f. R-307, op. 1, d. 28, l. 6 (from editor of prose department at *Znamia* (the journal where the first edition of the novel was published before it came out as a separate book), V. Katunov (and approved by chief editor, B. Suchkov), to Granin, 17 May 1962).
33 E. Iu. Bashilova and T. A. Golovkina, '"Kosmicheskie zori deistvitel'no prekrasny": letchik-kosmonavt SSSR G. S. Titov', in T. A. Golovkina and A. A. Chernobaev (eds.), *Kosmos. Vremia Moskovskoe: Sbornik dokumentov*, Moscow, 2019, 337–47 (338, 344).
34 Boris Pishchik et al., *Kosmanavty rasskazivaiut*, Moscow, 1964, 42.
35 See the photograph in Koroleva, *Zhit' nado*, 281.
36 Nami Mikoain and Feliks Medvedev, *Neizvestnaia Furtseva*, Moscow, 2013, 171.

NOTES TO PP. 90–104

37 Bulat Okudzhava, *Stikhotvoreniia*, Moscow, 2019, 27. Translation by author.

## CHAPTER 4: THE GLITTERING METROPOLIS

1 M. Posokhin, A. Mndoiants, N. Pekareva, *Kremlevskii dvorets s"ezdov*, Moscow, 1974, 191–3; Joseph A. Barome, 'The Bolshoi Theatre and Opera', *Russian Review* 24:1 (1965): 52–65 (62).
2 *Arkhitektura SSSR* 12:1 (1961).
3 Irina Rodimtseva, *The Moscow Kremlin: A Guide*, Leningrad, 1987, 14, 120.
4 Taubman, *Khrushchev*, 263.
5 Posokhin, *Kremlevskii dvorets*, 115; *Arkhitektura SSSR*, 12:4 (1961).
6 Iurii Gagarin, 'Metall i kharakter otlivaiutsia v trude', *Krasnaia zvezda*, 17 October 1961, in Gagarin, *Est' plamia! stat'i, rechi, pis'ma , interviu*, Moscow, 1968, 35–40 (40).
7 A. Iaroshevskaia, *Ekaterina Furtseva*, Moscow, 2013, 121–30.
8 Getty and Naumov, *Road to Terror*.
9 Stenogram of Presidium meeting of the CC KPSS, 17 June 1961, reproduced in A. A. Fursenko et al. (eds.), *Prezidium TsK KPSS 1954–1964*, vol. 1 of 2, Moscow, 2004, 510–16 (doc. 238).
10 Alexander Titov, 'The 1961 Party Programme and the Fate of Khrushchev's Reforms', in Ilic and Smith (eds.), *Soviet State and Society*, 8–25.
11 *XXII s"ezd Kommunisticheskoi partii Sovetskogo Soiuza: 17–31 oktiabria 1961 goda: stenograficheskii otchet*, vol. 3 of 3, Moscow, 1962.
12 Aleksandr Fokin, *'Kommunizm ne za gorami': Obrazy budushchego u vlasti i naseleniia SSSR na rubezhe 1950–1960-kh godov*, Moscow, 2017, 176.
13 Personal visit, November 2018. The house is open to the public and retains its original form and furnishings.
14 Andrew L. Jenks, *The Cosmonaut Who Couldn't Stop Smiling: The Life and Legend of Yuri Gagarin*, DeKalb, 2012 , 102.
15 Łukasz Stanek, *Architecture in Global Socialism: Eastern Europe, West Africa, and the Middle East in the Cold War*, Princeton, 2020.
16 This account draws on my earlier book *Property of Communists* (Wilson on 69–70; data on 101–3).
17 Interview with Posokhin's son: Il'ia Ivanov, 'Arkhitektor Mikhail Posokhin: "Posmotrite na Tverskuiu ulitsu – ona umerla"', *Moskvich*, 30 January 2020 (www.moskvichmag.ru).

18 Timothy J. Colton, *Moscow: Governing the Socialist Metropolis*, Cambridge, MA, 1995, 392.
19 Anna Bronovitskaia, Nikolai Malinin and Ol'ga Kazakova, *Moskva: arkhitektura sovetskogo modernizma 1955–1991*, Moscow, 2016, 91.
20 I.e. crafting an individual architectural sensibility onto the technologies of *tipovoe proektirovanie*, or standardized, prefabricated design. See Stephen V. Bittner, 'Remembering the Avant-Garde: Moscow Architects and the "Rehabilitation" of Constructivism, 1961–64', *Kritika* 2:3 (2001): 553–76 (560).
21 Vladimir Paperny, *Architecture in the Age of Stalin: Culture Two*, Cambridge, 2002.
22 My research on this is presented in more detail in my article 'Faded Red Paradise: Welfare and the Soviet City after 1953', *Contemporary European History* 24:4 (2015): 597–615 (608–12).
23 *Narodnoe khoziaistvo, statisticheskii ezhegodnik* (hereafter, *NKhSE*), Moscow, 1958: 906; 1960: 848; 1970: 734.
24 *NKhSE*, 1959: 796; 1965: 602; 1969: 592–3; 1972: 570. The data were openly published at the time and are open to interpretation, but their trajectory is plausible. Sums adjusted to allow for comparability after redenominations.
25 Leonard Kondrashenko, *Artek*, Simferopol', 1968, 17.
26 See my article 'Equality, Welfare, Myth, and Memory: The Artek Pioneer Camp at the Height of the Khrushchev Era', *Kritika* 23:2 (2022).

## CHAPTER 5: THE BOUNDARY BETWEEN TWO ENVIRONMENTS

1 Odd Arne Westad, *The Cold War: A World History*, London, 2017, ch. 1.
2 Ulitskaia's interview with Nikolai Solodnikov, 'Eshchenepozner' YouTube channel, 26 October 2019.
3 Sarah Davies, 'From Iron Curtain to Velvet Curtain? Peter Brook's *Hamlet* and the Origins of British–Soviet Cultural Relations during the Cold War', *Contemporary European History* 27:4 (2018): 601–26 (617).
4 The National Archives, London: FO 418/96. Hayter to Macmillan, 8 December 1955.
5 Christina Ezrahi, *Swans of the Kremlin: Ballet and Power in Soviet Russia*, Pittsburgh, 2012, 142, 154–5.
6 Smith, 'Peaceful Coexistence at all Costs', 537–58 (542, 544, and passim).

7 Philippe Vonnard and Kevin Marston, 'Building Bridges Between Separated Europeans: The Role of UEFA's Competitions in East–West Exchanges (1955–1964)', in Nicola Sbetti, Philippe Vonnard and Grégory Quin (eds.), *Beyond Boycotts: Sport During the Cold War in Europe*, Berlin, 2018, 85–108 (104).

8 Isabelle Gouarné, 'Mandatory Planning versus Indicative Planning? The Eastern Itinerary of French Planners (1960s–1970s)', in Michel Christian, Sandrine Kott and Ondřej Matějka (eds.), *Planning in Cold War Europe: Competition, Cooperation, Circulations (1950s–1970s)*, Berlin, 2018, 71–96 (76–6).

9 Sari Autio-Sarasmo, 'Soviet Economic Modernisation and Transferring Technologies from the West', in Markku Kangaspuro and Jeremy Smith (eds.), *Modernisation in Russia since 1900*, Helsinki, 2006, 104–23 (117–18).

10 See, e.g., Smith, *Property of Communists*, 76, 78, 88.

11 Natalia Tsvetkova, 'Universities During the Cultural Cold War: Mapping the Research Agenda', in Simo Mikkonen, Giles Scott-Smith and Jari Parkkinen (eds.), *Entangled East and West: Cultural Diplomacy and Artistic Interaction during the Cold War*, Berlin, 2019, 139–61 (158).

12 Rachel Applebaum, 'The Rise of Russian in the Cold War: How Three Worlds Made a World Language', *Kritika* 21:2 (2020): 347–70 (358, 364–6).

13 Petr Val' and Aleksandr Genis, *60-e: Mir sovetskogo cheloveka*, Moscow, 2013 [Ann Arbor, 1988], 58, 61–3.

14 Vladislav Zubok, *Zhivago's Children: The Last Russian Intelligentsia*, Cambridge, MA, 2009.

15 Susan E. Reid, 'Who Will Beat Whom? Soviet Popular Reception of the American National Exhibition in Moscow, 1959', *Kritika* 9:4 (2008): 855–904.

16 Eleonory Gilburd, *To See Paris and Die: The Soviet Lives of Western Culture*, Cambridge, MA, 2018, esp. chs. 3, 6 and epilogue.

17 Anne E. Gorsuch, *All This Is Your World: Soviet Tourism at Home and Abroad After Stalin*, Oxford, 2012, ch. 4.

18 O. S. Nagornaia et al., *Sovetskaia kul'turnaia diplomatiia v usloviiakh Kholodnoi voiny, 1945–1989gg*, Moscow, 2018, 313.

19 Alexander Hazanov, 'Porous Empire: Foreign Visitors and the Post-Stalin Soviet State', PhD dissertation, University of Pennsylvania, 2016, 47.

20 Shawn Salmon, 'Marketing Socialism: Inturist in the Late 1950s and Early 1960s', in Diane P. Koenker and Anne E. Gorsuch (eds.), *Turizm:*

*The Russian and East European Tourist under Capitalism and Socialism*, Ithaca, 2006, 186–204 (190).
21 Rósa Magnúsdóttir, *Enemy Number One: The United States of America in Soviet Ideology and Propaganda, 1945–1959*, Oxford, 2019, 129–33.
22 See, e.g., Stephen Kotkin, *Stalin*, vol. 2: *Waiting for Hitler, 1929–1941*, London, 2017, and James Harris, *The Great Fear: Stalin's Terror of the 1930s*, Oxford, 2016.
23 Khrushchev, *Vospominaniia*, vol. 2, 742, 760.
24 Molly Pucci, 'Translating the State: Czechoslovakia's Search for the Soviet Model of the Secret Police, 1945–1952', *Kritika* 18:2 (2017): 317–44 (esp. 324–8).
25 Johanna Conterio, 'Our Black Sea Coast: The Sovietization of the Black Sea Littoral Under Khrushchev and the Problem of Overdevelopment', *Kritika* 19:2 (2018): 327–61 (351).
26 Celia Donert, 'Feminism, Communism, and Global Socialism, 1968–1995: Encounters and Entanglements', in Juliane Fürst, Silvio Pons and Mark Selden (eds.), *The Cambridge History of Communism*, vol. 3, Cambridge, 2017.
27 Anne E. Gorsuch, '"Cuba, My Love": The Romance of Revolutionary Cuba in the Soviet Sixties', *American Historical Review* 120:2 (2015): 497–526.
28 See www.nobelprize.org/prizes/lists/all-nobel-prizes-in-physics.
29 Zhores A. Medvedev, *The Rise and Fall of T. D. Lysenko*, New York, 1969, 198, 204–5, 206–9.
30 Ulitskaia interview, 'Eshchenepozner'.
31 Kathleen E. Smith, *Moscow 1956: The Silenced Spring*, Cambridge, MA, 2017, ch. 7.
32 Loren R. Graham, *Lysenko's Ghost: Epigenetics and Russia*, Cambridge, MA, 2016, 139.
33 Jeff Eden, *God Save the USSR: Soviet Muslims and the Second World War*, Oxford, 2021.
34 Tatiana A. Chumachenko, *Church and State in Soviet Russia: Russian Orthodoxy from World War II to the Khrushchev Years*, ed. and trans. Edward E. Roslof, New York, 2002, 153–8.
35 Victoria Smolkin, *A Sacred Space Is Never Empty: A History of Soviet Atheism*, Princeton, 2018, 114 (and passim).
36 Geoffrey Hosking, *Rulers and Victims: The Russians in the Soviet Union*, Cambridge, MA, 2006, 281 and 279.
37 Kozlov, *Neizvestnyi SSSR*, 267–8.
38 Miriam Dobson, 'Child Sacrifice in the Soviet Press: Sensationalism and the "Sectarian" in the Post-Stalin Era', *Russian Review* 73:2 (2014): 237–59.

39 Numbers in this paragraph are from John Anderson, *Religion, State and Politics in the Soviet Union and Successor States, 1953–1993*, Cambridge, 1994, 55.
40 Judith Deutsch Kornblatt, *Doubly Chosen: Jewish Identity, the Soviet Intelligentsia, and the Russian Orthodox Church*, Madison, WI, 2004, ch. 3.
41 Cited in Smolkin, *A Sacred Space*, 60.
42 Miriam Dobson, 'Protestants, Peace and the Apocalypse: the USSR's Religious Cold War, 1947–62', *Journal of Contemporary History* 53:2 (2018): 261–90.
43 Miriam Dobson, 'The Social Scientist Meets the "Believer": Discussions of God, the Afterlife and Communism in the mid-1960s', *Slavic Review* 74:1 (2015): 79–103.
44 See Smith, 'Peaceful Coexistence at all Costs'.
45 Susan E. Reid, 'In the Name of the People: The Manège Affair Revisited', *Kritika* 6:4 (2005): 673–716 (esp. 705–10); Zubok, *Zhivago's Children*, 193–4, 209–10.

## CHAPTER 6: SLUSH

1 N. G. Tomilina, *Boi s 'ten'iu' Stalina. Prodolzhenie: Dokumenty i materialy ob istorii XXII s"ezda KPSS i vtorogo etapa destalinizatsii*, Moscow, 2015 (Doc. 1.1.2, Iz zakliuchitel'nogo slova pervogo sekretaria TsK KPSS N.S. Khrushcheva na XXII s"ezde KPSS, 62–85 (73, 75)).
2 Nanci Adler, *The Gulag Survivor: Beyond the Soviet System*, New Brunswick, 2002, 153, 159, 190.
3 Michael Scammell, *Solzhenitsyn: A Biography*, London, 1986, 270.
4 Scammell, *Solzhenitsyn*, 421.
5 Denis Kozlov, *The Readers of Novyi Mir: Coming to Terms with the Stalinist Past*, Cambridge, MA, 2013, 237.
6 Kozlov, *The Readers of Novyi Mir*, 210.
7 Franziska Exeler, *Ghosts of War: Nazi Occupation and Its Aftermath in Soviet Belarus*, Ithaca, 2022.
8 Yitzhak M. Brudny, *Reinventing Russia: Russian Nationalism and the Soviet State, 1953–1991*, Cambridge, MA, 1998.
9 Jones, *Myth, Memory, Trauma*, 170–71 and passim.
10 Anatoly Smeliansky, *The Russian Theatre After Stalin*, Cambridge, 1999, 30.
11 Diary entry, September 1964: Alla Demidova, *Vladimir Vysotskii: Kakim pomniu i liubliu*, Moscow, 2020, 79.

12 This account draws heavily on an interview given by Vysotskii in 1972. El'dar Riazanov, *Chetyre vechera s Vladimirom Vysotskim*, Moscow, 2004, 11–13.
13 Krivoi Rog is the Russian name for this largely Russophone city; it is Kryvyi Rih in Ukrainian.
14 Vladimir A. Kozlov (ed.), *Sedition: Everyday Resistance in the Soviet Union under Khrushchev and Brezhnev*, New Haven, 2011, 130.
15 Vladimir A. Kozlov, *Mass Uprisings in the USSR: Protest and Rebellion in the Post-Stalin Years*, Armonk, 2002. His work generally informs this section.
16 Kozlov (ed.), *Sedition*, 126.
17 Anatolii Strelianyi, 'Khrushchev and the Countryside', in William Taubman et al. (eds.), *Nikita Khrushchev*, New Haven, 2000, 113–37 (120).
18 Aaron Hale-Dorrell, *Corn Crusade: Khrushchev's Farming Revolution in the Post-Stalin Soviet Union*, Oxford, 2019, 1, 229.
19 Kozlov (ed.), *Sedition*, 137.
20 Stephen Kotkin, *Stalin*, vol 1: *Paradoxes of Power, 1878–1928*, London, 2014.
21 Nikolai Mitrokhin, 'The Rise of Political Clans in the Era of Nikita Khrushchev: The First Phase, 1953–1959', in Jeremy Smith and Melanie Ilic (eds.), *Khrushchev in the Kremlin: Policy and Government in the Soviet Union, 1953–1964*, Abingdon, 2011, 26–40 (34, 36).
22 Sergei Khrushchev, *Nikita Khrushchev and the Creation of a Superpower*, University Park, PA, 2000, 4, 16, 29–30, 38–9, 59, 129, 228, 231–2.
23 Laurent Coumel, 'The Scientist, the Pedagogue and the Party Official: Interest Groups, Public Opinion and Decision-Making in the 1958 Education Reform', in Ilic and Smith, *Soviet State and Society*; Jeremy Smith, 'Khrushchev and the Path to Modernisation Through Education', in Kangaspuro and Smith (eds.), *Modernisation in Russia*.
24 Jeremy Smith, 'The Battle for Language: Opposition to Khrushchev's Education Reform in the Soviet Republics, 1958–59', *Slavic Review* 76:4 (2017): 983–1002.
25 Nataliya Kibita, *Soviet Economic Management under Khrushchev: The Sovnarkhoz Reform*, London, 2013.
26 On the army, see chapter 8.
27 Taubman, *Khrushchev*, 13.
28 Author's translation of A. Solzhenitsyn, *Prusskye nochi*, Paris, 1974, 9, 26.
29 Author's translation of Bella Akhmadulina, 'Novaia tetrad'', in Akhmadulina, *Stikhotvoreniia*, Moscow, 2020, 38.

## CHAPTER 7: NEW YEAR WITH BREZHNEV

1. Iakub Zemliak, *S Novym Godom!*, Frunze, 1973 (not paginated).
2. Nataliia Lebina, *Passazhiry kolbasnogo poezda: etiudy k kartine byta rossiiskogo goroda: 1917–1991*, Moscow, 2019, 127–9.
3. E. Orlova, *S Novym Godom!*, Moscow, 1976, 3, 5, 53, 55, 74.
4. Example recipes are in Olga and Pavel Syutkin, *CCCP Cookbook: True Stories of Soviet Cuisine*, London, 2015.
5. Vas'kin, *Povsednevnaia zhizn'*, 463.
6. Christine Evans, *Between Truth and Time: A History of Soviet Central Television*, New Haven, p. 273, n. 34.
7. Evans, *Between Truth and Time*, ch. 3.
8. See chapters 8–9 for more on the later Gulag.
9. Ekaterina Emeliantseva Koller, 'Negotiating "Coldness": The Natural Environment and Community Cohesion in Cold War Molotovsk-Severodvinsk', in Julia Herzberg, Christian Kehrt and Franziska Torma (eds.), *Ice and Snow in the Cold War: Histories of Extreme Climatic Environments*, New York, 2019, 253–84 (257–9, 265).
10. See, e.g., Maya K. Peterson, *Pipe Dreams: Water and Empire in Central Asia's Aral Sea Basin*, Cambridge, 2019.
11. Andy Bruno, *The Nature of Soviet Power: An Arctic Environmental History*, Cambridge, 2016, 203.
12. Vladimir Dudintsev, *Novogodniaia skazka*, Moscow, 1965 (first published in *Novyi mir*, 1960).
13. S. Odnovalov and M. Tsimbal, 'Dlia krainego severa', *Sovetskaia arkhitektura* 17 (1965): 57.
14. Smith, *Property of Communists*.
15. Ekaterina Kalemeneva, 'From New Socialist Cities to Thaw Experimentation in Arctic Townscapes: Leningrad Architects Attempt to Modernise the Soviet North', *Europe-Asia Studies* 71:3 (2019): 426–49 (437).
16. Pey-Yi Chu, *The Life of Permafrost: A History of Frozen Earth in Russian and Soviet Science*, Toronto, 2020, ch. 5.
17. Paul R. Josephson, *The Conquest of the Russian Arctic*, Cambridge, MA, 2014, 242.
18. Yuri Slezkine, *Arctic Mirrors: Russia and the Small Peoples of the North*, Ithaca, 1994.
19. Aleksei Mikhailov, *Sneg: pervaia kniga stikhov*, Iakutsk, 1971, 17.
20. Anna Tikhomirova, 'Soviet Women and Fur Consumption in the Brezhnev Era', in David Crowley and Susan E. Reid (eds.), *Pleasures in Socialism: Leisure and Luxury in the Eastern Bloc*, Evanston, IL, 2010,

283–300 (288, 291, 294). On 'socialist luxury' as a concept: Ina Merkel, 'Luxury in Socialism: An Absurd Proposition?', in Crowley and Reid (eds.), *Pleasures in Socialism*, 53–70.

21 Aleksei Popov, 'Winter Tourism and Skiing in the Soviet Union: School of Courage, Source of Health, National Pastime', in Julia Herzberg, Andreas Renner and Ingrid Schierle (eds.), *The Russian Cold: Histories of Ice, Frost and Snow*, New York, 2021, 204–25 (213, 217).

22 This outline of Brezhnev's career draws on Susanne Schattenberg, *Brezhnev: The Making of a Statesman*, London, 2021, e.g. 93, 114, 125, 139–40, 142, 163.

23 Ekaterina Reznikova, 'Zolotye kletki', *Proekt media*, 10 February 2021.

24 Nicolaj Mitrohin, 'Back-Office Mikhaila Suslova ili kem i kak provodilas' ideologiia Brezhnevskogo vremeni', *Cahiers du monde russe* 54:3/4 (2013): 409–40.

25 Yoram Gorlizki and Oleg Khlevniuk, *Substate Dictatorship: Networks, Loyalty and Institutional Change in the Soviet Union*, New Haven, 2020, chs. 9 and 10.

26 Sergei Chuprinin, *Ottepel': Sobytiia. Mart 1953–avgust 1968 goda*, Moscow, 2020, 849.

27 Chuprinin, *Ottepel'*, 931–2. See also chapter 9.

28 Chuprinin, *Ottepel'*, 1019–20.

29 Chuprinin, *Ottepel'*, 1082–3.

30 Alexandra Oberländer, 'Hatching Money: The Political Economy of Eggs in the 1960s', *Cahiers du monde russe* 61 (2020): 1–2: 231–56.

31 See, e.g., T. H. Rigby, 'The Soviet Regional Leadership: The Brezhnev Generation', *Slavic Review* 37:1 (1978): 1–24.

32 A. N. Kosygin, *K velikoi tseli: izbrannye rechi i stat'i*, vol. 1 of 2, Moscow, 1979, 316–56.

33 Moshe Lewin, *Stalinism and the Seeds of Soviet Reform: The Debates of the 1960s*, London, 1974.

34 Simon Huxtable, 'In Search of the Soviet Reader: The Kosygin Reforms, Sociology, and Changing Concepts of Soviet Society, 1964–1970', *Cahiers du monde russe* 54 (2013): 304: 623–42.

35 Viktor Andriianov, *Kosygin*, Moscow, 2003, 177–81.

36 Mark Harrison, 'Economic Growth and Slowdown', in Edwin Bacon and Mark Sandle (eds.), *Brezhnev Reconsidered*, Basingstoke, 2002, 38–67 (54–9).

37 Martin Malia, *The Soviet Tragedy: A History of Socialism in Russia, 1917–1991*, New York, 1994.

38 Filina, '... Byl veku nuzhen Korolev', 148–51 (quotation on 150).

39 Koroleva, *Nado zhit'*, 289.

## CHAPTER 8: PEOPLE IN UNIFORM

1. Jenks, *Cosmonaut*, 244–7.
2. Nikita Barashev, 'U nas tol'ko odin Iura!', *Literaturnaia gazeta* 12:6636 (21–7 March 2018): 4–5 (5).
3. Jenks, *Cosmonaut*, 248–52 and ch. 11.
4. Jenks, *Cosmonaut*, 35, 67, 186–7.
5. On conceptualizing politics in the late Stalinist era as 'neopatrimonial', see Yoram Gorlizki and Oleg Khlevniuk, *Cold Peace: Stalin and the Soviet Ruling Circle, 1945–1953*, Oxford, 2004.
6. Iu. A. Vasil'ev, *Iurii Andropov: Na puti k vlasti*, Moscow, 2018, 4.
7. Gorbachev, *Memoirs*, 20–21.
8. A. I. Kokurin and N. V. Petrov (eds.), *Lubianka: organy VChK-OGPU-NKVD-NKGB-MGB-MVD-KGB, 1917–1991: spravochnik*, Moscow, 2003, 712–14 (Andropov, KGB report to CC CPSU, 3 July 1967). Cf. below for more on numbers.
9. Kokurin and Petrov (eds.), *Lubianka*, 718–19 (Andropov to Brezhnev, 6 May 1968, 714–23).
10. Sidney Bloch and Peter Reddaway, *Russia's Political Hospitals: The Abuse of Psychiatry in the Soviet Union*, London, 1977, 192–7.
11. Benjamin Nathans interview, 'Rights in Russia' YouTube channel, 23 November 2021.
12. Kokurin and Petrov (eds.), *Lubianka*, 719 (Andropov to Brezhnev, 6 May 1968, 714–23).
13. V. N. Khaustov, 'Deiatel'nost'' organov gosudarstvennoi bezopasnosti v 1950–1960-e gg', in R. N. Baiguzin (ed.), *Gosudarstvennaia bezopasnost' Rossii: istoriia i sovremennost'*, Moscow, 2004, 629–57 (655).
14. Edward Cohn, 'A Soviet Theory of Broken Windows: Prophylactic Policing and the KGB's Struggle with Political Unrest in the Baltic Republics', in *Kritika* 19:4 (2018): 769–92 (770, 779–80).
15. Khaustov, 'Deiatel'nost'' organov', 654.
16. Roi Medvedev, *Neizvestnyi Andropov*, Rostov on Don, 1999, 59–60.
17. Yuri Glazov, 'Yuri Andropov: A New Leader of Russia', *Studies in Soviet Thought* 26:3 (1983): 173–215 (184).
18. These numbers are notional and are estimates made by the journalist Yevgenia Albats for 1991. Albats, *KGB: State Within a State*, London, 1995, 23.

19 Kokurin and Petrov (eds.), *Lubianka*, 719 (Andropov to Brezhnev, 6 May 1968, 714–23).
20 Mark Harrison and Inga Zakšauskienė, 'Counter-Intelligence in a Command Economy', *Economic History Review* 69:1 (2016): 131–58 (142).
21 Harrison and Zakšauskienė, 'Counter-Intelligence in a Command Economy'.
22 Mark Harrison, 'Contracting for Counterintelligence: The KGB and Soviet Informers of the 1960s and 1970s', CAGE Working Paper, Department of Economics, University of Warwick, 2019, 8.
23 Geoffrey Hosking, *Trust: A History*, Oxford, 2014.
24 Smith, *Property of Communists*, 165.
25 Andrei Soldatov and Irina Borogan, *The New Nobility: The Restoration of Russia's Security State and the Enduring Legacy of the KGB*, New York, 2010, 10.
26 Mark Galeotti, '*Perestroika*, Perestrelka, Pereborka: Policing Russia in a Time of Change', *Europe–Asia Studies* 45:5 (1993): 769–86 (769–71).
27 Nikolai Zakharov, *Skvoz' gody*, Tula, 2003.
28 Judith Pallot, 'The Topography of Incarceration: The Spatial Continuity of Penality and the Legacy of the Gulag in Twentieth- and Twenty-First-Century Russia', *Laboratorium* 7:1 (2015): 26–50 (30–32).
29 Ivan Peshkov, 'The Communal Apartment Under "Special Surveillance": The Legacy of the Soviet Gulag in Multiethnic Criminal Subcultures in Eastern Siberian Prison Camps', *Laboratorium* 7:1 (2015): 71–91 (83 and passim).
30 Jeffrey S. Hardy, *The Gulag after Stalin: Redefining Punishment in Khrushchev's Soviet Union, 1953–1964*, Ithaca, 2016, 205–6.
31 Jonathan Haslam, *Near and Distant Neighbours: A New History of Soviet Intelligence*, Oxford, 2015, 8, 11.
32 Leonid Brezhnev, *Rabochie i dnevnikovye zapisi, 1964–1982*; 99, vol. 1 of 3, ed. S. V. Kudriashov et al., Moscow, 2016, 625.
33 Roger Reese, *The Soviet Military Experience: A History of the Soviet Army, 1917–1991*, London, 2000, 140.
34 John Erickson, 'Soviet Military Manpower Policies', *Armed Forces and Society* 1:1 (1974): 29–47.
35 Reese, *Soviet Military Experience*, 147.
36 Erica L. Fraser, 'Yuri Gararin and Celebrity Masculinity in Soviet Culture', in Philip E. Muehlenbeck (ed.), *Gender, Sexuality, and the Cold War*, Nashville, 2017, 270–89.
37 Erica L. Fraser, *Military Masculinity and Postwar Recovery in the Soviet Union*, Toronto, 2019, 37ff.

38 Maya Eichler, *Militarizing Men: Gender, Conscription and War in Post-Soviet Russia*, Stanford, 2020, 21.
39 Robert Dale, *Demobilized Veterans in Late Stalinist Leningrad: Soldiers to Civilians*, London, 2015.
40 Tarik Cyril Amar, 'Between James Bond and Iosif Stalin: *Seventeen Moments of Spring*, a Soviet Cultural Event of the Cold War and the Post-Thaw', *Kritika* 21:3 (2020): 627–58 (628).
41 Stephen Lovell, 'In Search of an Ending: *Seventeen Moments* and the Seventies', in Anne E. Gorsuch and Diane Koenker (eds.), *The Socialist Sixties: Crossing Borders in the Second World*, Bloomington, 2013, 303–21 (307).
42 Ol'ga Semenova, *Iulian Semenov*, Moscow, 2006.
43 E.g. Iulian Semenov, *Petrovka, 38 & Ogareva, 6*, St Petersburg, 2016 (*Ogareva, 6*, 1972), 411.
44 M. Mel'nichenko (ed.), *Sovetskii anekdot: ukazatel' siuzhetov*, Moscow, 2014, 669.
45 Mel'nichenko (ed.), *Sovetskii anekdot*, 665.

## CHAPTER 9: TO THE SQUARE

1 The first-hand account of the demonstration is Gorbanevskaya's, which she circulated in the form of a letter to the Western press, and which was reproduced in *The Chronicle of Current Events. Khronika tekushchikh sobytii* 1968 3:3 (28 August).
2 *Khronika tekushchikh sobytii* 1968 4:1 (9–11 October).
3 William Taubman observed similar meetings later in the Thaw when he was a visiting student at Moscow State University; Taubman, *The View from the Lenin Hills: Soviet Youth in Ferment*, London, 1968.
4 Natalya Gorbanevskaya, *Selected Poems with a Transcript of Her Trial and Papers Relating to Her Detention in a Prison Psychiatric Hospital*, ed. Daniel Weissbort, Oxford, 1972, 105–9.
5 Natal'ia Gorbanevskaia, 'Chto ia pomniu o demonstratsii', in Liudmila Ulitskaia et al., *Poetka: Kniga o pamiati: Natal'ia Gorbanevskaia*, Moscow, 2014, 289.
6 Liudmila Alexeeva, quoting the dissident Anatoly Marchenko, in Ludmilla Alexeyeva and Paul Goldberg, *The Thaw Generation: Coming of Age in the Post-Stalin Era*, Pittsburgh, 1993, 222.
7 Alexeyeva and Goldberg, *Thaw Generation*, 220.
8 Anna Krylova, 'The Tenacious Liberal Subject in Soviet Studies', *Kritika* 1:1 (2000): 119–46.

9 Other peoples in the Russian empire were involved in this process, notably from the Caucasus, and later from Ukraine.
10 Benjamin Nathans, 'Human Rights Defenders within Soviet Politics', in Riccardo Mario Cucciolla (ed.), *Dimensions and Challenges of Russian Liberalism: Historical Drama and New Prospects*, Charn, 2019.
11 Benjamin Nathans, 'The Dictatorship of Reason: Aleskandr Vol'pin and the Idea of Rights under "Developed Socialism"', *Slavic Review* 66:4 (2007): 630–63.
12 Rory Finnin, *Blood of Others: Stalin's Crimean Atrocity and the Poetics of Solidarity*, Toronto, 2022, 100–105.
13 Alexeyeva and Goldberg, *Thaw Generation*, 219.
14 Chuprinin, *Ottepel'*, 896–7.
15 Alexeyeva and Goldberg, *Thaw Generation*, 131.
16 Peter Reddaway, *The Dissidents: A Memoir of Working with the Resistance in Russia 1960–1990*, Washington, DC, 2020, ch. 4.
17 E.g. Hardy, *Gulag after Stalin*, 206.
18 Mark Harrison, *One Day We Will Live Without Fear: Everyday Lives under the Soviet Police State*, Stanford, 2016.
19 Kozlov, *Neizvestnyi SSSR*, 422–3, 427.
20 Sakharov's life story is told and analysed by himself in his *Memoirs* and by Jay Bergman, *Meeting the Demands of Reason: The Life and Thought of Andrei Sakharov*, Ithaca, 2009.
21 Andrei D. Sakharov, *Progress, Peaceful Coexistence and Intellectual Freedom*, New York, 1968, esp. 52–7.
22 Alexeyeva and Goldberg, *Thaw Generation*, 208.
23 Geoffrey Hosking, 'Trust and Distrust in the USSR: An Overview', *Slavonic and East European Review* 91:1 (2013): 1–25.
24 Tromly, *Making the Soviet Intelligentsia*, 250–56.
25 E.g. Protocol of meeting of bureau committee of MGU VLKSM, 7–8 December 1965, in D. Zubarev et al. (eds.), *5 Dekabria 1965 goda*, Moscow, 2005, 116–23.
26 Tromly, *Making the Soviet Intelligentsia*, 10.
27 Zubok, *Zhivago's Children*, 299.
28 Philip Boobbyer, *Conscience, Dissent and Reform in Soviet Russia*, Abingdon, 2005.
29 See the account of Medvedev in Barbara Martin, *Dissident Histories in the Soviet Union from De-Stalinization to Perestroika*, London, 2019.
30 See Benjamin Nathans, 'Thawed Selves: A Commentary on the Soviet First Person', *Kritika* 13:1 (2012): 177–83, which discusses Benjamin

Tromly, 'Intelligentsia Self-Fashioning in the Soviet Union: Revol't Pimenov's Political Struggle, 1949–57', op. cit.: 151–76.
31 Josephine von Zitzewitz, *The Culture of Samizdat: Literature and Underground Networks in the Late Soviet Union*, London, 2021, chs. 2–3.
32 Von Zitzewitz, *The Culture of Samizdat*, 174, 82.
33 Ann Komaromi, *Soviet Samizdat: Imagining a New Society*, Ithaca, 2022, ch. 4.
34 Serguei Alex. Oushakine, 'The Terrifying Mimicry of Samizdat', *Public Culture* 13:2 (2001): 191–214 (199).

## CHAPTER 10: SOCIALIST BODIES

1 Scammell, *Solzhenitsyn*, 637.
2 Scammell, *Solzhenitsyn*, 656.
3 Aleksandr I. Solzhenitsyn, *The Oak and the Calf: Sketches of Literary Life in the Soviet Union*, London, 1980, 1.
4 Scammell, *Solzhenitsyn*, 676.
5 *Khronika tekushchikh sobytii* 11 (31 December 1969).
6 Scammell, *Solzhenitsyn*, 77–8, 82.
7 Aleksandr Solzhenitsyn, *One Day in the Life of Ivan Denisovich*, London, 2000 (*Novyi mir*, 1962), 23.
8 *NkhSE*, 1963: 624; 1963: 734; 1970: 690; 1980: 496.
9 Michael Ryan, *Doctor and the State in the Soviet Union*, London, 1990, 3.
10 Ryan, *Doctor and the State*, 59–60.
11 Murray Feshbach and Alfred Friendly, *Ecocide in the USSR: Health and Nature in the USSR*, London, 1992, 183.
12 Murray Feshbach, 'Health in the USSR: Organization, Trends, and Ethics', in Hans-Martin Sass and Robert U. Massey (eds.), *Health Care Systems: Moral Conflicts in European and American Public Policy*, Dordrecht, 1988, 117–32 (119).
13 Ryan, *Doctor and the State*, 73.
14 B. V. Petrovskii, 'Okhrana zdorov'ia naroda – odna iz vazhneishikh zadach sovetskogo gosudarstva', in Petrovskii et al. (eds.), *60 let sovetskogo zdravookhraneniia*, Moscow, 1977, 7–36 (17–18).
15 Frances L. Bernstein, Christopher Burton and Dan Healey (eds.), *Soviet Medicine: Culture, Practice, and Science*, DeKalb, 2010, 11–12.
16 Vladimir Soloukhin, 'Sentenced: A Lyrical Documentary' (published in *Moskva*, 1975), in Soloukhin, *Scenes from Russian Life*, trans. David Martin, London, 1988, 37.

17 See Susan Grant, 'The *Fizkul'tura* Generation: Modernizing Lifestyles in Early Soviet Russia', *Soviet and Post-Soviet Review* 37 (2010): 142–65 (147).
18 Stephen P. Dunn and Ethel Dunn, 'Everyday Life of the Disabled in the USSR', in William O. McCagg and Lewis Siegelbaum (eds.), *The Disabled in the Soviet Union: Past and Present, Theory and Practice*, Pittsburgh, 1989, 199–234 (202).
19 Claire L. Shaw, *Deaf in the USSR: Marginality, Community and Soviet Identity, 1917–1991*, Ithaca, 2017.
20 William A. Knaus, *Inside Russian Medicine: An American Doctor's First-Hand Report*, New York, 1981, 313–23.
21 Aleksandr Solzhenitsyn, *Cancer Ward*, trans. Nicholas Bethell and David Burg, London, 1971, 18, 95, 99, 137, 247–51.
22 Michael Binyon, *Life in Russia*, London, 1983, 52.
23 Sakharov, *Memoirs*, 295–8.
24 Ryan, *Doctor and the State*, 38–42.
25 Soloukhin, 'Sentenced', 100.
26 V. I. Ivkin, *Gosudarstvennaia vlast' SSSR. Vysshie organy vlasti i upravleniia i ikh rukovoditeli 1923–1991: Istoriko-biograficheskii spravochnik*, Moscow, 1999, 349–50.
27 Mie Nakachi, 'Liberation Without Contraception? The Rise of the Abortion Empire and Pronatalism in Socialist and Postsocialist Russia', in Rickie Solinger and Mie Nakachi (eds.), *Reproductive States: Global Perspectives on the Invention and Implementation of Population Policy*, Oxford, 2016, 290–328 (307–8).
28 Yuliya Hilevych and Chizu Sato, 'Popular Medical Discourses on Birth Control in the Soviet Union During the Cold War: Shifting Responsibilities and Relational Values', in Ann-Katrin Gembries, Theresia Theuke and Isabel Heinemann (eds.), *Children by Choice? Changing Values, Reproduction and Family Planning in the Twentieth Century*, Munich, 2018, 99–122 (100, 103, 114).
29 Mie Nakachi, *Replacing the Dead: The Politics of Reproduction in the Postwar Soviet Union*, Oxford, 2021, 187.
30 Andrej A. Popov, Adriaan Ph. Visser and Evert Ketting, 'Contraceptive Knowledge, Attitudes, and Practice in Russia during the 1980s', *Studies in Family Planning* 24:4 (July–August 1993): 227–35 (227).
31 Siobhán Hearne, 'Sanitising Sex in the USSR: State Approaches to Sexual Health in the Brezhnev Era', *Europe-Asia Studies* 2022 (advance online), 11–12.

32 Siobhán Hearne, 'Selling Sex Under Socialism: Prostitution in the Postwar USSR', *European Review of History: Revue européenne d'histoire* 29:2 (2022): 290–310.
33 Nakachi, *Replacing the Dead*, 193, 196.
34 Nakachi, *Replacing the Dead*, 197.
35 Anna Rotkirch, '"What Kind of Sex Can You Talk About?" Acquiring Sexual Knowledge in Three Soviet Generations', in Daniel Bertaux, Paul Thompson and Anna Rotkirch (eds.), *On Living Through Soviet Russia*, London, 2004, 91–117 (112).
36 Sof'ia Chuikina, '"Byt neotdelim ot politiki": ofitsial'nye i neofitsial'nye normy "polovoi" morali v sovetskom obshchestve 1930–1980-x godov', in Elena Zdravomyslova and Anna Temkina (eds.), *V poiskakh seksual'nosti*, St Petersburg, 2002, 99–127 (126–7).
37 Igor S. Kon, *The Sexual Revolution in Russia: From the Age of the Czars to Today*, New York, 1995, 89, 92–3.
38 Rustam Alexander, *Regulating Homosexuality in Soviet Russia, 1956–91: A Different History*, Manchester, 2021, ch. 2.
39 Alexander, *Regulating Homosexuality*, 133, 138.
40 Dan Healey, *Russian Homophobia from Stalin to Sochi*, London, 2018, 35–6, 43, 47.
41 Healey, *Russian Homophobia*, 153, 169, 171–2.
42 Alexander, *Regulating Homosexuality*, ch. 3.
43 Healey, *Russian Homophobia*.
44 Arthur Clech, 'Between the Labor Camp and the Clinic: Tema or the Shared Forms of Late Soviet Homosexual Subjectivities', *Slavic Review* 77:1 (2018): 6–29 (18).
45 Francesca Stella, *Lesbian Lives in Soviet and Post-Soviet Russia: Post/Socialism and Gendered Sexualities*, Basingstoke, 2015, 49–51.
46 Mark B. Adams, 'The Soviet Nature-Nurture Debate', in Loren R. Graham (ed.), *Science and the Soviet Social Order*, Cambridge, MA, 1990, 94–138 (119 and passim.).
47 Graham, *Lysenko's Ghost*, 10–12 (and ch. 1 passim).

## CHAPTER 11: A STRING BAG

1 Sergei Khrushchev, *Khrushchev on Khrushchev: An Inside Account of the man and His Era By His Son*, ed. and trans. William Taubman, Boston, 1990, 205–6.
2 *NKhSE*, 1959: 645; 1964: 593.

3 Philip Hanson, *The Rise and Fall of the Soviet Economy: An Economic History of the USSR from 1945*, London, 2003, 73.
4 Natalya Chernyshova, *Soviet Consumer Culture in the Brezhnev Era*, London, 2013, 9.
5 Merlin Läänemets, 'The Rise of Status Consumption in the Estonian SSR: Socialist "Good Taste" and Western Influence', *Soviet and Post-Soviet Review*, 2023: 125 (13–15).
6 Mel'nichenko (ed.), *Sovetskii anekdot*, 568.
7 Mel'nichenko (ed.), *Sovetskii anekdot*, 568. The joke was sufficiently apposite to be used as the title of one of the major histories of Soviet material culture: Lebina, *Passazhiry kolbasnogo poezda*.
8 Elena Bogdanova, 'The Soviet Consumer – More Than Just a Soviet Man', in Timo Vihavainen and Elena Bogdanova (eds.), *Communism and Consumerism: The Soviet Alternative to the Affluent Society*, Leiden, 2016, 113–38 (120).
9 Bogdanova, 'The Soviet Consumer', 125.
10 Kirsten Bönker, 'Talking With the Consumer: Consumer Issues on Soviet Television', *Laboratorium* 8:1 (2016): 30–57.
11 Diane P. Koenker, 'The Smile Behind the Sales Counter: Soviet Shop Assistants on the Road to Full Communism', *Journal of Social History* 54:3 (2021): 872–96.
12 Diane P. Koenker and Benjamin Bamberger, 'Tips, Bonuses or Bribes: The Immoral Economy of Soviet Service Work in the Soviet 1960s', *Russian Review* 79:2 (2020): 246–68 (249).
13 Ol'ga Gurova, *Sovetskoe nizhnee bel'e: mezhdu ideologiei i povsednevnost'iu*, Moscow, 2008, 153–4.
14 Jenny Leigh Smith, 'Empire of Ice Cream', 149–50.
15 Kristy Ironside, *A Full-Value Ruble: The Promise of Prosperity in the Postwar Soviet Union*, Cambridge, MA, 2021.
16 Chernyshova, *Soviet Consumer Culture*, 82.
17 Jukka Gronow and Sergey Zhuravlev, *Fashion Meets Socialism: Fashion Industry in the Soviet Union after the Second World War*, Helsinki, 2016, 92–5.
18 Virginia Olmsted McGraw, '"Proletarian in Content, National in (Uni)form": Fashion, Modernization and National Identity in the Soviet Union', *Soviet and Post-Soviet Review*, 2022: 1–27 (19–20).
19 Larissa Zakharova, 'How and What to Consume: Patterns of Soviet Clothing Consumption in the 1950s and 1960s', in Vihavainen and Bogdanova (eds.), *Communism and Consumerism*, 85–112 (89–90).
20 Virginia Carter Olmsted McGraw, 'Soviet by Design: Fashion, Consumption

and International Competition during Late Socialism, 1948–1982', PhD dissertation, University of North Carolina at Chapel Hill, 2020, 311–18.
21 Merkel, 'Luxury in Socialism: An Absurd Proposition?'
22 On dacha life: see, e.g., Stephen Lovell, *Summerfolk: A History of the Dacha, 1710–2000*, Ithaca, 2003.
23 Yulia Karpova, *Comradely Objects: Design and Material Culture in Soviet Russia, 1960s–80s*, Manchester, 2020, 65–6, 87.
24 Serguei Alex. Oushakine, '"Against the Cult of Things": On Soviet Productivism, Storage Economy, and Commodities With No Destination', *Russian Review* 73:2 (2014): 198–236.
25 Alexey Golubev, *The Things of Life: Materiality in Late Soviet Russia*, Ithaca, 2021.
26 Susan E. Reid, 'Makeshift Modernity: DIY, Craft and the Virtuous Homemaker in New Soviet Housing of the 1960s', *International Journal for History, Culture and Modernity* 2:2 (2014): 87–124.
27 https://danilovskymarket.ru/about?part=history.
28 Anna Ivanova, *Magaziny 'Beryozka': paradoksy potrebleniia v pozdnem SSSR*, Moscow, 2017, 42–3, 48, 54–5, 67–70, 79, 85.
29 Mel'nichenko (ed.), *Sovetskii anekdot*, 571. Note that many Soviet and post-Soviet jokes feature Chukchi, describing either endearing naiveté or outright stupidity, and are a window onto Soviet racism (see chapter 14).
30 Khrushchev, *Khrushchev on Khrushchev*, 204–5, 207.
31 Bittner, *Many Lives*, 217.
32 Khrushchev, *Khrushchev on Khrushchev*, 190.
33 Khrushchev, *Khrushchev on Khrushchev*, 201.
34 *Arkhitektura SSSR* 11 (1973): 11–12.
35 *Arkhitektura SSSR* 4 (1967): 39–44 (44).
36 Lewis H. Siegelbaum, *Cars for Comrades: The Life of the Soviet Automobile*, Ithaca, 2008, 239.
37 For the general context of Soviet new towns, see Lewis H. Siegelbaum, 'Modernity Unbound: The New Soviet City of the Sixties', in Gorsuch and Koenker (eds.), *The Socialist Sixties*, 66–83.
38 Blair A. Ruble, *Soviet Trade Unions: Their Development in the 1970s*, Cambridge, 1981, 102.
39 Valentina Fava, 'Between Business Interests and Ideological Marketing: The USSR and the Cold War in Fiat Corporate Strategy, 1957–1972', *Journal of Cold War Studies* 20:4 (2018): 26–64 (26).
40 K. M. Gordeeva, *Gorod Tol'iatti*, Kuibyshev, 1987, 6–7, 79–80.
41 Guido Seche and Michele Cera, *Tolyatti: Exploring Post-Soviet Spaces*, Berlin, 2020, 14, 16.

42 Gordeeva, *Gorod Tol'iatti*, 174, 190, 195.
43 Catriona Kelly, *Refining Russia: Advice Literature, Polite Culture, and Gender from Catherine to Yeltsin*, Oxford, 2001, 322.
44 Amy Nelson, 'A Hearth for a Dog: The Paradoxes of Soviet Pet Keeping', in Siegelbaum (ed.), *Borders of Socialism*, 123–44 (126).
45 Khrushchev, *Khrushchev on Khrushchev*, 202.
46 Khrushchev, *Nikita Khrushchev and the Creation of a Superpower*, 38–41.
47 Brezhnev, *Rabochie i dnevnikovye zapisi*, vol. 2, 488.
48 Granin, *Prichudy pamiati*, 231.
49 On Khrushchev's death and the KGB search, see Khrushchev, *Khrushchev on Khrushchev*, 328–49.

## CHAPTER 12: ON STAGE, OFF STAGE

1 Alexeyeva and Goldberg, *Thaw Generation*, 237.
2 Khrushchev, *Khrushchev on Khrushchev*, 326–7.
3 Nikolai Novikov, *Ernst Neizvestnyi: Iskusstvo i realnost'*, New York, 1981, 14, 108 (and, e.g., 20, 38, 40–41).
4 Albert Leong, *Centaur: The Life and Art of Ernst Neizvestny*, Lanham, 2002, 158.
5 Ernst Neizvestny, *Govorit Neizvestnyi*, Frankfurt, 1984, 13, 16, 21.
6 Leong, *Centaur*, 160.
7 Viktor Turov, 'O druzhbe s nim ia molchal shestnadtsat' let', *Literaturnaia gazeta*, 28 January 1998, 10. Sergei Khrushchev knew little of the meeting but mentioned it in *Khrushchev on Khrushchev*, 221. They disagree about whether Vysotsky sang.
8 The metaphor of 'force fields' is sometimes used by historians of the USSR in different contexts, e.g. Mark Edele, *Stalinist Society, 1928–1953*, New York, 2011.
9 Demidova, *Vladimir Vysotsky*, 148.
10 Joshua First, *Ukrainian Cinema: Belonging and Identity During the Soviet Thaw*, London, 2015, 202–4.
11 Catriona Kelly makes this argument about the work of the Leningrad film studio, Lenfilm, in *Soviet Art House: Lenfilm Studio under Brezhnev*, Oxford, 2021, 10–11.
12 Samantha Sherry, *Discourses of Regulation and Resistance: Censoring Translation in the Stalin and Khrushchev Era Soviet Union*, Edinburgh, 2015, 44–6, 54, 55, 58.
13 Stephen Lovell, *The Russian Reading Revolution: Print Culture in the Soviet and Post-Soviet Eras*, Basingstoke, 2000, 49.

14 A. V. Blium, *Kak delalos' v Leningrade: Tsenzura v gody ottepeli, zastoia i perestroiki, 1953–1991*, St Petersburg, 2005, 70–73.
15 Smeliansky, *Russian Theatre After Stalin*, 99.
16 Alexander Gershkovich, *The Theater of Yuri Lyubimov: Art and Politics at the Taganka Theater in Moscow*, trans. Michael Yurieff, New York, 1989, 84.
17 Birgit Beumers, *Yury Lyubimov at the Taganka Theatre*, London, 2004, 49–81.
18 A. V. Anisimov, *Teatry Moskvy*, Moscow, 1984, 6.
19 Ellendea Proffer Teasley, *Brodsky Among Us: A Memoir*, Brighton, MA, 2017, 6.
20 Joseph Brodsky, 'In a Room and a Half', in *Less Than One: Selected Essays*, London, 1986.
21 *Survey* 74/5, printed in Andrei Amalrik, *Will the Soviet Union Survive until 1984?*, London, 1970.
22 Cf. Dina R. Spechler, *Permitted Dissent in the USSR: Novy Mir and the Soviet Regime*, New York, 1982.
23 Alexeyeva and Goldberg, *Thaw Generation*, 237.
24 Semen Ekshtut, *Iurii Trifonov: velikaia sila nedoskazannogo*, Moscow, 2014, 8.
25 Polly Jones, *Revolution Rekindled: The Writers and Readers of Late Socialist Biography*, Oxford, 2019, 202–14.
26 Rossiiskii gosudarstvennyi arkhiv literatury i iskusstva (Russian State Archive of Literature and Art, RGALI, Moscow), f. 1702, op. 10, d. 646, l. 1. She calls it a *povest'* rather than a novel (*roman*), reflecting its shorter length.
27 Simon Morrison, *Bolshoi Confidential: Secrets of the Russian Ballet from the Rule of the Tsars to Today*, London, 2016, ch. 6.
28 Solomon Volkov (ed.), *Testimony: The Memoirs of Dmitri Shostakovich*, London, 1979, 140–41.
29 Elizabeth Wilson, *Shostakovich: A Life Remembered*, London, 2006 (new edn), 474.
30 Dmitry Shostakovich, *About Himself and His Times*, Moscow, 1981 (1980 printing in Russian), 291.
31 Robert Edelman, *Serious Fun: A History of Spectator Sports in the USSR*, Oxford, 1993, 161, 171.
32 Aleksei Beliakov, *Alla Pugacheva*, Moscow, 2009, 32, 39–51, 62, 97.
33 E. Uvarova, *Arkadii Raikin*, Moscow, 1986, 248.
34 Stephen Lovell, *Russia in the Microphone Age: A History of Soviet Radio, 1919–1970*, Oxford, 2015, 208.

35 Kristin Roth-Ey, *Moscow Prime Time: How the Soviet Union Built the Media Empire That Lost the Cultural Cold War*, Ithaca, 2011, 273–4.
36 Alexander Solzhenitsyn, *Letter to Soviet Leaders*, London, 1974, 7, 42 and passim.
37 This account draws on Solzhenitsyn, *Oak and the Calf*, 407–52 (quotation on 452), and Scammell, *Solzhenitsyn*, 820–4, 829, 839–42.

## CHAPTER 13: OIL FIELDS AND SILVER BIRCHES

1 M. A. Suslov, 'Velikaia nauka pobezhdat', speech of 17 January 1973, in Suslov, *Marksizm-leninizm i sovremennaia epokha. Izbrannye rechi i stat'i v trekh tomakh*, vol. 3 of 3, Moscow, 1982, 18.
2 Suslov, 'Vernost' ideolam sotsialisticheskoi revoliutsii', speech of 17 September 1976, in Suslov, *Marksizm-leninizm i sovremennaia epokha*, vol. 3, 181.
3 Serguei Oushakine, 'Totality Decomposed: Objectalizing Late Socialism in Post-Soviet Biochronicles', in Choi Chatterjee et al. (eds.), *Everyday Life in Russia: Past and Present*, Bloomington, 2015, 279–310 (288).
4 It can be viewed on the 'Sovetskoe televidenie' YouTube channel.
5 Sakharov, *Memoirs*, 286–7.
6 Feliks Chuev, *140 besed s Molotovym: Vtoroi posle Stalina*, Moscow, 2020 (first published 1991), 511.
7 Arnold Bucholz, 'The Scientific-Technological Revolution (STR) and Soviet Ideology', *Studies in Soviet Thought* 30:4 (1985): 337–46 (342).
8 See Fokin, '*Kommunizm ne ze gorami*'.
9 Valentin Kataev, *Time, Forward!*, Evanston, 1995 (1932), 3.
10 See Elana Gomel, 'Our Posthuman Past: Subjectivity, History and Utopia in Late-Soviet Science Fiction', in Colleen McQuillen and Julia Vaingurt (eds.), *The Human Reimagined: Posthumanism in Russia*, Boston, 2018, 37–54 (39–40).
11 N. Sizov, 'Glubzhe osoznaval smysl epokhi', *Iskusstvo kino* 8 (1979): 34–51 (44).
12 Reinhart Koselleck, 'Historical Criteria of the Modern Concept of Revolution' (1969), in Koselleck, *Futures Past: On the Semantics of Historical Time*, Cambridge, MA, 1985, 39–54.
13 See, e.g., Linda Cook, *The Soviet Social Contract and Why It Failed: Welfare Policy and Workers' Politics from Brezhnev to Yeltsin*, Cambridge, MA, 1993; James R. Millar, 'The Little Deal: Brezhnev's Contribution to Acquisitive Socialism', *Slavic Review* 44:4 (1985): 694–706.

14 Alexei Yurchak, *Everything was Forever Until It Was No More: The Last Soviet Generation*, Princeton, 2005, 10, 14.
15 George W. Breslauer, *Five Images of the Soviet Future: A Critical Review and Synthesis*, Berkeley, 1978.
16 Svetlana Boym, *Common Places: Mythologies of Everyday Life in Russia*, Cambridge, MA, 1994.
17 Anatoly Kalashnikov, 'Historicist Architecture and Stalinist Futurity', *Slavic Review* 79:3 (2020): 591–612.
18 Katherine Zubovich, *Moscow Monumental: Soviet Skyscrapers and Urban Life in Stalin's Capital*, Princeton, 2020, 97–8, 109–10.
19 Suslov, 'Vtoroi s"ezd RSDRP i ego vsemirno-istoricheskoe znachenie', in Suslov, *Marksizm-leninizm i sovremennaia epokha*, vol. 3, 24–44.
20 Aleksei Kosygin, 'Imia i dela Lenina budut zhit' vechno', speech of 22 April 1970, in Kosygin, *K velikoi tseli*, vol. 1, 589.
21 Suslov, 'Uchenie i dela V. I. Lenina bessmertny', speech of 18 January 1974, in Suslov, *Marksizm-leninizm i sovremennaia epokha*, vol. 3, 59.
22 Stephen E. Hanson, *Time and Revolution: Marxism and the Design of Soviet Institutions*, Chapel Hill, 1997, 179.
23 Denis Kozlov, 'The Historical Turn in Late Soviet Culture: Retrospectivism, Factography, Doubt, 1953–91', *Kritika* 2:3 (2001): 577–600.
24 E. V. Gutnova, *Perezhitoe*, Moscow, 2001.
25 Jones, *Revolution Rekindled*.
26 Martin, *Dissident Histories*.
27 Transcribed from film of *Belorusskii vokzal*, Mosfilm, 1970.
28 Letter from Iu. I. Sidorenko of Kostroma to Brezhnev, 18.10.82, in N. G. Tomilina (ed.), *Pamiatnik Pobedy: Istoriia sooruzheniia memorial'nogo kompleksa pobedy na Poklonnoi gore v Moskve*, Moscow, 2005, 145 (doc. 60).
29 Jonathan Brunstedt, *The Soviet Myth of World War II: Patriotic Memory and the Russian Question in the USSR*, Cambridge, 2021, ch. 5. There was no straight line to the nationalist obsession about 1941–5 that shaped the propaganda justifying the invasion of Ukraine in 2022, which was a later and murderous confection; there were many dead ends, thoughtful interludes and periods of indifference on the way.
30 Ekaterina Mel'nikova, 'Rukami naroda: sledopytskoe dvizhenie 1960–1980-x gg. v SSRR', *Antropologicheskii forum* 37 (2018): 20–53.
31 A. Adamovich and D. Granin, *Blokadnaia kniga*, Moscow, 1979–83.
32 *Kino iskusstvo*, 12:80 (1985).
33 Cf. Lewis H. Siegelbaum and Leslie Page Moloch, *Broad Is My Native Land: Repertoires and Regimes of Migration in Russia's Twentieth Century*, Ithaca, 2014.

34 Mervyn Matthews, *The Passport Society: Controlling Movement in Russia and the USSR*, Boulder, CO, 1993.
35 Al'bert Baiburin, *Sovetskii pasport: istoriia, struktura, praktiki*, St Petersburg, 2017.
36 Thane Gustafson, *Crisis Amid Plenty: The Politics of Soviet Energy under Brezhnev and Gorbachev*, Princeton, 1989, 342.
37 *Pravda*, 31 October 1979, 2.
38 See Egor Gaidar, *Gibel' imperii: uroki dlia sovremennoi Rossii*, Moscow, 2006.
39 L. Brezhnev, 'Speech at Meeting With Workers at Likhachev Car Plant', 30 April, 1976, in n.a., *KPSS o formirovanii novogo cheloveka: Sbornik dokumentov i materialov (1965-1976)*, Moscow, 1976, 384–95 (385).
40 *XXV s"ezd Kommunisticheskoi partii Sovetskogo Soiuza: Stenograficheskii otchet*, vol. 1 of 3, Moscow, 1976, 105, 113 (Brezhnev's report at the Twenty-fifth Party Congress).
41 Michael Cotey Morgan, *The Final Act: The Helsinki Accords and the Transformation of the Cold War*, Princeton, 2018.
42 Sarah B. Snyder, *Human Rights Activism and the End of the Cold War: A Transnational History of the Helsinki Network*, Cambridge, 2011.
43 Daniel C. Thomas, *The Helsinki Effect: International Norms, Human Rights, and the Demise of Communism*, Princeton, 2001.
44 Benjamin Nathans, 'The Dictatorship of Reason: Aleksandr Vol'pin and the Idea of Rights Under "Developed Socialism"', *Slavic Review* 66:4 (2007): 630–63 (634 and passim).
45 *Pravda*, 25 May 1977, 1.
46 See, e.g., *Pravda*, 5 June 1977, 2.
47 Gorbanevskaya, *Selected Poems*, 62 (very slightly amended translation).
48 Jon Lawrence, *Me, Me, Me? The Search for Community in Postwar England*, Oxford, 2019, 2.

## CHAPTER 14: HAMMER AND SICKLE AS FAR AS THE EYE CAN SEE

1 Aleksei Leonov, *Vremia pervykh: sud'ba moia – ia sam*, Moscow, 2017, 122–3.
2 Leonov, *Vremia pervykh*, 43.
3 Leonov, *Vremia pervykh*, 246.
4 Westad, *The Cold War: A World History*, 365, 406–8, 414.
5 Andrew L. Jenks, *Collaboration in Space and the Search for Peace on Earth*, London and New York, 2022, 17–18.

6 Souvik Naha, '"The Russian Deadpan Expert" vs "America's White Hope": The Personal, the National and the Global in the "Cold War of Chess"', in Vonnard et al. (eds.), *Beyond Boycotts*, 179–93 (179, 192–3).
7 Sari Autio-Sarasmo, 'Transferring Western Knowledge to a Centrally Planned Economy: Finland and the Scientific-Technical Cooperation with the Soviet Union', in Christian et al. (eds.), *Planning in Cold War Europe*, 143–64 (149, 151, 156).
8 See Smith, *Property of Communists*; and, more recently, Ol'ga Iakushenko, 'Sovetskaia arkhitektura i zapad: otkrytie i assimiliatsiia zapadnogo opyta v sovetskoi arkhitekture kontsa 1950-kh–1960-kh godov', *Laboratorium* 8:2 (2016): 76–102.
9 Stanek, *Architecture in Global Socialism*. More broadly, see Mark, Betts et al., *Socialism Goes Global*.
10 Sergei Zhuk, *Soviet Americana: The Cultural History of Russian and Ukrainian Americanists*, London, 2018.
11 The approach was then historicized fruitfully by, inter alia, Kate Brown, *Plutopia: Nuclear Families, Atomic Cities, and the Great Soviet and American Plutonium Disasters*, Oxford, 2013.
12 Frithjof Benjamin Schenk, '"A Sixth Part of the World": The Career of a Spatial Metaphor in Russia and the Soviet Union (1837–2021)', *Kritika* 24:2 (2023): 349–80.
13 Frank Billé and Caroline Humphrey, *On the Edge: Life Along the Russia-China Border*, Cambridge, MA, 2021, 7.
14 Katerina Clark, *Moscow, the Fourth Rome: Stalinism, Cosmopolitanism and the Evolution of Soviet Culture, 1931–1941*, Cambridge, MA, 2011.
15 Saulius Grybkauskas, *Governing the Soviet Union's National Republics: The Second Secretaries of the Communist Party*, Abingdon, 2021.
16 Suslov, 'Druzhba i bratstvo svobodnykh narodov SSSR', speech of 28 November 1973, in Suslov, *Marksizm-leninizm i sovremennaia epokha*, vol. 3, 45.
17 Adrianne K. Jacobs, 'An Empire in Aspic: Popularizing National Cuisines in Late Soviet Russia', *Soviet and Post-Soviet Review* (2022): 1–32 (10).
18 Ronald Grigor Suny, *The Revenge of the Past: Nationalism, Revolution and the Collapse of the Soviet Union*, Stanford, 1993, ch. 3.
19 Yuri Slezkine, 'The USSR as a Communal Apartment, or How a Socialist State Promoted Ethnic Particularism', *Slavic Review* 53:2 (1994): 414–52.
20 Hosking, *Rulers and Victims*.
21 Jeremy Smith, *Red Nations: The Nationalities Experience in and after the USSR*, Cambridge, 2013, 217.

22 Mitrohin, 'Back-Office Mikhaila Suslova', 425–6, 430–31.
23 Hosking, *Rulers and Victims*, ch. 9.
24 Serhii Plokhy, *Lost Kingdom: A History of Russian Nationalism from Ivan the Great to Vladimir Putin*, London, 2017, esp. ch. 17.
25 Smith, *Red Nations*, 223–5.
26 Diane P. Koenker, 'The Taste of Others: Soviet Adventures in Cosmopolitan Cuisines', *Kritika* 19:2 (2018): 243–72 (256–7).
27 Elizabeth Schwall, 'A Spectacular Embrace: Dance Dialogues between Cuba and the Soviet Union, 1959–1973', *Dance Chronicle* 41:3 (2018): 275–302 (294).
28 Gorsuch, 'Cuba, My Love'.
29 Suslov, 'Kommunisticheskoe dvizhenie v avangarde bor'by za mir, sotsial'noe i natsial'noe osvobozhdenie', speech of 4 July 1974, in Suslov, *Marksizm-leninizm i sovremennaia epokha*, vol. 3, 142–9.
30 Haslam, *Near and Distant Neighbours* (on sovereignty).
31 Kokurin and Petrov (eds.), *Lubianka*, 725–9 (725): speech of Andropov at the April (1973) Plenum of the CC CPSU, 29 April 1973.
32 Thomas R. Loyd, 'Black in the USSR: African Students, Soviet Empire, and the Politics of Global Education during the Cold War, 1956–1976', PhD dissertation, Georgetown University, 2021, esp. ch. 5.
33 Constantin Katsakioris, 'Burden or Allies?: Third World Students and Internationalist Duty Through Soviet Eyes', *Kritika* 18:3 (2017): 539–67 (541, 560 (on student stipends)).
34 Abigail Judge Kret, '"We Unite With Knowledge": The Peoples' Friendship University and Soviet Education for the Third World', *Comparative Studies of South Asia, Africa and the Middle East* 33:2 (2013): 239–56.
35 Anika Walke, 'Was Soviet Internationalism Anti-Racist? Toward a History of Foreign Others in the USSR', in David Rainbow (ed.), *Ideologies of Race: Russia and the Soviet Union in Global Context*, Montreal and Kingston, 2019, 284–311 (305).
36 Cf. the USSR as a 'developmental state': Georgi M. Derluguian, *Bourdieu's Secret Admirer in the Caucasus: A World System Biography*, Chicago, 2005, 226.
37 Artemy M. Kalinovsky, *Laboratory of Socialist Development: Cold War Politics and Decolonization in Soviet Tajikistan*, Ithaca, 2018, ch. 5.
38 Kalinovsky, *Laboratory of Socialist Development*, 185, 294; chs. 5, 7.
39 Yuri Slezkine, *The Jewish Century*, Princeton, 2004.
40 Slava Gerovitch, '"We Teach Them to Be Free!": Specialized Maths Schools and the Cultivation of the Soviet Technical Intelligentsia', *Kritika* 20:4 (2019): 717–54 (734–5).

41 Adrienne Edgar, 'Children of Mixed Marriage in Soviet Central Asia: Dilemmas of Identity and Belonging', in Rainbow (ed.), *Ideologies of Race*, 208–33.
42 Jeff Sahadeo, *Voices from the Soviet Edge: Southern Migrants in Leningrad and Moscow*, Ithaca, 2019, ch. 4.
43 Zvi Gitelman, *A Century of Ambivalence: The Jews of Russia and the Soviet Union, 1881 to the Present*, New York, 1988, 280–81.
44 Ronald Grigor Suny, *Looking Toward Ararat: Armenia in Modern History*, Bloomington, 1993, 216–17, 228–9.
45 Adrienne Edgar, *Intermarriage and the Friendship of Peoples: Ethnic Mixing in Soviet Central Asia*, Ithaca, 2022, 11, 73–4.
46 This is part of the argument of Erik R. Scott, *Familiar Strangers: The Georgian Diaspora and the Evolution of Soviet Empire*, Oxford, 2016.

## CHAPTER 15: *HOMO SOVIETICUS*

1 Schattenberg, *Brezhnev*, 346.
2 Aleksandr Zinoviev, *Ispoved' otshchepentsa*, Moscow, 2005, 442.
3 Alexander Zinoviev, *Homo Sovieticus*, London, 1985 (1982), 39.
4 Zinoviev, *Homo Sovieticus*, 43.
5 Zinoviev, *Homo Sovieticus*, 67.
6 Alexander Zinoviev, *The Reality of Communism*, London, 1985 (1981), 87.
7 Paul R. Josephson, *New Atlantis Revisited: Akademgorodok, the Soviet City of Science*, Princeton, 1997; cf., for Chernogolovka in Moscow Region, Maria Rogacheva, *The Private World of Soviet Scientists from Stalin to Gorbachev*, Cambridge, 2017.
8 Larissa Titarenko and Elena Zdravomyslova, *Sociology in Russia: A Brief History*, Cham, 2017, ch. 4.
9 The best description and critique of the concept is Gulnaz Sharafutdinova, *The Afterlife of the 'Soviet Man': Rethinking Homo Sovieticus*, London, 2023.
10 Mikhail Heller (Geller), *Cogs in the Soviet Wheel: The Formation of Soviet Man* (trans. David Floyd), London, 1988.
11 Frank Ellis, 'The Media as Social Engineer', in Catriona Kelly and David Shepherd (eds.), *Russian Cultural Studies: An Introduction*, Oxford, 1998, 192–222 (208).
12 Vladimir Bukovsky, *To Build a Castle: My Life as a Dissenter*, New York: Viking, 1977, 430, 437.
13 Krylova, 'The Tenacious Liberal Subject'.

14 David Priestland, *Stalinism and the Politics of Mobilization: Ideas, Power and Terror in Interwar Russia*, Oxford, 2007.
15 Michael Voslensky, *Nomenklatura: Anatomy of the Soviet Ruling Class*, London, 1983 [1980], 183ff.
16 Ivanova, *Magaziny 'Beryozka'*, 202.
17 N. A. Aitov, 'The Dynamics of Social Mobility in the USSR' (originally published in *Sovetskaia sotsiologiia* 2 (1982): 197–210), in Murray Yanowitch (ed.), *The Social Structure of the USSR: Recent Soviet Studies*, Armonk, 1986, 254–70 (256, 266).
18 Chernyshova, *Soviet Consumer Culture*, 7.
19 *Bol'shaia Sovetskaia entsiklopediia*, Moscow, 1974, 3rd edn, vol. 18, 1974, 492.
20 Dzhamil' Gasanly, *Sovetskii Azerbaidzhan: Ot ottepeli k zamorozkam (1959–1969)*, Moscow, 2020, 648.
21 L. Gordon and E. Klopov, *Man After Work*, Moscow, 1975, 108–18.
22 Golubev, *Things of Life*, 32.
23 Alexandra Oberländer, 'Cushy Work, Backbreaking Leisure: Late Soviet Work Ethics Reconsidered', *Kritika* 18:3 (2017): 569–90 (573 and passim).
24 Ruble, *Soviet Trade Unions*, 2.
25 Wendy Z. Goldman, *Terror and Democracy in the Age of Stalin: The Social Dynamics of Repression*, Cambridge, 2007, 127–36.
26 Ruble, *Soviet Trade Unions*, 64.
27 Ruble, *Soviet Trade Unions*, 70–71.
28 Suslov, 'Krepnushchee edinstvo partii i naroda', speech of 9 June 1975, in Suslov, *Marksizm-leninizm i sovremennaia epokha*, vol. 3, 122–36.
29 'On progress to fulfilment by the Party organization of Georgia of the CC CPSU decree on the organizational and political work of the Tbilisi gorkom', 24 June 1976, in *KPSS o formirovanii novogo cheloveka*, 226–33 (229).
30 Mark Harrison, *Secret Leviathan: Secrecy and State Capacity under Soviet Communism*, Stanford, 2023.
31 Larissa Zakharova, 'Trust in Bureaucracy and Technology: The Evolution of Secrecy Policies and Practice in the Soviet State Apparatus (1917–91)', *Kritika* 21:3 (2020): 555–90 (586).
32 Asif Siddiqi, 'Soviet Secrecy: Towards a Social Map of Knowledge', *American Historical Review*, 2021: 1046–71.
33 See, e.g., Aleksandra Arkhipova and Anna Kirziuk, *Opasnye sovetskie veshchi: gorodskie legendy i strakhi v SSSR*, Moscow, 2020.

34 V. G. Afanasyev et al., *Soviet Democracy in the Period of Developed Socialism*, Moscow, 1979, 5.
35 Martin Conway, *Western Europe's Democratic Age, 1945–1968*, Princeton, 2020.
36 Hosking, *Trust*.
37 Ilya Kabakov, *Ten Characters*, London, 1989, e.g. 30–33; interview with David A. Ross in Boris Groys, David A. Ross and Iwona Blazwick (eds.), *Ilya Kabakov*, London, 1998, 6–28 (e.g. 11).

## CHAPTER 16: THE DANGER SOCIETY

1 Jenks, *Cosmonaut*, 254.
2 Donald Raleigh (trans. and ed.), *Russia's Sputnik Generation: Soviet Baby Boomers Talk About Their Lives*, Bloomington, 2006, 129, and cited in Mark B. Smith, 'The Withering Away of the Danger Society: The Pensions Reforms of 1956 and 1964 in the Soviet Union', *Social Science History* 39:1 (2015): 129–48 (129). The title of this chapter uses the same phrase as the title of this article, but only draws on the material in the article tangentially.
3 Brown, *Plutopia*, passim.
4 Paul R. Josephson, *Would Trotsky Wear a Bluetooth? Technological Utopianism under Socialism, 1917–1989*, Baltimore, 2010, 248.
5 *NKhSE*, 1958: 906; 1960: 848; 1970: 734; 1980: 527. Comparable figures allowing for redenomination.
6 V. A. Pertsev, *Sotsial'noe obespechenie i obsluzhivanie naseleniia RSFSR (vtoraia polovina 1950-kh–1980-e gody): na materialakh oblastei tsentral'nogo chernozem'ia*, Voronzezh, 2014, 367, 374.
7 Quotations are from Smith, 'Withering Away of the Danger Society', 142.
8 Paul P. Rogers, *Insurance in the Soviet Union*, New York, 1986.
9 Paul P. Rogers, 'The Structure of Soviet Insurance', *The Journal of Risk and Insurance* 32:2 (1965): 237–54.
10 Josephson, *Would Trotsky Wear a Bluetooth?*, 235.
11 Kirill Chunikhin, 'Risks and Respirators: The Hazardous Trajectories of Soviet Occupational Safety, 1940s–1980s', *Technology and Culture* 63:3 (2022): 603–33 (624).
12 Nigel A. Raab, *All Shook Up: The Shifting Soviet Response to Catastrophes, 1917–1991*, Montreal, 2017, 66–7.
13 Raab, *All Shook Up*, 67; http://iaspei.org/about/bios-obituaries/valentin-ivanovich-ulomov-1933-2017.

14 Raab, *All Shook Up*, 190.
15 Marc Elie, '"Au centre d'un double malheur": Le séisme du 7 décembre 1988 en Arménie et l'expulsion des sinistrés azéris de Spitak', *Revue d'études comparatives Est-Ouest* 44:1 (2013): 45–75.
16 Gerovitch, '"We Teach them to Be Free"', 746 and passim.
17 Alexandre Borovik, 'The Kolmogorov Reform of Mathematics Education in the USSR', in Dirk De Bock (ed.), *Modern Mathematics: An International Movement?*, Cham, 2023, 319–36.
18 Eglė Rindzevičiūtė, 'A Struggle for the Soviet Future: The Birth of Scientific Forecasting in the Soviet Union', *Slavic Review* 75:1 (2016): 52–76 (60, 62, 63, 70).
19 Ivan Boldyrev and Till Düppe, 'Programming the USSR: Leonid V. Kantorovich in Context', *The British Journal for the History of Science* 53:2 (2020): 255–78 (272).
20 Clemens Günther, 'The Cultural and Political Imaginary of Cybernetic Socialism', *Kritika* 24:2 (2023): 321–48.
21 Gregory Afinogenov, 'Andrei Ershov and the Soviet Information Age', *Kritika* 14:3 (2013): 561–84.
22 Ksenia Tatarchenko, 'Before the Collapse: Programming Cultures in the Soviet Union', in Mario Biagioli and Vincent Antonin Lépinay (eds.), *From Russia With Code: Programming Migrations in Post-Soviet Times*, Durham, NC, 2019, 38–58 (50).
23 Slava Gerovitch, 'InterNyet: Why the Soviet Union Did Not Build a Nationwide Computer Network', *History and Technology* 24:4 (2008): 335–50; Benjamin Peters, *How Not to Network a Nation: The Uneasy History of the Soviet Internet*, Cambridge, 2017, 13.
24 I. B. Orlov and A. D. Popov, *Skvoz' 'zheleznyi zanaves'. Russo turisto: sovetskii vyezdnoi turizm, 1955–1991*, Moscow, 2016, 103.
25 *Pravda*, 8 February 1981, 2.
26 B. S. Pushkarev, K. M. Aleksandrov, S. S. Balmasov et al., *Dve Rossii XX veka: obzor istorii 1917–1993*, Moscow, 2008, 411.
27 Steven E. Harris, 'Dawn of the Soviet Jet Age: Aeroflot Passengers and Aviation Culture Under Nikita Khrushchev', *Kritika* 21:3 (2020): 591–626 (614–15).
28 Vas'kin, *Povsednevnaia zhizn'*, next to 257 (inset photo and caption).
29 *Pravda*, 8 February 1981, 2.
30 *Pravda*, 9 February 1983, 2.
31 *Pravda*, 16 February 1977, 6.
32 Sakharov, *Memoirs*, 321–3.
33 Iulian Semenov, *Protivostoianie*, St Petersburg, 2015 (1979), 335.

34 http://www.airdisaster.ru/database.php?id=107; http://www.airdisaster.ru/database.php?id=60; https://www.baaa-acro.com/crash/crash-tupolev-tu-104a-pushkin-50-killed. All checked on 18 August 2023.

35 Note of Goskino USSR on articles in *Sovetskaia Rossiia* about the films *Moscow Doesn't Believe in Tears* and *Air Crew*, 3 November 1980, signed off by F. T. Ermash, chair of Goskino SSSR, in N. G. Tomilina et al. (eds.), *Apparat TsK KPSS i kul'tura, 1979–1984: Dokumenty*, Moscow, 2019, doc. 74, 417–19 (418).

36 Karl Lorentz Kleve, 'Making Iron Curtain Overflights Legal: Soviet-Scandinavian Aviation Negotiations in the Early Cold War', in Sune Bechmann Pedersen and Christian Noack (eds.), *Tourism and Travel During the Cold War: Negotiating Tourist Experiences Across the Iron Curtain*, London, 2019, 175–89.

37 Stephen F. Cohen, *Sovieticus: American Perceptions and Soviet Realities*, New York, 1986, 134–8.

38 Colton, *Moscow*, 555–6; Iu. S. Borisov et al. (eds), *Istoriia Moskvy s drevneishikh vremen do nashikh dnei*, vol. 3: XX vek, Moscow, 2000, 300.

39 Vas'kin, *Povsednevnaia zhizn'*, 71–2.

40 Gorbachev, *Memoirs*, ch. 1.

41 William Taubman, *Gorbachev: His Life and Times*, London, 2017, 129–33. This is the standard biography. I have relied on it and Gorbachev's own memoirs for biographical details.

42 Gorbachev, *Memoirs*, 15.

43 Gorlizki and Khlevniuk, *Substate Dictatorship*, 245.

44 Gorbachev, *Memoirs*, 12–15.

45 *Pravda*, 10 February 1979, 2.

46 Rudol'f Pikhoia, 'Ob usloviiakh priniatiia resheniia o vvode voisk v Afganistan', *Otechestvennaia istoriia* 6 (2019): 27–34 (29–30).

47 Artemy M. Kalinovsky, *A Long Goodbye: The Soviet Withdrawal from Afghanistan*, Cambridge, MA, 2011, 2 and ch. 1.

48 Chris Miller, *Chip War: The Fight for the World's Most Critical Technology*, New York, 2022, 147–8.

## CHAPTER 17: MISFITS

1 Donald J. Raleigh, '"Soviet" Man of Peace: Leonid Il'ich Brezhnev and His Diaries', *Kritika* 17:4 (2016): 837–68.

2 See, e.g., Juliane Fürst, 'Where Did All the Normal People Go? Another Look at the Soviet 1970s', *Kritika* 14:3 (2013): 621–40.

3 Andrei Soldatov and Irina Borogan, *The Red Web: The Struggle Between*

*Russia's Digital Dictators and the New Online Revolutionaries*, New York, 2015, 17–20.
4 N. G. Tomilina (ed.), *Piat' kolets pod kremlevskimi zvezdami: Dokumental'naia khronika Olimpiady 80 v Moskve*, Moscow, 2011, 758.
5 Colton, *Moscow*, 395.
6 *The Economist*, 26 July 1980, 45.
7 Colton, *Moscow*, 395.
8 Tomilina (ed.), *Piat' kolets*, 74, doc. 16; 82–3, doc. 20.
9 See the opening segment of Tamara Eidel'man's feature on Brezhnev on her YouTube channel, 15 April 2023.
10 Schattenberg, *Brezhnev*, 343–8.
11 Victor Dönninghaus and Andrei Savin, 'Leonid Brezhnev: Public Display Versus the Sacrality of Power', *Russian Studies in History* 52:4 (2014): 71–93 (74).
12 Schattenberg, *Brezhnev*.
13 Roi Medvedev, *Neizvestnyi Andropov*, Rostov-on-Don, 1999.
14 Shaun Morcom, 'Work and Soviet Society after Stalin: Discourses of "Labour Discipline" and the Law in the USSR, 1956–1991', *Slavonic and East European Review* 98:1 (2020): 106–38.
15 Hanson, *Rise and Fall*, 170–71.
16 *Pravda*, 18 February 1977, 2.
17 Mark Galeotti, *The Vory: Russia's Super Mafia*, New Haven, 2018, 81, 93–4.
18 Rhiannon Lee Dowling, 'Brezhnev's War on Crime: The Criminal in Soviet Society, 1963–1984', PhD dissertation, University of California, Berkeley, 2017.
19 Yana Skorobogatov, 'Killing the Soviet Man: The Death Penalty in the Soviet Union, 1954–1991', PhD dissertation, University of California, Berkeley, 2018, 4.
20 Yoram Gorlizki, 'Delegalization in Russia: Soviet Comrades' Courts in Retrospect', *American Journal of Comparative Law* 46 (1998): 403–25 (424).
21 Gerovitch, 'We Teach Them to be Free!'
22 Kelly, *Soviet Art House*, 332.
23 Juliane Fürst, *Flowers through Concrete: Explorations in Soviet Hippieland*, Oxford, 2021, 61–2, 64–9, 344.
24 Timothy W. Ryback, *Rock Around the Bloc: A History of Rock Music in Eastern Europe and the Soviet Union*, Oxford, 1990, 149.
25 Yurchak, *Everything Was Forever*, ch. 5.
26 Polly McMichael, '"After All, You're a Rock and Roll Star (At Least,

That's What They Say)": *Roksi* and the Creation of the Soviet Rock Musician', *Slavonic and East European Review* 83:4 (2005): 664–84 (669).
27 Ryback, *Rock Around the Bloc*, 153, 156.
28 Zbigniew Wojnowski, 'The Lives and Afterlives of a Soviet Misfit: Volodymyr Ivasiuk, the Emotional Crisis of Late Socialism and the Anti-Soviet Turn in Ukrainian Popular Culture', *Contemporary European History* 32:1 (2023): 61–78.
29 Catriona Kelly, *Socialist Churches: Radical Secularization and the Preservation of the Past in Petrograd and Leningrad, 1918–1988*, DeKalb, 2016, 234–5.
30 Birgit Menzel, 'Occult and Esoteric Movements in Russia from the 1960s to the 1980s', in Birgit Menzel, Michael Hagemeister and Bernice Glatzer Rosenthal (eds.), *The New Age of Russia: Occult and Esoteric Dimensions*, Munich, 2012, 151–85 (173).
31 Healey, *Russian Homophobia*, 99.
32 Maija Runcis and Lilita Zalkalns, 'Women's Role in the Alternative Culture Movements in Soviet Latvia, 1960–1990', in Melanie Ilic (ed.), *The Palgrave Handbook of Women and Gender in Twentieth-Century Russia and the Soviet Union*, London, 2018, 365–80.
33 Elena Zdravomyslova, 'The Café Saigon *Tusovka*: One Segment of the Informal-Public Sphere of Late-Soviet Society', in Robin Humphrey, Robert Miller and Elena Zdravomyslova (eds.), *Biographical Research in Eastern Europe: Altered Lives and Broken Biographies*, Aldershot, 2003, 141–77 (esp. 149, 151, 153, 156, 169, 172).
34 Medvedev, *Neizvestnyi Andropov*, 484.
35 Viktor Pribytkov, *Chernenko*, Moscow, 2009, 129.

## CHAPTER 18: THE LIFE CYCLE OF ETERNAL SOCIALISM

1 *Pravda*, 10 February 1981, 1.
2 Chris Miller, *The Struggle to Save the Soviet Economy: Mikhail Gorbachev and the Collapse of the USSR*, Chapel Hill, 2016, ch. 2.
3 Ninel' Ismailova, 'Evgenii Leonov', in V. Ia. Dubrovskii, *Evgenii Leonov: zhizn' i roli*, Rostov-on-Don, 1998, 38.
4 Interview with S. Dvoretskii, 'Sotsialisticheskaia industriia', 14 February 1976, in B. M. Poiurovskii (ed.), *Evgenii Leonov: dnevniki, pis'ma, vospominaniia*, Moscow, 2000, 270–74 (270).
5 Evgeny Leonov to Andrei Leonov, 30 September 1974: Evgenii Leonov, *Pis'ma sinu*, Moscow, 2018, 36–7.

6 Natal'ia Starosel'skaia, *Natal'ia Gundareva*, Moscow, 2018, 22.
7 Valery Tishkov, *Ethnicity, Nationalism and Conflict in and after the Soviet Union: The Mind Aflame*, London, 1997, 41.
8 Jessica Lovett, 'Turning Science into Fiction? Censoring Population Research in the Soviet Union, 1964–1982', *Contemporary European History* (2022) (First View).
9 Christel Lane, *The Rites of Rulers: Ritual in Industrial Society – the Soviet Case*, Cambridge, 1981, 69–70.
10 Caroline Humphrey, *Karl Marx Collective: Economy, Society and Religion in a Siberian Collective Farm*, Cambridge, 1983, 383–4.
11 Nakachi, *Replacing the Dead*, 199.
12 Anastasia Novkunskaya, Daria Litvina and Anna Temkina, 'Khamstvo', Global Informality Project: https://www.in-formality.com/wiki/index.php?title=Khamstvo_(USSR,_Russia).
13 Paula A. Michaels, *Lamaze: An International History*, Oxford, 2014, 3–7, 114–40, 141.
14 Evgeniia Albats, interview with Nikolai Solodnikov, 'Eshchenepozner' YouTube channel, 27 May 2021.
15 On adoption and fostering: Catriona Kelly, *Children's World: Growing Up in Russia, 1890–1991*, New Haven, 2007, 269.
16 Mirjam Galley, *Building Communism and Policing Deviance in the Soviet Union: Residential Childcare, 1958–1991*, Abingdon, 2021, 21–2.
17 Marko Dumančić, *Men Out of Focus: The Soviet Masculinity Crisis in the Long Sixties*, Toronto, 2021, chs. 2–3 and 207.
18 Sergei Kukhterin, 'Fathers and Patriarchs in Communist and Post-Communist Russia', in Sarah Ashwin (ed.), *Gender, State and Society in Soviet and Post-Soviet Russia*, London, 2000, 71–89 (76–7).
19 Zhanna Chernova, 'The Model of "Soviet" Fatherhood: Discursive Prescriptions', *Russian Studies in History* 51:2 (2012): 35–62 (43).
20 Anna Rotkirch, *The Man Question: Loves and Lives in Late 20th Century Russia*, Helsinki, 2000, 115–20.
21 Susan Grant and Isaac McKean Scarborough (eds.), *Geriatrics and Ageing in the Soviet Union: Medical, Political and Social Contexts*, London, 2023, 1.
22 Isaac McKean Scarborough, 'A New Science for an Old(er) Population: Soviet Gerontology and Geriatrics in International Comparative Perspective', *Social History of Medicine* 35:4 (2022): 1247–66.
23 Ol'ga Maksimova, 'Starost' ili "tretii vozrast"? diskursy sub"ektivnogo vospriiatiia individami sobstvennykh vozrastnykh izmenenii', *Laboratorium* 12:2 (2020): 22–44 (34).

24 Susan Grant, 'Age Matters: Health, Older People and Gerohygiene in the Late Soviet Union', *Medical History* 66:3 (2022): 207–24.
25 Alissa Klots and Maria Romashova, 'Lenin's Cohort: The First Mass Generation of Soviet Pensioners and Public Activism in the Khrushchev Era', *Kritika* 19:3 (2018): 573–97.
26 Alissa Klots and Maria Romashova, 'Young Minds – Young Bodies: The Emotional and the Physical in the Late Socialist Discourse on Aging', *Soviet and Post-Soviet Review* 48 (2021): 189–210.
27 Stephen Lovell, 'Soviet Russia's Older Generations', in Lovell (ed.), *Generations in Twentieth-Century Europe*, Basingstoke, 2007, 205–26 (212).
28 Victoria Sememova and Paul Thompson, 'Family Models and Transgenerational Influences: Grandparents, Parents and Children in Leningrad from the Soviet to the Market Era', in Daniel Bertaux, Paul Thompson and Anna Rotkirch (eds.), *On Living Through Soviet Russia*, London, 2004, 118–43 (127).
29 Susan Grant, 'A Comfortable Old Age: Designing Care Homes for Older Soviet Persons', in Grant and Scarborough (eds.), *Geriatrics and Ageing*, 91–112.
30 Christopher Mark Davis, 'Developments in the Health Sector of the Soviet Economy, 1970–90', in Joint Economic Committee, United States Congress, 'Gorbachev's Economic Plans, vol. 2: Study Papers Submitted to the Joint Economic Committee, Congress of the United States', Washington, DC, 1987, 317–18, 322.
31 *Narodnoe khoziaistvo SSSR za 70 let: Iubileinyi statisticheskii ezhegodnik*, Moscow, 1987, 409.
32 Riazanov, *Chetyre vechera*, 82 and 89.
33 Diary entry of 13 July 1980: Demidova, *Vladimir Vysotskii*, 106–7.
34 Joy Neumeyer, 'Late Socialism as a Time of Weeping: The Life, Death and Resurrection of Vladimir Vysotskii', *Kritika* 22:3 (2021): 511–33 (517, 530–32).
35 V. I. Novikov, *Vysotskii*, Moscow, 2002, 356–66.
36 Vladimir Soloukhin, 'Sentenced: A Lyrical Documentary' (published in *Moskva*, 1975), in Soloukhin, *Scenes from Russian Life*, trans. David Martin, London, 1988, 20.
37 Sergei Mokhov, 'Care for the Dying in the Late USSR (1970s–80s)', *Zhurnal issledovanii sotsial'noi politiki* 20:2 (2022): 323–34.
38 Riazanov, *Chetyre vechera*, 84.
39 Lane, *Rites of Rulers*, 84–5 and 283–4.
40 Sergei Mokhov, *Death and Funeral Practices in Russia*, London, 2022, 21–4.
41 Catriona Kelly, *St Petersburg: Shadows of the Past*, New Haven, 2014, 320.

## CHAPTER 19: THE LAST REVOLUTIONARY

1 Gorbachev, *Memoirs*, 212. Raisa Gorbacheva, *Ia nadeius'*, Moscow, 1991, 13. The Russian – 'Tak dal'she zhit' nel'zia' – is especially sonorous and rhythmical.
2 Raisa Gorbacheva, *Ia nadeius'*, 13.
3 Taubman, *Gorbachev*.
4 Archie Brown, *The Gorbachev Factor*, Oxford, 1996, 56–7.
5 Hanson, *Rise and Fall*, 5, 174–5.
6 M. V. Konotopov and S. I. Smetanin, *Razvitie ekonomiki Rossii v XVI – XX vekakh. Izbrannye Trudy*, vol. 3: *Istoriia otechestvennoi tekstil'noi promyshlennosti*, St Petersburg, 2018, 401–4.
7 Ryan, *Doctors and the State*, 98–9.
8 Moshe Lewin, *The Gorbachev Phenomenon: A Historical Interpretation*, London, 1988, 112.
9 Rustam Alexander, 'AIDS/HIV and Homophobia in the USSR, 1983–1990', *Kritika* 24:1 (2023): 121–50 (128–32, 149); Murray Feshbach, 'The Early Days of the HIV/AIDS Epidemic in the Former Soviet Union', in Judyth L. Twigg (ed.), *HIV/AIDS in Russia and Eurasia*, vol. 1, New York, 2006, 7–32 (9, 11, 13).
10 Stephen White, *Russia Goes Dry: Alcohol, State and Society*, Cambridge, 1996, 62.
11 *Pravda*, 18 April 1985, 1.
12 Davis, 'Developments', 315.
13 Mark Lawrence Schrad, *Vodka Politics: Alcohol, Autocracy, and the Secret History of the Russian State*, New York, 2014, 263, 265–6, 270, 275.
14 Abel Aganbegyan, *Moving the Mountain: Inside the Perestroika Revolution*, London, 1989, 20–21.
15 Schrad, *Vodka Politics*, 276–7.
16 Serhii Plokhy, *Chernobyl: History of a Tragedy*, London, 2018, 92, 132, 144, 151 and passim.
17 *Pravda*, 15 May 1986, 1.
18 Plokhy's *Chernobyl* makes the case that the disaster led to the collapse of the USSR precisely because of its impact on Ukrainian nationhood.
19 Schlögel, *Soviet Century*, 151.
20 Sonja D. Schmid, *Producing Power: The Pre-Chernobyl History of the Soviet Nuclear Industry*, Cambridge, MA, 2015, 161–2.
21 Schlögel, *Soviet Century*, 155.
22 *Pravda*, 10 June 1986.

23 Mikhail Gorbachev, *Perestroika: New Thinking for Our Country and the World*, London, 1987, 49–51.
24 *Materialy XXVII s"ezda kommunisticheskoi partii sovetskogo soiuza*, Moscow, 1986, 3, 91.
25 Aganbegyan, *Moving the Mountain*, 19.
26 Hanson, *Rise and Fall*, 204, 206, and ch. 7 passim.
27 Mokhov, *Death and Funeral Practices*, 23.
28 Ryan, *Doctor and State*, 104.
29 Vladislav Zubok, *Collapse: The Fall of the Soviet Union*, New Haven, 2021.
30 On Politburo reshuffles, see Taubman, *Gorbachev*, 219–22.
31 Timothy Colton, *Yeltsin: A Life*, New York, 2008, chs. 1–4 passim and esp. 71–3, 83, 99.
32 Boris Yeltsin, *Against the Grain: An Autobiography*, London, 1990, 82–3.
33 Dzarasov, *Moskovskaia pravda*, 3 June 1988, cited in R. W. Davies, *Soviet History in the Gorbachev Revolution*, London, 1989, 121–2.

## CHAPTER 20: PHONE CALL TO GORKY

1 Riazanov, *Chetyre vechera*, 24.
2 Riazanov, *Chetyre vechera*, 82.
3 Alexeyeva and Goldberg, *Thaw Generation*, 306–11.
4 Sakharov, *Memoirs*, 614–16.
5 *Izvestiia*, 6 April 1989.
6 *Pravda*, 8 April 1989.
7 *Izvestiia*, 5 April 1989, 1.
8 Brown, *Gorbachev Factor*, 264–5.
9 Bergman, *Meeting the Demands of Reason*, 372–82.
10 *Pravda*, 5 April 1988.
11 Anatoly Sobchak, *For a New Russia: The Mayor of St Petersburg's Own Story of the Struggle for Justice and Democracy*, London, 1991, 104–9.
12 M. Steven Fish, *Democracy from Scratch: Opposition and Regime in the New Russian Revolution*, Princeton, 1995.
13 M. Steven Fish, *Democracy Derailed in Russia: The Failure of Open Politics*, Cambridge, 2005, 4.
14 Angus Roxburgh, *The Second Russian Revolution*, London, 1991.
15 Bergman, *Meeting the Demands of Reason*, 384–90.
16 *Sovetskie profsoiuzy*, 1987, 15:28.
17 Galeotti, *The Vory*, 101.

18 Hanson, *Rise and Fall*, 205.
19 Yoram Gorlizki, 'Structures of Trust after Stalin', *Slavonic and East European Review* 91:1 (2013): 119–46.
20 Smith, *Property of Communists*, chs. 4 and 5.
21 On information asymmetry, incentivized opportunism and property relations, see Stephen Solnick, *Stealing the State: Control and Collapse in Soviet Institutions*, Cambridge, MA, 1999.
22 Stephen Kotkin, *Armageddon Averted: The Soviet Collapse, 1970–2000*, Oxford, 2001.
23 Michael Ellman, 'The Increase in Death and Disease under Catastroika', *Cambridge Journal of Economics* 18:4 (1994): 329–55: table 7.
24 Donald A. Filzer, *Soviet Workers and the Collapse of Perestroika: The Soviet Labour Process and Gorbachev's Reforms, 1985–1991*, Cambridge, 1994, 73.
25 Filtzer, *Soviet Workers and Perestroika*, 64.
26 Aganbegyan, *Moving the Mountain*, 174–5.
27 Aganbegyan, *Moving the Mountain*, 175.
28 Miller, *Struggle to Save the Soviet Economy*, 6.
29 https://www.nobelprize.org/prizes/peace/1990/gorbachev/acceptance-speech/.
30 Feliks Chuev, *Tak govoril Kaganovich: ispoved' stalinskogo apostola*, Moscow, 1992, 210, 201.
31 Anatol Lieven writes that it was an armoured personnel carrier (*The Baltic Revolution: Estonia, Latvia, Lithuania and the Path to Independence*, New Haven, 1994, 251); Lithuanian government publicity materials describe it as a tank.
32 Kristina Spohr, *Post Wall, Post Square: Rebuilding the World After 1989*, London, 2019, 569.

## CHAPTER 21: THE END OF SOVIET CIVILIZATION

1 Courtney Doucette, 'Glasnost in the Mailroom: the Soviet Subject in Gorbachev's *Perestroika*', *Soviet and Post-Soviet Review* 48 (2021): 171–88.
2 Natalia Roudakova, *Losing Pravda: Ethics and the Press in Post-Truth Russia*, Cambridge, 2017, ch. 1.
3 *Pravda*, 20 August 1991, 1.
4 N.a., *Putsch, The Diary: Three Days that Collapsed the Empire*, London, 54.
5 Archie Brown posited thirty years at a talk at the School of Slavonic and East European Studies, University College London, *c.* 2005.

6 The opposite argument is that de-Stalinization led directly to Soviet collapse thirty-five years later. Cf. the discussion in Stephen V. Bittner, 'What's in a Name? De-Stalinisation and the End of the Soviet Union', in Thomas M. Bohn, Rayk Einax and Michel Abesser (eds.), *De-Stalinisation Reconsidered: Persistence and Change in the Soviet Union*, Frankfurt-on-Main, 2014, 31–42.

7 Mariia Zezina, 'Nekotorye voprosy istoricheskoi rekonstruktsii sovetskoi zhizni', *Otechestvennaia istoriia*, 5 (2019): 19–24 (23).

8 See, e.g., Leon Aron, *Roads to the Temple: Truth, Memory, Ideas and Ideals in the Making of the Russian Revolution, 1987–1991*, New Haven, 2012.

9 See, e.g., Arkady Ostrovsky, *The Invention of Russia: The Journey from Gorbachev's Freedom to Putin's War*, London, 2016, chs. 1–5.

10 Tamara Eydelman, 'The Year of Utopias Realised: Schools, Teachers and Educational Reformers in 1990', in Irina Prokhorova (ed.), *1990: Russians Remember a Turning Point*, London, 2013, 74–102 (75).

11 Il'ia Ven'iavkin, 'Svidetel'stva kolpashevskogo iara', *Inliberty* blog, 9 November 2015, https://old.inliberty.ru/blog/2081-Svidetelstva-kolpashevskogo-yara (accessed 13 June 2021).

12 Chuev, *Tak govoril Kaganovich*, 66, 158.

13 Vladimir Shlapentokh, *A Normal Totalitarian Society: How the Soviet Union Functioned and How It Collapsed*, Armonk, 2001.

14 Feature on 'Sotsialisticheskii gorod. Kakim emu byt', *Arkhitektura SSSR* (September–October 1987): 30–37.

15 Kon, *Sexual Revolution in Russia*, 110–11.

16 John Bushnell, *Moscow Graffiti: Language and Subculture*, Winchester, MA, 1990, 140.

17 Dina Fainberg, *Cold War Correspondents: Soviet and American Reporters on the Ideological Frontlines*, Baltimore, 2020, 241–54.

18 Krista A. Goff, *Nested Nationalism: Making and Unmaking Nations in the Soviet Caucasus*, Ithaca, 2020.

19 Taubman, *Gorbachev*, 614–19.

20 Eugenia Belova and Valery Lazarev, *Funding Loyalty: The Economics of the Communist Party*, New Haven, 2012, p. 152.

21 Christopher Clark, *Revolutionary Spring: Fighting for a New World, 1848–1849*, London, 2023, 540.

22 Isaac McKean Scarborough, 'The Extremes It Takes to Survive: Tajikistan and the Collapse of the Soviet Union, 1985–1992', PhD dissertation, London School of Economics and Political Science, 2018, 205.

23 Victoria Clement, *Learning to Become Turkmen: Literacy, Language and Power, 1914–2014*, Pittsburgh, 2018, 119.
24 Clark, *Revolutionary Spring*, 541.
25 Serhii Plokhy, *The Last Empire: The Final Days of the Soviet Union*, London, 2014, 292–3.
26 Catherine Belton, *Putin's People: How the KGB Took Back Russia and then Took On the West*, London, 2020, ch. 2.
27 See Solnick, *Stealing the State*; and Kotkin, *Armageddon Averted*.
28 Plokhy, *The Last Empire*, 208–9.
29 E. Abeliuk and E. Leenson (eds.), *Taganka: lichnoe delo odnogo teatra*, Moscow, 2007, 359.

## AFTERWORD

1 Then and during the war which soon followed, essential voices describing Russia included the social scientists Grigory Yudin (Moscow School of Social and Economic Sciences) and Jeremy Morris (Aarhus University), the BBC's Steve Rosenberg, Ekaterina Gordeeva and her many interviewees on her YouTube channel, and the journalists of TV Rain and *Novaya gazeta*, whose editor, Dmitry Muratov, won the Nobel Peace Prize in 2021.

# *Acknowledgements*

This book draws directly and indirectly on many years of primary research in Moscow and elsewhere, but it also rests on a comprehensive (though inevitably incomplete) reading of the secondary literature. I make use of no material published after August 2023, when I completed the first extremely long draft of this book. I acknowledge my debt to the work of the many historians whom I cite in the endnotes and apologize for any inadvertent omissions, including to those not cited as I reduced the word-length but whose influence on my work remains. I am also grateful for the professionalism and kindness of the many librarians and archivists who made this project possible. Over the longer-than-expected period it took to write this book, I built up many debts to my editors for their patience, encouragement, wisdom and expertise: to Simon Winder at Penguin Books, and Dan Gerstle at Norton / Liveright. I am similarly indebted to Andrew Gordon of David Higham Associates and George Lucas of Inkwell Management. I owe thanks to David Watson, who copyedited the text, and Cecilia Mackay, who worked on the pictures, and to the teams who supported me at Penguin and Norton. I would like to thank colleagues in Cambridge who helped me with my Faculty work in the very difficult circumstances of 2021 and 2022, when this project was effectively suspended, including Alex Walsham and Bill Foster. Chris Clark kindly read the manuscript. My work depended on the enduring support of my parents, and above all on the everyday presence of my daughter Sonia, whose life-force and wit allowed me to complete the text.

I would not have written this book or become a historian were it not for my wife, Larisa (Laura) Shikova. She was diagnosed with cancer while I was working on my last book and died while I was writing this one. After her death, I decided hundreds of times to abandon *Exit Stalin*; in the way of grief, I completed it because I wanted to show it to her. This book is dedicated to the memory of Larisa Shikova with a sense of overwhelming loss, but also with endless love and gratitude, as the smallest tribute to her many brilliant qualities.

# Index

abdication, Nicholas II 20
abortion 24, 30, 229–30, 389
Abramov, Fyodor 262
Abu Dhabi 101
Academy of Sciences 117, 124–5, 199, 207, 211, 302, 321, 344, 356, 433, 461
   Academy of Medical Sciences 228
   Research Institute of Economics 344
   Research Institute of Genetics 82
   Research Institute of History 65
   Tsiolkovsky Gold Medal 80
Aeroflot 178, 275, 338 (illustration), 345–8, 354
Afghan War 191, 355–6, 406, 409, 434
agricultural collectivization 30, 32, 41, 43, 64, 157, 351, 371, 420
Akademgorodok 234, 315, 321
Akhmadulina, Bella 106, 152
Aksenov, Vasily 84
alcohol 19, 160, 221, 252, 260, 328, 370, 380, 395, 409–12, 422, 470
Aleksy (Patriarch) 126–7
Alexander II 57
Alexeyeva, Lyudmila 200, 205, 209–10, 258, 268

Alexievich, Svetlana 8
All-People's State 103
Alma-Ata (Almaty) 87, 165
Altai 88, 265
Amalrik, Aleksei 267–8, 286
American National Exhibition, Moscow 118
Andropov, Yuri 17, 165, 173, 180–9, 195, 213, 215, 247, 250, 254, 310, 317, 354–5, 357–8, 365–8, 381, 398, 406–7, 409–10, 419–20, 429, 455
Anti-Party Group 69, 158
antisemitism 38, 47, 128, 197, 207, 213, 307, 312
Aral Sea 161
Arbat (Moscow) 6, 105, 142, 189, 203–4, 249, 264, 349, 373
Arctic 10, 108, 122, 161–2, 254
Arkhangelsk 39, 161, 167, 248
Armenia 25, 150, 181, 304–5, 313–5, 317, 343, 394, 416, 463, 466
Armstrong, Neil 173
Artek Pioneer Camp 110–11, 122, 258
article 58 34, 54, 134, 371
Arzamas-16 207, 239
Ashkhabad 207, 258
Astrakhan 78

# INDEX

Aswan Dam 122
Azerbaijan 180, 327, 407, 463, 466

Babarinsk 205
Baberowski, Jörg 11
Babitsky, Konstantin 197
Baghdad 101, 302
bagmen 24
Baikal, Lake 128, 258, 293, 336
Baikal-Amur Railway (BAM) 281, 284, 324
Baikonur *see* Tyura-Tam
Bakhmut 21, 480
Baku 180, 251, 315, 354
*Ballad of a Soldier* (Grigory Chukrai) 140
Baltic (states, republics) 10, 12, 18, 38, 200, 206, 304, 306, 346, 371, 378, 445, 465–6
Barashev, Pavel 178
Barbarossa, Operation 36, 38
Barvikha (Moscow Region) 79
Bauman, Karl 33
Bayeva, Tatyana 197–8, 203
Belarus 8, 126, 140, 260, 291, 307, 466, 468, 470, 474, 476
Belgrade 89
Beria, Lavrenty 53–4, 59, 134, 179–80, 185–6, 258, 316, 366
Berlin 37, 40, 68
  Berlin Wall 121, 446
  East Berlin 308
*beryozka* shop 248, 326
Bessarabia 38
Bevin, Ernest 69
Binyon, Michael 225
Black Sea 79, 110, 119, 122, 150
blind people 223, 401
Bloody Sunday 3

Bogoraz, Larisa 197, 202, 204–5, 215, 429
Bolsheviks *see* Russian Social Democratic and Labour Party
Bonn 232, 276
Bonner, Elena 196 (illustration), 346–7, 356, 430, 437, 451
Brasilia 104
Bratsk 252, 258, 293
Brecht, Bertolt 143
Breslauer, George W. 286
Brest-Litovsk, Treaty of 22, 114
Brezhnev, Leonid 17, 130, 132 (illustration), 150–51, 156–8, 164–7, 169–71, 174, 180–82, 184, 190–91, 194, 208, 238, 240, 250, 254–5, 279, 282–3, 290, 294, 296, 301, 305, 307, 319–20, 322, 332, 334, 347, 349–50, 354–5, 361, 364–6, 370, 398, 401, 419, 445
Brezhnev, Yuri 156
Brezhnev Doctrine 295
Brezhnev generation 170, 181, 188, 191, 393
Brezhneva, Galina 156, 165, 370
Brezhneva, Viktoriya 156
Britain 52, 83–4, 86, 113, 116, 220, 297, 398, 465
  London 70, 115, 119, 130, 232
Brodsky, Joseph 167, 203, 214, 266–7
Brook, Peter 115
Bukhara 396
Bukharin, Nikolai, 22
Bulganin, Nikolai 59–61, 63, 70, 116
Bulgaria 10, 122, 308
Bulldozer exhibition 260–61
Bush, George H. W. 296, 365, 423, 468, 481
butter 1
*byt* 8

Cambridge, University of 83–4, 123
cancer 81, 136, 168, 172, 223–6, 235, 273, 339, 397–8, 473, 478
car production 252
le Carré, John 193
Caspian Sea 128
Castro, Fidel 122, 178
Caucasus 2, 5, 10, 18, 31, 37, 39, 79, 161, 219, 313, 351, 354, 379, 394, 409, 503n9
   Transcaucasian republic 25, 470
Central Asia 10, 25, 29, 39, 114, 126, 128, 161, 245, 273, 306, 311–3, 378–9, 387–8, 393–4, 396, 409, 463, 466
Central Committee
   Agriculture 355
   Culture Department 138
   International Department 177, 355
   Komsomol 300
   Plenum 103, 164, 171, 296, 310, 350
   Science Department 202
   Turkmenistan 258
   Ukraine 36
   USSR 63, 65, 67, 69, 94, 100, 125–6, 138, 147–8, 157, 165–7, 181–2, 248, 250, 273, 334, 353, 363, 407, 419, 421, 467
   Uzbekistan 422
central planning 1, 8, 29, 130, 171, 220, 222, 223, 240, 243, 244, 344, 345, 416, 417, 439, 443
Chair of Presidium of Supreme Soviet (head of state) *see* Supreme Soviet
Chechen-Ingush ASSR 39, 113, 134, 145, 315, 369
Chechnya *see* Chechen-Ingush ASSR

Cheka 21, 113–14, 179, 182, 185, 275, 366
Cherenkov, Pavel 123
Chernenko, Konstantin 17, 350, 354, 366, 381, 395, 398, 407
Chernyshova, Natalia 239
Chimkent 206
China 122, 273, 301, 303–4, 383, 408, 443
Chistopol 429
Chita 145
Christianity 20, 96, 127–8, 160, 316
   the Bible 20, 128, 178
*Chronicle of Current Events* 199, 214
Chukchi 163, 248, 508n29
Chukovskaya, Lydia 217
Chuvash ASSR 188
Civil War 22–4, 28, 31, 126, 135, 179, 192, 222, 291, 314, 393, 399, 423
Cliburn, Van 118
Cold War 10, 43–4, 80, 83, 97, 114, 117–19, 122, 129, 161, 190, 234, 279, 296, 308, 320, 348, 355, 357–8, 370, 413, 423, 446, 456, 469, 484n9
collective, *kollektiv* 42, 57, 59, 96, 169, 186, 227, 294, 330, 337, 362, 368, 408–9, 461, 478
collective farms 30, 52, 60, 66, 73–4, 88, 98, 108, 110, 127, 146, 150, 169, 171, 247, 272, 292, 353, 399, 421, 476
collective leadership 11, 59–60, 68–9
Commissariat of Enlightenment 26
communal apartments 25, 104, 169, 267, 272, 307

communes 24, 30, 360 (illustration)
comrades' courts 101, 230, 337, 372
Congress of People's Deputies 426 (illustration), 424, 434–6, 442, 454
conscription 190–91
Constituent Assembly 21
consumer goods, consumerism *see* consumption
consumption 8–9, 11, 60, 96, 118, 121, 150, 158, 160, 238–9, 240, 242–7, 253, 316, 328, 363, 367, 369, 378, 391, 411, 421, 442, 446
contraception 230, 389
convergence paradigm 106, 208, 234, 239, 303
convicts *see* zeks
corn *see* maize
Cossacks 1, 3, 22, 142
Council of Ministers 60–61, 69, 80, 100, 134, 166, 179–80, 226, 419
*Cranes are Flying, The* (Mikhail Kalatozov) 119, 140
Crick, Francis 123–4
Crimea 31, 37, 77, 89, 122, 139, 165, 364, 450
  Crimean Tartars 39, 134, 141, 202, 315
Cuba 10, 122, 177, 194, 309, 317
Cuban Missile Crisis 146–7, 301
cuisine 159, 306, 316
Czechoslovakia 10, 121, 167, 197, 200, 217, 232, 241, 308, 437

dachas 45, 53, 78–80, 149, 151, 164–5, 193, 217–18, 237, 246, 248–50, 253–5, 257, 260, 274, 328, 342, 355, 365, 369, 422, 440, 450

Dagestan 145
*Days and Nights* 142
*Days of Surgeon Mishkin, The* 227
deaf people 380
  All-Russian Society for the Deaf (VOG) 223, 336
decolonization *see* empire
*dedovshchina* 191
deficit 7, 30, 44, 100, 102, 105, 121, 146, 164, 169, 214, 221, 231, 239, 242, 244, 246, 248, 266, 316, 327, 387, 391, 395, 409, 411, 438, 441, 459
Dekulakization 30–31, 157, 265, 399
Delonye, Vadim 197, 215
Demidova, Alla 261, 264–5, 396
demobilization (1945–) 44, 190
democracy 19, 24, 35, 96, 117, 122, 200, 285–6, 322–3, 331–6, 415–16, 418, 424, 432, 434–6, 441, 443, 450, 452, 469
democratization 367, 432, 435–6, 443, 452
dentistry 221, 227, 408
department stores 241–2, 309, 410
deportations (national) 39, 41, 46, 114, 134, 141, 290, 315
de-Stalinization 9, 13, 53, 54–5, 61, 64, 66–9, 79, 81, 114, 117, 129, 142, 144–5, 167, 184, 189, 202–3, 209, 239, 255, 257–8, 335, 342, 352, 528n6
Dickens, Charles 85
*Die Welt* 121
Dneproderzhinsk 156–7
Dobkin, Aleksandr 214
Dobkina, Natalia, 214
Doctors' Plot 46–7, 53
Donbass 20–21, 24, 28

DOSAAF (Volunteer Society for the Army, Air Force and Navy) 191
Dremliuga, Vladimir 197
*druzhiny* (volunteer patrols) 101, 230, 337
Dubček, Alexander 167
Dubinin, Nikolai 234
Dudintsev, Vladimir 162
Duma, State (Russian empire) 19
Duma, State (Russian Federation) 476
Dunayeva, Lydia 224
Dushanbe 311
Dymshits, Mark 346
Dzerzhinsky, Feliks 179, 185
Dzhambul 224

East Germany *see* Germany
Eastern bloc 60, 62, 67, 101, 113, 119, 121–2, 171–2, 182, 240, 246, 308–9, 311, 357, 434, 457, 469
Edelman, Tamara 455
Eden, Sir Anthony 70, 116
education reform (1958) 149–50, 391
Efroimson, Vladimir 125
Ehrenburg, Ilya 57, 84, 118
Eisenhower, Dwight 121
electrification 26, 293, 392
empire (Soviet empire) 10–12, 106, 297, 300, 303–4, 306, 308, 311, 316–17, 395, 451, 463–4
  decolonization 10–12, 117, 446, 451, 463–4
  Russian empire 17–19, 22, 25, 73, 82, 156, 200, 212, 227, 313, 330, 449
Engels (town) 76
Engels, Frederick 280, 333
equality (social and economic) 14, 29, 109–11, 129–30, 149, 156,
165–6, 208, 246, 250, 254, 302, 306, 325–6, 370, 408
*uravnilovka* ('obsessive levelling') 109, 325
Erofeyev, Venedikt 252
Estonia 10, 150, 217, 228, 232, 239, 321, 363
evacuees (wartime) 36, 38, 45, 207, 291, 400
Exhibition of Economic Achievements *see* VDNKh

Fainberg, Viktor 197–8, 202
Falk, Robert 130
famine
  Civil War 23
  Kazakhstan 31, 41, 311
  Leningrad 48
  Moldavia 41
  Russian republic 31, 41
  Ukraine 31, 41, 64, 141
fatherhood 384–5, 391
Fedin, Konstantin 168
Feodosiya 89
Finland 38, 117, 181, 237, 279, 302, 463
Finnish Ingrians 463
First World War 19–20
Firyubin, Nikolai 99
Fonteyn, Margot 115
food prices 1, 146, 169, 173, 206, 238, 441
football 116, 179, 187, 271, 380
*Foreign Literature* (journal) 119
'former people' 24
Foundation to Combat Corruption 476
France 37, 117, 309, 390, 396, 460
Frank, Ilya 123

Frunze (city) 206
Fürst, Juliane 375
Furtseva, Ekaterina 88–90,94, 99–100, 120, 126, 132 (illustration), 133, 148, 266, 270, 309, 420

Gagarina, Anna 73–5
Gagarin, Yuri 72 (illustration), 73–6, 80, 87, 88–90, 93–4, 97–8, 127, 174, 177–8, 191, 197, 202, 299, 339, 352, 356
Gaitskell, Hugh 116
Galich, Aleksandr 202
Gandhi 200
GDR *see* Germany
genetics 82–3, 123–6, 233–5
Georgia 17, 25, 51, 53, 67, 145, 150, 219, 278 (illustration), 306–8, 313, 316, 370, 384, 416, 434, 454, 463, 466
Germany 11, 22, 36–7, 39–43, 48, 53, 56, 58, 73, 78, 81, 113–14, 119, 121, 134, 151, 156, 193, 209, 224, 229, 239, 254, 287, 351, 400, 477
    GDR 10, 121, 159, 185–6, 232, 308, 314
    West Germany 237, 275, 284, 302, 349, 357, 381, 413
Gerö, Ernö 67
Ginzburg, Aleksandr 199
*glasnost* 414–16, 424, 428, 435–6, 449, 452–4, 459–60, 469
Glavlit 263–4
Glitsiniya (State Dacha Number 1) 165
Gorbachev, Mikhail 7, 9–10, 12, 17, 51, 63, 170, 173, 202, 206, 280, 358, 365, 370, 401
    and Andropov 182, 366–8
    and Chernenko 350, 354, 381
    and the Cold War 423
    comes to power 405–7
    and human rights 296
    move to Moscow 350, 354–5
    and *perestroika* 409–12, 414–20, 424, 432, 434–6, 438–9
    and politics of 1990–91 442–6, 450, 452–4, 456–8, 464–7, 469–70
    and Sakharov 430–31, 434
    and Secret Speech 66, 352
    and Stavropol 252, 352–4
    and Yeltsin 420–22
    youth and family 308, 351–2
Gorbacheva, Raisa 308, 351–5, 405–6, 442, 464
Gorbanevskaya, Natalya 197–200, 202, 215, 297, 299
Gorky (city and region) 146, 231, 355–6, 406, 430–31, 434
Gorky Studio 192–3, 283
Nizhny Novgorod 18
Gorky, Maksim 266
Gorky Institute for World Literature, Moscow 269
Gorlovka-Shcherbinovka soviet 21
Gosbank 438
Goskino 262–3, 348
Gosplan 1, 29, 63, 117, 150
'goulash communism' 170
grain 30, 169, 238, 294, 361
grandmothers 101, 115, 159, 269, 392, 394
Granin, Daniil 57–9, 68, 85–8, 119, 125, 218, 291
Great Fatherland War 10, 42, 44, 126, 140–41, 179, 190, 192, 228, 290
Great Terror *see* Terror

Grossman, Vasily 6, 40–42
Grozny 145
GRU (military intelligence) 189–91, 309
Gruson, Claude 117
Gulag 6, 31, 41, 46, 50 (illustration), 52–4, 60, 66, 77–9, 124–5, 130, 134–9, 141, 152, 161, 179, 183, 187, 189, 205, 217–18, 232, 234, 273–4, 311, 321, 369, 371
Gzhatsk 73–4, 80

*habeas corpus* 65, 111
Havel, Václav 286, 437
Hayter, Sir William 70
healthcare 10, 45, 84, 107, 182, 219–22, 226, 229, 230
Helsinki 72 (illustration), 279, 302
   Helsinki Accords 279–80, 284, 294–6, 429
   Helsinki Watch 296
Hemingway, Ernest 119, 194
Hero
   Cities 290
   Mothers 30
   of Socialist Labour 79, 326, 356
   of the Soviet Union 177, 326
higher education institutes (*vuz*) 211
hockey 122, 253
*Holodomor see* famine: Ukraine
homosexuality 232–3, 363, 379
Hope, Bob 118
Hosking, Geoffrey 307
housing 7, 25, 43–5, 85, 95, 100–103, 107, 110, 134, 173, 187, 190, 221, 231, 237, 250–52, 269–70, 302, 327, 329, 363, 373, 386–7, 392, 394, 400, 439–40, 457, 459
Hughes, John 18

Hugo, Victor 85
Hungary 10, 170, 172, 181, 199, 308, 418
   Hungarian Revolution 10, 67–8, 116, 121, 185, 199

*I am Twenty* (*Ilyich's Gate*, Marlen Khutsiev) 203–4
*I Walk Around Moscow* 251–2
Ikramov, Kamil 142
indigenization 26
industrialization *see* industry
industry 7, 8, 18, 20–21 28–32, 34, 38, 43–5, 60, 64, 109–11, 158, 162, 171, 181, 186, 233, 238, 245–6, 291, 305, 311, 321, 324–5, 328–9, 340, 342, 367, 371, 383–4, 393, 399, 417, 420, 433, 439
inflation 173, 238, 244, 417
Ingushetia *see* Chechen-Ingush ASSR
Institute of Scientific Atheism 129
intelligentsia 13, 22, 85, 104, 118–19, 125, 128, 130, 150, 164, 167, 197, 200, 204–7, 210–12, 214, 249, 257, 260, 265, 268, 272, 313, 323, 330, 351–2, 367, 386, 392, 427–8, 430, 479
International Social Security Association (ISSA) 117, 302, 341
International Union of Architects 105
internationalism 96, 117, 312
Intourist 119
Irkusk 59, 348, 389, 394
*Irony of Fate or Congratulations on a Light Steam!, The* (Eldar Ryazanov) 160, 228, 238, 271, 427, 471

Islam 126, 128, 312, 356, 410
Italy 38, 271, 287, 309
Ivashutin, Pyotr 189

Jewish Anti-Fascist Committee 47
Jewish people 17, 28, 38, 41–2, 46–7, 83, 128, 141, 181, 193, 198–9, 203, 267, 312–15, 317, 344, 346, 377–8, 463
Jewish Theatre, Moscow 46, 203

Kaganovich, Lazar 28, 30–33, 55, 59, 62, 68–9, 100, 148, 444–6
Kalashnikov, Anatoly 286
Kalinovka 17–18, 23
Kamchatka 126
Kamenev, Lev 27
Kamenskoye *see* Dneproderzhinsk
Kapustin Yar 78–9
Kara-Murza, Vladimir 479
Karelia 162, 181, 463
Karetnikova, Anna 63, 66
Kataev, Valentin 33, 282, 297
Katyn massacre 38
Kazakhstan 26, 31, 39, 41, 69, 75, 136, 145, 155, 157, 165, 206, 228, 305, 311, 313, 315, 332
Kazan 17, 78, 128, 199, 347
Kazan Church (New Maiden, Leningrad) 378
Kazandzhik 59
Kekkonen, Urho 237
Kelly, Catriona 375
Kennedy, Edward (Ted) 194
Kennedy, John F. 121
KGB 2–5, 64, 67, 69, 70, 81, 102, 107, 113, 120, 127, 130, 146, 147, 167, 179, 179–89, 191, 193, 195, 197–200, 205–6, 210, 213–15, 217–18, 230, 232, 234, 247, 249, 255, 259–62, 267–8, 273–4, 303, 309–10, 316, 330, 344, 346, 352–4, 356, 358, 362–3, 366, 368, 376, 398, 405, 419, 421–2, 428, 430, 441, 450–51, 467–8
Khabarovsk 188, 248, 279, 347–8, 433
Kharkiv 28, 37
Khrushchev, Nikita 14, 69–70
  overcomes Anti-Party Group 68–9
  and army 146–7, 190
  childhood and youth 17–20
  and collective leadership 59–61
  communist vision 94–5, 107–8
  death 254–5
  on equality 149–50
  fall from power 150–52
  foreign interactions 116, 120–21, 130
  and Furtseva 89, 100
  and Gagarin 76
  on housing 101–4
  and Hungarian Revolution 67–8
  and KGB 180
  life and career before 1953 16 (illustration), 21–8, 31–7, 43–5, 48, 480
  and Lysenko 124
  at Manezh exhibition 130
  and maize (corn) 145
  mother 18–20
  and Neizvestny 258–9
  and Nixon 118
  Novocherkassk 3
  opposition to 144, 146–8, 365
  and Pasternak 81
  and religion 126, 129

in retirement 237, 248–50, 253
and Sakharov 207, 209
gives Secret Speech 61–5, 141; and at Twenty-second Congress 133
and Serov 113–4
and Solzhenitsyn 138–9
and Ukraine 17
and Vysotsky 259–60
and Yevtushenko 257–8
Khrushchev, Sergei (father) 18, 149
Khrushchev, Sergei (son) 120, 149, 249, 254–5, 259
Khrushcheva, Nina 32, 249, 260
Khrushcheva, Yefrosinia 19, 23
kindergarten 100, 251, 363, 384, 389, 481
King, Martin Luther 200
Kirgiz republic 206
Kishinev (Chișinău) 157
Kislovodsk 79, 135, 354
Kohl, Helmut 446
Kok-Terek 224
Kolesnikova, Maria 475
*kolkhoz see* collective farms
Kolyma 77
*kommunalka see* communal apartments
Komsomol 59, 66, 74, 135, 180–81, 211, 280, 285, 300, 333, 351–2, 385, 441
Konev, Ivan 36
Kopelev, Lev 136–8, 202
Kopyonkin, Aleksei 190
*korenizatsiia see* indigenization
Korolev, Sergei 74–80, 88–9, 98–100, 135, 173–4, 177
Kosior, Stanislav 31–2
Kostolevsky, Igor 192

Kosygin, Aleksei 166, 170–72, 174, 182, 250, 254, 288, 304, 344, 383, 419
economic reform 171–3, 238–9, 367, 416, 418
Kosygina, Klavdiya 172
Kotkin, Stephen 8, 286
Kovrigina, Maria 229
Kozhevnikov, Vadim 192
Kozlov, Frol 3, 5
Kozlov, Vladimir 145
Krasnodar 37, 145
Krasnoyarsk 92 (illustration)
Kremlin (Moscow) 1, 34, 36, 99, 100, 130, 207, 249, 250, 254, 264, 275, 290, 304, 350, 354, 379, 383, 386, 422, 470
Hall of the Supreme Soviet in Great Kremlin Palace 63
Kremlin Hospital 175, 226, 381
Kremlin Polyclinic Number 1 254
Kremlin Wall (burial place) 133, 365
New Year venue 93, 158
Palace of Congresses 93, 104, 154 (illustration), 158, 288, 415, 434
as political venue 18, 26, 62, 63, 68, 93, 98, 120, 121, 151, 174, 255, 294, 366, 415
as residence 27, 165
Krivoi Rog 145, 497n13
Kronstadt 23–4
Kryuchkov, Vladimir 184
*Kuban Cossacks, The* 142
Kudepsta 79
Kukharchuk, Nina *see* Khrushcheva, Nina
Kurochkin, B. N. 2
Kursk 17, 58, 87, 124, 156
Kuznetsov, Anatoly 141, 267–8

Kuznetsov, Eduard 346
Kyiv 16 (illustration), 18, 28, 32,
  35–6, 43, 45, 59, 77, 124, 141,
  149, 163, 239, 254, 267, 290,
  310, 344, 347, 394, 399, 412,
  433, 469

Lagos 101, 302
Laktionov, Aleksandr 130
Landau, Lev 123
late socialism 12, 474
Latvia 10, 33, 188, 228, 230, 232,
  243, 461
*Le Figaro* 129
Lebedev, Vladimir 138–9
legitimacy (political) 2, 9, 13, 21,
  85, 166, 173, 275, 295, 332,
  334, 370, 372, 437, 440, 446,
  456, 460, 476
Lenin, Vladimir xiv (illustration),
  11, 17, 21–2, 24–7, 51, 64,
  90, 129, 133, 155, 181, 266,
  280, 293, 333, 353, 365, 371,
  385, 392, 410, 415, 418,
  421–4
  Lenin Hills, Moscow 164, 250,
    287–8
  Lenin Prize 99, 140
  Lenin Stadium, Moscow, 363
  Lenin's Mausoleum 51, 133, 140,
    364
  Order of Lenin 46, 79, 113, 177,
    281, 326, 351, 354, 393
Leninakan 343
Leningrad 27, 36, 39, 44, 48, 52,
  57–9, 63, 66, 85–7, 119, 140,
  160, 162, 167, 183, 188, 199,
  214, 223, 232, 239, 245, 248,
  266–7, 281, 285, 288, 291,
  302, 306, 313, 321, 346–8,
  378–80, 383–5, 387, 407, 424,
  435–6, 462, 471
  Blockade 48, 66, 140
  Leningrad Affair 45, 66
  Petrograd 21, 23, 156, 449
  Piskarevskoye cemetery 140
  St Petersburg 18, 24, 73,
    170, 304
Leninism (see also Marxism-
  Leninism) 44, 48, 96, 101, 133,
  280, 284, 415, 418, 432
Leonov, Aleksei 299–301
Leonov, Yevgeny 168–9, 324–5,
  373, 383–5, 392
Levitan, Yuri 73, 272
Liberman, Yevsei 171
Lioznova, Tatyana 192
literacy 26, 33
Lithuania 10, 185–6, 228, 305, 445
Litvinov, Pavel 197–8, 200, 202–3
Lollobrigida, Gina 89–90
Lubyanka 6, 135, 182, 184–5, 189,
  195, 259, 366, 379
Lugansk / Luhansk *see*
  Voroshilovgrad
Lukashenko, Aleksandr 474–5
Lviv 4, 10, 45, 310, 378
Lysenko, Trofim 124–5, 234
Lyubimov, Yuri 142, 143, 262, 266,
  386, 428, 431, 471

Magadan 6, 77, 162
Magnitogorsk 8
maize (corn) 120, 145–6
Malenkov, Georgi, 46, 53–4, 59–61,
  68–9, 77, 100, 149
Manezh exhibition (1962) 130, 257,
  258, 260
Marchenko, Anatoly 205, 215, 423,
  429–31

Marxism-Leninism 8–9, 12, 18, 27, 32, 55–6, 67, 129, 211, 239, 251, 281–2, 293, 310–11, 373, 408, 452–3
masculinity 55, 89, 191, 227–8, 300, 348, 391
meat
  as cuisine 159
  consumption 442
  prices 1, 2
  production 95, 146
Medical-Labour Expert Commissions 223
Meir, Golda 46
Mensheviks *see* Russian Social Democratic and Labour Party
microdistricts 100, 251, 312, 373, 459
Mikhailov, Andrei 163
Mikhoels, Solomon 46
Mikoyan, Anastas 3–4, 59–60, 110, 139, 151
Ministry of Health 84, 229–30, 409
Ministry of Internal Affairs (MVD) 3, 187–8, 230, 363, 372
Minsk 45–6, 102, 135, 225, 237, 306, 368, 475
Moiseyenko, Konstantin 27
Moldavia 10, 41, 127, 157, 145, 165, 429, 466
Moldova *see* Moldavia
*Molodaia gvardiya* 141, 290
Molotov (city and region, Perm) 420
Molotov, Vyacheslav 27, 46–7, 53–5, 59, 62, 68–9, 100, 250, 282, 456
Molotov–Ribbentrop Pact *see* Nazi-Soviet Pact
Monchegorsk 161, 164

Mongolia 69, 122, 128, 250, 303, 389
*Morning Round* (Aida Manasarova) 228
Moscow (*also passim*)
  Bauman Institute 60, 77
  Baumansky raion 33
  Bolshoi Theatre 53, 63, 93, 115, 270, 350, 379
  Butyrka Prison 77, 200
  Danilovsky market 247
  Detsky Mir 159
  Dinamo district 203
  Dinamo Moscow 187
  Frunzensky raion 107
  Gorky Street 57, 99, 104, 204, 247–8, 350, 366, 422, 481
  Granovsky Street 99–100, 149, 172, 250, 254, 366, 383
  Hall of Columns 51, 288, 354
  Herzen Oncological Institute 228
  House of Government 34, 149, 188
  Industrial Academy 32
  Institute of Oriental Studies 193
  *Izvestiya* Building 104
  Kalinin Prospekt 105, 264
  Krasnopresnensky raion 33
  Kremlin *see* Kremlin
  Kutuzovsky Prospekt 165, 182, 250, 281, 366
  Marble Hall, Moscow Soviet 173
  Mayakovsky Square 107
  Mayakovsky Theatre 169, 385
  Metro 33, 165, 190, 251–2, 481
  Metropole Hotel 350
  Moscow Arts Theatre (MKhAT) 115, 142, 204, 227
  Moscow State Institute of International Relations (MGIMO) 211

Moscow – *cont'd*
  Moscow State University (MGU)
    51, 66, 81–2, 123–5, 198, 207,
    211, 234, 287, 313, 320, 351,
    354, 363, 420
  Moscow Uprising 19, 33
  Moskva Hotel 63, 350
  National Hotel 350
  Old Square 27, 181, 275, 421
  Pedagogical Institute of Foreign
    Languages (Maurice Thorèze)
    203
  People's Friendship University 117
  Perovo 145
  Polezhaevskaya 190
  Pushkin Square 104, 204, 211,
    385, 481
  Radio Street 77
  Red Square 54, 197, 200, 202–4,
    208, 215, 217, 219, 268–9,
    304, 349–50, 363, 386
  Rossiya Hotel, 349–50, 354
  Sokolniki Park 118
  Sovremennik Theatre 227
  Stanislavsky Theatre 169, 385
  Trubnaya Square 51
  Tverskaya-Yamskaya Street 421
  Tverskoi Boulevard 104
  Vakhtangov Theatre 142
  Yeliseevsky emporium 247
*Moskva* (journal) 228
motherhood 4, 18–20, 30, 40, 58,
  63, 73, 75–6, 78, 82, 108,
  156, 178, 198, 223, 231, 270,
  385–7, 389–92
Mozambique 10
Mukhina, Lena 98
Murmansk 52, 162, 375
MVD see Ministry of Internal
  Affairs

Nagorno-Karabakh 480
Nagy, Imre 67
Nasser, Abdel 121
Nathans, Benjamin 201
nationalism 10, 22, 315, 463–9
nationalities 25–6, 118, 126, 134,
  202, 213, 306–8, 315–6, 463–4
nationhood 47, 163, 212, 306–7,
  414, 465, 467, 525n18
NATO 60, 308–9, 357, 470
Navalny, Alexei 476–7, 479
Nazis 37–8, 40–44, 74, 140, 193,
  209, 267, 272, 287, 291, 308,
  346, 454
Nazi–Soviet Pact 37–8, 454, 465
Nehru, Jawaharlal 237
Neizvestny, Ernst 130, 258–60,
  378, 461
Nelina, Nina 53
New Economic Policy (NEP) 23,
  28, 109, 169, 418, 432, 454
New Russia Company 18
Nikolayev, A. G. 88
Nizhny Novgorod *see* Gorky
Nkrumah, Kwame 237
NKVD 6, 35, 39, 64, 77–8, 113–14,
  142, 147, 179, 188
Nobel Prize
  in Literature 8, 81, 94, 219, 267,
    269, 275
  in Physics 123–4
  Peace Prize 274, 444–5, 529n1
Nokia 117, 302
Nordhausen Institute 78
normality 5, 11, 13, 101, 106,
  284–6, 337, 347, 376, 381,
  451, 458–62, 471
North Caucasus Military District
  (Army) 5
North Ossetia 59

Novgorod 188
Novocherkassk uprising 1–5, 130, 144, 146, 173, 206
Novosibirsk 204–5, 234, 315, 321–2, 344
*Novyi mir* 56, 137, 138–41, 168, 202, 225, 270

Odesa 36, 76–7, 262
*Office Romance, An* (Eldar Ryazanov) 252
oil 169, 238, 293–4
Okudzhava, Bulat 81, 90, 290
old-age pensioners 408, 417
  *see also* pensions
Olenogorsk 162
Olympic Games (Moscow 1980) 346, 361–4, 397
Omsk 78, 102, 477
Order of Lenin *see under* Lenin, Vladimir
Orgburo 27
Orlova, Raisa 137–8, 202
Orthodox Church 20, 126–9, 174, 274, 304, 316, 378, 388, 399
  Council for the Affairs of the Russian Orthodox Church 127
Oshanin, Lev 392
Ostrovsky, Arkady 392
Ostrovsky, Nikolai 33
Oushakine, Serguei, 12, 215, 281
Oxford 116

palaces of culture 100, 264, 312
Pankratova, Anna 65–6
paradox 10–11, 38, 41, 59, 88, 105, 164, 225, 258–9, 262, 288, 291, 297, 303, 309, 328, 331, 336, 375, 377, 381, 390, 397, 438, 440, 451, 464, 468

Paradzhanov, Sergei 232
Paris 116, 118–19, 194, 204, 215, 244, 246, 272, 274, 287, 322, 396
Party Conferences
  Fourteenth 26–7
  Nineteenth 424, 456
Party Congresses
  Tenth 23, 24, 207
  Fourteenth 27
  Nineteenth 60
  Twentieth 61–3, 68, 111, 158, 202, 419
  Twenty-second 93, 111, 127, 133, 137
  Twenty-fifth 294
  Twenty-seventh 416
  Twenty-eighth 415
passports 128, 189, 292, 309, 313, 315, 379, 388, 396
Pasternak, Boris 80–82, 431
  *Doctor Zhivago* 81, 454
peasantry 17–18, 21–2, 26, 30–33, 39, 40, 43, 60, 73–4, 108, 136, 138–9, 145, 149, 163, 280, 293, 351, 399, 421, 449
Peenemünde 78
pensions 7, 45, 107–11, 117, 151, 210, 244, 249–50, 327, 339, 341, 393, 458
People's Commissariat of Internal Affairs see NKVD
people's democracies 10, *see also* Eastern bloc
Peredelkino 81, 217, 274
*perestroika* 6, 12, 40, 68, 129, 168, 184, 247, 322, 339, 343, 392, 405–6, 408–10, 414–16, 418, 420, 424, 427, 432, 435, 437, 441–5, 450, 452–3, 456, 458, 460–62, 468

periodization 11, 203, 209, 451–3
permafrost 101, 162
personhood 11–12, 129, 238, 294, 322–3, 398, 451, 458, 478
Petrograd *see* Leningrad
Petrovsky, Boris 221, 229
Petrovsky Clinic 226
pets 253–4
physical culture 222
Picasso, Pablo 118
Pioneers 110, 122, 158, 222, 244, 258
Pitsunda 150–51, 165, 250
Pivorarov, Valentin 148
Plisetskaya, Maya 115, 270
Podgorny, Nikolai 166, 254
Poland 10, 18, 37–8, 45, 67, 121, 135, 151, 200, 308, 357, 395, 434
police state 7, 11, 60, 67, 121, 184, 194–5, 206, 208, 210, 255, 292, 375–6
Polikarpov, Dmitry 138
Politburo 3, 12, 18, 22, 27–8, 31, 33, 35, 45–7, 53–4, 59, 61–2, 67–9, 80, 94, 99–100, 110, 113, 130, 144, 147–9, 151, 158, 166, 180, 254, 275, 280, 282, 307, 330, 332, 334, 340, 349–50, 354–5, 357, 361, 364–6, 381, 383, 390, 405–7, 410, 412–13, 419, 422–3, 455–6
polyclinics 223, 228, 251, 408
  Kremlin Polyclinic Number 1 *see* Kremlin
Pomerantsev, Vladimir 56
Ponomarev, Boris 95, 355, 175
Posokhin, Mikhail 104–5
Pospelov, Pyotr 61–2
Prague 308
Prague Spring 10, 142, 167, 192, 197, 200, 203, 209, 217, 266, 295

*Pravda* 46, 55, 61, 80, 151, 174, 193, 255, 274, 294, 347, 368, 413, 435, 470
*pravda* (truth, justice) 56
Presidium *see* Politburo
Presidium of Supreme Soviet *see* Supreme Soviet
prices 1–2, 48, 146, 169, 171, 173, 206, 238, 244, 438, 441, 449, 488n61
Primakov, Yevgeny 193–4
Primorsky krai 145
Pritykina, Tatyana 214
Procuracy 38, 77, 167, 232
Proletkult 26
promotees 32, 109, 113, 170–71, 188, 330
prophylaxis (healthcare) 107, 221–3, 394, 457
prophylaxis (KGB) 184, 230
*propiska* 189, 292
  '101st kilometre' 189
prosthetics 223
psychiatric hospitals (KGB) 183, 198–9
Purges *see* Terror
Pushkin, Aleksandr 427
Pushkin Square (and Statue), Moscow 104, 204, 211, 385, 481
Pushkin Theatre, Moscow, 142

Raikin, Arkady 271
Rákosi, Mátyás 67
Rasputin, Valentin 293
Reagan, Ronald 357, 365, 405, 423, 469
Rechulsky convent 127
Red Army 22, 24, 37, 39, 40, 44 133, 151

Reddaway, Peter 205
Reed, John 143
Reichsbahn 121
Reshetovskaya, Natalia 136
Riga 239, 380, 445
rights 5, 7, 13, 60, 65, 96, 103,
  110–11, 134, 198, 201, 204–5,
  215, 342, 372, 379, 390, 400,
  429, 432
  consumer rights 241–2
  human rights 200, 201, 208, 210,
    213, 279, 294–7, 423, 430–31,
    436–7, 457, 468–9
  national rights 15, 202, 445, 463
  property rights 102, 440–41
  social and economic rights 65,
    106, 255, 340, 442, 457
  voting rights 62
  women's rights 122
Roginsky, Arseny 214
Romania 10, 37, 122, 308
Rome 246
  'third Rome', 'fourth Rome' 304
Rossiia, Rossiya *see* RSFSR
Rostov 2, 37, 135
RSFSR 11, 17, 25, 31, 41, 66, 78,
  126, 128, 135, 150, 161, 181,
  188, 228–9, 232, 253, 262,
  273, 289, 304–7, 316, 331–2,
  347, 349 351, 353, 387, 391,
  435, 442, 446, 450, 463,
  465–6, 468, 470
Rudenko, Roman 167
rule of law 11, 184, 195, 322, 436,
  440
rules of the game 67, 186
Rusakova, Elena 214
Russian Federation 470
Russian language 59, 117–18, 150,
  273, 311, 315, 497n13

Russian people, Russian republic
  (see RSFSR)
Russian Social Democratic and
  Labour Party (RSDLP) 19, 95,
  287
  Bolsheviks 12, 19–24, 30, 34,
    40–41, 47–8, 60–62, 85, 95, 97,
    114, 133, 135, 156, 158, 174,
    179, 207, 222, 229–30, 273,
    280, 286, 288, 371–2, 387,
    454
  Mensheviks 19, 21, 47, 288
Russophone (see Russian language)
Rutchenko 21
Ryazan 39, 136–7, 146, 217–18
Ryazanov, Eldar 159–60, 168–9,
  238, 252, 271, 368, 427–8,
  461, 471
Rybinsk 135, 181, 183

Sakharov, Andrei 9, 52, 196
  (illustration), 207–9, 226, 239,
  281, 346, 355–6, 366, 406, 426
  (illustration), 430–31, 433–4,
  436–7, 444, 451
Sakharova, Klavdiya, 207, 226
sanatoria 79, 107, 122, 187, 222–3,
  325, 329
Saratov 74, 76, 280
Savitskaya, Svetlana 300
Sberbank 244, 438
*Science and Religion* (journal) 127
scissors crisis 24
Scofield, Paul 115
Scotland Yard 121
Second World War *see* Great
  Fatherland War
Secret Speech 9, 62–9, 133, 136,
  141, 145, 147, 198, 202–3,
  294, 352, 400, 420, 452, 481

Secretariat 27
Sedky, Aziz 121
Semashko, Nikolai 221
Semichastny, Vladimir 70, 167–8, 180
Semyonov, Yulian 192–4, 347, 369
　Kostenko novels 194, 347, 369
　*Seventeen Moments of Spring* 192–3
Seregin, Vladimir 177
Serov, Ivan 69, 113–14, 120, 180, 330
Sevastopol 37, 450
*Seventeen Moments of Spring* 192–3
Severodvinsk 161
sex workers 222, 230–31, 361, 409, 460, 462
*sharashka* 78, 135, 137–8
Shatrov, Mikhail 249
Shelepin, Aleksandr 130, 180, 254, 330
shock workers 29, 109
Sholokhov, Mikhail 94, 271
shortages *see* deficit
Shostakovich, Dmitry 270–71, 431
Shukshin, Vasily 265
Siberia 6, 10, 17, 22, 29, 38, 46, 58, 88, 92 (illustration), 128, 161, 169, 188, 215, 262, 267–8, 293, 308, 407, 420, 455
Simonov, Konstantin 140
Sinyavsky-Daniel case 168, 204–5, 208, 211, 258
Siuda, Pyotr 3
Slutsky, Boris 84
Smolensk 44, 59
snow 57, 158, 163–4, 168, 393
Snow, C. P. 83–4, 86
Sochi 48, 79, 248
social mobility 32, 109, 165, 170, 325–6, 330, 400

social welfare 43, 100, 106–9, 146, 150, 171, 190, 201, 222–3, 250–51, 285, 296, 302, 316, 325, 329, 339–42, 395, 408, 441, 457–8
　see also pensions
socialist justice 2, 415
socialist legality 56, 201, 372
socialist legality *see* socialist justice
socialist realism 33, 40, 56, 58–9, 130, 138, 140, 163, 219, 258, 263, 265, 269, 282, 296–7, 324
Socialist Revolutionaries 21–2
Soloukhin, Vladimir 228, 397
Solzhenitsyn, Aleksandr 134–40, 144, 151–2, 167–8, 202, 206–7, 217–19, 224–5, 234–5, 272–5, 290, 366, 371
Solzhenitsyna, Natalia (Svetlova) 274
*sovnarkhozy* 150, 166
Spain 116, 271
special settlements 31, 38
*Spring Call-Up* 192
Sputnik 80, 94, 282
St Petersburg *see* Leningrad
Stakhanov, Aleksei 29
Stakhanovites 29, 34, 109
Stalin, Joseph 17, 25–9, 31–2, 34, 36, 43, 45, 47–8, 55, 57, 60–64, 67, 69, 77, 79, 95, 116, 120, 124, 133, 140, 148, 151, 288, 305, 307, 314, 316, 322, 372, 424, 431, 452, 456, 474
　death of 51–3, 152
Stalinism 5, 8, 9, 11, 23, 40, 42, 43, 44, 54, 56, 59, 61–2, 64–5, 67–8, 79, 97, 109, 124, 137–40, 141–2, 146, 167, 172, 179, 184, 189, 202, 204–5, 208–10, 219, 235, 255,

257–9, 282, 284, 326, 351–2, 362, 371, 375, 415, 424, 452, 454–7
late (postwar) Stalinism (historiographical concept) 44–5, 47–8, 79, 81, 86, 108, 193, 217, 287, 390, 400, 407, 416
*Short Course* 61
Stalina, Svetlana 48
Stalinabad *see* Dushanbe
Stalingrad 37, 40, 68, 140
Star City 174, 177
State Planning Authority *see* Gosplan
Stavropol 17, 66, 181–2, 252, 350–54, 366, 407
Stevenson, Adlai 120
Sumgait 145
Supreme Rada 467
Supreme Soviet 60, 63, 89, 94, 146, 297, 332, 353, 433, 442
    Chair of Presidium of Supreme Soviet 60, 116, 158, 166, 329–30
    Presidium of Supreme Soviet 326
    Supreme Soviet (RSFSR) 442
    Supreme Soviet (Ukrainian republic) 467
Suslov, Mikhail 94, 126, 130, 165–6, 182, 254, 269, 280–81, 287–8, 305, 307, 309, 322, 332, 365
Sverdlovsk 69, 125, 348, 420–21
Sweden 117, 346
*Sword and the Shield, The* 192

Tabakov, Oleg 193
Taganka Theatre 142–4, 261–6, 269–70, 386, 395–8, 428, 431, 470–71, 481
Tajikistan 311–12, 315, 355–6, 387, 466, 480
Tallinn 232, 346, 376
Tambov 22, 347
Tamm, Igor 123
Tashkent 102, 224, 251, 319–20, 338 (illustration), 347
    earthquake 311, 342–3
Tass 46
Tbilisi 51–2, 66, 251, 271, 334, 399, 434, 445, 457
television 98, 115, 155, 159–61, 271–2, 343
Tendriakov, Vladimir 142, 219
Tereshkova, Valentina 88, 174, 300
Termitau 145
Terror (1936–8) 7, 14, 27, 33–5, 41–2, 45, 54, 61–2, 64–6, 115, 140–41, 147–8, 170, 179–80, 188, 198, 207, 257, 269, 289–90, 312, 393, 400, 454–5
Teush, Veniamin and Susanna 217
Thatcher, Margaret 410
Thaw 7, 12, 56, 57–9, 61, 80–82, 84–9, 97, 100, 105, 107, 110–11, 114, 117, 120, 122–4, 126, 128.9, 137, 139–43, 152, 158, 167–8, 184–5, 198, 200–204, 206–10, 212, 214, 217, 227, 229, 231, 234, 239, 245, 249, 251, 253, 255, 260, 262–3, 266, 268, 282, 284, 294, 321, 323, 328, 339–40, 351, 362, 364, 366–7, 372–4, 386, 391, 394, 400, 416, 419, 432, 456–7, 474
    Ilya Ehrenberg, *The Thaw* 57, 84, 118

Third Party Programme 95–6, 108, 127, 148
'Third World' 10, 96, 117, 122, 310–11
Tikhanovskaya, Svetlana (Sviatlana Tsikhanouskaya) 475
Tikhanovsky, Sergei 474
Tikhonov, Vyacheslav 192
Timashuk, Lydia 46
Timofeyev-Resovsky, Nikolai 125, 234
Titov, Gherman 75, 88, 90, 93, 127
Tolstoy, Leo 85, 138
Tomsk 455–6, 476–7
totalitarianism 41, 57, 106, 199, 267, 322–3, 330, 367, 371, 439, 458
trade unions 2, 32, 89, 297, 325, 328–31, 332, 333, 335, 336, 432, 433, 435
    All-Union Central Soviet of Trade Unions (VSTsSPS) 329–30
Transcaucasian republic *see* Caucasus
Trapeznikov, Sergei 209
Trifonov, Yuri 53, 219, 223, 268–70, 289, 398, 461
Trotsky, Leon 22, 24, 27–9
Tselikovskaya, Lyudmila 142
Tsepkalo, Veronika 475
Tsiolkovsky, Konstantin 76–7, 94
Tupolev aircraft 78, 347–8
Turkmenistan (Turkmen republic) 59, 258, 466
Turksib railway 29
Tvardovsky, Aleksandr 138–41, 168, 217–8, 225
Tver *guberniya* 88
Tyura-Tam (Baikonur) cosmodrome 75, 88, 300

*udarniki see* shock workers
UEFA 116
Ufa (illustration) xiv
Ukraine 10, 17–18, 25–6, 31, 36, 40–3, 45, 64–5, 76, 113, 124, 126, 136, 141, 145, 156–7, 163, 200, 232, 235, 251, 263, 273–4, 304–5, 307–8, 313, 315–6, 366, 378, 387, 407, 413–4, 446, 466–7, 469, 473, 478–9, 481
Ukrainian republic (see Ukraine)
Ulanova, Galina 115
Ulitskaya, Lyudmila 81–3, 115, 123–5, 128, 203, 374–5
Union of Writers 33, 167–8, 218, 222, 268–9, 271
United Kingdom *see* Britain
United Nations 117, 120, 147, 279, 470
United States of America 43, 46, 52, 114, 116–17, 120, 128, 205, 207–8, 220, 224, 230, 231, 259, 267–8, 279, 282–3, 285, 300, 303, 315–16, 323, 330, 345, 358, 371, 377, 379, 381, 390, 396, 408, 423, 468
USSR, foundation of 25
Uzbekistan 136, 224–5, 245, 273, 298 (illustration), 306, 310–11, 370, 387, 394, 422

VDNKh 98–9
Versailles, Treaty of 22
Vietnam
    North Vietnam 10, 309
    Vietnam War 356, 380
Village Prose 228, 262, 265, 307, 397
Vilnius 377, 445, 457
Virgin Lands 145, 157

Vladivostok 77
Vlasov, Andrei 40
VOG (All-Russian Society for the Deaf) see deaf people
Voinovich, Vladimir 219
Volga (river and region) 76, 113, 128, 135, 181
Volga Automobile Factory (VAZ) 252
Volga car 369
Volga Germans 134, 314
Volgograd 140, 383
  Mamayev Kurgan memorial 140
Voprosy istorii 65
Voronezh 102, 264, 340
Voroshilov, Kliment 51, 59, 62, 69, 116, 176 (illustration)
Voroshilovgrad 37, 271
Voznesensky, Andrei 107, 143, 268
VSTsSPS see trade unions
vydvyzhentsy see promotees
Vysotsky, Vladimir 142, 144, 256 (illustration), 259–62, 265, 272–3, 275, 340, 386, 395–8, 427–9, 431, 461, 481, 509n7

Warsaw Pact 10, 65, 167, 192, 295, 308–9, 357
Washington, DC 104, 194, 274, 287, 301, 355, 423, 469
Watson, James 123
welfare see social welfare
workers' control (kontrol', supervision) 21
World Festival of Youth 112 (illustration), 120, 199, 362

Yablonskaya, Tatyana (Tetiana Yablonska) 163

Yakovlev, Aleksandr 63, 65, 419
Yakutia 163, 281
Yakutsk 162
Yaroslavl 181, 183
Yashin, Ilya 479
Yefremov, Leonid 353
Yefremov, Oleg 89, 227
Yerevan 271, 395
Yeryomenko, Andrei 37
Yevtushenko, Yevgeny 140–41, 257–9, 261, 270, 396
Yezhov, Nikolai 35, 185
*Young People* (Nikolai Moskalenko) 163
youth novels 84
Yugoslavia 243, 309, 469
Yuzovka 18–19, 21–3, 25–8, 156

Zagorsk 135, 149
Zakharov, Nikolai 188
Zaporozh'e 157
*zeks* 6, 41, 134–6, 189, 219, 274
Zhdanov, Andrei 33, 46–8, 57, 480
Zhdanov, Yuri 48
Zhemchuzhina, Polina 47
Zhitomir 76
Zhukov, Georgi 36, 68–9, 147, 190
Zhutovsky, Boris 237
*Zigzag of Fortune* (Eldar Ryazanov) 168–9, 368
Zinoviev, Aleksandr 320–22, 331–2, 337
Zinoviev, Grigory 27
von Zitzewitz, Josephine 215
*Znamya* journal 57, 87
Znanie (All-Union Knowledge Society) 127
Zverev, Arseny 250